W9-BRV-035

MEET THE *SOUTHERN LIVING*® FOODS STAFF

Our test kitchens and photography studio operate five days a week testing, tasting, and photographing new recipes. This year, staffers prepared over 4,200 recipes – whisking approximately 730 pounds of flour, 234 dozen eggs, and 1,456 cups of sugar into the recipes in this book. Here we invite you to meet our staff.

Kaye Adams, Executive Editor; Wanda Stephens, Editorial Assistant (standing); Elle Barrett, Foods Editor

Assistant and Associate Foods Editors: (seated) Donna Florio, Andria Scott Hurst, Dana Adkins Campbell, Jackie Mills; (standing) Patty Vann, Jodi Jackson Loe, Susan Nash, Denise Gee

Test Kitchens Staff: Vanessa Ward, Mary Allen Perry, Judy Feagin, Vanessa Johnson

Photo Stylists: Mary Lyn Hill, Leslie Simpson

Test Kitchens Staff: Peggy Smith, Vie Warshaw, Diane Hogan, Margaret Monroe, Anna Fowler

Photographers: Charles Walton IV, Tina Evans, J. Savage Gibson

Southern Living®

1996 ANNUAL RECIPES

Oxmoor House®

Book Division of Southern Progress Corporation
P.O. Box 2463, Birmingham, Alabama 35201

Library of Congress Catalog Number: 79-88364
ISBN: 0-8487-1523-3
ISSN: 0272-2003

Manufactured in the United States of America
First printing 1996

WE'RE HERE FOR YOU!

We at Oxmoor House are dedicated to serving you with reliable information that expands your imagination and enriches your life. We welcome your comments and suggestions. Please write to us at:

Oxmoor House, Inc.
Editor, *Southern Living*® *Annual Recipes*
2100 Lakeshore Drive
Birmingham, AL 35209

To order additional copies of this book or any others, call 1-205-877-6560.

Cover: *Gift Box Cake (page 319)*
Back Cover: *Grilled Asian Chicken Salad (page 158), Herbed Tomato Tart (page 94), Chesapeake Bay Crab Cakes With Jalapeño Tartar Sauce (page 69), Beef Stew, a salad with Green Onion Dressing, Sour Cream Cornbread (pages 16, 17)*
Page 1: *Hopping John (page 272), Collard Greens (page 272)*
Page 4: *Spicy Blueberry Pie (page 147)*

Southern Living®

Executive Editor: Kaye Mabry Adams
Foods Editor: Elle Barrett
Foods/Travel Writer: Dana Adkins Campbell
Associate Foods Editors: Jackie Mills, R.D., Susan Hawthorne Nash
Assistant Foods Editors: Donna Florio, Denise Gee, Andria Scott Hurst, Jodi Jackson Loe, Patty M. Vann
Test Kitchens Director: Vanessa Taylor Johnson
Assistant Test Kitchens Directors: Judy Feagin, Peggy Smith
Test Kitchens Staff: Anna C. Fowler, Diane Hogan, Mary Allen Perry, Vanessa McNeil Ward, Vie Warshaw
Editorial Assistants: Karen Brechin, Wanda T. Stephens
Senior Foods Photographer: Charles Walton IV
Photographers: Tina Evans, J. Savage Gibson
Senior Photo Stylist: Leslie Byars Simpson
Assistant Photo Stylist: Mary Lyn Hill
Photo Services: Tracy Underwood
Production Manager: Kenner Patton
Assistant Production Manager: Bradford Kachelhofer
Editorial Contributor: Trinda Gage

Oxmoor House, Inc.

Editor-in-Chief: Nancy Fitzpatrick Wyatt
Senior Editor, Editorial Services: Olivia Kindig Wells
Art Director: James Boone

Southern Living® *1996 Annual Recipes*

Senior Foods Editor: Susan Carlisle Payne
Associate Foods Editor: Whitney Wheeler Pickering
Copy Editor: Donna Baldone
Editorial Assistant: Stacey Geary
Production and Distribution Director: Phillip Lee
Associate Production Manager: Theresa L. Beste
Production Assistant: Valerie L. Heard
Editorial Consultant: Jean Wickstrom Liles
Indexer: Mary Ann Laurens
Designer and Illustrator: Carol Middleton

Table of Contents

The chapters of this cookbook are arranged like the monthly pages of Southern Living® *magazine – celebrating the seasons and meeting the needs of your busy lifestyle.*

OCTOBER 231

NOVEMBER 261

DECEMBER 305

APPENDICES 337

RECIPE INDEX SECTION 342

FAVORITE RECIPES 367

It's easy to find any of the nearly 1,000 kitchen-tested recipes in this cookbook. Simply turn to our three cross-referenced indexes in the back of this cookbook, and you'll find every recipe indexed by title, month, food category, and main ingredient. Family-pleasing recipes are at your fingertips!

OUR YEAR AT SOUTHERN LIVING®

Dear Friends,

With this, our eighteenth volume of *Southern Living® Annual Recipes,* we look back on a year full of great tastes, inviting entertaining ideas, and helpful and healthful food tips, all here in one beautifully illustrated cookbook. The variety of recipes we highlight each year is astounding. From Roasted Quail Étouffée, page 34, to Elizabeth and Phoebe's Fresh Peach Pie, page 119, from Chesapeake Bay Crab Cakes, page 69, to Fig Preserves, page 195, our recipes reflect the bounties of the Southern land and seas and the pleasures of the Southern table.

Our thanks to those of you who so generously shared your favorite recipes – and the warm and wonderful recollections that often came with them.

Your stories and kitchen memories make us feel you've pulled up a chair at our tasting table. We think that reader bond brings a special warmth to the pages of *Southern Living* magazine. To those of you who have never contributed a recipe, please consider writing to us at the magazine next year. We'd love to add your special recipes to our files or hear about your favorite restaurant or local great cook.

This year, an unprecedented 24 recipes received our most coveted rating.

During our daily taste testings, all *Southern Living* recipes are rated on a 5-point scale. You can read about those recipes that received our highest rating on the pages that follow. We think these blue ribbon recipes are proof that the love of cooking is as strong as ever in the South and evolving to meet the time and taste demands of the nineties and beyond.

Whether you're planning a simple dinner for two or an elaborate buffet for 20, you'll find just the recipes you need within these pages. Thank you for celebrating another year with us.

Elle Barrett
Foods Editor

Elle joined the Foods Staff of Southern Living *in 1992. She was named Foods Editor this year. She is a member of the International Association of Culinary Professionals and Association of Food Journalists.*

1996's Best Recipes

We gather almost every day for taste testing. There we scrutinize our recipes and declare favorites.

Recipes prepared by our Test Kitchens Staff must be tasted, retested, if necessary, and "passed" before being published. After gaining our stamp of approval, we assign each recipe an in-house rating. We consider taste, as well as ease of preparation, broadness of appeal, and relevancy to today's standards.

This was a record year for great recipes at *Southern Living*. We tested more than 4,000 recipes during 1996, and a record-breaking 24 of them received our highest rating. These winners range from down-home favorites, such as greens and yeast rolls, to chefs' specialties and dishes that call out for the good china. They're sure to inspire rave reviews at your table, too.

Our highest-rated recipes follow, in the order of their appearance.

■ **CORN-BLACK BEAN SALSA** *(page 15):* Trade the same old gravy and bottled salad dressing for this Corn-Black Bean Salsa and get compliments every time. This versatile low-fat topping stirs up sassy flavor in pastas, omelets, meats, and salads. Lime juice and cilantro are key ingredients. A snap to prepare, this salsa's the secret to meals in minutes.

■ **SOUTHERN-STYLE CHILES RELLENOS** *(page 24):* Cheddar cheese grits and Country Ham Sauce, classics from the heart of Dixie, add a creamy richness to Southern-Style Chiles Rellenos. Whip up a batch of biscuits to soak up the extra sauce, and enjoy.

■ **CRÊPES CON QUESO** *(page 48):* Odile Besseau and Durfee Bedsole, owners of The Taylor House in Marshall, Texas, cook country French with a Southern accent. Their unique style gives this dish international appeal, while the cornmeal crêpes lend a familiar flavor. This is one of those recipes that makes our staff members too impatient to wait for their copy of the magazine. Most of them made a copy of this recipe to take home immediately after taste-testing.

■ **LUMP CRAB HASH WITH THREE-PEPPER HOLLANDAISE** *(page 52):* Chef Ken Vedrinski lends us his recipe for indulgence. He serves this luxurious dish for breakfast at Woodlands Resort and Inn in Summerville, South Carolina. This recipe gets its title from the blend of pink, green, and white peppercorns used in the hollandaise sauce. But if you don't have a peppercorn blend, you can substitute black pepper. At home, this dish can make an ordinary morning extraordinary.

■ **MORRISON HOUSE BRIOCHE** *(page 53):* Grace your plate morning, noon, or night with this rich buttery bread. A signature offering at the Morrison House in Alexandria, Virginia, it's a welcome treat with any meal. It makes a great substitute for sandwich bread and dinner rolls. And toasted and spread with jam, it's a comforting snack.

■ **CHEESE MUFFINS** *(page 54):* These melt-in-your-mouth Cheese Muffins are so light you'll almost think they're mini cheese soufflés. They're quick, easy, and a great companion to a cup of coffee or a bowl of chili. Just seven commonly found ingredients and less than 30 minutes from start to snack time, this recipe is homemade made easy.

■ **STONE CRAB BISQUE** *(page 86):* "Rich, rich, rich" is how one staffer described Stone Crab Bisque. Deliciously deserving of our top rating, it's chock-full of onions, mushrooms, and stone crab claw meat. Whether you're entertaining friends or you're in front of the fireplace with a significant other, this rich warming soup is what memories are made of.

■ **HERBED TOMATO TART** *(page 94):* Garden-fresh herbs and ruby tomatoes are showcased in this pretty-as-a-picture tart. Frozen puff pastry sheets make it a breeze to prepare, while fresh tomatoes say homemade.

■ **BLUE CHEESE CRISPS** *(page 106):* All-time favorite cheese wafers are updated with blue cheese lovers in mind. Replace boring crackers with Blue Cheese Crisps for an inventive new crunch. One editor's happy-hour menu suggestion: "These would be great with a dry martini!"

■ **ARTICHOKE AND SHRIMP PLATTER WITH BÉARNAISE SAUCE** *(page 132):* This appetizer is a welcome change from the ordinary. Fresh artichokes and shrimp are dolloped with an unbeatable classic Béarnaise Sauce. Serve this crowd-pleaser with plenty of crusty bread . . . yum.

■ **ORZO SALAD WITH SESAME DRESSING** *(page 137):* This unusual salad will be a showstopper at your next party. Sesame oil lends its distinct flavor to this easy-to-prepare dish. Layers of orzo, carrot, raisins, and sunflower kernels in a glass bowl move this healthy side dish to center stage.

▪ **EDNA'S GREENS** *(page 144):* Great Southern chefs Edna Lewis and Scott Peacock make simple greens spectacular. Just three ingredients, plus water, is all this recipe calls for. The tender and flavorful end result is worth the time it takes to wash all the greens. According to one longtime and distinctively Southern staff member, "Edna's greens are what Southern greens are all about."

▪ **VANILLA CUSTARD ICE CREAM** *(page 145):* Another hit from chefs Edna Lewis and Scott Peacock, this all-time favorite dessert brings back the flavor of days gone by. Authentic creamy custard ice cream like you probably haven't had in years, this recipe is a "must try" – and a "will never forget."

▪ **CRAB IMPERIAL** *(page 148):* Dig into the crust of golden browned breadcrumbs to uncover the creamy crab mixture that makes Crab Imperial really stand out among our recipes. Some may be left guessing, but you'll know that horseradish is the secret ingredient. Add a simple side dish, salad, and bread for a knockout meal that's sure to be a hit at home or a potluck.

▪ **VANILLA SOUFFLÉS WITH VANILLA CRÈME SAUCE** *(page 155):* First published two years ago, this recipe quickly became one of our most requested. A perfect ending to an elegant meal, Warm Vanilla Soufflés drizzled with cool Vanilla Crème Sauce is a match made in heaven. The sauce – if there's any left over – can also dress up fresh fruit, pound cake, and ice cream.

▪ **HERBED CHEESE-STUFFED MUSHROOMS** *(page 171):* Fresh from the garden or local herb shop, parsley, rosemary, and thyme are mixed with cream cheese and fresh Parmesan cheese to make simple stuffed mushrooms a big hit. Be sure to make enough for seconds or thirds. We guarantee they won't be around long.

▪ **FIGS WITH PROSCIUTTO, WALNUTS, AND CREAM** *(page 194):* With this recipe, Frank Stitt, owner and chef at Highlands in Birmingham, Alabama, proves once again that starting with simple, fresh ingredients leads to perfection. And even if you thought you didn't like figs, this recipe might just change your mind. Its presentation is beautiful, so remember this recipe when you're planning a meal to impress company.

▪ **CLASSIC TROUT AMANDINE** *(page 202):* Fresh trout and real butter are the basics behind this winning recipe. A touch of lemon juice and the addition of buttery sliced almonds turn plain fish into a timeless classic. We recommend this dish the next time you want to serve your guests a simple but spectacular entrée.

▪ **WARM GOAT CHEESE AND POTATO SALAD** *(page 234):* Miles James takes the close-to-the-earth foods of the Ozarks to new heights. Served at James At The Mill in Johnson, Arkansas, this dish is worth the extra time at home. The recipe may look intimidating, but our test kitchens staff assures you that it's very simple. Try it the next time you want to wow your guests.

▪ **SAMOSAS** *(page 239):* Try these crisp little fried pies from the heart of India, and you'll enjoy the best of both worlds – traditional earthy flavors in a no-fuss pastry. Convenient egg roll wrappers make these satisfying snacks quick and easy, while a dip in mango chutney defines their origin and doubles their deliciousness.

▪ **TABBOULEH COUSCOUS** *(page 251):* Parsley usually plays a supporting role in recipes, but this Middle Eastern-inspired recipe gives it star billing. Combined with couscous cooked in chicken broth and a medley of vegetables, the taste is a refreshing change from familiar side salads. Make it ahead so the flavors have time to develop, and you'll have one less thing to do at mealtime.

▪ **ITALIAN CREAM CAKE** *(page 262):* Thick layers of Nutty Cream Cheese Frosting studded with toasted chopped pecans and spread between delicate cake layers make a luscious dessert for any gathering. Coconut and even more pecans mingle in this unforgettable treat reminiscent of European bakery cakes. It's sure to become one of your all-time favorite recipes, too.

▪ **BOURBON-CHOCOLATE-PECAN TARTS** *(page 264):* These jewels are a wonderful twist on a favorite traditional Southern dessert. The cream cheese pastry combined with the chocolate morsels and pecan halves is oh-so-sinfully rich. And the shot of bourbon adds just the right kick. This recipe is a baker's dream and a dessert to savor; no one will be able to eat just one bite.

▪ **OVERNIGHT YEAST ROLLS** *(page 321):* A tour group visited our kitchens while these fluffy rolls were baking, and they were quick to comment on the heavenly aroma. You're the only one who'll know just how easy it is to make them. Plan ahead and make the dough the night before; it needs to chill 8 hours. The next day is as easy as pie; there's no kneading necessary, and the rolls require only one rise. Make a few adjustments to this recipe, and you can create Cinnamon Rolls or Orange Rolls.

JANUARY

SALSA: FLAVOR SENSATION

The holidays are over. There's no more turkey with giblet gravy, sausage stuffing, or pecan pie. It's time to trade gravy for salsa or chutney. These low-fat toppings add a flourish to meals and make it easier for you to win at the losing game.

SWEET-'N'-HOT APPLE CHUTNEY

(pictured on page 42)

Pair this chutney with potato pancakes, pork, ham, or lamb.

3 Granny Smith apples
2 serrano chile peppers, seeded
1 poblano chile pepper, seeded
½ red bell pepper
4 shallots
2 cups rice wine vinegar
¾ cup firmly packed brown sugar
2 teaspoons fresh lemon juice

• **Peel** and core apples; finely chop apples, peppers, and shallots.
• **Combine** vinegar and sugar in a saucepan; bring to a boil, stirring until sugar dissolves. Add apple, pepper, and shallot; boil 20 minutes or until most of liquid evaporates, stirring occasionally. Remove from heat, and stir in lemon juice; cool.
• **Serve** warm or at room temperature. Store in refrigerator up to 1 week in an airtight container. **Yield:** 2½ cups.

Chef Phillip Rice
Tex's Grill
San Antonio, Texas

PEACH SALSA

(pictured on page 42)

Chips, fish, or chicken will wake up to the fruity flavor of this salsa.

1 (16-ounce) can peaches in juice, drained and chopped
4 plum tomatoes, chopped
4 green onions, sliced
2 tablespoons chopped pickled jalapeño peppers
1 tablespoon finely chopped fresh cilantro
1 tablespoon olive oil
1 tablespoon lime juice
1 teaspoon honey
¼ teaspoon salt
¼ teaspoon pepper

• **Combine** all ingredients in a large bowl, stirring gently. Store in refrigerator up to 3 days in an airtight container. **Yield:** 3 cups.

Judy Carter
Winchester, Tennessee

TROPICAL SALSA

(pictured on page 42)

This exotic concoction turns mundane fish or chicken into a marvelous meal.

1 ripe mango, peeled, seeded, and chopped
½ cup chopped plum tomato
½ cup chopped red bell pepper
½ cup chopped purple onion
1 tablespoon minced garlic
1½ teaspoons minced jalapeño pepper
1 teaspoon ground cumin
1 tablespoon olive oil
1 tablespoon red wine vinegar
¼ cup fresh lime juice
½ teaspoon hot sauce
½ cup chopped fresh cilantro
¼ teaspoon salt
¼ teaspoon pepper

• **Combine** all ingredients. Store in refrigerator up to 3 days in an airtight container. **Yield:** 2½ cups.

Paul Stansel
Raleigh, North Carolina

Stir up sassy flavor with these salsas. They'll earn you compliments every time.

Salsa isn't just for Tex-Mex food anymore. Try these low-fat, high-flavor salsas as a fresh and colorful complement to pasta, omelets, sliced meat, and green salads. Adventuresome souls sometimes stir salsa into black-eyed peas and rice for a hopping John dish that gets raves.

AVOCADO-FETA SALSA

(pictured on page 42)

Serve this tangy version of guacamole with Tex-Mex combos, burgers, pasta, grilled fish, or chicken.

1 large avocado
2 plum tomatoes
¼ cup chopped purple onion
1 clove garlic, minced
1 tablespoon chopped fresh parsley
½ teaspoon chopped fresh oregano
1 tablespoon olive oil
½ tablespoon red wine vinegar
½ (4-ounce) package crumbled feta cheese

• **Peel** and seed avocado; chop avocado and tomatoes, and place in a large bowl. Add onion and next 5 ingredients, tossing to coat. Fold in cheese. Serve immediately. **Yield:** 2 cups.

Heather Riggins
Nashville, Tennessee

TOMATO SALSA

(pictured on page 42)

Pair this classic salsa with chips, pasta, or anything Tex-Mex.

1 (16-ounce) can crushed tomatoes, undrained
2 (14.5-ounce) cans diced tomatoes, undrained
1 (4.5-ounce) can chopped green chiles, undrained
1 medium onion, chopped
2 large jalapeño peppers, chopped
2 cloves garlic, minced
½ cup chopped fresh cilantro
2 tablespoons lime juice
1 tablespoon sugar

• **Combine** all ingredients. Store in refrigerator up to 3 days in an airtight container. **Yield:** 7 cups.

Sheila Fogle
Huntsville, Alabama

CORN-BLACK BEAN SALSA

(pictured on page 42)

This colorful salsa is good with just about anything.

1 (15-ounce) can black beans, rinsed and drained
1 cup frozen corn kernels, thawed
½ cup chopped red bell pepper
½ cup chopped fresh cilantro
8 green onions, sliced
3 tablespoons lime juice
2 tablespoons balsamic vinegar
½ teaspoon ground cumin
¼ teaspoon salt

• **Combine** all ingredients. Store in refrigerator up to 3 days in an airtight container. **Yield:** 4 cups.

Kenner Patton
Birmingham, Alabama

MIX-AND-MATCH MENUS

Looking for uncomplicated meals to prepare after long workdays? Then look no further. You can count on our "What's for Supper?" column each month for simple weeknight suppers. This month, we've included recipes you can mix and match for family-pleasing menus.

BEEF STEW

(pictured on page 38)

1 (2¾-pound) boneless chuck roast *
¼ cup all-purpose flour
2 tablespoons vegetable oil
4 cups water
1 tablespoon Worcestershire sauce
2 teaspoons salt
1 teaspoon garlic salt
¾ teaspoon pepper
¼ teaspoon ground allspice
2 bay leaves
4 carrots, scraped
2 stalks celery
4 medium-size red potatoes
3 small onions
2 green bell peppers
3 tablespoons all-purpose flour
3 tablespoons water

• **Trim** fat from roast; cut roast into 1-inch cubes. Place beef and ¼ cup flour in a plastic bag; seal bag, and shake vigorously to coat.

• **Pour** oil into a large Dutch oven; place over medium-high heat until hot. Add beef, and cook until browned, stirring occasionally.

• **Add** 4 cups water and next 6 ingredients; bring to a boil. Cover, reduce heat, and simmer 2 hours or until beef is tender. Remove and discard bay leaves.

• **Cut** carrots and celery into 2-inch lengths. Peel potatoes; cut potatoes and onions into eighths. Cut bell peppers into 1-inch pieces.

• **Add** carrot, celery, potato, onion, and bell pepper to beef mixture; cover and simmer 30 minutes or until vegetables are tender.

• **Combine** 3 tablespoons flour and 3 tablespoons water, stirring well; stir into stew. Bring to a boil; boil, stirring constantly, 1 minute or until thickened and bubbly. **Yield:** 6 to 8 servings.

* Substitute 2 pounds stew meat for roast.

Ann Winniford
Dallas, Texas

CHICKEN LASAGNA

1 (8-ounce) package medium egg noodles
½ cup butter or margarine
½ cup all-purpose flour
1 teaspoon dried basil
1 teaspoon salt
½ teaspoon pepper
4 cups chicken broth
4 cups chopped cooked chicken
1 (24-ounce) carton cottage cheese
1 large egg, lightly beaten
2 cups (8 ounces) shredded mozzarella cheese
¾ cup freshly grated Parmesan cheese

• **Cook** noodles according to package directions; drain and set aside.

• **Melt** butter in a large saucepan over medium heat; stir in flour and next 3 ingredients. Cook 1 to 2 minutes, stirring constantly.

• **Add** broth, stirring until smooth; bring to a boil. Reduce heat, and simmer 5 to 8 minutes or until thickened and bubbly. Stir in chicken; remove from heat.

• **Combine** cottage cheese and egg, stirring well.

• **Spoon** one-third chicken mixture into a lightly greased 13- x 9- x 2-inch baking dish. Top with half each of noodles, cottage cheese mixture, and mozzarella cheese. Repeat layers, ending with chicken mixture. Sprinkle with Parmesan cheese.

• **Bake** at 350° for 1 hour. **Yield:** 8 servings.

Yvonne M. Greer
Mauldin, South Carolina

GREEN ONION DRESSING

(pictured on page 38)

4 green onions, cut into 1-inch pieces
1 cup vegetable oil
½ cup red wine vinegar
2 tablespoons sugar
¾ teaspoon Worcestershire sauce
½ teaspoon dry mustard

• **Combine** all ingredients in container of an electric blender or food processor, and pulse 3 times or until onions are chopped. Cover and chill. **Yield:** 1¾ cups.

Kim Uding
Sainte Genevieve, Missouri

REFRIGERATOR BISCUITS

You can store this dough in the refrigerator up to 3 days, so you can bake fresh biscuits for each meal.

1 (8-ounce) package cream cheese, softened
½ cup margarine, softened
1 cup self-rising flour

• **Beat** cream cheese and margarine at medium speed with an electric mixer 2 minutes or until mixture is creamy. Gradually add flour, beating at low speed just until blended.
• **Spoon** dough into lightly greased miniature (1¾-inch) muffin pans, filling two-thirds full, or cover and store dough in the refrigerator up to 3 days.
• **Bake** at 400° for 17 minutes or until golden. Serve immediately. **Yield:** 2 dozen.

Mrs. John B. Wright
Greenville, South Carolina

SOUR CREAM CORNBREAD

(pictured on page 38)

3 large eggs, lightly beaten
1 cup self-rising cornmeal
1 (8¾-ounce) can cream-style corn
1 (8-ounce) carton sour cream
¼ cup vegetable oil

• **Heat** a lightly greased 8-inch cast-iron skillet in a 400° oven 5 minutes.
• **Combine** all ingredients, stirring just until moistened.
• **Remove** prepared cast-iron skillet from oven, and spoon batter into hot skillet.
• **Bake** at 400° for 20 minutes or until golden. **Yield:** 6 servings.

Note: You can bake batter in lightly greased hot cornstick pans for 16 to 18 minutes. **Yield:** 16 cornsticks.

Laura Morris
Bunnell, Florida

MAPLE NUT CAKE

1 cup shortening
½ cup firmly packed brown sugar
1 cup maple syrup
2 large eggs
2½ cups all-purpose flour
2 teaspoons baking powder
½ teaspoon baking soda
½ teaspoon salt
2 teaspoons ground nutmeg
½ cup hot water
½ cup sherry
1 cup chopped pecans, toasted
Maple Frosting
12 to 15 pecan halves

• **Beat** shortening at medium speed with an electric mixer until fluffy; gradually add sugar, beating well. Add syrup and eggs, beating until blended.
• **Combine** flour and next 4 ingredients in a bowl; add to shortening mixture alternately with hot water and sherry, beginning and ending with flour mixture. Beat at low speed until blended after each addition. Stir in 1 cup chopped pecans. Pour batter into a greased and floured 13- x 9- x 2-inch pan.
• **Bake** at 350° for 30 minutes or until a wooden pick inserted in center comes out clean. Cool cake completely in pan on a wire rack.
• **Spread** Maple Frosting on top of cake; place a pecan half on each serving. **Yield:** 12 to 15 servings.

Maple Frosting

¼ cup butter or margarine, softened
2¼ cups sifted powdered sugar, divided
2 to 3 tablespoons milk
½ teaspoon maple extract

• **Beat** butter at medium speed with an electric mixer until creamy; gradually add 1 cup powdered sugar, beating well. Add remaining sugar and milk, beating until spreading consistency. Beat in extract. **Yield:** 1 cup.

Sara Beebee
Atlanta, Georgia

BLUEBERRY DELIGHT

2 cups graham cracker crumbs
½ cup sifted powdered sugar
1 cup finely chopped pecans
½ cup butter or margarine, melted
1 (8-ounce) package cream cheese, softened
1 cup sugar
2 large eggs
2 tablespoons lemon juice
1 (21-ounce) can blueberry pie filling
1 (12-ounce) container frozen whipped topping, thawed

• **Combine** first 3 ingredients; add butter, stirring well. Press into a greased 13- x 9- x 2-inch pan.
• **Beat** cream cheese at medium speed with an electric mixer until smooth. Add 1 cup sugar, eggs, and lemon juice, mixing until smooth. Spread over crust.
• **Bake** at 350° for 25 minutes or until set. Cool completely.
• **Spread** pie filling over cream cheese mixture; spread whipped topping over filling. Cover and chill several hours. **Yield:** 12 to 15 servings.

Bunnie George
Birmingham, Alabama

Speed Under Pressure

Like some people, you might assume pressure cookers are for grandmothers and nothing a modern cook would ever use. But think again. A pressure cooker can take a three-hour production to a 15-minute meal. And if you have a fear of blow up, relax. Pressure can't build inside the pot unless the lid is locked into place. And you can't remove the lid until the pressure is released.

Once you dig into homemade chili that's almost as fast as opening a can, you'll be a convert.

Gee's Italian Pot Roast

"Mrs. Gee" is Carol Genusa's name on the Internet. We found her recipe in The Cooking Club on America Online.

2 tablespoons olive oil
1 (3- to 4-pound) boneless chuck roast
1 large onion, finely chopped
4 cloves garlic, minced
1 cup dry red wine
1 cup beef broth
2 (6-ounce) cans tomato paste
1 (15-ounce) can tomato sauce
1 teaspoon salt
1 teaspoon dried basil
1 teaspoon sugar
1 teaspoon hot sauce
12 ounces linguine, uncooked
½ cup grated Parmesan cheese

• **Pour** oil into a 6-quart pressure cooker; place over medium-high heat until hot. Add roast, and cook until browned on all sides. Remove roast, and set aside.
• **Add** onion and garlic to cooker, and cook, stirring constantly, until onion is tender. Add red wine and next 7 ingredients, and return roast to cooker.
• **Cover** cooker with lid, and seal securely; place pressure control over vent and tube. Cook over high heat until pressure control rocks back and forth quickly. Reduce heat until pressure control rocks occasionally; cook 45 additional minutes.
• **Remove** from heat; run cold water over cooker to reduce pressure. Carefully remove lid so that steam escapes away from you.
• **Cook** pasta according to package directions; serve roast and sauce over pasta. Sprinkle with cheese. **Yield:** 6 servings.

Carol Landry Genusa
Monroe, Louisiana

Cincinnati Chili

Because the meat in this chili is not browned and drained, use very lean ground beef.

2 pounds ground round
2 cups water
2 (6-ounce) cans no-salt-added tomato paste
1 large onion, finely chopped
1 clove garlic, minced
2 large bay leaves
3 tablespoons chili powder
1 tablespoon ground cumin
2 teaspoons ground allspice
1½ teaspoons ground cinnamon
1 teaspoon salt
1 teaspoon pepper
¼ teaspoon ground red pepper
1 teaspoon white wine vinegar
1 teaspoon Worcestershire sauce
Hot cooked spaghetti
Shredded Cheddar cheese
Chopped onion

• **Combine** beef and water in a 4-quart pressure cooker; stir with a fork until thoroughly blended. Stir in tomato paste and next 12 ingredients.
• **Cover** cooker with lid, and seal securely; place pressure control over vent and tube. Cook over high heat until pressure control rocks back and forth quickly. Reduce heat until pressure control rocks occasionally; cook 15 additional minutes.
• **Remove** from heat; run cold water over cooker to reduce pressure. Carefully remove lid so that steam escapes away from you.
• **Remove** and discard bay leaves. Stir chili well. Serve over hot spaghetti, and top with cheese and onion. Serve with oyster crackers. **Yield:** 6 to 8 servings.

Mary Blackmon
Lake Dallas, Texas

Pressure Points

▪ A pressure cooker cuts cooking time by about two-thirds. When the cooker reaches maximum pressure of 15 pounds, the boiling point of water increases from 212° to 250°, which decreases the cooking time.

▪ If you're buying a new pressure cooker, choose at least a 6-quart model. With most recipes, the pot can be filled only one-half to two-thirds full to allow for buildup of steam.

▪ Plan on spending about $50 for a 6-quart cooker. Look for one at hardware or department stores or kitchen specialty shops.

▪ If you're using an old pressure cooker, check the rubber gasket that fits inside the lid. If it isn't in good condition, buy a replacement gasket.

▪ Start the cooker over high heat to build up the pressure as quickly as possible. Once you reach full pressure, reduce heat, and start timing the cooking.

NAVY BEAN SOUP

If you love the taste of ham hocks, but can't afford the fat, follow the directions here to make a fat-free ham broth. Freeze the broth in ice cube trays, and use a few cubes to season beans, soups, or greens.

2 ham hocks *
7 cups water
1 pound dried navy beans
1 cup chopped celery
1 cup chopped onion
1 carrot, scraped and sliced diagonally
1 teaspoon dried basil
1 teaspoon dried oregano
½ teaspoon salt
½ teaspoon ground nutmeg
¼ teaspoon pepper

• **Combine** ham hocks and water in a 6-quart pressure cooker.
• **Cover** cooker with lid, and seal securely; place pressure control over vent and tube. Cook over high heat until pressure control rocks back and forth quickly. Reduce heat until pressure control rocks occasionally; cook 45 additional minutes.
• **Remove** from heat; run cold water over cooker to reduce pressure. Carefully remove lid so that steam escapes away from you.
• **Pour** broth into a fat strainer; let stand until fat rises to top. Pour broth into a large bowl; discard fat. Remove meat from ham hocks; discard skin, bones, and fat.
• **Combine** broth, meat, beans, and remaining ingredients in cooker. Cook soup as directed above 30 minutes. **Yield:** 9 cups.

* Substitute 1 cup cubed ham for ham hocks. Decrease salt, if desired, and reduce the broth cooking time to 30 minutes.

Deborah Moore Clark
Roanoke, Virginia

TIMESAVING VEGETABLES

Spending too much time washing and chopping fresh vegetables? Why bother when there's a whole garden of recipe-ready vegetables just waiting at the produce counter? You'll pay just a little more, but there's no waste, and your time is worth the difference.

CHICKEN-AND-VEGETABLE STIR-FRY

2 tablespoons vegetable oil
1 pound chicken breast strips
2 tablespoons water
1 (16-ounce) package broccoli stir-fry mix
1 purple onion, cut into strips
2 red bell peppers, cut into strips
1 (11.75-ounce) bottle stir-fry sauce
Hot cooked rice

• **Pour** oil around top of a preheated wok, coating sides; heat at medium-high (375°) for 2 minutes. Add chicken, and stir-fry 2 minutes or until lightly browned.
• **Add** water and vegetables, stirring gently. Cover and cook 8 minutes or until vegetables are crisp-tender, stirring once. Add sauce, and stir-fry 2 additional minutes. Serve over rice. **Yield:** 4 servings.

SKILLET SPINACH

4 slices bacon
2½ tablespoons balsamic vinegar
1 (10-ounce) package fresh spinach
2 tablespoons chopped pecans, toasted
¼ teaspoon salt
¼ teaspoon pepper
Pinch of sugar (optional)

• **Cook** bacon in a large skillet until crisp; remove bacon, reserving 1 tablespoon drippings in skillet. Crumble bacon, and set aside.
• **Add** vinegar to bacon drippings in skillet, and bring mixture to a boil over medium-high heat, stirring to loosen bacon particles.
• **Add** spinach to mixture in skillet, and cook, stirring constantly, 1 to 2 minutes or until spinach is limp. Stir in bacon, pecans, salt, pepper, and sugar, if desired. Serve immediately. **Yield:** 2 servings.

Joel Allard
San Antonio, Texas

FRIED VEGGIES

This appetizer is a great way to use leftover vegetables. The batter also works for sliced zucchini and yellow squash.

1 cup all-purpose flour
1½ teaspoons seasoned salt
2 large eggs, lightly beaten
⅔ cup milk
1 teaspoon vegetable oil
Vegetable oil
1 cup cauliflower flowerets
1 cup broccoli flowerets
1 cup whole mushrooms
1 cup baby carrots

• **Combine** flour and salt in a bowl, and stir well.
• **Combine** eggs, milk, and 1 teaspoon oil; add to flour mixture, stirring with a wire whisk until smooth.
• **Pour** oil to depth of 2 inches into a Dutch oven; heat to 375°.
• **Dip** vegetables in batter; fry, a few at a time, until golden. Drain on paper towels. Serve with Ranch-style salad dressing, if desired. **Yield:** 6 to 8 appetizer servings.

MUSHROOM DELUXE CASSEROLE

½ cup butter or margarine, divided
3 (8-ounce) packages sliced mushrooms
1½ cups herb-seasoned stuffing mix
2 cups (8 ounces) shredded sharp Cheddar cheese, divided
½ cup half-and-half

• **Melt** ¼ cup butter in a large skillet over medium-high heat; add mushrooms, and cook, stirring constantly, until tender. Stir in stuffing mix.
• **Spoon** half of mushroom mixture into an 8-inch square baking dish; sprinkle with half of cheese. Repeat layers; dot with remaining butter. Pour half-and-half over casserole.
• **Bake** at 325° for 30 minutes. **Yield:** 6 servings.

Arlene Cox
Elizabethton, Tennessee

TIME AND EFFORT

You'd have to:
▪ Wash and trim 1 pound of spinach for each 10-ounce package of leaves.

▪ Wash and trim at least 2 heads of broccoli for each 16-ounce package of flowerets.

▪ Wipe with a damp paper towel and slice at least a dozen whole mushrooms for each 8-ounce package of sliced mushrooms.

▪ Wash and trim a small cauliflower for each 16-ounce package of flowerets.

▪ Wash and tear at least 2 pounds of iceberg lettuce and shred 1 small head red cabbage plus 4 carrots for each 48-ounce package of salad mix.

SWEET BROCCOLI SLAW

1 cup sugar
½ cup apple cider vinegar
¼ cup water
½ teaspoon mustard seeds
½ teaspoon celery seeds
1 (16-ounce) package broccoli slaw mix

• **Combine** first 5 ingredients in a small saucepan; bring to a boil, stirring constantly, until sugar dissolves. Remove from heat. Pour over broccoli slaw mix, stirring gently.
• **Cover** and chill at least 4 hours, stirring occasionally. Serve with a slotted spoon. **Yield:** 4 to 6 servings.

Trenda Leigh
Richmond, Virginia

CHEATER'S CARROT CAKE

2 large eggs, lightly beaten
1 (8-ounce) can crushed pineapple, undrained
1 (8.25-ounce) package yellow cake mix
⅓ cup mayonnaise or salad dressing
1 cup shredded carrot
1 (2-ounce) package pecan pieces
1 teaspoon ground cinnamon
½ (12-ounce) container cream cheese frosting

• **Combine** first 7 ingredients in a large bowl, stirring until blended. Pour batter into a greased and floured 9-inch square pan.
• **Bake** at 350° for 30 minutes or until a wooden pick inserted in center of cake comes out clean. Cool completely in pan on a wire rack. Spread frosting over top of cake. **Yield:** one 9-inch cake.

Bill Jackson
Alpine, Alabama

FROM *THEIR* KITCHEN TO OURS

In honor of this year's Olympic Games, we're introducing a tribute series entitled "From *Their* Kitchen to Ours." This first story has us heading straight to the finish line for winning Greek desserts – a sweet start to a great year.

BAKLAVA

This dessert, pronounced BAHK-lah-vah, has a delicate flavor and texture and makes a wonderful gift. It also freezes well when stored in an airtight container.

2 cups sugar
1 cup water
¾ cup honey
2 tablespoons brandy
1 tablespoon fresh lemon juice
1 (3-inch) stick cinnamon
12 cups finely chopped pecans (3 pounds, shelled)
1 cup sugar
1 tablespoon ground cinnamon
1 teaspoon ground cloves
1 (16-ounce) package frozen phyllo pastry, thawed
1 pound unsalted butter, melted
Whole cloves

• **Combine** first 6 ingredients in a saucepan; bring to a boil over medium-high heat, stirring constantly. Immediately remove from heat; cool syrup completely.
• **Combine** pecans and next 3 ingredients, stirring well.
• **Cut** phyllo sheets in half crosswise; keep covered with a slightly damp towel.
• **Brush** two 13- x 9- x 2-inch pans with butter. Place 8 phyllo sheets in one pan, brushing each sheet with butter; top with 2 cups pecan mixture.
• **Place** 3 phyllo sheets over pecan mixture, brushing each sheet with butter;

top with 2 cups pecan mixture. Repeat with 3 more phyllo sheets and 2 cups pecan mixture; top with 6 phyllo sheets, brushing all but the top sheet with butter.

• **Repeat** procedure with remaining phyllo sheets, butter, and pecan mixture in second pan.

• **Cut** layers diagonally into ¾-inch diamonds; gently brush with remaining butter. Insert a clove in center of each diamond.

• **Bake** at 300° for 1 hour. Remove from oven, and pour syrup evenly over baklava. Cool completely in pans on wire racks.

• **Cut** again diagonally; remove from pans, and store in airtight containers at room temperature. **Yield:** about 10 dozen.

Jeannie Sfakianos
Birmingham, Alabama

FINIKIA

Pronounced fin-EE-key-ah, these cookies are similar to shortbread.

1 cup sugar
1 cup vegetable oil
1 cup orange juice
½ cup butter, softened
1 tablespoon ground cinnamon
4 teaspoons baking powder
1 teaspoon baking soda
6 to 6½ cups all-purpose flour
Honey Syrup
3 cups ground walnuts

• **Combine** first 5 ingredients in a large mixing bowl, and beat at medium speed with an electric mixer until well blended. Gradually add baking powder, baking soda, and enough flour to make a medium dough (mixture should not stick to your hands).

• **Turn** dough out onto a lightly floured surface, and knead several times. Shape dough into 1¼-inch balls, and flatten each into a 3- x 1-inch oval. Place on ungreased cookie sheets.

• **Bake** at 350° for 20 minutes or until lightly browned. Remove to wire racks to cool.

• **Dip** cookies into hot Honey Syrup with a slotted spoon; roll in ground walnuts, and place on wire racks to cool. **Yield:** 4¼ dozen.

Honey Syrup

2 cups sugar
1 cup water
1 cup honey
2 tablespoons lemon juice

• **Combine** sugar and water in a saucepan; bring to a boil over medium heat. Reduce heat, and simmer 10 minutes.

• **Add** honey and lemon juice, stirring well; return to a boil. Reduce heat, and simmer 5 minutes. **Yield:** 2¾ cups.

Mary Pappas
Richmond, Virginia

From Our Kitchen to Yours

TESTING THE WATERS

Looking for a new way to add pizzazz to a glass of water? Simply add slices of lemon, lime, orange, and – surprisingly – cucumber to a pitcher of iced water, stir, and let chill. (You can also add a few sprigs of fresh mint, if you like.) Then pour through a wire-mesh strainer into your glass so that only the flavor (and not the actual slices) goes in.

THAT'S THE WAY THE CAKE CRUMBLES

Company's due in an hour and your star cake dessert isn't living up to its reputation. Here's how to turn an "oops" into a "whew."

If your layers fail to come out of the cake pans evenly after you bake them in dutifully greased and floured pans, run a knife around the edges to loosen, and gently invert the first pan to free the layer, here's the solution.

Pull out your parfait glasses, crumble the cake, layer it with whipped cream frosting and colorful sliced fruit, and pretend that parfaits were the plan all along.

TAKE THE PLUNGE

So you forgot to chill the champagne, and party guests are knocking on the door. Instead of popping the bottle in the freezer or an ice bucket at the last second, submerge the bubbly in a mixture of half ice, half tap water. This will bring it to the right festive temperature more quickly than ice alone. (If you're already using your ice bucket, just send the champagne for a brisk dip in the kitchen sink instead.)

SEIZE THE DAY

Melting chocolate is usually easy: just stir constantly in a heavy saucepan over *low* heat. But every once in a while, the chocolate "seizes" (a fancy kitchen term for "clumps").

The cause? A drop of moisture found its way into the pan. The solution? Try stirring a tablespoon of vegetable oil or shortening (per 6 ounces of chocolate) into the gloppy mess (over low heat). Sometimes the extra fat will smooth things out.

TOOLING AROUND THE KITCHEN

You would never think that inanimate objects could possess a stubborn streak, but just look around the grocery store the next time you go. The place is full of items not easily tamed by the timid, including rugged rutabagas and a variety of wily winter squash.

Yet we load our carts with these treasures and head for the kitchen for the impending battle. After huffing and puffing our way through a drawer full of hefty knives, we eventually wrestle the fruit or veggie to the dinner plate.

Ah, but there's a better way. For instance, to cut open squash (acorn, butternut, and spaghetti), rutabagas, and jicama, use a clean handsaw and a large wooden cutting board.

And don't forget dessert. If your finale calls for crushed hard candies, roll them in a nonfuzzy dish towel and whack with a hammer on a sturdy counter, floor, or even the driveway.

PASS THE PLATE

Southern Living HALL OF FAME

Pass the Plate is one of the largest books in the *Southern Living* Cookbook Hall of Fame. It features both quick-and-easy recipes for family meals and extravagant menus for entertaining. And the kids cooking section will be a favorite if you have little hands that like to help in the kitchen.

The cookbook committee of Christ Episcopal Church of New Bern, North Carolina, has headed up *Pass the Plate* since it was first published in 1981. Proceeds from the sale of the cookbooks have benefited Habitat for Humanity, Prison Ministry, the Coastal Women's Shelter, and the Thompson Children's Home.

ARTICHOKE FLAN

½ (15-ounce) package refrigerated piecrusts
1 egg white
1 (9-ounce) package frozen artichoke hearts
3 large eggs, lightly beaten
1½ cups whipping cream
1½ cups (6 ounces) shredded Swiss cheese
½ teaspoon salt
¼ teaspoon dried thyme
Dash of ground red pepper

• **Fit** 1 piecrust into a 9-inch pieplate following package directions; fold edges of piecrust under, and crimp. Brush piecrust with egg white; set aside.
• **Cook** artichokes according to package directions; drain well.
• **Combine** eggs and next 5 ingredients in a bowl; pour mixture into prepared piecrust. Arrange artichokes over filling.
• **Bake** at 375° for 45 minutes or until a knife inserted in center comes out clean. **Yield:** 8 servings.

MIXER CHEESE BISCUITS

1 cup margarine, softened
2 cups (8 ounces) shredded extra-sharp Cheddar cheese
2 cups all-purpose flour
½ teaspoon salt
½ teaspoon ground red pepper
1 teaspoon lemon juice

• **Beat** margarine at medium speed with an electric mixer until creamy; gradually add cheese, beating well. Add flour, salt, and pepper; beat at low speed until blended. Add lemon juice, and beat at medium speed 20 minutes.
• **Pipe** or drop dough by level tablespoonfuls onto ungreased baking sheets.
• **Bake** at 300° for 20 minutes or until set. Transfer to wire racks to cool. **Yield:** 6 dozen.

INCREDIBLE PIMIENTO CHEESE

2 (8-ounce) packages mild Cheddar cheese
2 (8-ounce) packages sharp Cheddar cheese
1 (16-ounce) loaf process cheese spread
3 tablespoons sugar
½ teaspoon salt
½ teaspoon pepper
2 (4-ounce) jars diced pimiento, drained
2 cups mayonnaise or salad dressing

• **Position** shredding disc in food processor bowl; shred Cheddar cheeses. Cut cheese loaf into cubes. Position knife blade in processor bowl; add half of cheeses. Process until smooth, stopping once to scrape down sides. Transfer mixture to a bowl.
• **Add** remaining cheeses, sugar, salt, and pepper to processor bowl; process until smooth, stopping once to scrape down sides.
• **Stir** into cheese mixture in bowl. Stir in pimiento and mayonnaise. **Yield:** 2 quarts.

Note: This cheese spread may be frozen.

JANET'S CRUNCHY CHICKEN

4 skinned and boned chicken breast halves *
½ cup Italian salad dressing
2½ cups corn flakes, crushed

• **Place** chicken in a shallow dish or heavy duty, zip-top plastic bag; add salad dressing. Cover or seal; chill 1 hour. Remove chicken from marinade, discarding marinade.
• **Dredge** chicken in corn flakes; place on a rack in broiler pan.
• **Bake** at 375° for 45 minutes or until tender. **Yield:** 4 servings.

* You can substitute 4 (½-inch-thick) center-cut pork chops for chicken.

SAVVY SANDWICHES

When leftover turkey has lost its appeal, serve these easy, flavorful sandwiches for dinner.

BEEF, BACON, AND BLUE CHEESE SANDWICHES

½ (4-ounce) package crumbled blue cheese
¼ cup butter or margarine, softened
½ (8-ounce) package cream cheese
½ cup sour cream
1 tablespoon finely chopped onion
⅛ teaspoon ground white pepper
⅛ teaspoon garlic salt
1 (12-ounce) package bacon, cooked and crumbled
12 slices pumpernickel or sourdough bread, toasted
12 ounces thinly sliced cooked roast beef
1 tablespoon chopped fresh chives
2 tomatoes, thinly sliced
1 head endive, separated

• **Combine** blue cheese and butter; set aside.
• **Combine** cream cheese and next 4 ingredients in a small saucepan; cook over low heat, stirring constantly, until blended. Cool and stir in bacon.
• **Spread** blue cheese mixture over 6 bread slices; top evenly with roast beef.
• **Spread** cream cheese mixture on remaining 6 bread slices, and sprinkle with chives. Serve open-face with tomato slices and endive leaves. **Yield:** 6 servings.

Nancy Williams
Starkville, Mississippi

FALAFEL SANDWICHES

Falafel (feh-LAH-fehl) sandwiches are to Israelis what hot dogs are to Americans.

2 (15-ounce) cans chick-peas (garbanzo beans), rinsed and drained
½ cup fine, dry breadcrumbs
4 cloves garlic, pressed
½ cup chopped fresh parsley
2 tablespoons ground cumin
1 teaspoon salt
½ teaspoon ground red pepper
2 large eggs
Vegetable oil
5 (8-inch) pita bread rounds
Tahini Sauce
Cucumber Relish

• **Position** knife blade in food processor bowl; add first 8 ingredients. Process until mixture is smooth, stopping once to scrape down sides of bowl. Shape mixture into 10 (½-inch-thick) patties.
• **Pour** oil to depth of ½ inch into a large heavy skillet; place over medium heat until hot.
• **Fry** patties in hot oil 3 to 5 minutes or until golden, turning once. Drain on paper towels.
• **Cut** pita bread rounds in half, and place 1 patty into each pita half. Top with Tahini Sauce and Cucumber Relish, and serve immediately. **Yield:** 5 servings.

Tahini Sauce

⅔ cup tahini
½ cup lemon juice
¼ cup water
2 tablespoons olive oil
½ teaspoon salt
2 cloves garlic, minced

• **Combine** all ingredients in a small bowl, stirring until blended; cover and chill. **Yield:** 1¼ cups.

Note: You can find tahini (a thick paste made of ground sesame seeds) near the peanut butter or specialty foods in most supermarkets.

Cucumber Relish

1 large cucumber, peeled, seeded, and chopped
4 plum tomatoes, chopped
2 cloves garlic, pressed
¼ cup chopped fresh parsley
2 tablespoons lemon juice
¼ teaspoon salt
¼ teaspoon pepper

• **Combine** all ingredients; cover and chill. **Yield:** 2 cups.

Sarah W. Meriwether
Montgomery, Alabama

SOUTHWESTERN CHICKEN SANDWICHES

4 skinned and boned chicken breast halves
1 to 2 tablespoons fajita seasoning
⅓ cup mayonnaise or salad dressing
2 tablespoons chopped fresh cilantro
1½ teaspoons grated lime rind
1½ tablespoons fresh lime juice
1 jalapeño pepper, seeded and minced
1 tablespoon vegetable oil
4 hamburger buns
1 tomato, sliced
4 slices purple onion
1 green bell pepper, sliced

• **Place** chicken between two sheets of heavy-duty plastic wrap, flatten to ¼-inch thickness, using a meat mallet or rolling pin. Sprinkle chicken evenly with fajita seasoning; set aside.
• **Combine** mayonnaise and next 4 ingredients; set aside.
• **Pour** oil into a large skillet; place over medium-high heat until hot. Add chicken, and cook about 4 minutes on each side.
• **Spread** mayonnaise mixture evenly on bottom halves of buns. Top with chicken, tomato, onion, additional mayonnaise mixture, bell pepper, and top halves of buns. **Yield:** 4 servings.

Bruce Messer
Middlesboro, Kentucky

Mapping Out Chiles Rellenos

If you're continually searching for great chiles rellenos, you can stop now. Here we offer two recipes that won superior ratings in our Test Kitchens. We also give you ideas for making chiles rellenos in *your* neck of the woods. (To make great salsas to serve with them, see our recipes beginning on page 14.)

SOUTHERN-STYLE CHILES RELLENOS

We enjoyed the Southern flair of this batch. How can you go wrong with cheese grits and country ham?

8 large poblano or Anaheim chile peppers
Creamy Grits
3 large eggs, lightly beaten
½ cup whipping cream
1 cup all-purpose flour
1 cup yellow cornmeal
½ teaspoon salt
Peanut oil
Country Ham Sauce
Garnishes: shredded Cheddar cheese, sliced green onions

• **Place** peppers on an aluminum foil-lined baking sheet.
• **Broil** 5½ inches from heat (with electric oven door partially opened) about 5 minutes on each side or until peppers look blistered.
• **Place** peppers in a bowl or heavy-duty, zip-top plastic bag; cover bowl with plastic wrap or seal bag. Let stand 10 minutes to loosen skins.
• **Peel** peppers; carefully cut peppers lengthwise on 1 side, leaving stems attached. Remove seeds.
• **Spoon** Creamy Grits into a large heavy-duty, zip-top plastic bag; seal. Snip a hole in one corner of bag; squeeze grits into peppers. Secure stuffed peppers with wooden picks, if desired. Cover and chill until firm.
• **Combine** eggs and whipping cream, stirring well.
• **Combine** flour, cornmeal, and salt in a shallow dish; carefully dredge peppers in cornmeal mixture, and dip into egg mixture. Dredge in cornmeal mixture again.
• **Pour** peanut oil to depth of 1 inch into a large cast-iron or heavy skillet, and heat to 375°. Fry 2 peppers at a time, cut side up, 2 minutes, turning once. Drain on paper towels, and remove wooden picks.
• **Serve** with Country Ham Sauce; garnish, if desired. **Yield:** 4 servings.

Creamy Grits

3 (10¾-ounce) cans condensed chicken broth, undiluted
½ cup whipping cream
1 cup quick-cooking grits, uncooked
2 cups (8 ounces) shredded sharp Cheddar cheese

• **Combine** chicken broth and whipping cream in a large saucepan; bring to a boil. Stir in grits, and return to a boil. Cover, reduce heat, and simmer 5 to 7 minutes. Stir in cheese. Cool 10 minutes. **Yield:** 4 cups.

Country Ham Sauce

¼ cup butter or margarine
¼ cup all-purpose flour
1 (10¾-ounce) can condensed chicken broth, undiluted
¾ cup whipping cream
¼ cup water
¼ cup chopped country ham
1 teaspoon freshly ground pepper

• **Melt** butter in a heavy saucepan over low heat; add flour, stirring until smooth. Cook, stirring constantly, 3 to 5 minutes or until lightly browned.
• **Add** broth, whipping cream, and water gradually; cook over medium heat, stirring constantly with a wire whisk, until thickened and bubbly. Stir in ham and pepper. **Yield:** 2½ cups.

Terry L. Ward
Helena, Alabama

CHEESE CHILES RELLENOS

See our "Rellenos around the Region" list on the next page for tips on dressing up these easy, delicious stuffed peppers.

8 large poblano or Anaheim chile peppers
1 (8-ounce) package Monterey Jack cheese with peppers
2 large eggs, lightly beaten
¼ cup whipping cream
¾ cup all-purpose flour
¾ cup yellow cornmeal
¼ teaspoon salt
Peanut oil

• **Place** peppers on an aluminum foil-lined baking sheet.
• **Broil** 5½ inches from heat (with electric oven door partially opened) about 5 minutes on each side or until peppers look blistered.
• **Place** peppers in a bowl or heavy-duty, zip-top plastic bag; cover bowl with plastic wrap or seal bag. Let stand 10 minutes to loosen skins.
• **Peel** peppers; carefully cut peppers lengthwise on 1 side, leaving stems attached. Remove seeds.
• **Cut** cheese into 8 long pieces; place 1 piece in each pepper cavity. Secure peppers with wooden picks, if desired.
• **Combine** eggs and whipping cream, stirring well.
• **Combine** flour, cornmeal, and salt in a shallow dish; carefully dredge peppers in cornmeal mixture, and dip into egg mixture. Dredge peppers in cornmeal mixture again.
• **Pour** oil to depth of 1 inch into a large cast-iron or heavy skillet, and heat to 375°. Fry 2 peppers at a time, cut side up, 2 minutes, turning once. Drain on paper towels, and remove wooden picks. Serve immediately with salsa. **Yield:** 4 servings.

Rellenos Around the Region

When making chiles rellenos, think about what you have left over in your refrigerator that you can use in the fillings. Use these flavorful regional fillings for personalizing the recipe for Cheese Chiles Rellenos on the previous page.

You'll need about ½ cup filling per poblano (which is mild to moderately hot in flavor) and ¼ cup filling per Anaheim (milder; closer in flavor to a green bell pepper).

- **El Paso Rellenos (traditional):** ground beef or pork, raisins, olives, cinnamon, slivered almonds, garlic
- **Yazoo City (Mississippi) Rellenos:** catfish and wild rice
- **New Orleans Rellenos:** red beans and rice
- **Kansas City Rellenos:** shredded barbecued beef and baked beans
- **Chesapeake Bay Rellenos:** blue crab and corn
- **Louisville Rellenos:** pot roast and carrots
- **Breaux Bridge (Louisiana) Rellenos:** crawfish étouffée and rice
- **Chinatown (Washington, D.C.) Rellenos:** chicken-fried rice with sweet-and-sour sauce
- **Miami Rellenos:** stone crab and finely chopped Homestead tomatoes
- **Memphis Rellenos:** rib meat, dry rub, and cornbread
- **Vidalia (Georgia) Rellenos:** ham and chopped Vidalia onion
- **Greensboro (North Carolina) Rellenos:** barbecued chicken with vinegar slaw
- **Austin Rellenos:** red bean chili
- **Lafayette (Louisiana) Rellenos:** jambalaya
- **Key West Rellenos:** jerk pork and yellow rice
- **Santa Fe Rellenos:** black beans, goat cheese, pine nuts, roasted red bell pepper

Warm Up to Salads

Add warmth to your cool salads. Chicken Caesar Salad or Warm Potato-and-Sausage Salad can easily become the main course. So take the chill off with these recipes.

Warm Potato-and-Sausage Salad

3 pounds red potatoes
4 green onions, sliced
½ cup chopped dill pickle
¼ cup chopped fresh parsley
1 pound kielbasa sausage, sliced
½ cup olive oil, divided
¼ cup white wine vinegar
3 cloves garlic, pressed
1 tablespoon chopped fresh tarragon or 1 teaspoon dried tarragon
1 tablespoon Dijon mustard
1 teaspoon freshly ground pepper
½ teaspoon salt

• **Cook** potatoes in boiling water to cover in a Dutch oven 10 to 15 minutes or until tender; drain and cool slightly. Cut into 1-inch pieces.
• **Combine** potato, green onions, dill pickle, and parsley in a large bowl.
• **Cook** sausage in 1 tablespoon oil in Dutch oven over medium-high heat 4 minutes or until browned; drain. Stir sausage into potato mixture.
• **Combine** remaining oil, vinegar, and next 5 ingredients in Dutch oven; bring to a boil over medium heat. Pour over potato mixture; toss gently to coat. **Yield:** 6 servings.

Edith Askins
Greenville, Texas

BAKED GOAT CHEESE SALAD

(pictured on page 37)

"Goat cheese releases more flavor when it's warm and creamy," says Paula Lambert, founder of Mozzarella Company in Dallas.

3 sprigs fresh rosemary
3 sprigs fresh thyme
3 sprigs fresh oregano
½ cup olive oil
1 (11-ounce) log fresh goat cheese
½ teaspoon Dijon mustard
3 tablespoons balsamic vinegar
¼ teaspoon salt
¼ teaspoon freshly ground pepper
½ cup dry breadcrumbs
½ bunch watercress, trimmed
½ head Bibb lettuce, torn
1 small head radicchio, torn
Garnish: fresh thyme sprigs

• **Combine** first 4 ingredients in a small saucepan over medium-high heat. Bring to a boil; remove from heat, and let cool.
• **Cut** cheese log into 8 rounds, and place rounds on a plate; drizzle with oil mixture. Let stand 30 minutes.
• **Pour** oil from cheese into a bowl; discard herbs. Chill cheese rounds 15 minutes or until firm.
• **Add** mustard and next 3 ingredients to oil, stirring with a wire whisk.
• **Coat** cheese with breadcrumbs; place on a baking sheet. Bake at 350° for 10 minutes; set aside.
• **Combine** greens in a bowl; drizzle with oil mixture, tossing to coat. Place on four individual salad plates; top each serving with 2 cheese rounds. Garnish, if desired. **Yield:** 4 servings.

Paula Lambert
Mozzarella Company
Dallas, Texas

CHICKEN CAESAR SALAD

4 skinned and boned chicken breast halves
1½ teaspoons lemon-pepper seasoning
1 teaspoon garlic powder
¼ cup olive oil
2 tablespoons white wine vinegar
1 teaspoon Dijon mustard
½ teaspoon Worcestershire sauce
1 head romaine lettuce, torn
1 cup garlic croutons
¼ cup grated Parmesan cheese

• **Cut** chicken into ¼-inch strips; sprinkle with lemon-pepper seasoning and garlic powder.
• **Pour** olive oil into a large skillet, and place over medium-high heat until hot. Add chicken strips, and cook 4 to 5 minutes or until done. Remove chicken strips, and drain on paper towels, reserving drippings in skillet.
• **Combine** vinegar, mustard, and Worcestershire sauce; add to reserved drippings. Cook over medium heat, stirring until blended. Pour over romaine lettuce; add chicken, and toss gently. Sprinkle with croutons and cheese; serve immediately. **Yield:** 4 servings.

L. J. Richard
Church Point, Louisiana

NUT'N BETTER

Crack the case on ho-hum salads, crunchless breads, and dull appetizers with these nuttier-than-usual recipes. Nuts add flavor and crunch to otherwise ordinary foods. Toasting them heightens their flavor and crispness even more. To toast, spread chopped nuts on a shallow pan, and bake at 350° for 5 to 10 minutes (bake 10 to 15 minutes for halves and whole nuts). Stir occasionally and watch closely because they burn easily.

PINE NUT, RICE, AND FETA SALAD

1 (7-ounce) package long-grain-and-wild rice mix
1 (4-ounce) package crumbled feta cheese
½ cup chopped green bell pepper
½ cup chopped yellow bell pepper
½ cup chopped onion
⅔ cup pine nuts, toasted
1 (2-ounce) jar diced pimiento, drained
⅓ cup olive oil
2 tablespoons tarragon wine vinegar
⅛ teaspoon pepper
Lettuce leaves (optional)

• **Cook** rice according to package directions; let cool.
• **Combine** cheese, and next 5 ingredients in a large bowl; stir in rice.
• **Combine** oil, vinegar, and pepper, stirring well; pour over rice mixture. Toss gently. Cover and chill up to 24 hours. Serve on lettuce leaves, if desired. **Yield:** 6 to 8 servings.

Betty Joyce Mills
Birmingham, Alabama

CORN-AND-WALNUT SPREAD

2 (8-ounce) packages cream cheese, softened
¼ cup fresh lime juice
1 tablespoon ground cumin
1 teaspoon salt
1 teaspoon ground black pepper
½ teaspoon ground red pepper
1 (8-ounce) can whole kernel corn, drained
1 cup chopped walnuts, toasted
1 (4.5-ounce) can chopped green chiles, drained
4 green onions, chopped

• **Combine** all ingredients; cover and chill up to 8 hours. Serve with crackers, or use as a stuffing for celery or cherry tomatoes. **Yield:** 4 cups.

Carrie Easley
Dallas, Texas

JALAPEÑO NUT MIX

1 cup whole almonds
1 cup pecan halves
1 cup dry roasted peanuts
1 cup Brazil nuts
¼ cup butter or margarine
⅓ cup jalapeño pepper sauce
1 tablespoon hot sauce
1 tablespoon Worcestershire sauce
1½ teaspoons garlic powder
1½ teaspoons salt
1 teaspoon dry mustard

• **Combine** first 4 ingredients in a 15- x 10- x 1-inch jellyroll pan.
• **Bake** at 325° for 10 minutes.
• **Combine** butter and next 6 ingredients in a saucepan; cook over medium heat, stirring constantly, until butter melts.
• **Pour** butter mixture over nuts, stirring to coat. Bake 20 additional minutes, stirring once. Spread nuts on paper towels to cool. **Yield:** 4 cups.

BOURBON-PECAN BREAD

3 cups all-purpose flour
4 teaspoons baking powder
1½ teaspoons salt
1 cup sugar
¼ cup butter or margarine
2 teaspoons grated orange rind
1½ cups chopped pecans, divided
1 cup milk
½ cup bourbon
1 large egg, lightly beaten
2 tablespoons bourbon

• **Combine** first 4 ingredients in a bowl; cut in butter with pastry blender until mixture is crumbly. Add orange rind and 1¼ cups pecans.
• **Combine** milk, ½ cup bourbon, and egg, stirring well; add to dry ingredients, stirring just until moistened. Pour batter into a greased and floured 9- x 5- x 3-inch loafpan. Sprinkle with remaining ¼ cup pecans.
• **Bake** at 350° for 50 to 60 minutes or until a wooden pick inserted in center comes out clean. Cool in pan on a wire rack 10 minutes; remove from pan, and cool completely on wire rack.
• **Drizzle** with 2 tablespoons bourbon. **Yield:** one 9-inch loaf.

Mrs. L. Mayer
Richmond, Virginia

WAKE-UP CALLS WORTH CELEBRATING

A bountiful late-morning meal, simply presented, satisfies both family and friends. This collection of recipes puts an innovative spin on familiar breakfast favorites. The menu suggestions accompanying each recipe make the rest of your meals easy to plan. These recipes are worth getting up for.

BROCCOLI-CHICKEN MUFFINS

Hot baked apples are the perfect side dish with these hearty brunch muffins.

2 cups biscuit and baking mix
⅓ cup grated Parmesan cheese
½ teaspoon freshly ground pepper
¼ teaspoon salt
¼ teaspoon garlic powder
1 large egg, lightly beaten
1 cup buttermilk
2 tablespoons vegetable oil
1 cup chopped cooked broccoli
1 cup chopped cooked chicken

• **Combine** first 5 ingredients in a large bowl; make a well in center of mixture.
• **Combine** egg, buttermilk, and oil; add to dry ingredients, stirring just until moistened. Stir in broccoli and chicken. Spoon into greased muffin pan, filling to top.
• **Bake** at 425° for 20 to 22 minutes. Remove from pan immediately. **Yield:** 1 dozen.

GINGERBREAD PANCAKES

These pancakes received rave reviews in our Test Kitchens. Team them with parfaits made from fresh berries and yogurt.

1 cup all-purpose flour
2 teaspoons baking powder
½ teaspoon salt
1 tablespoon sugar
1 tablespoon ground cinnamon
½ teaspoon ground ginger
¼ teaspoon ground allspice
⅛ teaspoon ground nutmeg
⅛ teaspoon ground cloves
1 large egg, lightly beaten
1 cup buttermilk
3 tablespoons butter or margarine, melted
1 tablespoon molasses

• **Combine** first 9 ingredients in a large bowl; make a well in center of mixture.
• **Combine** egg and next 3 ingredients; add to dry ingredients, stirring just until moistened.
• **Spoon** about 2 tablespoons batter onto a hot, lightly greased griddle. Repeat procedure with remaining pancake batter.
• **Cook** pancakes until tops are covered with bubbles and edges look cooked; turn and cook other side. Serve with Orange Marmalade Syrup. **Yield:** 10 pancakes.

Orange Marmalade Syrup

⅔ cup maple syrup
⅓ cup orange marmalade

• **Combine** ingredients in a small saucepan, and bring to a boil, stirring constantly. **Yield:** 1 cup.

Joel Allard
San Antonio, Texas

BRUNCH POPOVER PANCAKE

Complete with fruit and the "pancake," this recipe needs little else served with it. If you want a heavier meal, consider serving it with scrambled eggs and bacon or thinly sliced ham.

4 large eggs, lightly beaten
1 cup milk
1 cup all-purpose flour
¼ teaspoon salt
⅓ cup butter or margarine, melted
3 tablespoons orange marmalade
3 tablespoons butter or margarine
1 tablespoon lemon juice
1 (16-ounce) package frozen sliced peaches, thawed and drained
1 cup frozen blueberries, thawed

• **Place** a well-greased 12-inch cast-iron skillet in a 425° oven for 5 minutes.
• **Combine** first 5 ingredients, stirring with a wire whisk until blended.
• **Remove** skillet from oven. Pour batter into hot skillet.
• **Bake** at 425° for 20 to 25 minutes. (This resembles a giant popover and will fall quickly after removing from oven.)
• **Combine** marmalade, 3 tablespoons butter, and lemon juice in a saucepan; bring to a boil. Add peaches, and cook over medium heat 2 to 3 minutes, stirring constantly.
• **Spoon** mixture on top of baked pancake. Sprinkle with blueberries. **Yield:** 4 servings.

Bunny Campbell
Gainesville, Florida

GRITS PUDDING

Serve slices of country ham with this cousin to rice pudding. Add blueberry muffins and fresh grapefruit juice to round out the menu. For more kick, add grenadine syrup to the grapefruit juice.

1 cup water
¼ teaspoon salt
¼ cup quick-cooking grits, uncooked
2 cups milk
1 tablespoon butter or margarine
2 large eggs
¼ cup sugar
⅓ cup raisins
Ground nutmeg (optional)

• **Bring** water and salt to a boil in a heavy saucepan; gradually stir in grits. Cook 4 to 5 minutes, stirring occasionally. Gradually stir in milk; return to a boil. Remove from heat. Add butter; set aside.
• **Beat** eggs and sugar until frothy. Gradually stir about one-fourth of hot mixture into eggs; add to remaining hot mixture, stirring constantly. Stir in raisins.
• **Pour** mixture into a lightly greased 1½-quart baking dish. Place in a large pan. Add hot water to pan to depth of 1 inch.
• **Bake** at 350° for 1 hour, stirring at 20-minute intervals. Sprinkle with nutmeg, if desired. **Yield:** 4 to 6 servings.

Ruth D. Whitehead
West Columbia, South Carolina

NUTMEG: A SPICE OF LIFE

Whole nutmeg, the warm, comforting spice that enhances many recipes, springs from the spice rack and begs to be grated. One whole nutmeg yields about 1 tablespoon of grated spice.

QUICK 'N' EASY CUSTARD PIE

2 cups milk
3 large eggs
½ cup sugar
¾ teaspoon vanilla extract
¼ teaspoon freshly ground nutmeg
Dash of salt
1 unbaked 9-inch pastry shell
Freshly ground nutmeg

• **Heat** milk in a medium saucepan until hot. (Do not boil.)
• **Combine** eggs and sugar; beat at high speed with an electric mixer until thickened. Add vanilla, ¼ teaspoon nutmeg, and salt; beat until blended. Gradually stir in hot milk, stirring constantly. Pour into pastry shell; sprinkle with additional nutmeg.
• **Bake** on lower oven rack at 400° for 25 minutes or until a knife inserted in center comes out clean. Cool on a wire rack; cover and chill at least 2 hours before serving. **Yield:** one 9-inch pie.

Claudine M. Moore
Lenoir, North Carolina

POP GRAHAM MUNCHIES

10 cups popped popcorn
3 cups honey graham cereal
2 cups miniature marshmallows
1½ cups golden raisins
½ cup butter or margarine
¼ cup firmly packed brown sugar
1½ teaspoons ground cinnamon
¼ teaspoon ground ginger
¼ teaspoon freshly ground nutmeg

• **Combine** first 4 ingredients in a large roasting pan. Set aside.
• **Combine** butter and next 4 ingredients in a small saucepan; cook over low heat, stirring constantly, until butter melts. Pour over popcorn mixture, tossing to coat.
• **Bake** at 325° for 20 minutes, stirring every 5 minutes.
• **Pour** onto wax paper, and let cool. **Yield:** about 3 quarts.

RESOLUTION SOLUTIONS

Now that the holidays are over, you may find yourself regretting the many trips you made to the Christmas buffet. But the high-fat habit will be easy to break when you make these flavorful, nearly fat-free recipes part of your New Year's resolution.

VEGETABLE STIR-FRY PASTA

8 ounces angel hair pasta, uncooked
¾ cup vegetable broth, divided
⅓ cup reduced-sodium soy sauce
3 tablespoons dry white wine
1 tablespoon cornstarch
2 teaspoons minced fresh ginger
1 teaspoon garlic powder
2 carrots
2 stalks celery
1 onion
1 red bell pepper
4 small yellow squash
8 mushrooms
3 green onions
1 teaspoon olive oil
2 cups broccoli flowerets

• **Cook** pasta according to package directions, omitting salt and fat; drain and keep warm.
• **Combine** ½ cup broth and next 5 ingredients, stirring well; set aside.
• **Cut** carrots, celery, onion, and bell pepper into thin slices; cut squash in half lengthwise, and cut into thin slices. Slice mushrooms and green onions.
• **Pour** oil around top of a wok or large nonstick skillet, coating sides; place over medium-high heat. Add carrot, celery, onion, and bell pepper; stir-fry 5 minutes.
• **Stir** in remaining ¼ cup broth, squash, mushrooms, green onions, and broccoli; stir-fry 5 additional minutes or until tender.
• **Stir** in broth mixture; boil 1 minute. Serve over pasta. **Yield:** 4 servings.

Tami Summerour
Little Mountain, South Carolina

❤ Per serving: Calories 326 (8% from fat)
Fat 3g (0.4g saturated) Cholesterol 0mg
Sodium 699mg Carbohydrate 64.2g
Fiber 7.5g Protein 12.7g

MARGE CLYDE'S BLACK BEAN SOUP

1 pound dried black beans
4 hot peppers in vinegar, finely chopped
½ cup chopped onion
¼ teaspoon minced garlic
½ cup fresh lemon juice
3 (14¼-ounce) cans reduced-sodium fat-free chicken broth
1½ cups chopped onion
1 tablespoon minced garlic
Vegetable cooking spray
1 (10-ounce) can diced tomatoes and green chiles, undrained
½ teaspoon pepper
½ teaspoon hot sauce
⅔ cup cooked rice

• **Sort** and wash beans; place beans in a large Dutch oven. Cover with water to depth of 2 inches above beans; let soak overnight. Drain beans, and set aside.
• **Combine** hot peppers and next 3 ingredients; cover and chill.
• **Cook** chicken broth and beans in Dutch oven over medium-high heat 2½ hours, adding hot water as needed to keep beans covered with liquid.
• **Cook** onion and garlic in a skillet coated with cooking spray over medium-high heat, stirring constantly, until tender. Reduce heat, and add tomatoes, pepper, and hot sauce; cook 5 additional minutes.
• **Position** knife blade in food processor bowl; add tomato mixture and 2 cups beans. Pulse 3 times or until blended; add to remaining beans.
• **Spoon** 2 tablespoons rice into each individual bowl; ladle 1½ cups soup over rice. Top each serving evenly with hot pepper mixture. **Yield:** 5 servings.

Marge Clyde
San Antonio, Texas

❤ Per serving: Calories 422 (5% from fat)
Fat 2.4g (0.4g saturated) Cholesterol 0mg
Sodium 520mg Carbohydrate 76.8g
Fiber 13.3g Protein 21.9g

Watch Out for Fat

FAT FREE, NOT CALORIE FREE

Don't be sold on every food label that screams fat free because labels can be misleading. Be sure that you always check these labels for the serving size and the number of calories. For 60 calories you can have one fat-free cookie that you probably will devour in only two bites. For the exact same number of calories and still no fat, you could have 2 whole cups of air-popped popcorn, 9 stalks of celery, or 20 cherry tomatoes.

▪ You probably won't solve your weight problem by eating just foods with less fat. People gain weight because they take in more calories than they actually burn off. Consume 3,500 extra calories and you'll be 1 pound heavier. *Extra* calories end up as *extra* weight, whether they're coming from butter, bananas, or fat-free cookies.

▪ Fresh vegetables and fruits have a tiny amount of fat because they contain many fat-soluble vitamins like E and K. But the quantity of fat in these foods is so minuscule that you're safe in assuming they are virtually fat free. (Avocados are the exception to this rule.)

BETTER LIVING

Linda Sutton of Winston-Salem, North Carolina, has always tried to eat healthy foods and exercise on a regular basis. But in the last year, she's stepped up her routine. Linda shares her suggestions for better living.

▪ The busier you are, the more energy you'll have. Try roller skating, bicycling, walking, Jazzercise, raking leaves, and washing windows. All these activities are easy and inexpensive, and they'll make you feel healthier.

▪ Cutting back on fat is a lot easier if you enjoy eating fruits, vegetables, and grains. If you feel you must have meat with every meal, gradually decrease the amount of meat and increase the vegetables and grains.

▪ Some of the hardest things to give up are things you love the most, like bread, butter, and sweets. Whatever you decide to give up, make it a reward when you've exercised more than usual.

▪ Drink lots of water throughout the day. It keeps you from becoming dehydrated during strenuous exercise and helps make you feel full.

▪ Cut back on buying processed foods. You'll save money and maximize nutrition. Quality produce, flavored vinegars, and salsas add diversity to meals.

CHEESECAKE WITH RASPBERRY-LEMON SAUCE

Vegetable cooking spray
¾ cup graham cracker crumbs, divided
3 (8-ounce) packages nonfat cream cheese, softened
1½ cups sugar, divided
1 cup egg substitute
1 tablespoon grated lemon rind
1 teaspoon vanilla extract
4 egg whites
⅓ cup nonfat sour cream
1 (12-ounce) package frozen unsweetened raspberries, thawed
1 teaspoon freshly grated lemon rind
1½ teaspoons fresh lemon juice

• **Coat** bottom and sides of a 9-inch springform pan with cooking spray; sprinkle with ½ cup graham cracker crumbs, and set aside.

• **Beat** cream cheese at medium speed with an electric mixer until smooth. Gradually add ¾ cup sugar to cream cheese, beating well. Add egg substitute, lemon rind, and vanilla, beating until blended.

• **Beat** egg whites at high speed until soft peaks form; gently fold into cream cheese mixture. Pour batter into prepared pan.

• **Bake** at 350° for 45 minutes or until lightly browned.

• **Combine** ¼ cup sugar and sour cream; spread over cheesecake, and sprinkle with remaining ¼ cup graham cracker crumbs.

• **Bake** at 450° for 5 minutes. Remove from oven; let cool completely. Gently run a knife around edge of pan to release sides; cover and chill at least 4 hours.

• **Combine** raspberries and ½ cup sugar in a small saucepan; cook over medium-low heat, stirring constantly, until sugar dissolves. Pour mixture through a wire-mesh strainer into a bowl, discarding solids. Stir in lemon rind and lemon juice. Serve sauce with cheesecake. **Yield:** 8 servings.

Sandi Pichon
Slidell, Louisiana

♥ Per serving: Calories 308 (4% from fat)
Fat 1.4g (0.2g saturated) Cholesterol 15mg
Sodium 542mg Carbohydrate 56.3g
Fiber 3.4g Protein 18.5g

FEBRUARY

A NEW LOOK AT MEAT & POTATOES

What a pity that these Southern supper mainstays – meat and potatoes – often get a bad rap. Sure, they're comforting, but they're usually bland, overcooked, heavy, or *boring,* some scoff. These recipes might change that.

ROASTED PORK LOIN

You'll love what the garlic-ginger marinade does for this tender pork.

½ cup soy sauce
¼ cup vegetable oil
2 tablespoons molasses
1 tablespoon ground ginger
2 teaspoons dry mustard
6 cloves garlic, minced
1 (4- to 5-pound) rolled boneless pork loin roast

• **Combine** first 6 ingredients in a bowl, stirring with a wire whisk until blended.
• **Remove** pork loin halves from elastic net. (There should be 2 pieces.) Trim excess fat from pork. Place pork in a shallow dish or heavy-duty, zip-top plastic bag; pour soy sauce mixture over pork, turning to coat. Cover and chill at least 8 hours.
• **Remove** pork loin from marinade, reserving marinade. Place pork loin halves together, and secure with string. Place in a greased roasting pan.
• **Bake** at 325° for 2 hours or until meat thermometer inserted in thickest portion registers 160°, brushing with remaining marinade during first hour of cooking. **Yield:** 10 to 12 servings.

Myrna M. Ruiz
Marietta, Georgia

FILLET OF BEEF WITH RED PEPPER BUTTER

⅓ cup butter, softened
¼ cup finely chopped red bell pepper
¾ teaspoon seasoned salt
¼ to ½ teaspoon ground red pepper
2 (2½-inch-thick) beef tenderloin steaks

• **Combine** first 4 ingredients, stirring well. Shape into 4 (2-inch) rounds on a wax paper-lined baking sheet; cover and chill 1 hour or until firm.
• **Place** beef tenderloin steaks on a rack in broiler pan.
• **Broil** 5½ inches from heat (with electric oven door partially opened) 6 minutes. Turn steaks over, and top each with a butter round.
• **Broil** 6 to 7 additional minutes (with electric oven door partially opened) or until a meat thermometer registers 145° (rare), 160° (medium), or to desired degree of doneness. Turn steaks over, and transfer to a serving platter; top with remaining butter rounds. **Yield:** 2 servings.

Kira F. Giffin
Houston, Texas

FLAVORFUL FLANK STEAK

1 tablespoon butter or margarine
¼ cup chopped onion
1 clove garlic, minced
½ teaspoon chili powder
½ cup tomato sauce
2 tablespoons white vinegar
1 tablespoon honey
¼ teaspoon salt
¼ teaspoon pepper
1 (1½-pound) flank steak (¾ inch thick)

• **Melt** butter in a medium saucepan over medium-high heat; add onion, garlic, and chili powder, and cook, stirring constantly, until onion is tender.
• **Stir** in tomato sauce and next 4 ingredients; bring to a boil. Reduce heat, and simmer 5 minutes or until slightly thickened; cool.
• **Make** ¼-inch-deep cuts on both sides of steak; place steak in a shallow dish or heavy duty, zip-top plastic bag. Pour tomato sauce mixture over steak, turning to coat. Cover or seal, and chill at least several hours.
• **Cook** steak, without grill lid, over medium-hot coals (350° to 400°) about 7 minutes on each side or to desired degree of doneness. Slice diagonally across grain to serve. **Yield:** 4 servings.

Karen Peacock
Black Mountain, North Carolina

ORANGE MASHED POTATOES

¼ cup butter or margarine
2 cups finely chopped onion
3 pounds baking potatoes
½ cup sour cream
¾ cup orange juice
1 teaspoon salt
Garnish: orange zest

• **Melt** butter in a large skillet over medium-high heat; add onion, and cook, stirring constantly, until browned. Set aside.
• **Peel** potatoes; cut into fourths.
• **Cook** potato in boiling water to cover 15 minutes or until potato is tender; drain.
• **Beat** potato, sour cream, and orange juice at medium speed with an electric mixer until mixture is fluffy. Stir in onion and salt. Garnish, if desired. **Yield:** 8 servings.

Margert Stewart
Murfreesboro, Tennessee

These flavor-packed recipes grant you permission to indulge.

We're sure that after pairing your favorite meat with your favorite potato dish, all you closet meat-and-potatoes lovers will be pleased and redeemed.

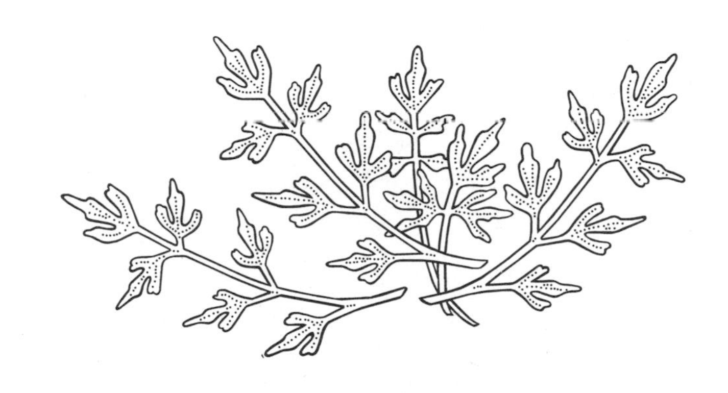

SOUTHWESTERN POTATO BOATS

3 baking potatoes (about 1½ pounds)
1 (14.5-ounce) can chili-style stewed tomatoes, drained
½ cup chopped purple onion
2 tablespoons chopped fresh cilantro
2 tablespoons minced jalapeño pepper
¾ teaspoon salt
¼ teaspoon pepper
1½ teaspoons vegetable oil
1½ teaspoons white vinegar
¼ teaspoon minced garlic
¼ pound bacon, cooked and crumbled
1 (8-ounce) package shredded colby-Monterey Jack cheese blend

• **Pierce** potatoes with a fork, and bake at 350° for 1 hour or until done. Let potatoes cool to touch.
• **Cut** potatoes in half lengthwise, and scoop out pulp, leaving ¼-inch-thick shells. Reserve pulp for another use.
• **Combine** tomatoes and next 8 ingredients; stir in bacon and cheese.
• **Bake** potato shells at 350° for 5 to 8 minutes or until lightly browned; spoon tomato mixture evenly into shells. Bake 10 to 15 additional minutes or until cheese melts. **Yield:** 6 servings.

CHEESY SCALLOPED POTATOES

2½ pounds red potatoes
3 tablespoons butter or margarine
⅓ cup chopped green onions
⅓ cup chopped red bell pepper
1 clove garlic, minced
¼ teaspoon ground red pepper
2 cups whipping cream
¾ cup milk
¾ teaspoon salt
¼ teaspoon freshly ground pepper
1 cup (4 ounces) shredded Swiss cheese
¼ cup grated Parmesan cheese

• **Cut** potatoes into ⅛-inch-thick slices; set aside.
• **Melt** butter in a Dutch oven over medium-high heat; add green onions and next 3 ingredients. Cook 2 minutes, stirring constantly. Add whipping cream and next 3 ingredients, stirring mixture well.
• **Add** potato slices; bring to a boil over medium heat, and cook 15 minutes or until potato slices are tender, stirring gently. Spoon into a lightly greased 11- x 7- x 1½-inch baking dish; sprinkle with cheeses.
• **Bake** at 350° for 45 minutes or until bubbly and golden. Let stand 15 minutes before serving. **Yield:** 8 servings.

Lee Wells
Knoxville, Tennessee

Handing Down Cornbread: From "Ma E" To Me

Chef Johnny Earles of the Florida Panhandle goes home to Louisiana, where his passion for cooking – and his hankering for cornbread – began. There, the chef-owner of the famed Criolla's restaurant near Destin, pays tribute to his grandmother Mildred Earles.

SOUFFLÉ CORNBREAD

(pictured on page 40)

Don't be scared by the term soufflé. It just means Johnny separates the eggs and folds the beaten whites into the batter as you would in a soufflé. He also "juices" the corn with a food processor: "There's so much flavor locked up in those kernels."

1 (28-ounce) package frozen whole kernel corn, thawed *
6 tablespoons butter or margarine, softened
2 large eggs, separated
½ cup whipping cream
1½ cups yellow cornmeal
1 cup all-purpose flour
1 tablespoon baking powder
1½ teaspoons salt
⅓ cup sugar
Vegetable cooking spray

• **Position** knife blade in food processor bowl; add corn to bowl. Process 1 to 2 minutes or until juicy. Pour corn through a wire-mesh strainer into a 2-cup liquid measuring cup, discarding solids in strainer. (You'll need 1¼ cups corn liquid. If liquid doesn't readily separate from solids in processing, combine ¾ cup processed corn and ½ cup milk.)
• **Beat** butter and egg yolks in a large mixing bowl at medium speed with an electric mixer until smooth. Add corn liquid and whipping cream, stirring well. (Mixture will be lumpy.)
• **Combine** cornmeal and next 4 ingredients; add to corn mixture, stirring until blended.
• **Heat** a 10-inch cast-iron skillet in a 375° oven for 5 to 10 minutes.
• **Beat** egg whites at high speed until stiff peaks form; fold into cornmeal mixture.
• **Remove** skillet from oven; coat with cooking spray. Pour cornmeal mixture into skillet.
• **Bake** at 375° for 25 minutes or until golden. **Yield:** 8 servings.

* Substitute 2 (15¼-ounce) cans whole kernel corn or 5½ cups fresh corn kernels (8 to 10 ears) for frozen corn.

ROASTED QUAIL ÉTOUFFÉE

(pictured on page 40)

Johnny gives this oven method for roasting quail, but when he has time, he loves to put them on the smoker. If you don't hunt your own quail, you can mail-order them from Quail International at 1-800-843-3204.

1 medium potato, peeled and cut into ½-inch pieces
1 large fresh leek, chopped
4 cups loosely packed fresh spinach
1 tablespoon vegetable oil
½ teaspoon salt
¼ teaspoon ground black pepper
8 quail, dressed
8 large plum tomatoes
½ cup vegetable oil
½ cup all-purpose flour
1½ cups chopped onion
½ cup finely chopped green bell pepper
½ cup finely chopped celery
2 cloves garlic, minced
4 bay leaves
3 cups chicken broth
2 teaspoons salt
2 teaspoons fresh thyme or ¾ teaspoon dried thyme
1 teaspoon Worcestershire sauce
½ teaspoon sugar
⅓ cup chopped green onions
2 tablespoons chopped fresh parsley
2 teaspoons ground black pepper
½ teaspoon ground red pepper
2 teaspoons hot sauce
Soufflé Cornbread (see recipe)

• **Cook** potato in boiling water to cover 8 minutes or until tender; drain and cool.
• **Cook** leek and spinach in 1 tablespoon oil in a large skillet over medium heat, stirring constantly, 3 minutes or until wilted; cool.
• **Combine** potato, leek mixture, ½ teaspoon salt, and ¼ teaspoon pepper; spoon into cavities of quail. Place 1 leg over the other, and secure with a

wooden pick. Place quail and tomatoes in a large roasting pan.

• **Bake** at 400° for 45 minutes; cool tomatoes slightly. Chop tomatoes, reserving liquid; set aside.

• **Pour** ½ cup oil into a large skillet or Dutch oven; place over medium-high heat until very hot. Add flour, and cook, stirring constantly, 2 to 3 minutes or until golden (do not burn).

• **Add** 1½ cups onion and next 4 ingredients; cook 4 to 5 minutes or until onion is tender. Gradually add chicken broth, stirring constantly.

• **Add** tomato, reserved liquid, 2 teaspoons salt, and next 3 ingredients; bring to a boil. Reduce heat, and simmer, uncovered, 1 hour.

• **Stir** in green onions and next 4 ingredients. Add quail, breast side up; simmer 15 minutes. Remove and discard bay leaves. Serve quail mixture over Soufflé Cornbread. **Yield:** 8 servings.

VICKSBURG CORNBREAD

(pictured on page 40)

Johnny named this for his memories of the years when he traveled from his childhood home in Vicksburg, Mississippi, to visit "Ma E" just to get some of her cornbread.

2 tablespoons bacon drippings
1 cup all-purpose flour
1 cup yellow cornmeal
1 tablespoon baking powder
1 teaspoon salt
1 cup milk
1 large egg
5 ounces Gouda cheese, cut into cubes (optional)
¼ cup finely chopped green onions (optional)

• **Place** bacon drippings in a 10-inch cast-iron skillet, tilting pan to coat bottom evenly; heat in a 375° oven for 10 minutes.

• **Combine** flour and next 3 ingredients in a bowl. Combine milk and egg, stirring well. Add to flour mixture, stirring just until dry ingredients are moistened. Stir in cheese and green onions, if desired.

• **Pour** hot drippings from skillet into batter; stir until blended. Pour batter into skillet.

• **Bake** at 375° for 20 minutes or until done. Immediately remove from skillet. **Yield:** 8 servings.

Note: Omit the cheese and green onions when preparing cornbread for dressing.

"MA E"'S LEGACY

"Ma E," as she is affectionately called, made food the center of Johnny's life. When you dine at Criolla's, that grandmotherly influence is elusive. From ambience to menu, this refined yet relaxed place is the essence of Caribbean/Creole, offering adventurous dishes no one's ever seen at Sunday dinner. But amid a plate of glorious fresh seafood, tropical fruits and vegetables, and exotic spices, you'll likely find the surprisingly comfortable foods Johnny grew up eating at Ma E's table: mashed potatoes, cheese grits, and cornbread. That's when you get a glimpse into this chef's soul.

On a trip back to Bogalusa, Louisiana, to cook with Ma E, Johnny studied his family's evolution of cornbread from Ma E's traditional oyster-cornbread dressing to his creations that combine cornbread with some of his favorite childhood ingredients, like quail and butterbeans. Here he shares his favorites.

MA E'S TRADITIONAL OYSTER-CORNBREAD DRESSING

½ cup butter or margarine
½ cup chopped onion
¾ cup chopped green bell pepper
½ cup chopped celery
2 teaspoons minced garlic
3 bay leaves
1 (12-ounce) container fresh oysters, undrained
1 cup chicken broth
¼ cup chopped green onions
½ teaspoon ground black pepper
½ teaspoon ground white pepper
2 tablespoons finely chopped fresh parsley
2 teaspoons salt
2 teaspoons hot sauce
½ teaspoon dried thyme
3 large eggs
1½ cups milk
Vicksburg Cornbread (see recipe)

• **Melt** butter in a large skillet over medium-high heat; add onion and next 4 ingredients, and cook, stirring constantly, 5 minutes or until vegetables are tender.

• **Drain** oysters, reserving liquid; set oysters aside.

• **Add** oyster liquid, broth, and green onions to skillet; bring to a boil. Reduce heat, and simmer 5 minutes, stirring occasionally; remove from heat.

• **Stir** in oysters, black pepper, and next 5 ingredients. Remove and discard bay leaves.

• **Beat** eggs and milk in a bowl. Crumble cornbread into milk mixture. Add oyster mixture, stirring well. Pour into a lightly greased 11- x 7- x 1½-inch baking dish.

• **Bake** at 350° for 45 minutes or until top is lightly browned. **Yield:** 8 to 10 servings.

BUTTERBEANS, BACON, AND TOMATOES
(pictured on page 40)

3 slices bacon, chopped
1 cup finely chopped onion
3 cloves garlic, minced
1 bay leaf
¾ cup chopped green bell pepper
7 plum tomatoes, seeded and chopped
4 cups chicken broth
4 cups fresh or frozen butterbeans, thawed
2 tablespoons finely chopped fresh parsley
1 teaspoon salt
1 teaspoon pepper
1 teaspoon Worcestershire sauce
½ teaspoon hot sauce
Vicksburg Cornbread (see recipe, page 35)

• **Cook** bacon in a skillet over medium heat, stirring constantly, 8 minutes or until crisp. Add onion, garlic, and bay leaf; cook 3 minutes or until onion is tender, stirring often.
• **Add** bell pepper; cook 3 minutes, stirring often. Add tomato, and cook 3 minutes, stirring constantly.
• **Add** broth and butterbeans; bring to a boil. Cover, reduce heat, and simmer 30 minutes, stirring occasionally.
• **Simmer,** uncovered, 20 minutes, stirring often. Stir in parsley and next 4 ingredients. Cook 5 minutes, stirring often. Remove and discard bay leaf. Serve over Vicksburg Cornbread. **Yield:** 6 servings.

ROOT OF THE MATTER

Add gusto to meals with parsnips, beets, and turnips. They're easy on the budget and available year-round. Here are new ways to try these often overlooked vegetables as side dishes.

Surprise your family with Fried Parsnips instead of French fries, and serve Beet Fritters instead of hash browns. Your family will love the flavors, and you'll be glad you unearthed buried treasures.

FRIED PARSNIPS

12 medium parsnips (about ¾ pound), scraped
¾ cup fine, dry breadcrumbs
¾ teaspoon salt
1 teaspoon pepper
Vegetable oil

• **Cook** whole parsnips in boiling water to cover 20 minutes or until tender; drain. Cut parsnips into 3- x ½-inch strips.
• **Combine** breadcrumbs, salt, and pepper in a large heavy-duty, zip-top plastic bag; add parsnips, a few at a time, shaking bag to coat.
• **Pour** oil to depth of 3 inches into a Dutch oven, and heat to 375°. Fry parsnips, a few at a time, 1 minute. Drain on paper towels; serve immediately. **Yield:** 4 servings.

Sibyl White
Woodstock, Georgia

PARSNIP-CARROT MEDLEY

¾ cup water
1 pound carrots, scraped and shredded
1 pound parsnips, scraped and shredded
2 tablespoons butter or margarine
1 tablespoon maple syrup
1 teaspoon dried tarragon
½ teaspoon salt
¼ teaspoon pepper

• **Bring** water to a boil in a large saucepan; add carrot and parsnip. Cover and cook 5 to 7 minutes or until crisp-tender, stirring twice. Stir in butter and remaining ingredients; serve immediately. **Yield:** 8 servings.

Cathy Darling
Grafton, West Virginia

TURNIP-AND-CARROT STIR-FRY

1 pound turnips
2 carrots
1 medium onion
2 tablespoons butter or margarine
2 tablespoons sugar

• **Peel** turnips, and cut into thin slices. Scrape carrots; cut carrots and onion into slices.
• **Melt** butter in a large skillet over medium-high heat; add turnip, carrot, and onion. Cook, stirring constantly, 15 minutes or until tender.
• **Stir** in sugar, and cook, stirring constantly, until vegetables are lightly glazed. Serve immediately. **Yield:** 3 servings.

Jean Brodhagen
Tulsa, Oklahoma

BEET FRITTERS

2 cups peeled, shredded beet (about ⅔ pound) *
¼ cup finely chopped onion
½ cup soft breadcrumbs
1 large egg, beaten
¼ teaspoon ground ginger
¼ teaspoon salt
⅛ teaspoon pepper
Vegetable oil
Sour cream

• **Combine** first 7 ingredients in a bowl; toss well.
• **Pour** oil to depth of ¼ inch into a large heavy skillet; cook over medium-high heat until hot. Spoon ¼ cup beet mixture into hot oil; flatten slightly. Repeat with remaining beet mixture.
• **Cook** 4 to 5 minutes on each side or until done. Drain on paper towels; top with sour cream. **Yield:** 8 fritters.

* Substitute 2 cups peeled, shredded rutabaga for beets.

Agnes L. Stone
Ocala, Florida

You'll love the contrast of warm cheese and crisp, cool greens in Baked Goat Cheese Salad (recipe, page 26).

Beef Stew, a salad with Green Onion Dressing, and Sour Cream Cornbread will satisfy the heartiest appetites. (Recipes begin on page 16.)

Above: *Cozy up to the fire with Cream of Pimiento Soup and Seasoned Breadsticks. (Recipes begin on page 45.) The soup recipe doubles easily if you want to invite friends.*

Left: *Crunchy Sprout Salad (recipe, page 45) tumbles from a colorful, leafy bowl of radicchio.*

Right: *Two Southern favorites, Roasted Quail Étouffée with Soufflé Cornbread (recipes, page 34), team up for a comforting down-home meal.*

Cornbread moves from the bread basket to center stage when rich Butterbeans, Bacon, and Tomatoes (recipe, page 36) are served over hot-from-the-skillet Vicksburg Cornbread (recipe, page 35).

With cooked rice as the star ingredient, Spicy Shrimp Casserole (top) dazzles with ease and creamy flavor, while Hoppin' John Salad rings of fluffy tradition. (Recipes begin on page 62.)

Tropical Salsa, recipe, page 14

Tomato Salsa, recipe, page 15

Peach Salsa, recipe, page 14

Avocado-Feta Salsa, recipe, page 15

Sweet-'n'-Hot Apple Chutney, recipe, page 14

Corn-Black Bean Salsa, recipe, page 15

Left: *Gazpacho Aspic (recipe, page 65) brings chopped vegetables into clear, delicious view.*

Below: *In Marshall, Texas, Crêpes Con Queso (recipe, page 48) are The Taylor House's signature dish. And no wonder – the spicy cheese filling makes them fabulous.*

A great catch, Chesapeake Bay Crab Cakes With Jalapeño Tartar Sauce (recipe, page 69), make living light easy.

A Warm Winter Supper

Put another log on the fire and plump up the pillows: This easy dinner for four is served by the hearth – with no knives required.

Set the stage by opening the meal with a delicious rosy Cream of Pimiento Soup. Then bring forth the rest of the meal, course by course, for a cozy and leisurely evening.

CREAM OF PIMIENTO SOUP

(pictured on page 39)

1 (4-ounce) jar diced pimiento, undrained
2 tablespoons butter or margarine
2½ tablespoons all-purpose flour
1 (14½-ounce) can ready-to-serve chicken broth
1½ cups half-and-half
2 teaspoons grated onion
½ teaspoon salt
¼ teaspoon hot sauce

• **Place** pimiento in container of an electric blender, and process until smooth, stopping once to scrape down sides. Set pimiento aside.
• **Melt** butter in a heavy saucepan over low heat; add flour, and stir until mixture is smooth. Cook 1 minute, stirring constantly.
• **Add** chicken broth and half-and-half gradually to flour mixture; cook over medium heat, stirring constantly, until mixture is thickened and bubbly.
• **Stir** in pimiento, onion, salt, and hot sauce; cook over low heat, stirring constantly, until thoroughly heated. **Yield:** 3¾ cups.

Note: You can easily double the recipe to serve 8.

Eugenia W. Bell
Lexington, Kentucky

SALMON-AND-VEGETABLE RAGOÛT

2 tablespoons olive oil, divided
2 tablespoons butter or margarine, divided
4 (6-ounce) salmon fillets (1½ inches thick)
⅛ teaspoon salt
⅛ teaspoon pepper
⅓ cup chopped purple onion
¼ cup chopped green bell pepper
2 green onions, cut diagonally into 1-inch pieces
2 tablespoons minced garlic
1 tablespoon chopped fresh cilantro
1 (11-ounce) can diced tomatoes and green chiles, undrained
1 (8-ounce) bottle clam juice
½ cup dry white wine
½ teaspoon salt
⅛ teaspoon pepper
Hot cooked rice
Garnishes: sliced green onions, chopped fresh cilantro, lemon wedges

• **Combine** 1 tablespoon olive oil and 1 tablespoon butter in an 11- x 7- x 1½-inch baking dish; place in a 375° oven for 5 minutes or until butter is lightly browned.
• **Sprinkle** fillets with ⅛ teaspoon salt and ⅛ teaspoon pepper; place salmon in baking dish, skin side up.
• **Bake** at 375° for 15 to 20 minutes or until fish flakes easily when tested with a fork, turning once. Remove and discard skin; break salmon into 1½-inch pieces.
• **Heat** remaining 1 tablespoon olive oil and 1 tablespoon butter in a heavy saucepan over medium-high heat until butter melts; add purple onion and next 3 ingredients, and cook, stirring constantly, 3 minutes or until tender.
• **Stir** cilantro and next 5 ingredients into onion mixture; bring to a boil. Cook 10 to 15 minutes or until reduced to 1½ cups, stirring occasionally.
• **Add** salmon, and cook just until thoroughly heated, stirring gently. Serve over rice; garnish, if desired. **Yield:** 4 servings.

Carolynn St. Pierre
Winter Haven, Florida

CRUNCHY SPROUT SALAD

(pictured on page 39)

1 (3-ounce) package chicken ramen noodle soup mix
¼ cup vegetable oil
1½ tablespoons rice wine vinegar
1 tablespoon sesame oil
1 teaspoon chili-flavored oil
1 (3.2-ounce) package enoki mushrooms
2 carrots, scraped and shredded
1 cucumber, peeled, seeded, and chopped
½ cup bean sprouts
¼ pound fresh snow pea pods, cut into thin strips
1 avocado, peeled, seeded, and chopped
4 leaves radicchio or red cabbage
¼ cup sesame seeds, toasted

• **Place** noodles in a 9-inch square pan; discard seasoning packet.
• **Bake** at 375° for 7 minutes or until browned, stirring twice. Cool.
• **Combine** vegetable oil and next 3 ingredients, stirring with a wire whisk until blended.
• **Combine** half of noodles, mushrooms, and next 5 ingredients. Add oil mixture; toss gently to coat.
• **Place** radicchio on individual serving plates; spoon vegetable mixture evenly on radicchio. Sprinkle with remaining noodles and sesame seeds. **Yield:** 4 servings.

Daisy Trippeer
Germantown, Tennessee

LOTS OF VEGETABLES

Sue George's creamed corn, made from frozen shoepeg corn, lets you prepare a family favorite on a weeknight. Or serve Betsi Goode's bean salad for supper tonight, and then have the leftovers with chips for lunch tomorrow. With these vegetable dishes added to your repertoire, you can liberate yourself from frozen fries and canned peas.

SEASONED BREADSTICKS

(pictured on page 39)

1 (11-ounce) can refrigerated breadsticks
Olive oil
1 teaspoon chili powder
½ teaspoon ground cumin

• **Unroll** dough onto a large cutting board; cut dough crosswise into thirds. Separate dough into 24 pieces; stretch each piece to 11 inches, and place ¼ inch apart on cutting board. Brush dough lightly with olive oil.
• **Combine** chili powder and cumin; sprinkle evenly over dough. Twist ends of dough pieces in opposite directions 3 or 4 times. Place breadsticks 1 inch apart on ungreased baking sheets, pressing ends securely.
• **Bake** at 350° for 12 to 14 minutes or until golden. Transfer to wire racks to cool. **Yield:** 2 dozen.

Caryn Hogan
Birmingham, Alabama

BANANAS GLACÉ

⅓ cup light rum
⅓ cup apricot preserves
2 tablespoons butter or margarine
2 large firm bananas
Vanilla ice cream
Garnishes: dried apricot halves, fresh mint leaves

• **Combine** first 3 ingredients in a small skillet; cook over medium heat until butter melts.
• **Peel** bananas, and cut in half lengthwise. Cut each half into 6 pieces; add to skillet.
• **Cook** over low heat until thoroughly heated, stirring occasionally. Serve banana mixture immediately over vanilla ice cream; garnish, if desired. **Yield:** 4 servings.

Rita W. Cook
Corpus Christi, Texas

FREEZER-FRESH CREAMED CORN

3 (16-ounce) packages frozen shoepeg corn, partially thawed and divided
½ cup butter or margarine
1¾ to 2 cups milk
1½ to 2 teaspoons salt
½ teaspoon pepper

• **Position** knife blade in food processor bowl; add 1 package corn. Process until smooth, stopping once to scrape down sides.
• **Melt** butter in a heavy skillet over medium heat; stir in pureed corn, remaining 2 packages corn, milk, salt, and pepper. Bring to a boil, stirring constantly; reduce heat, and simmer 20 minutes or until desired thickness, stirring often. **Yield:** 10 to 12 servings.

Sue George
Birmingham, Alabama

HOME-COOKED POLE BEANS

2 pounds fresh pole beans, trimmed
3 slices bacon
1 cup water
1 teaspoon salt
¼ teaspoon pepper
¼ teaspoon sugar

• **Cut** beans into 1½-inch pieces, and set aside.
• **Cook** bacon in a large saucepan until crisp; remove bacon, reserving 2 tablespoons drippings in pan. Crumble bacon, and set aside.
• **Add** water and next 3 ingredients to saucepan; bring to a boil over high heat. Add beans; cover, reduce heat to medium, and cook 15 minutes or to desired degree of doneness. Sprinkle with crumbled bacon. **Yield:** 6 to 8 servings.

Louise Crawford
Coldwater, Mississippi

SPICY BEAN SALAD

1 (15-ounce) can Great Northern beans, rinsed and drained
1 (15-ounce) can black beans, rinsed and drained
4 plum tomatoes, chopped
1 medium-size green bell pepper, chopped
¾ cup chopped green onions
½ cup salsa
¼ cup red wine vinegar
2 tablespoons chopped fresh cilantro
½ teaspoon salt
½ teaspoon pepper

• **Combine** all ingredients; cover and chill 2 hours. **Yield:** 6 servings.

Betsi Goode
Arlington, Texas

PINEAPPLE-ORANGE SWEET POTATOES

1½ pounds sweet potatoes
1 (15¼-ounce) can sliced pineapple, drained
½ cup orange juice
½ cup orange marmalade
¼ cup raisins (optional)

• **Bake** sweet potatoes at 400° for 50 minutes or until done; cool.
• **Peel** and cut sweet potatoes into ⅓-inch slices; cut pineapple slices in half. Alternate sweet potato and pineapple

slices in a lightly greased 8-inch square baking dish.
• **Combine** orange juice, marmalade, and raisins, if desired, in a small saucepan; cook over low heat 5 minutes, stirring occasionally. Pour over sweet potato and pineapple slices.
• **Bake** at 350° for 15 minutes. **Yield:** 6 servings.

Feast Without Meat

These meatless main dishes are every bit as satisfying as meat-laden entrées. Whether you're looking for a cooktop supper solution that's quick or a make-ahead brunch idea for visitors, these three recipes are guaranteed to charm even the staunchest meat lover.

MUSHROOM CASSEROLE

¼ cup butter or margarine
1½ pounds fresh mushrooms, sliced *
1 large onion, chopped
½ cup chopped celery
½ cup chopped green pepper
½ cup mayonnaise or salad dressing
8 slices white bread, cut into 1-inch pieces
2 large eggs, lightly beaten
1½ cups milk
1 (10¾-ounce) can cream of mushroom soup, undiluted
1 cup freshly grated Romano cheese

• **Melt** butter in a large skillet or Dutch oven. Add mushrooms and next 3 ingredients, and cook over medium heat, stirring constantly, until tender; drain well. Stir in mayonnaise.
• **Place** half of bread evenly into a lightly greased 13- x 9- x 2-inch baking dish. Spoon mushroom mixture evenly over bread. Top with remaining bread.
• **Combine** eggs and milk; pour over bread pieces. Cover and chill at least 8 hours.
• **Pour** soup over casserole; top with cheese.
• **Bake** at 350° for 1 hour or until thoroughly heated and bubbly. **Yield:** 6 servings.

* You can substitute gourmet mushrooms like shiitake, crimini, and portabello. Be sure to chop the portabello mushrooms.

Yvonne M. Greer
Mauldin, South Carolina

VEGETABLE LASAGNA

Sunny Tiedemann serves any leftover slices of this garden-fresh favorite chilled. "It's even better the second day," she says.

10 lasagna noodles, uncooked
2 cups sliced fresh mushrooms
1 cup grated carrot (about 1 large)
½ cup chopped onion
1 tablespoon olive oil
1 (15-ounce) can tomato sauce
1 (12-ounce) can tomato paste
1 (4¼-ounce) can chopped ripe olives, drained
1 (4½-ounce) can chopped green chiles, undrained
1½ teaspoons dried oregano
2 cups cottage cheese
1 (10-ounce) package frozen chopped spinach, thawed and well drained
4 cups (16 ounces) shredded Monterey Jack cheese
1 (3-ounce) package refrigerated grated Parmesan cheese

• **Cook** noodles according to package directions. Drain and set aside.
• **Cook** mushrooms, carrot, and onion in olive oil over medium-high heat, stirring constantly, until tender. Stir in tomato sauce and next 4 ingredients.
• **Place** half of cooked lasagna noodles in a greased 13- x 9- x 2-inch baking dish or pan. Layer with half each of cottage cheese, spinach, tomato sauce mixture, Monterey Jack cheese, and Parmesan cheese. Repeat layers.
• **Bake** at 375° for 45 minutes or until bubbly. Let stand 10 minutes before serving. **Yield:** 8 servings.

Sunny Tiedemann
Bartlesville, Oklahoma

PASTA WITH GREENS

Toasted pine nuts add satisfying crunch to this meatless entrée.

1 (8-ounce) package fettuccine
1 (16-ounce) package frozen collards or other greens
2 to 3 cloves garlic, minced
3 tablespoons olive oil
½ teaspoon salt
¼ teaspoon freshly ground pepper
½ cup freshly grated Parmesan cheese
⅓ cup pine nuts, toasted
Garnishes: freshly grated Parmesan cheese, toasted pine nuts

• **Cook** pasta according to package directions; drain and set aside.
• **Cook** greens according to package directions; drain and set aside.
• **Cook** garlic in olive oil in a large skillet over medium-high heat until tender, but not brown. Add greens, salt, and pepper; cook until heated.
• **Combine** pasta, greens, ½ cup Parmesan cheese, and ⅓ cup pine nuts in a large serving bowl. Garnish, if desired. **Yield:** 2 main-dish or 4 side-dish servings.

Melinda Clement
Kingsville, Texas

DINING AT THE TAYLOR HOUSE

In Marshall, Texas, the flavors of France mingle with the taste of Texas. There at The Taylor House, Odile Besseau and Durfee Bedsole serve country French cooking with a Southern accent.

CRÊPES CON QUESO

(pictured on page 43)

1 cup all-purpose flour
½ cup yellow cornmeal
1 tablespoon chili powder
1 teaspoon salt
1 cup chicken broth
3 large eggs
Vegetable cooking spray
Crêpe Filling
1 cup (4 ounces) shredded Cheddar cheese
Garnish: fresh cilantro sprig

• **Position** knife blade in food processor; add first 6 ingredients. Process until smooth. Chill at least 2 hours.
• **Coat** an 8-inch nonstick skillet with cooking spray; place over medium heat until hot. Pour ⅓ cup batter into pan; quickly tilt pan in all directions so batter covers bottom of pan. Cook 1 minute or until crêpe can be shaken loose from pan. Turn crêpe over; cook about 30 seconds. Place on a towel to cool. Repeat with remaining batter.
• **Spoon** about ½ cup Crêpe Filling on half of each crêpe; roll up, and place, seam side down, in a lightly greased 13- x 9- x 2-inch baking dish. Sprinkle crêpes evenly with cheese.
• **Bake** at 300° for 5 minutes or until cheese melts. Garnish, if desired. **Yield:** 4 servings.

Crêpe Filling

1 tablespoon butter or margarine
1 large onion, coarsely chopped
1 green bell pepper, coarsely chopped
1 red bell pepper, coarsely chopped
1 bunch green onions, sliced
4 cloves garlic, minced
2 (4½-ounce) cans chopped green chiles, drained
1½ cups whipping cream
1 cup (4 ounces) shredded Swiss cheese
2½ cups shredded cooked chicken
2 teaspoons Cajun poultry seasoning blend
¼ teaspoon salt
¼ teaspoon pepper

• **Melt** butter in a large skillet over medium heat; add chopped onion and next 4 ingredients, and cook, stirring constantly, 5 minutes or until tender.
• **Stir** in chiles and whipping cream; bring to a boil. Reduce heat, and simmer 15 minutes.
• **Stir** in cheese and remaining ingredients; cook 3 minutes. **Yield:** 4 cups.

Note: For Cajun poultry seasoning blend, we used Chef Paul Prudhomme's Poultry Magic.

TAYLOR HOUSE MUFFINS

Serve these with apple butter, butter, and strawberry preserves.

2½ cups all-purpose flour
1 tablespoon baking powder
½ teaspoon salt
⅓ cup sugar
2 large eggs, lightly beaten
½ cup milk
½ cup vegetable oil
1 teaspoon vanilla extract

• **Combine** first 4 ingredients in a bowl; make a well in center.
• **Combine** eggs and next 3 ingredients, stirring mixture well; add to dry ingredients, and stir just until moistened. Spoon batter into greased muffin pans, filling two-thirds full.
• **Bake** at 350° for 20 minutes. Remove from pans immediately; cool on wire racks. **Yield:** 1 dozen.

DURFEE'S BREAD PUDDING

1 (16-ounce) loaf French bread
½ cup raisins
6 large eggs, lightly beaten
4 cups milk
2 tablespoons butter or margarine, melted
1½ cups sugar
½ teaspoon almond extract
¼ teaspoon vanilla extract
⅓ cup slivered almonds, toasted

• **Cut** bread into 1¼-inch-thick slices; place in a single layer in a lightly greased 13- x 9- x 2-inch baking dish. Sprinkle with raisins.
• **Combine** eggs and next 5 ingredients; pour over bread, and let stand 30 minutes.
• **Sprinkle** almonds over egg mixture; place dish in a large pan. Add hot water to pan to depth of 1 inch.
• **Bake** at 350° for 45 minutes or until a knife inserted in center comes out clean, shielding with aluminum foil after 30 minutes to prevent excessive browning. Serve warm with whipped cream. **Yield:** 12 to 15 servings.

QUICK & EASY

A Flash in the Pan

You're just home from work, and you need dinner in a flash. Any of these entrées will be ready in the time it takes to microwave the frozen vegetables.

SCALLOPS IN VERMOUTH-CREAM SAUCE

1 pound sea scallops
2 tablespoons all-purpose flour
2 tablespoons butter or margarine
¼ cup dry vermouth
½ cup whipping cream
¼ teaspoon salt
⅛ teaspoon pepper

• **Coat** scallops with flour; set aside.
• **Melt** butter in a large skillet over medium heat; add scallops. Cook 3 to 4 minutes or until scallops are opaque, stirring occasionally. Remove scallops from skillet.
• **Add** vermouth to skillet, stirring to loosen particles from bottom of skillet. Bring to a boil; cook 3 minutes or until reduced by half. Stir in whipping cream, salt, and pepper; reduce heat to low. Add scallops; cook just until thoroughly heated. **Yield:** 2 main-dish servings or 4 appetizer servings.

Elaine C. Heintz
Staunton, Virginia

LEMON CHICKEN

4 skinned and boned chicken breast halves
½ cup all-purpose flour
¼ cup butter or margarine
2 tablespoons minced garlic
1 cup apple juice
2 tablespoons lemon juice
½ teaspoon pepper

• **Coat** chicken with flour; set aside.
• **Melt** butter in a large skillet over medium heat; add chicken and garlic. Cook 8 minutes or until chicken is browned on both sides, turning once. Remove chicken from skillet, and keep warm.
• **Add** apple juice, lemon juice, and pepper to skillet, stirring to loosen particles from bottom of skillet. Bring to a boil; cook 10 minutes or until reduced to ½ cup. Pour over chicken; serve immediately. **Yield:** 4 servings.

Marge Killmon
Annandale, Virginia

TURKEY-BASIL PICCATA

2 tablespoons all-purpose flour
¼ teaspoon salt
¼ teaspoon pepper
1 (¾-pound) package turkey cutlets
2 tablespoons olive oil
4 cloves garlic, minced
1½ teaspoons dried basil or 1½ tablespoons chopped fresh basil
½ cup dry white wine
1½ tablespoons fresh lemon juice
1 lemon, sliced

• **Combine** first 3 ingredients in a shallow dish; dredge cutlets in flour mixture, shaking off excess.
• **Pour** olive oil into a large skillet; place over medium-high heat until hot. Add cutlets, and cook 1½ minutes or until done, turning once. Remove cutlets from skillet.
• **Add** garlic and basil to skillet; cook 45 seconds, stirring to loosen particles from bottom of skillet. Add wine, lemon juice, and lemon slices; cook 45 seconds, stirring constantly. Return cutlets to pan; cook just until thoroughly heated. Serve immediately. **Yield:** 3 to 4 servings.

Deborah Holley
Patterson, Louisiana

KUNG PAO PORK

1 small red bell pepper
½ small onion
¾ pound lean pork
¼ cup soy sauce, divided
¼ cup water
2 tablespoons lemon juice
2 tablespoons sugar
2 teaspoons cornstarch
¼ teaspoon dried crushed red pepper
2 tablespoons olive oil
2 cloves garlic, minced
¼ cup unsalted roasted peanuts
Hot cooked rice

• **Cut** bell pepper and onion into 1-inch pieces; set aside. Cut pork into ½-inch cubes; drizzle with 2 tablespoons soy sauce.
• **Combine** remaining 2 tablespoons soy sauce, water, and next 4 ingredients, stirring until blended; set aside.
• **Pour** olive oil around top of a preheated wok or large skillet, coating sides; heat at medium-high (375°) 2 minutes. Add pork and garlic; stir-fry 3 minutes or until lightly browned. Add bell pepper and onion; stir-fry 3 minutes or until vegetables are tender.
• **Add** soy sauce mixture; stir-fry 2 minutes or until thickened. Stir in peanuts, and serve over rice. **Yield:** 3 servings.

Sandra Enwright
Winter Park, Florida

TIME-SAVERS

■ Use 1 teaspoon dried herbs for 1 tablespoon chopped fresh herbs.

■ Buy precut packaged meats for marinating and stir-frying.

■ Cook more pasta or rice than you need. Drain and toss excess lightly with oil, and store in zip-top plastic bags in refrigerator up to three days. To serve, reheat in boiling water just until heated.

KNEAD TO DO BREADS

Spend time kneading, punching, rolling, and shaping dough. Then be prepared to share. When you make Saffron Bread, Whole Wheat Rolls, or Oatmeal-Cinnamon-Pecan Rolls, the tantalizing aroma will lure everyone within range.

SAFFRON BREAD

Saffron is the world's most expensive spice. To be economical substitute 2 teaspoons turmeric for 1/4 teaspoon saffron in this recipe. We liked both versions.

2½ cups warm milk (105° to 115°), divided
2 packages active dry yeast
8 cups all-purpose flour, divided
1½ cups sugar
¼ teaspoon salt
¼ teaspoon ground saffron
¾ cup butter, melted
1 large egg, lightly beaten
1 cup slivered almonds
1 cup golden raisins
2 tablespoons butter, melted
2 teaspoons sugar
Additional slivered almonds (optional)

• **Combine** ½ cup warm milk and yeast in a 1-cup liquid measuring cup; let stand 5 minutes.
• **Combine** remaining 2 cups milk, 1 cup flour, sugar, and next 4 ingredients; add almonds and raisins. Stir in yeast mixture.
• **Add** remaining flour, 1 cup at a time, stirring after each addition until smooth. Place dough in a large well-greased bowl, turning to grease top.
• **Cover** and let rise in a warm place (85°), free from drafts, 2 hours or until doubled in bulk.
• **Turn** dough out onto a well-floured surface, and knead 5 minutes or until smooth.
• **Divide** dough in half. Divide each half into 3 portions. Shape each portion into an 18-inch rope. Pinch loose ends of ropes at 1 end to seal; braid ropes. Repeat procedure with remaining half of dough. Place braids on greased baking sheets.
• **Cover** and let rise in a warm place (85°), free from drafts, 30 minutes or until doubled in bulk.
• **Brush** braids with 2 tablespoons melted butter; sprinkle with 2 teaspoons sugar and additional slivered almonds, if desired.
• **Bake** at 400° for 25 to 30 minutes, covering with aluminum foil after 20 minutes to prevent excessive browning. **Yield:** 2 loaves.

Note: For a variation, shape dough into 3 dozen S-shaped rolls. Bake at 400° for 10 to 13 minutes.

Kathy Seaberg
St. Petersburg, Florida

WHOLE WHEAT ROLLS

2 packages active dry yeast
½ cup warm water (105° to 115°)
2¾ cups all-purpose flour
2 cups whole wheat flour
¼ cup firmly packed brown sugar
2 teaspoons salt
2 large eggs
1 (12-ounce) container small-curd cottage cheese
3 tablespoons butter, softened

• **Combine** yeast and warm water in a 1-cup liquid measuring cup; let stand 5 minutes.
• **Combine** flours, brown sugar, and salt; set aside.
• **Combine** eggs, cottage cheese, and butter in a large bowl; beat at medium speed with an electric mixer until well blended. Add yeast mixture; gradually beat in flour mixture to make a soft dough.
• **Turn** dough out onto a well-floured surface, and knead until smooth and elastic (about 5 minutes). Place dough in a well-greased bowl, turning to grease top.
• **Cover** and let rise in a warm place (85°), free from drafts, 2 hours or until doubled in bulk.
• **Punch** dough down, and divide into thirds. Shape each portion of dough into 12 balls. Place dough in greased muffin pans.
• **Cover** and let rise in a warm place (85°), free from drafts, 30 minutes or until doubled in bulk.
• **Bake** at 375° for 12 minutes. **Yield:** 3 dozen.

Note: Store Whole Wheat Rolls in an airtight container up to 1 month.

Marie P. Stone
Wicomico Church, Virginia

OATMEAL-CINNAMON-PECAN ROLLS

1 package active dry yeast
¼ cup warm water (105° to 115°)
1 cup milk
1 cup sugar, divided
1 teaspoon salt
⅓ cup butter
2 large eggs
4 to 4½ cups all-purpose flour
1 cup quick-cooking oats, uncooked
⅓ cup butter, melted
⅓ cup dark corn syrup
1¼ cups firmly packed brown sugar, divided
¾ cup chopped pecans, toasted
2 tablespoons butter or margarine, softened
2 teaspoons ground cinnamon

• **Combine** yeast and warm water in a 1-cup liquid measuring cup; let stand 5 minutes.
• **Combine** milk, ½ cup sugar, salt, and ⅓ cup butter in a saucepan; cook over low heat until butter melts, stirring occasionally. Cool to 105° to 115°.

• **Combine** yeast mixture, milk mixture, eggs, and 1 cup flour in a mixing bowl; beat at medium speed with an electric mixer until well blended. Gradually stir in oats and enough remaining flour to make a soft dough.
• **Turn** dough out onto a well-floured surface, and knead until smooth and elastic (about 10 minutes). Place dough in a well-greased bowl, turning to grease top.
• **Cover** and let rise in a warm place (85°), free from drafts, 1 hour or until doubled in bulk.
• **Punch** dough down; cover and let rest 10 minutes.
• **Combine** ⅓ cup melted butter, corn syrup, and ¾ cup brown sugar, stirring until blended. Spoon evenly into two 9-inch square pans. Sprinkle with pecans.
• **Divide** dough in half. Roll each portion into a 12-inch square. Spread each with 1 tablespoon softened butter, leaving a ½-inch border.
• **Combine** cinnamon, remaining ½ cup sugar, and remaining ½ cup brown sugar; sprinkle over dough.
• **Roll** up dough, jellyroll fashion, pressing firmly to eliminate air pockets; pinch seams to seal. Cut each roll into 12 (1-inch) slices, and place in prepared pans.
• **Cover** and let rise in a warm place (85°), free from drafts, 45 minutes or until doubled in bulk.
• **Bake** at 375° for 20 minutes or until golden. Invert onto plates. **Yield:** 2 dozen.

Donna Campbell
Huntsville, Alabama

From Our Kitchen to Yours

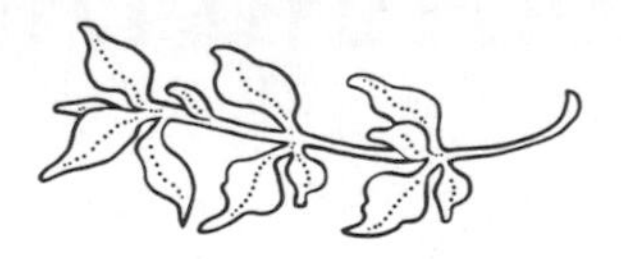

BAYING AT THE SPOON

To ease the task of fishing out elusive bay leaves in soup pots with a spoon, try these reader hints. Lila Hughes of Richardson, Texas, suggested using ground bay leaves. She orders the product from Pendery's (1-800-533-1870).

Jacqueline T. Graves sent our favorite comment: "Why remove them? We've had a fun tradition at our house for many years. Whoever finds the bay leaf in the soup bowl gets 24 hours of good luck or an extra piece of dessert, finder's choice. (But a less amusing technique is to take a mortar and pestle to the leaves before cooking.)"

GO AHEAD: BUY A LEMON

▪ Buy a whole bag while you're at it. Not only can you drop a wedge of citrus flavor into a drink anytime, but you can also use lemons for routine kitchen cleanup.

▪ After chopping garlic and onions for dinner, your hands sometimes still bear the evidence hours later. Squeeze and rub a lemon half over your fingers right after handling the strong scents for a quick recovery.

▪ After squeezing fresh lemons for recipes, grind the rinds in the garbage disposal to clean out that impossible-to-reach appliance.

▪ Atlanta reader Fay Brewer makes a "lemon scrubbie" to clean her wooden cutting boards. She fills a squeezed lemon half with salt and vigorously rubs it, cut side down, over the board for an abrasive, citrusy natural cleaner. Finish with soap and hot water.

GRATE SAVE

When you're busy trying to get a meal on the table, some of the last-minute details you forget are the ones you can't see – such as the rolls or biscuits hiding in a dark oven. Just as a scorched reminder wafts its way to the table, someone looks at you and states the obvious: "Is something burning?"

If you can't convince them that black-bottomed biscuits are the latest rage, gently scrape the flat, burned undersides against a fine-toothed grater to remove most of the mistake. Do this over the sink; it's messy.

A FINE-TINED FINISH

Whether you serve dessert on fine china or on casual plates, an easy garnish of sifted powdered sugar or cocoa will dress up a sweet finale.

Simply spoon a tablespoon or so of powdered sugar or cocoa into a fine wire-mesh strainer or sifter, lay a fork on the front of the plate, and gently shake the powder over it. Carefully lift the fork straight up to avoid smearing the design; then set a slice of pie or cake on the blank part of the plate. And just to avoid an optical confusion, go ahead and put the *real* dessert forks at each place before bringing out the plates.

P.S. For a little variety to your design, check the baking aisle at the grocery store for Domino's flavored powdered sugars in 1-pound boxes: chocolate (light brown), lemon (off-white), and strawberry (pale pink).

Rise and Dine

One of the best things about a weekend away is indulging in breakfast at your leisure. These signature recipes from bed-and-breakfasts and country inns across the South give you a taste of that luxury – even if you have to cook it yourself. Pair the recipes with ideas for a Bloody Mary bar, and you've got a party.

LUMP CRAB HASH WITH THREE-PEPPER HOLLANDAISE

(pictured on page 77)

This recipe gets its title from the blend of pink, green, and white peppercorns Chef Ken Vedrinski uses in the hollandaise sauce. If you don't have a peppercorn blend, substitute black pepper.

1 large red potato, peeled and cubed
1 medium-size sweet potato, peeled and cubed
1 large red bell pepper
2 tablespoons butter
1 cup chopped purple onion
1 large tomato, peeled, seeded, and chopped
1 pound fresh jumbo lump crabmeat, drained
2 green onions, chopped
¾ teaspoon salt
¾ teaspoon pepper
8 poached eggs
Three-Pepper Hollandaise

• **Cook** potatoes in boiling water to cover 4 to 5 minutes or until almost tender; drain and set aside.

• **Place** bell pepper on an aluminum foil-lined baking sheet.

• **Broil** pepper 5½ inches from heat (with electric oven door partially opened) about 5 minutes on each side or until pepper looks blistered.

• **Place** pepper in a plastic bag; seal and let stand 10 minutes to loosen skin. Peel pepper; remove and discard seeds. Coarsely chop pepper, and set aside.

• **Melt** butter in a skillet or Dutch oven over medium-high heat; add potato and 1 cup onion, and cook, stirring constantly, until onion is tender.

• **Add** bell pepper, tomato, and next 4 ingredients; cook until thoroughly heated. Spoon hash onto individual serving plates; place poached eggs onto hash, and top with Three-Pepper Hollandaise. **Yield:** 4 servings.

Three-Pepper Hollandaise

3 egg yolks, lightly beaten
⅓ cup dry white wine
1 tablespoon lemon juice
1 teaspoon Worcestershire sauce
1 teaspoon freshly ground mixed peppercorns
1 cup butter, melted

• **Combine** first 5 ingredients in top of a double boiler; bring water to a boil over high heat. Reduce heat to low; cook, stirring constantly with a wire whisk, 4 minutes or until a thermometer registers 160°. Remove from heat immediately.

• **Add** butter in a thin stream, whisking until blended. **Yield:** 1 cup.

Chef Ken Vedrinski
Woodlands Resort and Inn
Summerville, South Carolina

STUFFED FRENCH TOAST

Texans Gail Drago and Ann Ruff discovered this wonderful recipe when researching their book, Texas Historic Inns Cookbook.

1 (8-ounce) package cream cheese, softened
¼ cup crushed pineapple
½ cup chopped pecans, toasted
1 (16-ounce) loaf French bread
4 large eggs
1 cup whipping cream
½ teaspoon vanilla extract
1 teaspoon ground ginger
1 (12-ounce) jar apricot preserves
½ cup orange juice

• **Beat** cream cheese and pineapple at medium speed with an electric mixer until light and fluffy; stir in pecans.

• **Cut** bread into 12 (1½-inch-thick) slices; cut a pocket through top crust of each slice. Stuff each slice evenly with cream cheese mixture.

• **Combine** eggs and next 3 ingredients, stirring well with a wire whisk. Dip bread slices in egg mixture, coating all sides.

• **Cook** on a lightly greased griddle over medium-high heat 3 minutes on each side or until golden.

• **Combine** preserves and orange juice in a saucepan; cook over low heat, stirring constantly, until melted. Serve with hot toast. **Yield:** 6 servings.

Annie's Bed and Breakfast
Big Sandy, Texas

MORRISON HOUSE BRIOCHE

(pictured on page 77)

Don't limit this buttery bread to breakfast. It's also delicious as a sandwich or dinner roll.

4⅓ cups all-purpose flour
2 tablespoons sugar
½ package active dry yeast (1½ teaspoons)
¼ cup warm water (105° to 115°)
2 teaspoons salt
8 large eggs
1¼ cups unsalted butter, chilled and cut into pieces
1 large egg, lightly beaten

- **Combine** flour and sugar in a large mixing bowl. Make a well in center of mixture; add yeast and water in center. Let stand 5 minutes.
- **Beat** at low speed with an electric mixer until blended; add salt and 8 eggs, one at a time, beating until blended after each addition. Add butter gradually, beating well (small bits of butter will be visible). Cover and chill at least 8 hours (dough will be sticky).
- **Divide** dough into 12 portions; pinch off a 1-inch ball of dough from each portion, and set aside.
- **Roll** larger pieces into balls on a lightly floured surface; place in well-greased individual brioche molds or a muffin pan. Place molds or muffin pan on a baking sheet.
- **Make** a well in center of each ball. Shape remaining dough pieces into balls, and place in wells.
- **Brush** brioche with beaten egg; let stand 30 minutes.
- **Bake** at 350° for 30 minutes. Cool in molds 10 minutes; remove from molds. **Yield:** 1 dozen.

Morrison House
Alexandria, Virginia

BUILD A BLOODY MARY BAR

A Bloody Mary bar is a great idea for an at-home brunch buffet. Set out glasses, ice, and a dozen or more ingredients along with the vodka and tomato juice, and let guests be creative with their cocktails. Try these suggestions for your own Bloody Mary bar.

- Celery salt, margarita salt, Cajun seasoning, or dillweed can go in the drink or on the rim of the glass.
- Spice things up with hot sauces, horseradish, freshly ground black pepper, jalapeño peppers, or pepper vodka.
- Be creative with garnishes. Try lime wedges, olives, pepperoncini, green onions, pickled cherry peppers, carrot sticks, pickles, pickled mixed vegetables, cucumber spears, and, of course, celery sticks.

ARKANSAS GERMAN-BAKED PANCAKE

Innkeeper Crescent Dragonwagon published this recipe and hundreds more in her book, The Dairy Hollow House Cookbook.

3 large eggs
¾ cup milk
½ teaspoon vanilla extract
¾ cup all-purpose flour
½ teaspoon salt
1½ tablespoons butter or margarine
Apple Filling
Sifted powdered sugar
Whipped cream

- **Heat** a 12-inch cast-iron skillet in a 450° oven for 5 minutes.
- **Combine** first 3 ingredients in a mixing bowl; beat at medium speed with an electric mixer until smooth. Add flour and salt; beat 5 minutes.
- **Melt** butter in skillet; pour batter into hot skillet.
- **Bake** at 450° for 15 minutes; reduce heat to 350°, and bake 8 additional minutes or until puffed and browned. Remove from oven; spoon Apple Filling over pancake (pancake will deflate).
- **Sprinkle** with powdered sugar, and dollop with whipped cream. Cut into wedges, and serve immediately. **Yield:** 4 servings.

Apple Filling

¼ cup butter or margarine
4 large Granny Smith apples, cored and sliced
¼ cup honey

- **Melt** butter in a large skillet over medium-high heat; add apples, and cook, stirring constantly, 12 minutes or until tender. Gently stir in honey; cook just until thoroughly heated. Serve warm. **Yield:** 4 servings.

Dairy Hollow House
Eureka Springs, Arkansas

Welcoming Mugs 'N' Muffins

Bill and Tricia Kelly often play host to casual, bring-the-kids Mugs 'n' Muffins parties – "a way of meeting our neighbors and having them meet us," says Tricia.

We think that's a great idea. And for those of us outside the Kellys' corner of Greenville, South Carolina, try this muffin care package idea they sent to share. It's perfect for your own party.

RASPBERRY-STREUSEL MUFFINS

The streusel (German for "sprinkle") – a crumbly topping of flour, butter, sugar, and, in this recipe, chopped pecans – makes a delicious crown for these sweet muffins.

1¾ cups all-purpose flour, divided
2 teaspoons baking powder
½ cup sugar
1 large egg, lightly beaten
½ cup milk
½ cup butter, melted
1 cup frozen unsweetened raspberries
2 tablespoons butter or margarine, melted
¼ cup chopped pecans
¼ cup firmly packed brown sugar

• **Combine** 1½ cups flour, baking powder, and sugar in a large bowl; make a well in center of mixture.
• **Combine** egg, milk, and ½ cup butter; add to dry ingredients, stirring just until moistened. Fold in raspberries. Spoon into greased muffin pans, filling two-thirds full.
• **Combine** remaining ¼ cup flour, 2 tablespoons butter, pecans, and brown sugar; sprinkle over muffins.
• **Bake** at 375° for 20 to 25 minutes. **Yield:** 1 dozen.

ORANGE BLOSSOM MUFFINS

2 cups biscuit and baking mix
¼ cup sugar
1 large egg, lightly beaten
½ cup orange juice
2 tablespoons vegetable oil
½ cup orange marmalade
½ cup chopped pecans
3 tablespoons sugar
1 tablespoon all-purpose flour
½ teaspoon ground cinnamon
¼ teaspoon ground nutmeg

• **Combine** biscuit mix and ¼ cup sugar in a large bowl; make a well in center of mixture.
• **Combine** egg, orange juice, and oil; add to biscuit mixture, stirring just until moistened. Stir in marmalade and pecans.
• **Place** paper baking cups in muffin pans; spoon batter into cups, filling two-thirds full.
• **Combine** 3 tablespoons sugar and next 3 ingredients; sprinkle evenly over batter.
• **Bake** at 400° for 18 minutes or until done. **Yield:** 1 dozen.

CHEESE MUFFINS

These golden pillowy muffins get top marks for ease, taste, and versatility.

2 tablespoons butter or margarine, divided
½ cup chopped onion
1½ cups biscuit and baking mix
1 cup (4 ounces) shredded sharp American cheese, divided
1 large egg, lightly beaten
½ cup milk
1 tablespoon sesame seeds, toasted

• **Melt** 1 tablespoon butter in a skillet over medium-high heat; add onion, and cook, stirring constantly, 3 minutes or until tender.
• **Combine** onion, biscuit mix, and ½ cup cheese in a large bowl. Combine egg and milk; add to onion mixture, stirring just until moistened.
• **Spoon** batter into greased muffin pans, filling half-full. Sprinkle with remaining ½ cup cheese and sesame seeds; dot with remaining 1 tablespoon butter.
• **Bake** at 400° for 13 minutes or until golden. Remove muffins from pans immediately, and serve warm. **Yield:** 1 dozen.

Start With Biscuit Mix

It may already be on your shelf. If not, you can find it with the flour at your grocery store. It's so unassuming, you might not think of it as versatile and speedy, but it is. So bring out the biscuit mix and whip up one of these recipes for dinner tonight. There's a lot of good food in that box.

QUICK ROLLS

2¼ cups biscuit and baking mix, divided
1 (8-ounce) carton sour cream
½ cup butter, melted

• **Combine** 2 cups biscuit mix, sour cream, and butter, stirring well.
• **Sprinkle** remaining ¼ cup biscuit mix over work surface. Drop dough by level tablespoonfuls onto biscuit mix, and roll into balls. Place 3 balls into each of 12 greased muffin cups.
• **Bake** at 350° for 15 to 20 minutes or until rolls are golden. **Yield:** 1 dozen.

Carolyn W. Olah
Crawfordville, Florida

DILLY CHEESE MUFFINS

3 cups biscuit and baking mix
1½ cups (6 ounces) shredded Swiss cheese
1 tablespoon sugar
1 large egg
1¼ cups milk
1 tablespoon vegetable oil
1 tablespoon chopped fresh dill
½ teaspoon dry mustard
Vegetable cooking spray

• **Combine** first 3 ingredients in a large bowl; make a well in center of mixture.
• **Combine** egg and next 4 ingredients, stirring well; add to dry ingredients, stirring just until moistened.
• **Place** paper baking cups in muffin pans, and coat with cooking spray; spoon batter into cups, filling two-thirds full.
• **Bake** at 350° for 25 to 28 minutes. Remove from pans immediately, and cool on wire racks. **Yield:** 1½ dozen.

Kathy Jones
Montreal, Missouri

CHICKEN DUMPLING PIE

3 cups chopped cooked chicken or turkey
2 (10¾-ounce) cans cream of chicken soup, undiluted
1 (10½-ounce) can condensed chicken broth, undiluted
1 (15-ounce) can mixed vegetables, drained
½ teaspoon poultry seasoning
2 cups biscuit and baking mix
1 (8-ounce) carton sour cream
1 cup milk

• **Combine** first 5 ingredients in a large bowl, and pour chicken mixture into a lightly greased 13- x 9- x 2-inch baking dish.
• **Combine** biscuit mix, sour cream, and milk in a medium bowl; pour over chicken mixture.
• **Bake** at 350° for 50 to 60 minutes or until topping is golden. **Yield:** 6 to 8 servings.

Lilann Taylor
Savannah, Georgia

PEANUT BLOSSOM COOKIES

1 (14-ounce) can sweetened condensed milk
¾ cup creamy peanut butter
1 teaspoon vanilla extract
2 cups biscuit and baking mix
⅓ cup sugar
1 (9-ounce) package milk chocolate kisses, unwrapped

• **Combine** milk and peanut butter, stirring until smooth; stir in vanilla. Add biscuit mix, stirring well.
• **Shape** dough into 1-inch balls; roll in sugar, and place on ungreased cookie sheets. Make an indentation in the center of each ball with thumb or spoon handle.
• **Bake** at 375° for 8 to 10 minutes or until lightly browned. Remove cookies from oven, and press a kiss in center of each cookie. Remove to wire racks to cool completely. **Yield:** 4 dozen.

Ann Elsie Schmetzer
Madisonville, Kentucky

PRETTY IN PINK

Bring the sunshine inside with pink grapefruit. Although its color ranges from very pale pink to ruby red, the sweet-tart flavor is always refreshing. Sample this juicy citrus fruit in these recipes.

And do something different for your valentine this year – bake Grapefruit Meringue Pie. It gives the lemon version some serious competition with its sweet pucker power.

BROILED GRAPEFRUIT

3 large pink grapefruit
½ cup apricot preserves
1 tablespoon brown sugar
½ cup flaked coconut

• **Peel,** section, and seed grapefruit; place in four lightly greased individual baking dishes. Place dishes on a large baking sheet.
• **Combine** apricot preserves and sugar in a small bowl, stirring well; spoon over grapefruit.
• **Broil** 5½ inches from heat (with electric oven door partially opened) 2 to 3 minutes or until bubbly.
• **Sprinkle** with coconut; broil 1 additional minute or until coconut is lightly toasted. **Yield:** 4 servings.

SPICED PINK GRAPEFRUIT

2 large pink grapefruit
1 large lemon
⅔ cup water
¼ cup sugar
1 (3-inch) stick cinnamon, broken
4 whole cloves

• **Cut** 2 (3- x 1-inch) strips of rind from each grapefruit and lemon; set aside.
• **Peel** grapefruit, and cut into ½-inch-thick slices. Discard seeds, and place slices in an 8-inch square dish; set aside.
• **Squeeze** 2 tablespoons juice from lemon, and set juice aside. Reserve lemon for another use.
• **Scrape** white pith from rind strips. Combine rind strips, water, and next 3 ingredients in a small saucepan. Bring to a boil; reduce heat, and simmer 3 minutes.
• **Stir** in lemon juice; pour mixture over grapefruit in dish. Cover and chill at least 4 hours. Remove cinnamon sticks, cloves, and rind strips. **Yield:** 2 servings.

Elizabeth R. Drawdy
Spindale, North Carolina

GRAPEFRUIT-WHITE WINE SPRITZERS

4 cups pink grapefruit juice cocktail, chilled
1 (750-milliliter) bottle Sauterne or other sweet wine, chilled
⅔ cup sugar
1 pink grapefruit, thinly sliced
2 cups club soda, chilled
Garnish: grapefruit sections or rind strips

• **Combine** first 3 ingredients, stirring until sugar dissolves; add grapefruit. Add club soda just before serving. Pour over ice, and garnish, if desired. Serve immediately. **Yield:** 11 cups.

GRAPEFRUIT MERINGUE PIE

1 large pink grapefruit
1 tablespoon sugar
1½ cups sugar
⅓ cup cornstarch
¼ teaspoon salt
1¾ cups fresh grapefruit juice
¾ cup water
3 egg yolks
2 tablespoons butter or margarine
1 (9-inch) baked pastry shell
5 egg whites
½ teaspoon cream of tartar
⅔ cup sugar

• **Peel,** section, and seed grapefruit; sprinkle with 1 tablespoon sugar, stirring gently. Chill.
• **Combine** 1½ cups sugar, cornstarch, and salt in a large heavy saucepan; gradually stir in grapefruit juice and water.
• **Beat** egg yolks lightly; stir into juice mixture. Add butter; bring to a boil over medium heat, stirring constantly. Boil 1 minute, stirring constantly. Pour into pastry shell.
• **Beat** egg whites and cream of tartar at high speed with an electric mixer until foamy. Add ⅔ cup sugar, 1 tablespoon at a time, beating until stiff peaks form and sugar dissolves (2 to 4 minutes). Spread meringue over hot filling, sealing to edge of pastry.
• **Bake** at 325° for 25 to 28 minutes or until golden. Cool on a wire rack. Serve with grapefruit sections. **Yield:** one 9-inch pie.

TASTES OF CARNIVAL

Jami Gaudet of Macon, Georgia, captures the spirit of Mardi Gras in one bowl. "Green and yellow soups topped with purple cabbage are a tasty treat for the eyes and the palate," Jami says. "These Mardi Gras colors symbolize faith (green), justice (gold), and power (purple)."

Follow the soup with traditional dishes like red beans and rice and jambalaya. Then serve Jami's King Cake Fruit Tart as a sweet ending to a delicious mealtime parade. These make-ahead recipes will quickly put you in the spirit of Carnival.

MARDI GRAS SOUP

English Pea Soup
Roasted Yellow Bell Pepper Soup
Shredded red cabbage

• **Pour** ¾ cup of each soup simultaneously down the sides of 5 shallow soup bowls, taking care not to mix soups. Place red cabbage on top. **Yield:** 5 servings.

English Pea Soup

6 tablespoons unsalted butter
1½ cups chopped onion
3 cups vegetable or chicken broth
2 (1-pound) packages frozen English peas
¼ teaspoon salt
⅛ teaspoon ground white pepper

• **Melt** butter in a Dutch oven over medium heat; add onion, and cook, stirring constantly, until tender. Add broth, and bring to a boil.
• **Stir** in peas, salt, and pepper; reduce heat, and simmer 5 to 10 minutes or until peas are tender. Cool slightly.
• **Position** knife blade in food processor bowl; add soup, and process until smooth.
• **Pour** soup through a wire-mesh strainer into Dutch oven, discarding solids; cook over low heat just until soup is thoroughly heated. **Yield:** 4 cups.

Roasted Yellow Bell Pepper Soup

3 yellow bell peppers
2 tablespoons unsalted butter
½ cup chopped onion
½ cup chopped leek
¼ teaspoon salt
¼ teaspoon freshly ground pepper
1 medium-size red potato, peeled and sliced
2½ cups vegetable or chicken broth

• **Cut** bell peppers in half; remove and discard seeds. Place peppers, cut side down, on an aluminum foil-lined baking sheet.
• **Broil** 5½ inches from heat (with electric oven door partially opened) about 5 minutes or until bell peppers look blistered.
• **Place** bell peppers in a heavy-duty, zip-top plastic bag; seal and let stand 10 minutes to loosen skins. Peel peppers, and coarsely chop; set aside.
• **Melt** butter in a Dutch oven over medium heat; add onion and next 3 ingredients, and cook, stirring constantly, 10 minutes or until tender.
• **Add** chopped bell pepper, potato, and broth; bring to a boil. Reduce heat, and simmer 10 minutes or until potato is tender, stirring occasionally. Cool slightly.
• **Position** knife blade in food processor bowl; add soup, and process until smooth. Return to Dutch oven, and cook over low heat just until soup is thoroughly heated. **Yield:** 4 cups.

KING CAKE FRUIT TART

1 (20-ounce) package refrigerated sliceable sugar cookie dough
1 (8-ounce) package cream cheese, softened
1 (3-ounce) package cream cheese, softened
1 cup sifted powdered sugar
1 teaspoon vanilla extract
4 to 6 kiwifruit, peeled and sliced
4 to 6 carambola (star fruit), sliced
1 cup blueberries
1 cup seedless purple grapes, cut in half
1 (8-ounce) can pineapple chunks, drained
¾ cup apple jelly
2 tablespoons water
¼ cup chopped pecans, toasted

• **Line** two 9-inch round cakepans with 12-inch squares of aluminum foil, allowing corners to extend outside pans.
• **Cut** cookie dough into ⅛-inch-thick slices; line each prepared pan with half of slices, pressing edges of dough together to seal.
• **Bake** at 325° for 15 to 20 minutes or until lightly browned; cool completely in pans on wire racks.
• **Remove** cookie crusts from pans, using foil corners. Remove foil from crusts; place crusts on serving plates.
• **Combine** cream cheese, powdered sugar, and vanilla; beat at medium speed with an electric mixer until smooth and fluffy. Spread evenly over each crust. Arrange kiwifruit and next 4 ingredients on top.
• **Combine** apple jelly and 2 tablespoons water in a small saucepan; cook over medium heat, stirring constantly, until jelly melts. Remove from heat, and drizzle evenly over each tart. Sprinkle with pecans. Cover and chill at least 1 hour. **Yield:** 2 (9-inch) tarts.

CHOCOLATE: LIGHT AT LAST

Our Foods staff loves chocolate so much that, left to our own devices, we'd plan a story on this luscious sweet for every issue. Since 1979, we've published 946 chocolate dessert recipes. Chocolate definitely has a grip on us that no other food can match. Unfortunately, indulging in its pleasures can leave a lasting bulge on the waistline. This month, we've opened our cupboard to share a collection of light chocolate desserts that won't leave you looking large.

FROZEN CHOCOLATE BROWNIE PIE

¼ cup margarine
⅔ cup firmly packed brown sugar
½ cup egg substitute
¼ cup buttermilk
¼ cup all-purpose flour
⅓ cup cocoa
¼ teaspoon salt
1 teaspoon vanilla extract
Vegetable cooking spray
½ gallon vanilla nonfat frozen yogurt, softened
1 quart chocolate nonfat frozen yogurt, softened
¾ cup chocolate syrup
Garnishes: fresh strawberries, chocolate curls

• **Melt** margarine in a large saucepan over medium-high heat; add brown sugar, stirring with a wire whisk to blend. Remove from heat, and let cool slightly.
• **Add** egg substitute and buttermilk to pan, stirring well.
• **Combine** flour, cocoa, and salt; add to buttermilk mixture, stirring until blended. Stir in vanilla. Pour into a 9-inch springform pan lightly coated with cooking spray.
• **Bake** at 350° for 15 minutes. Cool completely in pan on a wire rack.
• **Spread** half of vanilla yogurt over brownie; cover and freeze until firm. Spread chocolate yogurt over vanilla yogurt; cover and freeze until firm. Top with remaining vanilla yogurt. Cover and freeze at least 8 hours.
• **Remove** sides of pan. Serve each wedge with 1 tablespoon syrup; garnish, if desired. **Yield:** 12 servings.

Karen Moneyhun
Centreville, Virginia

❤ Per serving: Calories 258 (17% from fat)
Fat 4.8g (1g saturated) Cholesterol 0mg
Sodium 205mg Carbohydrate 46.2g
Fiber 0.1g Protein 6.9g

TRIPLE CHOCOLATE TORTE

½ cup sugar
¼ cup cocoa
3 tablespoons all-purpose flour
¼ teaspoon baking powder
1 (4-ounce) bar bittersweet chocolate, finely chopped
½ cup boiling water
2 egg yolks
2 tablespoons chocolate liqueur
4 egg whites
½ cup sugar
Sifted powdered sugar

• **Combine** first 4 ingredients in a large bowl; add chocolate and boiling water, stirring until chocolate melts. Stir in egg yolks and liqueur.
• **Beat** egg whites at high speed with an electric mixer until foamy. Add ½ cup sugar, 1 tablespoon at a time, beating until stiff peaks form and sugar dissolves (2 to 4 minutes).
• **Stir** one-third of egg whites into chocolate mixture; fold in remaining egg whites. Pour into a lightly greased 8-inch springform pan.
• **Bake** at 375° for 28 minutes or until a wooden pick inserted in center comes out clean. Cool in pan on a wire rack 10 minutes; remove sides of pan, and cool completely (cake will be cracked on top). Sprinkle with powdered sugar.
Yield: 10 servings.

Sharon O'Dell
St. George Island, Florida

❤ Per serving: Calories 171 (24% from fat)
Fat 4.7g (2.5g saturated) Cholesterol 44mg
Sodium 37mg Carbohydrate 31.5g
Fiber 0.1g Protein 2.9g

PLAN FOR A HEALTHY LIFESTYLE

Jeremy J. Barker of Sarasota, Florida, has enjoyed the benefits of exercise and healthful eating since childhood. He shares tips from his fine-tuned plan for a healthy lifestyle.

▪ Your body won't wear away from too much exercise, but it *will* waste away from lack of activity.

▪ The key to staying fit is to exercise consistently and regularly.

▪ Any amount of activity is better than none at all.

▪ Choose a type of exercise because you enjoy it, not because doing it burns the most calories.

▪ Exercise with someone. If you don't show up, you'll be damaging both your health plan and your social graces.

▪ Once you make eating low-fat foods a routine, your body will let you know when you're going astray. Stop eating drive-through food and you'll need to eat a hamburger only once every two years just to remind yourself that you didn't need it after all.

CONFECTION QUESTION

"How much chocolate can I have for 100 calories or less?"

Carolyn Fowler
Calhoun, Georgia

Not much. But these are the best choices we found.

▪ 1 snack-size Almond Joy bar
▪ 8 pieces Butterfinger BB's candy
▪ 3 pieces Dove dark chocolate Promises candy
▪ 4 Hershey's kisses
▪ 30 plain M&M's
▪ 1 Fun Size 3 Musketeers bar
▪ 1 Fun Size Snickers bar
▪ 8 Tootsie Roll midgees
▪ 1 miniature York peppermint patty
▪ 1 SnackWell's Chocolate Truffle Cookie Cake
▪ 6 chocolate graham crackers
▪ 5 Keebler bite-size Chips Deluxe cookies
▪ 2 cups Suisse Mocha instant coffee
▪ 1 cup artificially sweetened hot cocoa
▪ ½ cup low-fat chocolate milk
▪ 1 Jell-O Fat-Free Chocolate Pudding Snack
▪ ½ cup chocolate nonfat frozen yogurt

MARCH

A Slice of Spring

Pound cakes are no longer one pound each of flour, butter, sugar, and eggs. Fruit, spices, nuts – even Cheddar cheese and cornmeal – add depth. These moist, full-flavored confections need no ice cream or sauce to enhance their appeal.

LEMONY POUND CAKE

1 cup vegetable oil
2½ cups sugar
1 cup buttermilk
4 egg whites
1 large egg, lightly beaten
1 teaspoon vanilla extract
1 teaspoon butter flavoring
½ teaspoon lemon extract
3 cups all-purpose flour
¼ teaspoon baking soda
¼ teaspoon salt

• **Beat** oil and sugar at medium speed with an electric mixer 2 minutes.
• **Combine** buttermilk and next 5 ingredients, stirring until blended.
• **Combine** flour, soda, and salt; add to oil mixture alternately with buttermilk mixture, beginning and ending with flour mixture. Beat at low speed just until blended after each addition. Pour batter into a greased and floured 10-inch tube pan.
• **Bake** at 325° for 1 hour or until a wooden pick inserted in center comes out clean.
• **Cool** cake in pan on a wire rack 10 to 15 minutes; remove from pan, and let cool completely on wire rack. **Yield:** 1 (10-inch) cake.

Pretty and Pink Pound Cake Loaf: Prepare batter; divide into thirds. Spread 1 portion into a greased and floured 9- x 5- x 3-inch loafpan. Stir ¼ cup seedless raspberry jam and, if desired, 2 drops of red liquid food coloring into second portion; spread gently over first layer. Spoon remaining batter over top. Bake at 325° for 1 hour and 35 minutes or until a wooden pick inserted in center comes out clean. **Yield:** 1 (9-inch) loaf.

Joseph L. Whitten
Odenville, Alabama

BANANA POUND CAKE

1 cup shortening
½ cup butter, softened
3 cups sugar
5 large eggs
3 ripe bananas, mashed
3 tablespoons milk
2 teaspoons vanilla extract
3 cups all-purpose flour
1 teaspoon baking powder
½ teaspoon salt

• **Beat** shortening and butter at medium speed with an electric mixer about 2 minutes or until creamy. Gradually add sugar, beating 5 to 7 minutes. Add eggs, one at a time, beating just until yellow disappears.
• **Combine** banana, milk, and vanilla.
• **Combine** flour, baking powder, and salt; add to shortening mixture alternately with banana mixture, beginning and ending with flour mixture. Beat at low speed just until blended after each addition. Pour batter into a greased and floured 10-inch tube pan.
• **Bake** at 350° for 1 hour and 20 minutes or until a wooden pick inserted in cake comes out clean.
• **Cool** cake in pan on a wire rack 10 to 15 minutes; remove from pan, and let cool completely on wire rack. **Yield:** 1 (10-inch) cake.

Janet Bean
Charlotte, North Carolina

BROWN SUGAR-RUM POUND CAKE

1½ cups butter, softened
1 (16-ounce) package light brown sugar
1 cup sugar
5 large eggs
¾ cup milk
¼ cup dark rum
2 teaspoons vanilla extract
3 cups all-purpose flour
1 teaspoon baking powder
¼ teaspoon salt
1 cup chopped pecans

• **Beat** butter at medium speed with an electric mixer about 2 minutes or until creamy. Gradually add sugars, beating

5 to 7 minutes. Add eggs, one at a time, beating mixture just until yellow disappears.
• **Combine** milk, rum, and vanilla.
• **Combine** flour, baking powder, and salt; add to butter mixture alternately with milk mixture, beginning and ending with flour mixture. Beat at low speed just until blended after each addition. Fold in chopped pecans. Pour batter into a greased and floured 13-cup Bundt pan.
• **Bake** at 325° for 1 hour and 20 minutes or until a wooden pick inserted in center comes out clean.
• **Cool** cake in pan on a wire rack 10 to 15 minutes; remove from pan, and let cool completely on wire rack. Serve slices with sweetened whipped cream, if desired. **Yield:** 1 (10-inch) cake.

Denise Allen
Birmingham, Alabama

Flavors and textures by the pound

Pound cakes are traditionally smooth-grained, vanilla-flavored loaves with crusty tops. Sometimes called "plain" cakes, they're simple and unadorned.

BLACK PEPPER POUND CAKE

Serve this sweet pound cake for a different dessert. The pepper and nutmeg add a surprising kick.

1 cup butter, softened
1 cup sugar
4 large eggs
1½ cups all-purpose flour
¼ teaspoon salt
½ teaspoon cream of tartar
¾ teaspoon freshly ground pepper
¼ teaspoon ground nutmeg or mace
1 tablespoon lemon juice
1 teaspoon vanilla

• **Beat** butter at medium speed with an electric mixer about 2 minutes or until creamy. Gradually add sugar, beating 5 to 7 minutes. Add eggs, one at a time, beating just until yellow disappears.
• **Combine** flour and next 4 ingredients; gradually add to butter mixture. Mix at low speed just until blended after each addition. Stir in lemon juice and vanilla.
• **Spoon** batter into a greased and floured 6-cup Bundt pan or a 9- x 5- x 3-inch loafpan.
• **Bake** at 325° for 50 to 55 minutes or until a wooden pick inserted in cake comes out clean.
• **Cool** cake in pan on a wire rack 10 to 15 minutes; remove from pan, and let cool completely on wire rack. **Yield:** 1 (8-inch) cake or 1 (9-inch) loaf.

Ruby G. Tomlin
Andalusia, Alabama

AZTEC POUND CAKE

1 cup butter, softened
1 tablespoon grated orange rind
2 cups sugar
6 large eggs, separated
2 cups all-purpose flour
1 cup yellow cornmeal
½ teaspoon baking soda
¼ teaspoon salt
1 (8-ounce) carton sour cream
1 teaspoon vanilla extract

• **Beat** butter and orange rind at medium speed with an electric mixer about 2 minutes until creamy; gradually add sugar, beating well. Add egg yolks, one at a time, beating just until yellow disappears.
• **Combine** flour, cornmeal, soda, and salt; add to butter mixture alternately with sour cream, beginning and ending with flour mixture. Beat at low speed just until blended after each addition. Stir in vanilla.
• **Beat** egg whites at high speed until stiff peaks form; fold into batter. Pour batter into two greased and floured 8½- x 4½- x 2½-inch loafpans.
• **Bake** at 325° for 1 hour and 5 minutes or until a wooden pick inserted in center comes out clean.
• **Cool** cakes in pans on a wire rack 10 minutes; remove from pans, and let cool completely on wire rack. **Yield:** 2 loaves.

Mrs. Joel Allard
San Antonio, Texas

CHEESY POUND CAKE

Traditional pound cake takes on added flavor with a surprise ingredient – Cheddar cheese.

1½ cups butter, softened
1 (8-ounce) package cream cheese, softened
3 cups sugar
6 large eggs
3 cups all-purpose flour
Dash of salt
2 cups (8 ounces) finely shredded sharp Cheddar cheese
1 tablespoon vanilla extract

• **Beat** butter and cream cheese at medium speed with an electric mixer about 2 minutes or until creamy. Gradually add sugar, beating 5 to 7 minutes. Add eggs, one at a time, beating just until yellow disappears.
• **Combine** flour and salt; gradually add to butter mixture. Beat at low speed just until blended after each addition. Stir in Cheddar cheese and vanilla. Pour batter into a greased and floured 10-inch tube pan.
• **Bake** at 325° for 1 hour and 45 minutes or until a wooden pick inserted in center comes out clean.
• **Cool** cake in pan on a wire rack 10 to 15 minutes; remove from pan, and let cool completely on wire rack. Serve with apple butter, if desired. **Yield:** 1 (10-inch) cake.

LaDonna Funderburk
Moultrie, Georgia

RICE TWICE

Next time you've got leftover rice, give it a second chance: Send it packing to the freezer. Rice is just as good the second go-round, maybe even better. Let these recipes, ideas, and storage tips lead the way to delicious rice *déjà vu*.

SPICY SHRIMP CASSEROLE

(pictured on page 41)

2 pounds unpeeled medium-size fresh shrimp
3 cups cooked long-grain-and-wild rice mix
1 cup (4 ounces) shredded longhorn Cheddar cheese
1 (10¾-ounce) can cream of mushroom soup, undiluted
1 tablespoon butter or margarine
½ cup chopped green onions
2 teaspoons Worcestershire sauce
½ teaspoon dry mustard
½ teaspoon freshly ground pepper
¼ cup milk
1 teaspoon Cajun seasoning
Garnishes: green onions, peeled cooked shrimp

• **Peel** shrimp, and devein, if desired.
• **Combine** rice, shrimp, cheese, and soup in a bowl.
• **Melt** butter in a large skillet over medium-high heat, and add green onions; cook, stirring constantly, until tender.
• **Stir** green onions, Worcestershire sauce, and next 4 ingredients into rice mixture. Spoon mixture into a lightly greased 11- x 7- x 1½-inch or 2-quart baking dish.
• **Bake** at 375° for 45 minutes. Garnish, if desired. **Yield:** 6 servings.

Judy Grimes
Brandon, Mississippi

SMOKY CAJUN JAMBALAYA

1 pound andouille or Cajun-style sausage
4 skinned and boned chicken breast halves
2 tablespoons peanut oil
1 cup chopped cooked ham
2 teaspoons Cajun seasoning
1 large onion, finely chopped
1 medium-size green bell pepper, chopped
½ cup chopped celery
3 cloves garlic, minced
1 (14½-ounce) can Cajun-style stewed tomatoes, undrained
½ cup chicken broth
1 tablespoon Worcestershire sauce
½ teaspoon hot sauce
3 cups hot cooked rice
1 cup finely chopped green onions

• **Cut** sausage into ½-inch slices; cut chicken into ½-inch pieces.
• **Cook** sausage in oil in a large Dutch oven over medium-high heat 3 minutes or until browned. Add chicken, and cook, stirring constantly, 3 minutes or until browned.
• **Stir** in ham, and cook until thoroughly heated. Remove meat mixture, reserving 1 tablespoon drippings in Dutch oven. Return meat mixture to Dutch oven; stir in Cajun seasoning and next 5 ingredients. Cook 5 minutes, stirring constantly.

• **Stir** in chicken broth and remaining ingredients; cook, stirring constantly, 2 minutes or until thoroughly heated. **Yield:** 6 servings.

Margaret Jones
Birmingham, Alabama

EASY TURKEY EMPANADAS

1 (15-ounce) package refrigerated piecrusts
2 cups cooked yellow rice
1 cup chopped smoked turkey
1 cup (4 ounces) shredded Monterey Jack cheese with jalapeño peppers
½ cup sliced green onions
1 (2.25-ounce) can sliced ripe olives, drained
1 to 2 teaspoons fajita seasoning
Cornmeal

• **Unfold** piecrusts, and press out fold lines.
• **Combine** rice and next 5 ingredients; spoon evenly onto half of each piecrust. Fold piecrusts over filling, pressing edges to seal. Crimp edges with a fork. Place on a baking sheet sprinkled with cornmeal.
• **Bake** at 400° for 25 minutes or until golden. Cut in half, and serve with sour cream and picante sauce. **Yield:** 4 servings.

Sandra Stewart
Northport, Alabama

SAVORY SUCCOTASH

4 thick slices bacon
1 medium onion, chopped
½ teaspoon rubbed sage
1 (10-ounce) package frozen whole kernel corn, partially thawed
1 (10-ounce) package frozen lima beans, partially thawed
1½ cups half-and-half
1 teaspoon sugar
¼ to ½ teaspoon salt
¼ to ½ teaspoon pepper
3 cups hot cooked rice
1 cup chopped cooked ham

• **Cook** bacon in a large skillet until crisp; remove bacon, reserving 2 tablespoons drippings in skillet. Crumble bacon, and set aside.
• **Add** onion and sage to drippings; cook, stirring constantly, 3 to 5 minutes or until crisp-tender. Drain and return to skillet.
• **Add** corn and lima beans; cook, stirring constantly, 5 to 7 minutes or until tender. Add half-and-half and next 3 ingredients; reduce heat, and simmer until liquid is slightly reduced, stirring occasionally.
• **Stir** in rice and ham; cook 2 to 3 minutes or until thoroughly heated. Sprinkle with bacon, and serve immediately. **Yield:** 6 to 8 servings.

Stanlay Webber
Winston-Salem, North Carolina

RETHINKING RICE

WHAT'S IN STORE

▪ Store rice in the refrigerator up to seven days or in the freezer in a heavy-duty, zip-top plastic freezer bag up to six months.

▪ When refrigerating rice, be sure to cover the rice tightly so the grains won't dry out or absorb the flavors of other foods.

▪ To reheat rice, add 2 tablespoons liquid for each cup of leftover rice. Cover and reheat over medium-low heat 4 to 5 minutes. Or microwave, covered, at HIGH about 1½ minutes per cup.

▪ Leftover rice is a great soup thickener.

▪ Give leftover rice a polished look: Firmly pack it in a well-oiled mold, cover with plastic wrap, and weight it down. Chill about an hour before unmolding onto a serving plate. Serve chilled.

CHEAP TRICKS

For full flavor enhancement, don't just cook rice in water. Substitute one of the following for all or part of the cooking water: apple, orange, or pineapple juice; chicken, vegetable, or beef stock; wine; beer; sherry; cream; or milk. Label and freeze small bags of leftover rice, and reheat when needed (1-cup bags are great for solo diners).

Boost the flavor and appearance of reheated rice by adding the following:

▪ Chopped dates and toasted nuts
▪ Sliced mushrooms, green onions, or shallots
▪ Chopped asparagus, bell pepper, broccoli, carrots, celery, green beans, onion, or tomato
▪ Chopped ham, bacon, pork, or seafood (nice for fried rice – just add an egg, a bit of oil and soy sauce, and scramble in a wok or large skillet)
▪ Chopped cilantro, parsley, or other fresh herbs; minced fresh ginger or garlic
▪ Crushed pineapple, sliced mandarin oranges, chopped red or green apples, or raisins
▪ Sliced ripe or pimiento-stuffed olives
▪ Grated Romano or Parmesan cheese, or crumbled feta cheese

HOPPIN' JOHN SALAD

(pictured on page 41)

The mint in this Southern black-eyed pea and rice salad makes it exceptionally original.

2 cups cooked black-eyed peas
3 cups cooked long-grain rice
½ cup chopped purple onion
¼ cup chopped celery
1 jalapeño pepper, seeded and minced
¼ cup loosely packed fresh chervil or parsley
¼ cup loosely packed fresh mint
1 clove garlic
½ teaspoon salt
3 tablespoons fresh lemon juice
¼ cup olive oil
¼ teaspoon freshly ground pepper

• **Combine** the first 5 ingredients in a large bowl.
• **Place** herbs and garlic on a cutting board, and sprinkle evenly with salt; finely chop herbs and garlic. Sprinkle over rice mixture, and stir gently.
• **Combine** lemon juice, olive oil, and pepper in a bowl; stir into rice mixture. **Yield:** 6 cups.

John Martin Taylor
Charleston, South Carolina
The New Southern Cook
(Bantam)

QUICK CALAS

Pronounced "kah-LAHS," these fried rice cakes, similar to beignets, are named from an African word for rice. They've been popular in New Orleans for more than a century.

2 cups cooked long-grain rice
2 cups biscuit and baking mix
2 tablespoons sugar
1 teaspoon ground cinnamon
1 teaspoon ground nutmeg
2 large eggs, lightly beaten
½ cup evaporated milk
1 teaspoon vanilla extract
Vegetable oil
Sifted powdered sugar

• **Combine** first 5 ingredients in a bowl. Combine eggs, milk, and vanilla; add to dry ingredients, stirring well. Cover and chill 1 hour.
• **Pour** oil to depth of 2 inches into a Dutch oven or electric fryer; heat to 350°. Drop batter by tablespoonfuls into hot oil. Fry calas, a few at a time, 2 minutes or until golden, turning once. Drain on paper towels. Sprinkle with powdered sugar; serve warm. **Yield:** about 4 dozen.

GARDEN-FRESH SALADS

When you're choosing lettuce, there are several varieties beyond the familiar iceberg to turn your head.

Butterhead lettuces, which include Boston and Bibb, have small loosely packed, pale-green heads and a buttery texture. Leaf lettuces, such as Oak Leaf, Salad Bowl, Red Leaf, and Green Leaf, do not form heads, but rather have medium- to dark-green leaves growing from a center stalk. Some varieties have red-tipped leaves. Leaf lettuces are full flavored and crispy. Romaine lettuce has an elongated head with dark-green leaves outside and paler leaves inside.

COMPANY'S COMING SALAD

8 cups mixed salad greens
1 (11-ounce) can mandarin oranges, drained
1 green onion, sliced
Orange Vinaigrette (see recipe, page 65)
Glazed Almonds

• **Combine** first 3 ingredients; drizzle with Orange Vinaigrette, and toss gently. Sprinkle with Glazed Almonds. **Yield:** 8 servings.

Glazed Almonds

1 egg white
¼ cup sugar
1 cup sliced almonds
2 tablespoons butter, melted

• **Beat** egg white at high speed with an electric mixer until foamy; gradually add sugar, beating until stiff peaks form. Fold in almonds.
• **Combine** butter and almonds in an 8-inch square baking dish; stir to coat.
• **Bake** at 325° for 20 minutes, stirring every 5 minutes. Cool. **Yield:** 1 cup.

Lori Cook
Wichita Falls, Texas

GREEK CAESAR SALAD

¾ cup olive oil
¼ cup lemon juice
¼ cup egg substitute
2 cloves garlic, pressed
1 teaspoon dried oregano
¼ teaspoon salt
⅛ teaspoon pepper
1 head romaine lettuce, torn
¾ cup kalamata olives, pitted
1 small purple onion, thinly sliced
½ cup crumbled feta cheese
Pita Croutons

• **Combine** first 7 ingredients in a small bowl, stirring with a wire whisk. Cover and chill.
• **Combine** lettuce and next 3 ingredients in a large bowl; gradually add enough dressing to coat leaves, tossing gently. Sprinkle with Pita Croutons, and serve with remaining dressing. **Yield:** 6 servings.

Pita Croutons

2 tablespoons olive oil
1 teaspoon dried oregano
¼ teaspoon crushed garlic
Dash of salt
1 (8-inch) pita bread round, split into 2 circles

• **Combine** first 4 ingredients, and brush olive oil mixture over the inside of each pita bread circle.

• **Cut** each pita bread circle into bite-size pieces, and place on a baking sheet.
• **Bake** at 400° for 5 to 7 minutes or until golden. **Yield:** 1⅓ cups.

LEMON-HONEY VINAIGRETTE

1 cup white wine vinegar
¾ cup vegetable oil
¼ cup honey
1 tablespoon grated lemon rind
3 tablespoons fresh lemon juice
1 teaspoon salt
2 cloves garlic, minced

• **Combine** all ingredients in a jar; cover tightly, and shake vigorously. Chill. **Yield:** 2 cups.

ORANGE VINAIGRETTE

⅓ cup olive oil
2 tablespoons red wine vinegar
½ teaspoon grated orange rind
1½ teaspoons fresh orange juice
¼ teaspoon poppy seeds
¼ to ½ teaspoon salt
⅛ teaspoon pepper

• **Combine** all ingredients in a jar; cover tightly, and shake vigorously. Chill. **Yield:** ½ cup.

BASIL-RED WINE VINAIGRETTE

⅔ cup olive oil
⅓ cup red wine vinegar
1½ teaspoons salt
1 teaspoon sugar
1 teaspoon dried basil
½ teaspoon pepper

• **Combine** all ingredients in a jar; cover tightly, and shake vigorously. Chill. **Yield:** 1 cup.

Patricia Ryan
Sarasota, Florida

ASPIC WITH AN ATTITUDE

If the thought of serving aspic reminds you of the boring opaque aspics served in ladies' tea rooms, think again. These recipes represent the best of classic aspics. They bring vegetables and fruits into clear, delicious view.

GAZPACHO ASPIC

(pictured on page 43)

A twist on traditional tomato aspic, this recipe is brimming with vegetables.

1 envelope unflavored gelatin
1 tablespoon sugar
¼ teaspoon salt
1 beef-flavored bouillon cube
1¼ cups water, divided
3 tablespoons lemon juice
⅛ teaspoon hot sauce
1 (14.5-ounce) can diced Italian-style tomatoes, well drained
½ cup finely chopped celery
¼ cup finely chopped green bell pepper
2 tablespoons sliced green onions
Lettuce leaves
Mayonnaise (optional)

• **Combine** first 4 ingredients and ¼ cup water in a small saucepan; let stand 1 minute. Cook over low heat, stirring until gelatin and bouillon cube dissolve. Remove from heat.
• **Combine** remaining 1 cup water, lemon juice, hot sauce, and gelatin mixture in a bowl; chill until consistency of unbeaten egg white.
• **Stir** in tomatoes and next 3 ingredients; spoon into six lightly oiled ½-cup molds. Chill until firm.
• **Unmold** onto lettuce leaves; dollop each serving with mayonnaise, if desired. **Yield:** 6 servings.

Becky Schuford
Wilmington, North Carolina

ASPARAGUS ASPIC

1 pound fresh asparagus *
2 envelopes unflavored gelatin
1¼ cups cold water, divided
¼ cup red wine vinegar
1 tablespoon lemon juice
¾ cup sugar
1 cup chopped celery
½ cup chopped pecans, toasted
¼ cup chopped pimiento-stuffed olives
¼ cup chopped onion
Lettuce leaves

• **Snap** off tough ends of asparagus; remove scales with a vegetable peeler, if desired.
• **Arrange** asparagus in a steamer basket over boiling water; cover and steam 8 minutes or until crisp-tender.
• **Plunge** asparagus into ice water to stop the cooking process; drain. Cut into ½-inch slices; chill.
• **Sprinkle** gelatin over ¼ cup cold water in a medium bowl; stir and let stand 1 minute.
• **Combine** remaining 1 cup water, wine vinegar, lemon juice, and sugar in a small saucepan; bring to a boil, stirring constantly. Add to gelatin mixture, stirring until gelatin dissolves; chill until consistency of unbeaten egg white.
• **Stir** in chilled asparagus, celery, and next 3 ingredients. Pour into six lightly oiled ½-cup molds. Cover and chill until firm.
• **Unmold** onto lettuce leaves. **Yield:** 6 servings.

* Substitute 1 (10-ounce) package frozen asparagus spears, cooked, for fresh.

Sarah Bondurant
Hernando, Mississippi

BLUE CHEESE ASPIC

1 (3-ounce) package lemon-flavored gelatin
1¼ cups boiling water
¼ cup dry white wine
½ cup sour cream
1 cup finely chopped Rome apple
¼ cup crumbled blue cheese

• **Dissolve** gelatin in boiling water; stir in wine. Add sour cream, stirring well with a wire whisk.
• **Chill** until gelatin mixture is consistency of unbeaten egg white. Fold in apple and cheese. Spoon mixture into a lightly oiled 3-cup mold; cover and chill until firm.
• **Unmold** onto a serving platter. **Yield:** 6 servings.

Charlotte Pierce
Greensburg, Kentucky

SATISFYING SOUPS

Soup is pure, soothing contentment. These recipes make natural sandwich partners, great solo suppers, and perfect openers for elegant dinners.

CREAM OF WATERCRESS SOUP

¼ cup butter or margarine
2 cups chopped onion
½ cup finely chopped shallot
2 (14½-ounce) cans ready-to-serve chicken broth
1 medium potato, peeled and finely chopped
1¼ pounds watercress, trimmed
1 cup whipping cream
¼ teaspoon salt
¼ teaspoon freshly ground black pepper
⅛ teaspoon ground red pepper
Pinch of ground nutmeg

• **Melt** butter in a Dutch oven; add chopped onion and shallot. Cook over medium-high heat 3 to 5 minutes, stirring constantly.
• **Add** broth and potato; bring to a boil. Cover, reduce heat, and simmer 15 minutes or until potato is tender.
• **Add** watercress; remove from heat. Let stand, covered, 5 minutes.
• **Pour** broth mixture through a large wire-mesh strainer into a bowl, reserving vegetable pulp in strainer.
• **Position** knife blade in food processor bowl; add reserved vegetable pulp and about 1 cup strained broth. Process 30 seconds, stopping once to scrape down sides.
• **Return** pureed vegetable mixture and remaining strained broth to Dutch oven; add whipping cream and remaining ingredients.
• **Cook** over low heat 5 minutes or until thoroughly heated (do not boil). **Yield:** 7 cups.

Rublelene Singleton
Scotts Hill, Tennessee

TOMATO SOUP WITH HERBED YOGURT AND PARMESAN TOASTS

1 orange
1 tablespoon olive oil
3 medium onions, sliced
6 cloves garlic, minced
1½ tablespoons dried basil, crushed
1½ tablespoons dried marjoram, crushed
1½ teaspoons ground cumin
¼ teaspoon dried crushed red pepper
3 (14.5-ounce) cans no-salt-added whole tomatoes, undrained
3 cups ready-to-serve reduced-sodium fat-free chicken broth
½ teaspoon salt
¼ teaspoon pepper
Herbed Yogurt
Parmesan Toasts

• **Remove** rind from orange, using a vegetable peeler, being careful not to cut into white membrane; cut rind into thin strips. Reserve orange pulp for another use.
• **Heat** oil in a large heavy saucepan over medium heat; add orange rind, onion, and garlic. Cover, reduce heat, and cook 30 minutes or until onion is tender, stirring occasionally.
• **Add** basil and next 3 ingredients; cook 5 minutes, stirring constantly.
• **Add** tomatoes and broth; bring to a boil over high heat. Cover, reduce heat, and simmer 20 minutes. Remove from heat. Cool slightly.
• **Place** about one-third of mixture into container of an electric blender or food processor; process until smooth. Return to saucepan; repeat procedure with remaining mixture. Stir in salt and pepper.
• **Ladle** soup into individual soup bowls; top evenly with Herbed Yogurt, and serve each with 2 Parmesan Toasts. **Yield:** 9½ cups.

Herbed Yogurt

¾ cup plain nonfat yogurt
2 green onions, finely chopped
1 tablespoon dried basil
1 clove garlic, minced

• **Combine** all ingredients; stir until blended. **Yield:** about 1 cup.

Parmesan Toasts

Vegetable cooking spray
¾ cup coarsely grated Parmesan cheese
2 tablespoons all-purpose flour

• **Cover** a baking sheet with aluminum foil, and coat with cooking spray.
• **Combine** cheese and flour, tossing gently; place in a colander to remove excess flour. Spoon mixture by tablespoonfuls into 3-inch circles on baking sheet.
• **Bake** at 350° for 5 minutes or until edges are lightly browned. Remove to wire racks; cool completely. **Yield:** 12 toasts.

Charlene Funkhouser
Cascado, Idaho

VIRGINIA COOKERY, PAST AND PRESENT

Virginia Cookery, Past and Present, dates back much further than its 1957 publication. It contains the recipes and an original cookbook manuscript from the Bailey Washington and Richard Bland Lee families submitted by the great-great-granddaughter of Lee.

This book, published by the Olivet Episcopal Church Women in Franconia, Virginia, first raised money to help the church build a new sanctuary. But the churchwomen underestimated the longevity of the book. Since that time, the church has built and furnished new additions and purchased office and kitchen equipment with the continuing proceeds.

CHICKEN SALAD

2 cups chopped cooked chicken
1 cup chopped celery
1 cup seedless grapes, cut in half
½ cup chopped almonds, toasted
1 (11-ounce) can mandarin oranges, drained
½ cup mayonnaise
1 teaspoon grated onion
¼ teaspoon salt (optional)
Lettuce leaves

• **Combine** the first 5 ingredients in a bowl.
• **Combine** mayonnaise, onion, and, if desired, salt; add to chicken mixture, stirring gently. Spoon onto lettuce leaves. **Yield:** 4 cups.

FRENCH BREAKFAST PUFFS

⅓ cup butter or margarine, melted
½ cup sugar
1 large egg
1½ cups all-purpose flour
1½ teaspoons baking powder
½ teaspoon salt
¼ teaspoon ground nutmeg
½ cup milk
¼ cup sugar
½ teaspoon ground cinnamon
2 tablespoons butter or margarine, melted

• **Beat** first 3 ingredients at medium speed with an electric mixer until creamy and well blended.
• **Combine** flour and next 3 ingredients; add to butter mixture alternately with milk, beginning and ending with flour mixture. Beat at low speed until blended after each addition. Spoon into greased miniature (1¾-inch) muffin pans, filling two-thirds full.
• **Bake** at 350° for 14 to 16 minutes. Remove from pans immediately.
• **Combine** ¼ cup sugar and cinnamon. Dip tops of muffins in 2 tablespoons melted butter and then in sugar mixture. **Yield:** 28 miniature muffins.

Note: If using regular muffin pans, bake 20 to 25 minutes. **Yield:** 10 muffins.

APPLESAUCE CAKE

¾ cup shortening
2 cups sugar
3 large eggs
3 cups all-purpose flour
1½ teaspoons baking soda
½ teaspoon salt
1 teaspoon ground cinnamon
½ teaspoon ground cloves
¼ teaspoon ground nutmeg
1½ cups applesauce
1 cup raisins
1 cup chopped walnuts or pecans

• **Beat** shortening at medium speed with an electric mixer 2 minutes or until fluffy. Gradually add sugar, beating mixture 5 to 7 minutes. Add eggs, one at a time, beating just until yellow disappears.
• **Combine** flour and next 5 ingredients; add to shortening mixture alternately with applesauce, beginning and ending with flour mixture. Beat at low speed just until blended after each addition. Stir in raisins and chopped nuts.
• **Pour** batter into a greased and floured 12-cup Bundt pan.
• **Bake** at 350° for 1 hour or until a wooden pick inserted in center comes out clean, shielding with aluminum foil after 45 minutes to prevent excessive browning.
• **Cool** cake in pan on a wire rack 10 to 15 minutes; remove from pan, and cool completely on wire rack. **Yield:** 1 (10-inch) cake.

living *light*

Savor the Flavor of Spa Cuisine

We visited two of South Florida's most talented spa chefs, ate in their restaurants, and came back with their best recipes. Here's your chance to experience the taste without the expense of taking the trip.

SKILLET-SEARED ORANGE CHICKEN

¾ cup fine, dry breadcrumbs
1½ teaspoons chopped fresh mint
1½ teaspoons chopped fresh cilantro
1½ teaspoons chopped fresh basil
4 (5-ounce) skinned and boned chicken breast halves
Vegetable cooking spray
1 cup broccoli flowerets
1 cup cauliflower flowerets
1 cup sliced carrot
½ cup shiitake mushrooms
¼ pound fresh spinach, torn
½ cup coarsely chopped purple onion
Blended Rice
Mandarin-Teriyaki Sauce

• **Combine** first 4 ingredients in a shallow dish. Dredge chicken in mixture.
• **Place** a large cast-iron skillet over medium-high heat until very hot. Remove from heat; carefully coat with cooking spray, and return to heat. Add chicken, and cook 4 to 5 minutes on each side. Remove from heat, and keep warm.
• **Arrange** broccoli and next 3 ingredients in a steamer basket over boiling water; cover and steam 8 minutes or until crisp-tender.
• **Cook** spinach in a small amount of boiling water 5 to 8 minutes or until tender; drain well.
• **Place** chicken on individual serving plates; arrange steamed vegetables, spinach, and purple onion evenly on plates. Serve with Blended Rice and Mandarin-Teriyaki Sauce. **Yield:** 4 servings.

Blended Rice

½ cup basmati rice, uncooked
½ cup wild rice, uncooked
Vegetable cooking spray
½ cup peeled, finely chopped plum tomato
½ cup sliced green onions
¼ cup reduced-sodium soy sauce

• **Cook** basmati and wild rice according to package directions.
• **Coat** a skillet with cooking spray; add cooked rice, tomato, and remaining ingredients. Cook over medium heat, stirring constantly, until thoroughly heated. **Yield:** 2½ cups.

Mandarin-Teriyaki Sauce

1 tablespoon cornstarch
½ cup reduced-sodium soy sauce
1 cup unsweetened pineapple juice
2 tablespoons brown sugar
1 tablespoon minced garlic
1 tablespoon minced fresh ginger
1 tablespoon chopped fresh cilantro
2 (11-ounce) cans mandarin oranges, drained

• **Combine** cornstarch and soy sauce, stirring until smooth. Set aside.
• **Combine** pineapple juice and next 4 ingredients in a skillet; bring to a boil over medium-high heat, stirring constantly. Stir in cornstarch mixture; boil 1 minute, stirring constantly. Remove from heat; stir in oranges. Cool. **Yield:** 3 cups.

PGA National Resort & Spa
Palm Beach Gardens, Florida

♥ Per serving: Calories 566 (8% from fat)
Fat 4.8g (1g saturated) Cholesterol 60mg
Sodium 1760mg Carbohydrate 94.8g
Fiber 7.6g Protein 37.8g

CHILLED POACHED SALMON SALAD

2 (14½-ounce) cans vegetable broth
½ cup chopped carrot
¼ cup chopped onion
1 sprig fresh parsley
1 bay leaf
2 tablespoons dry white wine
4 (5-ounce) salmon fillets
4 new potatoes
8 asparagus spears
8 baby carrots
1 cup cauliflower flowerets
4 cups gourmet salad greens
2 Roma tomatoes, cut into fourths
4 radishes
½ red bell pepper, cut into thin strips
8 black olives
Lemon-Caper Dressing
Garnish: grated lemon rind

• **Combine** first 6 ingredients in a large skillet; place over medium heat. Bring to a boil. Reduce heat, and add salmon; cover and simmer 8 minutes or until tender. Drain; chill salmon at least 2 hours.

• **Cook** potatoes in boiling water to cover 15 minutes or until tender. Drain; chill at least 1 hour.

• **Snap** off tough ends of asparagus; remove scales with a vegetable peeler, if desired. Cook asparagus, carrots, and cauliflower in a small amount of boiling water 3 minutes. Drain; immediately plunge vegetables into ice water to stop the cooking process.

• **Arrange** salad greens onto four individual plates. Top greens evenly with vegetables and olives, and place a salmon fillet over vegetables; drizzle each serving with 2 tablespoons Lemon-Caper Dressing. Garnish, if desired. **Yield:** 4 servings.

Lemon-Caper Dressing

At 42 calories and 4.5 fat grams per tablespoon, this flavorful dressing adds life to vegetables and salads.

1/3 cup hot water
1/3 cup chopped fresh dill
1/4 cup chopped fresh parsley
2 tablespoons capers
2 tablespoons lemon juice
2 shallots, quartered
2 cloves garlic
2 teaspoons Dijon mustard
1/2 teaspoon salt
1/2 teaspoon freshly ground pepper
2/3 cup olive oil

• **Combine** all ingredients except olive oil in container of an electric blender, and process until smooth. Turn blender on high, and gradually add oil in a slow, steady stream; process until thickened. Cover and chill up to 3 days. **Yield:** 2 cups.

Doral Golf Resort and Spa
Miami, Florida

♥ Per serving: Calories 418 (37% from fat) Fat 17.5g (2.7g saturated) Cholesterol 61mg Sodium 326mg Carbohydrate 38.4g Fiber 5.6g Protein 28.5g

CHESAPEAKE BAY CRAB CAKES WITH JALAPEÑO TARTAR SAUCE

(pictured on page 44)

1 large egg, lightly beaten
2 tablespoons nonfat mayonnaise
2 tablespoons finely chopped green bell pepper
1 (2-ounce) jar diced pimiento, drained
1 1/2 tablespoons finely chopped purple onion
1 1/2 teaspoons lemon juice
1 teaspoon Dijon mustard
1/2 teaspoon Old Bay seasoning
1/2 cup fresh whole-grain breadcrumbs
1 pound fresh lump crabmeat, drained
Vegetable cooking spray
Jalapeño Tartar Sauce
Garnishes: finely chopped red and green bell peppers, alfalfa sprouts, lemon wedges

• **Combine** first 8 ingredients; fold in breadcrumbs and crabmeat. Divide crabmeat mixture into 12 portions, and shape each portion into a patty.

• **Coat** a large nonstick skillet with cooking spray; place over medium-high heat until hot. Add crab cakes, and cook 3 to 4 minutes or until golden, turning once. Serve with Jalapeño Tartar Sauce; garnish, if desired. **Yield:** 4 appetizer servings.

Jalapeño Tartar Sauce

1/2 cup nonfat mayonnaise
1 small jalapeño pepper, seeded and finely chopped
3 tablespoons finely chopped, unpeeled English cucumber
2 tablespoons finely chopped purple onion
1 tablespoon lemon juice
1/4 teaspoon Worcestershire sauce

• **Combine** all ingredients; cover and chill. **Yield:** 1 cup.

PGA National Resort & Spa
Palm Beach Gardens, Florida

♥ Per serving: Calories 210 (20% from fat) Fat 4.5g (0.8g saturated) Cholesterol 169mg Sodium 956mg Carbohydrate 13.5g Fiber 2.2g Protein 25.6g

DINING TIPS FROM THE DORAL

▪ Revamp your pantry and throw away fatty foods. If you don't offer your family high-fat food options, then they can't make high-fat choices.

▪ Enhance flavors in soups, pasta dishes, muffins, and desserts with citrus rind. Zesting citrus can be time-consuming, so make it in batches and freeze.

▪ Eat foods as close to their natural state as possible.

▪ Tape this reminder to your refrigerator door: The fat that you put into your body is the fat that you wear on your body.

▪ Take steps to reduce the stress in your life. For most people, additional stress means more snacks.

▪ Hang in there. It takes at least a month to incorporate a lifestyle change into your daily routine.

LOW-FAT COOKING TIPS FROM THE PGA NATIONAL

■ Enjoy the flavors of simply prepared fresh foods without covering them up with heavy sauces. Make salsas that accentuate your meals instead of gravies that blanket them in fat.

■ Don't fry fish or chicken. Instead sharpen your skills at broiling, grilling, and poaching.

■ Give up the bread and butter habit.

■ Plan several vegetarian meals each week and limit red meat to just one meal. Be sure to always fill your plate with more vegetables, salad, and pasta than meat.

■ Take the time to make every meal a dining experience. Spend at least half an hour at the dinner table, conversing with family and savoring each bite of the food.

CITRUS GAZPACHO

1 large grapefruit
2 large oranges
1 cup chopped plum tomatoes
½ cup chopped green bell pepper
¼ cup chopped English cucumber *
¼ cup chopped tomatillo
2 tablespoons chopped purple onion
2 tablespoons chopped fresh cilantro
2 cloves garlic, minced
½ cup reduced-sodium vegetable juice
½ cup reduced-sodium tomato juice
¼ cup ready-to-serve reduced-sodium, fat-free chicken broth
2 tablespoons fresh lime juice
1 teaspoon hot sauce
Garnish: fresh cilantro sprigs

• **Peel,** section, and seed grapefruit and oranges. Coarsely chop sections, and place in a bowl. Add tomato and next 11 ingredients; cover and chill 4 hours. Garnish, if desired. **Yield:** 4 cups.

* Substitute ¼ cup peeled, chopped cucumber for English cucumber.

PGA National Resort & Spa
Palm Beach Gardens, Florida

❤ Per 1-cup serving: Calories 99 (5% from fat) Fat 0.7g (0g saturated) Cholesterol 0mg Sodium 24mg Carbohydrate 23.2g Fiber 5.2g Protein 2.8g

FROM *THEIR* KITCHEN TO OURS

For this month's nod to the Olympic Games, we look to the lively food of Jamaica. These Caribbean islanders love a good time, as well as their Olympic contenders – including the Atlanta-bound track squad and Winter Olympic bobsled team. (Bobsledding in Jamaica? Yes, *anything's* possible.)

To get into the rhythm of the island, enjoy a taste of the country with this Jamaican menu.

MONTEGO BAY GRILLED FISH WITH CARIBBEAN SALSA

(pictured on page 80)

3 tablespoons chopped fresh cilantro
1 roasted jalapeño pepper, chopped *
2 tablespoons fresh lime juice
1 tablespoon minced garlic
1 tablespoon minced fresh ginger
Vegetable cooking spray
4 amberjack or grouper fillets (about 1½ pounds)
Caribbean Salsa

• **Combine** first 5 ingredients; set aside.
• **Coat** a grill tray with cooking spray, and place on food rack. Heat, covered with grill lid, over hot coals (400° to 500°) 10 minutes. Place fish on hot grill tray.
• **Cook,** covered with grill lid, 10 minutes. Turn fish, and spread with cilantro mixture. Cook, covered, 10 minutes or until fish flakes easily when tested with a fork. Serve with Caribbean Salsa. **Yield:** 4 servings.

Caribbean Salsa

1 large ripe banana, peeled and chopped
½ cup finely chopped red bell pepper
½ cup finely chopped green bell pepper
½ cup chopped fresh cilantro
3 green onions, finely chopped
1 roasted jalapeño pepper, chopped *
1 tablespoon minced fresh ginger
2 tablespoons brown sugar
3 tablespoons fresh lime juice
1 tablespoon olive oil
¼ teaspoon salt
⅛ teaspoon pepper

• **Combine** all ingredients, tossing gently to coat; cover and chill 2 hours. **Yield:** 2½ cups.

* To roast jalapeños, place on an aluminum foil-lined baking sheet. Broil 5½ inches from heat (with electric oven door partially opened) about 5 minutes on each side or until blistered. Place in a heavy-duty, zip-top plastic bag; seal and let stand 10 minutes to loosen skins. Peel peppers; remove and discard seeds.

NOT SO FAST, BUT OH SO EASY

Call them Crock-Pots™ or slow cookers. By any name they cook deliciously slow. You can walk the dog, buy the groceries, pick up the kids, and set the table all before you dish up dinner. So, dig out your slow cooker from the corner cabinet because these recipes are too good to let wait.

SWEET JAMAICAN RICE

(pictured on page 80)

2 cups hot cooked rice
1 (11-ounce) can mandarin oranges, drained and chopped
1 (8-ounce) can crushed pineapple, drained
½ cup chopped red bell pepper
½ cup slivered almonds, toasted
⅓ cup sliced green onions
¼ cup flaked coconut, toasted
2 tablespoons hot mango chutney
¼ teaspoon ground ginger

• **Combine** all ingredients in a large skillet; cook over medium-high heat, stirring constantly, 5 minutes or until thoroughly heated. **Yield:** 4 servings.

Andy Jones
New Port Richey, Florida

REGGAE RUNDOWN

(pictured on page 80)

A rundown is a Jamaican dish reduced by slow cooking. This vegetable stew gets its kick from a Caribbean Scotch bonnet pepper.

1 (8-ounce) sweet potato
1 (8-ounce) baking potato
1 (14-ounce) can coconut milk
3 carrots, scraped and sliced
3 green onions, chopped
2 cloves garlic, minced
½ teaspoon salt
¼ teaspoon ground allspice
⅛ teaspoon dried thyme
1 cup peeled, chopped tomato
⅛ teaspoon minced Scotch bonnet or habanero pepper

• **Peel** potatoes; cut into ¾-inch cubes.
• **Bring** coconut milk to a boil in a large heavy saucepan over medium heat, stirring often; stir in potato, carrot, and next 5 ingredients. Return to a boil, stirring often; reduce heat, and simmer 7 minutes or until vegetables are almost tender, stirring often.
• **Stir** in tomato and pepper; cook 5 minutes or until thoroughly heated, stirring often. **Yield:** 4 servings.

CHUCK ROAST BARBECUE

1 (2- to 2½-pound) boneless chuck roast, trimmed
2 medium onions, chopped
¾ cup cola-flavored carbonated beverage
¼ cup Worcestershire sauce
1 tablespoon apple cider vinegar
2 cloves garlic, minced
1 teaspoon beef-flavored bouillon granules
½ teaspoon dry mustard
½ teaspoon chili powder
¼ teaspoon ground red pepper
½ cup ketchup
2 teaspoons butter or margarine
6 hamburger buns

• **Combine** roast and onion in a 4-quart slow cooker.
• **Combine** cola and next 7 ingredients; reserve ½ cup in refrigerator. Pour remaining mixture over roast and onion.
• **Cook,** covered, on HIGH 6 hours or until roast is very tender; drain and shred roast. Keep warm.
• **Combine** reserved ½ cup cola mixture, ketchup, and butter in a small saucepan; cook over medium heat, stirring constantly, just until thoroughly heated. Pour over shredded roast, stirring gently. Spoon onto buns, and serve with potato chips and pickle spears, if desired. **Yield:** 6 servings.

Lee Stearns
Mobile, Alabama

CHILI BEAN SOUP

½ pound lean ground beef
1 small onion, finely chopped
1 (15-ounce) can pinto beans, undrained
1 (10-ounce) can diced tomatoes and green chiles, undrained
¼ cup dry red wine
2 teaspoons chili powder
¼ teaspoon garlic salt

• **Cook** beef and onion in a large skillet until browned, stirring until meat crumbles; drain well.
• **Combine** beef mixture, beans, and remaining ingredients in a 1-quart slow cooker.
• **Cook,** covered, 3 hours. Serve with a green salad and cornbread, if desired. **Yield:** 2 servings.

Note: A 1-quart slow cooker has no LOW or HIGH setting, only off and on.

PORK CHOPS AND GRAVY

½ cup all-purpose flour
1½ teaspoons dry mustard
½ teaspoon salt
½ teaspoon garlic powder
6 (1-inch-thick) lean pork chops
1 (10¾-ounce) can condensed chicken broth, undiluted
2 tablespoons vegetable oil

• **Combine** first 4 ingredients in a shallow dish; dredge pork chops in flour mixture, and set aside.
• **Combine** remaining flour mixture and chicken broth in a 3½-quart slow cooker.
• **Pour** oil into a large skillet; place over medium-high heat until hot. Cook chops in hot oil just until browned on both sides; place in slow cooker.
• **Cook,** covered, on HIGH 2 to 2½ hours or until chops are tender. Serve with hot rice or mashed potatoes. **Yield:** 6 servings.

Carol S. Noble
Burgaw, North Carolina

SLOW SECRETS

- Read the instruction booklet that comes with your appliance.

- Slow cookers come in sizes ranging from 1 to 6 quarts. Be sure to consider the convenience of removable stoneware liners. In addition, 1-quart slow cookers have no LOW or HIGH setting, only off and on.

- Choose the right size slow cooker for the recipe, and always fill the slow cooker at least half full for best results.

- Coat the inside of the stoneware liner with vegetable cooking spray to make cleanup easier and quicker.

- To make a favorite recipe in a slow cooker, reduce the amount of liquid by half, except when you're preparing soups.

- Milk and other dairy products may separate during long cooking, so add them near the end of cooking time or substitute an undiluted cream soup.

- Use half the amount of herbs you usually would. Add ground herbs and spices during the last hour of cooking.

- Always cook with the cover on, and don't peek inside until it's time to stir.

- Use the LOW setting for all-day cooking. One hour on HIGH equals 2 to 2½ hours on LOW. There's no need to preheat.

SLOW-SIMMERED SPAGHETTI SAUCE

This sauce tastes every bit as good as ones prepared on the cooktop. You just don't have to stir it.

2 cloves garlic, minced
1 large onion, chopped
4 (14.5-ounce) cans Italian-style tomatoes, undrained and chopped
1 (15-ounce) can tomato sauce
1 (12-ounce) can tomato paste
2 to 3 teaspoons dried basil
2 to 3 teaspoons dried oregano
½ teaspoon dried crushed red pepper

• **Combine** all ingredients in a 4-quart slow cooker.
• **Cook,** covered, on HIGH 6 hours. Serve over spaghetti, chicken, or pork. **Yield:** 2½ quarts.

Note: You can freeze the spaghetti sauce in airtight containers up to 2 weeks.

Cindy Sullivan
Tallahassee, Florida

SAUCY APPLES 'N' PEARS

When entertaining, serve this directly from the slow cooker so that the fruit stays warm.

3 cooking apples (1½ pounds)
3 ripe pears (1½ pounds)
1 tablespoon lemon juice
¼ cup butter or margarine, melted
½ cup firmly packed dark brown sugar
2 (3-inch) sticks cinnamon
¼ cup raisins
½ cup chopped pecans
½ cup maple syrup
1 tablespoon cornstarch
2 tablespoons water

• **Core** and slice apples and pears; place in a 5-quart slow cooker. Sprinkle with lemon juice, tossing to coat well.
• **Combine** butter and brown sugar; spoon over fruit. Add cinnamon sticks, raisins, and pecans; drizzle with maple syrup, and stir gently.
• **Cook,** covered, on LOW 3 hours.
• **Combine** cornstarch and water, stirring well; stir into fruit mixture.
• **Cook,** covered, on LOW 3 hours or until fruit is tender. Remove and discard cinnamon sticks; serve topping over ice cream or pound cake. **Yield:** 8 servings.

CARAMEL PIE

If you don't own a 1-quart slow cooker, borrow one and make this recipe. But don't try this in a 4- or 5-quart slow cooker – the caramel might burn. It's so easy and wildly delicious, we gave it our best rating.

2 (14-ounce) cans sweetened condensed milk *
1 (9-inch) graham cracker crust
1 (8-ounce) container frozen whipped topping, thawed
1 (1.4-ounce) English toffee candy bar, coarsely chopped

• **Pour** condensed milk into a 1-quart slow cooker.
• **Cook,** covered, 6 to 7 hours or until mixture is the color of peanut butter, stirring with a wire whisk every 30 minutes.
• **Pour** into graham cracker crust; cool. Spread whipped topping over top, and sprinkle with chopped candy bar. Cover and chill. **Yield:** 1 (9-inch) pie.

* Substitute 2 (14-ounce) cans nonfat sweetened condensed milk for regular.

Note: A 1-quart slow cooker has no LOW or HIGH setting, only off and on.

Marla Highbaugh
Louisville, Kentucky

Macaroni and Cheese, Please

If macaroni has become mundane, be sure to try these simple, satisfying variations on the old standby. These recipes are worth the time it takes you to make real macaroni and cheese from scratch.

MACARONI MOUSSE

Hilda Rutherford's mother gave her this recipe in the fifties. To this day no one seems to know why it's called "mousse."

½ (8-ounce) package macaroni
1 small onion, finely chopped
1½ cups (6 ounces) shredded sharp Cheddar cheese
1 (2-ounce) jar diced pimiento, drained
2 tablespoons chopped green bell pepper
2 teaspoons dried parsley flakes
3 tablespoons butter or margarine
½ teaspoon salt
¼ teaspoon pepper
1 large egg, lightly beaten
4 slices white bread, crusts removed
½ cup slivered almonds (optional)
1½ cups milk

• **Cook** macaroni according to package directions; drain. Place macaroni in a lightly greased 2-quart baking dish.
• **Combine** onion and next 9 ingredients; stir in almonds, if desired.
• **Cook** milk in a small saucepan over low heat just until heated; stir into onion mixture (bread should dissolve). Pour over macaroni.
• **Bake** at 350° for 45 to 50 minutes. **Yield:** 6 servings.

Hilda Rutherford
Charlotte, North Carolina

MEXICAN MACARONI

1 (8-ounce) package macaroni
1 (14½-ounce) can Mexican-style tomatoes, undrained and chopped
1 (10¾-ounce) can cream of mushroom soup, undiluted
1 (8-ounce) carton sour cream
1 (4.5-ounce) can chopped green chiles
1 cup (4 ounces) shredded Monterey Jack cheese
1 cup (4 ounces) shredded Cheddar cheese

• **Cook** macaroni according to package directions; drain.
• **Combine** macaroni, tomatoes, and next 3 ingredients; stir in half of cheeses. Pour into a lightly greased 2-quart baking dish; top with remaining cheeses.
• **Bake** at 350° for 30 minutes. **Yield:** 6 servings.

Jane Rutland
Guntersville, Alabama

MACARONI PRIMAVERA

In this recipe the vegetables and macaroni cook together in the same pot, making cleanup a breeze.

4 quarts water
1 (8-ounce) package macaroni
3 large carrots, scraped and sliced
2 cups fresh broccoli flowerets
1 cup coarsely chopped fresh yellow squash
1 cup cottage cheese
½ (8-ounce) package cream cheese, softened
1 tablespoon prepared mustard
½ teaspoon salt
½ teaspoon pepper
¼ teaspoon hot sauce
1 cup sliced fresh mushrooms
1 cup (4 ounces) shredded mozzarella cheese
1 cup (4 ounces) shredded Cheddar cheese
3 tablespoons freshly grated Parmesan cheese

• **Bring** 4 quarts water to a boil in a large Dutch oven; add macaroni, and cook 4 minutes.
• **Add** carrot, and cook 2 minutes; add broccoli, and cook 2 minutes. Stir in squash, and cook 1 minute; drain.
• **Combine** cottage cheese and next 5 ingredients in a large bowl; stir in pasta mixture, mushrooms, mozzarella cheese, and half of Cheddar cheese.
• **Spoon** into a lightly greased 2-quart baking dish; sprinkle with Parmesan cheese and remaining Cheddar cheese.
• **Bake** at 375° for 20 minutes, shielding with aluminum foil after 15 minutes to prevent overbrowning, if necessary. **Yield:** 6 to 8 servings.

Lora Sheridan
Winston-Salem, North Carolina

Macaroni Twists

▪ If you favor lots of different cheeses, try substituting them in any of these recipes for a twist on an old favorite.

▪ By using new low-fat products on the market, you can lighten your favorite macaroni and cheese recipe considerably.

▪ You can reduce the amount of sodium in any pasta dish by cooking the pasta in unsalted water.

▪ Regular macaroni is tube shaped, but surprise your family with interesting variations like shells, ribbons, or twists.

KNIFE-AND-FORK SANDWICHES

A sandwich is a good choice when it's your night to cook. All these hot and hefty options come to the table in 15 to 30 minutes; the hard part is choosing just one. You could tackle these single-handedly, but we recommend using a knife and fork.

GIANT HAM-AND-PEPPER SANDWICH

2 Anaheim chile peppers
1 red bell pepper
1 green bell pepper
3 green onions
1 tablespoon butter or margarine
1 (10-ounce) can refrigerated pizza dough
1¼ pounds thinly sliced cooked ham
⅓ cup Thousand Island salad dressing
1½ cups (6 ounces) shredded sharp Cheddar cheese

• **Cut** peppers into thin strips; slice green onions.
• **Melt** butter in a 10-inch cast-iron skillet over medium-high heat; add peppers and green onions, and cook, stirring constantly, until tender. Remove from skillet; wipe drippings from skillet, and set skillet aside to cool.
• **Unroll** pizza dough, stretching to a 14½-inch square (do not tear dough). Gently place dough in cooled skillet, allowing edges to overhang.
• **Place** ham, pepper mixture, salad dressing, and cheese on dough; bring corners and sides of dough over cheese. Twist corners together in center, forming a knot, and pinch seams to seal.
• **Bake** at 425° for 15 to 20 minutes or until golden. Let sandwich stand 5 minutes before cutting into wedges. **Yield:** 6 servings.

Lee Barnett
Helena, Alabama

TURKEY-ASPARAGUS SANDWICHES

4 (1-ounce) slices Cheddar cheese
2 English muffins, split and toasted
½ pound thinly sliced turkey
½ pound fresh asparagus *
1 (0.9-ounce) package hollandaise sauce mix
Paprika (optional)

• **Place** a cheese slice on each muffin half; top evenly with turkey.
• **Cut** asparagus spears to fit muffin halves; place in a steamer basket over boiling water. Cover and steam 3 to 4 minutes or until asparagus is tender. Top each sandwich with 2 or 3 asparagus spears; reserve remaining asparagus for another use.
• **Prepare** sauce mix according to package directions; pour evenly over sandwiches. Sprinkle with paprika, if desired. **Yield:** 4 servings.

* Substitute 1 (10-ounce) package frozen asparagus spears, cooked, for fresh.

Toni Simmons
Apex, North Carolina

HOT CHICKEN SALAD SANDWICHES

2 (5-ounce) cans chunk white chicken, drained and flaked
1 (8-ounce) can pineapple tidbits, drained
1 cup (4 ounces) shredded Cheddar cheese
¼ cup finely chopped green bell pepper
2 tablespoons finely chopped celery
1 tablespoon finely chopped onion
⅓ cup mayonnaise or salad dressing
1 teaspoon salt
3 kaiser rolls, split

• **Combine** first 8 ingredients, stirring well; set aside.

• **Place** rolls, cut side up, on a baking sheet. Broil 5½ inches from heat (with electric oven door partially opened) until lightly browned.
• **Spread** filling evenly over rolls. Bake at 350° for 5 minutes or until thoroughly heated. **Yield:** 6 servings.

Nancy Williams
Starkville, Mississippi

Dinner in a Piecrust

Gather your dinner ingredients under a flaky crust for one terrific meal. All you need is one of these all-in-one-dish recipes.

CHICKEN POT PIE

¼ cup butter or margarine
¼ cup all-purpose flour
1½ cups chicken broth
1½ cups half-and-half
¾ teaspoon salt
½ teaspoon freshly ground pepper
2 tablespoons butter or margarine
1 (8-ounce) package sliced fresh mushrooms
1 small onion, chopped
3 stalks celery, sliced
3½ cups chopped cooked chicken
2 hard-cooked eggs, chopped
1 (15-ounce) package refrigerated piecrusts

• **Melt** ¼ cup butter in a heavy saucepan over low heat; add flour, stirring until smooth. Cook 1 minute, stirring constantly. Gradually add chicken broth and half-and-half; cook over medium heat, stirring constantly, until thickened and bubbly. Stir in salt and pepper; set sauce aside.
• **Melt** 2 tablespoons butter in a skillet over medium-high heat; add mushrooms, onion, and celery, and cook, stirring constantly, until vegetables are tender. Drain and stir vegetable mixture, chicken, and chopped egg into sauce.
• **Fit** 1 piecrust into a 9-inch deep-dish pieplate according to package directions. Spoon filling into crust; top with remaining piecrust. Trim off excess pastry. Fold edges under, and flute. Cut slits in top.
• **Bake** at 375° for 30 to 40 minutes or until top is golden, covering edges with strips of aluminum foil after 20 minutes to prevent excessive browning. **Yield:** 6 servings.

Angie Williams
Montgomery, Alabama

HAM-AND-CHEESE PIE

1 (8-ounce) can refrigerated crescent rolls
1½ cups finely chopped ham
1 (8-ounce) package Monterey Jack cheese, cubed
2 tablespoons grated Parmesan cheese
2 tablespoons finely chopped onion
2 large eggs, lightly beaten

• **Unroll** crescent rolls, and separate into 8 triangles. Fit 5 triangles into a 9-inch pieplate, pressing edges together to seal.
• **Combine** chopped ham and next 4 ingredients; spoon into pieplate.
• **Cut** remaining 3 triangles into thin strips; arrange over mixture.
• **Bake** on lower oven rack at 325° for 1 hour. Let stand 5 minutes before serving. **Yield:** 6 servings.

Kathy Miller
Olney, Maryland

CONTINENTAL MEAT PIE

1 large egg, lightly beaten
¾ pound ground chuck
¾ pound ground pork
1 teaspoon dried Italian seasoning
3 tablespoons all-purpose flour
3 tablespoons vegetable oil
½ pound Italian hot link sausage, cut into ½-inch slices (optional)
3 cups water
1 (1⅝-ounce) package dry spaghetti sauce mix
1 (6-ounce) can tomato paste
1 pound carrots, scraped
1½ pounds small zucchini
1 (16-ounce) jar whole white onions, drained
½ (15-ounce) package refrigerated piecrusts
1 large egg, lightly beaten

• **Combine** first 4 ingredients; shape into 2-inch balls, and roll in flour.
• **Pour** oil in a large skillet, and place over medium-high heat until hot. Add meatballs, and cook until browned, stirring occasionally. Add sausage, if desired, and cook until browned; drain well.
• **Add** water, sauce mix, and tomato paste to meatball mixture, stirring well; cook over low heat 15 minutes.
• **Cut** carrots and zucchini into 1-inch pieces; place in a saucepan, and cover with water. Bring to a boil over medium heat; cover, reduce heat, and simmer 10 minutes or until tender. Drain well; spoon vegetables into a 13- x 9- x 2-inch baking dish. Add meatball mixture and onions.
• **Roll** piecrust into a 14- x 10-inch rectangle on a lightly floured surface; cut lengthwise into 9 strips. Place 3 pastry strips lengthwise over meatball mixture; weave 3 pastry strips crosswise over meatball mixture. Cover rim of dish with remaining 3 pastry strips, pressing to seal. Brush pastry strips with beaten egg.
• **Bake** at 425° for 30 minutes or until golden. **Yield:** 6 servings.

Mrs. Michael Dryden
Pollock, Louisiana

GREEK APPETIZER

Volunteer to bring appetizers to your next potluck party. You can make this version of tiropita, a Greek cheese pie wrapped in phyllo, ahead because it freezes well. And if you've never worked with phyllo, go ahead and try – it's easier than you think.

GREEK SPINACH-AND-CHEESE PASTRIES

2 large eggs, lightly beaten
2 (10-ounce) packages frozen chopped spinach, thawed and drained
2 cups (8 ounces) shredded sharp Cheddar cheese
1 cup (4 ounces) crumbled feta cheese
¾ cup thinly sliced green onions
1½ tablespoons dried dillweed or ½ cup chopped fresh dill
½ cup chopped fresh flat-leaf parsley
½ teaspoon salt
¼ teaspoon pepper
1 (16-ounce) package frozen phyllo pastry (22 sheets), thawed
Vegetable cooking spray

• **Combine** first 9 ingredients in a large bowl; set aside.
• **Unfold** phyllo, and cover with a slightly damp towel to prevent pastry from drying out.
• **Place** 1 sheet of phyllo on a flat surface covered with wax paper; coat with cooking spray. Top with another sheet of phyllo; coat with cooking spray. Cut crosswise into 6 (2½-inch-wide) strips.
• **Place** 1 tablespoon spinach mixture at base of each strip; fold right bottom corner over to form a triangle. Continue folding back and forth into a triangle, gently pressing corners together.
• **Place** triangles, seam side down, on ungreased baking sheets; coat triangles lightly with cooking spray.
• **Repeat** procedure with remaining phyllo sheets, cooking spray, and spinach mixture.
• **Bake** pastries at 350° for 12 to 14 minutes or until golden. Serve immediately. **Yield:** 5½ dozen.

Note: Freeze unbaked pastries on baking sheets; store in freezer in airtight containers up to 2 weeks. Bake, unthawed, as directed.

FROM OUR KITCHEN TO YOURS

GOURMET GOOF, SUPER SAVE

Soup or stew too salty or too fiery? Stir a few large chunks of raw potato into pots and remove them before serving. Those starchy tubers will absorb some of the excess heat or counteract a heavy hand with the salt, if that's your problem.

A SOFT TOUCH

It's tough to guess the perfect moment in the life of an avocado. You finally pick one, set it faithfully on your kitchen window ledge, and give it a daily squeeze. Come Mexican night, it's sometimes still hard as a rock.

There's one last-ditch solution: Peel, seed, and microwave it at HIGH for 30 seconds or so. Sometimes, it'll give up and get soft enough to eat. (Not awe-inspiringly ripe, just soft.) And sometimes, it just won't. Your safety net? Add an extra-large carton of sour cream to the grocery list to make up for the irresistible fat you may have to throw out in a stubborn avocado.

TAKE A WHACK AT IT

Some of our favorite recipes use candy bars made of English toffee wrapped in milk chocolate, but breaking them up to mix into other ingredients has been a mess. After battling them with rolling pins, sharp knives, and warm hands, we've had more chocolate on the counter and ourselves than in the mixing bowl.

The solution? Just whack a still-wrapped candy bar against the edge of the countertop a few times until it breaks into chunks.

HANDS OFF

If you squeamishly back away from a bowl of gooey meat loaf-to-be or a vat of cookie dough, take a tip from Dorothy Gunn of Pinehurst, North Carolina. Instead of getting elbow deep in the stuff and then scrubbing her hands for hours, she keeps a supply of disposable gloves in her kitchen to handle such jobs. When the deed is done, she just peels off the gloves into the garbage. As a bonus, the disposable gloves are more sanitary.

EASY AS PIE . . . CRUST

And we're not talking homemade. We mean the kind of crust you buy folded up in the box in your grocer's refrigerated section. Just unwrap, unfold, cut with fun cookie cutters, and bake quickly for some eye-catching salad croutons.

If you don't have many shaped cutters in your kitchen, cut free-form triangles or diamonds with a knife, and straight or curvy strips with a fluted pastry wheel for a wavy edge. Bake at 400° for 4 to 6 minutes, and then cool the shapes and put them on delicate greens.

Serving a salad with a sweet dressing? Brush the cutouts with milk or egg white; then sprinkle them with sugar before baking.

Top a pecan pie with a pile of pastry leaves or a holiday dessert with Christmas-themed shapes sprinkled with red or green sugar crystals.

Right: *Lump Crab Hash With Three-Pepper Hollandaise and Morrison House Brioche (recipes, page 52) are two of the best breakfast recipes we've ever published.*

Create a springtime spread worthy of a family reunion or church picnic with Lemony Pecan Chicken, Stuffed Tomatoes, Roasted Caraway Potatoes, and Squash Tart. (Recipes begin on page 82.)

Left: *When piped onto vegetables, this spread becomes Roasted Garlic Canapés (recipe, page 95) – edible art. For easy piping ideas, see our tips on page 96.*

Below: *Easy baked Snapper Fingers With Banana Salsa (recipe, page 85) gets your party off to a great start.*

Montego Bay Grilled Fish With Caribbean Salsa meets its spicy match with Sweet Jamaican Rice and Reggae Rundown, a traditional Jamaican vegetable dish. *(Recipes begin on page 70.)*

APRIL

FEEDING BODY AND SOUL

The faithful parishioner sits in his usual pew, but today is special – the annual church picnic. What a fine day for it. Spangles of sunlight shining through new leaves dapple the windows, and like the squirming toddler in front of him, this parishioner is ready to sprint outside. Eventually the minister winds down and gives the benediction. It's time to head outside, grab a plate, and beat the kids to the biggest piece of fried chicken. Amen, amen.

LEMONY PECAN CHICKEN

(pictured on page 78)

1 cup chopped fresh parsley
½ cup grated Parmesan cheese
½ cup chopped pecans
2 cloves garlic
1 tablespoon dried basil
3 tablespoons lemon juice
⅓ cup peanut oil
6 skinned and boned chicken breast halves
⅛ teaspoon salt
Garnishes: lemon slices and wedges, fresh parsley sprigs

• **Combine** first 3 ingredients; reserve ⅔ cup parsley mixture.
• **Combine** remaining parsley mixture, garlic, basil, and lemon juice in container of an electric blender; process until smooth, stopping once to scrape down sides.
• **Turn** blender on high; gradually add oil in a slow, steady stream. Process until blended.
• **Arrange** chicken breast halves in an ungreased 11- x 7- x 1½-inch baking dish; sprinkle with salt. Pour mixture from blender over chicken; sprinkle with reserved ⅔ cup parsley mixture.
• **Bake** at 350° for 30 minutes or until chicken is done; garnish, if desired.
Yield: 6 servings.

Rita Williams
Mount Juliet, Tennessee

ROASTED CARAWAY POTATOES

(pictured on page 78)

3 pounds new potatoes, unpeeled and quartered
2 medium onions, sliced
¼ cup olive oil
1 tablespoon caraway seeds
1½ teaspoons salt
1 teaspoon pepper

• **Combine** all ingredients in a large bowl or large heavy-duty, zip-top plastic bag. Stir mixture in bowl or seal bag, and shake well to coat. Place potato mixture in an ungreased 13- x 9- x 2-inch pan.
• **Bake** at 400° for 1 hour or until potato is tender, stirring occasionally.
Yield: 8 servings.

Jeanne Dobson
New Orleans, Louisiana

STUFFED TOMATOES

(pictured on page 78)

1 (10-ounce) package frozen whole kernel corn
10 plum tomatoes
1 (16-ounce) can kidney beans, rinsed and drained
1 (4.5-ounce) can chopped green chiles, undrained
3 tablespoons vegetable oil
3 tablespoons apple cider vinegar
2 tablespoons finely chopped fresh cilantro or 2 teaspoons ground coriander *
1½ teaspoons finely chopped fresh oregano or ½ teaspoon dried oregano
¼ teaspoon salt
¼ teaspoon pepper
Dash of sugar
Garnish: fresh cilantro or parsley sprigs

• **Cook** corn according to package directions; cool.
• **Cut** tomatoes in half lengthwise; scoop out pulp to form shells. Place tomato shells, cut side down, on paper towels to drain.
• **Combine** corn, beans, and chiles in a large bowl. Combine oil and next 6

ingredients in a jar; cover tightly, and shake vigorously. Pour over corn mixture, stirring gently to coat. Cover and chill.
• **Spoon** corn mixture into tomato shells, using a slotted spoon; garnish, if desired. **Yield:** 10 servings.

* Substitute 2 tablespoons chopped fresh parsley for fresh cilantro or 2 teaspoons dried parsley flakes for ground coriander.

Lula Bell Hawks
Newport, Arkansas

The young and young-at-heart will enjoy taking these home-cooked favorites to church picnics. They're sure to disappear in a hurry, and you'll go home happy.

SQUASH TART

(pictured on page 78)

½ (15-ounce) package refrigerated piecrusts
2 yellow squash, sliced (about ¾ pound)
2 zucchini, sliced (about ¾ pound)
1½ cups water
1 teaspoon salt
¼ cup butter or margarine, melted
2 large eggs, lightly beaten
1 (8-ounce) carton sour cream
½ cup finely chopped onion
½ teaspoon salt
¼ teaspoon pepper

• **Fit** piecrust into a 9-inch pieplate following package directions; fold edges under, and crimp. Line pastry with aluminum foil, and fill with pie weights or dried beans.
• **Bake** at 450° for 6 minutes; remove pie weights and foil. Bake 1 additional minute; set aside.
• **Combine** yellow squash and next 3 ingredients in a skillet; bring to a boil. Cover, reduce heat, and simmer 3 to 4 minutes or until crisp-tender; drain.
• **Combine** butter and half of squash mixture in a large bowl; coarsely mash. Stir in egg and next 4 ingredients; pour into prepared pastry. Arrange remaining squash and zucchini slices on top.
• **Bake** at 350° for 35 to 40 minutes or until a knife inserted in center comes out clean. **Yield:** 1 (9-inch) pie.

Esther Harmon
Banner Elk, North Carolina

CHEDDAR-APPLE BREAD

½ cup shortening
½ cup sugar
1 large egg
1 (21-ounce) can apple pie filling
2½ cups all-purpose flour
1 teaspoon baking soda
1 teaspoon baking powder
1 teaspoon salt
1 teaspoon apple pie spice
½ cup milk
1 cup (4 ounces) shredded Cheddar cheese
½ cup chopped walnuts

• **Beat** shortening at medium speed with an electric mixer until fluffy. Gradually add sugar, beating well. Add egg, beating until blended. Stir in pie filling.
• **Combine** flour and next 4 ingredients; gradually add to apple mixture alternately with milk, beginning and ending with flour mixture. Stir well after each addition. Stir in Cheddar cheese and walnuts. Spoon batter into a greased 9- x 5- x 3-inch loafpan.
• **Bake** at 350° for 50 minutes or until a wooden pick inserted in center comes out clean. Cool in pan on a wire rack 10 minutes; remove bread from pan, and cool completely on wire rack. **Yield:** 1 loaf.

Note: You can freeze bread in an airtight container up to 3 months.

Lynn Aigner
Woodsboro, Texas

PINEAPPLE BAKE

This side dish goes good with sliced ham, pork, chicken, or turkey.

2 (20-ounce) cans sliced pineapple in juice, undrained
2 cups (8 ounces) shredded sharp Cheddar cheese
⅔ cup sugar
⅓ cup all-purpose flour
1 cup round buttery cracker crumbs
¼ cup butter or margarine, melted

• **Drain** sliced pineapple, reserving ⅓ cup juice.
• **Place** pineapple in a lightly greased 11- x 7- x 1½-inch baking dish; sprinkle with cheese.
• **Combine** reserved pineapple juice, sugar, and flour; pour over cheese. Combine cracker crumbs and butter; sprinkle over flour mixture.
• **Bake** at 350° for 25 minutes or until bubbly. **Yield:** 8 servings.

Sheryl Jennings
Uvalde, Texas

FRESH STRAWBERRY COBBLER

¼ cup butter or margarine, softened
¾ cup sugar
1 large egg
1 teaspoon vanilla extract
1¼ cups all-purpose flour
1¼ teaspoons baking powder
½ teaspoon salt
½ cup milk
3 cups fresh strawberries, cut in half lengthwise
¼ cup all-purpose flour
¼ cup sugar
¼ cup butter or margarine, chilled

• **Beat** ¼ cup softened butter at medium speed with an electric mixer; gradually add ¾ cup sugar, beating well. Add egg and vanilla, beating well.
• **Combine** 1¼ cups flour, baking powder, and salt; add to butter mixture alternately with milk, beginning and ending with flour mixture. Spoon mixture into a greased 8-inch square baking dish. Arrange strawberries on top, cut side down.
• **Combine** ¼ cup flour and ¼ cup sugar; cut in ¼ cup chilled butter with pastry blender until crumbly. Sprinkle over strawberries.
• **Bake** at 350° for 1 hour or until a wooden pick inserted in center comes out clean. Serve warm with ice cream or sweetened whipped cream. **Yield:** 8 servings.

FIRST-TIMER'S FOCACCIA

Ed Cromwell of Jacksonville, Florida, admits that he's no baker. But his daughter, Liz Lorber, somehow manages to get him into the kitchen for an occasional journey into the unknown.

You, too, can make this Italian bread that's as good as Ed's, even if you've never baked bread before.

FOCACCIA WITH ROSEMARY

Use focaccia for sandwiches or serve it when you want to add an authentic Italian touch to any meal. Cube and toast leftovers to make flavorful croutons.

2 packages active dry yeast
2 cups warm water (105° to 115°)
6 cups all-purpose flour, divided
½ cup unsalted butter, softened
½ cup finely chopped fresh rosemary leaves, divided
1 teaspoon salt
½ cup olive oil, divided
8 cloves garlic, minced
2 teaspoons kosher salt
½ teaspoon freshly ground pepper

• **Combine** yeast and water in a 2-cup liquid measuring cup, and let stand 5 minutes.
• **Place** 4 cups flour in a large bowl; make a well in center. Add yeast mixture; stir until a soft dough forms.
• **Cover** and let rise in a warm place (85°), free from drafts, 1 hour or until doubled in bulk.
• **Sprinkle** remaining 2 cups flour on a flat surface. Turn dough out onto floured surface, and knead until flour is incorporated to make a firm dough. Gradually knead in butter, ¼ cup rosemary, and salt.
• **Knead** until dough is smooth and elastic (about 5 minutes), adding additional flour, if necessary.
• **Brush** two 15- x 10- x 1-inch jellyroll pans with 2 tablespoons olive oil. Set aside.
• **Divide** dough in half. Roll each portion into a 15- x 10-inch rectangle. Place in prepared pans. Using fingertips, press small indentations in top of dough; sprinkle with garlic and remaining ¼ cup rosemary. Drizzle with remaining 6 tablespoons olive oil, and sprinkle with kosher salt and pepper.
• **Cover** and let rise in a warm place (85°), free from drafts, 30 to 45 minutes or until almost doubled in bulk.
• **Bake** at 375° for 25 to 30 minutes or until golden. Cut into squares. **Yield:** 2 loaves.

> *"Focaccia? I didn't even know what it was. But it turned out great, and all I did was stand there and follow Liz's recipe."*
>
> *Ed Cromwell*
> *Jacksonville, Florida*

Spring Celebrations

A FLORIDIAN FEAST

Nita Norman checks her Tropical Pork Loin and a pot of Miami Rice – contributions to the evening's meal. A fruity aroma fills her spacious kitchen, a sure sign of good things – and good friends – to come.

FLORIDIAN FEAST
Serves Eight

Snapper Fingers With Banana Salsa **Fresh Baby Vegetables and Ranch-Style Dressing**
Hearts of Palm Salad **Stone Crab Bisque**
Tropical Pork Loin
Miami Rice **Asparagus With Warm Citrus Dressing**
Stuffed Homestead Tomatoes
Key Lime Cheesecake With Strawberry-Butter Sauce

Mack and Delia Brown, Bill and Marilyn Motley, and Don and Ann Murray arrive late afternoon at Nita and Harold Norman's historic home on the Coral Gables Waterway.

"This is one of the nicest feelings," Nita says. "We all talk about the South, our lives, the places we've traveled – and, of course, the food we adore. That's why we have so much fun. We're like family."

After appetizers on the patio, the couples sit down to a tropical feast. Welcome to their party.

SNAPPER FINGERS WITH BANANA SALSA

(pictured on page 79)

1½ cups crushed potato chips
¼ cup grated Parmesan cheese
1 teaspoon ground thyme
1 pound snapper or grouper fillets, cut into strips
¼ cup milk
Banana Salsa
Garnishes: fresh parsley sprigs

• **Combine** first 3 ingredients in a shallow dish; dip fish in milk, and dredge in potato chip mixture. Place fish in a single layer on a greased baking sheet.
• **Bake** at 500° for 8 to 10 minutes. Serve fish with Banana Salsa. Garnish, if desired. **Yield:** 8 servings.

Banana Salsa

2 medium-size ripe bananas, chopped
½ cup chopped green bell pepper
½ cup chopped red bell pepper
3 green onions, chopped
1 tablespoon chopped fresh cilantro
2 tablespoons light brown sugar
3 tablespoons fresh lime juice
1 tablespoon vegetable oil
¼ teaspoon salt
¼ teaspoon pepper
1 small jalapeño pepper, seeded and chopped (optional)

• **Combine** first 10 ingredients, stirring gently. Add jalapeño pepper, if desired. Cover and chill at least 3 hours. **Yield:** 8 servings.

HEARTS OF PALM SALAD

1 bunch red leaf lettuce
1 green bell pepper
1 red bell pepper
1 ripe avocado
1 (7.7-ounce) can hearts of palm, drained
1 (8-ounce) bottle Caesar vinaigrette

• **Separate** lettuce leaves; arrange on individual salad plates.
• **Cut** bell peppers into thin strips; peel and slice avocado.
• **Arrange** bell peppers, avocado, and hearts of palm over lettuce. Drizzle evenly with dressing. **Yield:** 8 servings.

STONE CRAB BISQUE

½ cup butter or margarine, divided
½ cup finely chopped onion
½ cup finely chopped green bell pepper
2 green onions, finely chopped
¼ cup chopped fresh parsley
1 (8-ounce) package fresh mushrooms, chopped
¼ cup all-purpose flour
2 cups milk
2 teaspoons salt
¼ teaspoon pepper
1 teaspoon hot sauce
3 cups half-and-half
2½ cups stone crab claw meat (22 medium claws) *
¼ cup dry sherry

• **Melt** ¼ cup butter in a Dutch oven over medium-high heat; add onion and next 4 ingredients, and cook, stirring constantly, 5 minutes or until tender. Remove from Dutch oven, and set aside.
• **Melt** remaining ¼ cup butter in Dutch oven over low heat; add flour, stirring until smooth. Cook 1 minute, stirring constantly. Gradually stir in milk. Cook over medium heat, stirring constantly, until thickened and bubbly.
• **Stir** in onion mixture, salt, and next 3 ingredients. Bring to a boil, stirring constantly; reduce heat, and gently stir in crab claw meat. Simmer 5 minutes, stirring often. Stir in sherry. **Yield:** 8 servings.

* Substitute 2½ cups flaked, back-fin crabmeat for claw meat.

Note: Stone crab is in season October 15 to May 15. You can mail-order it from Joe's Stone Crab in Miami Beach, 1-800-780-2722. The medium stone crab claws come in orders of six. Market prices vary, so call for specific prices. There's an additional charge for packing and shipping.

TROPICAL PORK LOIN

2 (15-ounce) cans sliced mangoes, drained
1 small onion, chopped
2 cloves garlic, minced
½ cup honey
⅓ cup soy sauce
¼ cup chopped crystallized ginger
¾ cup lemon-lime carbonated beverage
1 (2½- to 3-pound) boneless pork loin roast, well trimmed
¼ cup flaked coconut, toasted

• **Position** knife blade in food processor bowl; add mangoes. Process until smooth, stopping once to scrape down sides. Pour 2 cups mango puree into a large shallow dish or heavy-duty, zip-top plastic bag; chill remaining puree.
• **Add** onion and next 5 ingredients to dish or bag, stirring well; add roast, turning to coat. Cover or seal, and marinate in refrigerator 6 to 8 hours, turning roast occasionally.
• **Remove** roast, reserving ½ cup marinade. Place roast on a rack in a lightly greased broiler pan; pour reserved ½ cup marinade over roast.
• **Bake** at 325° for 1½ hours or until a meat thermometer inserted in thickest part registers 160°.
• **Broil** 5½ inches from heat (with electric oven door partially opened) 5 minutes or until lightly browned. Remove roast to a serving platter, and keep warm; reserve ¼ cup drippings in broiler pan.
• **Add** remaining mango puree to reserved pan drippings; cook over medium heat until sauce is thoroughly heated, stirring occasionally.
• **Sprinkle** coconut over roast; serve with sauce. **Yield:** 8 servings.

MIAMI RICE

1⅓ cups orange juice
1½ cups water
1 (10-ounce) package yellow rice
1 cup chopped dates

• **Bring** orange juice and water to a boil in a saucepan; stir in rice.
• **Cover,** reduce heat, and simmer 25 minutes or until liquid is absorbed and rice is cooked. Stir in dates. **Yield:** 8 servings.

ASPARAGUS WITH WARM CITRUS DRESSING

2 pounds fresh asparagus
½ cup butter or margarine
2 teaspoons grated lime rind
2 tablespoons fresh lime juice

• **Snap** off tough ends of asparagus. Remove scales from stalks with a vegetable peeler, if desired.
• **Place** asparagus in an 11- x 7- x 1½-inch dish. Cover tightly with heavy-duty plastic wrap, and fold back a small corner to allow the steam to escape.
• **Microwave** at HIGH 6 to 7 minutes or until crisp-tender, giving dish a half-turn after 3 minutes. Set aside.
• **Place** butter in a 2-cup liquid measuring cup; microwave at HIGH 1 minute or just until melted. Stir in lime rind and juice; pour over asparagus. **Yield:** 8 servings.

STUFFED HOMESTEAD TOMATOES

The tomatoes grown in Homestead, Florida, are some of the freshest and most flavorful we've ever tried. If they aren't available where you live, use your region's best and brightest to bring out the full flavor of this dish.

8 medium-size firm ripe tomatoes *
1 cup Italian-seasoned breadcrumbs
⅓ cup chopped green onions
¼ cup chopped fresh parsley
1 tablespoon chopped fresh thyme
2 cloves garlic, minced
½ teaspoon salt
¼ teaspoon pepper
¼ cup olive oil

• **Cut** a ¼-inch slice from top of each tomato; scoop out pulp into a bowl, leaving tomato shells intact. Place shells upside down on paper towels to drain.
• **Add** breadcrumbs and next 7 ingredients to tomato pulp, stirring well; spoon mixture into tomato shells, and place in a lightly greased 13- x 9- x 2-inch baking dish.
• **Bake** at 450° for 10 minutes. **Yield:** 8 servings.

* Substitute 12 plum tomatoes, cut in half lengthwise, for 8 medium-size ones.

KEY LIME CHEESECAKE WITH STRAWBERRY-BUTTER SAUCE

2 cups graham cracker crumbs
¼ cup sugar
½ cup butter or margarine, melted
3 (8-ounce) packages cream cheese, softened
1¼ cups sugar
6 large eggs, separated
1 (8-ounce) carton sour cream
1½ teaspoons grated lime rind
½ cup Key lime juice
Strawberry-Butter Sauce

• **Combine** first 3 ingredients, and firmly press mixture on bottom and 1 inch up sides of a buttered 9-inch springform pan.
• **Bake** at 350° for 8 minutes; cool.
• **Beat** cream cheese at medium speed with an electric mixer until fluffy; gradually add 1¼ cups sugar, beating well. Add egg yolks, one at a time, beating after each addition. Stir in sour cream, lime rind, and lime juice.
• **Beat** egg whites at high speed until stiff peaks form; fold into cream cheese mixture. Pour batter into crust.
• **Bake** at 350° for 1 hour and 5 minutes; turn oven off. Partially open oven door; let cheesecake cool in oven 15 minutes. Remove from oven, and immediately run a knife around edge of pan to release sides.
• **Cool** completely in pan on a wire rack; cover and chill 8 hours. Serve with Strawberry-Butter Sauce. **Yield:** 1 (9-inch) cheesecake.

Strawberry-Butter Sauce

1¼ cups fresh strawberries, hulled
¼ cup butter or margarine, melted
½ cup sifted powdered sugar
1½ teaspoons grated lime rind

• **Position** knife blade in food processor bowl; add strawberries. Process until smooth, stopping once to scrape down sides. Stir in butter and remaining ingredients. **Yield:** 1 cup.

GREEK EASTER DINNER

Toni Spanos Nordan and her husband, Clay, of Birmingham, Alabama, are hosting the family's Greek Orthodox Easter celebration. The day is observed according to the preGregorian calendar; therefore, the Orthodox holiday falls one week later than Easter.

Join the Nordans and experience a delicious taste of Greek tradition.

GREEK EASTER MENU
Serves Eight

Roasted Peppers-Feta Cheese Crostini
Egg-Lemon Soup
Grilled Leg of Lamb
Orzo
Greek-Style Squashes
Green Pea Salad
Easter Egg Bread
Bunny Cake

ROASTED PEPPERS-FETA CHEESE CROSTINI

1 (8-ounce) package feta cheese
1 (16-ounce) jar roasted red bell peppers, drained
1 tablespoon olive oil
1 French baguette, thinly sliced

• **Cut** cheese into 24 equal pieces; cut bell peppers into 1-inch strips. Wrap pepper strips around cheese pieces; secure with wooden picks, and place in an 8-inch square baking dish. Drizzle with olive oil.
• **Bake** at 325° for 20 minutes; remove wooden picks, and serve warm on bread slices. **Yield:** 2 dozen.

Laura Leatherwood
Birmingham, Alabama

EGG-LEMON SOUP

Margie Spanos, Toni's mother, has been making this soup for years. "The kids called it grass soup because of all the herbs," she says.

2 quarts chicken broth
1 cup rice, uncooked
½ cup chopped green onions
½ cup chopped fresh parsley
1 tablespoon chopped fresh dill
1 tablespoon chopped fresh mint
6 large eggs
⅓ cup lemon juice
Garnish: fresh dill sprigs

• **Bring** broth to a boil in a Dutch oven over medium-high heat; add rice. Cover, reduce heat, and simmer 20 minutes or until rice is tender.
• **Stir** green onions and next 3 ingredients into broth mixture.
• **Beat** eggs with a wire whisk until frothy; gradually add lemon juice, stirring constantly.
• **Add** 2 cups hot broth mixture gradually to egg mixture, stirring constantly; gradually add to remaining broth mixture, stirring constantly. Cook over medium heat 5 minutes or until thermometer registers 160° (do not boil). Garnish each serving, if desired. **Yield:** 8 cups.

Margie Spanos
Birmingham, Alabama

ORZO, GRECIAN STYLE

To give orzo the flavor of the season, prepare it according to package directions, substituting chicken broth for half of the water. Sprinkle with grated kasseri (a sharp Greek cheese made from sheep's or goat's milk) or Parmesan cheese. **Yield:** 8 servings.

GRILLED LEG OF LAMB

Toni's brother, Michael, always prepares the lamb. This is one of his best recipes.

1 head garlic
1 (6- to 7-pound) leg of lamb, trimmed
1 (750-milliliter) bottle dry red wine
¼ cup olive oil
1 tablespoon dried oregano
1 tablespoon dried rosemary
2 teaspoons paprika

• **Peel** garlic; cut 5 cloves into thin slices, and crush remaining cloves.
• **Make** 1-inch-deep cuts into lamb, using a small paring knife; insert a garlic slice into each cut. Place lamb in a large shallow dish.
• **Combine** crushed garlic, wine, and next 4 ingredients; reserve 1 cup wine mixture, and chill. Pour remaining wine mixture over lamb; cover and marinate in refrigerator 8 hours, turning occasionally.
• **Remove** lamb from marinade, discarding marinade.
• **Cook** over low coals (under 300°) for 1½ hours or until a meat thermometer inserted in thickest portion, making sure it does not touch fat or bone, registers 145°, turning and basting with reserved wine mixture every 15 minutes. Remove from heat; cover and let stand 30 minutes or until meat thermometer registers 150° (medium-rare). **Yield:** 8 servings.

Michael Spanos
Birmingham, Alabama

GREEK-STYLE SQUASHES

4 large zucchini
4 large yellow squash
½ cup olive oil
¼ cup lemon juice
2 tablespoons chopped fresh parsley
2 tablespoons chopped fresh dill
1 teaspoon salt
½ teaspoon freshly ground pepper

• **Cut** zucchini and yellow squash diagonally into ¼-inch-thick slices, and arrange slices in a steamer basket over boiling water. Cover and steam 5 minutes or until crisp-tender.
• **Combine** oil and next 5 ingredients, stirring well; pour over vegetables, tossing to coat. **Yield:** 8 servings.

GREEN PEA SALAD

This recipe halves easily.

2 (16-ounce) packages frozen English peas, thawed
2 green onions, sliced
2 (8-ounce) cans sliced water chestnuts, drained
⅔ cup reduced-fat sour cream
⅔ cup reduced-fat mayonnaise
1 teaspoon freshly ground black pepper
Garnishes: sliced green onions, cashew halves

• **Combine** first 6 ingredients. Garnish, if desired. **Yield:** 8 servings.

EASTER EGG BREAD

Margie bakes enough loaves to send one home with each family member. If you start baking about a week ahead of time, you can do it, too.

2 cups sugar
1½ cups milk
1 cup butter or margarine
3 packages active dry yeast
1 tablespoon all-purpose flour
1 teaspoon sugar
⅓ cup warm water (105° to 115°)
6 large eggs, lightly beaten
9 cups all-purpose flour
2 hard-cooked eggs, unshelled and dyed
1 large egg, lightly beaten
1 teaspoon sesame seeds

• **Combine** first 3 ingredients in a large saucepan; cook over medium heat until butter melts. Cool milk mixture to 105° to 115°.

• **Combine** yeast and next 3 ingredients in a large bowl; let stand 5 minutes. Stir in 6 lightly beaten eggs. Gradually add 9 cups flour alternately with milk mixture, stirring well.

• **Turn** dough out onto a well-floured surface, and knead until smooth and elastic (about 5 minutes). Place dough in a well-greased bowl, turning to grease top.

• **Cover** and let rise in a warm place (85°), free from drafts, 1 hour.

• **Punch** dough down, and divide in half; divide each half into 3 portions. Shape each portion into a 2½-foot rope. Pinch 3 ropes together at 1 end to seal; braid ropes. Place braid on a lightly greased baking sheet, and shape into a circle. Place 1 hard-cooked egg where braids meet, shaping dough around egg. Repeat procedure with remaining 3 ropes of dough.

• **Cover** braids; let rise in a warm place (85°), free from drafts, 30 minutes.

• **Brush** bread with 1 beaten egg, and sprinkle with sesame seeds.

• **Bake** at 350° for 30 minutes or until golden. **Yield:** 2 loaves.

Margie Spanos
Birmingham, Alabama

Bunny Cake

A family tradition started in the 1940s, this dessert is always the hit of the party. Toni and her best friend, Melissa McDonald, decorate the Bunny Cake with a construction theme, depicting the renovations to the Nordans' house.

Start your own Bunny Cake tradition with your favorite frosted layer cake. Come up with a theme that spotlights a current family event.

To make bunnies for the cake, cut large marshmallows in half for bodies and heads. Cut additional large marshmallows into fourths to make ears. Cut miniature marshmallows into quarters for hands.

Gently press cut marshmallows into frosting of cake to resemble bunnies.

Dip a wooden pick in liquid food coloring, and press into the marshmallow to make faces and whiskers. Using a small paintbrush and liquid food coloring, paint the bunnies as desired. Add other decorations to complete your theme.

On the Hunt

Entertain children with an egg hunt and luncheon. Our easy, kid-pleasing menu gets a jump start with frozen potatoes and chicken breast strips. Hide plastic eggs and include a golden one; award a prize to the person who finds it.

Finger Chicken

1 (16-ounce) carton plain yogurt
1½ teaspoons garlic powder
⅛ teaspoon paprika
1¼ pounds chicken breast strips
2 cups white cornmeal
1 teaspoon salt
Vegetable oil
Tangy Peach Sauce

• **Combine** first 3 ingredients in a large shallow dish. Add chicken, tossing to coat; cover and chill at least 1 hour.

• **Combine** cornmeal and salt in a shallow dish. Remove chicken from marinade, discarding marinade; dredge chicken in cornmeal mixture.

• **Pour** oil to depth of 3 inches into a Dutch oven or electric fryer; heat to 400°. Fry chicken, a few strips at a time, 4 to 5 minutes or until golden, turning once. Drain on paper towels; serve with Tangy Peach Sauce. **Yield:** 6 servings.

Tangy Peach Sauce

1 (10-ounce) jar peach preserves
3 tablespoons Dijon mustard
1½ teaspoons soy sauce

• **Combine** all ingredients in a small saucepan; cook over medium heat, stirring constantly, just until thoroughly heated. **Yield:** 1½ cups.

Something "Eggstra"

Cut out egg shapes from cardboard and distribute with the invitations. Ask the guests to decorate the eggs and bring them to the party. Award a prize to the person with the most original egg. Later, use the decorated eggs as place cards.

Baked Potato Fries

1 cup Italian-seasoned breadcrumbs
1 (28-ounce) package frozen dinner fries
2 large eggs, lightly beaten
3 tablespoons butter or margarine, melted
1 teaspoon salt

• **Place** breadcrumbs in a shallow dish. Dip fries into egg, and dredge in breadcrumbs. Place fries in a single layer on an ungreased 15- x 10- x 1-inch jellyroll pan; drizzle with butter.
• **Bake** at 400° for 25 minutes or until golden, turning once. Sprinkle with salt, and serve warm. **Yield:** 8 servings.

Jennifer Schair
Woodstock, Georgia

Sunny Day Salad

6 canned peach halves
1 head leaf lettuce
¾ cup shredded carrot
1 (8-ounce) can pineapple tidbits, drained
12 raisins
2 maraschino cherries

• **Place** 1 peach half, cut side down, in center of each lettuce-lined salad plate.
• **Arrange** shredded carrot to resemble hair; arrange pineapple tidbits to resemble sunrays. Arrange raisins to resemble eyes.
• **Cut** cherries into slivers; arrange slivers to resemble mouths. Chill 30 minutes. **Yield:** 6 servings.

Jane Marion
Cary, North Carolina

Peanut Butter Spread

1 (8-ounce) package cream cheese, softened
1½ cups creamy peanut butter
½ cup sifted powdered sugar
1 tablespoon milk
⅓ cup chopped dry roasted peanuts

• **Combine** first 4 ingredients in a small mixing bowl; beat at medium speed with an electric mixer 1 minute or until smooth. Shape mixture to resemble an egg; press peanuts onto egg. Serve spread with apple wedges or graham crackers. **Yield:** 2 cups.

Fran Pointer
Kansas City, Missouri

Egg on Your Plate

There's more than one way to stuff an egg. Try cutting some of the eggs crosswise, instead of lengthwise, for a different look. To make them stand upright, cut a thin slice off the bottom of each half before adding the stuffing. Forget the pickle relish this year, and stuff Easter's leftovers with new flavors.

Green Eggs and Ham

Guacamole-stuffed eggs are topped with country ham in this recipe.

6 ounces thinly sliced country ham
12 large hard-cooked eggs
1 ripe avocado, peeled and mashed
2 tablespoons finely chopped onion
1 clove garlic, minced
2 tablespoons mayonnaise or salad dressing
1½ to 2 tablespoons fresh lime juice
1 teaspoon hot sauce
1 small tomato, peeled, seeded, and finely chopped

• **Cook** ham in a nonstick skillet over medium heat 5 minutes or until lightly browned, turning once. Drain and finely chop.
• **Cut** eggs in half lengthwise, and carefully remove yolks. Mash yolks with a fork; add avocado and next 5 ingredients, stirring well. Fold in tomato, and spoon into egg whites. Top with ham. **Yield:** 2 dozen.

Black-and-Blue Eggs

12 large hard-cooked eggs
1 (4-ounce) package crumbled blue cheese
¼ cup half-and-half
2 tablespoons lime juice
1 tablespoon black caviar

• **Cut** eggs in half lengthwise, and carefully remove yolks. Mash yolks with a fork; add cheese, half-and-half, and lime juice, stirring until smooth. Spoon or pipe into egg whites, and top each evenly with caviar. **Yield:** 2 dozen.

J. McGrath
Opa-Locka, Florida

DRESSY VEGGIES

The ham has been picked up from the grocery store, and you've figured out what you're going to serve for dessert. Here are some vegetable ideas that will make your meal complete. In these recipes, onions, brussels sprouts, and celery get dressed up for company.

MARBLEIZED GARLIC-CHEESE-STUFFED EGGS

Marbleize hard-cooked eggs for any recipe, using the beet juice method described here. Don't worry about a flavor clash – you won't taste beet flavor in the egg white if you use plain, not pickled, beets.

1 (15-ounce) can whole beets, undrained
6 large hard-cooked eggs
1 head garlic
1 teaspoon olive oil
1 cup (4 ounces) shredded Monterey Jack cheese
2 tablespoons olive oil
1/8 teaspoon salt
1/4 teaspoon freshly ground pepper
1/4 teaspoon chopped fresh rosemary
1/4 teaspoon chopped fresh thyme
Garnish: fresh thyme or rosemary sprigs

• **Drain** beets, reserving liquid in an 11- x 7- x 1½-inch baking dish; reserve beets for another use. Crack egg shells with back of a spoon; do not peel. Place eggs in beet liquid; add enough water to cover eggs. Cover and store in refrigerator at least 8 hours.
• **Cut** off pointed end of garlic head, and spread cloves apart, leaving tight outer covering intact; place, cut side up, on a square of aluminum foil. Drizzle with 1 teaspoon olive oil, and wrap in foil.
• **Bake** garlic at 350° for 30 minutes.
• **Remove** eggs from beet liquid, discarding beet liquid. Dry eggs with paper towels, and peel.
• **Cut** eggs in half lengthwise, and carefully remove yolks.
• **Position** knife blade in food processor bowl; squeeze pulp from garlic cloves into processor bowl. Add cheese; pulse several times. Add egg yolks, 2 tablespoons olive oil, salt, and pepper; process until smooth. Stir in chopped rosemary and thyme; spoon or pipe into egg whites. Garnish, if desired. **Yield:** 1 dozen.

RATATOUILLE-STUFFED ONIONS

6 large onions, cut in half crosswise
1½ cups finely chopped green bell pepper
3/4 cup peeled and finely chopped eggplant
3/4 cup finely chopped zucchini
3/4 cup thinly sliced fresh mushrooms
1/4 cup olive oil
1½ cups peeled, seeded, and chopped tomato
1/2 cup dry white wine
1/4 cup tomato paste
1½ teaspoons dried thyme
1 teaspoon dried rosemary
1/2 teaspoon salt
1/2 teaspoon freshly ground pepper
1/2 teaspoon garlic powder
1/3 cup pine nuts, toasted and divided
2 tablespoons grated Parmesan cheese

• **Cut** a thin slice from bottom of onion halves, if necessary, for onions to sit upright. Scoop out onions, leaving a ½-inch-thick shell. Chop onion centers to measure 1½ cups; reserve remaining onion for another use.
• **Place** shells, upright, in a 13- x 9- x 2-inch baking dish; add hot water to dish to depth of 1 inch.
• **Cover** and bake at 400° for 35 minutes or until tender. Remove shells; drain and keep warm.
• **Cook** reserved 1½ cups chopped onion, bell pepper, and next 3 ingredients in oil in a large skillet over medium-high heat, stirring constantly, 3 minutes or until tender.
• **Add** tomato and next 7 ingredients; bring to a boil, stirring constantly. Reduce heat, and simmer 12 minutes or until most of liquid evaporates, stirring often. Remove from heat; stir in 3 tablespoons pine nuts.
• **Spoon** evenly into onion shells; sprinkle with Parmesan cheese and remaining pine nuts. Serve immediately. **Yield:** 12 servings.

BRUSSELS SPROUTS DIJON

2/3 cup mayonnaise or salad dressing
2/3 cup sour cream
1/4 cup Dijon mustard
1/2 teaspoon garlic salt
1 tablespoon Worcestershire sauce
Dash of hot sauce
4 (10-ounce) packages frozen brussels sprouts
3 tablespoons butter or margarine, melted
1/4 cup finely chopped pecans, toasted

• **Combine** first 6 ingredients in a small saucepan; cook over low heat until heated, stirring often. Keep warm.
• **Cook** brussels sprouts according to package directions 5 minutes, and drain well.
• **Combine** brussels sprouts, butter, and pecans, tossing to coat; serve with sauce. **Yield:** 12 servings.

Note: To save 84 calories and 9.6 fat grams, substitute reduced-fat mayonnaise and sour cream for the regular versions, and substitute reduced-calorie margarine for regular margarine. Analysis below is for lightened version.

❤ Per serving: Calories 124 (58% from fat)
Fat 8.5g (1.9g saturated) Cholesterol 10mg
Sodium 352mg Carbohydrate 9.6g
Fiber 3.6g Protein 4.3g

CELERY CASSEROLE

4 cups chopped celery
1 (10¾-ounce) can cream of celery soup, undiluted
1 (8-ounce) can sliced water chestnuts, drained
1 (2-ounce) jar diced pimiento, drained
½ teaspoon dried basil
¼ cup fine, dry breadcrumbs
¼ cup slivered almonds

• **Combine** first 5 ingredients, stirring well; pour into a lightly greased 8-inch square baking dish. Sprinkle with breadcrumbs and almonds.
• **Bake** at 350° for 45 minutes. **Yield:** 6 servings.

Ilene Culpepper
Marianna, Florida

SPRING'S ONIONS

Cooks tend to cast green onions in a supporting role, sprinkling their freshness on soups and baked potatoes. But used in abundance, they offer a mild flavor that is the highlight of these dishes – not the garnish.

HOISIN CRAB POT STICKERS

½ pound fresh lump crabmeat
5 fresh mushrooms, finely chopped
⅔ cup sliced green onions
3 tablespoons hoisin sauce
1 tablespoon dark sesame oil
1 teaspoon grated fresh ginger
1 (12-ounce) package wonton wrappers
2 tablespoons vegetable oil, divided
1 cup chicken broth, divided

• **Drain** crabmeat, and remove any bits of shell. Combine crabmeat and next 5 ingredients.
• **Place** 1 teaspoon crabmeat mixture in center of each wonton wrapper; moisten edges of wrappers with water. Fold wrappers in half, forming triangles; pinch edges to seal. Stand pot stickers on folded edge; press down to flatten slightly.
• **Pour** 1 tablespoon oil into a large nonstick skillet; place over medium-high heat until hot. Fry half of pot stickers in hot oil about 3 minutes or until golden on bottom. Add ½ cup chicken broth; reduce heat to medium.
• **Cover** and cook 8 minutes until tender. Repeat procedure with remaining pot stickers, oil, and broth. Serve with soy sauce, if desired. **Yield:** 4 dozen.

LoriAnn Glen
Overland, Missouri

MIDDLE EASTERN MAHIMAHI

1 tablespoon butter or margarine
1 cup sliced green onions
½ cup finely chopped yellow bell pepper
2 teaspoons minced garlic
1½ cups currant jelly
¼ cup water
1 teaspoon ground cinnamon
1 teaspoon ground cumin
½ teaspoon ground red pepper
½ teaspoon lemon juice
2 bay leaves
6 mahimahi steaks (3 pounds)
1½ cups finely chopped tomato
1 teaspoon paprika
½ teaspoon seasoned salt

• **Melt** butter in a skillet over medium-high heat; add green onions and next 9 ingredients, and cook 2 minutes, stirring occasionally. Remove from heat.
• **Place** fish in a lightly greased 13- x 9- x 2-inch baking dish; pour green onion mixture over fish. Top with chopped tomato, and sprinkle with paprika and seasoned salt.
• **Bake** at 425° for 20 to 30 minutes or until fish flakes easily when tested with a fork. Discard bay leaves. Serve fish immediately. **Yield:** 6 servings.

Marion Hall
Knoxville, Tennessee

ORIENTAL CHICKEN SALAD

3 tablespoons soy sauce
2 teaspoons grated fresh ginger
2 skinned and boned chicken breast halves
5 cups coarsely chopped mixed salad greens
1 cup fresh bean sprouts
1 cup fresh snow pea pods, trimmed
½ green bell pepper, thinly sliced
½ red bell pepper, thinly sliced
1 cucumber, thinly sliced
1 cup sliced green onions
1 (3-ounce) package ramen noodles
Oriental Salad Dressing
2 teaspoons sesame seeds, toasted
Spicy Peanut Sauce

• **Combine** soy sauce and ginger in a shallow dish or heavy-duty, zip-top plastic bag; add chicken. Cover or seal, and marinate in refrigerator up to 4 hours.
• **Remove** chicken from marinade, discarding marinade. Place chicken on a rack in a broiler pan.
• **Broil** 4 inches from heat (with electric oven door partially opened) 7 minutes on each side or until tender. Cool slightly, and slice.
• **Combine** salad greens and next 6 ingredients. Break uncooked noodles into small pieces, and sprinkle on top; reserve seasoning packet for another use. Add ½ cup Oriental Salad Dressing, tossing to coat.
• **Arrange** chicken on top; pour remaining Oriental Salad Dressing over chicken. Serve with Spicy Peanut Sauce. **Yield:** 4 servings.

Oriental Salad Dressing

⅓ cup pineapple juice
¼ cup rice vinegar
1 tablespoon reduced-sodium soy sauce
2 teaspoons brown sugar
1½ teaspoons sesame oil
¼ teaspoon pepper

• **Combine** all ingredients in a jar; cover tightly, and shake vigorously. **Yield:** ⅔ cup.

Spicy Peanut Sauce

½ cup chunky peanut butter
⅓ cup coconut milk
2 tablespoons reduced-sodium soy sauce
1 tablespoon grated fresh ginger
1 tablespoon sesame oil
¼ teaspoon dried crushed red pepper
¼ cup chicken broth

• **Combine** all ingredients in a bowl, stirring well with a wire whisk. **Yield:** 1⅓ cups.

Fran Pointer
Kansas City, Missouri

GREEN ONION CROSTINI

4 cups sliced green onions
¼ teaspoon pepper
1 (3-ounce) package cream cheese, softened
¼ cup mayonnaise
¼ cup sour cream
1 French baguette, sliced and toasted
1 pound bacon, cooked and crumbled

• **Combine** first 5 ingredients, mixing well. Spread green onion mixture on baguette slices, and top with bacon. **Yield:** 3 dozen.

Peggy Fowler Revels
Woodruff, South Carolina

TEMPURA-BATTERED GREEN ONIONS

4 bunches green onions
1 cup cold water
1 large egg
1 cup all-purpose flour
Peanut oil
1 teaspoon salt

• **Cut** onions into 2- or 4-inch lengths, discarding roots and top portions. Cut several slits in each end, cutting almost to, but not through, center.

• **Place** onions in ice water, and chill until ends curl (about 1 hour). Dry with paper towels.

• **Combine** 1 cup cold water and egg, stirring mixture well; add flour, stirring until mixture is blended. (Mixture will be lumpy.)

• **Pour** oil to depth of 3 inches into a Dutch oven or electric fryer; heat to 375°. Dip green onions in batter, and fry in hot oil 1 minute or until golden. Drain on paper towels. Sprinkle with salt, and serve immediately. **Yield:** about 2 dozen.

TAKE A FRESH LOOK AT GREEN ONIONS

Green onions are indispensable in food preparation. Added to a recipe, green onions can produce a choice of flavors – pungent or subtle, strong or mild, sweet or tangy.

IDENTIFYING

▪ Onions are classified as green or dry. Bulb formations usually identify green onion varieties. Dry onions such as white, red, or the famous Vidalia are more fully developed than the green onion variety and are easily identified by their brittle, papery outer skins. Shallots and garlic are also types of dry onions.

▪ Members of the green onion group are scallions, spring green onions, leeks, and chives. Scallions have tender green tops and a firm, white base with straight sides, not bulb shaped. Spring green onions have tubular green stems and a small, white bulb-shaped base. Scallions are milder in flavor than spring green onions. Leeks have a thick white cylindrical stalk, bulb base, and broad, flat green leaves. Chives have slender green hollow stems. Leeks and chives have a mild onion taste.

SELECTING

When purchasing green onion varieties, make sure the bunches are crisp and tender. Look for white stalks up to about 3 inches from the roots.

TIPS FOR USING GREEN ONIONS

▪ For more flavor, cook chopped onion in a small amount of fat before adding to other ingredients. A teaspoon of sugar added to the butter or oil before adding the onion gives a caramelized flavor.

▪ Add chopped onion to a salad dressing 1 to 2 hours before mixing with other salad ingredients for more flavor.

▪ **Spring Green Onion Garnish:** Trim off the bulb end and most of the green top of the onion. Slice both ends lengthwise at ⅛-inch intervals, leaving a 1-inch uncut space in the center. Place in ice water for at least 1 hour or until tips curl.

▪ To rid your hands of onion odor, rub them with vinegar, lemon juice, or parsley. Then wash your hands in soapy water.

Fresh, Quick Menus

If the thought of cooking for company gives you butterflies, check out these two menus. Choose the Casual Menu when you want comfort to be the theme of the evening. Our Fresh Menu is spiffed up a little and will impress your guests. Only you'll know how easy the recipes are, and you're not telling, are you?

Casual Menu
Serves Four

Chicken-and-Three-Cheese French Bread Pizzas
Garden Salad With Buttermilk Dressing
Congo Squares

CHICKEN-AND-THREE-CHEESE FRENCH BREAD PIZZAS

½ cup butter or margarine, softened
½ cup (2 ounces) shredded Cheddar cheese
⅓ cup freshly grated Parmesan cheese
1 clove garlic, pressed
¼ teaspoon dried Italian seasoning
1 (16-ounce) loaf sliced French bread
1 (10-ounce) can white chicken, drained and flaked *
1 cup (4 ounces) shredded mozzarella cheese
¼ cup chopped red bell pepper
¼ cup chopped green onions

• **Combine** first 5 ingredients in a small bowl, and spread evenly over bread slices. Top with chicken; sprinkle with mozzarella cheese, bell pepper, and green onions.
• **Bake** at 350° for 10 minutes or until cheese melts. **Yield:** 6 servings.

* Substitute 1½ cups chopped cooked chicken breast for canned.

M. B. Quesenbury
Dugspur, Virginia

GARDEN SALAD WITH BUTTERMILK DRESSING

¾ cup mayonnaise or salad dressing
½ cup buttermilk
1 tablespoon chopped fresh parsley
1 tablespoon finely chopped onion
1 clove garlic, minced
¼ teaspoon salt
Dash of pepper
4 cups mixed salad greens

• **Combine** first 7 ingredients; stir with a wire whisk until blended. Cover and chill 2 hours. Serve with salad greens. **Yield:** 4 servings.

Janice M. France
Louisville, Kentucky

CONGO SQUARES

¾ cup butter or margarine, softened
1 (16-ounce) package brown sugar
2 large eggs
1 teaspoon vanilla extract
2¾ cups all-purpose flour
2½ teaspoons baking powder
½ teaspoon salt
1 cup (6 ounces) semisweet chocolate morsels
1 cup pecan pieces

• **Beat** butter and sugar at medium speed with an electric mixer until mixture is creamy. Add eggs and vanilla, beating well.
• **Combine** flour, baking powder, and salt; gradually add to butter mixture, beating well. Stir in chocolate morsels and pecans; spoon into a greased 13- x 9- x 2-inch pan.
• **Bake** at 350° for 30 minutes. Cool in pan on a wire rack (center will fall as it cools). Cut into squares. **Yield:** 3 dozen.

Cathy Robinson
Columbia, South Carolina

Fresh Menu
Serves Four

Herbed Tomato Tart
Asparagus and Bean Sprouts
Strawberry-Orange Sauce With Pound Cake

HERBED TOMATO TART
(pictured on page 152)

1 (17¼-ounce) package frozen puff pastry sheets, thawed
4 plum tomatoes, thinly sliced
1 teaspoon salt
1 (8-ounce) package shredded mozzarella cheese
1 (4-ounce) package crumbled feta cheese
¼ cup chopped onion
1 clove garlic, minced
¼ cup finely chopped mixed fresh herbs
1 tablespoon olive oil

• **Roll** 1 pastry sheet into a 14-inch square on a lightly floured surface; place on an ungreased baking sheet. Cut 4 (12- x 1-inch) strips from

remaining pastry sheet, and place along edges on top of pastry square, forming a border. Reserve remaining pastry for another use.
• **Bake** at 400° for 10 minutes or until golden. Transfer pastry shell to a wire rack to cool.
• **Place** tomato slices in a single layer on paper towels; sprinkle evenly with salt. Let stand 20 minutes.
• **Place** baked pastry shell on baking sheet; sprinkle with mozzarella cheese and next 3 ingredients. Arrange tomato slices in a single layer on top. Sprinkle with herbs; drizzle with oil.
• **Bake** at 400° for 15 minutes or until cheese melts; serve immediately. **Yield:** 4 servings.

Note: For the mixed fresh herbs, we combined oregano, basil, chives, sage, tarragon, rosemary, thyme, and dill. You can substitute 1 tablespoon mixed dried herbs for fresh.

ASPARAGUS AND BEAN SPROUTS

1 pound fresh asparagus
1/4 teaspoon salt
1/4 teaspoon garlic powder
1/4 teaspoon ground ginger
2 tablespoons butter or margarine, divided
2 tablespoons sliced green onions
1/2 to 3/4 cup fresh bean sprouts
1/4 cup slivered almonds, toasted

• **Snap** off tough ends of asparagus; remove scales from stalks with a vegetable peeler, if desired. Set aside.
• **Combine** salt, garlic powder, and ginger; set spice mixture aside.
• **Cook** asparagus in a small amount of boiling water in a large skillet 3 minutes; drain and set aside.
• **Add** 1 tablespoon butter and half of spice mixture to skillet; add asparagus, and cook over medium-high heat 1 minute, stirring constantly. Remove asparagus to a serving platter.
• **Add** remaining 1 tablespoon butter and spice mixture to skillet; add green onions, and cook 2 minutes, stirring constantly.
• **Add** bean sprouts to skillet, and cook 1 minute or until thoroughly heated. Spoon over asparagus; sprinkle with almonds. **Yield:** 4 servings.

Kay C. Cooper
Madison, Alabama

STRAWBERRY-ORANGE SAUCE

1 (15.25-ounce) jar unsweetened strawberry spread
2 tablespoons grated orange rind
1/3 cup fresh orange juice
1 tablespoon orange liqueur (optional)
1 cup sliced fresh strawberries

• **Combine** first 3 ingredients. Stir in liqueur, if desired. Add strawberries, stirring gently. Serve over pound cake slices. **Yield:** 2 cups.

Renee A. Butner
Winston-Salem, North Carolina

PIPE DREAMS

Piping – be it mashed potatoes on a casserole or frosting on a cake – can be simple. For example, take our Whipped Cream Cake on the following page. To make it, you'll need a piping tip, a heavy-duty, zip-top plastic bag or decorating bag, and three 6- x 2-inch round cakepans. Look for the supplies in kitchen shops, and baking supply and crafts stores. You can order the cakepans (item number 2105-C-2185) for $5.49 each, plus shipping, from Wilton Industries at 1-800-772-7111.

Soon you'll know just how easy it is to pipe like a pro, and with these recipes and the tips on the next page, we're convinced that you can, too.

ROASTED GARLIC CANAPÉS

(pictured on page 79)

Don't save this for fancy canapés. It's just as good served as a spread for crackers.

2 heads garlic
2 tablespoons olive oil
2 (8-ounce) packages cream cheese, softened
1/2 cup butter or margarine, softened
3/4 teaspoon salt
Assorted fresh vegetables and toasted breads
Garnishes: assorted fresh herbs, sliced citrus wedges, and olives

• **Cut** off pointed end of garlic heads, leaving tight outer covering intact. Place garlic heads, cut side up, on a square of aluminum foil or in a garlic roaster. Drizzle with olive oil; wrap in foil or cover with lid.
• **Bake** at 350° for 1 hour or until golden. Cool.
• **Squeeze** out pulp from each clove.
• **Position** knife blade in food processor bowl; add garlic pulp. Process until smooth, stopping once to scrape down sides. Add cream cheese, and pulse 2 or 3 times, stopping once to scrape down sides.
• **Add** butter and salt; process 1 minute or until smooth, stopping once to scrape down sides. Store in the refrigerator in an airtight container up to 5 days. Pipe onto vegetables and breads. Garnish, if desired **Yield:** 2 2/3 cups.

Note: To prepare garlic ahead, roast as directed. Cool and separate into cloves. Freeze in an airtight container up to 3 months. The cloves will thaw in minutes.

WHIPPED CREAM CAKE

This petite cake is perfect for luncheons, anniversary dinners, teas, or birthday parties. Plan on it serving 6 to 8 people. And if you want a decorator look without the trouble of a homemade cake, follow the baking and assembling directions here, using 1 (18.25-ounce) package white cake mix and 2 (16-ounce) containers vanilla ready-to-spread frosting.

1 cup whipping cream
2 large eggs
1 cup sugar
1 teaspoon vanilla extract
1½ cups sifted cake flour
2 teaspoons baking powder
¼ teaspoon salt
Buttercream Frosting

• **Grease** three 6- x 2-inch round cakepans; line with wax paper. Grease and flour wax paper; set aside.
• **Beat** whipping cream with a wire whisk until foamy; set aside.
• **Beat** eggs with a wire whisk until foamy; add sugar and vanilla extract. Gradually stir whipping cream into egg mixture.
• **Combine** flour, baking powder, and salt; fold into whipping cream mixture. Pour batter into prepared pans.
• **Bake** at 350° for 18 minutes or until a wooden pick inserted in center comes out clean. Cool in pans on wire racks 10 minutes; remove from pans, and cool completely on wire racks.
• **Spread** 2½ cups Buttercream Frosting between layers and on top and sides of cake.
• **Spoon** about 1 cup frosting into a decorating or heavy-duty, zip-top plastic bag fitted with a No. 5 round tip; pipe curly lines over top and sides of cake. Do not overlap lines.
• **Spoon** remaining frosting into a decorating or heavy-duty, zip-top plastic bag fitted with a No. 2B large basketweave tip; pipe a ruffle around base of cake. **Yield:** 1 (3-layer) cake.

Note: If you have only one 6- x 2-inch round cakepan, bake layers one at a time. Cover the remaining batter and set aside while each layer bakes. Wash, dry, and prepare pan again before baking each remaining layer.

Buttercream Frosting

1½ cups butter
1 (16-ounce) package powdered sugar, sifted
2 tablespoons milk
1 teaspoon vanilla extract

• **Beat** butter at medium speed with an electric mixer until creamy; gradually add sugar, beating until light and fluffy. Add milk and vanilla, beating to desired consistency. **Yield:** about 4 cups.

Helen Walker
Edmond, Oklahoma

READY, AIM, SQUEEZE

If piping has never been your bag, try these tips for certain success.

▪ Disposable decorating bags are available for about 25 cents each at most crafts stores and Wal-Mart stores. A reusable plastic one costs from $2 to $5. But, with all but the thickest foods, you can use a heavy-duty, zip-top plastic bag.

▪ To fit a tip into a disposable decorating bag, cut off the end of the bag one half the length of the tip, and place the tip into the opening from the inside of the bag. You can do the same thing with the corner of a heavy-duty, zip-top plastic bag.

▪ To fill a decorating bag, fold the top down to make a cuff, and fill the bag about halfway. Open the cuff, and fold the top of the bag closed. As you pipe, fold the bag down so that the food you're piping doesn't come out of the top.

▪ These recipes don't require it, but you can use a plastic coupler to let you change tips on the same bag.

▪ Practice piping on wax paper before trying it on a cake or canapé. You can spoon the piped food back into the decorating bag once you get a feel for piping the design you want.

▪ To decorate the Whipped Cream Cake, recipe at left, fit a No. 5 round tip into a decorating bag and squeeze, making curly lines that cover the cake, but do not overlap. To make the frosting ribbon, fit a No. 2B large basketweave tip into a decorating bag, and hold the bag at a 45-degree angle at the base of the cake. Squeeze the decorating bag and lift the tip slightly, then pull the tip down and away to create a ruffle. Pipe each ruffle separately around the cake.

▪ To pipe Roasted Garlic Canapés (on previous page), use a No. 2D flower decorating tip. To make flowers, hold the bag straight up, and squeeze close to the surface, letting the tip touch the piped garlic spread; pull the tip away. To pipe rosettes, hold the bag straight up, and make a flower, but instead of pulling the tip away, continue squeezing and move the tip to make a half-circle around the flower.
To pipe lines, hold the bag at a 45-degree angle; squeeze, pulling the bag to make a line as you pipe.

Brunch Basics

When busy evening schedules hamper your party plans, have a weekend brunch. Those who usually skip breakfast and have lunch on the run will enjoy the pleasant change of pace.

Your menu can be as elaborate as time will allow. Start with these easy recipes, and then add fresh fruit and a spirited beverage for a terrific party that eases you into the afternoon.

Weekend Brunch Menu

Serves Six

Layered Eggs
Quick Cheese Grits
Easy Banana Bread

Layered Eggs

1 tablespoon butter or margarine
½ cup chopped onion
½ cup chopped green bell pepper
1 clove garlic, minced
1 (14.5-ounce) can diced tomatoes
½ teaspoon chili powder
2 tablespoons butter or margarine
2 tablespoons all-purpose flour
1 cup milk
¼ teaspoon salt
¼ teaspoon pepper
8 hard-cooked eggs, sliced
½ cup (2 ounces) shredded Cheddar cheese
½ cup soft breadcrumbs
1 tablespoon butter or margarine, melted

• **Melt** 1 tablespoon butter in a large skillet over medium-high heat. Add onion, bell pepper, and garlic; cook, stirring constantly, until tender. Add tomatoes and chili powder. Reduce heat to medium-low, and cook 8 minutes or until thickened; set aside.

• **Melt** 2 tablespoons butter in a saucepan. Stir in flour, and cook 2 minutes or until light brown. Gradually stir in milk, salt, and pepper with a wire whisk. Cook mixture 2 minutes or until thickened and bubbly. Stir into tomato mixture.

• **Layer** half of egg slices in a lightly greased 8-inch square baking dish. Top with half of tomato mixture. Repeat layers. Sprinkle with cheese.

• **Combine** breadcrumbs and melted butter; sprinkle over casserole.

• **Bake** at 350° for 15 minutes or until bubbly. Let stand 5 minutes before serving. **Yield:** 6 servings.

Mrs. Robert W. Meyer
Seminole, Florida

Quick Cheese Grits

3 cups water
¾ teaspoon salt
¾ cup quick-cooking yellow grits, uncooked
¼ cup (1 ounce) shredded Cheddar cheese

• **Bring** water and salt to a boil in a large saucepan. Gradually stir in grits. Cook 4 to 5 minutes, stirring often. Remove from heat; cover grits, and let stand 1 to 2 minutes or until desired thickness.

• **Pour** into individual serving bowls; sprinkle with shredded cheese. **Yield:** 6 servings.

Easy Banana Bread

4 large eggs
1 (18.25-ounce) package yellow cake mix without pudding
1 (3.4-ounce) package banana instant pudding mix
1 cup water
¼ cup vegetable oil
3 bananas, mashed
½ cup chopped walnuts or pecans

• **Beat** eggs at medium speed with an electric mixer until thick and pale; add cake mix and next 3 ingredients, mixing well. Stir in bananas and walnuts.

• **Pour** batter into two greased and floured 8½- x 4½- x 3-inch loafpans.

• **Bake** at 350° for 1 hour or until a wooden pick inserted in center comes out clean. Cool in pans on wire racks 10 minutes; remove from pans, and cool completely on wire racks. **Yield:** 2 loaves.

New Beginnings With Brunch

Remember when you moved into the neighborhood? Over time all the new faces became new friends. So don't let the new neighbors on the block wish they'd moved to another subdivision. Welcome them with a Weekend Brunch in their honor.

▪ Invite a couple of friends over for a cozy brunch, or call in a crowd; the Weekend Brunch Menu doubles easily for a get-together for the whole block.

▪ Make a boxful of goodies for a housewarming gift. Start with a hat box or basket, and add breakfast items like gourmet coffees, flavored syrups, and preserves. Include a map of the new city and brochures suggesting things to do around town. For a homemade touch, bake an extra recipe of Easy Banana Bread; give one loaf as a gift and keep one for yourself. And don't forget to include the recipe!

Louisiana Light

Cooks really take food seriously in Louisiana, using butter, roux, and cream with abandon. That's why everyone loves – but limits – indulgence in their signature dishes. The state's most celebrated foods see the light in these low-fat recipes. Now you won't have to deny yourself the pleasures of Seafood Gumbo, Crawfish Fettuccine, or Bananas Foster. So, enjoy!

SEAFOOD GUMBO

2½ cups all-purpose flour
1 tablespoon olive oil
2 cups chopped celery
1 cup chopped green bell pepper
1 cup chopped onion
1 cup chopped green onions
5 cloves garlic, pressed
1 tablespoon gumbo filé
7 (14½-ounce) cans ready-to-serve, no-salt-added, fat-free chicken broth
1 tablespoon salt
½ teaspoon black pepper
½ teaspoon ground red pepper
1 tablespoon hot sauce
1 (10-ounce) package frozen cut okra
3 pounds unpeeled large fresh shrimp
2 pounds fresh crabmeat
1 pound crawfish meat
2 (12-ounce) containers fresh oysters, undrained
Gumbo filé
Hot cooked rice

• **Sprinkle** flour evenly in a 15-x 10- x 1-inch pan.

• **Bake** at 400° for 20 minutes or until caramel colored (do not burn), stirring often; cool.

• **Pour** oil into a 12-quart stockpot; place over medium heat until hot. Add celery and next 5 ingredients; cook, stirring constantly, 5 to 7 minutes or until tender.

• **Add** toasted flour, broth, salt, pepper, red pepper and hot sauce; bring to a boil. Reduce heat, and simmer, uncovered, 30 minutes. Add okra, and simmer, uncovered, 30 minutes.

• **Peel** shrimp, and devein, if desired. Drain and flake crabmeat, removing any bits of shell.

• **Add** shrimp, crabmeat, crawfish, and oysters to stockpot; cook 15 to 20 minutes or just until seafood is done. Stir in additional gumbo filé, if desired. Spoon over rice and serve immediately. **Yield:** 9 quarts.

Beth Ann Spracklen
Arlington, Texas

♥ Per serving (1 cup gumbo and ½ cup rice):
Calories 223 (9% from fat)
Fat 2.1g (0.4g saturated) Cholesterol 82mg
Sodium 333mg Carbohydrate 32.2g
Fiber 0.6g Protein 16.2g

CRAWFISH FETTUCCINE

If you prefer, you can use shrimp instead of crawfish in this recipe.

2 pounds crawfish meat
2 teaspoons Cajun seasoning
1 (12-ounce) package fettuccine
2 (½-ounce) envelopes butter-flavored granules
1 teaspoon chicken bouillon granules
¾ cup water
2 medium onions, chopped
1 green bell pepper, chopped
3 cloves garlic, pressed
½ teaspoon dried basil
½ teaspoon dried thyme
1 tablespoon cornstarch
1 (12-ounce) can evaporated skimmed milk
½ (16-ounce) loaf reduced-fat process cheese spread, cubed
¼ cup chopped fresh parsley
3 tablespoons freshly grated Parmesan cheese
Garnish: chopped fresh parsley

• **Combine** crawfish and Cajun seasoning; cover and chill 30 minutes.

• **Cook** pasta according to package directions; drain and keep warm.

• **Combine** butter granules, bouillon granules, and water in a large deep skillet or Dutch oven; cook over medium heat until granules dissolve.

• **Add** onion, bell pepper, and garlic; cook over medium-high heat, stirring constantly, 10 minutes or until tender. Stir in crawfish mixture, basil, and thyme; cook 5 minutes.

• **Combine** cornstarch and evaporated milk, stirring well; stir into crawfish mixture. Add cheese spread, stirring well. Bring to a boil over medium heat; boil 1 minute, stirring constantly.

• **Stir** in pasta and ¼ cup chopped parsley. Serve immediately; sprinkle servings evenly with Parmesan cheese. Garnish, if desired. **Yield:** 8 servings.

Holli Cramm
Tomball, Texas

♥ Per serving: Calories 400 (13% from fat)
Fat 5.9g (2.8g saturated) Cholesterol 171mg
Sodium 844mg Carbohydrate 48.6g
Fiber 2.1g Protein 37.4g

LOUISIANA LIFESTYLES

DANCING TAKES A TURN

Gerald and Carol Trahan of Lafayette, Louisiana, were loyal health club members until they dis covered that Cajun dancing was great aerobic exercise and much more fun than pedaling a stationary bike. Their enthusiasm will inspire you to discover a type of exercise that's a pleasure and not a burden.

"We dance four or five nights a week," Carol says. "We're addicted, and it helps us stay fit."

Don't doubt that the Trahans are getting a workout. "When zydeco is playing, you'll be out on the dance floor for nearly 10 minutes before you get a break," Gerald says. "And, oh, you huff and you puff. That's when you find out if you're in shape."

The Trahans dance at clubs and restaurants, but they aren't tempted by the rich food. "When you go dancing, you can't eat too much," Gerald says. "You just can't cut a rug when you're carrying an extra load."

THE BIG EASY'S GONE BANANAS

On a typical morning, Chef Mike Rousseau and his staff prepare 400 servings of Bananas Foster for breakfast at Brennan's. "We flame about 35,000 pounds of bananas a year," Mike says, as if he's talking about grains of rice instead of crates of fruit. "It's such an easy dessert," he says. "Some days, we'll make as many as 2,500 servings."

Brennan's first chef, Paul Blange, created the dessert in 1951 at the request of owner Owen Edward Brennan. Chef Paul named it after Richard Foster, a frequent customer and a friend of Owen's.

"People come to the restaurant from all over the world and that's the dessert they're looking for," Mike says.

If you're visiting New Orleans, be sure you don't miss sampling Brennan's world-famous, 650-calorie dessert. In the meantime, try our lightened version that has just half the calories.

BANANAS FOSTER

In this light version the amounts of butter and sugar are decreased and the ice cream is replaced with nonfat frozen yogurt. But the flavor and the flames are as authentic as the original.

1 tablespoon butter
¼ cup firmly packed dark brown sugar
⅛ teaspoon ground cinnamon
4 bananas, quartered
¼ cup banana liqueur
¼ cup dark rum
12 ounces nonfat vanilla frozen yogurt

• **Melt** butter in a large skillet over medium-high heat; add brown sugar and next 3 ingredients. Cook, stirring constantly, 2 minutes or until bananas are tender.

• **Pour** rum over bananas, and ignite with a long match; cook until flames disappear. Serve immediately over frozen yogurt. **Yield:** 4 servings.

♥ Per serving: Calories 323 (16% from fat) Fat 5.8g (3.5g saturated) Cholesterol 8mg Sodium 110mg Carbohydrate 64.9g Fiber 3.5g Protein 5.5g

SPICE UP WITH GINGER

Although ginger is not yet a staple in Southern cooking, its pungent flavor gives a boost to the region's traditional foods. Try this versatile root fresh, crystallized, chocolate-dipped, pickled, ground, or in a syrup. In each form, it undergoes a change. Its spicy-sweet flavor can impart a gentle, refreshing glow or an intense afterburn.

GINGER BEEF WITH BOK CHOY

1¼ pounds flank steak
3 cloves garlic, minced
2 tablespoons minced fresh ginger
1 tablespoon reduced-sodium soy sauce
1 tablespoon rice wine vinegar
½ teaspoon dried crushed red pepper
2 tablespoons peanut oil
4 cups shredded bok choy
¼ teaspoon salt
¼ teaspoon pepper
Hot cooked rice

• **Freeze** steak 30 minutes; trim any fat. Slice steak diagonally across grain into ¼-inch strips.

• **Combine** garlic and next 4 ingredients in a bowl; add steak, tossing to coat. Cover and marinate in refrigerator 20 minutes.

• **Pour** 1 tablespoon oil into a large skillet; place over high heat until hot. Add half of steak mixture, and cook, stirring constantly, 3 to 4 minutes or until browned. Remove from skillet; repeat procedure with remaining oil and steak mixture.

• **Combine** steak mixture and bok choy in skillet; cook 2 to 3 minutes, stirring constantly. Add salt and pepper; toss gently. Serve with rice. **Yield:** 4 servings.

Jean Hoffman
Durham, North Carolina

GINGER PORK RIBS

1 tablespoon butter or margarine
1 medium onion, chopped
1 cup ginger marmalade or preserves
¼ cup soy sauce
2½ tablespoons honey
2½ tablespoons dry sherry
1 tablespoon grated fresh ginger
1 tablespoon grated orange rind
4 to 5 pounds baby-back pork ribs

• **Melt** butter in a large skillet over medium-high heat; add onion, and cook, stirring constantly, until tender. Add marmalade and next 5 ingredients; cook over medium heat, stirring constantly, until thoroughly heated.
• **Arrange** ribs in a shallow dish; pour ginger mixture over ribs. Cover and chill at least 8 hours.
• **Remove** ribs from marinade, discarding marinade. Place ribs on a rack in a roasting pan.
• **Bake** at 350° for 45 minutes or until tender. **Yield:** 4 servings.

Mike Singleton
Memphis, Tennessee

Note: You can find ginger marmalade at specialty supermarkets.

GINGER TEA

2 quarts water
½ cup grated fresh ginger
⅓ cup fresh lemon juice
¼ cup honey
4 regular-size green tea bags
1½ cups sugar

• **Combine** first 4 ingredients in a large Dutch oven; bring mixture to a boil. Reduce heat, and simmer 5 minutes, stirring occasionally. Remove mixture from heat.
• **Add** tea bags; cover and let stand 5 minutes. Remove tea bags; stir in sugar, and let cool.
• **Pour** tea through a wire-mesh strainer into a pitcher; serve over ice. **Yield:** 2 quarts.

GINGERY GINGERBREAD

½ cup butter, softened
½ cup sugar
1 large egg
1 cup molasses
½ cup finely grated fresh ginger
2½ cups all-purpose flour
1½ teaspoons baking soda
½ teaspoon baking powder
1 teaspoon ground cinnamon
1 teaspoon ground ginger
½ teaspoon ground cloves
1 cup hot water

• **Beat** butter at medium speed with an electric mixer until creamy; gradually add sugar, beating well. Add egg and molasses, beating until blended. Add fresh ginger, beating until blended.
• **Combine** flour and next 5 ingredients; add to butter mixture alternately with hot water, beginning and ending with flour mixture. Beat at low speed until blended after each addition; beat 1 additional minute or until very smooth. Pour batter into a greased 13- x 9- x 2-inch pan.
• **Bake** at 350° for 40 minutes or until a wooden pick inserted in center comes out clean. Cool in pan on a wire rack 10 minutes; remove from pan, and cool completely on wire rack.
• **Cut** into squares; serve with vanilla ice cream. **Yield:** 12 servings.

Milton Hurst
Birmingham, Alabama

GETTING TO KNOW GINGER

■ Look for fresh ginger that has a smooth skin. Wrinkled skin indicates that it's dry. Keep fresh ginger cool and dry.

■ Use thin slices for subtle flavor; mince or grate for direct flavor.

■ To extract ginger juice – the most potent part of the root – wrap grated ginger in cheesecloth, and squeeze. Use in marinades and sauces.

■ To mince fresh ginger, use a garlic press.

■ Desperately seeking ginger? Don't waste time roaming every aisle of the store. For crinkle-cut ginger (item number 47266), call Williams-Sonoma at 1-800-541-2233.

For crystallized ginger (item number 10673) or Ginger Beer Syrup (item number 12099), call Norm Thompson at 1-800-547-1160.

For chocolate-covered ginger or a free mail-order catalog, call Fran's Chocolates at 1-800-422-3726.

IT'S A WRAP

Turn your next stir-fry dinner into an event with homemade egg rolls. The little bundles are made from basic ingredients, but yield exotic results. Look for egg roll wrappers in your grocer's produce section. And instead of ordering takeout, stay in and get rolling.

VIETNAMESE EGG ROLLS

½ (3¾-ounce) package cellophane noodles
½ pound lean boneless pork
1 pound unpeeled large fresh shrimp
3 cloves garlic, pressed
1 tablespoon sesame oil
6 green onions, chopped
2 tablespoons chopped fresh cilantro
2 teaspoons grated fresh ginger
20 egg roll wrappers
Vegetable oil

• **Soak** noodles in hot water to cover 10 minutes or until soft; drain. Cut into 2-inch pieces; set aside.
• **Trim** excess fat from pork, and cut into 1-inch pieces; set aside.
• **Peel** shrimp, and devein, if desired.
• **Position** knife blade in food processor bowl, and add pork. Process until pork is coarsely chopped. Add shrimp, and process until mixture is finely chopped.
• **Cook** meat mixture and garlic in 1 tablespoon oil in a wok or large skillet over medium-high heat 5 minutes, stirring until pork crumbles and shrimp turn pink.
• **Add** noodles, green onions, cilantro, and ginger; cook 2 to 3 minutes. Cool completely.
• **Spoon** ¼ cup mixture in center of each egg roll wrapper. Fold top corner of wrapper over filling, tucking tip of corner under filling; fold left and right corners over filling. Lightly brush remaining corner with water; tightly roll filled end toward remaining corner, and gently press to seal.
• **Pour** oil to depth of 2 inches into a wok or Dutch oven; heat to 375°. Fry, a few at a time, until golden, turning once; drain. **Yield:** 20 egg rolls.

Agnes Nguyen
Birmingham, Alabama

CHINESE EGG ROLLS

½ pound lean boneless pork
½ pound lean ham
3 tablespoons peanut oil
1 (8-ounce) package mushrooms, chopped
1 cup chopped bean sprouts
¼ cup finely chopped green onions
¼ cup finely chopped water chestnuts
1 tablespoon soy sauce
2 teaspoons cornstarch
16 egg roll wrappers
Peanut oil

• **Position** knife blade in food processor bowl; add pork and ham. Process until finely chopped. Cook meat mixture in 3 tablespoons oil in a large nonstick skillet over medium-high heat, stirring until it crumbles; drain.
• **Add** mushrooms and next 3 ingredients; cook, stirring constantly, until tender.
• **Combine** soy sauce and cornstarch, stirring well; add to meat mixture. Cook 2 to 3 minutes or until thickened and bubbly.
• **Spoon** ¼ cup meat mixture in center of each egg roll wrapper. Fold top corner of wrapper over filling, tucking tip of corner under filling; fold left and right corners over filling. Lightly brush remaining corner with water; tightly roll filled end toward remaining corner, and gently press to seal.
• **Pour** peanut oil to depth of 2 inches into a wok or Dutch oven; heat to 375°. Fry, a few at a time, until golden, turning once; drain. **Yield:** 16 egg rolls.

Nora Henshaw
Okemah, Oklahoma

SCRUMPTIOUS EGG ROLLS

1 (0.5-ounce) package dried shiitake mushrooms
1 (0.35-ounce) package dried oyster mushrooms
4 cups grated cabbage
1 stalk celery, finely chopped
2 green onions, sliced
1 carrot, scraped and grated
1 tablespoon peanut oil
1½ tablespoons soy sauce
¼ teaspoon salt
¼ teaspoon sugar
1½ teaspoons ground ginger
½ teaspoon garlic powder
12 egg roll wrappers
Peanut oil

• **Combine** mushrooms and boiling water to cover; let stand 5 minutes. Drain and chop mushrooms.
• **Cook** cabbage and next 3 ingredients in 1 tablespoon oil in a wok or large skillet over medium-high heat, stirring constantly, until tender. Remove from heat. Stir in mushrooms, soy sauce, and next 4 ingredients.
• **Spoon** ¼ cup cabbage mixture in center of each egg roll wrapper. Fold top corner of wrapper over filling, tucking tip of corner under filling; fold left and right corners over filling. Lightly brush remaining corner of wrapper with water; tightly roll filled end toward remaining corner, and gently press to seal.
• **Pour** peanut oil to depth of 2 inches into a wok or Dutch oven; heat to 375°. Fry, a few at a time, until golden, turning once; drain. **Yield:** 12 egg rolls.

Debra S. Baker
Greenville, North Carolina

Sausage: A Link To Dinner

If you've got sausage, then you've got supper. Bulk or link, mild or hot, it delivers huge flavor without much fuss.

SAUSAGE BURGERS

6 (6-inch) French sandwich rolls
1½ pounds mild Italian link sausage
¼ cup chopped onion
1 large egg, lightly beaten
1 teaspoon dried oregano
4 red or green bell peppers, cut into thin strips
1 medium onion, thinly sliced
2 tablespoons vegetable oil
½ teaspoon salt
⅛ teaspoon pepper
1 tablespoon white vinegar

• **Cut** a ¾-inch slice from top of each roll; set tops aside.
• **Scoop** out bottoms of rolls, leaving ½-inch shells; tear bread pieces to measure ½ cup fresh breadcrumbs. Set shells and breadcrumbs aside.
• **Remove** and discard casings from sausage; crumble sausage into a large bowl. Add reserved breadcrumbs, chopped onion, egg, and oregano; knead with your hands to mix well. Divide mixture into 6 equal portions, and shape into 5- x 2-inch oval patties.
• **Cook,** covered with grill lid, over medium-hot coals (350° to 400°) 7 minutes on each side or until done. Remove from grill, and keep warm.
• **Cook** bell pepper strips and sliced onion in oil in a skillet over medium-high heat, stirring constantly, 5 minutes or until crisp-tender. Stir in salt, pepper, and vinegar; spoon evenly into bread shells. Top with sausage patties and bread tops; serve immediately. **Yield:** 6 servings.

Janie Wallace
Seguin, Texas

SAUSAGE-STUFFED SHELLS

½ (12-ounce) package jumbo pasta shells (about 20)
1 pound mild Italian link sausage
1 large egg, lightly beaten
¾ cup Italian-seasoned breadcrumbs
1 (30-ounce) jar spaghetti sauce
¼ cup grated Parmesan cheese

• **Cook** pasta shells according to package directions; drain and set aside.
• **Remove** and discard casings from sausage. Brown sausage in a large skillet, stirring until it crumbles; drain.
• **Combine** sausage, egg, and breadcrumbs in skillet; set aside.
• **Spread** 1 cup spaghetti sauce in bottom of a lightly greased 13- x 9- x 2-inch baking dish. Spoon sausage mixture into shells, and place in baking dish. Pour remaining sauce over stuffed shells.
• **Cover** and bake at 350° for 15 minutes; sprinkle with cheese, and bake, uncovered, 5 additional minutes or until thoroughly heated. **Yield:** 4 to 6 servings.

Note: To make ahead, store stuffed shells in the refrigerator, without sauce or cheese, at least 8 hours. Assemble shells and sauce in baking dish as directed, and let stand at room temperature 30 minutes. Cover and bake at 350° for 20 minutes; sprinkle with cheese, and bake, uncovered, 5 additional minutes or until thoroughly heated.

Christine Johnston
Bossier City, Louisiana

SAUSAGE-VEGETABLE SKILLET

1 tablespoon butter or margarine
1 pound kielbasa sausage, cut into ½-inch slices
1 head cauliflower, broken into flowerets
3 zucchini, thinly sliced
3 carrots, scraped and thinly sliced
1 medium onion, thinly sliced
½ teaspoon salt
¼ teaspoon pepper
1 cup (4 ounces) shredded Monterey Jack cheese

• **Melt** butter in a 12-inch skillet over medium-high heat; add sausage, and cook until browned, stirring often. Remove with a slotted spoon, reserving drippings in skillet; set sausage aside.
• **Add** cauliflower and next 3 ingredients to skillet; cook, stirring constantly, 5 minutes or until crisp-tender. Stir in salt and pepper; cover, reduce heat, and simmer 5 minutes. Stir in sausage; cook just until thoroughly heated.
• **Spoon** mixture into individual baking dishes, and sprinkle with cheese. Cover and let stand until cheese melts. **Yield:** 6 servings.

Betty Levine
Loudon, Tennessee

Sausage Savvy

Sausage is made of ground meat, (usually pork), mixed with fat, salt, seasonings, and fillers like cereals, soybean flour, and dried milk solids. The mixture is then enclosed in a tubelike casing.

Sausage flavors vary with seasoning combinations or curing techniques. Modern times, however, have changed little, except for the processing speed and, well, the casing. In the past, the sausage mixture was fitted into either pig's or sheep's intestines, but, to the relief of some, most of today's casings are made of synthetic material.

QUICK & EASY

Capitalize on Canned Soups

Canned cream soup is a staple for most cooks. In fact, cooks use more than one million cans of soup in recipes every day. They speed up your dinner preparation and give your recipes flavor and creaminess straight from the can. Plus, when prepared according to label directions, they make a pretty darn good bowl of soup. Try our new ideas for inventive additions.

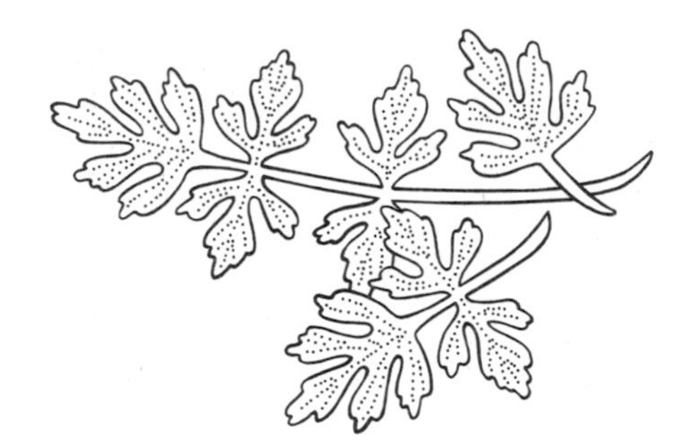

QUICKER ENCHILADAS

1 pound ground chuck
1 small onion, chopped
1 (10¾-ounce) can cream of mushroom soup, undiluted
2 (4.5-ounce) cans chopped green chiles, undrained and divided
8 (8-inch) flour tortillas
1 (8-ounce) package shredded colby-Monterey Jack cheese blend, divided
1 (10¾-ounce) can Cheddar cheese soup, undiluted

• **Brown** ground chuck and onion in a large skillet, stirring until meat crumbles; drain. Stir in mushroom soup and 1 can green chiles.
• **Spoon** ½ cup beef mixture down center of each tortilla; sprinkle each with 2½ tablespoons cheese blend. Roll up tortillas, and place each, seam side down, in a lightly greased 13- x 9- x 2-inch baking dish. Pour Cheddar cheese soup over tortillas.
• **Drain** remaining can green chiles; sprinkle chiles and remaining ¾ cup cheese over soup.
• **Cover** and bake at 350° for 20 minutes; uncover and bake 5 additional minutes. Serve with salsa. **Yield:** 4 servings.

Mrs. Joe Ford
Hamlin, Texas

HAM-AND-POTATO CASSEROLE

1 (26-ounce) package frozen shredded potatoes
1 (1-pound) ham slice, cut into bite-size pieces
1 (10¾-ounce) can cream of potato soup, undiluted
½ teaspoon pepper
¼ cup grated Parmesan cheese
1 cup (4 ounces) shredded Cheddar cheese
Paprika

• **Combine** first 4 ingredients in a large bowl; spoon into a lightly greased 13- x 9- x 2-inch baking dish.
• **Bake** at 400° for 25 minutes; sprinkle with cheeses and paprika, and bake 5 additional minutes or until thoroughly heated. **Yield:** 4 to 5 servings.

TUNA CASSEROLE

Cook noodles up to 3 days ahead; toss with 1 teaspoon of oil, and store in the refrigerator until needed.

1 (5-ounce) package egg noodles
1 (10¾-ounce) can cream of mushroom soup, undiluted
1 (5-ounce) can evaporated milk
⅓ cup finely chopped onion
1 (6-ounce) can solid white tuna in spring water, drained and flaked
1 cup (4 ounces) shredded Cheddar cheese
1 (8.5-ounce) can English peas, drained
½ teaspoon pepper
1 cup tiny fish-shaped crackers

• **Cook** noodles according to package directions; drain. Stir in soup and next 6 ingredients; pour into a lightly greased 8-inch square baking dish.
• **Bake** at 350° for 25 minutes. Sprinkle with crackers; bake 5 additional minutes or until thoroughly heated. **Yield:** 4 to 6 servings.

Chicken Casserole: Substitute 1 (10¾-ounce) can cream of chicken soup, 1 (5-ounce) can chunk white chicken, and 1 cup buttery animal-shaped crackers.

Note: For fish-shaped crackers, we used Pepperidge Farm Original Goldfish; for animal-shaped crackers, we used Ritz Ark Animals.

CHICKEN PACKETS

These bundles might seem hard to make, but they're really a snap.

2 tablespoons olive oil
4 skinned and boned chicken breast halves, cut into 1-inch pieces
1 cup chopped onion
½ cup chopped green bell pepper
½ cup sour cream
½ (10¾-ounce) can cream of mushroom soup, undiluted
½ teaspoon garlic salt
¼ teaspoon pepper
3 (8-ounce) cans refrigerated crescent dinner rolls
1 cup (4 ounces) shredded mozzarella cheese
Garnish: fresh parsley sprigs

• **Pour** oil into a medium skillet, and place over medium-high heat until hot. Add chicken, onion, and bell pepper; cook, stirring constantly, 5 minutes or until chicken is tender. Drain.
• **Combine** chicken mixture, sour cream, and next 3 ingredients in a small bowl, stirring well.
• **Unroll** crescent rolls, and separate into 12 rectangles; press perforations to seal. Spoon 2 tablespoons chicken mixture in center of each rectangle, and sprinkle evenly with cheese. Bring corners of rectangles together and twist, pinching seams to seal; place on lightly greased baking sheets.
• **Bake** at 350° for 20 minutes or until lightly browned. Garnish, if desired. **Yield:** 1 dozen.

Note: You can freeze unbaked packets in airtight containers up to 3 days. Remove from freezer, and bake, unthawed, at 350° for 30 minutes or until lightly browned.

Cathy Ruark
Brandon, Mississippi

SHRIMP SPREAD

1 (6-ounce) can tiny cocktail shrimp, rinsed and drained
1 (8-ounce) package cream cheese, softened
1 (10¾-ounce) can cream of shrimp soup, undiluted
¼ cup chopped red bell pepper
2 tablespoons finely chopped onion
Dash of hot sauce

• **Chop** shrimp, and set aside.
• **Beat** cream cheese at medium speed with an electric mixer until fluffy; gradually add soup, beating well after each addition.
• **Stir** in shrimp, bell pepper, and remaining ingredients; chill at least 2 hours. Serve with crackers or toasted French baguette slices. **Yield:** 2½ cups.

SOUP SELECTIONS

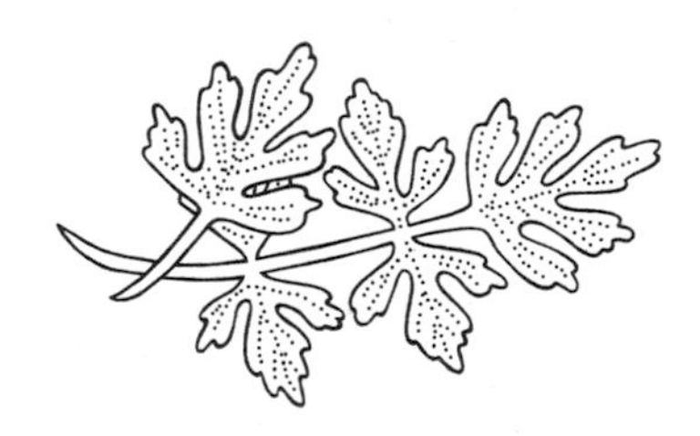

There are at least eight different flavors of cream soup, including asparagus, broccoli, celery, chicken, chicken and broccoli, mushroom, potato, and shrimp. The three most popular flavors – mushroom, chicken, and celery – come in reduced-fat versions. A low-sodium cream of mushroom soup is also available. As a rule, the reduced-fat and low-sodium versions are interchangeable with the regular ones.

If you're out of mushroom soup, substitute cream of chicken or celery in the recipe. You'll get the same creamy consistency with a new flavor twist.

SHERRIED MUSHROOM SOUP

2 tablespoons butter or margarine
1 small onion, chopped
¼ teaspoon garlic powder
2 (10½-ounce) cans condensed chicken broth, undiluted
3 (10¾-ounce) cans cream of mushroom soup, undiluted
1 cup milk
2 tablespoons sour cream
1 tablespoon chopped fresh parsley
1 teaspoon chopped fresh thyme
1 cup quick brown rice, uncooked
½ cup dry sherry
¼ teaspoon pepper
1 (8-ounce) package sliced fresh mushrooms
Garnish: toast points

• **Melt** butter in a 3-quart saucepan over medium-high heat; add onion and garlic powder, and cook, stirring constantly, until tender. Add broth; reduce heat, and simmer 5 minutes.
• **Combine** soup and next 4 ingredients, stirring with a wire whisk until blended; stir into broth mixture. Add rice and next 3 ingredients; cook 20 to 30 minutes or until rice is tender and soup is thickened. Garnish, if desired. **Yield:** 2 quarts.

Marilyn W. Godsey
Fort Myers, Florida

For Liver Lovers

Liver brings out the passion in everyone – you either love it or you hate it. If you love liver, then you've probably had it crisp and brown on the outside with a moist, pink center. If you don't, then you've probably had it tough, dry, and overcooked.

Fry chicken livers for an inexpensive dinner or grind them for a tasty spread. Those who love liver will love these recipes. For those who don't, one bite might change your mind.

FRIED CHICKEN LIVERS

1 pound chicken livers
2 cups all-purpose flour
1½ teaspoons seasoned salt
1 teaspoon pepper
1 cup buttermilk
Vegetable oil

• **Pierce** chicken livers several times with a fork.
• **Combine** flour, salt, and pepper in a shallow dish; dredge livers in flour mixture. Dip livers into buttermilk, and dredge in flour mixture again.
• **Pour** oil to depth of 2 inches into a Dutch oven or electric fryer; heat to 365°. Cook livers, a few at a time, 4 to 5 minutes or until golden. Serve immediately. **Yield:** 4 to 5 servings.

GARLIC CHICKEN LIVERS

¼ cup chopped fresh parsley
1 teaspoon salt
1 teaspoon pepper
1 teaspoon garlic powder
½ cup fine, dry breadcrumbs
½ pound chicken livers
9 slices bacon, cut in half

• **Combine** first 5 ingredients in a shallow dish, and dredge livers in breadcrumb mixture. Wrap a piece of bacon around each liver, and secure with a wooden pick. Place livers on a rack in a roasting pan.
• **Bake** at 400° for 20 minutes or until bacon is crisp. Serve immediately. **Yield:** 1½ dozen.

Vance McNeil
Houston, Texas

GRANDMA ROSE'S CHOPPED CHICKEN LIVERS

Art Meripol shares his grandmother's recipe. Although the original uses schmaltz – rendered chicken fat – olive oil makes a fine substitute.

2 tablespoons olive oil
1 pound chicken livers
2 cloves garlic, minced
1 medium onion, chopped and divided
1 hard-cooked egg, chopped
¼ teaspoon salt
¼ teaspoon pepper

• **Pour** oil into a large skillet; place over medium-high heat until hot. Add livers, garlic, and half of onion; cook, stirring constantly, 10 minutes or until livers are done. Remove from heat.
• **Position** knife blade in food processor bowl; add remaining onion, liver mixture, egg, salt, and pepper. Pulse 5 times or until livers are chopped. Cover and chill. Serve with rye or pumpernickel bread. **Yield:** ¾ cup.

Art Meripol
Birmingham, Alabama

Creative Crackers

Most people won't bake their own crackers – why bother when they can buy perfectly good ones at the grocery store? But these same ones diligently squeeze cheese straws out of cookie presses and agonize over whether to use medium or sharp Cheddar cheese. Granted, cheese straws aren't ordinary crackers, but neither are these easy recipes.

Serve Vegetable Crackers when you would saltines, offer Blue Cheese Crisps in place of traditional cheese straws, and grab a handful of Soup Nuts instead of oyster crackers.

VEGETABLE CRACKERS

5½ cups all-purpose flour, divided
2 (0.9-ounce) envelopes spring vegetable soup mix
1 teaspoon baking soda
2 tablespoons butter or margarine, softened
1 large egg
2 cups buttermilk
½ teaspoon salt

• **Combine** 4½ cups flour, soup mix, and soda in a large mixing bowl; add butter and egg, beating at medium speed with an electric mixer until blended. Add buttermilk, beating well.
• **Stir** in enough remaining flour to form a soft dough. Turn dough out onto a lightly floured surface, and knead 4 or 5 times.
• **Divide** dough into fourths; roll each portion into a 10- x 12-inch rectangle (about 1/16 inch thick). Cut into 2-inch squares, using a pastry wheel or pizza cutter, and place on lightly greased baking sheets. Prick with a fork; sprinkle with salt.
• **Bake** at 400° for 12 to 15 minutes or until golden. Transfer to wire racks to cool completely. **Yield:** 10 dozen.

Note: For spring vegetable soup mix, we used Knorr.

Spring Fever for Flavor

Rachel and John Kilpatrick and their Houston supper club friends mark their calendars for a sow-and-grow dinner theme early each spring. Although fresh fruits and veggies aren't yet overflowing in their own backyard patches, their small patio gardens and the grocery store supply plenty for a preseason celebration.

After sipping mint juleps, the group feasts on recipes brightened by colorful produce and delicate herbs. Then it's home with the party favors – gloves, trowels, and small potted herbs – to garden on a grand scale.

BLUE CHEESE CRISPS

These updated cheese wafers received the highest rating our taste-testing panel ever gives.

2 (4-ounce) packages crumbled blue cheese
½ cup butter or margarine, softened
1⅓ cups all-purpose flour
⅓ cup poppy seeds
¼ teaspoon ground red pepper

• **Beat** cheese and butter at medium speed with an electric mixer until creamy. Add flour, poppy seeds, and pepper; beat until blended.
• **Divide** dough in half; shape each portion into a 9-inch log. Cover and chill 2 hours.
• **Cut** each log into ¼-inch-thick slices, and place on ungreased baking sheets.
• **Bake** at 350° for 13 to 15 minutes or until golden. Transfer to wire racks to cool completely. **Yield:** 6 dozen.

Shirley M. Draper
Winter Park, Florida

SOUP NUTS

Keep plenty of these little jewels on hand. They're great for snacking.

2 cups all-purpose flour
½ cup grated Parmesan cheese
1 teaspoon garlic salt
½ teaspoon dried Italian seasoning
3 large eggs
3 tablespoons olive oil

• **Combine** first 4 ingredients in a large mixing bowl; add eggs and oil, beating at medium speed with an electric mixer until blended.
• **Turn** dough out onto a lightly floured surface; knead lightly 3 or 4 times (dough may be crumbly). Divide dough into 6 portions. Shape each portion into a 12-inch log; cut each roll into ¼-inch-thick slices, and place on ungreased baking sheets.
• **Bake** at 375° for 12 minutes or until lightly browned. Transfer to wire racks to cool completely. **Yield:** 3 cups.

PASTA-VEGGIE SALAD

1 (9-ounce) package refrigerated cheese-filled tortellini, uncooked
3 ounces fettuccine, uncooked
2 cups fresh snow pea pods, trimmed
2 cups broccoli flowerets
1 pint cherry tomatoes, cut in half
2 cups sliced fresh mushrooms
1 (7.5-ounce) can pitted whole ripe olives, drained
2 tablespoons freshly grated Parmesan cheese
Herbed Pasta Salad Dressing
Garnish: freshly grated Parmesan cheese

• **Cook** tortellini and fettuccine according to package directions; drain and set aside.
• **Cook** snow peas in boiling water to cover 1 minute; remove and plunge peas immediately into cold water to stop the cooking process. Repeat procedure with broccoli.
• **Combine** snow peas, broccoli, cherry tomatoes, mushrooms, and olives in a large bowl; add pasta and 2 tablespoons cheese, tossing to combine. Add Herbed Pasta Salad Dressing, and toss well. Cover and chill. Garnish, if desired. **Yield:** 8 to 10 servings.

Herbed Pasta Salad Dressing

½ cup chopped fresh chives
2 tablespoons chopped fresh parsley
2 tablespoons chopped fresh basil
1 tablespoon chopped fresh dill
2 cloves garlic, minced
1 teaspoon salt
½ teaspoon pepper
½ teaspoon sugar
½ teaspoon chopped fresh oregano
½ teaspoon Dijon mustard
⅓ cup red wine vinegar
⅔ cup olive oil

• **Combine** all ingredients in a jar; cover tightly, and shake vigorously. **Yield:** 1¼ cups.

Rachel Kilpatrick
Houston, Texas

MUSHROOM-STUFFED TOMATOES

If the regular tomatoes are big but still pitifully pale, skip them and use plum tomatoes instead. You'll probably need 8 or 10; cut them in half lengthwise to stuff.

4 large or 6 medium-size ripe tomatoes
2 tablespoons butter or margarine
1 (8-ounce) package fresh mushrooms, chopped
¼ cup chopped onion
½ cup sour cream
2 egg yolks, lightly beaten
½ cup fine, dry breadcrumbs
1 teaspoon salt
¼ teaspoon pepper
¼ teaspoon dried thyme
1½ tablespoons fine, dry breadcrumbs
2 to 3 teaspoons butter or margarine, cut into 4 or 6 pieces

• **Cut** a ¼-inch slice from tops of tomatoes; scoop out pulp into a bowl, leaving tomato shells intact. Chop enough

pulp to measure 1 cup; drain on paper towels. Drain shells upside down on paper towels.
• **Melt** 2 tablespoons butter in a large skillet over medium-high heat; add mushrooms and onion. Cook, stirring constantly, 3 minutes or until tender.
• **Stir** in 1 cup chopped tomato pulp, sour cream, and next 5 ingredients; spoon evenly into tomato shells, and place in a greased 8-inch square baking dish. Sprinkle tomato shells evenly with 1½ tablespoons breadcrumbs, and dot with 2 to 3 teaspoons butter.
• **Bake** at 375° for 25 minutes or until thoroughly heated. **Yield:** 4 servings.

John Kilpatrick
Houston, Texas

A Bunch of Carrot Ideas

Dangle these carrots and lure your family back to the golden roots. The great taste and texture of our recipes outweigh promises of improved vision and good health.

BRAISED CARROTS, APPLES, AND CELERY

3 carrots, scraped and cut into thin 2-inch strips
3 stalks celery, diagonally sliced
1 purple onion, chopped
1 teaspoon olive oil
2 Granny Smith apples, cored and thinly sliced
1 cup currants
½ cup apple juice
¼ cup cider vinegar
¼ cup honey
2 tablespoons Dijon mustard
2 tablespoons chopped fresh basil
¼ teaspoon salt
¼ teaspoon freshly ground pepper

• **Cook** first 3 ingredients in hot oil in a large skillet over medium-high heat 10 minutes or until vegetables begin to caramelize, stirring often.
• **Add** sliced apple and next 5 ingredients; cover, reduce heat to medium, and cook 10 minutes. Uncover and cook until liquid is absorbed and vegetables are glazed.
• **Add** basil and remaining ingredients. **Yield:** 6 servings.

SCALLOPED CARROTS

4 cups sliced carrot
3 tablespoons butter or margarine
1 medium onion, chopped
1 (10¾-ounce) can cream of celery soup, undiluted
½ teaspoon salt
⅛ teaspoon pepper
½ cup (2 ounces) shredded Cheddar cheese
2 cups herb-seasoned stuffing mix
⅓ cup butter or margarine, melted

• **Cook** carrot in a small amount of boiling water 10 minutes or until tender; drain. Melt 3 tablespoons butter in a skillet over medium-high heat; add onion, and cook until tender, stirring constantly.
• **Stir** in soup and next 3 ingredients; spoon into a lightly greased 2-quart baking dish.
• **Combine** stuffing mix and ⅓ cup melted butter; spoon evenly over carrot mixture.
• **Bake** at 350° for 20 minutes or until thoroughly heated. **Yield:** 6 servings.

Carrie Triechel
Johnson City, Tennessee

CARROT MARMALEMON

1 pound carrots
3 lemons
3 cups sugar
1 cup water
1 teaspoon ground cinnamon
½ teaspoon ground cloves

• **Scrape** and shred carrots. Cut a thin slice from both ends of lemons, and cut each lemon into 8 wedges, removing seeds and any tough membranes.
• **Combine** lemon wedges, carrot, sugar, and 1 cup water in a saucepan; bring to a boil over medium-high heat, stirring constantly. Reduce heat, and simmer 30 minutes or until slightly thickened, stirring occasionally. Remove from heat; cool 30 minutes.
• **Position** knife blade in food processor; add carrot mixture. Process until smooth, stopping once to scrape down sides. Return mixture to saucepan; stir in cinnamon and cloves. Bring to a boil; reduce heat, and simmer 5 minutes or until thickened, stirring often.
• **Pour** mixture into hot, sterilized jars, filling to ¼ inch from top; wipe jar rims. Cover immediately with metal lids, and screw on bands. Process jars in boiling-water bath 10 minutes; cool on a wire rack. **Yield:** 3 half-pints.

CARROT HASH BROWNS

4 carrots, scraped and shredded
2 medium potatoes, peeled and shredded
½ small onion, grated
1 teaspoon salt
1 teaspoon pepper
3 tablespoons butter or margarine

• **Combine** first 5 ingredients, stirring mixture well.
• **Melt** butter in a large nonstick skillet over high heat; add carrot mixture, pressing firmly with a spatula or wooden spoon. Cook 5 to 6 minutes or until browned on bottom.
• **Invert** hash browns onto a plate, and slide back into skillet. Cook 5 to 6 additional minutes or until browned on bottom.
• **Transfer** to a serving plate carefully, and cut into wedges. Serve immediately. **Yield:** 8 to 10 servings.

Quick Carrot Fixes

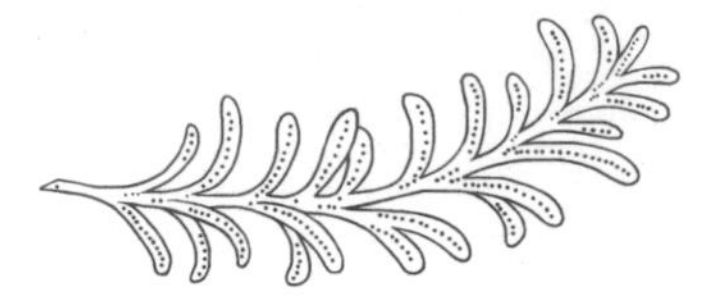

Start with 4 large carrots, scraped and cut into thin strips, and choose one of the following:

- Melt 1½ tablespoons butter in a skillet over medium-high heat; add carrot and 1 tablespoon brown sugar. Cook 5 minutes, stirring constantly.

- Combine carrot and 1 cup orange juice in a small saucepan; bring to a boil. Cover, reduce heat, and simmer 8 minutes.

Start with 2 cups of sliced cooked carrot, and choose one of the following:

- Stir in ¼ cup orange marmalade and 2 tablespoons brown sugar.

- Stir in 2 tablespoons honey, 1 tablespoon butter or margarine, and 2 teaspoons fresh lime juice.

- Mash the carrot; stir in 2 tablespoons butter or margarine, ¼ cup whipping cream, ¼ teaspoon salt, and ¼ teaspoon pepper.

- Stir in 1 (2-ounce) package honey mustard-flavored sauce mix for carrots.

- Stir in 1½ teaspoons butter or margarine, ½ teaspoon lemon juice, ¼ teaspoon salt, and ½ teaspoon ground ginger.

- Stir in 1 cup orange yogurt and 1 (5½-ounce) can pineapple tidbits, drained; cover and chill.

APRICOT-ORANGE-CARROT COOLER

1 medium carrot, scraped and sliced
½ cup water
1 cup orange juice, chilled
1 (12-ounce) can apricot nectar, chilled

• **Combine** carrot and water in a small saucepan; bring to a boil. Cover, reduce heat, and simmer 12 minutes or until tender. Remove from heat; cool.
• **Combine** carrot mixture, orange juice, and apricot nectar in container of an electric blender; process until smooth. **Yield:** 5 cups.

CARROT-PECAN SPREAD

1 pound carrots, scraped and sliced
1 cup pecan pieces, toasted
1 (8-ounce) package cream cheese, softened
½ teaspoon salt
½ teaspoon ground white pepper
3 to 4 tablespoons whipping cream

• **Position** knife blade in food processor bowl; add sliced carrot and pecans. Pulse 3 or 4 times or until mixture is finely chopped. Add cream cheese, salt, and white pepper; process until smooth, stopping once to scrape down sides.
• **Pour** whipping cream through food chute with processor running, blending just until spreading consistency. Serve with assorted crackers or as a sandwich spread. **Yield:** about 3 cups.

Fried Pies: Grandma's or Yours?

Stir up some fun tonight – cook plump, juicy fried pies. Prepare the fillings ahead of time, and then get everyone involved in assembling and frying. Purchased piecrusts and wonton wrappers or our foolproof pastry make these easier than the ones your grandmother made from scratch. We've expanded the flavors and included a savory beef pie you can serve as an entrée.

FRIED BEEF PIES

For a great entrée, spoon this filling into the Fried Pies pastry.

¾ pound lean ground beef
2 large plum tomatoes, chopped
1 small green bell pepper, chopped
1 small onion, chopped
1 small carrot, scraped and coarsely shredded
1 stalk celery, thinly sliced
¼ cup currants
1 tablespoon capers
1 teaspoon salt
1½ teaspoons pepper
48 wonton wrappers
Vegetable oil

• **Brown** ground beef in a large skillet, stirring until it crumbles; drain well, and place in a large bowl.
• **Add** tomato and next 5 ingredients to skillet; cook over medium heat, stirring constantly, 5 minutes or until vegetables are tender. Add to beef.
• **Stir** in capers, salt, and pepper.
• **Spoon** 1 tablespoon beef mixture onto half of each wonton wrapper. Moisten edges with water; fold wrapper over filling, forming a triangle, and press edges to seal.
• **Pour** oil to depth of 1 inch into a large heavy skillet or Dutch oven; heat

to 375°. Fry pies in hot oil 1 to 2 minutes or until golden, turning once. Drain well on paper towels, and serve immediately. **Yield:** 4 dozen.

FRIED PIES

3 cups all-purpose flour
1 teaspoon salt
¾ cup shortening
1 large egg, lightly beaten
¼ cup water
1 teaspoon white vinegar
2 cups fruit filling (see recipes)
Vegetable oil
Sugar (optional)

• **Combine** flour and salt in a large bowl; cut in shortening with pastry blender until crumbly.
• **Combine** egg and water, stirring with a fork; drizzle over flour mixture. Add vinegar, and stir with a fork just until dry ingredients are moistened.
• **Divide** pastry into thirds; roll each portion to ¼-inch thickness on a lightly floured surface, and cut each into 5-inch circles.
• **Spoon** 2½ tablespoons fruit filling onto half of each pastry circle. Moisten edges with water; fold dough over fruit filling, pressing edges to seal. Crimp edges with a fork dipped in flour.
• **Pour** oil to depth of ½ inch into a large heavy skillet. Fry pies in hot oil over medium-high heat 6 to 8 minutes or until golden, turning once. Drain well on paper towels. Sprinkle with sugar, if desired. **Yield:** about 1 dozen.

MIXED FRUIT FRIED PIE FILLING

1 cup chopped dried mixed fruit
¾ cup apple juice
¼ cup sugar
½ teaspoon vanilla extract
¼ cup chopped walnuts
¼ teaspoon ground cinnamon

• **Combine** dried fruit and apple juice in a small saucepan; let stand 30 minutes. Bring to a boil over medium-high heat; reduce heat, and cook 10 minutes or until fruit is tender and liquid evaporates, stirring often.
• **Remove** from heat; add sugar and remaining ingredients, stirring until sugar dissolves. Cool. **Yield:** 1¾ cups.

Note: Filling recipe makes 11 pies with Fried Pies recipe.

DRIED CHERRY FRIED PIE FILLING

2 (3-ounce) packages dried Bing cherries, chopped
1 cup water
½ cup sugar
¼ teaspoon vanilla extract
¼ teaspoon almond extract
½ cup chopped almonds

• **Combine** cherries and water in a medium saucepan; let stand 30 minutes. Bring to a boil over medium heat; reduce heat, and simmer 20 minutes or until liquid evaporates, stirring often.
• **Remove** from heat; add sugar and remaining ingredients, stirring until sugar dissolves. Cool. **Yield:** 1¾ cups.

Note: Filling recipe makes 11 pies with Fried Pies recipe.

ORANGE-PINEAPPLE FRIED PIE FILLING

⅔ cup chopped dried pineapple
½ cup orange juice
¼ cup water
⅓ cup sugar
½ teaspoon ground cinnamon
¼ teaspoon vanilla extract

• **Combine** first 3 ingredients in a saucepan; let stand 1 hour. Bring to a boil over medium heat; reduce heat, and cook 15 minutes or until tender and liquid evaporates, stirring often.
• **Remove** fruit from heat; add sugar, cinnamon, and vanilla, stirring until sugar dissolves. Cool. **Yield:** ⅔ cup.

Note: Triple filling recipe to use in Fried Pies recipe.

COOL-KITCHEN APPETIZERS

Take several blocks of cream cheese and a handful of pantry staples and you've got the ingredients for a no-cook, make-ahead appetizer buffet. There's Ginger Fruit Dip to serve with fresh fruit, Vegetable Cheesecake to spread on bread or crackers, and Ham Stack-Ups to lend a savory accent to the mix of recipes.

With such unique flavors, these three appetizers can be served at the same party and no one will guess that they all sprang from humble blocks of cream cheese.

HAM STACK-UPS

10 (8-inch) flour tortillas
1 (8-ounce) package cream cheese, softened
1 (2¼-ounce) can deviled ham
⅔ cup coarsely chopped green bell pepper
4 green onions, coarsely chopped
1 tablespoon mayonnaise or salad dressing
1½ teaspoons Worcestershire sauce
½ teaspoon garlic powder
Dash of hot sauce
¼ cup finely chopped pecans

• **Stack** tortillas; cut tortillas into 6-inch squares. Set aside.
• **Position** knife blade in food processor; add cream cheese and next 7 ingredients. Process until smooth, stopping once to scrape down sides.
• **Layer** tortillas, spreading each evenly with about 3 tablespoons cream cheese mixture and ending with cream cheese mixture. Sprinkle top with pecans.
• **Cover** and chill 8 hours.
• **Cut** into 1-inch squares; insert a wooden pick into each square. **Yield:** 3 dozen.

Paige Carroll
Charlotte, North Carolina

GINGER FRUIT DIP

1 (3-ounce) package cream cheese, softened
1 cup marshmallow cream
½ cup mayonnaise or salad dressing
1 teaspoon ground ginger
1 teaspoon grated orange rind
Garnish: fresh mint sprig

• **Beat** cream cheese at medium speed with an electric mixer until smooth; add marshmallow cream and next 3 ingredients, stirring until smooth. Garnish, if desired, and serve with fresh fruit. **Yield:** 1 cup.

Sue-Sue Hartstern
Louisville, Kentucky

VEGETABLE CHEESECAKE

1 (5-ounce) package thin vegetable crackers
⅓ cup butter or margarine, melted
2 (8-ounce) packages cream cheese, softened
½ cup finely chopped broccoli flowerets
½ cup finely chopped red bell pepper
¼ cup finely chopped green onions
⅓ cup grated Parmesan cheese
2 teaspoons Ranch-style salad dressing mix
¼ teaspoon garlic powder
Dash of Worcestershire sauce

• **Position** knife blade in food processor bowl; add crackers. Process until crackers become fine crumbs (about 1½ cups crumbs).
• **Combine** crumbs and butter; press mixture in bottom of a 9-inch springform pan.
• **Beat** cream cheese at medium speed with an electric mixer until smooth; add broccoli and next 6 ingredients, mixing well. Spread mixture over crust.
• **Cover** and chill 8 hours.
• **Remove** sides of pan; place pan on a serving platter. Serve with bread or crackers. **Yield:** 12 appetizer servings.

WING IT

Many believe wings are the best part of the chicken. They have lots of flavor and are just the right size. While wings make perfect appetizers, they're great for supper, too. Let these recipes help you spread *your* wings in new directions.

CURRIED CHICKEN WINGS

10 chicken wings
¼ cup butter, melted
¼ cup honey
¼ cup prepared mustard
1 to 1½ teaspoons curry powder

• **Cut** off wingtips, and discard; cut wings in half at joint.
• **Combine** melted butter and next 3 ingredients in a large heavy-duty, zip-top plastic bag; add chicken, and seal. Chill at least 2 hours, turning chicken occasionally.
• **Remove** chicken from marinade, discarding marinade; place chicken in a lightly greased 13- x 9- x 2-inch baking dish.
• **Bake** at 375° for 1 hour. **Yield:** 20 appetizers or 2 to 3 main-dish servings.

Diane Winger
Kansas City, Missouri

SWEET-AND-SOUR CHICKEN WINGS

16 chicken wings
2 teaspoons salt
2 large eggs, lightly beaten
1 cup cornstarch
Vegetable oil
1½ cups sugar
1 cup apple cider vinegar
½ cup ketchup
2 tablespoons soy sauce

• **Cut** off wingtips, and discard; cut wings in half at joint. Sprinkle chicken with salt; dip in egg, and dredge with cornstarch.
• **Pour** oil to depth of 2 inches into a Dutch oven; heat to 375°. Fry chicken, a few at a time, for 8 minutes or until golden; drain on paper towels.
• **Line** a 13- x 9- x 2-inch baking dish with aluminum foil, and add chicken.
• **Combine** sugar and next 3 ingredients in a small saucepan; bring to a boil over medium heat, stirring constantly. Remove from heat. Reserve ½ cup sugar mixture; pour remaining mixture over chicken.
• **Bake** at 400° for 30 minutes. Serve chicken wings with reserved sugar mixture. **Yield:** 32 appetizers or 3 main-dish servings.

Linda Heath
Bolivar, Missouri

TANDOORI CHICKEN WINGS

Look for tandoori paste, an Indian spice blend, among the sauces at your supermarket.

10 chicken wings
1 (8-ounce) carton plain nonfat yogurt
¼ cup tandoori paste
2 tablespoons lemon juice
1 medium onion, sliced

• **Cut** off wingtips, and discard; cut wings in half at joint. Make small slits in chicken with a sharp knife.
• **Combine** yogurt and tandoori paste in a large heavy-duty, zip-top plastic bag; add chicken, and seal. Chill at least 2 hours, turning chicken occasionally.
• **Remove** chicken from marinade, discarding marinade; place chicken in a lightly greased 13- x 9- x 2-inch pan.
• **Bake** at 400° for 10 minutes; reduce heat to 375°, and bake 20 to 25 additional minutes. Transfer chicken to a serving platter.
• **Sprinkle** lemon juice over onion slices; toss gently to coat. Arrange over chicken. **Yield:** 20 appetizers or 2 to 3 main-dish servings.

Manoja Pasala
Huntsville, Alabama

WHAT A FLAKE

If you're a potato purist, convinced that the instant variety tastes like wallpaper paste, then these recipes will make an instant potato believer out of you. Not only do the tasty packaged spuds come to dinner in a flash, they're perfect in a variety of recipes. Grab a box and see what you've been missing.

CHINESE CHICKEN WINGS

10 chicken wings
½ cup red plum sauce
3 tablespoons soy sauce
2 tablespoons prepared horseradish
1 tablespoon hot sauce
1 tablespoon prepared mustard

• **Cut** off wingtips, and discard; cut wings in half at joint.
• **Combine** red plum sauce and next 4 ingredients in a large heavy-duty, zip-top plastic bag; add chicken, and seal. Chill 3 to 4 hours, turning the chicken occasionally.
• **Line** a 13- x 9- x 2-inch pan with aluminum foil; add chicken and marinade.
• **Bake** at 425° for 45 minutes; drain. Serve with Chinese mustard. **Yield:** 20 appetizers or 2 to 3 main-dish servings.

Paula McCollum
Springtown, Texas

GRILLED HONEY CHICKEN WINGS

10 chicken wings
½ cup soy sauce
¼ cup dry sherry
¼ cup honey
¼ teaspoon garlic powder
¼ teaspoon ground ginger
3 tablespoons butter

• **Cut** off wingtips, and discard; cut wings in half at joint.
• **Combine** soy sauce and next 5 ingredients in a small saucepan; cook, stirring constantly, over medium heat until thoroughly heated. Reserve ¼ cup marinade, and chill.
• **Pour** remaining marinade into a large heavy-duty, zip-top plastic bag; add chicken, and seal. Chill 2 hours, turning chicken occasionally.
• **Remove** chicken from marinade, discarding marinade. Cook chicken, covered with grill lid, over medium-hot coals (350° to 400°) 20 minutes, turning once and basting with reserved ¼ cup marinade. **Yield:** 20 appetizers or 2 to 3 main-dish servings.

Sharon Chapman
Aiken, South Carolina

IRISH TATER BREAD BOWLS

These bowls are perfect for serving hearty stews, thick soups, green salads, or creamy dips.

Vegetable cooking spray
1 (16-ounce) package hot roll mix
1 cup instant potato flakes
1 tablespoon dried chives
1 teaspoon instant minced onion
1⅓ cups hot water (120° to 130°)
2 tablespoons butter or margarine, melted
1 large egg, lightly beaten

• **Invert** six 10-ounce custard cups onto a large baking sheet. Coat outside of cups generously with cooking spray, and set aside.
• **Combine** hot roll mix, yeast packet from mix, potato flakes, chives, and onion in a large bowl; add hot water, butter, and egg, stirring until dough pulls away from sides of bowl.
• **Turn** dough out onto a floured surface; shape into a ball with greased hands. Knead 5 minutes or until smooth. Cover; let rest 5 minutes.
• **Divide** dough into 6 portions; shape each portion over custard cup. Cover loosely, and let rise in a warm place (85°), free from drafts, 30 minutes.
• **Bake** at 375° for 20 to 30 minutes or until golden. Cool 5 minutes; remove from custard cups. Bake, right side up, 5 additional minutes, if desired, for extra crispness. **Yield:** 6 bowls.

Ada M. Johnson
Memphis, Tennessee

CHOCOLATE-SPICE POTATO CAKE

1 cup butter or margarine, softened
2 cups sugar
4 large eggs
2 cups all-purpose flour
2 teaspoons baking powder
1 teaspoon ground cinnamon
1 teaspoon ground cloves
1 teaspoon ground nutmeg
¼ cup cocoa
½ cup milk
⅔ cup instant potato flakes
1 cup (6 ounces) semisweet chocolate morsels
1 cup chopped pecans

• **Beat** butter at medium speed with an electric mixer about 2 minutes or until creamy; gradually add sugar, beating 5 to 7 minutes. Add eggs, one at a time, beating just until yellow disappears.
• **Combine** flour and next 5 ingredients; add to butter mixture alternately with milk, beginning and ending with flour mixture. Set batter aside.
• **Prepare** potato flakes according to package directions. Add mashed potato to batter, and beat until blended. Stir in semisweet chocolate morsels and pecans. Pour batter into a greased and floured 10-inch tube pan.
• **Bake** at 350° for 1 hour and 20 minutes or until a wooden pick inserted in center comes out clean. Cool in pan on a wire rack 10 minutes; remove from pan, and cool completely on wire rack. **Yield:** 1 (10-inch) cake.

Anna Rucker
Norfolk, Virginia

BEERQUICK SUGAR CAKE

4 cups biscuit and baking mix
½ cup instant potato flakes
¼ cup sugar
¼ cup nonfat dry milk powder
2 large eggs, lightly beaten
3 tablespoons vegetable oil
1 (12-ounce) can beer at room temperature
1 cup butter or margarine, melted
2 cups firmly packed brown sugar
1¼ teaspoons ground cinnamon

• **Combine** first 4 ingredients in a large bowl; make a well in center of mixture.
• **Combine** eggs, oil, and beer; add to dry ingredients, stirring just until moistened.
• **Spoon** batter into a greased 15- x 10- x 1-inch jellyroll pan, and let stand 10 minutes.
• **Combine** butter, brown sugar, and cinnamon; spread half of butter mixture over top of cake.
• **Bake** at 350° for 15 minutes. Remove cake from oven; spread with remaining butter mixture. Bake 10 additional minutes. Serve immediately. **Yield:** 15 to 18 servings.

Laura Greene Knapp
Cary, North Carolina

FROM OUR KITCHEN TO YOURS

PICKY, PICKY, PICKY

You've always heard it's easy to find out if a cake has finished baking. Just insert a wooden pick in the center and if it comes out clean, it's done. That's it, right? Well, not exactly.

Your average wooden pick works great in a shallow cake layer, but not in a deep Bundt or tube cake. If you use a 2-inch wooden pick, you may find that the outer portion of the cake is done, but what about the center? Instead, use a long wooden skewer made for kabobs or a metal cake tester. Both are available at grocery or discount housewares stores.

MEALED WITH A KISS

Many Southern church communities have a stock-the-freezer program to provide meals on short notice for members who have become ill or have experienced other temporary crises. But there are times when troubling situations call for more personal and permanent answers.

A reader recently put her heart into lightening the load for an older, longtime fellow choir member whose wife is no longer able to cook. Wanting the couple to have at least one enjoyable, home-cooked dinner each week, she rounded up choir and other church members to form "Mealed With a Kiss," a group with about 15 volunteers. Each volunteer prepares a meal and delivers it to the couple's home just once every three months; then the cycle repeats. This reader sends each member of the group a quarterly calendar with names, telephone numbers, and weeks assigned. That allows the group members to plan ahead and call someone else on the list to swap times if needed.

HAPPY DAY, MOM

Get a head start on Mother's Day, but don't get her slippers or perfume again this year. If she's a cook, we have a gift suggestion that doesn't involve deciphering pastry bags from parchment paper in a gadget-filled kitchen store.

Call your local bookstore for a copy of *The Good Cook's Book of Days: A Food Lover's Journal* by Michele Anna Jordan ($25). This beautifully illustrated volume is waiting to be filled with your mom's best recipes and menus, notes from memorable meals with friends, important dates, food likes and dislikes of guests, as well as information on and phone numbers of her favorite restaurants, markets, and cookware shops. She'll also find food quotes throughout and charts of storage times, measurement equivalents, and uses for flavored mustards and vinegars.

GOT YA COVERED

When your cheesecake turns out with a giant crevice, it's not your "fault." This often happens and is just the nature of the beast. Some think it's because the oven heat is too dry, causing the cheesecake's moisture to evaporate too quickly. (One tip we've heard – but haven't tried yet – is to place a pan of hot water on the bottom oven shelf while baking.)

There may be little you can do to prevent the crack, but here's a quick fix. Before serving the cheesecake, mound several fresh, colorful berries strategically over the split. Then combine ½ to 1 cup sour cream and a tablespoon or two of milk in a heavy-duty, zip-top plastic bag. Knead the bag with your hands to mix; then snip a tiny hole in one corner of the bag with scissors. Drizzle mixture over the berries and that crack in the cheesecake will soon be forgotten.

MULTIPLICATION TABLES

Let's see . . . *seven* women in *one* kitchen at *one* time, each preparing *seven* casseroles makes . . . a mess? Well, maybe. But it also makes 49 meals for the freezer in one evening *and* a fun time for the cooks.

Lisa Summerford and six of her Hartselle, Alabama, friends call themselves the "Kitchen Sisters." The group picks one night each month to descend upon a volunteer's kitchen. Each brings along a favorite recipe and enough ingredients to make it seven times.

They assign areas of the kitchen and dining room for chopping, mixing, cooking, and assembling. The Sisters put their casseroles into serving dishes, then they wrap and label each for the freezer.

Lisa says that they divide the costs for all ingredients equally, and they usually average $35 – and a whole lot of fun – per cook.

With our updated version of a bridesmaids' luncheon tradition – the charm or trinket cake – attendants pull ribbons with symbolic charms attached from the center of Orange Blossom Cake and from under Pineapple Upside-Down Cake Roll (recipes, page 162).

Right: *Serve reader-favorite Vanilla Soufflés With Vanilla Crème Sauce (recipe, page 155) for a dreamy dessert.*

Above: *Serve a split by the slice with Banana Split Terrine (recipe, page 164), which adds crystallized ginger to the traditional flavors of chocolate, strawberry, and vanilla.*

Right: *Learn how easy it is to make candied violets with our Peaches-and-Cream Cake. Then relax in a rocker and sample these springtime treats, including Chocolate Midnight or Orange Curd Miniature Tarts. (Recipes begin on page 118.)*

Show off the first peaches of the season with Elizabeth and Phoebe's Fresh Peach Pie (recipe, page 119).

MAY

DESSERT ON THE VERANDA

Marion Sullivan, a consummate Southerner from Charleston, South Carolina, has some sweet tricks up her sleeve. She's a master at disguising decadence beneath an elegant veil of chocolate curls or buttery frosting.

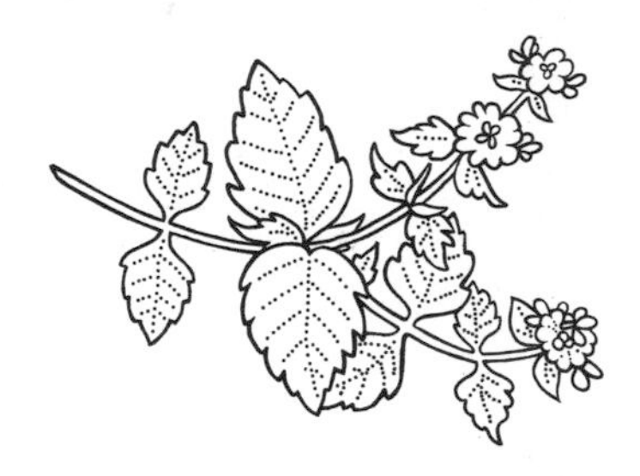

Cut a slice of her pansy-sprinkled Peaches-and-Cream Cake and you'll find a layer of peaches *and* a layer of meringue. To counter the cake's incredibly rich flavor, she recommends that you serve it with an assortment of fresh fruit.

With just one bite into one of her pretty little tarts, you'll experience an explosion of either orange or chocolate flavor.

Here Marion generously shares some of her favorite dessert recipes with us. Now you, too, can enjoy these delicious sweets on your own front porch.

FUSSY ABOUT SOFT WHEAT FLOUR

Soft wheat flour makes a difference in these recipes. We've found that White Lily flour works best, but regular all-purpose flour makes an acceptable substitute. You can order White Lily flour by mail. To receive a catalog, send a self-addressed, stamped, business-size envelope to White Lily, P.O. Box 871, Knoxville, TN 37901.

PEACHES-AND-CREAM CAKE

(pictured on page 115)

"When I started candying flowers 15 years ago, I thought it was the most wonderful thing in the world. They make a dessert special," says Marion.

1 cup unsalted butter, softened
2 cups sugar
6 large eggs
3 cups soft wheat flour (see note at left)
1 teaspoon baking powder
½ teaspoon baking soda
1 teaspoon salt
1 cup buttermilk
2 teaspoons vanilla extract
1 to 2 teaspoons sugar
1 cup chopped pecans, toasted
¾ cup sugar
4 egg whites
⅛ teaspoon cream of tartar
Pinch of salt
Peach Filling
Butter Whip Frosting
Candied and plain pansies

• **Beat** butter at medium speed with an electric mixer until creamy; gradually add 2 cups sugar, beating well. Add eggs, one at a time, beating until blended after each addition.

• **Combine** flour and next 3 ingredients; add to butter mixture alternately with buttermilk, beginning and ending with flour mixture. Beat at low speed until blended after each addition. Stir in vanilla. Pour batter into two greased and floured 10-inch round cakepans or springform pans.

• **Bake** at 325° for 30 to 35 minutes or until a wooden pick inserted in center comes out clean; cool in pans on wire racks 10 minutes. Remove from pans, and cool completely on wire racks.

• **Grease** a 10-inch springform pan; line bottom of pan with aluminum foil. Grease foil; sprinkle foil and sides of pan with 1 to 2 teaspoons sugar. Set pan aside.

• **Position** knife blade in food processor bowl; add pecans and ¾ cup sugar. Process until pecans are ground, stopping once to scrape down sides; set aside.

• **Combine** egg whites, cream of tartar, and pinch of salt; beat at high speed with an electric mixer until soft peaks form. Fold in pecan mixture, and spread in prepared pan.

• **Bake** at 250° for 1 hour and 30 minutes to 1 hour and 45 minutes or until thoroughly dry. Cool completely in pan on a wire rack; remove from pan.

• **Place** 1 cake layer on a cake plate; spread with half of Peach Filling. Spread 1 cup Butter Whip Frosting over filling, and top with meringue layer.

• **Spread** remaining filling over meringue layer, and spread 1½ cups frosting over filling; top with remaining cake layer. Spread top and sides of cake with remaining frosting, as desired. Chill 2 to 3 hours; decorate with pansies. **Yield:** 1 (10-inch) cake.

Note: To make candied pansies, sprinkle 2 envelopes unflavored gelatin over 2 cups warm water; stir with a wire whisk until gelatin dissolves. Dip pansies into gelatin mixture, shaking to remove excess; sprinkle all sides of pansies with superfine sugar, covering completely. Place pansies on baking sheets, and let stand 30 minutes or until dry and firm.

Peach Filling

1¾ cups dried peaches
1½ cups water
¼ cup sugar
2 tablespoons light corn syrup

• **Combine** peaches and 1½ cups water in a medium saucepan; bring to a boil. Cover, remove from heat, and let stand 30 minutes or until peaches are soft.
• **Add** sugar and syrup; bring to a boil. Reduce heat, and simmer 30 minutes or until most of liquid evaporates; remove from heat.
• **Position** knife blade in food processor bowl; add peach mixture. Process until mixture is smooth, stopping once to scrape down sides; cool. **Yield:** 2 cups.

Butter Whip Frosting

1¼ cups unsalted butter, softened
2 (16-ounce) packages powdered sugar, sifted
2 teaspoons vanilla extract
¼ teaspoon almond extract
1½ cups whipping cream

• **Combine** butter, 1 cup powdered sugar, and vanilla and almond extracts; beat at medium speed with an electric mixer until combined.
• **Add** remaining powdered sugar alternately with whipping cream, beating well after each addition. Beat at high speed until smooth and spreading consistency. **Yield:** about 6 cups.

"Desserts don't have to be hard to be good."

Marion Sullivan

"I learned to love desserts at a very young age," Marion Sullivan says, while reminiscing about the brownies and hot chocolate soufflés of her youth.

Her passion for food goes beyond desserts though. She turned a love of cooking into a livelihood by writing about food and operating a catering company. Marion now works as a consultant to restaurants and chefs.

Don't be intimidated by her impressive resumé. She's down to earth when it comes to what's realistic for the home cook.

"The Peaches-and-Cream Cake is more complicated than a plain layer cake, but it's not that difficult, and it's a pretty special dessert," she reassures.

If the sweets Marion has shared leave you longing for more, you can order a set of six of her "cookbooklets" to appease your appetite. Published by Wellspring, they contain a total of 150 recipes. To order the collection for $25 (price includes shipping; South Carolina residents add 6% sales tax), call Hoppin' John's Books About Food in Charleston; (803) 577-6404.

ELIZABETH AND PHOEBE'S FRESH PEACH PIE

(pictured on page 116)

"Betty Edge was my college roommate. I named this pie after her daughters. Assemble it at the last minute so the crust will remain crisp," Marion advises.

¼ cup unsalted butter, softened
1 cup sifted powdered sugar
1 tablespoon brandy
1 baked (9-inch) pastry shell
6 large fresh peaches, peeled and sliced
3 tablespoons fresh lemon juice
¼ cup sugar
1½ cups whipping cream
3 tablespoons sifted powdered sugar
1 teaspoon vanilla extract

• **Beat** butter at medium speed with an electric mixer until creamy; gradually add 1 cup powdered sugar and brandy, beating well. Spread into bottom of pastry shell; chill.
• **Combine** peaches, lemon juice, and ¼ cup sugar; cover and chill.
• **Beat** whipping cream at high speed with an electric mixer until foamy; gradually add 3 tablespoons powdered sugar and vanilla, beating until soft peaks form. Cover and chill.
• **Drain** peaches; arrange over butter mixture. Dollop whipped cream mixture over peaches; serve immediately. **Yield:** 1 (9-inch) pie.

MINIATURE TARTS

(pictured on page 115)

3 cups soft wheat flour (see note, page 118)
1 teaspoon sugar
½ teaspoon salt
1 cup unsalted butter, cut into small pieces and chilled
2 large eggs
1 teaspoon apple cider vinegar
Chocolate Midnight Filling or Orange Curd Filling

• **Position** knife blade in food processor bowl; add first 4 ingredients. Pulse 4 or 5 times or until mixture is crumbly.
• **Add** eggs and vinegar, and process until mixture forms a ball, stopping once to scrape down sides. Flatten dough slightly, and wrap in plastic wrap; chill 1 hour.
• **Spoon** 1 rounded teaspoon dough into a lightly greased 1½-inch fluted tart pan, and press into tart pan. Fit another tart pan over dough, and press gently. (Fitting another tart pan over dough and pressing gently ensures that pastry remains thin and even during baking.) Place tart pan on a baking sheet. Repeat procedure with remaining dough, and chill 1 hour. Place a baking sheet on top of tart pans.
• **Bake** at 350° for 10 minutes; remove top baking sheet and top tart pans. Bake 6 to 8 additional minutes or until tart shells are lightly browned. Carefully remove shells from pans, and cool on wire racks.
• **Spoon** Chocolate Midnight Filling or Orange Curd Filling into tart shells; garnish, if desired. **Yield:** 5½ dozen.

Chocolate Midnight Filling

⅔ cup water
3 tablespoons ground regular coffee
1 cup firmly packed brown sugar
1½ cups European (Dutch process) cocoa
⅔ cup whipping cream
3 tablespoons unsalted butter
4 egg yolks, lightly beaten
Garnishes: white and dark chocolate curls

• **Combine** water and coffee in a small saucepan; bring to a boil. Boil 1 minute; pour through a fine wire-mesh strainer into a cup, discarding coffee grounds.
• **Combine** brown sugar and cocoa in a heavy saucepan; gradually add coffee and whipping cream. Cook over low heat, stirring constantly with a wire whisk, until thoroughly heated.
• **Add** butter, stirring until it melts. Using a wire whisk, gradually stir about one-fourth of hot mixture into egg yolks; add to remaining hot mixture, stirring constantly.
• **Cook** over low heat, stirring constantly, 5 minutes or until mixture thickens; cool. **Yield:** 2 cups.

Orange Curd Filling

5 large eggs
3 egg yolks
½ cup sugar
5 tablespoons frozen orange juice concentrate, thawed and undiluted
2 tablespoons finely chopped orange rind
⅛ teaspoon salt
1 cup unsalted butter, cut into small pieces
2 tablespoons orange liqueur
2 tablespoons orange extract
Garnish: orange rind strips

• **Combine** first 6 ingredients in top of a double boiler; bring water to a boil. Reduce heat to low; cook, stirring constantly with a wire whisk, until thickened. Add butter, a few pieces at a time, stirring constantly. Stir in liqueur and extract.
• **Spoon** into a nonaluminum bowl, and cool completely.
• **Cover** and store any remaining curd in refrigerator, and serve with pound cake or use as a filling for a layer cake. **Yield:** 3 cups.

TAKE YOUR THYME

When Simon and Garfunkel penned "parsley, sage, rosemary, and thyme," they saved the best for last. Fresh thyme gives so much flavor to ordinary foods with so little effort.

More grocery stores now carry fresh herbs in their produce sections, so you can simply toss a small bunch of thyme into your basket and then into your dinner. Or grow your own in a flowerpot on your patio. Then snip a few sprigs and try them in these recipes.

JAMAICAN JERK CHICKEN

The distinguishing flavors in Jamaican jerk seasoning are thyme, allspice, and pepper. Rub the seasoning on chicken or pork, and pan-fry or grill. (As a bonus, the seasoning is fat free.)

½ cup coarsely chopped onion
6 green onions, chopped
2 cloves garlic, coarsely chopped
1 to 2 jalapeño peppers, unseeded and coarsely chopped
2 tablespoons fresh thyme leaves
1 tablespoon light brown sugar
1 teaspoon salt
1 teaspoon freshly ground pepper
1 teaspoon ground allspice
½ teaspoon ground cinnamon
¼ teaspoon ground nutmeg
6 skinned and boned chicken breast halves or boneless pork loin chops
Vegetable cooking spray

• **Position** knife blade in food processor bowl; add first 11 ingredients, and process until blended.
• **Rub** 1 tablespoon mixture onto each chicken breast. Cover and chill 1 hour.
• **Cook** chicken in a nonstick skillet coated with cooking spray 5 to 7 minutes on each side; or cook, without grill lid, over medium coals (300° to 350°) 10 minutes on each side or until chicken is done. **Yield:** 6 servings.

THYME-POTATO BAKE

- 3½ pounds red potatoes, peeled and coarsely chopped
- 2 (14½-ounce) cans ready-to-serve vegetable or chicken broth
- 1 tablespoon butter or margarine
- 2 cloves garlic, minced
- 2 large eggs, lightly beaten
- ½ cup freshly grated Parmesan cheese
- 1 to 2 tablespoons fresh thyme leaves
- ¾ teaspoon salt
- ¼ teaspoon pepper
- 2 tablespoons soft breadcrumbs
- 1 teaspoon butter or margarine, melted

• **Combine** potato and broth in a Dutch oven; cook over medium-high heat 10 minutes or until tender. Drain, reserving broth; mash potato.
• **Melt** 1 tablespoon butter in a small skillet over medium-high heat; add garlic, and cook, stirring constantly, until tender.
• **Combine** mashed potato, garlic, and next 5 ingredients in a large bowl, stirring until smooth. (Stir in ⅓ cup of reserved broth, if necessary.)
• **Spoon** potato mixture into a lightly greased 8-inch square baking dish.
• **Combine** breadcrumbs and melted butter; sprinkle over potato mixture.
• **Bake** at 350° for 35 minutes. **Yield:** 6 servings.

SHALLOT-THYME SAUCE

Try this delicate yet rich sauce with grilled veal, lamb, or chicken, or steamed vegetables.

- 8 sprigs fresh thyme
- 2 shallots, finely chopped
- 1 clove garlic, minced
- 1 cup dry white wine
- ½ cup whipping cream
- 1 cup cold butter, cut into 8 pieces
- Dash of salt
- Dash of pepper

• **Combine** first 4 ingredients in a medium skillet, and cook over medium-high heat 15 minutes or until liquid is reduced to ⅓ cup.
• **Reduce** heat to simmer. Stir in whipping cream, and simmer 10 minutes or until mixture is reduced by half.
• **Remove** mixture from heat; immediately add butter, a few pieces at a time, stirring constantly with a wire whisk until smooth. If necessary, place skillet over low heat for a few seconds to melt butter. (Do not melt butter before adding to sauce.)
• **Pour** sauce through a wire-mesh strainer into a bowl, discarding solids. Stir in salt and pepper. Serve immediately. (Do not reheat the sauce or it will separate.) **Yield:** 1⅓ cups.

THYME-LEMON BUTTER

Put a pat on hot-off-the-grill pork chops, steak, or fish, or use it to top a baked potato or dinner roll. You can shape the butter, slice it, and freeze. Take out a little as you need it.

- 2 tablespoons fresh thyme leaves
- 1 cup butter, softened
- 1 teaspoon grated lemon rind
- 1 tablespoon fresh lemon juice

• **Position** knife blade in food processor bowl; add thyme, and pulse 10 times. Add butter and remaining ingredients. Process until mixture is smooth, stopping once to scrape down sides.
• **Spoon** butter mixture onto plastic wrap. Shape mixture into a 1-inch diameter log by folding wrap over mixture and rolling. (Work quickly to keep butter from melting.) Seal in wrap, and chill 4 hours or store in refrigerator up to 1 week. **Yield:** about 1 cup.

THYME MAYONNAISE

A little fresh thyme gives oomph to regular mayonnaise in potato salad, deviled eggs, and sandwiches. You can also brush it on fish, chicken, or pork chops before broiling or grilling.

- 1 cup mayonnaise
- 2 tablespoons fresh thyme leaves, chopped

• **Combine** mayonnaise and thyme; chill 1 hour or store in refrigerator up to 1 week. **Yield:** about 1 cup.

"THYMELY" TIP

Need a new idea for a Mother's Day gift? Head to your neighborhood garden shop and assemble an herb basket. Choose several fresh herbs – thyme, parsley, oregano, and others great for cooking – in cell packs or small pots, and tuck them, along with growing tips, into a pretty basket.

TIME FOR AN OIL CHANGE

You've admired all the expensive flavor-infused oils in specialty grocery stores and dipped bread into bowls of them in restaurants. Now you can make these treasures at home.

We give you basic instructions for making the oils and easy recipes to get you started. Don't be timid about turning your kitchen into a laboratory. Try blending two or more herbs, herbs and garlic, or herbs and peppercorns for variations on the basic recipe. Making infused oils isn't rocket science – it's the start of a great meal.

TIPS FOR INFUSING OIL

- Start with fresh herbs and fresh oil. Wash and thoroughly dry the herbs before starting the infusion.
- Canola oil is pale, has no flavor, and stays liquid in the refrigerator. This makes it perfect for infusing.
- Extra virgin olive oil can make infused oils a special treat, but pair it with stronger flavoring ingredients like basil, rosemary, black pepper, or garlic. Olive oil will solidify in the refrigerator, but returns to liquid at room temperature. This can be a bonus. When the olive oil is solidified, it spreads easily on toasted bread.
- Making infused oils isn't an exact science. Vary the amounts of the flavoring ingredients to suit your taste.
- If your infused oil is cloudy, strain it through several thicknesses of cheesecloth. Don't worry if the oil doesn't clear; the flavor will not be affected.
- Don't use infused oils for frying. If heated, the flavor compounds can break down and become bitter. Add infused oils at the end of cooking or use them in cold dishes.
- Look for decorative decanters at kitchen specialty shops to showcase the infused oils.
- An infused oil makes a thoughtful housewarming or hostess gift, but be sure to let the recipient know to discard any remaining oil after 2 weeks to prevent possible food poisoning.

MAKING INFUSED OILS

Basic Recipe: Place herb or spice in a heavy saucepan; add 1 cup canola oil. Warm over low heat 20 minutes, stirring occasionally; cool at least 8 hours. Pour through a wire-mesh strainer, discarding solids. Cover and store in refrigerator up to 2 weeks; then discard.

Basil Oil: Use 1 cup chopped fresh basil.

Black Pepper Oil: Use ½ cup coarsely ground black pepper.

Chile Pepper Oil: Crumble 2 dried red chile peppers, and place in a heatproof container. Heat oil, and pour over chiles.

Chive Oil: Use 1 cup chopped fresh chives; reduce oil to ¾ cup.

Dill Oil: Use 1 cup chopped fresh dill.

Ginger Oil: Place ⅓ cup chopped fresh ginger in a heatproof container. Heat oil, and pour over ginger.

Mint Oil: Use 1 cup chopped fresh mint leaves.

Oregano Oil: Use 1 cup chopped fresh oregano.

Roasted Garlic Oil: Place 8 heads garlic on a sheet of aluminum foil. Drizzle garlic with ¼ cup canola oil; seal foil over garlic. Bake at 400° for 45 minutes; cool. Squeeze pulp from each clove into a heatproof container. Heat oil; pour over garlic. Then pour through a wire-mesh strainer. After straining oil, add the garlic pulp to mashed potatoes or tomato sauce.

Rosemary Oil: Use ½ cup chopped fresh rosemary.

Sage Oil: Use ½ cup chopped fresh sage leaves.

Thyme Oil: Use 1 cup fresh thyme leaves.

EASY RECIPES USING INFUSED OILS

Cheese Spread: Combine 1 (4-ounce) package crumbled feta cheese and 3 tablespoons Rosemary or Sage Oil in food processor; process until smooth. Cover spread, and chill at least 1 hour; serve with assorted crackers. **Yield:** ½ cup.

White Bean Spread: Combine 2 (15.5-ounce) cans Great Northern beans, drained; ¼ cup Roasted Garlic Oil; ½ teaspoon salt; and ¼ cup lemon juice in food processor; process until smooth. Stir in 2 tablespoons chopped fresh sage; serve spread with crudités or crackers. **Yield:** 2 cups.

Herb-and-Tomato Pasta: Combine 8 ounces hot cooked pasta; ¼ cup Basil, Oregano, Thyme, or Rosemary Oil; 2 cloves garlic, minced; 4 large ripe tomatoes, peeled and chopped; ¼ teaspoon salt; and ¼ teaspoon freshly ground pepper. Serve pasta immediately. **Yield:** 8 cups.

Mediterranean Pasta: Combine 8 ounces hot cooked pasta; ¼ cup Basil, Oregano, Thyme, or Rosemary Oil; 2 cloves garlic, minced; 4 large tomatoes, peeled and chopped; 1 (4-ounce) package crumbled feta cheese; ½ cup niçoise or kalamata olives, pitted and chopped; ¼ teaspoon salt; and ¼ teaspoon freshly ground pepper. Serve pasta immediately. **Yield:** 8 cups.

Herbed Rice Salad: Combine 2 cups cooked long-grain rice; ¾ cup chopped fresh parsley; 1 bunch green onions, sliced; 3 tablespoons any herb-flavored Infused Oil; ¼ cup lemon juice; 1 cup chopped fresh tomato; ½ teaspoon salt; and ¼ teaspoon freshly ground pepper. Cover and chill at least 2 hours. **Yield:** 3 cups.

Grilled Vegetables: Combine 6 cups sliced or quartered fresh vegetables, like zucchini, yellow squash, onion, eggplant, or bell pepper; 2 cloves garlic, minced; ¼ cup Roasted Garlic Oil or any herb-flavored Infused Oil; ¼ teaspoon salt; and ¼ teaspoon freshly ground pepper in a large heavy-duty, zip-top plastic bag. Seal and chill 1 hour, turning occasionally. Remove vegetables from marinade, reserving marinade. Spray a grill basket with vegetable cooking spray; place vegetables in basket, and cook, covered with grill lid, over medium-hot coals (350° to 400°) 10 to 15 minutes, turning occasionally. Toss vegetables with reserved marinade. **Yield:** 6 servings.

Infused Oil Vinaigrette: Combine ¼ cup white wine vinegar, ¼ teaspoon salt, ¼ teaspoon freshly ground pepper, and ¾ cup any flavor Infused Oil in a jar; cover tightly, and shake vigorously. Chill. **Yield:** 1 cup.

Soy-Ginger Salad Dressing: Combine ½ teaspoon dark sesame oil, 2 tablespoons soy sauce, 2 tablespoons rice vinegar, and 2 tablespoons lime juice. Stir in ¼ cup Ginger Oil with a wire whisk. **Yield:** about 1 cup.

Flavored Mayonnaise: Combine ⅓ cup egg substitute, ½ teaspoon dry mustard, 2 tablespoons white wine vinegar, and ½ cup any flavor Infused Oil in the container of an electric blender; process just until mixture is combined. With blender on high, add an additional ½ cup Infused Oil in a slow, steady stream. Cover mayonnaise; store in refrigerator up to 2 weeks, and then discard any remaining. **Yield:** 1½ cups.

Minted Melon: Combine 1½ cups cantaloupe balls, 1½ cups honeydew balls, ¼ cup fresh lime juice, and 2 tablespoons Mint Oil in a large heavy-duty, zip-top plastic bag; seal bag, and chill at least 8 hours. **Yield:** 4 servings.

Quick Uses for Infused Oil

Experiment with these easy ideas for using infused oils.

- Savor them at their simplest as a dip for French bread.
- Drizzle any herb-infused oil over a platter of sliced tomatoes, and garnish the tomatoes with a sprig of the same herb.
- Toss cooked pasta or rice with a sprinkling of any infused oil.
- Drizzle your choice of oil over baked or mashed potatoes, steamed vegetables, or fresh mozzarella or goat cheese.
- Marinate niçoise or kalamata olives, covered, in **Oregano, Rosemary,** or **Roasted Garlic Oil** at least 8 hours.
- Pop popcorn in **Chile Pepper Oil** for a spicy snack.
- Marinate slices of fresh mozzarella or goat cheese by covering them with any herb-infused oil and refrigerating for a day or two. Use the cheese as an appetizer or serve a slice atop a green salad.
- Punch up the flavor of commercial pasta sauce with a few spoonfuls of **Roasted Garlic, Rosemary, Oregano,** or **Basil Oil.**
- Sprinkle **Dill Oil** over cooked zucchini, green beans, or new potatoes.
- Make scrambled eggs, using **Black Pepper Oil,** but warn your family to taste their eggs before adding more pepper.
- Substitute **Roasted Garlic Oil** for the vegetable oil in your favorite Caesar salad dressing recipe.
- Brush any infused oil on fish, chicken, scallops, or shrimp before grilling.
- If you never serve a fine wine with salad because of the acidity of the salad dressing, toss salad greens with any herb-flavored infused oil, salt, and pepper. The oil alone will be enough to flavor the greens, and the salad won't clash with your wine.
- Take a tip from restaurant chefs: Place one of the more colorful oils like **Chile Pepper, Black Pepper,** or **Sage** in a squeeze bottle. Decorate an entrée or salad plate with dots or drizzles of the oil.
- For a special dinner, make several infused oils and place fresh herbs or garlic in the bottles. They'll look beautiful on your table and guests can choose the flavor of their choice for dipping bread.

Cooking With Lemon Herbs

A backyard bounty of herbs is one of summer's greatest rewards. While walking through the garden, pick a handful of fragrant lemon herbs for transforming an average meal into something special.

LEMON SHRIMP AND PASTA

Look for fish sauce in the Asian section of your grocery store.

1½ pounds unpeeled medium-size fresh shrimp
6 stalks lemon grass, thinly sliced (white part only)
1 tablespoon peanut oil
1 cup coconut milk
1½ teaspoons fish sauce
¼ cup thinly sliced green onions
1 tablespoon chopped fresh cilantro
Hot cooked angel hair pasta

• **Peel** shrimp, and devein, if desired; set aside.
• **Cook** lemon grass in oil in a skillet over medium heat 1 minute, stirring occasionally. Add coconut milk; cook over low heat until reduced by half, stirring occasionally.
• **Add** shrimp; cook 5 minutes or until shrimp turn pink. Stir in fish sauce, green onions, and cilantro; serve immediately with pasta. **Yield:** 5 to 6 servings.

CREAM OF TOMATO SOUP WITH LEMON BASIL

3 pounds tomatoes, cut into fourths
¼ cup chopped fresh lemon basil
2 tablespoons butter or margarine
2 tablespoons all-purpose flour
2 cups half-and-half
1 teaspoon sugar
1 teaspoon salt
¼ teaspoon freshly ground pepper
2 tablespoons chopped fresh lemon basil

• **Combine** tomato and ¼ cup lemon basil in a large heavy saucepan; bring to a boil. Reduce heat, and simmer 10 to 15 minutes or until tomato is soft.
• **Pour** mixture through a wire-mesh strainer into a bowl, pressing mixture against sides of strainer with back of a spoon; discard pulp. Set tomato liquid aside.
• **Melt** butter in saucepan over low heat; add flour, stirring until smooth. Cook 1 minute, stirring constantly. Gradually add half-and-half; cook over medium heat, stirring constantly, until mixture is thickened and bubbly.
• **Stir** in sugar, salt, and pepper; gradually stir in tomato liquid and 2 tablespoons lemon basil. Cook just until thoroughly heated (do not boil). Serve immediately. **Yield:** 5½ cups.

LEMON THYME COOKIES

1 cup butter or margarine, softened
1½ cups sugar
2 large eggs
2½ cups all-purpose flour
2 teaspoons cream of tartar
½ teaspoon salt
½ cup chopped fresh lemon thyme

• **Beat** butter at medium speed with an electric mixer until creamy; gradually add sugar, beating well. Add eggs, one at a time, beating until blended after each addition.
• **Combine** flour, cream of tartar, and salt; gradually add to butter mixture. Beat at low speed until blended after each addition. Stir in lemon thyme.
• **Shape** dough into 2 (10-inch) rolls; wrap each in wax paper, and chill at least 2 hours.
• **Unwrap** dough; cut each roll into ½-inch-thick slices, and place on lightly greased cookie sheets.
• **Bake** at 350° for 10 minutes. Cool on wire racks. **Yield:** 3½ dozen.

CULINARY CULTIVATION

Lemon Honey: Coarsely chop ½ cup fresh lemon balm or lemon verbena; place in a saucepan with 1 cup honey. Cook over low heat 15 minutes. Pour through a wire-mesh strainer, discarding solids.

Lemon Butter: Stir 2 tablespoons chopped fresh lemon basil or lemon thyme leaves into ½ cup softened butter. Cover and chill.

Lemon Vinegar: Bring 2 cups white wine vinegar and 2 cups fresh lemon verbena to a boil. Remove from heat, and let cool. Pour vinegar mixture into a glass jar, and let stand at room temperature 1 week. Pour through a wire-mesh strainer, discarding herbs. Store vinegar in a glass jar at room temperature.

IN A LEAGUE OF THEIR OWN

The Junior League of Houston has published a third cookbook, *Stop and Smell the Rosemary: Recipes and Traditions to Remember.* Eleven women – some of whom had never met – guided the project.

The group's diversity (it includes an art director, a caterer and foods stylist, an editor, an accountant, a marketing specialist, and some full-time moms) guaranteed success. Each cooks nearly every day. Beverle Grieco, a member of the committee, says, "We're not gourmet cooks; we're *good* cooks."

In the midst of the planning and recipe testing, the committee received a tempting offer to visit member Nancy Abendshein's family ranch near San Antonio. Not surprisingly, the retreat soon evolved into a tryout for several decorating ideas and recipes for the cookbook. The dinner included mild-flavored flautas, created with children in mind. Those folks who enjoy spicy flavors added their favorite picante sauce to heat up the flautas. Baked Spicy Rice and Black Bean-Corn Salsa rounded out the main course.

By the time the weekend ended, they were all fast friends, and the project had taken a giant step forward. "We had a clearer vision of the cookbook and how the recipes and entertaining section would fit together. We had proof that our ideas would work," said Beverle.

Here are some of the best recipes from their ranch retreat.

RANCHO RAMILLETE FLAUTAS

(pictured on page 151)

If you can find them, try panela cheese instead of mozzarella and Mexican cream in place of the sour cream-whipping cream mixture.

1 (5-pound) beef brisket
1 medium onion, unpeeled
1 head garlic, unpeeled
2 teaspoons salt
⅔ cup sour cream
¼ cup whipping cream
20 (8-inch) flour tortillas
1 cup vegetable oil
1 head leaf lettuce, shredded
8 ounces fresh mozzarella or Monterey Jack cheese, shredded
1 bunch radishes, shredded
2 plum tomatoes, cut in half and sliced
Picante sauce
Garnish: waffle-cut radish slices

• **Trim** fat from brisket; place brisket in a Dutch oven, and add water to cover. Add onion, garlic, and salt; bring to a boil. Cover, reduce heat, and simmer 4 to 5 hours or until tender, adding more water as needed.
• **Remove** brisket from Dutch oven, and chill until cool. Shred brisket with a fork; set aside.
• **Combine** sour cream and whipping cream; chill.
• **Cover** tortillas with damp paper towels, and microwave at HIGH 1 minute. Keep warm.
• **Spoon** ½ cup shredded brisket down center of each tortilla; roll up tortillas, and place, seam side down, in a 13- x 9- x 2-inch baking dish. Cover and keep warm.
• **Pour** oil into a 12-inch skillet; place over medium-high heat until hot. Place filled tortillas, seam side down, in hot oil; cook until golden on both sides, turning once. Drain on paper towels.
• **Serve** warm with sour cream mixture, lettuce, cheese, radish, tomato, and picante sauce. Garnish, if desired. **Yield:** 6 to 8 servings.

Note: Double recipe to serve 12; however, 1 (5-pound) brisket will be enough to make 12 servings. Freeze any remaining brisket in an airtight container up to 2 weeks.

BAKED SPICY RICE

(pictured on page 151)

1 cup long-grain rice, uncooked
2 (10-ounce) cans diced tomatoes and green chiles, undrained
1 cup water
1 teaspoon salt
⅔ cup pimiento-stuffed olives, sliced
¼ cup vegetable oil
½ cup chopped onion
1 cup (4 ounces) shredded Monterey Jack cheese

• **Combine** all ingredients in a shallow greased 2-quart baking dish.
• **Cover** and bake at 350° for 45 minutes. Stir well, and bake, uncovered, 15 additional minutes or until liquid is absorbed and rice is tender. **Yield:** 6 to 8 servings.

Note: To double recipe, prepare it in 2 batches, and bake in separate baking dishes.

BLACK BEAN-CORN SALSA

(pictured on page 151)

This salsa won our highest rating when tested.

3 ears fresh white corn
¾ cup water
3 medium tomatoes, peeled, seeded, and finely chopped
2 jalapeño peppers, seeded and minced
2 (15-ounce) cans black beans, rinsed and drained
1 cup chopped fresh cilantro
⅓ cup fresh lime juice
¼ teaspoon salt
¼ teaspoon freshly ground pepper
2 avocados, peeled, seeded, and finely chopped

• **Cut** corn from cob into a saucepan; add water, and bring to a boil. Cover, reduce heat, and simmer 6 to 7 minutes or until tender. Drain corn; transfer to a large bowl.
• **Add** tomato and next 6 ingredients to corn, stirring mixture gently. Cover and chill.
• **Stir** avocado into corn mixture, and serve with tortilla chips. **Yield:** 8 cups.

Note: Recipe may be doubled.

MANGO MARGARITAS

This fruity drink also won our highest rating when tested.

1 (26-ounce) jar sliced mangoes, undrained
Colored decorator sugar
1 (6-ounce) can frozen limeade concentrate, thawed and undiluted
1 cup gold tequila
½ cup Triple Sec or Cointreau
¼ cup Grand Marnier
Crushed ice

• **Spoon** 3 tablespoons mango liquid into a saucer; pour mangoes and remaining liquid into container of an electric blender.
• **Place** sugar in a saucer; dip rims of glasses into mango liquid, and then sugar. Set aside.
• **Add** limeade concentrate and next 3 ingredients to blender container; process until smooth, stopping once to scrape down sides.
• **Pour** half of mixture into a small pitcher, and set aside.
• **Add** ice to remaining mixture in blender to bring it to 5-cup level; process until slushy, stopping once to scrape down sides. Pour into prepared glasses; repeat with remaining mango mixture and ice. Serve immediately. **Yield:** 10 cups.

KAHLÚA GINGERBREAD WITH KEY LIME CURD

½ cup butter or margarine, softened
¾ cup sugar
⅓ cup firmly packed dark brown sugar
1 large egg
2 cups all-purpose flour
1½ teaspoons baking soda
1½ teaspoons ground ginger
1 teaspoon ground cinnamon
1 teaspoon ground cloves
½ teaspoon salt
1 cup molasses
⅔ cup hot water
⅓ cup Kahlúa
2 tablespoons brewed coffee
Key Lime Curd
Whipped cream
Garnishes: fresh mint sprig, Key lime rind

• **Beat** butter at medium speed with an electric mixer until creamy; gradually add sugars, beating well. Add egg, beating until blended.
• **Add** flour and next 9 ingredients; beat at medium speed until smooth. Pour into a greased and floured 13- x 9- x 2-inch pan.
• **Bake** at 325° for 35 minutes or until a wooden pick inserted in center comes out clean. Cut into triangles; serve warm or at room temperature with Key Lime Curd and whipped cream. Garnish, if desired. **Yield:** 12 servings.

Key Lime Curd

2 cups sugar
1 cup butter or margarine, cut up
⅔ cup fresh Key lime juice
1 tablespoon grated Key lime rind (optional)
4 large eggs, lightly beaten

• **Combine** first 3 ingredients, and lime rind, if desired, in a heavy saucepan; cook over medium heat, stirring constantly, until butter melts. Gradually stir one-fourth of hot mixture into eggs; add to remaining hot mixture, stirring constantly.
• **Cook** over low heat, stirring constantly, 10 minutes or until lime mixture thickens and coats a spoon. Remove from heat; cool. Cover and chill at least 2 hours. **Yield:** 3 cups.

A SETTING TO SAVOR

Your backyard or the nearest lawn-and-garden store can bring summer to your table. From the entertaining section of *Stop and Smell the Rosemary: Recipes and Traditions to Remember* come these ideas for your next special dinner.

■ Center table with pots of herbs. Set plants in large clay pots. Tuck moss around base of each plant. Tie several strands of raffia into bows around plants as an accent.

■ Ring napkins with long stems of herbs or other greenery; tuck in a few blossoms for added color.

■ Mark guests' places at table with small pots of herbs and attach place cards to the potted herbs.

■ Tie aprons onto the backs of chairs. If guests congregate in the kitchen, give them aprons, and put them to work. White chef's aprons are available at restaurant-supply stores.

Pineapple Paradise

If fresh pineapple is your passion, nothing could be sweeter than these recipes. For best flavor, select yellow pineapples with green leaves.

To prepare the fruit, first cut off the leaves. Then cut off the rind on the bottom. Stand the pineapple upright, cut off the remaining rind, and trim away any brown spots. Cut in half lengthwise, and trim the core; chop as desired. A 2-pound pineapple yields about 3 cups of chunks.

TROPICAL CHICKEN SALAD

4 skinned and boned chicken breast halves
1 cantaloupe
1 fresh pineapple
1 papaya
1 pear
2 cups seedless green grapes
Ginger Dressing
¼ cup sliced almonds, toasted

• **Place** chicken on a lightly greased rack; place rack in broiler pan.
• **Broil** 5½ inches from heat (with electric oven door partially opened) 4 to 5 minutes on each side or until done. Cool to touch.
• **Cut** chicken into 1½-inch pieces. Cover and chill at least 1 hour.
• **Cut** cantaloupe in half; remove and discard seeds. Scoop out balls, using a melon baller, reserving shells. Set melon balls aside. Trim shells, leaving as much pulp as possible; discard trimmings. Cut each shell in half; set aside.
• **Cut** pineapple lengthwise into quarters, leaving green top attached; remove and discard core. Remove pineapple pulp, and cut into 1-inch pieces, leaving ½-inch-thick shells; set aside.
• **Peel** papaya; cut papaya and pear into wedges.
• **Combine** cantaloupe balls, pineapple, papaya, pear, and grapes; toss fruit gently with ½ cup Ginger Dressing.
• **Combine** chopped chicken and ¼ cup Ginger Dressing.
• **Place** pineapple and cantaloupe shells on lettuce-lined plates; spoon chicken and fruit mixtures evenly into shells. Sprinkle with almonds, and serve with remaining Ginger Dressing. **Yield:** 8 servings.

Ginger Dressing

1 cup olive oil
⅓ cup orange juice
3 tablespoons red wine vinegar
2 tablespoons grated fresh ginger
2 tablespoons chopped fresh chives or frozen chives
1 tablespoon Dijon mustard
¼ teaspoon freshly ground pepper

• **Combine** all ingredients in container of an electric blender; process until smooth, stopping once to scrape down sides. **Yield:** 1½ cups.

PIÑA COLADAS

For your next party, serve Piña Coladas in fresh pineapple shells and garnish with a fruit kabob.

1 cup chopped fresh pineapple *
2 cups pineapple juice
1 cup dark rum
1 (16-ounce) can cream of coconut
1 quart rum-raisin or vanilla ice cream, divided
2 cups crushed ice, divided
Pineapple Shells (optional)
Garnishes: pineapple chunks, maraschino cherries

• **Combine** first 4 ingredients in a bowl, stirring well.
• **Combine** 1¼ cups pineapple mixture, 1 cup ice cream, and ½ cup ice in container of an electric blender; process until smooth. Repeat procedure 3 times with remaining ingredients. Serve immediately in pineapple shells, if desired. Garnish, if desired. **Yield:** about 9 cups.

Pineapple Shells: Cut off green tops of pineapples; cut a thin slice from bottoms, if necessary, to stand upright. Carefully remove pulp with a sharp knife, leaving ½-inch-thick shells.

* Substitute 1 (8-ounce) can crushed pineapple for 1 cup fresh.

William Moreno
Richmond, Virginia

PINEAPPLE-MINT DESSERT

1 fresh pineapple
1 quart vanilla ice cream or pineapple sherbet
Mint Sauce

• **Cut** off green top of pineapple; cut a thin slice from bottom of pineapple. Stand pineapple upright, and remove rind. Cut pineapple pulp crosswise into ½-inch-thick slices; remove center core with a 1-inch round cutter.
• **Arrange** pineapple slices in 8 individual bowls; top each slice with a scoop of ice cream and Mint Sauce. **Yield:** 8 servings.

Mint Sauce

½ cup chopped fresh mint
¾ cup pineapple juice
1½ tablespoons cornstarch
2 tablespoons water
½ cup light corn syrup

• **Combine** mint and pineapple juice in a small saucepan. Bring to a boil; reduce heat, and simmer 5 minutes. Pour mixture through a wire-mesh strainer into a 1-cup liquid measuring cup, discarding mint. Add enough water to equal ½ cup, if necessary.
• **Combine** cornstarch and water in saucepan, stirring well; stir in pineapple juice mixture and corn syrup. Cook over medium heat, stirring constantly, until mixture is thickened. Cover and chill. **Yield:** 1 cup.

living *light*

STIR-FRY LIGHT

Flavor comes easy to stir-fry recipes. Fresh ginger, garlic, or sesame oil perfumes the plate and makes your taste buds sing. Stir-frying is easy, too. Once you chop the ingredients, dinner is ready in minutes. Best of all, it takes just a smattering of fat to stir-fry light.

STIR-FRY CHICKEN WITH VEGETABLES

Look for Oriental broth near the canned chicken and beef broth at your grocery store.

1 tablespoon cornstarch
¼ cup ready-to-serve Oriental broth
1 tablespoon reduced-sodium soy sauce
4 (4-ounce) skinned and boned chicken breast halves, cut into ½-inch strips *
⅓ cup ready-to-serve Oriental broth
¼ cup reduced-sodium soy sauce
2 tablespoons dry sherry
1 tablespoon rice vinegar
1 tablespoon dark sesame oil
1 tablespoon chili puree with garlic
1 tablespoon cornstarch
2 teaspoons sugar
4 teaspoons canola oil, divided
2 large carrots, scraped and thinly sliced
1 green bell pepper, sliced
1 red bell pepper, sliced
1 onion, cut into thin strips
1 tablespoon minced fresh ginger
4 green onions, chopped
Garnish: green onions

• **Combine** first 3 ingredients; add chicken, stirring to coat. Cover and chill 30 minutes.
• **Combine** ⅓ cup broth and next 7 ingredients; set aside.
• **Remove** chicken from marinade, discarding marinade.
• **Heat** 2 teaspoons canola oil in a large nonstick skillet over high heat; add chicken, and stir-fry 5 minutes until tender. Remove chicken from skillet, and set aside.
• **Heat** remaining 2 teaspoons canola oil in skillet; add carrot, and stir-fry 2 to 3 minutes. Add green bell pepper and next 4 ingredients; stir-fry 3 additional minutes.
• **Stir** in broth mixture; bring to a boil. Boil 1 minute or until thickened. Stir in chicken, and garnish, if desired. **Yield:** 4 servings.

* Substitute 1 pound fresh turkey breast for chicken breast halves.

L. Hedrick
Annandale, Virginia

♥ Per serving: Calories 287 (32% from fat)
Fat 9.8g (1.3g saturated) Cholesterol 66mg
Sodium 1070mg Carbohydrate 18.3g
Fiber 2.7g Protein 28.9g

SWORDFISH STIR-FRY

If you can't find cellophane noodles, substitute a package of low-fat ramen noodles minus the seasoning packet. Substitute shrimp or chicken breasts for the swordfish.

1 (4-ounce) package cellophane noodles
1 tablespoon cornstarch
½ cup ready-to-serve, no-salt-added, fat-free chicken broth
3 tablespoons fresh lime juice
1 tablespoon fish sauce
1 tablespoon sugar
1 teaspoon chili puree with garlic
Vegetable cooking spray
½ pound boneless swordfish fillet, cut into 1-inch pieces
1 teaspoon canola oil
½ red bell pepper, thinly sliced
2 cloves garlic, pressed
1 tablespoon minced fresh ginger
1 large cucumber, peeled, seeded, and sliced
⅓ cup chopped green onions
¼ cup chopped fresh cilantro
Hot cooked noodles

• **Cook** noodles according to package directions; drain and set aside.
• **Combine** cornstarch and next 5 ingredients; set aside.
• **Coat** a large nonstick skillet with cooking spray, and place over medium-high heat until hot; add fish, and stir-fry 2 to 3 minutes or until tender. Remove fish from skillet; set aside.
• **Pour** oil into skillet; add bell pepper, garlic, and ginger, and stir-fry, 1 minute. Add cucumber, and stir-fry 30 additional seconds.
• **Stir** in broth mixture; bring to a boil. Boil 1 minute. Return fish to skillet; add green onions and cilantro, stirring until coated. Serve over hot cooked noodles. **Yield:** 2 servings.

Chloe Dowling
Birmingham, Alabama

♥ Per serving: Calories 457 (17% from fat)
Fat 8.7g (1.6g saturated) Cholesterol 44mg
Sodium 757mg Carbohydrate 69g
Fiber 1.4g Protein 24.8g

STIR-FRY SHRIMP

1 tablespoon cornstarch
1/3 cup fresh lime juice
1/3 cup dry sherry
3 tablespoons hoisin sauce
1 tablespoon chili puree with garlic
2 teaspoons dark sesame oil
2 pounds unpeeled medium-size fresh shrimp
2 teaspoons canola oil
4 cloves garlic, minced
2 tablespoons minced fresh ginger
3 carrots, scraped and thinly sliced
1 red bell pepper, thinly sliced
1/2 pound fresh snow pea pods
1/4 pound fresh bean sprouts
2 bunches green onions, sliced
3 cups hot cooked rice

• **Combine** first 6 ingredients in a small bowl; set lime juice mixture aside.
• **Peel** shrimp, and devein, if desired; set aside.
• **Pour** canola oil into a large nonstick skillet; place over high heat until hot. Add garlic and next 4 ingredients; stir-fry 3 minutes. Add shrimp and bean sprouts; stir-fry 3 additional minutes or until shrimp turn pink.
• **Add** green onions and lime juice mixture; bring to a boil. Boil 1 minute or until thickened. Serve immediately over hot cooked rice. **Yield:** 4 servings.

♥ Per serving: Calories 472 (15% from fat)
Fat 7.5g (1.1g saturated) Cholesterol 172mg
Sodium 540mg Carbohydrate 64.7g
Fiber 5.5g Protein 31.5g

STIR-FRY BEEF SALAD

1 pound boneless round steak
2 cloves garlic, minced
3 tablespoons minced fresh ginger, divided
2 tablespoons reduced-sodium soy sauce, divided
3 cloves garlic, minced
3 tablespoons white vinegar
2 tablespoons creamy peanut butter
1 tablespoon molasses
1/2 teaspoon dark sesame oil
1 teaspoon canola oil
1/2 cup fresh cilantro leaves
8 cups mixed salad greens
1 red bell pepper, cut into strips
1/2 cup fresh bean sprouts
4 cherry tomatoes, quartered

• **Trim** excess fat from steak; cut steak into thin strips.
• **Combine** 2 cloves garlic, 1 tablespoon ginger, and 1 tablespoon soy sauce in a heavy-duty, zip-top plastic bag; add steak. Seal and chill at least 1 hour, turning steak occasionally.
• **Combine** remaining 2 tablespoons ginger, 1 tablespoon soy sauce, 3 cloves garlic, and next 4 ingredients in container of an electric blender; process until smooth, stopping once to scrape down sides. Set aside.
• **Remove** steak from marinade, discarding marinade.
• **Pour** canola oil into a large nonstick skillet; place over medium-high heat until hot. Add steak, and stir-fry 1 to 2 minutes or until browned.
• **Combine** cilantro and salad greens; divide evenly onto individual serving plates. Top with steak, bell pepper strips, bean sprouts, and tomato; drizzle with ginger mixture. **Yield:** 4 servings.

♥ Per serving: Calories 267 (36% from fat)
Fat 10.8g (1.9g saturated) Cholesterol 65mg
Sodium 361mg Carbohydrate 12.5g
Fiber 1.5g Protein 30.8g

POLICING FAT

Melody Trivisone of Alpharetta, Georgia, has two children, ages 11 and 12, who play a big part in her awareness of the importance of eating healthy foods. "They're my fat police," she says. Here Melody shares child-approved tips to help your family eat healthy.

▪ Make a game out of reading labels in the grocery store and making low-fat substitutions in the kitchen.

▪ Introduce your family to low-fat snack alternatives like popcorn, raisins, and yogurt.

▪ Cut back on snack foods like potato chips and cookies. Rid your mind that these things exist, and rid your pantry of them, too.

▪ Seek out recipes for low-fat chicken and pasta. "I must have 365 recipes of my own that use chicken," Melody says. "Red meat should be an occasional treat."

▪ Do not punish yourself *or* your children. "Pizza beckons us once a week," Melody says. "It's the family's favorite indulgence."

SOY-AND-GINGER MARINADE

Patsy Bell Hobson uses this versatile marinade on chicken before grilling it. It's also good for meat and seafood.

1/2 cup reduced-sodium soy sauce
1/2 cup coarsely chopped onion
2 cloves garlic
2 tablespoons coarsely chopped fresh ginger
1/2 teaspoon ground cinnamon
1/2 teaspoon ground allspice
1/4 teaspoon ground cloves

• **Combine** all ingredients; add meat, poultry or seafood. Cover and chill 30 minutes.
• **Remove** from marinade, discarding marinade. Grill as desired.

Patsy Bell Hobson
Liberty, Missouri

ORIENT SUCCESS

Low-fat and uniquely flavored, these unfamiliar Asian ingredients are definitely worth seeking out in the ethnic section of your grocery store. If you're watching your salt intake, be aware that many Asian condiments are high in sodium.

▪ **Cellophane noodles**, sometimes labeled rice noodles, have no fat, cook in less than 5 minutes, and soak up the flavor of anything you pour over them.

▪ Just a spoonful of concentrated **chili puree with garlic** adds heat and flavor to stir-fries.

▪ Try **dark sesame oil** once and you'll make it a pantry staple. A half-teaspoon of this oil gives robust flavor to a plateful of food.

▪ **Hoisin sauce** is also referred to as Peking sauce. Its sweet and spicy flavor enriches stir-fries, pastas, and marinades.

▪ A little bit of **fish sauce** goes a long way. Its salty fish flavor is the "secret" ingredient in many Asian recipes.

▪ **Oriental broth** has a hint of ginger and soy; use it to add more flavor to stir-fry recipes.

SPICY ORIENTAL EGGPLANT

Serve this as a side dish, or toss it with pasta for a quick weeknight dinner.

½ cup ready-to-serve Oriental broth
1 large eggplant, peeled and cut into cubes (1 pound)
2 tablespoons reduced-sodium soy sauce
2 teaspoons chili puree with garlic
1 teaspoon sugar
1 teaspoon red wine vinegar
1 teaspoon dark sesame oil
2 cloves garlic, minced
2 tablespoons minced fresh ginger
1 bunch green onions, chopped

• **Combine** broth and eggplant in a large nonstick skillet; cover and cook over high heat 3 to 4 minutes or until tender. Drain and set aside. Wipe out skillet with paper towels.
• **Combine** soy sauce, chili puree, sugar, and vinegar in a small bowl, and set mixture aside.
• **Heat** oil in nonstick skillet; add garlic and ginger, and stir-fry 1 minute. Add eggplant and soy sauce mixture; stir-fry 2 additional minutes. Stir in green onions. **Yield:** 2 servings.

Betty Levine
Loudon, Tennessee

♥ Per serving: Calories 130 (19% from fat)
Fat 2.8g (0.4g saturated) Cholesterol 0mg
Sodium 902mg Carbohydrate 25.3g
Fiber 4.9g Protein 5g

SNEAK IN GOOD NUTRITION

Ann Birkmire of Reston, Virginia, plays a little trick in her kitchen. "I have two small children, both of whom tend to avoid vegetables. These recipes camouflage healthy ingredients like zucchini, spinach, and sweet potatoes. And the children just love them."

ZUCCHINI LOAVES

You can freeze these loaves up to 1 month; drizzle with glaze after thawing.

3 large eggs, lightly beaten
1½ cups sugar
3 cups shredded zucchini (1½ pounds)
¾ cup vegetable oil
2 teaspoons vanilla extract
2 cups all-purpose flour
1 cup whole wheat flour
½ cup wheat germ
¼ cup nonfat dry milk powder
1 teaspoon baking powder
1 teaspoon baking soda
1 teaspoon salt
2 teaspoons ground cinnamon
½ teaspoon ground nutmeg
¼ teaspoon ground cloves
1 cup sifted powdered sugar
½ teaspoon vanilla extract
2 tablespoons milk
¼ cup chopped pecans, toasted

• **Combine** first 5 ingredients in a large bowl, stirring well.
• **Combine** all-purpose flour and next 9 ingredients, stirring well. Add to zucchini mixture, stirring just until blended. Spoon batter evenly into two greased and floured 8- x 4- x 2½-inch loafpans.
• **Bake** at 350° for 45 to 50 minutes or until a wooden pick inserted in center comes out clean. Cool in pans on

a wire rack 10 minutes; remove from pans, and let cool completely on wire rack.
- **Combine** powdered sugar, ½ teaspoon vanilla, and milk, stirring until smooth. Drizzle evenly over loaves; sprinkle with pecans. **Yield:** 2 loaves.

SPINACH MEAT LOAF

We added the steak sauce to Ann's recipe; it helps to keep the meat loaf moist.

2 large eggs, lightly beaten
1½ pounds ground round
½ cup regular oats, uncooked
½ cup wheat germ
½ cup shredded carrot
¼ cup chopped onion
1 (10-ounce) package frozen chopped spinach, thawed and well drained
½ cup milk
1 teaspoon salt
½ teaspoon pepper
½ cup steak sauce

- **Combine** first 10 ingredients, stirring well; shape into a 9- x 5- x 3-inch loaf, and place on a lightly greased rack in broiler pan.
- **Bake** at 350° for 40 minutes. Spread steak sauce over meat loaf; bake 20 additional minutes or until a meat thermometer inserted in center registers 160°. **Yield:** 6 to 8 servings.

SWEET POTATO PIE

Serve this pie chilled with low-fat ice cream for a cooling dessert.

1 (14½-ounce) can mashed sweet potatoes
¾ cup milk
¾ cup firmly packed brown sugar
2 large eggs
1 tablespoon butter or margarine, melted
½ teaspoon salt
½ teaspoon ground cinnamon
1 unbaked (9-inch) pastry shell

- **Combine** first 7 ingredients in container of an electric blender; process until smooth, stopping once to scrape down sides. Pour into pastry shell.
- **Bake** at 400° for 10 minutes. Reduce heat to 350°, and bake 35 additional minutes or until a knife inserted in center comes out clean, shielding edges with aluminum foil after 20 minutes to prevent excessive browning. **Yield:** 1 (9-inch) pie.

FROM *THEIR* KITCHEN TO OURS

If sharing cultures is part of the Olympic spirit, then Jerry Mauri deserves a gold medal. He spends his days teaching the cooking of his Italian homeland to professional students at the Baltimore International Culinary College. Try Jerry's delicious versions of risotto, one of Italy's classic dishes.

RISOTTO WITH SHELLFISH AND PEAS

Leave a few of the mussels and clams in their shells to use as a garnish.

3 pounds fresh mussels
2 dozen fresh littleneck clams
1 cup dry white wine, divided
2 (14½-ounce) cans ready-to-serve vegetable broth
1 medium onion, finely chopped
1 clove garlic, finely chopped
2 tablespoons olive oil
1½ cups Arborio rice, uncooked
1 cup frozen English peas, thawed
⅛ teaspoon threads of saffron
Pinch of ground red pepper
¼ cup chopped fresh Italian parsley
½ teaspoon salt
½ teaspoon freshly ground black pepper

- **Scrub** mussels and clams with a brush, removing beards from mussels. Discard any opened shells.
- **Bring** ½ cup wine to a boil in a large saucepan; add mussels and clams, and cook just until shells open. Reserve cooking liquid. Discard any unopened shells. Remove mussels and clams from shells, and set aside.
- **Pour** cooking liquid through a fine wire-mesh strainer into a liquid measuring cup, and add enough water to measure 1 cup; return to saucepan. Add vegetable broth; bring to a boil over medium-high heat. Reduce heat, and simmer.
- **Cook** onion and garlic in oil in a large saucepan over medium-low heat, stirring constantly, 10 minutes or until tender (do not brown).
- **Add** rice, and cook over medium-high heat 3 minutes, stirring constantly. Add remaining ½ cup wine, and cook until liquid evaporates.
- **Add** ½ cup hot broth mixture to rice; cook, stirring constantly, until liquid is absorbed. Repeat procedure with remaining broth mixture, ½ cup at a time. Add peas, saffron, and red pepper after 15 minutes.
- **Stir** in mussels, clams, parsley, salt, and black pepper. **Yield:** 3 main-dish servings or 6 appetizer servings.

CREATE A STIR

Risotto is a creamy rice dish prepared by gradually adding small amounts of hot broth to the rice while stirring constantly.

Arborio rice is traditionally used to make risotto. It has the ability to absorb more liquid than other types of rice and its plump grains remain firm in the center when cooked. This type of rice will guarantee the creamy consistency and *al dente* texture of a good risotto.

Use a wooden spoon to stir risotto; a metal spoon can break the grains.

RISOTTO WITH GREENS

If you can't find peppery arugula, use more watercress in its place.

1 tablespoon butter or margarine
1 tablespoon olive oil
1 small onion, chopped
1 clove garlic, minced
1½ cups Arborio rice, uncooked
½ cup dry white wine
1 cup fresh watercress, chopped
1 cup fresh arugula, chopped
3 (14½-ounce) cans ready-to-serve chicken or vegetable broth, heated
5 plum tomatoes, seeded and chopped
1 teaspoon chopped fresh thyme
1 teaspoon chopped fresh oregano
1 teaspoon chopped fresh mint
½ cup freshly grated Parmesan cheese
2 tablespoons butter or margarine
½ teaspoon freshly ground pepper

• **Melt** 1 tablespoon butter in a large saucepan over medium-low heat; add oil, onion, and garlic, and cook 10 minutes or until tender (do not brown), stirring often.
• **Add** rice; cook over medium-high heat 3 minutes, stirring constantly. Stir in wine, and cook 2 to 3 minutes or until liquid evaporates. Stir in watercress and arugula.
• **Add** ½ cup hot broth; cook, stirring constantly, until liquid is absorbed. Repeat procedure with remaining broth, ½ cup at a time.
• **Stir** in tomato and remaining ingredients. **Yield:** 3 main-dish servings or 6 appetizer servings.

RICE WITH SPRING VEGETABLES

Substitute Swiss or Parmesan cheese for the fontina and Gruyère cheeses.

2 tablespoons unsalted butter
1 small onion, finely chopped
1 clove garlic, chopped
1½ cups Arborio rice, uncooked
½ cup 1-inch fresh asparagus pieces
½ cup small Sugar Snap peas
½ cup finely chopped leek
½ cup thinly sliced carrot
3 (14½-ounce) cans ready-to-serve chicken or vegetable broth
1 teaspoon chopped fresh mint
2 ounces prosciutto or cooked ham, cut into thin strips
⅓ cup grated Parmesan cheese
½ cup (2 ounces) shredded fontina cheese
2 ounces grated Gruyère cheese
¼ teaspoon freshly ground pepper
Pinch of ground nutmeg
Garnishes: fresh Italian parsley and thyme sprigs

• **Melt** butter in a large skillet over medium-low heat; add onion and garlic, and cook, stirring constantly, 10 minutes or until tender.
• **Stir** in rice and next 5 ingredients; cook over medium-high heat 25 minutes, stirring often.
• **Add** mint; cook 5 minutes or until liquid evaporates and rice is tender, stirring often.
• **Stir** in prosciutto and next 5 ingredients; garnish, if desired. **Yield:** 3 main-dish servings or 6 appetizer servings.

GET TO THE HEART OF THE MATTER

Baby artichokes, the petite version of the full-size delicacy, grow lower on the plant and, sheltered from the sun, yield a smaller size. The leaves are tender, so you can eat the whole thing with the exception of a few rough outer leaves.

Artichoke plants produce year-round, but spring is prime time, with a second, smaller peak in October. The crop is harvested by hand, which is why they're sometimes more expensive than less jazzy produce. But they're definitely worth the higher price. Try these recipes and see for yourself.

QUICK 'N' EASY WHOLE COOKED ARTICHOKES

4 artichokes
1 cup water

• **Hold** each artichoke by stem, and wash by plunging up and down in cold water. Cut off stem ends, and trim about ½ inch from top of each artichoke. Remove any loose bottom leaves.
• **Stand** artichokes in an 11- x 7- x 1½-inch baking dish, and add 1 cup water to dish. Cover dish with heavy-duty plastic wrap.
• **Microwave** at HIGH 15 to 20 minutes, giving dish a quarter-turn halfway through cooking time. Let stand 5 minutes. (When done, the petal near the center will pull out easily.) Serve with melted butter or desired dipping sauce. **Yield:** 4 servings.

ARTICHOKE AND SHRIMP PLATTER WITH BÉARNAISE SAUCE

3 cups water
1 pound unpeeled medium-size fresh shrimp
4 Quick 'n' Easy Whole Cooked Artichokes, chilled (see recipe)
Béarnaise Sauce

• **Bring** water to a boil; add shrimp, and cook 3 to 5 minutes or until shrimp turn pink. Drain well; rinse with cold water. Peel shrimp, and devein, if desired. Chill.
• **Arrange** artichokes and shrimp on a serving platter. Serve with Béarnaise

Sauce and French bread. **Yield:** 4 appetizer servings.

Béarnaise Sauce

¼ cup tarragon vinegar or white wine vinegar
¼ cup dry white wine or dry vermouth
¼ cup finely chopped shallot
3 egg yolks, lightly beaten
2 tablespoons chopped fresh tarragon or 1 teaspoon dried tarragon
½ cup butter or margarine, cut into thirds
½ teaspoon chopped fresh tarragon (optional)

• **Combine** first 3 ingredients in a saucepan; bring to a boil over medium heat. Reduce heat to low, and simmer until reduced to 1 tablespoon (about 10 minutes). Pour through a wire-mesh strainer, reserving liquid and discarding solids. Cool liquid slightly.
• **Combine** reserved liquid, egg yolks, and 2 tablespoons tarragon in a small saucepan. Add one-third of butter; cook over low heat, stirring constantly with a wire whisk, until butter melts.
• **Add** another third of butter, stirring constantly; as sauce thickens, stir in remaining butter. Cook, stirring constantly, until thickened. Stir in ½ teaspoon tarragon, if desired. Serve immediately. **Yield:** ¾ cup.

HERBED ARTICHOKE SAUTÉ

10 baby artichokes
1 tablespoon olive oil
1 red bell pepper, seeded and cut into thin strips
1 tablespoon fresh thyme leaves
½ cup dry white wine
½ teaspoon salt
2 tablespoons chopped shallot
2 cloves garlic, minced
2 tablespoons butter

• **Hold** each artichoke by stem, and wash by plunging up and down in cold water. Cut off stem ends. Remove dark-green outer leaves from baby artichokes until light-green leaves appear. Place artichokes in a large Dutch oven; cover with water, and bring to a boil. Cook 12 to 15 minutes or until tender; drain and cool slightly.
• **Cut** artichokes in half lengthwise.
• **Cook** artichokes in oil in a large nonstick skillet over medium-high heat 2 minutes, stirring constantly. Add bell pepper strips and thyme leaves. Cook 3 additional minutes, stirring constantly. Remove artichoke mixture from skillet; set aside.
• **Combine** wine and next 3 ingredients in skillet; bring to a boil over medium-high heat. Reduce heat to low, and simmer until reduced to 2 tablespoons (about 5 minutes).
• **Stir** in butter; add artichoke mixture, and cook until thoroughly heated. **Yield:** 2 servings.

CHICKEN-AND-ARTICHOKE CASSEROLE

If you don't have time for fresh artichokes, try this recipe, which uses canned ones.

Vegetable cooking spray
8 skinned and boned chicken breast halves, cut into bite-size pieces
2 (14-ounce) cans quartered artichoke hearts, drained
1 (10¾-ounce) can reduced-sodium, reduced-fat cream of chicken soup, undiluted
1 cup reduced-fat mayonnaise
1 teaspoon lemon juice
½ teaspoon curry powder
¼ teaspoon ground white pepper
1 cup (4 ounces) shredded reduced-fat sharp Cheddar cheese
1¼ cups bread cubes
2 tablespoons butter or margarine, melted
Paprika

• **Coat** a large skillet with cooking spray; place over medium-high heat until hot. Add chicken, and cook, stirring constantly, 3 to 4 minutes or until tender; drain and set aside.
• **Drain** artichoke hearts well, and press gently between layers of paper towels.
• **Coat** an 11- x 7- x 1½-inch baking dish with cooking spray, and place artichokes in dish; top with chicken.
• **Combine** soup and next 4 ingredients; spread over chicken, and sprinkle with cheese.
• **Combine** bread cubes and butter, tossing to coat; sprinkle evenly over cheese.
• **Bake** at 350° for 25 minutes. **Yield:** 8 servings.

Barbara Cirilli
Greenville, Mississippi

THE WAY TO A WOMAN'S HEART

An artichoke is actually a flowerbud that's harvested before it blooms. Perhaps that explains why two famous women were drawn to the artichoke.

In the 1500s Catherine de Medici brought the delicacy to France when she married the heir to the French throne. Artichokes soon caught on and were even rumored to be an aphrodisiac.

In 1947 Marilyn Monroe was the first woman to be crowned California Artichoke Queen. Growers believe her reign inspired more people than ever to eat the exotic produce.

Holiday Picnic

Celebrate Memorial Day with your family and friends. Pack up this picnic menu and head outside to a shady spot.

Serve Rolled Pork with Rhubarb Sauce hot or cold. Slice the pork before you pack it to make serving a breeze. Toss the tortellini salad as much as 8 hours ahead – the flavors only get better. And just for the fun of it, freeze the ice cream at your picnic site.

Outdoor Menu
Serves 10

Rolled Pork With Rhubarb Sauce
Terrific Tortellini Salad
Butter-Pecan Ice Cream
Pineapple-Citrus Punch

Rolled Pork With Rhubarb Sauce

1 (3-pound) rolled boneless pork loin roast
2 tablespoons chopped fresh rosemary, divided
2 tablespoons chopped fresh thyme, divided
3 cloves garlic, cut into fourths
Olive oil-flavored cooking spray
2 cups fresh or frozen sliced rhubarb, thawed
1 (10-ounce) jar seedless raspberry preserves
⅔ cup honey
2 tablespoons apple cider vinegar
½ teaspoon dry mustard
¼ teaspoon ground cloves
Garnishes: fresh rosemary and thyme sprigs

• **Remove** string from pork roast; trim fat. Sprinkle half of chopped rosemary and thyme on top of half of pork roast; place other half of roast on top, and tie at 2-inch intervals with heavy string.

• **Place** roast in a shallow roasting pan. Cut 12 small slits in roast; insert garlic pieces. Sprinkle with remaining chopped rosemary and thyme, and coat with cooking spray.

• **Bake** at 325° for 1 hour.

• **Combine** rhubarb and next 5 ingredients in a saucepan; bring to a boil over medium heat. Reduce heat, and simmer 10 minutes; cool slightly.

• **Position** knife blade in food processor bowl; add rhubarb mixture, and pulse 4 times or until smooth. Reserve ⅔ cup mixture. Brush roast with remaining mixture.

• **Bake** roast 20 additional minutes or until meat thermometer inserted in thickest portion registers 160°. Let roast stand 10 minutes. Serve with reserved rhubarb mixture. **Yield:** 10 servings.

Terrific Tortellini Salad

2 (14-ounce) packages frozen cheese tortellini
1 green bell pepper, chopped
1 red bell pepper, chopped
1 cucumber, chopped
1 (14-ounce) can artichoke hearts, rinsed and drained
1 (8-ounce) bottle Caesar salad dressing
1 tomato, cut into wedges

• **Prepare** tortellini according to package directions; drain. Rinse with cold water; drain.

• **Combine** tortellini and next 5 ingredients in a large bowl; cover and chill 2 hours.

• **Arrange** tomato wedges over salad. **Yield:** 8 to 10 servings.

Tracy Russell
Greensboro, North Carolina

Butter-Pecan Ice Cream

¼ cup butter or margarine
2 cups chopped pecans
7 cups milk, divided
1 (14-ounce) can sweetened condensed milk
2 cups sugar
6 large eggs, lightly beaten
1 (5.1-ounce) package vanilla instant pudding mix
1 teaspoon vanilla extract

• **Melt** butter in a large heavy saucepan over medium-high heat; add pecans, and cook, stirring constantly, 3 minutes or until lightly browned. Drain and set aside.

• **Combine** 1 cup milk and next 3 ingredients in saucepan; cook over medium heat, stirring constantly, 5 minutes or until mixture coats back of a spoon. Cool. Stir in remaining 6 cups milk, pudding mix, and vanilla; add pecans, stirring well.

• **Pour** mixture into freezer container of a 5-quart hand-turned or electric freezer. Freeze according to manufacturer's instructions.

• **Pack** freezer with additional ice and rock salt; let stand 1 hour before serving. **Yield:** 1 gallon.

Tammy Sewell
Fort Benning, Georgia

Pineapple-Citrus Punch

1 (46-ounce) can pineapple juice
1 quart apple juice
1 (1-liter) bottle lemon-lime carbonated beverage
1 (6-ounce) can frozen lemonade concentrate, thawed and undiluted
1 orange, sliced
1 lime, sliced

• **Combine** first 4 ingredients, and add orange and lime slices. Serve over ice cubes. **Yield:** 3½ quarts.

Louise Mayer
Richmond, Virginia

MEATLESS AND MARVELOUS

You don't have to be a vegetarian to enjoy a dinner without meat. Vegetable plates and pasta have been popular at restaurants and summer kitchen tables for decades. Now it's easier than ever for you to make mouth-watering meatless entrées.

SPAGHETTI WITH FRESH TOMATO SAUCE

4 large tomatoes, peeled and finely chopped
3 tablespoons chopped fresh parsley
1 tablespoon olive oil
1½ teaspoons chopped fresh basil or ½ teaspoon dried basil
¼ teaspoon salt
¼ teaspoon freshly ground pepper
1 clove garlic, minced
1 (12-ounce) package linguine
⅓ cup freshly grated Parmesan cheese

• **Combine** first 7 ingredients in a large bowl, and set aside.
• **Cook** linguine according to package directions; drain and place in a large serving bowl.
• **Top** linguine with tomato mixture, and sprinkle with Parmesan cheese. **Yield:** 4 servings.

EGGPLANT SAUTÉ

1 (12-ounce) package fettuccine
1 to 2 tablespoons olive oil
1 medium onion, chopped
3 cloves garlic, minced
1 medium eggplant, peeled and cubed
1 large red bell pepper, sliced
2 (14½-ounce) cans pasta-style tomatoes, undrained
½ cup freshly grated Parmesan cheese

• **Cook** fettuccine according to package directions; drain. Place in a large serving bowl, and keep warm.
• **Pour** oil into a large skillet; place over medium-high heat until hot. Add onion and next 3 ingredients; cook, stirring constantly, 10 minutes or until vegetables are tender.
• **Stir** in tomatoes; spoon mixture over fettuccine, and sprinkle with Parmesan cheese. **Yield:** 4 servings.

Michelle Henderson
Birmingham, Alabama

TORTILLA PIE

(pictured on page 150)

1 (16-ounce) can refried beans
1 teaspoon chili powder
½ teaspoon ground cumin
8 (8-inch) flour tortillas
½ (16-ounce) jar chunky salsa
2 (4-ounce) cartons guacamole
1 (8-ounce) package shredded Mexican cheese blend
Garnishes: fresh cilantro sprigs, sour cream

• **Combine** first 3 ingredients in a small bowl, stirring well; set aside.
• **Place** 1 tortilla in a lightly greased 9-inch round cakepan; spread with half of bean mixture, and top with another tortilla. Spread with half of salsa, and top with another tortilla. Spread with half of guacamole, and top with another tortilla. Sprinkle with half of cheese, and top with another tortilla.
• **Repeat** layers with remaining ingredients, ending with cheese; cover with aluminum foil.
• **Bake** at 350° for 20 minutes or until thoroughly heated. Cut pie into wedges; garnish, if desired. **Yield:** 6 servings.

EAT OUT WITHOUT MEAT

When you're eating meatless dishes away from home, the following will fit right in:

- bean burritos
- vegetable salads
- grilled cheese sandwiches
- vegetable pitas
- cheese pizza
- chiles rellenos
- no-meat chili
- and of course, peanut butter sandwiches

BASIL-CHEESE PASTA

1 (12-ounce) package rotini
2 cloves garlic, minced
2 tablespoons olive oil
1 (3-ounce) package cream cheese, softened
½ cup cottage cheese
⅓ cup grated Parmesan cheese
½ cup dry white wine
½ cup chopped fresh basil

• **Cook** rotini according to package directions; drain and keep warm.
• **Cook** garlic in oil in a skillet over medium-high heat 1 minute, stirring constantly. Add cheeses; reduce heat and cook, stirring constantly, until blended.
• **Stir** in wine and basil; cook 3 minutes or until mixture is slightly thickened, stirring often. Spoon over rotini. **Yield:** 4 servings.

Betty Rabe
Plano, Texas

HURRY-SCURRY DINNERS

If speedy weeknight dinner ideas are what you've been searching for, here are some tasty options.

STEAK SANDWICHES

Add lots of hot, crisp steak fries for a casual meal.

3 tablespoons butter or margarine
3 large onions, thinly sliced
3 tablespoons garlic oil
12 wafer-thin breakfast steaks
6 hoagie sandwich rolls, toasted
1 (8-ounce) jar picante sauce

• **Melt** butter in a large skillet over medium-high heat; add onion, and cook, stirring constantly, until tender and browned. Remove onion from skillet, and set aside. Wipe drippings from skillet.
• **Pour** garlic oil into skillet; place over medium-high heat until hot. Fry steaks 2 to 3 minutes, turning occasionally.
• **Place** 2 steaks on each roll bottom; top with onion, picante sauce, and roll tops. **Yield:** 6 servings.

VEGETABLES AND COUSCOUS

Couscous cooks in just 5 minutes; it's a quick alternative to rice. Look for it next to the rice and pasta mixes at grocery stores. Add a salad of sliced tomato, purple onion, and cucumber, and dinner's ready.

1¼ cups chicken broth
1 tablespoon butter or margarine
¾ cup couscous, uncooked
1 tablespoon chopped fresh parsley
¼ teaspoon black pepper
1 small zucchini, sliced
1 small yellow squash, sliced
1 small red bell pepper, cut into 1-inch squares
1 tablespoon vegetable oil
¼ teaspoon salt
¾ teaspoon chopped fresh basil or ¼ teaspoon dried basil
2 to 4 tablespoons freshly grated Parmesan cheese

• **Combine** chicken broth and butter in a medium saucepan; bring to a boil. Stir in couscous, parsley, and pepper. Cover, remove from heat, and let stand 5 to 6 minutes or until liquid is absorbed. Set aside.
• **Cook** zucchini, squash, and bell pepper in oil in a nonstick skillet over medium-high heat, stirring constantly, until crisp-tender. Stir in salt and basil.
• **Spoon** couscous mixture onto a serving platter; top with vegetables, and sprinkle with cheese. Serve immediately. **Yield:** 2 to 3 servings.

Mary Helen Hackney
Richmond, Virginia

CREAMY FETTUCCINE

Add a salad topped with your favorite vinaigrette and crusty bread to make a hearty dinner.

1 (8-ounce) package fettuccine
1 (1.8-ounce) package white sauce mix
2 cups milk
2 (3-ounce) packages refrigerated grated Parmesan cheese
1 tablespoon dried parsley flakes
1 teaspoon coarsely ground pepper
1 teaspoon garlic powder
½ teaspoon salt

• **Cook** pasta according to package directions; drain and keep warm.
• **Combine** sauce mix and milk in a saucepan, and cook according to package directions.
• **Stir** in cheese and next 4 ingredients; add pasta, tossing to coat. **Yield:** 4 servings.

REFRIED BEAN SOUP

(pictured on page 150)

This dish is so filling, you need to add only tortilla chips and salsa to round out the meal.

1 small onion, chopped
2 cloves garlic, minced
1 tablespoon vegetable oil
1 (31-ounce) can refried beans
1 (16-ounce) can diced tomatoes, undrained
1 (10-ounce) can diced tomatoes and green chiles, undrained
1 (14½-ounce) can ready-to-serve chicken broth
2 tablespoons chopped fresh cilantro (optional)
6 corn tortillas
2 cups (8 ounces) shredded Monterey Jack cheese
1 (8-ounce) carton sour cream

• **Cook** onion and garlic in oil in a Dutch oven over medium-high heat, stirring constantly, until tender. Add beans and next 3 ingredients, stirring until smooth; bring to a boil. Reduce heat, and simmer 15 minutes. Stir in cilantro, if desired.

• **Cut** tortillas into thin strips; spread in a single layer on a baking sheet. Bake at 350° for 15 minutes or until browned, stirring every 5 minutes. Cool.

• **Ladle** soup into individual soup bowls; top with tortilla strips, cheese, and sour cream. Serve immediately. **Yield:** 7 cups.

Shirley M. Draper
Winter Park, Florida

SHOW-OFF SALADS

Hold it – don't toss that salad. Instead, arrange the ingredients in layers to highlight their flavors, textures, and colors. You'll end up with a delicious make-ahead side dish that has a lot of eye appeal.

ORZO SALAD WITH SESAME DRESSING

1 pound orzo, uncooked
1 tablespoon sesame oil
4 carrots, cut into thin strips
2 cups raisins
1 cup sunflower kernels, toasted
Sesame Dressing
2 tablespoons chopped fresh parsley
2 tablespoons sliced green onions

• **Cook** orzo in boiling salted water to cover 8 minutes or until tender; drain. Rinse with cold water; drain. Combine orzo and oil, tossing gently.

• **Spoon** half of orzo into a large glass bowl; top with half each of carrot strips, raisins, and sunflower kernels. Repeat layers; drizzle 1 cup Sesame Dressing over top.

• **Combine** parsley and green onions; sprinkle evenly over salad. Serve with remaining Sesame Dressing. **Yield:** 10 servings.

Sesame Dressing

3/4 cup corn oil
1/2 cup rice vinegar
1/4 cup sesame oil
1 tablespoon salt
1 tablespoon sugar
2 tablespoons grated orange rind
1 teaspoon pepper
1 teaspoon minced fresh ginger
1 teaspoon soy sauce
1/2 teaspoon minced garlic
1/4 teaspoon dried crushed red pepper

• **Place** all ingredients in container of an electric blender or food processor. Process until smooth, stopping once to scrape down sides. **Yield:** 1 2/3 cups.

Sally Harris Whatley
Margate, Florida

CAULIFLOWER WITH PARMESAN AND BACON

1 small head iceberg lettuce, torn (8 cups)
1/2 head cauliflower, coarsely chopped (3 cups)
1 purple onion, chopped
1 cup mayonnaise or salad dressing
1 tablespoon sugar
1/2 teaspoon dried thyme, crushed
1/2 cup grated Parmesan cheese
1/2 pound bacon, cooked and crumbled

• **Layer** first 3 ingredients in a large glass bowl.

• **Combine** mayonnaise, sugar, and thyme, stirring well; spoon mayonnaise mixture over vegetables, and sprinkle evenly with grated Parmesan cheese. Cover and chill 3 to 4 hours. Sprinkle with crumbled bacon just before serving. **Yield:** 6 to 8 servings.

S. Ramsey
Peoria, Arizona

TURKISH SALAD

6 cups thinly sliced spinach
3 cups shredded red cabbage
1/2 cup small pitted ripe olives, sliced
1/2 cup large pimiento-stuffed olives, sliced
1/2 cup currants
1/2 cup finely chopped gherkins
1/2 cup capers, drained
1/2 cup sliced almonds, toasted
2 tablespoons fresh lemon juice
3 oranges, sectioned
Balsamic Dressing

• **Place** half of spinach in a large glass bowl; top with cabbage and next 4 ingredients. Reserve 1 tablespoon capers and almonds; sprinkle remaining capers and almonds over gherkins. Top with remaining spinach, and drizzle with lemon juice.

• **Arrange** orange sections on top, and sprinkle with reserved capers and almonds. Cover and chill, if desired; serve with Balsamic Dressing. **Yield:** 6 to 8 servings.

Balsamic Dressing

1/2 cup balsamic vinegar
1/4 cup sugar
1/2 teaspoon salt
1 cup olive or vegetable oil

• **Place** first 3 ingredients in container of an electric blender or food processor. Process until blended. With blender on high, add oil in a slow, steady stream; process until smooth. Cover and chill. **Yield:** 1 1/4 cups.

Pamela W. Copenhaver
Springfield, Illinois

MEAL IN A BOWL

4 cups mixed salad greens
1 (15½-ounce) can garbanzo beans, drained
1 cup sliced fresh mushrooms
1 cup cherry tomatoes, halved
1 small cucumber, thinly sliced
½ small purple onion, thinly sliced and separated into rings
½ cup coarsely chopped walnuts, toasted
3 large hard-cooked eggs, cut into wedges
Avocado Dressing

• **Layer** first 7 ingredients in a large glass bowl; arrange hard-cooked eggs on top. Serve with Avocado Dressing. **Yield:** 6 to 8 servings.

Avocado Dressing

1 large avocado, peeled, seeded, and mashed
1 (8-ounce) carton sour cream
2 tablespoons lemon juice
2 cloves garlic, pressed
½ teaspoon ground cumin
¼ teaspoon salt
¼ teaspoon ground red pepper

• **Combine** all ingredients; cover and chill. **Yield:** about 1½ cups.

Note: Avocado Dressing doubles as a dip for fresh vegetables or tortilla chips.

Daisy Cotton
Karnes City, Texas

POTATO PANCAKES

Flip some potato pancakes to go with dinner tonight. Start with mashed potatoes for pancakes with crisp edges and smooth interiors, or chop or grate raw potatoes for thick and chunky ones. Either way, they'll be a comforting change from baked potatoes or French fries.

POTATO-HAM PANCAKES

6 medium potatoes
1 small onion
1 small green bell pepper
1 cup finely chopped cooked ham
2 large eggs, lightly beaten
1 clove garlic, minced
1¼ cups all-purpose flour
½ teaspoon salt
½ teaspoon pepper
¼ cup milk
¼ cup vegetable oil

• **Peel** potatoes; finely chop potatoes, onion, and bell pepper.
• **Combine** chopped vegetables, ham, and next 6 ingredients; shape into 12 patties.
• **Pour** oil into a large skillet; place over medium-high heat until hot. Cook patties, a few at a time, 3 minutes on each side or until golden. Drain on paper towels, and serve immediately. **Yield:** 12 (4-inch) pancakes.

Beverly Garner
Anderson, South Carolina

OLD-FASHIONED POTATO PANCAKES

3 cups mashed potatoes
2 large eggs, lightly beaten
1 small onion, chopped
⅛ teaspoon ground nutmeg
¼ cup all-purpose flour
3 tablespoons vegetable oil
Chopped fresh parsley

• **Combine** first 4 ingredients, and shape into 10 patties. Dredge in flour.
• **Pour** oil into a large skillet; place over medium-high heat until hot. Cook patties, a few at a time, 3 minutes on each side or until golden, turning once. Drain on paper towels; sprinkle with parsley, and serve immediately. **Yield:** 10 (4-inch) pancakes.

Mrs. Chris Bryant
Johnson City, Tennessee

LEFTOVER POTATO PANCAKES

(pictured on page 152)

1 (16-ounce) package frozen whole kernel corn, thawed
1 small onion, finely chopped
½ cup chopped green onions
2 teaspoons vegetable oil
2 cups mashed potatoes
½ cup all-purpose flour
2 large eggs, lightly beaten
¾ teaspoon salt
½ teaspoon freshly ground pepper
Vegetable cooking spray

• **Cook** first 3 ingredients in hot oil in a large nonstick skillet over medium-high heat, stirring constantly, until crisp-tender. Remove from heat.
• **Combine** mashed potatoes, flour, and eggs, stirring well; stir in corn mixture, salt, and pepper.
• **Coat** a large skillet with cooking spray. Place skillet over medium heat until hot. Drop mixture by rounded tablespoonfuls into skillet; cook 3 minutes on each side or until golden, wiping skillet with a paper towel as necessary. Drain; serve with salsa. **Yield:** 14 (4-inch) pancakes.

Gwen Louer
Roswell, Georgia

ONE POTATO-TWO POTATO PANCAKES

1 cup hot mashed potatoes
2 tablespoons butter or margarine
2 large eggs, lightly beaten
3 small potatoes, peeled and shredded
½ cup all-purpose flour
2 teaspoons baking powder
1 teaspoon caraway seeds
½ teaspoon salt
¼ teaspoon pepper
¼ cup milk
3 tablespoons butter or margarine

• **Combine** mashed potatoes and 2 tablespoons butter, stirring until butter melts. Stir in eggs and next 6 ingredients; add milk, stirring until blended.

• **Melt** 1 tablespoon butter in a large nonstick skillet over medium heat; drop potato mixture into skillet, 2½ tablespoonfuls at a time; flatten slightly. Cook 3 to 4 minutes on each side or until golden, adding remaining 2 tablespoons butter as needed. Drain on paper towels; serve immediately. **Yield:** 10 (4-inch) pancakes.

SPICY GRILLED CHEESE

A kid-pleaser becomes a grown-up taste-teaser when you take this classic to new heights. Place pepper cheese, tomato, and a sprinkle of cumin between thick slices of French bread for a hot, sassy sandwich.

GRILLED CHILI CON QUESO SANDWICHES

4 ounces process cheese spread with peppers
1 tablespoon butter or margarine, softened
4 (1-inch-thick) slices French bread
¼ teaspoon ground cumin
6 plum tomato slices

• **Cut** cheese into 4 slices. Spread butter evenly on 1 side of bread slices; sprinkle with cumin.

• **Place** a nonstick skillet or griddle over medium heat until hot; place 2 bread slices, buttered side down, in skillet. Top each bread slice with a cheese slice, 3 tomato slices, second cheese slice, and remaining bread slice, buttered side up.

• **Cook** until browned on both sides, turning sandwiches once. **Yield:** 2 servings.

BURGERS AND FRIES

Forget the drive-through and head home for hefty burgers and fries. They'll be hot and fresh – and there's no charge for seconds.

BEEF-AND-CHEESE BURGERS

3 tablespoons butter or margarine
½ cup chopped onion
½ cup sliced fresh mushrooms
1 clove garlic, minced
1 pound ground round
1 teaspoon salt
¼ teaspoon pepper
1 cup (4 ounces) shredded Swiss and Cheddar cheese blend
2 tablespoons milk
4 French rolls, toasted

• **Melt** butter in a large skillet over medium-high heat, and add onion, mushrooms, and garlic; cook, stirring constantly, 5 minutes or until tender.

• **Combine** onion mixture, ground round, and next 4 ingredients; shape into 4 oval patties the size of French rolls.

• **Place** a large nonstick skillet over medium heat until hot; add patties, and cook 8 minutes or until desired degree of doneness, turning once. Serve on rolls with lettuce, tomato, mustard, and ketchup. **Yield:** 4 servings.

Bobbie Groenewegen
St. Louis, Missouri

TUNA BURGERS

Take a break from beef burgers, and try tuna.

2 large eggs, lightly beaten
2 (9-ounce) cans solid white tuna in spring water, undrained and flaked
1 cup fresh breadcrumbs
½ cup finely chopped green bell pepper
¼ cup finely chopped celery
¼ cup finely chopped onion
¼ cup milk
½ teaspoon salt
¼ teaspoon pepper
1½ cups fine, dry breadcrumbs
8 hamburger buns, toasted

• **Combine** first 9 ingredients in a large bowl; shape into 8 patties. Coat patties with breadcrumbs, and place on a lightly greased 15- x 10- x 1-inch jellyroll pan.

• **Bake** at 350° for 35 minutes or until lightly browned. Serve patties on buns with tomato, lettuce, onion, and tartar sauce. **Yield:** 8 servings.

Beverly Garver
Anderson, South Carolina

GOLDEN POTATOES

¼ cup grated Parmesan cheese
¼ cup all-purpose flour
1 teaspoon garlic salt
½ teaspoon salt
¼ teaspoon pepper
6 medium potatoes
½ cup butter or margarine

• **Combine** first 5 ingredients in a large heavy-duty, zip-top plastic bag. Cut potatoes lengthwise into fourths; add to bag, and shake gently to coat. Set aside.

• **Place** butter in a 15- x 10- x 1-inch jellyroll pan; place pan in a 425° oven until butter melts. Add potato to pan, and return to oven.

• **Bake** 30 minutes, turning once. **Yield:** 4 to 6 servings.

Frances Christopher
Iron Station, North Carolina

MIXED VEGETABLE FRIES

2 medium potatoes
2 medium turnips
2 large beets
2 large carrots
2 cups all-purpose flour
½ cup cornstarch
1 teaspoon salt
½ teaspoon ground red pepper
Vegetable oil

• **Peel** potatoes, turnips, beets, and carrots; cut vegetables into thin strips. Cover with cold water, and let stand 10 minutes. Drain.
• **Boil** vegetables in water to cover, 2 minutes; drain and plunge into cold water to stop the cooking process. Drain and pat dry. Set vegetables aside.
• **Combine** flour and next 3 ingredients in a large heavy-duty, zip-top plastic bag; add vegetables, and shake bag to coat.
• **Fry** vegetables, a few at a time, in deep hot oil (380°) in a Dutch oven 4 to 6 minutes or until golden. Drain on paper towels; serve immediately. **Yield:** 6 servings.

FROM OUR KITCHEN TO YOURS

GET A GRIP

You can make beautiful desserts in springform pans, but unfortunately the pan creates a serving problem. You release the ring and remove it to reveal a tall, straight-sided cheesecake or other confection, but the bottom of the pan barely shows from beneath. That's just a little too plain.

So you put the cheesecake, springform pan bottom and all (removing the bottom often mangles the dessert), on a cake stand or tray. Then you start slicing the dense dessert, and it promptly slides around – or even off – the cake stand. Lovely.

We solved this problem with duct tape. Fold strips of duct tape (Scotch or masking tapes are too wimpy for this job) into loops with the sticky side out, and then conceal the loops between the springform pan and cake stand. That'll put the cheesecake in its place every time.

COMING ON THROUGH

Linda Gregory sent us relief from her kitchen in Appomattox, Virginia, for slicing soft cookie or yeast roll dough. To take care of this sticky situation, trade the knife for a piece of clean dental floss about 15 inches long. Hold it with both hands, and cut with a sawing motion similar to flossing your teeth.

"ORANGE" YOU GLAD?

When recipes call for grated orange rind, don't groan over the thought of tediously grating the fruit, and possibly even your knuckles, by hand. And don't whimper over the price of bottled orange rind.

Instead, take this suggestion from our Test Kitchens. The next time you grab an orange for a snack, don't peel it by hand as usual. Use a paring knife or a vegetable peeler (getting just the orange rind and not the white part), and drop the big pieces into a food processor. Add 1½ teaspoons sugar per orange peeled, and pulse two or three times; then process about a minute.

Put the grated orange rind into a heavy-duty, zip-top plastic bag in the freezer, and then you'll have fresh, inexpensive rind anytime you need it.

WHAT A GASP

Here's a handy tip for bagging leftovers and baked goods. After you put food in a heavy-duty, zip-top plastic bag, stick a straw into the bag just above the food and take a deep breath. The sides of the bag will suction and you can seal the bag. Then pull out the straw. Now that's airtight.

DINING DILEMMAS

Some people slide into elegant restaurant dining and all its ritual like a comfy pair of slippers. The less experienced dread it. We've asked a wine steward and a maître d' about some common "fancy dinner jitters."

There's no need to whine over the wine list. Greg Harrington of Emeril's in New Orleans, and other wine stewards are there to answer questions. "I walk up and say, 'Hi, I'm the wine guy. Can I help you pick a wine tonight?' We try to make it fun," says Greg.

The big lesson for diners is to relax and ask questions. "I don't think people know what they're getting when they open the wine list and just pick a $35 bottle." But a wine steward can tell you. It's the steward's job to share opinions and make sure you have a good experience.

Wayne Broadwell, maître d' of The Mansion on Turtle Creek in Dallas, adds, "A good restaurant is going to have good wines at inexpensive prices as well. A 5-star restaurant is going to have a good house wine."

Tips on tipping? Wayne says the standard for the waiter is 15%, not 20, and anything over 15 is a generous gesture for outstanding service. If your food isn't good, that's a problem with the kitchen, not the waiter. Unhappy with the service? Don't just dock the tip and leave in a huff. Discreetly talk with the manager to possibly salvage your evening.

Wayne suggests the standard $1 tip for the valet and $1 to the coat checker for each item. If you ask the maître d' for special touches, such as a favorite dessert for a birthday or anniversary, reward his or her efforts.

JUNE

THE GOSPEL OF GREAT SOUTHERN FOOD

Chefs Edna Lewis and Scott Peacock are committed to keeping Southern foodways honest by "rescuing old recipes and nursing them back to healthiness." True Southern food, they both believe, is the enjoyment of the land. And here we offer some of their classic Southern favorites.

VIRGINIA PAN-FRIED CHICKEN

2 quarts cold water
½ cup kosher salt or coarse-grain sea salt
1 (3½-pound) whole chicken, cut up
1 quart buttermilk
¾ cup all-purpose flour
2 tablespoons cornstarch
2 tablespoons potato starch *
¾ teaspoon fine-grain sea salt or salt
¼ teaspoon freshly ground pepper
1 pound lard
½ cup unsalted butter
4 slices bacon

• **Combine** water and kosher salt in a large bowl; add chicken. Cover and chill 4 to 8 hours. Drain chicken, and pat dry; rinse bowl.
• **Return** chicken pieces to bowl; add buttermilk. Cover chicken, and chill 4 to 8 hours.
• **Drain** chicken on a wire rack; discard buttermilk.
• **Combine** flour and next 4 ingredients in a heavy-duty, zip-top plastic bag; add 2 pieces of chicken. Seal and shake to coat. Remove chicken; repeat procedure with remaining chicken pieces.
• **Place** lard, unsalted butter, and bacon evenly in two large cast-iron or heavy skillets; heat to 350°. Remove and discard bacon.
• **Add** chicken, skin side down (fat will come halfway up sides of chicken). Cook over medium-high heat 10 to 12 minutes on each side or until chicken is done. Drain on paper towels. **Yield:** 4 to 6 servings.

* We used Manischewitz potato starch, but you can substitute all-purpose flour.

Note: Crush coarse-grain sea salt in a heavy-duty, zip-top plastic bag with a rolling pin to use for fine-grain sea salt.

BUTTERMILK BISCUITS WITH VIRGINIA HAM

4 cups all-purpose flour
2 tablespoons Single-Acting Baking Powder
1½ teaspoons salt
½ cup lard, chilled and cut up
1½ cups buttermilk
Unsalted butter, softened
½ pound cooked Virginia country ham, thinly sliced

• **Combine** first 3 ingredients in a large bowl; cut in lard with pastry blender until mixture is crumbly. Add buttermilk, stirring just until dry ingredients are moistened.
• **Turn** dough out onto a lightly floured surface; knead 3 or 4 times.
• **Roll** dough to ½-inch thickness; cut dough with a 2½-inch round cutter, and place on an ungreased baking sheet.
• **Bake** at 500° for 8 to 10 minutes or until lightly browned. Split and spread with butter; serve with ham. **Yield:** 1½ dozen.

Single-Acting Baking Powder

This baking powder releases its gases when moistened, making it different from the more popular and readily available double-acting variety, which releases some gases when wet and the rest when it's heated.

¼ cup cream of tartar
3 tablespoons cornstarch
2 tablespoons baking soda

• **Combine** all ingredients in a jar; cover tightly, and shake vigorously. Store at room temperature up to 1 month. **Yield:** ½ cup.

"We've always thought that until you've tasted a tomato warmed by the sun in your own garden, you haven't lived."

Chefs Edna Lewis and Scott Peacock

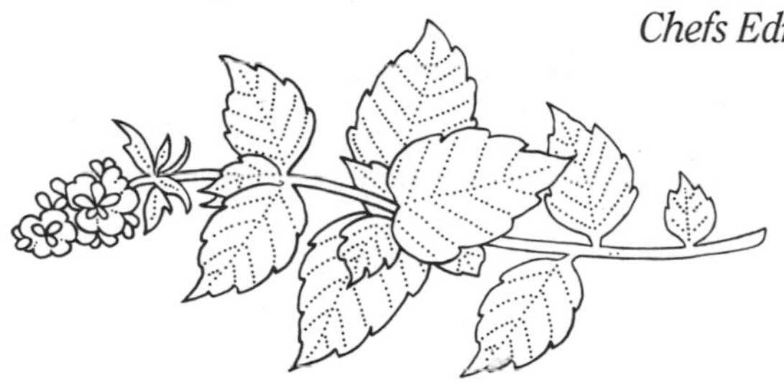

He calls her "amazing, an incredible teacher." She calls him "the next great Southern chef." Celebrated chef Edna Lewis and protégé chef Scott Peacock have been almost inseparable the past eight years, via telephone or on working trips together throughout the South, even Italy. Both are devoted to the Southern foodways they hold dear, and to the Society for the Revival and Preservation of Southern Food, an organization they founded.

SOUTHERN FOOD DEVOTEES

More than 150 cooks and authors dedicate their time to the Society by promoting the South's freshest, most flavorful cookery through conferences and field projects. Their dream is to create a Southern Food Cultural Center, with a farm filled with organic and heirloom produce, a cooking school, a restaurant, and a culinary heritage research center.

The "revival" is easy: Southern food is sought after from New York City to San Francisco, with transplanted Southern chefs no longer finding their culinary roots a yee-haw embarrassment. It's the "preservation" part that's proving difficult. "There needs to be an understanding of where things came from," Scott comments. "That Colonel Sanders did *not* invent fried chicken, and that not all vegetables come from a can."

At 80, Miss Lewis has been the doyenne of regional American cooking for more than 50 years, with venerable works like *The Edna Lewis Cookbook* (Ecco Press, 1972), *The Taste of Country Cooking* (Alfred A. Knopf, 1976), and *In Pursuit of Flavor* (Alfred A. Knopf, 1988). She's renowned not just in New York City for having spent a good deal of her life at legendary restaurants Gage & Tollner and Cafe Nicholson, but also throughout the Southern region, where she's made a considerable mark at dining establishments like Middleton Place outside Charleston and Fearrington House near Chapel Hill. In 1993, she moved to Atlanta to advise Harry's Gourmet Markets and the Horseradish Grill, write more cookbooks, and, of course, be near friend and colleague Scott.

FOOD PURIST AT HEART

Like her memories, her culinary convictions run deep. She shudders at the idea of "soul food" ("that's hard-times food in Harlem – not true Southern food"), marshmallows atop sweet potatoes, and barbecue not cooked on a pit. And she scoffs at what some chefs are doing with Southern food, such as serving grits with lemongrass gravy.

"When I grew up, everyone had a garden, and we ate bountiful foods – vegetables, fruits, grains, beans, and more fish than meat. People didn't know any better than to be good cooks, and good food bonded us together."

At 33, Scott is of the generation she's most worried about, though he's a stellar exception. As one of Public Broadcasting Service's 15 "Rising Star Chefs," he catapulted the Horseradish Grill into the limelight for two years by making unadorned fare such as fried chicken and greens seem, well, chic. He has left the restaurant to further pursue the Society's goals, as well as his own – to write cookbooks and produce an authentic product line of Southern foods.

EMPHASIS ON FRESH

"Southern food is so simple. It's either on or off," Scott says. "You can't hide it behind tortilla strips." Like Miss Lewis, he emphasizes fresh, home-grown ingredients with only the barest of embellishments to enhance the food's natural flavors. "The truest Southern food is immediate. It's harvested, fussed over, then eaten that day. I was lucky that my dad only allowed us to eat picked corn if it was less than a day old; otherwise, it went to the horses. These days there's no telling how old it is by the time it gets to the grocery stores. Most people miss its real flavor."

Healthy? Using lard? "Absolutely," Southern chef Scott Peacock says. "Of course, everything should be eaten in moderation. But if food fried in lard is cooked at the right temperature, it won't absorb as much oil as from other fats. It's only bad cooks who've given Southern cooking a bad rap – deep-frying foods instead of pan-frying; using canned vegetables instead of fresh."

DEFINING SOUTHERN CLASSICS

■ **Lard:** Pork fat that's used for baking, frying, and seasoning. Miss Lewis and Scott swear by it. It lends itself to flakier crusts, and it's a denser, better fat for frying foods (providing more flavor and crisper textures). It's best bought refrigerated to ensure freshness, but the sure test is smelling it to check for rancidity. Calories per tablespoon: lard – 120; butter – 100.

■ **Greens:** Collard, mustard, and turnip greens are traditionally boiled and seasoned with streak of lean. Miss Lewis's secret to great greens is to make a highly seasoned broth from cured and smoked pork shoulder or salt pork, and then cook the greens in that broth, uncovered (so they won't turn brown).

■ **Streak of lean:** A small portion of salted pork fat that has only a streak of lean meat. It's great for flavoring collard, mustard, and turnip greens.

■ **Virginia ham:** Also known as a Smithfield ham, it's the premier country-cured ham – much less salty and richer in color than an ordinary country ham. "If you have one in the house you can face any situation," Miss Lewis says.

EDNA'S GREENS

We gave this recipe the highest rating our Test Kitchens gives.

4½ pounds fresh greens (collard, mustard, or turnip)
1 pound salt pork (streak of lean) or smoked pork shoulder
3 quarts water
¼ teaspoon freshly ground pepper

• **Remove** and discard stems and discolored spots from greens. Wash greens thoroughly; drain and cut greens into strips. Set aside.
• **Slice** salt pork at ¼-inch intervals, cutting to, but not through, the skin.
• **Combine** salt pork, water, and pepper in a large Dutch oven; bring mixture to a boil. Cover, reduce heat, and simmer 1 hour.
• **Add** greens, and cook, uncovered, 17 minutes or until tender. Serve with a slotted spoon. **Yield:** 2 to 4 servings.

LANE CAKE

1 cup unsalted butter, softened
2 cups sugar
3½ cups all-purpose flour
1 tablespoon baking powder
¼ teaspoon salt
1 cup milk
8 egg whites
Lane Cake Filling

• **Beat** butter at medium speed with an electric mixer until creamy; gradually add sugar, beating well. Combine flour, baking powder, and salt; add to butter mixture alternately with milk, beginning and ending with flour mixture. Beat at low speed after each addition until blended.
• **Beat** egg whites at high speed until stiff. Stir one-third of egg whites into batter; gently fold in remaining egg whites. Spoon into three greased and floured 9-inch round cakepans.
• **Bake** at 325° for 25 minutes or until a wooden pick inserted in center comes out clean. Cool in pans on wire racks 10 minutes; remove from pans, and cool completely on wire racks.
• **Spread** Lane Cake Filling between layers and on top and sides of cake. **Yield:** 1 (3-layer) cake.

Lane Cake Filling

12 egg yolks
1½ cups sugar
¾ cup unsalted butter, melted
1½ teaspoons vanilla extract
½ cup bourbon
1½ cups finely chopped pecans
1½ cups finely chopped raisins
1½ cups flaked coconut

• **Beat** egg yolks at medium speed with an electric mixer 3 minutes; gradually add sugar, beating until blended. Beat 3 minutes. Gradually add butter; beat at low speed until blended.
• **Pour** mixture into top of a double boiler; bring water to a boil. Cook, stirring constantly, 20 minutes or until mixture thickens and candy thermometer registers 185°. Remove from heat; stir in vanilla and remaining ingredients. Cool slightly. **Yield:** 5 cups.

VANILLA CUSTARD ICE CREAM

This recipe is the real thing – a must-try. Like Edna Lewis's greens, it also scored our highest rating.

2 cups milk
1 vanilla bean, split
8 egg yolks
¾ cup sugar
½ teaspoon salt
¼ cup (2 ounces) vanilla extract
2 cups whipping cream
Garnishes: crumbled pralines, fresh mint sprigs

• **Cook** milk in a heavy saucepan over medium heat, just until bubbles appear, stirring often; remove from heat. Add vanilla bean; cover and let stand 20 minutes. Remove and discard vanilla bean.
• **Combine** egg yolks and next 3 ingredients in a large bowl; whisk until mixture is thick and pale. Gradually whisk in warm milk; return mixture to saucepan.
• **Cook** over very low heat, stirring constantly, 5 to 7 minutes or until mixture coats a spoon. Remove from heat; pour through a wire-mesh strainer into a bowl. Cool, stirring occasionally.
• **Stir** in whipping cream; cover and chill at least 1 hour.
• **Pour** chilled mixture into container of a 1-gallon hand-turned or electric ice cream freezer, and freeze according to manufacturer's instructions. Garnish, if desired. **Yield:** 2 quarts.

CATS' TONGUES

These crisp, slightly sweet cookies are long and thin and resemble their name in shape.

¼ cup unsalted butter, softened
⅓ cup sugar
2 egg whites
⅛ teaspoon vanilla extract
⅓ cup all-purpose flour
Pinch of salt

• **Beat** butter at medium speed with an electric mixer until fluffy; gradually add sugar, beating well. Add egg whites and vanilla, beating just until blended.
• **Combine** flour and salt; gradually add to butter mixture, beating just until blended after each addition. Drop batter by level teaspoonfuls onto lightly greased cookie sheets; pull a knife through batter until each cookie is about 5 inches long (one end will be wider).
• **Bake** at 425° for 4 to 5 minutes or until edges are lightly browned. Immediately remove from cookie sheets; transfer to wire racks to cool. **Yield:** 2½ dozen.

Note: If cookies harden on cookie sheets, return them to oven briefly to soften.

MY BLUE HEAVEN

For a heavenly experience, find a place in your area to pick blueberries. To celebrate your adventure, try our marmalade or Spicy Blueberry Pie on page 147. Still more recipes await on the following pages. The time is ripe for fresh blueberries, so don't miss them. And don't forget to freeze some for later.

BLUEBERRY MARMALADE

If you've never "put up" anything before, try this easy recipe. It uses only 4 cups of berries and makes 6 half-pints.

1 medium orange
1 lemon
¾ cup water
⅛ teaspoon baking soda
4 cups fresh blueberries, crushed
5 cups sugar
1 (6-ounce) package liquid fruit pectin

• **Peel** orange and lemon; finely chop rind, and place in a Dutch oven. Chop orange and lemon pulp, and set aside. Add water and baking soda to rind; bring to a boil. Reduce heat, and simmer 10 minutes, stirring occasionally.
• **Add** chopped orange and lemon pulp, blueberries, and sugar; return to a boil. Reduce heat, and simmer 5 minutes. Remove from heat, and cool 5 minutes.
• **Add** pectin; return to a boil. Boil 1 minute, stirring constantly; remove from heat, and skim off foam with a metal spoon.
• **Pour** into hot, sterilized jars, filling to ¼ inch from top; wipe jar rims. Cover at once with metal lids, and screw on bands.
• **Process** in boiling-water bath 10 minutes. **Yield:** 6 half-pints.

Adelyn Whiting
Albany, Georgia

HANDLING THE BLUES

Whether you pick your own or buy them from the market, here's how to handle fresh blueberries.

■ Do *not* wash berries before storing and freezing.

■ Store in refrigerator, tightly covered, as soon as possible.

■ Freeze in heavy-duty, zip-top plastic bags. Thaw only the amount of berries that you need for a specific recipe.

■ Wash berries, and remove any stems when ready to use.

BLUEBERRY TEA BREAD

2 tablespoons sifted cake flour
2 tablespoons sugar
½ teaspoon ground cinnamon
1 tablespoon chopped almonds
½ cup butter or margarine, divided
1½ cups fresh or frozen blueberries
3 cups sifted cake flour, divided
1½ cups sugar
2 teaspoons baking powder
½ teaspoon salt
1 large egg, lightly beaten
1 cup milk
1 tablespoon vanilla extract

• **Combine** first 4 ingredients; add 1 teaspoon butter, stirring until crumbly. Set almond mixture aside.
• **Combine** blueberries and 2 tablespoons cake flour, tossing gently to coat; set aside.
• **Combine** remaining cake flour, sugar, baking powder, and salt in a large bowl; cut in remaining butter with pastry blender until mixture is crumbly.
• **Combine** egg, milk, and vanilla, stirring well; add to flour mixture, stirring until dry ingredients are moistened. Add blueberry mixture, stirring gently (batter will be thin and lumpy).
• **Pour** batter into a greased and floured 9- x 5- x 3-inch loafpan, and sprinkle almond mixture evenly over batter.
• **Bake** at 350° for 1 hour and 10 minutes or until a wooden pick inserted in center comes out clean. Cool in pan on a wire rack 10 minutes; remove from pan, and let cool completely on wire rack. **Yield:** 1 loaf.

Wendy Dotson
Houston, Texas

BLUEBERRY-STREUSEL MUFFINS

¼ cup slivered almonds
¼ cup firmly packed brown sugar
1 tablespoon all-purpose flour
2 tablespoons butter or margarine
½ cup regular oats, uncooked
2 cups all-purpose flour
½ cup sugar
2 teaspoons baking powder
¼ teaspoon baking soda
¼ teaspoon salt
2 teaspoons grated lemon rind
1½ cups fresh or frozen blueberries
1 large egg, lightly beaten
¾ cup buttermilk
¼ cup vegetable oil

• **Position** knife blade in food processor bowl; pulse almonds 2 or 3 times or until chopped. Add brown sugar and 1 tablespoon flour; process 5 seconds. Add butter; pulse 5 times or until mixture is crumbly. Stir in oats; set aside.
• **Combine** 2 cups flour and next 5 ingredients in a large bowl; add blueberries, tossing gently. Make a well in center of mixture.
• **Combine** egg, buttermilk, and oil; add to flour mixture, stirring just until moistened. Spoon batter into greased muffin pans, filling two-thirds full; sprinkle with oat mixture.
• **Bake** at 400° for 15 to 20 minutes or until golden. Remove from pans immediately; cool on wire racks. **Yield:** 1 dozen.

BLUEBERRY UPSIDE-DOWN COBBLER

2½ cups fresh blueberries
1½ cups water
¼ cup shortening
1½ cups sugar, divided
1 cup all-purpose flour
2 teaspoons baking powder
⅛ teaspoon salt
½ cup milk
½ teaspoon ground nutmeg
Pinch of salt
3 tablespoons butter or margarine, cut into pieces
1 tablespoon lemon juice

• **Combine** blueberries and water in a nonaluminum saucepan; bring to a boil. Boil 5 minutes; cool. Pour mixture through a wire-mesh strainer into a bowl; reserve blueberries and juice separately.
• **Beat** shortening and 1 cup sugar in a large mixing bowl at medium speed with an electric mixer until mixture is smooth.
• **Combine** flour, baking powder, and ⅛ teaspoon salt in a bowl; add to shortening mixture alternately with milk, beginning and ending with flour mixture.
• **Pour** batter into a greased 11- x 7- x 1½-inch baking dish; spoon reserved berries over batter.
• **Combine** remaining ½ cup sugar, nutmeg, and pinch of salt; sprinkle over berries. Dot with butter.
• **Combine** reserved blueberry juice and lemon juice, and pour over top of batter.
• **Bake** at 375° for 35 to 40 minutes. **Yield:** 6 servings.

Sandra Russell
Gainesville, Florida

BLUEBERRY CRUNCH

This favorite from the Alabama Blueberry Association uses fresh or frozen berries. There's no need to thaw frozen berries for this recipe.

1 (20-ounce) can crushed pineapple in juice, undrained
1 (18.25-ounce) package yellow cake mix
3 cups fresh or frozen blueberries
½ cup sugar
½ cup butter or margarine, melted
1 cup chopped pecans

• **Spread** pineapple in a lightly buttered 13- x 9- x 2-inch baking dish; sprinkle with cake mix, blueberries, and sugar. Drizzle with butter, and top with pecans.
• **Bake** at 350° for 45 minutes or until bubbly. **Yield:** 10 servings.

BLUEBERRY NAPOLEONS

Stack crisp phyllo squares with blueberry sauce and creamy custard as the grand finale for your next dinner party.

3 sheets frozen phyllo dough, thawed
Butter-flavored cooking spray
1/3 cup sugar, divided
1 tablespoon cornstarch
Pinch of salt
1 cup whipping cream
1/2 teaspoon vanilla extract
3 cups fresh or frozen blueberries, thawed and divided
1/4 cup sifted powdered sugar
3 tablespoons orange liqueur
1/2 cup plain yogurt
1 tablespoon honey
2 teaspoons powdered sugar

• **Place** 1 sheet of phyllo on a flat surface. (Keep remaining phyllo sheets covered with a slightly damp towel.) Lightly coat phyllo with cooking spray; sprinkle with 1 tablespoon sugar. Fold phyllo in half; coat with cooking spray, and fold in half again.
• **Cut** phyllo into 4 squares, and place on a baking sheet. Repeat procedure twice with remaining phyllo sheets and 2 tablespoons sugar.
• **Bake** phyllo at 375° for 3 minutes or until lightly browned. Remove to wire racks to cool.
• **Whisk** together remaining sugar, cornstarch, and next 3 ingredients in a heavy saucepan. Bring to a boil over medium heat, stirring constantly; boil 1 minute, stirring constantly. Remove from heat, and cover with heavy-duty plastic wrap, pressing wrap directly onto custard; chill.
• **Process** 2 cups blueberries, 1/4 cup powdered sugar, and liqueur in an electric blender or food processor until smooth, stopping to scrape down sides. Pour through a fine wire-mesh strainer into a bowl, discarding skins; cover and chill.
• **Combine** yogurt and honey, stirring mixture well.
• **Spoon** blueberry mixture onto individual serving plates; top each with 1 phyllo square. Spoon custard on top of phyllo squares, and sprinkle evenly with half of remaining blueberries. Top each with another phyllo square; spoon yogurt mixture on top, and sprinkle with remaining blueberries. Top each with remaining phyllo squares, and sprinkle evenly with 2 teaspoons powdered sugar. Serve immediately. **Yield:** 4 servings.

BLUEBERRY PIZZA

1 1/2 cups all-purpose flour
2 tablespoons sugar
1 cup chopped pecans
3/4 cup butter or margarine, melted
1 (8-ounce) package cream cheese, softened
2 cups sifted powdered sugar
1 (8-ounce) container frozen whipped topping, thawed
5 to 6 cups fresh or frozen blueberries, thawed and divided
2/3 cup sugar
2 tablespoons cornstarch
2 tablespoons water

• **Combine** first 3 ingredients; add butter, stirring until well blended. Spread into a 12-inch pizza pan.
• **Bake** at 375° for 10 to 12 minutes or until lightly browned. Cool crust in pan on a wire rack.
• **Beat** cream cheese at medium speed with an electric mixer until creamy. Gradually add powdered sugar, beating until smooth; fold in whipped topping. Spread over crust.
• **Mash** 2 cups blueberries in a medium saucepan; stir in 2/3 cup sugar. Bring to a boil over medium heat, and boil 2 minutes.
• **Whisk** together cornstarch and water; stir into blueberry mixture. Return to a boil, stirring constantly; boil 1 minute. Cool.
• **Spread** over cream cheese mixture; top with remaining blueberries. **Yield:** 1 (12-inch) pizza.

Doris Glance
Rutherfordton, North Carolina

SPICY BLUEBERRY PIE

(pictured on page 4)

Discover the thrill of picking your own blueberries. Enjoy them by the handful or, even better, served under a hot, flaky crust in this easy-to-make pie.

3/4 cup sugar
1/4 cup firmly packed brown sugar
1/2 cup all-purpose flour
1/2 teaspoon ground cinnamon
1/4 teaspoon ground allspice
5 cups fresh blueberries
1 tablespoon lemon juice
1 tablespoon butter or margarine, melted
1 (15-ounce) package refrigerated piecrusts
1 tablespoon milk
1 teaspoon sugar

• **Combine** first 8 ingredients, tossing gently.
• **Fit** 1 piecrust into a 9-inch pieplate according to package directions. Spoon blueberry mixture into pastry shell.
• **Roll** remaining piecrust to 1/8-inch thickness; cut into 6 (2 1/2-inch-wide) strips. Arrange strips in a lattice design over filling; fold edges under, and crimp. Brush pastry with milk; sprinkle with 1 teaspoon sugar.
• **Bake** at 400° for 40 to 45 minutes or until golden, shielding edges with strips of aluminum foil during last 20 minutes of baking to prevent excessive browning. **Yield:** 1 (9-inch) pie.

Nan Ferguson
Atlanta, Georgia

HEAD FOR AN ISLAND

If you can't stand the heat, then come indoors – and bring your friends. A kitchen island can be the perfect place to enjoy a cool meal when the weather is steaming.

PLAN-AHEAD MENU
Serves Four

Crab Imperial
Dilled Summer Squash
Green Salad With Vinaigrette
Dinner Rolls
Coffee Pie

We've kept our menu seasonal and simple so you can enjoy fresh food without fuss. And most of the work can be done a day ahead, leaving you free to adopt a relaxed island attitude. Make the Coffee Pie a day before your gathering. Crab Imperial and Dilled Summer Squash can be put together shortly before your guests arrive.

CRAB IMPERIAL

1 pound fresh lump crabmeat
¼ cup butter or margarine
3 tablespoons all-purpose flour
1½ cups half-and-half
2 teaspoons chopped fresh parsley
1½ teaspoons dry mustard
¾ teaspoon salt
1 tablespoon lemon juice
2 teaspoons prepared horseradish
1 teaspoon Worcestershire sauce
1 cup soft breadcrumbs
2 tablespoons butter or margarine, melted

• **Drain** crabmeat, removing any bits of shell; set aside.
• **Melt** ¼ cup butter in a large heavy saucepan over low heat; add flour, stirring until mixture is smooth. Cook 1 minute, stirring constantly. Gradually add half-and-half; cook over medium heat, stirring constantly, until thickened and bubbly.
• **Stir** in parsley and next 5 ingredients; add crabmeat, stirring gently. Spoon into greased baking shells.
• **Combine** breadcrumbs and 2 tablespoons butter; sprinkle evenly over crabmeat mixture.
• **Bake** at 350° for 30 minutes or until bubbly. **Yield:** 6 servings.

Jane Maloy
Wilmington, North Carolina

DILLED SUMMER SQUASH

2 tablespoons butter or margarine
2 cloves garlic, minced
2 teaspoons chopped fresh dill
6 green onions, cut into 1-inch pieces
2 yellow squash, thinly sliced
2 zucchini, thinly sliced
½ green bell pepper, sliced
⅓ cup water
¼ teaspoon salt
¼ teaspoon pepper

• **Melt** butter in a large skillet; add garlic, dill, and green onions, and cook over medium-high heat 1 minute, stirring constantly. Add squash and zucchini; cook 1 minute, stirring constantly.
• **Add** bell pepper and remaining ingredients; cook 2 minutes, stirring constantly. Cover, reduce heat, and simmer 3 minutes or until crisp-tender. **Yield:** 4 servings.

Deborah D. Forster
Atascosa, Texas

COFFEE PIE

Make-ahead tip: This pie holds up well in the refrigerator overnight. Top it with dollops of whipped cream an hour before serving, and keep chilled until guests arrive.

1 cup water
1 tablespoon instant coffee granules
1 tablespoon butter or margarine
30 large marshmallows, cut into fourths
1 cup whipping cream, whipped
1 baked 9-inch pastry shell
½ cup chopped walnuts or pecans, toasted
Garnishes: whipped cream, chocolate-covered coffee beans

• **Bring** water to a boil in a heavy saucepan; add coffee granules, stirring to dissolve. Add butter and marshmallows to pan.
• **Cook** over low heat until marshmallows melt, stirring occasionally. Cool completely.
• **Fold** whipped cream into coffee mixture; spoon into pastry shell. Sprinkle evenly with walnuts. Cover and chill at least 8 hours. Garnish, if desired. **Yield:** 1 (9-inch) pie.

Jodie McCoy
Tulsa, Oklahoma

A cool summer supper is a cinch with this light Grilled Asian Chicken Salad (recipe, page 158).

Right: *Refried Bean Soup (recipe, page 136) tastes like burritos in a bowl. You can prepare this thick, full-flavored soup in less than 30 minutes.*

Far right: *Mild-flavored Rancho Ramillete Flautas were created with children in mind. Black Bean-Corn Salsa and Baked Spicy Rice accentuate the meal. (Recipes begin on page 125.)*

Help yourself to a wedge of Tortilla Pie (recipe, page 135) layered with refried beans, salsa, guacamole, and cheese.

Right: *Add green onions and frozen corn to yesterday's mashed potatoes for Leftover Potato Pancakes (recipe, page 138).*

Below: *Puff pastry sheets make the gourmet crust for Herbed Tomato Tart (recipe, page 94).*

Fry a Batch of Fritters

Fat watchers, these fritter recipes are not for you. They're fried, loaded with fat – and taste wonderful! And you'll never be able to eat just one.

But if you can afford the calories, pancake-style Corn-Jalapeño Fritters can't be beat. Honey Puffs offers a sweet choice. For a different twist on a Southern favorite, try hand-formed Cheese-Stuffed Potato Fritters.

No matter what shape you make them, fritters are a delicious excuse for eating fried food.

CORN-JALAPEÑO FRITTERS

2 cups milk, divided
1 cup quick-cooking yellow grits
3 tablespoons butter or margarine, softened
1 teaspoon baking powder
1 teaspoon salt
2 large eggs, lightly beaten
¼ cup finely chopped red bell pepper
½ cup finely chopped green onions
1 to 2 teaspoons minced, seeded jalapeño pepper
2 tablespoons finely chopped fresh basil
1 cup fresh corn, cut from cob (about 2 ears)
¼ cup all-purpose flour
2 tablespoons olive oil, divided
Garnish: sour cream

• **Combine** ½ cup milk and grits.
• **Heat** remaining 1½ cups milk in a medium saucepan over medium-high heat until boiling. Add grits mixture, stirring constantly with a wire whisk. Cook 2 minutes or until thickened.
• **Remove** from heat, and pour into a large bowl; cool slightly. Add butter and next 9 ingredients, stirring well.
• **Heat** 1 tablespoon olive oil in a large nonstick skillet or griddle over medium heat until hot.
• **Pour** 1 tablespoon batter for each fritter into hot skillet, and cook fritters until tops are covered with bubbles and edges look cooked; turn and cook other side. Repeat procedure with remaining olive oil and batter. Garnish, if desired. **Yield:** 2 dozen.

Helen H. Maurer
Christmas, Florida

CHEESE-STUFFED POTATO FRITTERS

2 pounds baking potatoes, peeled and cut into eighths
⅓ cup butter or margarine, softened
5 egg yolks
2 tablespoons finely chopped fresh parsley
1 teaspoon salt
½ teaspoon pepper
Pinch of ground nutmeg
½ (8-ounce) package mozzarella cheese, cut into 10 slices
All-purpose flour
2 large eggs, lightly beaten
1½ cups Italian-seasoned breadcrumbs
Vegetable oil

• **Cook** potato in boiling water to cover 15 minutes or until potato is tender; drain.
• **Combine** potato and butter in a large mixing bowl; beat at medium speed with an electric mixer until smooth. Let cool.
• **Add** egg yolks and next 4 ingredients to potato, stirring well.
• **Divide** potato mixture into 10 portions. Wrap each portion around a cheese slice, shaping into an oval. Lightly dust each with flour; dip into beaten egg, and dredge in breadcrumbs. Cover and chill 20 minutes.
• **Pour** oil to depth of 4 inches into a Dutch oven; heat to 340°. Fry, a few at a time, 8 minutes, turning once. Serve immediately. **Yield:** 10 fritters.

Barbara Carson
Tifton, Georgia

HONEY PUFFS

2 packages active dry yeast
1 cup warm water (105° to 115°)
2 cups warm milk (105° to 115°)
¼ cup sugar
1 teaspoon salt
1 large egg
4 cups all-purpose flour
Vegetable oil
Honey
Ground cinnamon

• **Combine** yeast and warm water in a 2-cup liquid measuring cup; let stand 5 minutes.
• **Combine** yeast mixture, milk, and next 3 ingredients; stir with a wooden spoon until well blended.
• **Add** flour, 1 cup at a time, stirring until smooth after each addition.
• **Cover** and let rise in a warm place (85°), free from drafts, 1 hour or until doubled in bulk.
• **Pour** oil to depth of 4 inches into a Dutch oven; heat to 375°. Drop dough by tablespoonfuls into oil, and fry until golden, turning once. Drain on paper towels; keep warm. Repeat procedure with remaining dough.
• **Drizzle** with honey, and sprinkle with cinnamon; serve immediately. **Yield:** 4 dozen.

Jean Voan
Shepherd, Texas

OIL CHANGE

Want to add pizzazz to foods fried in vegetable oil? Opt for one of the many flavored oils on the market. Garlic-, Pepper-, Sesame-, and Butter-flavored oils are just a few that can accent the flavor of any food.

TABLE FOR TWO

When the Southern sunlight softens and the sultry air finally abates, we fall gladly into a summer trance. A gloriously decorated table for two sets an outdoor stage for a romantic evening. And this menu of sumptuous fare, delicate and inviting, is the perfect complement.

A SPLENDID SUMMER REPAST

Serves Two

Artichoke Oysters
Gingered Tenderloin Steak
Lemon Couscous
Sesame Asparagus
Vanilla Soufflés With Vanilla Crème Sauce

ARTICHOKE OYSTERS

1 (4-ounce) jar marinated artichoke hearts, drained
Rock salt
6 fresh oysters (in the shell)
3 tablespoons fine, dry breadcrumbs
2 tablespoons grated Parmesan cheese
½ teaspoon paprika
Garnishes: fresh parsley sprigs, lemon curls

• **Position** knife blade in food processor bowl; process artichoke hearts until smooth, stopping once to scrape down sides.
• **Sprinkle** a layer of rock salt in a 15- x 10- x 1-inch jellyroll pan; set aside.
• **Scrub** oyster shells, and open, discarding tops. Arrange shell bottoms (containing oysters) over rock salt. Top oysters with pureed artichokes.
• **Combine** breadcrumbs, Parmesan cheese, and paprika; sprinkle evenly over oysters.
• **Broil** 4 inches from heat (with electric oven door partially opened) 3 minutes or until tops are golden. Garnish, if desired. **Yield:** 2 servings.

GINGERED TENDERLOIN STEAK

For its full flavor, look for ginger that has smooth skin. Wrinkled skin means it's dry and less flavorful.

¼ teaspoon salt
1 teaspoon pepper
1 tablespoon minced fresh ginger
2 cloves garlic, minced
2 (8-ounce) beef tenderloin steaks (1½ inches thick)
1 tablespoon butter
1 tablespoon vegetable oil
⅓ cup dry white wine
1 jalapeño pepper, seeded and minced

• **Combine** first 4 ingredients; rub on all sides of steaks. Cover and chill 2 hours.
• **Melt** butter and oil in a heavy skillet over medium-high heat; add steaks, and cook 4 minutes on each side or to desired degree of doneness. Remove steaks from skillet, and keep warm.
• **Add** wine and jalapeño pepper to skillet; cook 2 minutes, stirring constantly. Pour mixture over steaks. **Yield:** 2 servings.

LEMON COUSCOUS

1 tablespoon grated lemon rind
2 tablespoons fresh lemon juice
1 tablespoon butter or margarine
⅛ teaspoon salt
1 cup chicken broth
⅔ cup couscous, uncooked
2 tablespoons pecan pieces, toasted
2 tablespoons chopped fresh parsley
2 tablespoons finely chopped red bell pepper
Garnishes: fresh mint sprigs, lemon slices

• **Combine** first 5 ingredients in a saucepan; bring to a boil over medium-high heat. Add couscous, stirring well; cover, remove from heat, and let stand 10 minutes. Stir in pecans, parsley, and bell pepper. Garnish, if desired. **Yield:** 2 servings.

SESAME ASPARAGUS

½ pound fresh asparagus
3 tablespoons red wine vinegar
1 tablespoon dark sesame oil
1 tablespoon sesame seeds, toasted

• **Snap** off tough ends of asparagus; remove scales with a vegetable peeler, if desired.
• **Cover** and cook asparagus in a small amount of boiling water 2 minutes or until crisp-tender. Drain and rinse with cold water; drain well.
• **Combine** vinegar, oil, and sesame seeds in a large heavy-duty, zip-top plastic bag; add asparagus. Seal and chill 2 hours, turning occasionally.
• **Remove** asparagus from marinade, reserving marinade. Arrange asparagus on plates; drizzle with marinade. **Yield:** 2 servings.

VANILLA SOUFFLÉS WITH VANILLA CRÈME SAUCE

(pictured on page 114)

This top-rated dessert, first published two years ago, is one of our most requested recipes.

Vegetable cooking spray
Sugar
1½ tablespoons butter or margarine
1½ tablespoons all-purpose flour
6 tablespoons half-and-half
2 tablespoons sugar
2 large eggs, separated
1 tablespoon vanilla extract
1 tablespoon sugar
Sifted powdered sugar
Vanilla Crème Sauce

• **Coat** the bottom and sides of two 6-ounce baking dishes with cooking spray; sprinkle with sugar. Set aside.
• **Melt** butter in a small saucepan over medium heat; add flour, stirring until smooth. Cook flour mixture 1 minute, stirring constantly.
• **Add** half-and-half, stirring constantly; stir in 2 tablespoons sugar. Cook over medium heat, stirring constantly, until thickened. Remove from heat; set aside.
• **Beat** egg yolks until thick and pale. Gradually stir about half of hot mixture into egg yolks; add to remaining hot mixture, stirring constantly. Cook over medium heat 2 minutes; stir in vanilla. Cool 15 to 20 minutes.
• **Beat** egg whites at high speed with an electric mixer until foamy. Gradually add 1 tablespoon sugar, beating until soft peaks form. Gradually fold egg whites into half-and-half mixture. Spoon into prepared baking dishes.
• **Bake** at 350° for 25 minutes or until puffed and set. Sprinkle with powdered sugar, and serve immediately with Vanilla Crème Sauce. **Yield:** 2 servings.

Vanilla Crème Sauce

½ teaspoon vanilla extract
½ cup sugar
1 teaspoon cornstarch
1 cup whipping cream
4 egg yolks

• **Combine** first 3 ingredients in a heavy saucepan; gradually stir in whipping cream. Cook over low heat, stirring constantly, until sugar dissolves. Set aside.
• **Beat** egg yolks until thick and pale. Gradually stir about half of hot whipping cream mixture into yolks; add to remaining hot mixture, stirring constantly. Cook over medium heat, stirring constantly, until thickened.
• **Pour** through a wire-mesh strainer into a small bowl, discarding lumps. Cover and store in refrigerator up to 3 days. Serve with Vanilla Soufflés, fresh fruit, pound cake, or ice cream. **Yield:** 1½ cups.

WHAT'S FOR SUPPER?

CHICKEN WITH FRUIT

Create something sweet with chicken tonight – add fruit. Fresh, frozen, or canned fruits are terrific accessories for poultry. Whether you want your supper to be hot or cold, these chicken dishes make refreshing summer meals.

GRILLED CHICKEN-AND-FRUIT SALAD

¾ cup orange marmalade
3 tablespoons soy sauce
3 tablespoons lemon juice
3 teaspoons chopped fresh ginger
4 skinned and boned chicken breast halves
1 pineapple
2 medium jícamas
Vegetable cooking spray
2 cups fresh strawberry halves
1 cup fresh raspberries
Orange-Raspberry Vinaigrette
Lettuce leaves

• **Combine** first 4 ingredients; reserve ¼ cup mixture, and chill. Pour remaining mixture into a heavy-duty, zip-top plastic bag; add chicken. Seal and chill 8 hours, turning occasionally.
• **Peel,** core, and cut pineapple into spears; peel jícamas, and cut into ½-inch-thick slices. Combine reserved ¼ cup marmalade mixture, pineapple, and jícama, tossing to coat. Set aside.
• **Coat** a grill basket with cooking spray; place on grill over hot coals (400° to 500°). Remove chicken from marinade, discarding marinade.
• **Add** chicken and fruit mixture to basket; cook, covered with grill lid, 3 minutes on each side or until chicken is done. Remove from grill, and cool.
• **Cut** chicken and jícama into thin strips; cut pineapple into bite-size pieces.
• **Combine** chicken, jícama, pineapple, strawberries, and raspberries; drizzle with Orange-Raspberry Vinaigrette, and toss gently. Serve in a lettuce-lined bowl. **Yield:** 4 servings.

Orange-Raspberry Vinaigrette

Always wear rubber gloves when seeding and chopping a member of the pepper family. Pepper oils contain a fiery heat that can irritate even a small cut and is difficult to wash away with soap and water.

½ cup orange marmalade
¼ cup raspberry vinegar
1 medium jalapeño pepper, seeded and minced
2 tablespoons finely chopped fresh cilantro
2 tablespoons olive oil

• **Whisk** together all ingredients in a bowl. **Yield:** 1 cup.

Conveniently Light

If you think that cooking with prepackaged foods means having a meal that tastes like it's out of a can, guess again. You'll open a convenience product for each of these recipes, but the addition of fresh ingredients and flavorful seasonings lets you have homemade taste in a hurry.

BANANA CHICKEN WITH BLACK BEAN SAUCE

This unusual combination of ingredients is a delicious surprise – part southwestern, part tropical.

2 large medium-ripe bananas
1 tablespoon ground cumin, divided
4 skinned and boned chicken breast halves
2 teaspoons vegetable oil
½ cup chopped red bell pepper
½ cup chopped green onions
1 medium tomato, chopped
2 cloves garlic, minced
1 (11-ounce) can black bean soup, undiluted *
¼ teaspoon pepper
¼ teaspoon dried oregano
½ teaspoon chicken bouillon granules
½ cup water

• **Cut** bananas in half crosswise, and then in half lengthwise; sprinkle with ½ teaspoon cumin.
• **Sprinkle** chicken with remaining cumin; set aside.
• **Heat** oil in a large nonstick skillet over medium-high heat; add bananas, and cook until lightly browned, turning often. Transfer to a serving platter; keep warm.
• **Add** chicken to skillet; cook 4 to 5 minutes on each side or until done. Add to bananas; keep warm.
• **Add** bell pepper and next 3 ingredients to skillet; cook, stirring constantly, 2 to 3 minutes or until almost crisp-tender.
• **Add** soup and next 4 ingredients; cook, stirring constantly, until thoroughly heated. Spoon over chicken and bananas. **Yield:** 4 servings.

* Substitute 1 (15-ounce) can black beans, drained, for black bean soup.

Peggy Fowler Revels
Woodruff, South Carolina

PESTO-CRUSTED ORANGE ROUGHY

Try this flavorful herbed crust on any mild-flavored fish like cod, catfish, snapper, or grouper.

2 tablespoons pesto
½ cup fine, dry breadcrumbs
¼ teaspoon pepper
4 (4-ounce) orange roughy fillets
Vegetable cooking spray

• **Combine** pesto, breadcrumbs, and pepper in a shallow dish. Dredge fillets in breadcrumb mixture, and place in an 11- x 7- x 1½-inch baking dish coated with cooking spray. Coat fillets with cooking spray.
• **Bake** at 400° for 15 minutes or until fish flakes easily when tested with a fork. **Yield:** 4 servings.

♥ Per serving: Calories 190 (34% from fat)
Fat 7g (1g saturated) Cholesterol 24mg
Sodium 274mg Carbohydrate 11.3g
Fiber 1g Protein 19.4g

MEDITERRANEAN PICNIC LOAF

1 (16-ounce) round loaf peasant-style bread
3 large tomatoes
1 large purple onion, thinly sliced
1 green bell pepper, thinly sliced
4 ounces crumbled feta cheese
1 (6⅛-ounce) can solid white tuna in spring water, drained and flaked
½ cup kalamata olives, sliced
1 cup firmly packed fresh basil, chopped
2 tablespoons capers, rinsed and drained
2 tablespoons balsamic vinegar
1 tablespoon Dijon mustard
1 tablespoon olive oil
2 cloves garlic, minced

• **Cut** bread in half horizontally; hollow out center of bottom half, leaving a 1-inch-thick shell. Slice tomatoes; cut slices into fourths.
• **Layer** tomato, onion, bell pepper, and cheese in bread shell. Place tuna and next 3 ingredients in bread shell.

• **Combine** vinegar and next 3 ingredients; drizzle over mixture in bread shell, and cover with bread top.
• **Wrap** filled loaf in aluminum foil, and chill 2 hours. Cut into wedges to serve.
Yield: 6 servings.

Janice Elder
Charlotte, North Carolina

❤ Per serving: Calories 311 (27% from fat)
Fat 9.2g (3.6g saturated) Cholesterol 30mg
Sodium 976mg Carbohydrate 40.1g
Fiber 3.3g Protein 16.8g

SHRIMP-AND-COUSCOUS SALAD

4¼ cups water
1 lemon, sliced
1¼ pounds unpeeled large fresh shrimp
½ cup couscous, uncooked
½ red bell pepper, chopped
1 (14-ounce) can artichoke hearts, drained and coarsely chopped
¼ cup reduced-fat mayonnaise
⅓ cup fresh lemon juice
3 tablespoons chopped fresh dill
¼ teaspoon salt
½ teaspoon pepper

• **Combine** water and lemon slices in a Dutch oven; bring to a boil. Add shrimp, and cook 3 to 5 minutes or until shrimp turn pink. Drain, discarding lemon; rinse shrimp with cold water. Peel shrimp, and devein, if desired. Cut shrimp in half lengthwise. Cover and chill.
• **Cook** couscous according to package directions; place in a large bowl to cool. Stir with a fork; add shrimp, bell pepper, and artichoke hearts.
• **Combine** mayonnaise and next 4 ingredients, stirring well. Pour dressing over shrimp mixture, tossing to coat. Cover and chill at least 2 hours. **Yield:** 4 servings.

Janil K. Miller
Beaufort, North Carolina

❤ Per serving: Calories 234 (24% from fat)
Fat 6.2g (1g saturated) Cholesterol 113mg
Sodium 367mg Carbohydrate 25.7g
Fiber 0.7g Protein 19g

KEEPING OFF THE POUNDS

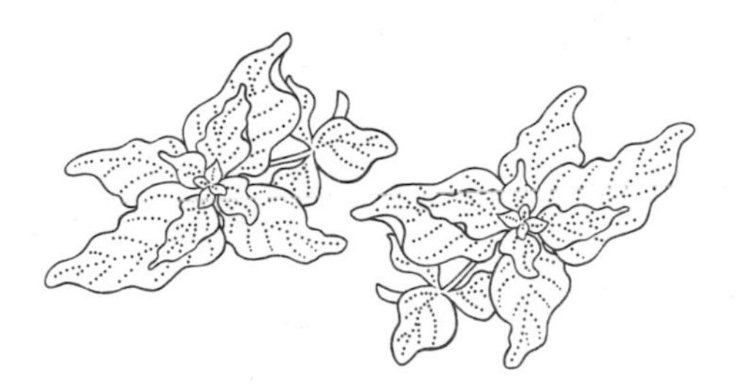

Celeste Powers of Mobile, Alabama, controls her weight by tightening the reins whenever she's more than 10 pounds over her ideal weight. Take her advice for keeping off the pounds.

▪ "I haven't fried anything in years," she says. "My husband and I grill everything from fresh tuna to fresh vegetables."

▪ Grow herbs during the summer months. "You won't miss the butter on your vegetables if you mix them with lemon zest and fresh herbs."

▪ Take your lunch to work. "If you go out to eat, you'll eat more and be tempted by foods that aren't good for you."

▪ Find a low-fat cookbook that you enjoy. "Healthy cooking is easier when you use recipes that you know are light, instead of trying to alter high-fat recipes."

COOL CONVENIENCE

Instead of a shake, try one of these creamy mango coolers (each has under 200 calories per serving), and sip into summer.

Tropical Refresher: Freeze 1 banana, cut into fourths, 1 cup refrigerated sliced mango, and 1 cup fresh pineapple chunks on a baking sheet 30 minutes. Combine frozen fruit, 1 cup skim milk, 1 cup vanilla low-fat yogurt, 2 tablespoons honey, 1 teaspoon lime juice, and ½ teaspoon vanilla extract in a blender, and process until smooth. **Yield:** 4 servings.

Erma Jackson
Huntsville, Alabama

Fruit Slush: Process 1 cup refrigerated sliced mango, 1 cup plain low-fat yogurt, 1 sliced banana, and 1 tablespoon honey in a blender until smooth. Add enough ice to bring mixture to 3½-cup level, and process until smooth. **Yield:** 3 servings.

Kiki Ellenby
Homestead, Florida

EASY-BAKE BISCUITS

Serve these biscuits with breakfast or as an accompaniment with a fruit salad for lunch. Each biscuit has only 125 calories.

Combine 3½ cups reduced-fat biscuit and baking mix, 3 tablespoons sugar, 3 tablespoons orange breakfast drink mix, and 2½ teaspoons ground cinnamon. Add 1¼ cups skim milk, and stir until dry ingredients are moistened. Drop by rounded tablespoonfuls onto a baking sheet coated with cooking spray. Bake at 425° for 10 minutes or until golden. While biscuits bake, prepare an orange glaze by stirring together 1½ cups sifted powdered sugar, 2 tablespoons water, ½ teaspoon orange extract, and ¼ teaspoon vanilla extract. Remove biscuits from oven, and drizzle with glaze; serve warm. **Yield:** 22 biscuits.

Susan C. Wise
Statesville, North Carolina

GRILLED ASIAN CHICKEN SALAD

(pictured on page 149)

4 (4-ounce) skinned and boned chicken breast halves
1 (3-ounce) package reduced-fat ramen noodles
1 tablespoon sesame seeds
½ cup white wine vinegar
⅓ cup honey
2 tablespoons hoisin sauce
1 tablespoon dark sesame oil
1 yellow tomato
1 tomato
6 cups mixed salad greens
½ head Chinese cabbage, shredded
½ bunch fresh cilantro, chopped
Garnish: whole green onions

• **Cook** chicken, covered with grill lid, over medium-hot coals (350° to 400°) 6 minutes on each side or until done; cool. Cut into thin slices; set aside.
• **Crumble** noodles into a 9-inch round cakepan, discarding seasoning packet; add sesame seeds to cakepan. Bake at 350° for 5 minutes or until lightly browned, stirring once; cool. Set aside.
• **Combine** vinegar and next 3 ingredients, stirring well; reserve ⅓ cup dressing. Combine remaining dressing with chicken in a large bowl. Cover and chill at least 1 hour.
• **Peel,** seed, and chop tomatoes. Combine tomato, salad greens, cabbage, and cilantro; drizzle with reserved ⅓ cup dressing, tossing to coat. Arrange salad and chicken on serving plates, and sprinkle with noodles. Garnish, if desired. **Yield:** 6 servings.

Karen Harper
Johnston, Iowa

❤ Per serving: Calories 428 (19% from fat)
Fat 8.8g (1.6g saturated) Cholesterol 75mg
Sodium 477mg Carbohydrate 57.2g
Fiber 4.9g Protein 33.3g

HUMMUS

Use ½ cup of this creamy bean spread inside each pita to make a sandwich. Or serve it as a dip with pita chips or vegetables.

1 (15-ounce) can chick-peas, drained
¼ cup tahini
2 tablespoons chopped fresh parsley
1 clove garlic
⅓ cup lemon juice
1½ teaspoons ground cumin
¼ teaspoon ground red pepper
2 tablespoons chopped onion
1 tablespoon reduced-sodium soy sauce

• **Position** knife blade in food processor; add all ingredients, and process until smooth. **Yield:** 2 cups.

Joan Ranzini
Waynesboro, Virginia

❤ Per ½-cup serving:
Calories 195 (41% from fat)
Fat 9.2g (1.2g saturated) Cholesterol 0mg
Sodium 385mg Carbohydrate 23.1g
Fiber 6.9g Protein 7g

SHE STANDS BY HER PAN

As a former backup singer for Tammy Wynette and opening act for Don Williams, Diane Pfeifer knows the highways and low ways of country music life. When the Atlanta resident wasn't onstage, she most likely was in some greasy spoon "eating bad food and getting indigestion."

She left the road in 1982 and detoured into advertising, singing jingles. And then she discovered a knack for cookbook writing. Her newest book, *Stand By Your Pan* (à la Tammy Wynette's "Stand By Your Man"), pays tribute to country music and is packed with easy-to-cook vegetarian fare. Here we feature some of those recipes; they're as great as their titles.

Look for *Stand By Your Pan* ($9.95) at B. Dalton Bookseller or Cracker Barrel. For information call 1-800-875-7242.

❤ BASTED DATES AND BASTED RICE (DATE-NUT RICE)

3 tablespoons butter or margarine
1 cup rice, uncooked
1 (14½-ounce) can ready-to-serve vegetable broth
½ cup chopped dried tomatoes
1 teaspoon dried parsley flakes
½ teaspoon salt
⅛ teaspoon ground cinnamon
⅛ teaspoon ground cumin
½ cup chopped dates
¼ cup pine nuts or slivered almonds, toasted

• **Melt** butter in a medium saucepan over medium-high heat; add rice, and cook 1 minute, stirring constantly.
• **Add** broth and next 5 ingredients; bring to a boil. Cover, reduce heat, and simmer 20 minutes or until rice is tender. Stir in dates and pine nuts. **Yield:** 4 to 6 servings.

FOUR-PART HOMINY (CHEESY HOMINY CASSEROLE)

3 (16-ounce) cans white hominy, drained
1 (8-ounce) carton reduced-fat sour cream
1 (4.5-ounce) can chopped green chiles, undrained
2 cups (8 ounces) shredded Cheddar cheese

• **Combine** all ingredients, and spoon hominy mixture into an ungreased 8-inch square baking dish.
• **Bake** at 350° for 25 minutes. Serve immediately. **Yield:** 6 servings.

BOOT SCOOT TABBOULI (TABBOULEH SALAD)

Mint and parsley are essential ingredients in this Lebanese favorite. Serve it with a crisp bread such as lavosh to scoop up every delicious morsel.

2 cups boiling water
1 teaspoon salt
1 cup bulgur wheat
1 cup finely chopped fresh parsley
½ cup finely chopped green onion tops
2 tablespoons finely chopped fresh mint or 2 teaspoons dried mint
¼ cup olive oil
¼ cup fresh lemon juice
½ teaspoon salt
¼ teaspoon pepper
1 cup peeled, finely chopped tomato

• **Combine** boiling water and 1 teaspoon salt; pour over bulgur. Let stand 30 minutes.
• **Drain** bulgur; add chopped parsley and next 6 ingredients, stirring well. Gently fold in chopped tomato; cover and chill salad at least 4 hours. **Yield:** 4¾ cups.

YOU LIMA MY LIFE (PAPRIKA LIMA SALAD)

One of our Foods Staff interns gave this dish a vote of confidence: "I hate lima beans, but I'll eat this," asking for seconds.

2 (15¼-ounce) cans lima beans, drained
1 clove garlic, pressed
3 tablespoons chopped fresh cilantro or parsley
2 teaspoons paprika
1 teaspoon dried dillweed
¼ teaspoon salt
⅛ teaspoon pepper
2 tablespoons lemon juice
2 tablespoons olive oil
1 tablespoon capers (optional)

• **Combine** all ingredients; cover and chill. **Yield:** 4 to 6 servings.

CAKY FLAKY TART (TART LEMON TART)

A good rule of thumb: One medium lemon yields about 3 tablespoons of juice and 2 to 3 teaspoons zest or grated rind.

1½ cups sugar
1 tablespoon all-purpose flour
1 tablespoon cornmeal
3 large eggs
3 tablespoons butter or margarine, melted
3 tablespoons milk
1½ teaspoons grated lemon rind
½ cup fresh lemon juice
1 (9-inch) unbaked pastry shell
Garnishes: whipped cream, fresh mint leaves

• **Combine** first 4 ingredients in a large bowl, stirring well. Stir in melted butter and next 3 ingredients. Pour into unbaked pastry shell.
• **Bake** at 375° for 35 minutes or until filling is set, shielding edges with strips of aluminum foil after 25 minutes to prevent excessive browning. Cool on a wire rack. Garnish, if desired. **Yield:** 1 (9-inch) pie.

I FALL TO PEACHES (PEACH COBBLER)

½ cup butter or margarine
1 cup all-purpose flour
1 teaspoon baking powder
1 teaspoon baking soda
½ teaspoon salt
1 cup sugar
1 cup milk
1 (21-ounce) can peach pie filling

• **Place** butter in a 13- x 9- x 2-inch baking dish. Bake at 350° until melted.
• **Combine** flour and next 4 ingredients; stir in milk. Pour batter evenly over butter. Spoon pie filling over batter (do not stir).
• **Bake** at 350° for 30 to 35 minutes or until browned. **Yield:** 6 servings.

QUICK & EASY

SPEEDY TACO SUPPER

Our south-of-the-border feast is fast enough for weeknights and easy enough for beginning cooks. And for a truly simple Mexican dessert just stir 1 teaspoon ground cinnamon into 1 quart vanilla or chocolate ice cream.

EASY TACOS

1 pound ground chuck
2 to 3 teaspoons Taco Seasoning Blend
¼ cup water
12 taco shells
Condiments: chopped onion and tomato, shredded lettuce and cheese

• **Brown** ground chuck in a large skillet over medium heat, stirring until it crumbles; drain. Add Taco Seasoning Blend and ¼ cup water, stirring well.
• **Cook** over medium heat 3 to 5 minutes or until liquid evaporates. Spoon meat mixture into taco shells; top with condiments as desired. **Yield:** 1 dozen.

Taco Seasoning Blend

3 tablespoons chili powder
1 tablespoon salt
1 tablespoon garlic powder
1½ teaspoons ground black pepper
¾ teaspoon ground red pepper

• **Combine** all ingredients. Store mixture in an airtight container up to 1 month. Use with beef or chicken. **Yield:** ⅓ cup.

Patricia Lawler
Euless, Texas

REFRIED BEANS

1 (31-ounce) can refried beans
½ cup Texas Salsa (see recipe)
1 cup (4 ounces) shredded Mexican cheese blend

• **Combine** beans and Texas Salsa in a saucepan; cook over medium heat until thoroughly heated. Sprinkle with cheese, and serve immediately. **Yield:** 4 servings.

Charlotte Pierce Bryant
Greensburg, Kentucky

GUACAMOLE

2 (6-ounce) packages frozen avocado dip, thawed
¼ cup chopped onion
¼ cup Texas Salsa (see recipe)
2 tablespoons chopped fresh cilantro
1½ tablespoons fresh lime juice
¼ teaspoon salt

• **Combine** all ingredients, stirring well. **Yield:** 2 cups.

Patsy Hobson
Liberty, Missouri

TEXAS SALSA

1 large tomato, quartered
½ purple onion, halved
1 clove garlic
¼ cup loosely packed fresh cilantro
½ teaspoon salt
1 (4.5-ounce) can chopped green chiles, undrained

• **Position** knife blade in food processor, and add first 5 ingredients. Process until chopped. Add chiles; pulse once or until mixture is combined. **Yield:** 2 cups.

Erin Whiteley
Annapolis, Maryland

SALSA VERDE

½ cup coarsely chopped purple onion
¼ cup loosely packed fresh cilantro
1 jalapeño pepper, seeded
½ teaspoon salt
2 (11-ounce) cans tomatillos, drained

• **Position** knife blade in food processor; add all ingredients. Process until finely chopped. **Yield:** 2 cups.

Ginny Munsterman
Garland, Texas

FROM OUR KITCHEN TO YOURS

FROM DAYS OF OLD

If you haven't met chefs Edna Lewis and Scott Peacock, proponents of Southern kitchen traditions (see story beginning on page 142), don't miss this sampling of the past. Testing these recipes took us back a few decades.

Those of us with the most birthdays under our belts wrinkled noses at the faintly familiar, but perhaps forgotten, smell of lard. And those too young to remember television before *The Brady Bunch* met this foreign cooking ingredient with wide eyes and pursed lips.

Be sure when you buy lard that it's good. Smell it to make sure it's not rancid. Beware: Because few people buy lard, grocers occasionally leave it on their shelves too long.

If you just can't bring yourself to cook with lard, use it instead for removing tar from your daughter's prom formal when she drags the hem through a freshly paved parking lot. But that's another story.

DOWN THROUGH THE PAGES

Here's a good habit to adopt while making meals. Jot down notes near the recipes in your cookbooks. Everytime you make dishes for a family gathering or special occasion, note it in the cookbook margins.

One day you can go back and see what you prepared, when you did it, and for whom. Make a note if it was for your child's first Christmas, Thanksgiving, or other occasion. It's a special way to make memories.

TOMATO PASTE WASTE

Here's an idea that's a great save for tomato paste. Put the can in the freezer for a couple of hours, take it out, and then open it at both ends. Push the "tomato popsicle" out into a heavy-duty, zip-top plastic bag, and put it back in the freezer. When you need a tablespoon or two for a recipe, just slice off a little, and return the rest to its icy haven till next time.

FLIPPED YOUR LID?

Pot lids tend to disappear to never-never land with those errant stray socks in the laundry. Try using metal mixing bowls or cookie or baking sheets over pots and pans on the cooktop. If you need a tight-fitting lid for boiling liquids that threaten to sneak out, put a heavy Dutch oven on top of the cookie sheet to weigh it down. But a word of caution: It's best not to tempt fate with these makeshift lids on a brimful pot or you'll end up with a mess instead of a meal.

WHAT TANGLED WEBS WE WEAVE

Smooth, creamy soups are such elegant appetizers, but they can look so disappointingly plain in the bowl. With a little flair, you can easily turn drab into dramatic.

If you've ever thought it must take as long to make a web design as a spider spends spinning one, here's a secret. Squirt a spiral of sour cream, thinned with a little milk, on top of the soup. (Use a pastry bag or heavy-duty, zip-top plastic bag with a tiny hole snipped in one corner.) Draw a wooden pick from the rim of the bowl toward the center four times, making an "X." Then pull the pick in the opposite direction (from the center toward the rim) four times, halfway between the original four lines.

Refreshing Lemonade

Lemonade is perfect for entertaining good friends outdoors. It's also the ultimate refreshment after washing your car or weeding the flowerbeds. When your taste buds crave a different kind of tingle, make one of our flavored sugar syrups to sweeten the beverage. And if you don't need a whole pitcher of this satisfying lemony drink, follow our simple directions to make Lemonade by the Glass. Aahhh.

SUGAR SYRUP

Lemon juice keeps the syrup from forming crystals.

1 cup water
2 cups sugar
¼ teaspoon lemon juice

• **Combine** all ingredients in a small saucepan; cook over low heat until sugar dissolves. Bring to a boil; reduce heat, and simmer 1 minute. Remove from heat; cool. Store in an airtight container at room temperature up to 2 weeks. **Yield:** 2 cups.

Mint Syrup: Add 1 cup loosely packed mint leaves to saucepan, and cook as directed. Cool. Discard mint.

Ginger Syrup: Add ¼ cup chopped fresh ginger to saucepan, and cook as directed. Cool. Remove and discard ginger; use syrup immediately. Do not store.

Berry Syrup: Substitute ½ cup seedless raspberry or strawberry jam for ½ cup sugar, and cook as directed. Cool.

Orange Syrup: Remove rind from 2 oranges, using a vegetable peeler; add to saucepan, and cook as directed. Cool. Remove and discard rind.

SWEET-TART LEMONADE

2 cups Sugar Syrup (see recipe)
1¾ to 2 cups fresh lemon juice
3 cups cold water

• **Combine** all ingredients, stirring well. Serve over ice. **Yield:** 7 cups.

Lemonade by the Glass: Combine 3 tablespoons Sugar Syrup, ¼ cup fresh lemon juice, and ¾ cup cold water; stir mixture well.

LEMON BITES

- Christopher Columbus introduced lemons to the New World in 1493. Lemonade was invented in Paris in 1630.
- A lemon contains more vitamin C than any other citrus fruit, which once made its juice the best prevention of scurvy.
- When buying a lemon, choose fruit that's heavy for its size and has smooth skin that's free of soft spots.
- Store lemons at room temperature 7 to 10 days or in the refrigerator 4 to 6 weeks.
- Squeeze 5 to 6 lemons for 1 cup lemon juice. If you don't want to squeeze a dozen lemons to make Sweet-Tart Lemonade, try using frozen lemon juice (not lemonade concentrate). One bottle has 7.5 ounces, just 1 tablespoon shy of a cup.

Showy Salad

"Antipasto" is Italian for "before the pasta," but you can enjoy this salad with almost any entrée. If you serve wine, consider an Italian pino grigio or an American sauvignon blanc to accompany the appetizer. Buon appetito!

SALAD ANTIPASTO

½ (8-ounce) package mozzarella cheese
18 slices salami
12 cherry tomatoes, halved
3 dozen whole ripe olives
12 pickled banana peppers
1 small purple onion, thinly sliced and separated into rings
½ cup olive oil
¼ cup lemon juice
¼ cup white wine vinegar
4 cloves garlic, minced
2 tablespoons dried oregano
½ teaspoon salt
¼ teaspoon pepper
½ cup (2 ounces) crumbled feta cheese
Fresh spinach leaves

• **Cut** mozzarella cheese into 18 thin sticks. Wrap each with a salami slice; secure with a wooden pick. Place in a shallow container. Add tomatoes and next 3 ingredients.
• **Whisk** together oil and next 6 ingredients. Drizzle over salad ingredients. Cover and chill at least 8 hours, turning ingredients occasionally. Drain.
• **Arrange** salad ingredients and feta on a spinach-lined plate. Serve with breadsticks. **Yield:** 6 servings.

HIDDEN CHARMS

It's something old, nothing new. Sometimes borrowed, and seldom blue – the charm cake (or trinket cake) is a delightful bridal custom. This bridesmaids' luncheon dessert is usually frosted in white or pink with delicate, enticing ribbons dangling from the layers. (Here we offer easier, no-frost versions.) Before cutting the cake, each attendant pulls a ribbon from the cake to discover a symbolic charm at the end.

ORANGE BLOSSOM CAKE

(pictured on page 113)

1 cup butter or margarine, softened
1 cup sugar
1 tablespoon grated orange rind
2 large eggs
1½ cups all-purpose flour
1½ teaspoons baking powder
¼ teaspoon salt
½ cup orange juice
1 teaspoon lemon juice
1 tablespoon orange liqueur *
½ teaspoon vanilla extract
Candied Orange Rind

• **Beat** butter in a large mixing bowl at medium speed with an electric mixer 2 minutes or until creamy; gradually add sugar, beating 5 to 7 minutes. Add orange rind and eggs, one at a time, beating just until yellow disappears.
• **Combine** flour, baking powder, and salt; add to butter mixture alternately with orange juice, beginning and ending with flour mixture. Beat at low speed until blended after each addition.
• **Stir** in lemon juice, liqueur, and vanilla. Pour batter into a greased and floured small (6-cup) Bundt pan.
• **Bake** at 350° for 35 to 40 minutes or until a long wooden pick inserted in center comes out clean (cake will rise above pan).
• **Cool** cake in pan on a wire rack 10 minutes; remove from pan, and let cool completely on wire rack. Sprinkle cake with Candied Orange Rind. **Yield:** 1 (8-inch) cake.

* Substitute 1 tablespoon orange juice for liqueur.

Candied Orange Rind

1 large orange
3 tablespoons light corn syrup
¼ cup sugar

• **Peel** orange, and cut rind into ⅛-inch strips. Reserve orange sections for another use.
• **Combine** rind and corn syrup in a small saucepan; bring to a boil over medium heat. Reduce heat, and cook 3 to 4 minutes.
• **Combine** rind and sugar, tossing to coat; spread on wax paper to dry. **Yield:** about ⅔ cup.

Adelyne Smith
Dunnville, Kentucky

PINEAPPLE UPSIDE-DOWN CAKE ROLL

(pictured on page 113)

1 (20-ounce) can crushed pineapple in juice
1 (2.25-ounce) package sliced almonds, toasted
¼ cup butter or margarine
¾ cup firmly packed brown sugar
3 large eggs
1 cup sugar
¼ cup warm water
1 teaspoon vanilla extract
1 cup all-purpose flour
1 teaspoon baking powder
¼ teaspoon salt
¼ cup sifted powdered sugar, divided
Gingered Crème Chantilly

• **Drain** crushed pineapple, pressing between layers of paper towels; set aside.
• **Reserve** 1 tablespoon sliced almonds; chop remaining almonds, and set aside.
• **Melt** butter in a small saucepan over medium-low heat. Add brown sugar, and cook, stirring constantly, 1 minute or until blended; stir in pineapple. Spread evenly in a lightly greased 15- x 10- x 1-inch jellyroll pan; sprinkle with chopped almonds. Set aside.
• **Beat** eggs in a large mixing bowl at medium-high speed with an electric mixer 3 minutes; gradually add 1 cup sugar, beating well after each addition. Add warm water and vanilla; beat 5 minutes or until thick and creamy.
• **Combine** flour, baking powder, and salt; sprinkle over batter, and fold into batter. Pour evenly over pineapple mixture, spreading to edges of pan.
• **Bake** at 375° for 13 minutes or until cake springs back when lightly touched in center. Cool in pan on a wire rack 5 minutes; loosen from sides of pan with a knife.
• **Sift** 3 tablespoons powdered sugar in a 15- x 10-inch rectangle on a cloth towel or work surface; turn cake out onto sugar. Starting at narrow end, roll up cake (without towel), and place, seam side down, on a wire rack to cool completely.
• **Transfer** to a serving platter; sprinkle lightly with remaining 1 tablespoon

Charmed, I'm Sure

The charm cake custom started in medieval times when a bridegroom supposedly bribed the bridesmaids with trinkets to let him see his hidden bride before the ceremony. There's also a reference to the cake in Emily Post's 1923 *Etiquette*.

Pulling the prized ring charm means that bridesmaid will be the next to marry; an anchor foretells that someone will soon "anchor" her heart; a baby predicts that the stork will visit her first; and a bow clues that a special friend will become a "beau." And there are plenty more.

Color-coded ribbons are attached to the charms so singles, marrieds, and junior bridesmaids will pull ones with appropriate messages – pale pink for the unwed, white for the already married, and hot pink for the young girls.

The trinkets come sealed in tiny plastic bags with the ribbons hanging out. When they're pulled from the frosting, the bag is messy, but not the charm. You can either have a caterer make the cake and insert the charms before frosting or make your own cake.

We opted for less mess with these homemade, no-frost cakes. You can drop the charms into the center of the Orange Blossom Cake, letting the ribbons hang over the cake stand. Conceal the charms with blossoms if you like. Or for Pineapple Upside-Down Cake Roll, lay the charms on the serving tray and place the cake on top of the charms, allowing the ribbons to extend over edge of tray.

CHARMS FOR CHARGE

You can order silver charms (in tiny bags with ribbons already attached) for $8 each and the novelty/plastic ones for $3 from Weddings, Etc., 2843 18th Street South, Birmingham, AL 35209; (205) 870-5299.

Winterthur Catalog offers a set of six sterling charms on satin ribbons (item #3199) for $45 plus tax and shipping. To order, call 1-800-767-0500.

powdered sugar. Top with reserved sliced almonds; serve with Gingered Crème Chantilly. **Yield:** 1 cake roll.

Gingered Crème Chantilly

You'll find crystallized ginger on your grocer's spice rack.

1 cup whipping cream
2 tablespoons powdered sugar
3 tablespoons minced crystallized ginger

• **Beat** whipping cream at high speed with an electric mixer until foamy; gradually add powdered sugar, beating until soft peaks form. Fold in ginger. **Yield:** 2 cups.

Corile W. Wilhelm
Terra Alta, West Virginia

Split Decisions

Few desserts make a more lasting impression than the banana split. The basic recipe requires no cooking – just the easy assembly of purchased ingredients like ice cream, syrups, and delicious toppings like nuts and ever-popular maraschino cherries. But you know we couldn't just leave it that way. These deliciously different variations will give you a whole new perspective on banana splits. The only decisions you'll have to make are which one to try first and whether to share the treat or devour it solo.

Baked Bananas

Build your banana split on a hot foundation of bananas flavored with honey and cream sherry.

6 medium bananas
3 tablespoons lime juice
⅓ cup honey
⅓ cup cream sherry
2 tablespoons butter or margarine, cut up
1 pint vanilla ice cream
1 pint chocolate ice cream
1 (5-ounce) jar walnut or pecan topping with syrup
6 maraschino cherries with stems

• **Place** bananas in a lightly greased 11- x 7- x 1½-inch baking dish, and brush with lime juice.
• **Combine** honey and cream sherry, stirring until blended; pour over bananas. Dot with butter.
• **Bake** at 400° for 30 minutes or until lightly browned. Cut bananas in half lengthwise, and place in individual serving dishes. Top each with vanilla and chocolate ice cream; drizzle with walnut topping. Top each with a cherry, and serve immediately. **Yield:** 6 servings.

Shelby Adkins
Penhook, Virginia

BANANA SPLIT TERRINE

(pictured on page 114)

½ gallon chocolate ice cream, softened
2 pints strawberry ice cream, softened
1 pint vanilla ice cream, softened
1 banana, chopped
3 tablespoons chopped maraschino cherries
2 tablespoons chopped crystallized ginger
1 (5-ounce) jar pecan topping with syrup
Garnish: maraschino cherries with stems

• **Line** a 9- x 5- x 3-inch loafpan with heavy-duty plastic wrap, smoothing wrinkles as much as possible.
• **Spread** chocolate ice cream on bottom and up sides of pan, and freeze until firm.
• **Spread** strawberry ice cream on top and up sides of chocolate ice cream, and freeze until firm.
• **Combine** vanilla ice cream and next 3 ingredients; spread over strawberry ice cream, and freeze until firm.
• **Remove** terrine from pan; peel off plastic wrap. Cut terrine into 6 wedges. Drizzle with pecan topping, and garnish, if desired. **Yield:** 6 servings.

FRENCH TOAST BANANA SPLITS

3 large eggs
½ cup whipping cream
1½ to 2 teaspoons ground cinnamon
½ cup hazelnut liqueur
1 teaspoon vanilla extract
½ cup sugar
2 large bananas, sliced
2 teaspoons unsalted butter
6 croissants
1 (5-ounce) jar hot fudge topping
1 quart vanilla ice cream
½ cup chopped hazelnuts, toasted

• **Whisk** together eggs and whipping cream. Stir in cinnamon, liqueur, and vanilla. Pour into a shallow dish.
• **Place** sugar in a separate shallow dish; dredge banana in sugar.
• **Melt** butter in a nonstick skillet over medium heat; add banana, and cook until lightly browned, turning once. Remove from skillet, and keep warm.
• **Cut** croissants in half horizontally; dip in egg mixture, coating well. Cook in skillet over medium heat, 3 or 4 halves at a time, until lightly browned, turning once. Place on individual serving plates.
• **Remove** lid from hot fudge topping; microwave topping at HIGH 1 minute, stirring after 30 seconds.
• **Top** croissants with ice cream; drizzle with topping. Spoon bananas over top, and sprinkle with toasted hazelnuts. Serve immediately. **Yield:** 6 servings.

Note: For hazelnut liqueur we used Frangelico.

Caroline Kennedy
Lighthouse Point, Florida

BANANA SPLIT-BROWNIE PIZZA

1 (21-ounce) package brownie mix
1 (8-ounce) can pineapple tidbits
2 (8-ounce) packages cream cheese, softened
⅔ cup sugar
3 bananas, sliced
1 pint strawberries, sliced
½ cup chopped pecans, toasted
1 (1-ounce) square semisweet chocolate
1 tablespoon butter or margarine

• **Prepare** brownie mix according to package directions; spread batter into a greased 15-inch pizza pan.
• **Bake** at 375° for 15 to 20 minutes or until a wooden pick inserted in center comes out clean. Cool completely in pan on a wire rack.
• **Drain** pineapple tidbits well, pressing between layers of paper towels to remove excess juice.
• **Beat** cream cheese and sugar in a medium mixing bowl at medium speed with an electric mixer until smooth. Spread mixture over cooled brownie crust; arrange pineapple, banana, strawberries, and pecans on top.
• **Combine** chocolate and butter in a 1-cup liquid measuring cup; microwave at HIGH 1 minute, stirring after 30 seconds. Drizzle over fruit; chill 1 hour, and serve immediately. **Yield:** 16 servings.

Note: For brownie mix we used Duncan Hines.

Carrie Treichel
Johnson City, Tennessee

ORANGE SYRUP

2 cups sugar
1 tablespoon grated orange rind
½ cup orange juice
⅓ cup light corn syrup
¼ cup orange liqueur
2 tablespoons butter or margarine
1 teaspoon clear vanilla extract

• **Combine** all ingredients in a heavy saucepan; bring to a boil over medium heat. Reduce heat to low; simmer 5 minutes or until sugar dissolves, stirring occasionally.
• **Pour** through a wire-mesh strainer into a small pitcher, discarding orange rind. Serve with orange sections over ice cream or waffles. **Yield:** 2 cups.

Beverly Justice
Columbiana, Alabama

MARASCHINO-ORANGE SAUCE

2 tablespoons sugar
1 tablespoon cornstarch
1 cup orange juice
1 teaspoon butter or margarine
⅓ cup drained maraschino cherries

• **Whisk** together first 3 ingredients in a small saucepan. Bring to a boil over medium heat, stirring constantly; boil 1 minute, stirring constantly. Remove from heat.
• **Add** butter and cherries, stirring gently until butter melts; cool completely. Cover and chill 1 hour. Serve with ice cream. **Yield:** 1¼ cups.

JULY

Corn: A Southern Sweetheart

It's the vegetable that whispers before it's born. Stand among the soldierlike rows of a Southern cornfield and you're on magical ground. Listen. The long, broad leaves rustle in the breeze like Mother Nature's taffeta skirts.

SUNNY CORN MUFFINS

- 2 ears fresh corn in husks
- 2 tablespoons butter or margarine
- ¼ cup finely chopped onion
- 1 cup all-purpose flour
- 1 cup yellow cornmeal
- 2 tablespoons sugar
- 1½ teaspoons baking powder
- ½ teaspoon baking soda
- 1 teaspoon salt
- 1 cup buttermilk
- 1 large egg
- ¼ cup butter or margarine, melted
- 1 cup (4 ounces) shredded Cheddar cheese
- 1 (4.5-ounce) can chopped green chiles, drained
- ¼ cup sunflower kernels

• **Remove** husks from corn; tear husks into ½-inch strips, and soak in hot water 15 minutes; drain. Cut corn kernels from cobs.
• **Melt** 2 tablespoons butter in a large skillet over medium-high heat; add corn and onion, and cook until tender, stirring often. Set aside.
• **Combine** flour and next 5 ingredients in a large bowl; make a well in center of mixture.
• **Combine** buttermilk, egg, and ¼ cup melted butter; add to dry ingredients, stirring just until moistened. Stir in corn mixture, cheese, and chiles.
• **Arrange** 4 husk strips across each lightly greased muffin cup to resemble spokes; spoon batter into cups, filling each three-fourths full. Sprinkle with sunflower kernels.
• **Bake** at 375° for 18 to 20 minutes or until muffins are golden (corn husks will brown deeply). Remove from pans; cool on wire racks. **Yield:** 1 dozen.

SOUTHERN CORN-AND-BACON CHOWDER

- 1 pound bacon, chopped
- 1 large onion, thinly sliced
- 10 ears fresh corn
- 2 (14½-ounce) cans ready-to-serve chicken broth
- 1 medium potato, peeled and cut into ½-inch cubes
- 2 carrots, shredded
- ¼ cup all-purpose flour
- 1½ cups milk
- 1½ cups half-and-half
- 1 tablespoon lemon juice
- ¼ teaspoon hot sauce
- 2 teaspoons salt
- ½ teaspoon pepper

• **Cook** bacon in a Dutch oven until crisp; remove bacon, reserving drippings. Set aside.
• **Cook** onion in 3 tablespoons reserved drippings in Dutch oven until tender; drain.
• **Cut** tips of corn kernels into a large bowl; scrape milk and remaining pulp from cobs. Add corn and next 3 ingredients to onion in Dutch oven.
• **Bring** to a boil; reduce heat, and simmer 10 minutes or until potato is tender. Set aside.
• **Whisk** together ⅓ cup reserved bacon drippings and flour in a 10-inch heavy skillet, and cook over medium-low heat, stirring constantly, 10 minutes or until browned. Remove from heat, and set aside.
• **Add** milk and half-and-half to vegetable mixture; cook over medium heat, whisking often, until thoroughly heated. Stir in lemon juice and next 3 ingredients. Whisk in flour mixture and three-fourths of cooked bacon.
• **Cook** until thickened, stirring often. Sprinkle with remaining bacon. **Yield:** about 3½ quarts.

Note: You can freeze chowder up to 1 month.

Gail Laughlin
Memphis, Tennessee

BUTTERMILK FRIED CORN

You can serve this as a side dish or sprinkle it on salads, soups, or casseroles.

2 cups fresh corn, cut from cob
1½ cups buttermilk
⅔ cup all-purpose flour
⅔ cup cornmeal
1 teaspoon salt
½ teaspoon pepper
Corn oil

• **Combine** corn and buttermilk in a large bowl; let stand 30 minutes. Drain.
• **Combine** flour and next 3 ingredients in a large heavy-duty, zip top plastic bag. Add corn to flour mixture, a small amount at a time, and shake bag to coat corn.
• **Pour** oil to depth of 1 inch in a Dutch oven; heat to 375°. Fry corn, a small amount at a time, in hot oil 2 minutes or until golden. Drain on paper towels. **Yield:** 2 cups.

Summer's golden trophy delivers sunshine in a husk. Join us as we salute a favorite Southern kernel.

It's a wistful vision of one of summer's sweetheart vegetables. From steamer to skillet, cornbread to chowder, fresh corn has sustained American cultures for centuries – and still brings ear-to-ear grins when it's placed on the table.

Ever wonder how corn lines up? The average ear of corn has 800 kernels, arranged in 16 rows. If you find yourself with more ears than you can eat in one sitting, refrigerate the extras in the husk in a plastic bag and use as soon as possible.

When corn is picked, its natural sugars immediately begin to turn to starch, so swiftness in cooking is key. Mark Twain recommended putting a kettle of water in the middle of a cornfield, building a fire under it, and shucking the ears of corn directly into the boiling water. Slathered with butter, it would be pretty unbeatable.

MONROE COUNTY CORN BOIL

Look for 25-pound lard cans at large feed and supply stores and some hardware stores. Cans are sold empty.

15 to 18 ears fresh corn in husks
30 small new potatoes
15 to 18 medium onions
3 (1-pound) packages smoked sausage, cut into 2-inch lengths
6 cups water

• **Punch** a ¼-inch hole in lid of a 25-pound lard can; set aside.
• **Remove** husks from corn. Cut off 1 inch from pointed end of corn, and discard. Stand corn, cut end up, in lard can. Place potatoes and onions over corn; place sausage on top of vegetables. Pour 6 cups water over sausage; cover with lid.
• **Place** lard can over medium-high heat, and place a clear glass over hole in lid. When steam condenses on the glass (mixture is boiling), reduce heat to medium-low, and simmer 1½ hours or until onions are tender. Serve with butter. **Yield:** 15 servings.

Ty Acton
Franklin, Alabama

MEXICAN CORN ON THE COB

8 slices bacon
8 ears fresh corn
¼ cup chili powder

• **Wrap** a bacon slice around each ear of corn; place each on a sheet of heavy-duty aluminum foil. Sprinkle with chili powder, and wrap in foil.
• **Cook,** covered with grill lid, over medium-hot coals (350° to 400°) 15 to 20 minutes, turning once. **Yield:** 8 servings.

Margie Kloeppel
Dallas, Texas

CONFETTI CORN SALAD

(pictured on page 187)

2 cups fresh corn, cut from cob
¾ cup water
1 (14½-ounce) can black beans, rinsed and drained
½ cup sliced green onions
½ cup chopped red bell pepper
1 small cucumber, seeded and chopped
2 cloves garlic, minced
¼ cup chopped fresh cilantro
1 teaspoon sweet red pepper flakes
¼ teaspoon salt
¼ teaspoon ground ginger
2 tablespoons corn oil
2 tablespoons rice vinegar
1 tablespoon sesame oil
1 tablespoon lime juice

• **Combine** corn and ¾ cup water in a saucepan; bring to a boil. Cover, reduce heat, and simmer 7 to 8 minutes or just until tender. Drain. Combine corn kernels, black beans, and next 5 ingredients in a large bowl.
• **Whisk** together red pepper flakes and next 6 ingredients until blended; pour over corn mixture. Cover and chill at least 2 hours. **Yield:** 4 to 6 servings.

Kitty Jones
Greeneville, Tennessee

TOMATO TRIMMINGS

The tomato may be the only produce that's as good unripe as it is fully matured. In these recipes you'll find both red and green ones shining as condiment ingredients. You don't believe green tomatoes can taste like raspberry jam? Just try our three-ingredient Mock Raspberry Jam.

Prepare these toppers while there's an abundance of fresh tomatoes at the market. Then any time of year you can enjoy a spoonful of summer with each dip in a jar.

RANCHERO SAUCE

2 tablespoons butter or margarine
10 green onions, finely chopped (1 cup)
¼ cup finely chopped green bell pepper
1 ripe tomato, peeled and chopped
1 (10-ounce) can diced tomatoes and green chiles, undrained
¼ teaspoon garlic powder
¼ teaspoon chili powder
⅛ to ¼ teaspoon dried crushed red pepper
½ teaspoon Worcestershire sauce

• **Melt** butter in a large skillet over medium-high heat. Cook green onions and bell pepper in butter until tender. Stir in chopped tomato and remaining ingredients.
• **Bring** to a boil; reduce heat, and simmer 20 minutes. Cool. Spoon into an airtight container; store in refrigerator up to 3 days. Serve with scrambled eggs, black-eyed peas, burritos, tacos, or polenta. **Yield:** 2 cups.

Carole Drennan
Abilene, Texas

GREEN TOMATO RELISH

6½ pounds green tomatoes, cored and quartered
1½ pounds yellow onions, peeled and quartered
½ pound green bell peppers, seeded and cut into 1-inch pieces
¼ cup salt
3 cups sugar
½ cup mustard seeds
1 tablespoon ground cinnamon
1 tablespoon whole cloves
1 tablespoon ground allspice
2 cups white vinegar (5% acidity)

• **Position** knife blade in food processor bowl; add first 3 ingredients. Process until finely chopped, stopping once to scrape down sides.
• **Pour** chopped vegetables into a large bowl; stir in salt. Cover and chill 8 hours.
• **Spoon** tomato mixture into a colander lined with cheesecloth, and let drain.
• **Combine** tomato mixture, sugar, and remaining ingredients in an 8-quart nonaluminum Dutch oven. Bring to a boil; reduce heat, and simmer 1 hour.
• **Spoon** hot mixture into hot jars, filling to ¼ inch from top. Remove air bubbles, and wipe jar rims. Cover at once with metal lids, and screw on bands.
• **Process** jars in a boiling-water bath 15 minutes. Store up to 1 year. Serve relish with hot dogs, hamburgers, or black-eyed peas. **Yield:** 5 pints.

Jana S. Collins
Mount Pleasant, Texas

MOCK RASPBERRY JAM

2½ cups chopped green tomatoes
1½ cups sugar
1 (3-ounce) package raspberry-flavored gelatin

• **Combine** tomato and sugar in a large saucepan; bring to a boil over medium heat, stirring often. Reduce heat, and simmer, uncovered, 20 minutes. Remove from heat.
• **Add** gelatin, stirring 2 minutes or until gelatin dissolves.
• **Pour** mixture into airtight containers, and store in refrigerator up to 1 week or freeze up to 6 months. **Yield:** 2 half-pints.

Patricia Andrews
McAlester, Oklahoma

summer suppers®

Centennial Supper

Maybe you couldn't get tickets to the Summer Olympic Games. Or maybe you just couldn't arrange a vacation to Atlanta. You can still be a part of the festivities. Celebrate the Olympic Games at your house with recipes from some of the South's competing athletes.

Olympic Celebration
Serves Eight

Smoked Turkey From a Deli
Ham-and-Pineapple Pizza
Southwestern Nachos
Pesto Primavera
Gorgonzola-Walnut Salad
Key Lime Pie
Spiced White Grape Punch

We started with a smoked turkey from the deli and added a refreshing punch. Then we asked Olympic contenders from the South to share recipes from their own families and kitchens. The result is a winning party menu that's long on fun and short on effort.

We made keepsake menu cards for the occasion using blank cards from a stationery shop and tied them with a red-white-and-blue ribbon. For our All-American centerpiece, we arranged sunflowers with American flags – talk about easy. So, invite a few friends to join you and your family for this Olympic celebration right in your own backyard.

HAM-AND-PINEAPPLE PIZZA

Weight lifter Bryan Jacob of Alpharetta, Georgia, opts for this sweet-and-savory pizza based on his favorite selection at Everybody's Pizza, near Emory University in Atlanta. Sliced into thin wedges, it's a crowd-pleasing appetizer.

1 (12-inch) refrigerated baked pizza crust
2 teaspoons olive oil
1 cup pizza sauce
2 cups chopped smoked ham
1 (20-ounce) can pineapple tidbits, well drained
½ cup (2 ounces) shredded mozzarella cheese
1 cup (4 ounces) shredded provolone cheese

• **Brush** pizza crust with olive oil, and spread pizza sauce evenly over crust. Top sauce evenly with ham and pineapple; sprinkle with cheeses.
• **Bake** at 425° for 10 minutes or until cheese melts and crust is lightly browned. **Yield:** 1 (12-inch) pizza.

Note: For pizza crust, we used Mama Mary's, available in the refrigerator section of your local supermarket.

SOUTHWESTERN NACHOS

The youngest Olympic softball player, 18-year-old Christa Williams of Houston, Texas, claims any and all types of Mexican food as her favorites. A spicy homemade guacamole stars in this appetizer.

½ (16-ounce) can refried beans
1 (10-ounce) package tortilla chips
1 cup Guacamole
½ cup sour cream
1 cup (4 ounces) shredded Cheddar cheese

• **Spread** refried beans evenly on 2 dozen tortilla chips; top each with Guacamole and sour cream, and place in a single layer on a lightly greased baking sheet. Sprinkle with cheese.
• **Bake** on highest rack in oven at 475° for 5 to 7 minutes or until cheese melts and edges are lightly browned; serve immediately. **Yield:** 6 to 8 appetizer servings.

Guacamole

Got a stubborn avocado that won't ripen? Seal it in a paper bag with an apple at room temperature for 1 to 3 days to speed up the ripening process.

1 avocado, peeled, seeded, and cut into pieces
1 green onion, cut into thirds
½ (4.5-ounce) can chopped green chiles
2 tablespoons chopped fresh cilantro or 2 teaspoons dried cilantro
1 teaspoon garlic salt
1 tablespoon mayonnaise
1½ teaspoons lemon juice
¼ teaspoon hot sauce
1 tomato, quartered

• **Position** knife blade in food processor bowl; add first 8 ingredients. Process until smooth, stopping once to scrape down sides. Add tomato; pulse until coarsely chopped. **Yield:** 1 cup.

PESTO PRIMAVERA

Rower Ruth Davidon captures the season's freshness in her Arlington, Virginia, kitchen with this vegetable-packed dish.

3 quarts water
1 cup sliced carrot
1 cup dried tomatoes, cut into fourths
1 (16-ounce) package linguine
2 yellow squash, cut into thin strips
1 red bell pepper, cut into thin strips
⅓ cup Ruth's Pesto
Toasted pine nuts

• **Bring** water to a boil in a large Dutch oven; add carrot, tomato, and linguine; cook 8 minutes.
• **Add** squash and bell pepper; cook 2 minutes. Drain well, and stir in ⅓ cup Ruth's Pesto. Sprinkle with pine nuts, and serve immediately. **Yield:** 8 servings.

Ruth's Pesto

4 cups loosely packed fresh basil leaves
1½ cups olive oil
1 cup freshly grated Parmesan cheese
½ cup pine nuts, toasted
3 cloves garlic
¼ teaspoon pepper

• **Combine** all ingredients in container of an electric blender or food processor, and process until smooth, stopping once to scrape down sides. **Yield:** 2 cups.

Note: Freeze pesto in 2-tablespoon portions in sections of ice cube trays. Allow 1 cube per 2 ounces pasta.

GORGONZOLA-WALNUT SALAD

Yachtsman Kevin Burnham of Coral Gables, Florida, includes this salad among his favorite training foods.

4 ounces Gorgonzola cheese, crumbled
¼ cup olive oil
1 tablespoon red wine vinegar
½ teaspoon salt
¼ teaspoon freshly ground pepper
1 medium head romaine lettuce, torn
1 cup walnut pieces, toasted

• **Combine** first 5 ingredients in container of an electric blender; process until smooth, stopping once to scrape down sides.
• **Combine** lettuce and walnuts in a serving bowl. Serve with Gorgonzola cheese mixture. **Yield:** 8 servings.

SPICED WHITE GRAPE PUNCH

You can prepare and chill this punch in advance.

3 cups boiling water
5 regular-size tea bags
1 teaspoon whole allspice
2 (3-inch) sticks cinnamon, broken in half
1½ cups sugar
9 cups water
2 cups white grape juice
1 cup orange juice
½ cup lemon juice

• **Pour** 3 cups boiling water over tea bags, allspice, and cinnamon sticks; cover and steep 5 minutes. Remove and discard tea bags and spices.
• **Stir** in sugar and remaining ingredients; cover and chill. Serve over ice. **Yield:** 1 gallon.

Note: Freeze a portion of punch in a small (6-cup) Bundt pan to use as a nondiluting ice ring for punch bowl.

Dinner, Dusk, and Daisies

Take the time to stop and smell the roses . . . and the daisies, zinnias, and fresh herbs. Invite friends for a relaxing supper amidst the fragrance of flowers and the knee-weakening aroma of dinner on the grill.

Late in the morning, marinate the chicken and prepare the green beans, potato salad, and tea. Later, slice the peaches and tomatoes, stuff the mushrooms, and pick some flowers for the table centerpiece.

Dinner in the Garden

Serves Eight

Herbed Cheese-Stuffed Mushrooms
Grilled Herbed Chicken Quarters
Dilled Green Beans
Tomato Wedges
Red Potato Salad
Peach Dumplings
Sparkling Summer Tea

Herbed Cheese-Stuffed Mushrooms

¾ pound large fresh mushrooms
1 (3-ounce) package cream cheese, softened
½ cup freshly grated Parmesan cheese
1 tablespoon chopped fresh parsley
1½ teaspoons chopped fresh rosemary
1½ teaspoons chopped fresh thyme
¼ teaspoon Worcestershire sauce
Pinch of salt
Pinch of pepper
Pinch of ground nutmeg

- **Clean** mushrooms with damp paper towels. Remove and discard stems or reserve for another use.
- **Combine** cream cheese and next 8 ingredients in a small bowl. Spoon or pipe cream cheese mixture evenly into mushroom caps, and place in a lightly greased 13- x 9- x 2-inch pan.
- **Bake** at 350° for 20 minutes. **Yield:** about 1½ dozen.

Barkley Shreve
Mobile, Alabama

Grilled Herbed Chicken Quarters

Although sherry adds a sweet kiss to this recipe, you can substitute less-expensive soy sauce with good results.

2 (0.75-ounce) envelopes garlic-and-herb salad dressing mix
½ cup vegetable oil
½ cup dry sherry
2 (2½- to 3-pound) whole chickens, quartered and skinned

- **Combine** first 3 ingredients in a shallow dish or heavy-duty, zip-top plastic bag; add chicken. Cover or seal; chill 8 hours or overnight, turning chicken occasionally.
- **Remove** chicken from marinade, discarding marinade.
- **Cook,** covered with grill lid, over medium-hot coals (350° to 400°) 50 to 60 minutes or until a meat thermometer inserted in thickest portion of chicken registers 180°, turning occasionally. **Yield:** 8 servings.

Note: For salad dressing mix we used Good Seasons.

Rita W. Cook
Corpus Christi, Texas

Key Lime Pie

Miami-based yachtsman Morgan Reeser's idea of an excellent evening is joining friends for a meal that's finished with this refreshing Floridian dessert.

1¾ cups graham cracker crumbs
2 tablespoons sugar
6 tablespoons butter, melted
3 large eggs, separated
1 (14-ounce) can sweetened condensed milk
½ cup fresh Key lime juice *
1 tablespoon lemon juice
2 teaspoons grated Key lime rind *
2 tablespoons sugar
1 cup whipping cream
1 tablespoon powdered sugar
½ teaspoon vanilla extract
Garnish: quartered lime slices

- **Combine** first 3 ingredients; press onto bottom and 1 inch up sides of a 9-inch springform pan. Cover and chill at least 1 hour.
- **Whisk** egg yolks; add condensed milk and next 3 ingredients, whisking until smooth.
- **Beat** egg whites at high speed with an electric mixer until foamy; gradually add 2 tablespoons sugar, beating until soft peaks form. Fold into yolk mixture; spoon into prepared crust.
- **Bake** at 325° for 15 to 20 minutes or until set and lightly browned. Cool on a wire rack; cover and chill 8 hours.
- **Beat** whipping cream at high speed with electric mixer until slightly thickened; add powdered sugar and vanilla, beating until soft peaks form.
- **Remove** sides of springform pan, and dollop whipped cream around top of pie. Garnish, if desired. **Yield:** 1 (9-inch) pie.

* You can substitute regular (Persian) lime juice and rind for the Key lime variety.

DILLED GREEN BEANS

2 pounds small fresh green beans
1 cup white wine vinegar
¼ cup chopped fresh dill
3 tablespoons sugar
2 cloves garlic, crushed
½ teaspoon salt
½ teaspoon pepper

• **Place** beans in boiling water to cover; reduce heat, and simmer 8 minutes or until crisp-tender. Drain; plunge beans into ice water to stop the cooking process, and drain again. Place beans in a large shallow dish.
• **Combine** vinegar and next 5 ingredients, stirring until sugar dissolves; pour over beans, stirring to coat. Cover and chill 8 hours, stirring occasionally. Serve with a slotted spoon. **Yield:** 8 servings.

Irene Smith
Covington, Georgia

RED POTATO SALAD

3 pounds small round red potatoes
½ cup chopped fresh chives or frozen chives
1 tablespoon grated onion
1 teaspoon sugar
1 teaspoon salt
½ teaspoon ground white pepper
½ cup sour cream
½ cup plain low-fat yogurt
2 to 3 tablespoons mayonnaise
2 teaspoons lemon juice
2 teaspoons Dijon mustard
Radicchio leaves
Garnish: fresh basil sprigs

• **Cook** potatoes in boiling water to cover 30 minutes or until tender. Drain and cool slightly. Peel potatoes; cut into thin slices.
• **Combine** chives and next 9 ingredients in a large bowl; add potato slices, tossing gently to coat. Cover and chill 2 to 3 hours. Serve on radicchio leaves; garnish, if desired. **Yield:** 10 servings.

Lisbeth McKeon
Southport, Connecticut

PEACH DUMPLINGS

1 cup sugar
2 cups water
2 tablespoons lemon juice
5 large fresh peaches, peeled and sliced (2 pounds)
1 cup pancake mix
¼ cup firmly packed brown sugar
¼ teaspoon ground nutmeg
½ cup milk
2 tablespoons vegetable oil
Vanilla ice cream
Garnishes: unpeeled peach slices, fresh mint sprigs

• **Combine** first 4 ingredients in a Dutch oven; bring to a slow boil.
• **Combine** pancake mix, brown sugar, and nutmeg. Add milk and oil; stir until dry ingredients are moistened. Drop by tablespoonfuls into boiling peach mixture.
• **Cover**, reduce heat to low, and cook 15 minutes (do not uncover). Serve warm with ice cream; garnish, if desired. **Yield:** 8 servings.

Charlotte Pierce
Greensburg, Kentucky

SPARKLING SUMMER TEA

1 quart boiling water
2 family-size tea bags
½ cup sugar
1 (12-ounce) can frozen lemonade concentrate, thawed and undiluted
1 quart water
1 (1-liter) bottle ginger ale
Garnishes: fresh mint leaves, lemon and lime slices

• **Pour** 1 quart boiling water over tea bags; cover and steep 15 minutes.
• **Remove** tea bags, squeezing gently. Stir in sugar, lemonade concentrate, and 1 quart water; chill.
• **Stir** in ginger ale, and serve over crushed ice; garnish, if desired. **Yield:** about 3½ quarts.

Mimi Davis
Owensboro, Kentucky

GREAT STEAKS

Imagine the perfect steak. Maybe it's a seared filet mignon, slightly pink in the center, meltingly tender, complemented by Red Wine-Butter Sauce. The flavor would be rich, full, indescribably wonderful. Dreams of such a steak might make a vegetarian repent, but we would probably rush unashamedly to the supermarket.

For a perfect steak, follow our guidelines. Purists will want to eat theirs plain. But if you prefer gilding the lily, try one of our classic sauces. All are high-calorie, butter-based concoctions offered without remorse. We hope you enjoy them in the same spirit.

PAN-GRILLED STEAKS

2 (1¼-inch-thick) steaks
¼ teaspoon salt
¼ teaspoon pepper

• **Sprinkle** steaks with salt and pepper; set aside.
• **Place** a large seasoned cast-iron skillet over medium heat 3 to 5 minutes or until very hot. Add steaks to skillet, and cook 16 minutes (medium) or to desired degree of doneness, turning occasionally. **Yield:** 2 servings.

Note: You can use a cast-iron skillet with ridges.

Broiled Steaks: Preheat broiler 5 minutes. Place steaks on a rack in a broiler pan; broil 5½ inches from heat (with electric oven door partially opened) 6 minutes on each side (medium) or to desired degree of doneness.

Grilled Steaks: Cook steaks, covered with grill lid, over hot coals (400° to 500°) 7 to 8 minutes on each side (medium) or to desired degree of doneness.

Grilled Vegetables: Place coarsely chopped onion, sliced fresh mushrooms, and minced garlic cloves on heavy-duty aluminum foil; dot with butter, and sprinkle with salt and pepper. Seal foil, and cook with grilled steaks.

Note: If using a gas grill, set heat selector on HIGH. Add wet hickory or other wood chips for a smoky flavor.

RED WINE-BUTTER SAUCE

Pan-Grilled Steaks (see recipe)
¼ cup dry red wine
¼ cup butter

• **Transfer** Pan-Grilled Steaks to a serving dish; keep warm. Add wine to skillet; stir to loosen browned bits that cling to bottom. Cook wine over medium-high heat until reduced to 1 tablespoon, stirring often. Stir in butter, and drizzle sauce over steaks. **Yield:** ¼ cup.

HERB-GARLIC BUTTER

½ cup butter or margarine, softened
1 tablespoon chopped fresh parsley
1 tablespoon lemon juice
½ teaspoon dried basil
¼ teaspoon garlic powder

• **Combine** all ingredients, stirring well. Serve with steak, corn on the cob, or bread. Store in refrigerator up to 1 week, or freeze up to 3 months. **Yield:** about ⅔ cup.

Patty Renwick
Mount Airy, Maryland

RAISING THE STEAKS

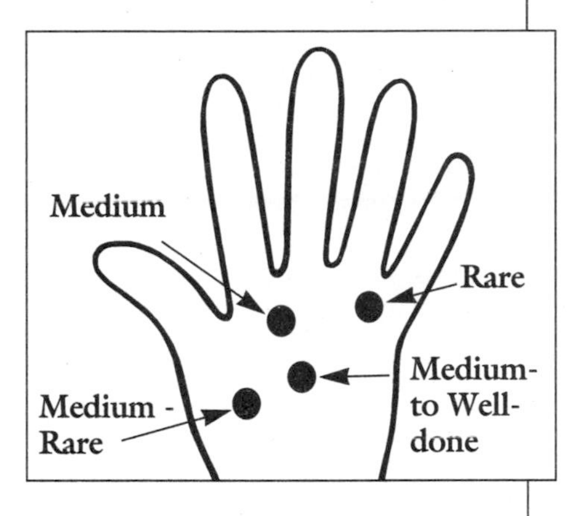

THE BASICS

Creating a great steak at home requires two things – a good piece of beef and the right cooking method. After extensive research, we determined our favorite methods are cooktop pan-grilling and grilling over hot coals. The results were outstanding – meat that was evenly browned, yet juicy, tender, and flavorful.

Grilling over hot coals gave us a tender steak with smoky flavor and handsome grill marks. Steaks cooked on a gas grill, however, had less flavor. We solved the problem by simply placing an aluminum foil pan with wet hickory or other wood chips on the lava rocks.

THE KINDEST CUT

If you're seeking perfection, buy the best steaks you can afford. The tenderest are filet mignon (tenderloin), chuck top blade steak, New York strip (top loin steak), porterhouse/T-bone, rib steak, rib-eye steak, and top sirloin. (Tip: Purchase your favorite cut on sale, and freeze it to enjoy later.)

▪ Purchase whole beef tenderloins on sale. Have the butcher cut the ends into steaks (filet mignon), and leave the center as a tenderloin roast. Properly wrapped beef can be frozen up to six months.

▪ Vacuum-packed beef may be a darker, purple-red color because of a lack of oxygen due to packaging. It should brighten once the meat is removed from the package.

AS YOU LIKE IT

There are several ways to tell when a steak is done. Chefs often press a finger against the meat while it's on the grill. Those less skilled may cut the steak and peek inside. Chef Richard Chamberlain of Chamberlain's Prime Chop House in Dallas, Texas, has an unusual technique for testing doneness: Compare pressure points on your hand to the firmness of the cooked meat. This is how it works: Turn your palm up, spreading fingers as far apart as possible. Press the center of your palm – that's what a medium to well-done steak should feel like. Below your index finger feels like a medium steak, below your thumb is medium-rare, and beneath your little finger is rare.

If you're uncomfortable with the hand method, cut into the steak for a quick look at the interior. Here's how to tell when your steak is ready. These guidelines are for steaks cut ¾ inch thick and grilled over hot coals, covered with grill lid.

Medium-rare: Center is very pink, slightly brown toward the exterior; cook 5 to 6 minutes per side.

Medium: Center is light pink, outer portion is brown; cook 7 to 8 minutes per side.

Well-done: Meat is uniformly brown throughout; cook 9 to 10 minutes per side.

STEAK HOUSE SELECTIONS

Here's how some Southern favorites get that great flavor.

■ At **Alabama Steaks** in Birmingham, Alabama, aged beef is cut in-house daily. The steaks are cooked on a very hot gas grill with hickory chunks added for smoky flavor.

■ The **Angus Barn** in Raleigh, North Carolina, serves only certified Angus beef from Kansas that has been aged three weeks. Steaks are grilled over very high heat on either charcoal or gas.

■ **Bern's Steakhouse** in Tampa, Florida, named the best steak house in the country by *The Wine Spectator* magazine, uses only Prime Midwest beef, which is aged in-house. The steaks are grilled over charcoal, basted with butter, and topped with garlic butter.

■ **Chops** in Atlanta, Georgia, serves only Prime beef to its customers. The meat is seasoned and cooked under a broiler at *1400°*.

■ At **Doe's Eat Place** in Greenville, Mississippi, steaks are broiled in a hot gas oven with a drip pan; drippings are then poured back over the meat.

■ In **Outback Steakhouse** restaurants, steaks are cut to the company's specifications, seasoned, and seared in butter on a very hot, flat griddle.

■ **Ruth's Chris Steak House** restaurants use Prime beef from the Corn Belt. The steaks are seasoned with salt and pepper and cooked under an *1800°* broiler. (That's no misprint – *1800°*!) Butter is placed on the meat when served.

■ **Ryan's Family Steak House** ages its beef and cuts its steaks in-house. The steaks are seasoned with secret ingredients and cooked over an open flame.

BÉARNAISE SAUCE

3 tablespoons white wine vinegar
3 tablespoons dry white wine
10 peppercorns, crushed
3 shallots, finely chopped
1 tablespoon chopped fresh tarragon
1 tablespoon water
3 egg yolks
1/4 teaspoon salt
Pinch of ground red pepper
3/4 cup unsalted butter, melted and cooled
1 tablespoon chopped fresh chervil or parsley

• **Bring** the first 5 ingredients to a boil over medium-high heat, and cook, whisking constantly, until mixture is reduced to 1 tablespoon. Remove from heat, and whisk in water and next 3 ingredients.
• **Cook** over low heat, whisking constantly, 4 minutes or until pale yellow. Remove from heat; add butter in a slow, steady stream, whisking constantly, until thickened.
• **Pour** sauce through a wire-mesh strainer into a bowl, discarding shallot; stir in chervil, and serve warm with steak. **Yield:** 1 cup.

SAIL-AWAY MENUS

Sailor or landlubber, anyone can be a galley gourmet. These recipes can be made ahead, chilled, and then served on the water – or on dry land.

For a midday jaunt, feed the crew a shrimp sandwich, along with chips that are better than any you'll buy in a bag. Or set sail for a dinner cruise, and serve shrimp, salmon, and potato salad – all chilled.

DINNER ON DECK
Serves Four

Shrimp Cocktail
Mint-Marinated Salmon Steaks
Green Bean-Red Potato Salad
Bakery Cheesecake

SHRIMP COCKTAIL

If you cook and peel your own shrimp, start with 2 pounds in the shell to yield 1 pound for this appetizer recipe.

3/4 cup chili sauce
2 to 4 tablespoons lemon juice
1 to 2 tablespoons prepared horseradish
2 teaspoons Worcestershire sauce
1/2 teaspoon grated onion
2 or 3 drops of hot sauce
1 pound cooked peeled shrimp
Lettuce leaves

• **Combine** first 6 ingredients; cover and chill.
• **Arrange** shrimp on lettuce leaves; top with sauce. **Yield:** 4 to 6 servings.

Marie A. Davis
Charlotte, North Carolina

MINT-MARINATED SALMON STEAKS

Cut into the salmon steaks near the center to test for doneness. Grilling time for the steaks will vary, depending upon weather conditions.

½ cup white wine
¼ cup olive oil
2 cloves garlic, minced
½ teaspoon salt
¼ teaspoon pepper
1 tablespoon lemon juice
¼ cup chopped fresh mint
4 (¾-inch-thick) salmon steaks
Vegetable cooking spray

• **Combine** first 7 ingredients. Place salmon steaks in a large shallow dish, and pour wine mixture over salmon. Cover and chill 2 hours, turning salmon occasionally.
• **Remove** salmon from marinade, discarding marinade.
• **Coat** grill rack or fish basket with cooking spray, and place salmon on rack or in basket.
• **Cook,** covered with grill lid, over medium coals (300° to 350°) 10 minutes on each side or until done. Remove from heat; cover and chill. **Yield:** 4 servings.

GREEN BEAN-RED POTATO SALAD

Leave the skins on the red potatoes for pretty color and to help them keep their shape after they're cooked.

1½ pounds round red potatoes
1 (9-ounce) package frozen whole green beans
2 tablespoons white vinegar
1 tablespoon sugar
¾ cup mayonnaise
2 tablespoons chopped onion
½ teaspoon dried dillweed or 1½ teaspoons finely chopped fresh dill

• **Cook** potatoes in boiling salted water to cover 10 minutes or until tender. Drain potatoes, and cool to touch. Cut into slices.
• **Cook** green beans according to package directions; drain and rinse with cold water.
• **Combine** potato slices and green beans in a bowl. Combine vinegar and next 4 ingredients; pour over potato mixture, and toss gently. Cover and chill 4 hours. **Yield:** 4 servings.

Linda Kirkpatrick
Westminster, Maryland

LUNCH ON THE LAKE
Serves Six to Eight

Shrimp Salad on Croissants
Potato Crisps
Marinated Vegetables
Fresh Fruit

SHRIMP SALAD ON CROISSANTS

Purchase large, sandwich-size croissants from the deli and cooked shrimp from the seafood department to save time.

3 cups cooked peeled shrimp
1 cup finely chopped celery
½ cup sliced ripe olives
½ cup sliced green onions
3 large hard-cooked eggs, finely chopped (optional)
Dressing
Leaf lettuce
8 large croissants, split

• **Combine** first 4 ingredients; stir in eggs, if desired. Add Dressing; toss gently. Cover and chill.
• **Line** croissant bottom with leaf lettuce; spread shrimp mixture over lettuce. Add croissant top. **Yield:** 8 servings.

Dressing

¾ cup mayonnaise
2 tablespoons chili sauce
2 teaspoons prepared horseradish, drained
¼ teaspoon salt

• **Combine** all ingredients. **Yield:** about 1 cup.

Jeanne S. Hotaling
Augusta, Georgia

POTATO CRISPS

We made these crunchy chips a day ahead and stored them in airtight containers. They were wonderful.

12 small baking potatoes, peeled (3 pounds)
Vegetable oil
Seasoned salt (optional)

• **Slice** potatoes thinly, and place in salted ice water until slicing is completed. Drain well on paper towels.
• **Pour** oil to depth of 2 inches into a Dutch oven; heat to 360°. Fry potato slices, a few at a time, 1 to 2 minutes or until golden and crisp, removing potatoes as they brown. Drain on paper towels. Sprinkle with seasoned salt, if desired. **Yield:** 8 servings.

MARINATED VEGETABLES

This recipe easily doubles to serve a crowd.

½ cup vegetable oil
⅓ cup cider vinegar
1½ teaspoons sugar
1 teaspoon dried dillweed
½ teaspoon garlic salt
¼ teaspoon salt
¼ teaspoon pepper
½ pound fresh broccoli, cut into flowerets
1 small cauliflower, cut into flowerets
3 small yellow squash, thinly sliced
3 medium carrots, scraped and diagonally sliced
3 medium fresh mushrooms, sliced

• **Combine** first 7 ingredients in a jar. Cover tightly, and shake vigorously. Set aside.
• **Combine** broccoli and next 4 ingredients in a large bowl.
• **Pour** oil mixture over vegetables, stirring gently to coat. Cover and chill 24 hours, stirring vegetables occasionally. **Yield:** 8 servings.

Carol Snyder
Monroe, North Carolina

BANK ON CRAB CAKES

Excitement about crab cakes is a matter of your purse's perspective – they certainly aren't routine weeknight fare.

Living near the water means crabbing with string, chicken necks, and a net. In the city, you'll need your credit card when you go crabbing. But after a meal of crab cakes, the smiles tell it all – it was worth it.

BAKED CRAB CAKES WITH CRESS SAUCE

For a special evening, serve these crab cakes. They're worth every penny.

¼ cup butter or margarine
¾ cup finely chopped celery
1 medium onion, finely chopped
4 slices white bread, trimmed and cubed
¼ cup milk
1 pound fresh lump crabmeat, drained
1 large egg, lightly beaten
⅓ cup chopped fresh parsley
½ teaspoon freshly ground black pepper
½ teaspoon ground red pepper
½ teaspoon dry mustard
1 cup fine, dry breadcrumbs
Cress Sauce

• **Melt** butter in a skillet over medium heat. Add celery and onion, and cook 10 minutes, stirring often; set aside.
• **Combine** bread cubes and milk in a large bowl; let stand 5 minutes. Drain and stir in celery mixture, crabmeat, and next 5 ingredients.
• **Shape** into 1-inch balls, and roll in breadcrumbs. Cover and chill up to 8 hours, if desired. Place on a lightly greased baking sheet, and flatten slightly.
• **Bake** at 400° for 15 minutes or until golden. Serve with Cress Sauce. **Yield:** 3 dozen.

Cress Sauce

1 bunch fresh watercress, stemmed and chopped
1 green onion, finely chopped
1½ tablespoons lemon juice
1 cup mayonnaise
⅛ teaspoon ground red pepper
½ cup whipping cream, whipped

• **Combine** all ingredients; cover and chill. **Yield:** 2 cups.

Joan Powell
Dallas, Texas

CRAB CAKES WITH GREENS AND DIJON DRESSING

¾ cup soft breadcrumbs
1 egg white, lightly beaten
2 tablespoons mayonnaise
1 tablespoon chopped fresh parsley
½ teaspoon prepared mustard
¼ teaspoon celery salt
¼ teaspoon freshly ground pepper
⅛ teaspoon salt
1 pound fresh lump crabmeat, drained
1 tablespoon vegetable oil
6 cups mixed salad greens
Dijon Dressing
Garnish: lemon slices

• **Combine** first 9 ingredients. Shape into 6 patties; cover and chill 1 hour.
• **Cook** patties in oil in a nonstick skillet over medium heat 3 minutes on each side or until golden. Drain on paper towels. Chill, if desired.
• **Arrange** salad greens and crab cakes on individual plates; top with Dijon Dressing. Garnish, if desired. **Yield:** 3 to 6 servings.

Dijon Dressing

1 cup mayonnaise
¼ cup Dijon mustard
1 teaspoon Worcestershire sauce

• **Combine** all ingredients; cover and chill. **Yield:** 1¼ cups.

Alma Madanick
Chincoteague Island, Virginia

Bumper-to-Bumper Crops

All the way there you promise you won't do it again. With resolve, you park, approach the bins, and focus. You calmly bag just a couple of tomatoes, a straggly fistful of green beans, the smallest cantaloupe. Then you snap, like a child diving in one of those giant playpens of colorful balls.

On the drive home, calculation replaces resolve as you rehearse excuses aloud: "No this isn't the same corn dish the sixth night in a row. Really."

Well we're here to help you. Go ahead and tear out this page. Be sure to keep it in your glove compartment, just in case. The next time you lose control at a produce stand, you'll be ready to fool your family and friends with these tasty new recipes.

STIR-FRIED OKRA

3 tablespoons vegetable oil
1 pound fresh okra, sliced
1 large onion, finely chopped
1 large green bell pepper, finely chopped
1 cup finely chopped celery
¼ teaspoon salt
¼ teaspoon pepper
½ teaspoon dried thyme, crushed
3 tablespoons soy sauce

• **Place** oil in a large skillet over medium-high heat until hot. Add okra and next 6 ingredients, and stir-fry mixture 8 to 10 minutes or until okra is crisp-tender.
• **Add** soy sauce to vegetable mixture, and cook, stirring constantly, 2 minutes or until okra is tender. **Yield:** 6 to 8 servings.

Sherida Eddlemon
Memphis, Tennessee

GREEN BEANS VINAIGRETTE

2 pounds fresh green beans
½ cup olive oil
2 teaspoons lemon zest strips or grated lemon rind
¼ cup fresh lemon juice
2 cloves garlic, minced
½ teaspoon salt
¼ teaspoon crushed red pepper flakes

• **Cook** beans in boiling water to cover 12 to 15 minutes or until tender; drain and cool.
• **Combine** oil and next 5 ingredients in a jar; cover tightly, and shake vigorously. Place beans in a large heavy-duty, zip-top plastic bag; add oil mixture. Seal and chill 2 hours, turning occasionally. **Yield:** 6 to 8 servings.

Mary Pappas
Richmond, Virginia

ASIAN CUCUMBERS AND PASTA

Tired of green salad? Try cucumbers warm in this pasta side dish.

2 cloves garlic
1 tablespoon grated fresh ginger
⅓ cup creamy peanut butter
¼ cup soy sauce
2 tablespoons fresh lime juice
1 tablespoon molasses
8 ounces angel hair pasta, uncooked
3 medium cucumbers, peeled, seeded, and coarsely chopped
½ cup sliced green onions

• **Combine** first 6 ingredients in container of an electric blender; process until smooth, stopping once to scrape down sides.
• **Cook** pasta according to package directions; drain and return to pan. Add peanut butter mixture, and toss gently.
• **Spoon** onto a serving platter; top with cucumber and green onions. **Yield:** 4 servings.

Margaret Springer
Killen, Alabama

EGGPLANT À LA CREOLE

1 pound unpeeled medium-size fresh shrimp
2 medium eggplants
3 tablespoons butter or margarine
1 large onion, finely chopped
1 cup sliced fresh mushrooms
½ teaspoon salt
½ teaspoon pepper
1 teaspoon dried thyme, crushed
1 (10¾-ounce) can cream of mushroom soup, undiluted
½ cup dry sherry
1 cup fine, dry breadcrumbs
½ cup grated Parmesan cheese, divided
2 tablespoons finely chopped fresh parsley

• **Peel** shrimp, and devein, if desired; set aside.
• **Cut** eggplants in half lengthwise. Scoop out and chop pulp, leaving ½-inch shells. Cook shells in boiling water to cover 2 to 3 minutes; drain and place in a lightly greased 13- x 9- x 2-inch baking dish.
• **Melt** butter in a large Dutch oven over medium-high heat; add chopped eggplant, onion, and next 4 ingredients, and cook 5 minutes, stirring often.
• **Add** shrimp, and cook 3 to 5 minutes or just until shrimp turn pink, stirring often. Stir in soup and sherry; remove from heat, and stir in breadcrumbs and ¼ cup Parmesan cheese.
• **Spoon** evenly into eggplant shells; sprinkle with remaining ¼ cup Parmesan cheese and parsley.
• **Bake** shells at 350° for 15 to 20 minutes or until thoroughly heated. **Yield:** 4 servings.

Ruth Sherrer
Fort Worth, Texas

SKILLET ZUCCHINI COMBO

(pictured on page 186)

3 ears fresh corn
1 medium onion, quartered and sliced
1 red bell pepper, cut into ½-inch squares
1 clove garlic, minced
2 tablespoons vegetable oil
3 medium zucchini, sliced (about 1 pound)
1 large tomato, peeled and chopped
2 jalapeño peppers, seeded and minced
1½ teaspoons chopped fresh basil or ½ teaspoon dried basil
½ teaspoon dried Italian seasoning
½ teaspoon salt
¼ cup freshly grated Parmesan cheese

• **Cut** corn kernels from cobs, and set aside.
• **Cook** onion, bell pepper, and garlic in oil in a large skillet 5 minutes, stirring often.
• **Add** zucchini; cook 7 minutes, stirring often.
• **Add** corn, tomato, and next 4 ingredients; cover and cook over low heat 7 minutes, stirring often. Sprinkle with Parmesan cheese, and serve immediately. **Yield:** 6 side-dish or 3 main-dish servings.

Janice Rinks
Bluff City, Tennessee

CHECKERBOARD VEGETABLE SQUARES

Fines herbes (FEEN erb) is a French term for a blend of four herbs, usually chives, parsley, tarragon, and chervil. You can often find it in dried form in a jar in your grocer's spice section.

1 cup cream-style cottage cheese
25 saltine crackers, coarsely crushed (1½ cups)
1 teaspoon dried fines herbes
2 to 4 tablespoons butter or margarine, divided
3 medium-size yellow squash, thinly sliced (about ½ pound)
1 (10-ounce) package fresh spinach
3 medium tomatoes, sliced
4 slices mozzarella cheese, cut into strips

• **Combine** first 3 ingredients, and set aside.
• **Melt** 2 tablespoons butter in a large skillet over medium-high heat; add sliced squash, and cook 2 minutes. Spoon mixture into a lightly greased 8-inch square baking dish, and spread half of cottage cheese mixture evenly over squash.
• **Place** spinach in skillet, and cook 2 to 3 minutes, adding 1 tablespoon butter, if necessary, to prevent sticking. Spoon evenly over cottage cheese mixture; spread remaining cottage cheese mixture over spinach.
• **Add** sliced tomato to skillet, and cook 1 minute, adding 1 tablespoon butter, if necessary, to prevent sticking. Spoon tomato evenly over cottage cheese mixture.
• **Bake** at 350° for 20 minutes. Arrange mozzarella cheese strips on top to resemble a checkerboard, and bake 10 additional minutes.
• **Remove** from oven, and let stand 10 minutes; cut into squares. Serve immediately. **Yield:** 6 servings.

Ursula Wulff
Orlando, Florida

SOUTH-OF-THE-BORDER SQUASH

2 pounds yellow squash, sliced (about 6 medium)
2 cups crushed tortilla chips
1 (10¾-ounce) can Cheddar cheese soup, undiluted
1 (10¾-ounce) can cream of mushroom soup, undiluted
1 (4.5-ounce) can chopped green chiles
¼ cup chopped onion
2 large eggs, lightly beaten
2 tablespoons taco seasoning
1 cup (4 ounces) shredded sharp Cheddar cheese
4 slices bacon, cooked and crumbled

• **Cover** and cook squash in a small amount of boiling water in a medium saucepan 8 minutes or until tender; drain. Press squash between paper towels to remove excess moisture.
• **Combine** squash, tortilla chips, and next 6 ingredients, stirring gently; spoon into a lightly greased 13- x 9- x 2-inch baking dish. Sprinkle evenly with cheese and bacon.
• **Bake** at 450° for 30 minutes. **Yield:** 8 servings.

Janet M. Newman
Marietta, Georgia

SALAD GREENS AND VEGGIES WITH FRIED OKRA CROUTONS

(pictured on page 187)

2 cups fresh corn kernels *
¾ cup white self-rising cornmeal
2½ teaspoons Creole seasoning, divided
2 cups sliced fresh okra *
Vegetable oil
1 pound romaine lettuce, torn
2 medium tomatoes, seeded and finely chopped
¼ cup vegetable oil
2 tablespoons white wine vinegar
2 cloves garlic, minced

• **Spread** corn kernels in a single layer on a lightly greased baking sheet.

• **Bake** at 400° for 10 minutes or until browned, and set aside.
• **Combine** cornmeal and 2 teaspoons Creole seasoning in a large heavy-duty, zip-top plastic bag; add okra, shaking to coat.
• **Pour** oil to depth of 3 inches into a heavy saucepan; heat to 375°. Fry okra until golden; drain on paper towels, and keep warm.
• **Place** lettuce on plates, and top with chopped tomato and fried okra.
• **Combine** remaining ½ teaspoon Creole seasoning, ¼ cup oil, vinegar, and garlic in a jar; cover tightly, and shake vigorously. Drizzle over salads; sprinkle with corn. **Yield:** 4 servings.

* You can substitute 2 cups frozen whole kernel corn and sliced okra, thawed, for fresh.

No-Cook Summer Desserts

If the heat is slowing everything except your craving for dessert, these treats are just your speed. Maintain a relaxed pace with recipes of few ingredients and make-ahead convenience. Both you and your kitchen stay cool while preparing these no-cook desserts. Go ahead and bring dinner to a delicious finish . . . with no sweat.

WATERMELON GRANITA

Granita is an Italian type of fruity, icy dessert. We consider it a snow cone for adults.

4 cups cubed watermelon, seeded
2 tablespoons lemon juice
½ cup sugar

• **Combine** all ingredients in container of an electric blender or food processor; process until smooth and sugar dissolves, stopping once to scrape down sides.
• **Pour** into an 8-inch square pan. Cover and freeze 2 hours or until almost firm, stirring occasionally.
• **Remove** from freezer 5 minutes before serving; stir, if necessary. Serve immediately. **Yield:** 4 to 6 servings.

Donna Presley
Perrytown, Arkansas

COOKIES AND CREAM

10 chocolate chip cookies
¼ cup milk
1 (8-ounce) container frozen whipped topping, thawed
Toppings: hot fudge sauce, chopped pecans, and maraschino cherries

• **Dip** each cookie quickly in milk. Dollop whipped topping into five dessert glasses, and top each with a cookie. Repeat layers, ending with whipped topping. Cover and chill at least 1 hour.
• **Add** toppings to each serving as desired. **Yield:** 5 servings.

Note: To make 1 large dessert, dip 1 (12-ounce) package chocolate chip cookies in ⅔ cup milk. Arrange a single layer of cookies in a 9-inch square pan, and spread with one-third of whipped topping. Repeat layers, ending with whipped topping. Cover and chill 1 hour. Spoon evenly into individual serving dishes, and let guests add toppings to each serving as desired. **Yield:** 9 servings.

Lisa Montgomery
Knoxville, Tennessee

FROZEN MOCHA DELIGHT

This works well for large gatherings and can be made up to three days in advance.

3 cups cream-filled chocolate sandwich cookie crumbs (about 30 cookies, crushed)
¼ cup butter or margarine, melted
½ gallon coffee ice cream, slightly softened
1 (16-ounce) container ready-to-spread chocolate frosting
1 (8-ounce) container frozen whipped topping, thawed
¼ cup sliced almonds, toasted

• **Combine** cookie crumbs and butter; press into bottom of a 13- x 9- x 2-inch dish or pan. Set aside.
• **Cut** ice cream into slices; arrange slices over crust, cutting to fit. Spread evenly with frosting and whipped topping. Sprinkle topping with almonds.
• **Freeze** 1 hour. Cover and return to freezer. Remove from freezer 20 minutes before serving. **Yield:** 12 to 15 servings.

Marge Killmon
Annandale, Virginia

Quick Eats, Cool Treats

Just in case you have leftover desserts . . .

▪ Layer crumbled brownie, chocolate pudding, and whipped topping in parfait glasses for a chocolate lover's dessert.

▪ Leftover pound or angel food cake makes the perfect trifle when crumbled and soaked with a liqueur. Layer cake slices or cubes in a trifle bowl alternately with fruit and whipped topping for a refreshing dessert.

Let the Games Begin

A patriotic pool party – with events such as ring relay and synchronized splashing – will get your kids in the spirit of the Summer Olympic Games. (Landlubbers can hold poolside orange passing or beach ball games.) No matter the game, cheer on the athletes and enjoy a red-white-and-blue party.

Swim Party Buffet

Serves 12

Power Munch
Five-Ring Pizzas
Banana Pudding Parfait Pops
Olympic Medal Cookies
Champions' Cooler

POWER MUNCH

6 cups crispy corn cereal squares
1 cup dry-roasted peanuts
3 tablespoons butter or margarine, melted
3 tablespoons honey
½ cup finely chopped dried apricots

• **Combine** cereal and peanuts in a 13- x 9- x 2-inch pan. Combine butter and honey. Drizzle over cereal mixture, tossing gently to coat.
• **Bake** at 300° for 10 minutes, stirring once. Add apricots; bake 10 additional minutes, stirring twice. Cool on wax paper; store in airtight containers. **Yield:** 6 cups.

Note: We used Corn Chex for the crispy corn cereal squares.

Barbara Barnard
Birmingham, Alabama

FIVE-RING PIZZAS

1 (14-ounce) jar pizza sauce
1 teaspoon dried Italian seasoning
1 pound ground beef
3 (10-ounce) cans refrigerated biscuits
½ cup (2 ounces) shredded Cheddar cheese
½ cup (2 ounces) shredded mozzarella cheese
½ cup chopped onion (optional)
¼ cup chopped green bell pepper (optional)
1 (2.5-ounce) can sliced mushrooms (optional)

• **Combine** pizza sauce and Italian seasoning; set aside.
• **Brown** ground beef in a large nonstick skillet, stirring until it crumbles; drain.
• **Separate** biscuits, and flatten to ¼-inch thickness on baking sheets; spread each with 1 tablespoon pizza sauce mixture. Top evenly with ground beef and cheeses; if desired, add onion, bell pepper, and mushrooms.
• **Bake** at 400° for 10 to 12 minutes. **Yield:** 30 mini pizzas.

Allison Mendoza
Arlington, Texas

The Spirit of Competition

Get your kids into the Olympic spirit with their own Summer Games.

Divide guests into teams with inexpensive color-coded T-shirts. After an hour of competition, serve this Olympic-themed spread. Instead of gold, silver, or bronze medals, each child wins a munchable medal – a cookie on a patriotic ribbon. Send kids home with their T-shirts and memories of poolside fame.

BANANA PUDDING PARFAIT POPS

1 (3.4-ounce) package vanilla pudding mix
1 (8-ounce) container frozen whipped topping, thawed
2 bananas, peeled and chopped
1 tablespoon lemon juice
12 (5-ounce) paper cups
¾ cup vanilla wafer crumbs
12 wooden craft sticks

• **Prepare** pudding mix according to package directions; fold in whipped topping. Combine banana and lemon juice (to prevent browning); fold into pudding mixture. Spoon ¼ cup into each paper cup.
• **Sprinkle** each with 1 tablespoon wafer crumbs, and top with another ¼ cup pudding mixture. Insert a wooden craft stick into center of each cup; freeze until firm. **Yield:** 12 servings.

OLYMPIC MEDAL COOKIES

This recipe calls for a big bowl, a big spoon, and a big appetite, but no mixer. Just add the ingredients, one at a time, and keep stirring.

6 large eggs
1 (16-ounce) package brown sugar
2 cups sugar
1½ teaspoons light corn syrup
2 cups (12 ounces) semisweet chocolate morsels
1 tablespoon baking soda
1 cup butter or margarine, softened
1 (28-ounce) jar creamy peanut butter
9 cups regular oats, uncooked
1 (12-ounce) package small jelly beans
45 large paper clips
Ribbon

• **Combine** first 10 ingredients, one at a time, in a large bowl, stirring well after each addition.

• **Pack** dough into a ¼-cup measure. Drop dough 2 inches apart on lightly greased cookie sheets; flatten slightly. Insert a large paper clip halfway into side of each cookie, leaving a loop wide enough to hold a ribbon.
• **Bake** at 350° for 12 minutes or until lightly browned. Cool on cookie sheets 10 minutes. Remove to wire racks to cool completely. Thread ribbon through loops; tie ends. **Yield:** 45 cookies.

Jeanne Maier
Stafford, Virginia

CHAMPIONS' COOLER

1 cup sugar
1 quart water
⅔ cup fresh orange juice (about 2 oranges)
3 tablespoons fresh lemon juice (1 lemon)
2 tablespoons fresh lime juice (1 lime)
1 orange, sliced
1 lemon, sliced
1 lime, sliced
Ice

• **Combine** sugar and 2 cups water in a microwave-safe bowl, and microwave at HIGH 2 minutes; stir until sugar dissolves.
• **Stir** in remaining 2 cups of water, orange juice, and next 5 ingredients. Add ice to bowl just before serving. **Yield:** 7½ cups.

Patricia Clarke
Baton Rouge, Louisiana

CENTERS OF ATTENTION

If your car heads to the florist on automatic pilot every time you need a centerpiece, it's time for a new direction. These casual ideas start at the grocery store, the nursery, your yard, a discount store, even the pet shop. And the best news is that you don't need any arranging talent.

EARTHLY DELIGHTS

Your local nursery (or perhaps grocery store) sells potted herbs like basil, mint, dill, and rosemary. Tie big squares of natural-toned burlap around the pots with twine, and group the pots in the middle of the table. Then string beads from a dime store or discount store onto more twine, and lay the bead garlands around the pots. Set your table with earthenware plates and dark goblets.

SUNNY DAYS

You may have access to a backyard patch of cheerful sunflowers. If not, check a farmers market or florist. Empty a bright can of tomatoes (perhaps into a skillet for the start of a fresh pasta sauce) and fill the can with a loose handful of the bold blooms. Tie a few long strands of raffia around the can, and stack it on top of two full cans. Use bright plates and napkins to complete the color scheme.

WAYS WITH WATERMELON

A typical picnic calls for watermelon served on newspaper. But the usually humble fruit brings this picnic table up a notch – with the help of china, crystal, and delicate blossoms. Just before serving the meal, slice a watermelon into various shapes and arrange casually on the table. Then insert the stems of summer flowers directly into the juicy fruit. After all, a watermelon is mostly water, so skip the vase. (Do not eat the melon.) Top plates with a soft melon-colored napkin.

CAN-DO CENTERPIECE

This tribute to the late Andy Warhol draws from his pop art look at soup cans. We stacked six soup cans, pyramid style. We opened and emptied the top can, and then filled it with asparagus spears cut to different lengths for varying heights. Stainless steel tumblers and colorful soup bowls add to this easy setting.

GO FISH

Kids love a special table, too, especially for a birthday bash. Add goldfish to the guest list, and give them the seat of honor – in the center of the table. Be sure to follow instructions from the pet store for helping the fish adapt to a new bowl.

Just before the celebration, carefully tuck the ends of ribbon from a few helium balloons into the rocks in the bowl. (Or you can put the ribbon ends under the fishbowl itself, letting the balloons float up around it.) Let the birthday boy or girl keep the goldfish as pets, or send them home with guests as either a prize for winning a game or a party favor.

living *light*

NATURE'S HARVEST

Summer's prized produce is as fleeting as a thunderstorm. It blows in to refresh us for a few sultry weeks and then disappears as fast as the lightning. Now's the time to get your fill of fuzzy peaches, fragrant basil, and tomatoes that taste like tomatoes. Try these easy low-fat recipes to temper your insatiable appetite for the season's bounty.

GRILLED CHICKEN SALAD WITH MANGO CHUTNEY

1 tablespoon olive oil
1 tablespoon reduced-sodium soy sauce
1 tablespoon balsamic vinegar
1 tablespoon rice wine vinegar
1 tablespoon dry sherry
1 tablespoon grated fresh ginger
1 teaspoon ground cinnamon
¼ teaspoon ground red pepper
4 (4-ounce) skinned and boned chicken breast halves
⅓ cup rice wine vinegar
2 tablespoons sugar
8 cups mixed salad greens
Mango Chutney

• **Combine** first 8 ingredients in a shallow dish or heavy-duty, zip-top plastic bag; add chicken. Cover or seal; chill 1 hour, turning chicken occasionally.
• **Remove** chicken from marinade, discarding marinade.
• **Cook** chicken, without grill lid, over medium-hot coals (350° to 400°) 5 to 6 minutes on each side or until tender.
• **Combine** ⅓ cup vinegar and sugar, stirring until sugar dissolves. Place salad greens on individual serving plates; drizzle evenly with vinegar mixture. Place chicken over salad greens; top with ½ cup Mango Chutney. **Yield:** 4 servings.

Mango Chutney

1 large mango, peeled, seeded, and finely chopped
1 large cucumber, peeled, seeded, and finely chopped
1 large jalapeño pepper, seeded and minced
¼ cup chopped purple onion
1 teaspoon grated fresh ginger
1 tablespoon chopped fresh basil
1 tablespoon rice wine vinegar
1 tablespoon balsamic vinegar
1½ teaspoons olive oil

• **Combine** all ingredients, stirring well. **Yield:** 3 cups.

Karl Harvey
Baton Rouge, Louisiana

♥ Per serving: Calories 211 (20% from fat)
Fat 4.9g (0.8g saturated) Cholesterol 48mg
Sodium 125mg Carbohydrate 22.2g
Fiber 2.1g Protein 21.4g

HERBED CHEESE SANDWICHES WITH ARTICHOKE-TOMATO SALSA

1 (15-ounce) carton part-skim ricotta cheese
1 (7-ounce) package crumbled feta cheese
½ cup chopped fresh parsley
2 tablespoons chopped green onions
1 teaspoon chopped fresh dill
16 slices rye bread
Artichoke-Tomato Salsa
8 lettuce leaves

• **Combine** first 5 ingredients, and spread on half of bread slices. Top with Artichoke-Tomato Salsa, lettuce, and remaining bread slices. Serve immediately. **Yield:** 8 sandwiches.

Artichoke-Tomato Salsa

2 medium tomatoes, chopped
1 (14-ounce) can artichoke hearts, drained and chopped
2 teaspoons olive oil
2 cloves garlic, minced
3 tablespoons chopped fresh basil

• **Combine** all ingredients; cover and chill. Serve with a slotted spoon. **Yield:** 3 cups.

Sarah Ryder
Lexington, Kentucky

♥ Per serving: Calories 294 (34% from fat)
Fat 11.4g (6.6g saturated) Cholesterol 39mg
Sodium 653mg Carbohydrate 35g
Fiber 3.8g Protein 15.6g

ROASTED SALSA VERDE

10 Anaheim chile peppers
1 large jalapeño pepper
3 cloves garlic, unpeeled
1 large onion, unpeeled
1 large tomato
½ cup fresh cilantro leaves
½ cup fresh lime juice
2 teaspoons jalapeño pepper sauce
½ teaspoon salt
½ teaspoon sugar
½ teaspoon ground cumin

• **Place** first 5 ingredients on an aluminum foil-lined baking sheet.
• **Broil** 5½ inches from heat (with electric oven door partially opened) 5 minutes on each side or just until peppers are blistered and remaining vegetables are browned; cool.
• **Remove** stems and seeds from peppers; peel garlic and onion. Remove core from tomato; cut tomato and onion into quarters.
• **Position** knife blade in food processor bowl; add vegetables, cilantro, and remaining ingredients. Process until mixture is finely chopped, stopping once to scrape down sides of bowl. Serve salsa with baked tortilla chips. **Yield:** 4 cups.

Carol Lundy
New Tazewell, Tennessee

❤ Per ¼-cup serving:
Calories 20 (5% from fat)
Fat 0.1g (0g saturated) Cholesterol 0mg
Sodium 154mg Carbohydrate 4.9g
Fiber 0.8g Protein 0.8g

PEACH MELBA MERINGUES WITH BUTTERMILK CUSTARD SAUCE

(pictured on page 188)

4 egg whites
¼ teaspoon cream of tartar
1 cup sugar
Buttermilk Custard Sauce
5 cups sliced fresh peaches
1 cup fresh raspberries
Raspberry Sauce

• **Beat** egg whites and cream of tartar at high speed with an electric mixer until foamy. Add sugar, 1 tablespoon at a time, beating until stiff peaks form and sugar dissolves (2 to 4 minutes).
• **Drop** mixture ½ cup at a time onto a baking sheet lined with parchment paper; shape with a spoon to resemble shallow bowls.
• **Bake** at 250° for 1 hour. Turn oven off, and let stand in oven 1½ hours. Remove from oven, and cool completely; remove from paper.
• **Pour** Buttermilk Custard Sauce evenly onto serving plates; top with meringue shells. Spoon peaches and raspberries into shells.
• **Place** ¼ cup Raspberry Sauce in a heavy-duty, zip-top plastic bag; seal. Snip a tiny hole in one corner of bag; squeeze small circles of sauce onto Buttermilk Custard Sauce around meringue shells. Pull a wooden pick through circles in several directions to make a design.
• **Drizzle** remaining Raspberry Sauce over fruit, if desired, and serve immediately. **Yield:** 8 servings.

Buttermilk Custard Sauce

3 cups buttermilk
¾ cup sugar
1 tablespoon cornstarch
4 egg yolks, lightly beaten
1 teaspoon vanilla extract

• **Whisk** together first 4 ingredients in a heavy saucepan. Bring to a boil over medium heat, whisking constantly; cook 1 minute, whisking constantly. Remove from heat; stir in vanilla. Cover and chill. **Yield:** 3 cups.

Raspberry Sauce

1 (12-ounce) package frozen unsweetened raspberries, thawed and undrained
2 tablespoons sugar
2 tablespoons raspberry liqueur
1 teaspoon cornstarch
1 tablespoon water

• **Combine** first 3 ingredients in container of an electric blender; process until smooth, stopping once to scrape down sides. Pour through a wire-mesh strainer into a small saucepan, pressing with back of a spoon; discard seeds.
• **Combine** cornstarch and water, stirring until smooth. Stir into raspberry mixture. Bring to a boil over medium heat; boil 1 minute, stirring constantly. **Yield:** 1 cup.

Susan H. Clark
Greer, South Carolina

❤ Per serving: Calories 344 (10% from fat)
Fat 3.8g (1.3g saturated) Cholesterol 113mg
Sodium 127mg Carbohydrate 73.1g
Fiber 6g Protein 7.4g

BRIGHT BELLS

Yellow or red bell peppers and reduced-fat cream cheese make a colorful, creamy sauce with very little fat. Serve the sauce with grilled fish or chicken, toss it with pasta, or chill it to use as a dip for assorted vegetables. A ¼-cup serving has 40 calories and 2 grams of fat.

Creamy Roasted Pepper Sauce: Place 2 large bell peppers; 1 small onion, quartered; and 3 cloves garlic on an aluminum foil-lined baking sheet. Bake at 500° for 10 to 15 minutes or until peppers are blistered, turning once. Place peppers in a heavy-duty, zip-top plastic bag; seal and let stand 10 minutes to loosen skins. Peel peppers; remove and discard seeds. Puree peppers, onion, and garlic in a blender. Add ½ (8-ounce) package reduced-fat cream cheese, ¼ teaspoon salt, ¼ teaspoon freshly ground pepper, and ½ cup chopped fresh basil. **Yield:** 2¼ cups.

A Salad Sampler

Tonight, when your family asks about the supper menu, you and the kitchen can stay cool. Serve one or all of these make-ahead salads. Your family will love the variety and you'll love how easy they are to prepare. Add crackers and a tall pitcher of iced tea for a refreshing meal.

SMOKED TURKEY SALAD

1 (10-ounce) package fresh spinach
1 pound smoked turkey, chopped
1 red bell pepper, cut into strips
4 green onions, diagonally sliced
½ cup walnut halves
½ cup vegetable oil
¼ cup raspberry or red wine vinegar
1 teaspoon seasoned salt
1 teaspoon dried Italian seasoning
¼ teaspoon freshly ground pepper

• **Remove** stems from spinach; wash leaves thoroughly, and pat dry. Set spinach aside.
• **Combine** turkey and next 3 ingredients in a large bowl. Combine oil and next 4 ingredients in a jar; cover tightly, and shake vigorously. Pour over turkey mixture; toss to coat. Cover and chill.
• **Place** spinach on individual salad plates; top with turkey mixture. **Yield:** 4 servings.

Peggy Fowler Revels
Woodruff, South Carolina

BROCCOLI-CHEESE-PASTA SALAD

(pictured on page 187)

8 ounces rigatoni, uncooked
4 cups fresh broccoli flowerets
4 ounces mozzarella cheese, cubed
⅓ cup chopped fresh parsley
2 tablespoons chopped fresh basil
Mustard Vinaigrette
Lettuce leaves
Garnish: cherry tomato halves

• **Cook** pasta according to package directions; drain. Rinse with cold water; drain.
• **Cook** broccoli in a small amount of boiling water 2 to 3 minutes or until slightly tender; drain. Rinse with cold water; drain.
• **Combine** pasta, broccoli, mozzarella cheese, and herbs in a large bowl; toss gently with Mustard Vinaigrette, and serve on a lettuce-lined platter. Garnish, if desired. **Yield:** 8 servings.

Mustard Vinaigrette

½ cup vegetable oil
⅓ cup lemon juice
2 teaspoons Dijon mustard
3 cloves garlic, minced
½ teaspoon salt
½ teaspoon pepper

• **Combine** all ingredients in a jar; cover tightly, and shake vigorously. Cover and chill. **Yield:** about 1 cup.

Heather Check
Oxford, Alabama

MEXICORN-BEAN SALAD

1 (11-ounce) can Mexican-style corn, drained
1 (15-ounce) can dark red kidney beans, rinsed and drained
1 cup thinly sliced celery
1 cup chopped sweet onion
¼ cup apple cider vinegar
¼ cup salsa
3 tablespoons vegetable oil
2 teaspoons prepared mustard
3 yellow bell peppers
Radicchio leaves

• **Combine** first 8 ingredients in a large bowl; cover and chill.
• **Cut** peppers in half lengthwise; remove and discard seeds. Spoon salad into peppers, and serve on radicchio leaves. **Yield:** 6 servings.

Mary Alice Adams
Kingsport, Tennessee

CREATE YOUR OWN SALAD

The makings of a great supper salad are right in your pantry and refrigerator. Add one or more of these ingredients to personalize our recipes, or toss any combination of these with your choice of dressings to create your own.

- Sliced or shredded vegetables
- Pasta
- Grated or shredded cheese
- Canned chicken or tuna
- Sliced ripe or green olives
- Chopped hard-cooked egg
- Canned fruits
- Toasted nuts
- Croutons
- Leftover cooked chicken, turkey, or ham cut into cubes
- Crumbled cooked bacon

Mashed avocado adds creamy texture to this two-handed Chicken-Avocado Dagwood sandwich (recipe, page 200).

Make the most of summer's supply of garden-fresh vegetables. Skip the meat, and make a meal from the bounty with Skillet Zucchini Combo (recipe, page 178).

Above: *We've updated the Southern vegetable plate. Try the usual okra, corn, and tomatoes in unusual Salad Greens and Veggies With Fried Okra Croutons (recipe, page 178).*

Top left: *Looking for a make-ahead salad for summer get-togethers? Try Confetti Corn Salad (recipe, page 168).*
Top right: *Tangy Mustard Vinaigrette dresses up Broccoli-Cheese-Pasta Salad (recipe, page 184).*

You can make Peach Melba Meringues With Buttermilk Custard Sauce (recipe, page 183) a day ahead and assemble just before serving for a cool finish to a hot day.

QUICK & EASY

FIVE-INGREDIENT FABULOUS

You can count the ingredients on one hand . . . one, two, three, four, five. Stirring up fabulous flavor with ingredients on hand has never been easier. Come on, let's go to the kitchen.

PEACHY GLAZED HAM

1 (16-ounce) can sliced peaches in light syrup, undrained
2 tablespoons dark brown sugar
2 to 3 teaspoons Dijon mustard
1 (1-pound) center-cut ham slice
⅓ cup sliced green onions

• **Drain** peaches, and reserve ½ cup syrup in a large skillet; set peaches aside.
• **Add** sugar and mustard to skillet; bring to a boil over medium-high heat. Cook 2 minutes or until mixture is slightly reduced.
• **Add** ham, and cook 2 minutes on each side. Add peaches and green onions; cover and cook over low heat 3 minutes or until peaches are thoroughly heated. **Yield:** 3 to 4 servings.

Robin Creed
Glade Valley, North Carolina

HONEY-LIME GRILLED CHICKEN

½ cup honey
⅓ cup soy sauce
¼ cup lime juice
4 skinned and boned chicken breast halves

• **Combine** first 3 ingredients in a heavy-duty, zip-top plastic bag; add chicken, turning to coat. Seal bag, and chill 30 minutes.
• **Remove** chicken from marinade, discarding marinade.
• **Cook** chicken, without grill lid, over medium-hot coals (350° to 400°) 5 to 6 minutes on each side or until done. **Yield:** 4 servings.

Karen Lapidus
Hampton, Alabama

MEXICORN

Helen Dowling of Birmingham, Alabama, shares her technique for keeping supper interesting – different variations of one basic recipe.

1 (14.5-ounce) can Mexican-style stewed tomatoes
1 (15¼-ounce) can whole kernel corn, drained
1 teaspoon chili powder

• **Combine** all ingredients in a saucepan; cook over medium heat until mixture is thoroughly heated. **Yield:** 3 to 4 servings.

Black Bean Mexicorn: Add 1 (15-ounce) can black beans, drained and rinsed. **Yield:** 4 servings.

Mexihominy: Substitute 1 (15.5-ounce) can yellow hominy for corn. **Yield:** 4 servings.

Mexicorn Main Dish: Add 1 pound ground beef, cooked, crumbled, and well drained; increase chili powder to 2 teaspoons, and top with 1 cup shredded Cheddar cheese. **Yield:** 4 to 6 servings.

GOOEY TURTLE BARS

½ cup butter, melted
1½ cups vanilla wafer crumbs
2 cups (12 ounces) semisweet chocolate morsels
1 cup pecan pieces
1 (12-ounce) jar caramel topping

• **Combine** butter and wafer crumbs in a 13- x 9- x 2-inch baking pan; press into bottom of pan. Sprinkle with chocolate morsels and pecans.
• **Remove** lid from caramel topping; microwave at HIGH 1 to 1½ minutes or until hot, stirring after 30 seconds. Drizzle over pecans.
• **Bake** at 350° for 12 to 15 minutes or until morsels melt; cool in pan on a wire rack. Chill at least 30 minutes; cut into squares. **Yield:** 2 dozen.

PINK PUNCH

This punch is supposed to be slushy, so prepare it at least 8 hours before you serve it.

3 (6-ounce) cans frozen pink lemonade concentrate, thawed and undiluted
2 (750-milliliter) bottles pink sparkling wine
3 (2-liter) bottles lemon-lime carbonated beverage, divided

• **Combine** lemonade concentrate, wine, and 2 bottles carbonated beverage in an airtight container, stirring well; cover and freeze 8 hours or until mixture is firm.
• **Let** stand at room temperature 10 minutes; place in a punch bowl. Add remaining bottle carbonated beverage, stirring until slushy. **Yield:** 2½ gallons.

Kathy Bowes
Metairie, Louisiana

DO-LITTLE DIPS

Whip up a dip or two and you've got the makings for a small summer gathering. Our dips offer great flavor, using few ingredients and minimal effort. Even better, they can all be made the day before you use them. So save those complicated recipes for autumn – a do-little dip will keep you and your kitchen cool.

ORANGE FRUIT DIP

1 (14-ounce) can reduced-fat sweetened condensed milk
1 (6-ounce) can frozen orange juice concentrate, thawed and undiluted
3 tablespoons grated orange rind

• **Combine** all ingredients in a small bowl, stirring until blended; cover and chill. Serve with fresh fruit or sugar cookies. **Yield:** 1¼ cups.

Carla Delle Harrigan
Lexington, Kentucky

APPLE DIP

This easy dip makes a great snack or light dessert for adults as well as children.

1 (3-ounce) package cream cheese, softened
1 cup sifted powdered sugar
½ cup caramel topping
2 tablespoons finely chopped dry roasted peanuts
3 large apples
3 tablespoons lemon juice

• **Beat** cream cheese and sugar at medium speed with an electric mixer until smooth. Spread into a 6-inch round in center of a serving plate; cover and chill 30 minutes.
• **Place** caramel topping in a 1-cup liquid measuring cup; microwave at HIGH 1 minute, stirring after 30 seconds. Drizzle over cream cheese mixture; sprinkle with peanuts.
• **Cut** apples into wedges; toss with lemon juice, and arrange on serving plate. **Yield:** 6 servings.

Nancy Matthews
Grayson, Georgia

TASTY TUNA DIP

1 (6-ounce) can solid white tuna in spring water, drained and flaked
1 (0.6-ounce) envelope Italian salad dressing mix
1 (8-ounce) carton sour cream

• **Combine** all ingredients, stirring until blended; cover and chill 8 hours. Serve with corn chips or melba rounds. **Yield:** 1½ cups.

Nancy Banks
Atlanta, Georgia

SAUCE NIÇOISE

This richly flavored dip is also wonderful with traditional salade niçoise ingredients – potatoes, tuna, and fresh green beans.

2 cups mayonnaise
1 (2-ounce) can anchovies, drained
¾ cup medium pitted ripe olives
1 tablespoon capers
2 cloves garlic

• **Position** knife blade in food processor bowl; add all ingredients. Pulse until finely chopped, stopping once to scrape down sides. Cover and chill at least 3 hours. Serve with fresh vegetables. **Yield:** about 2 cups.

Greg Fernald
Kingwood, Texas

INDONESIAN DIP

This sweet and spicy dip is equally at home with grilled chicken satay, a favorite Thai dish.

⅔ cup chunky peanut butter
½ cup firmly packed light brown sugar
½ cup fresh lemon juice
¼ cup chili-garlic paste
1 teaspoon soy sauce

• **Combine** all ingredients; cover and chill 24 hours. Serve dip with snow peas, Belgian endive, red bell pepper strips, and blanched asparagus. **Yield:** 1½ cups.

Mrs. Paul Smith
Longboat Key, Florida

FROM *THEIR* KITCHEN TO OURS

Fresh breads and pastries are divine in any country, but France has a knack for producing exquisite baked treats. We have simplified some techniques in these classic French recipes, and your results will taste as wonderful as what you'd get in Paris.

CRÊPES

French for "pancake," the paper-thin crêpe is one of the most versatile recipes to cross the Atlantic. This savory recipe is perfect for a filling of chicken or vegetables.

1 cup all-purpose flour
¼ teaspoon salt
1¼ cups milk
2 large eggs
⅔ cup butter, melted and divided

• **Beat** first 3 ingredients at medium speed with an electric mixer until smooth. Add eggs, beating well; stir in 2 tablespoons melted butter. Cover and chill at least 1 hour.
• **Brush** bottom of a 6-inch nonstick skillet with melted butter; place over medium heat until hot.
• **Pour** 2 tablespoons batter into pan; quickly tilt in all directions so batter covers bottom of pan. Cook 1 minute or until crêpe can be shaken loose from pan. Turn and cook about 30 seconds. Cool. Repeat procedure with remaining batter. Spoon shrimp salad or creamed chicken down center of each crêpe; roll up. **Yield:** 16 (6-inch) crêpes.

Note: You can make crêpes ahead by stacking them between sheets of wax paper and placing in an airtight container. Store in the refrigerator up to 2 days or freeze up to 3 months.

FRENCH BREAD

Crusty French Bread served with seasoned olive oil can double easily as an appetizer not just the bread for the meal. See our flavored-oil recipes on page 122 for some delicious dipping.

2 packages rapid-rise yeast
2 tablespoons sugar
2½ cups warm water (105° to 115°)
1 tablespoon salt
1 tablespoon butter, softened
6½ to 7 cups all-purpose flour, divided
1 egg white
1 tablespoon cold water

• **Combine** first 3 ingredients in a 1-quart liquid measuring cup; let stand 5 minutes.
• **Stir** together yeast mixture, salt, and butter in a large bowl. Gradually stir in enough flour to make a soft dough. Place in a well-greased bowl, turning to grease top.
• **Cover** and let rise in a warm place (85°), free from drafts, 40 minutes or until doubled in bulk.
• **Punch** dough down; turn out onto a lightly floured surface. Knead lightly 5 times. Divide dough in half. Roll 1 portion into a 15- x 10-inch rectangle. Roll up dough, starting at long side, pressing firmly to eliminate air pockets. Pinch ends to seal; turn under.
• **Place** dough, seam side down, on a greased baking sheet sprinkled with cornmeal. Repeat procedure with remaining dough.
• **Cover** and let rise in a warm place, free from drafts, 30 minutes or until doubled in bulk. Make 4 or 5 (¼-inch-deep) cuts on top of each loaf with a sharp knife.
• **Bake** at 400° for 25 minutes.
• **Combine** egg white and water; brush over loaves, and bake 5 additional minutes. **Yield:** 2 loaves.

Nancy P. Mumpower
Bristol, Virginia

CHOCOLATE ÉCLAIRS

1 (5.1-ounce) package vanilla instant pudding mix
2½ cups milk
1¾ cups frozen whipped topping, thawed
Cream Puff Pastry
½ cup butter
⅓ cup buttermilk
3 tablespoons cocoa
1 (16-ounce) package powdered sugar, sifted

• **Whisk** together pudding mix and milk in a large bowl, and chill 5 minutes. Fold in whipped topping. Spoon into a heavy-duty, zip-top plastic bag; seal and chill.
• **Place** Cream Puff Pastry in a heavy-duty, zip-top plastic bag; seal. Cut ½ inch off one corner, making a 1-inch-wide hole. Squeeze pastry into 4½-inch-long strips, 2 inches apart, on ungreased baking sheets.
• **Bake** at 400° for 30 to 40 minutes. Transfer to wire racks to cool.
• **Bring** butter, buttermilk, and cocoa to a boil over medium heat; remove from heat. Gradually add powdered sugar; stir until smooth.
• **Cut** a ½-inch hole in 1 end of each éclair with a sharp knife. Cut ¼ inch off one corner of bag with pudding mixture, making a ½-inch-wide hole. Squeeze pudding into éclairs. Spread frosting over tops. **Yield:** 12 to 15 éclairs.

Myrna Story
Waynesboro, Mississippi

Cream Puff Pastry

1 cup water
½ cup butter
1 cup all-purpose flour
4 large eggs

• **Bring** water and butter to a boil over medium heat; reduce heat to low. Add flour, and beat with a wooden spoon until mixture leaves sides of pan. Remove from heat. Add eggs, one at a time, beating until mixture is smooth. **Yield:** enough for 16 éclairs.

Terry Anderson
Brooksville, Florida

From Our Kitchen to Yours

WHACKING A WATERMELON

A big bowl of seedless watermelon chunks is so refreshing – when someone else does the carving. But we don't mind; we noticed that the seeds generally run in rows, so we adopted a linear method to carving, rather than the usual round route or haphazard approach.

First, slice off the rounded ends of the watermelon so it will stand up on end. (If the melon is huge and unwieldy, cut it in half crosswise and then cut the ends off.) With a boning knife, cut off the rind in long strips, from top to bottom.

Then cut the watermelon "meat" from top to bottom into several long planks, about 1½ inches square. At this stage, the rows of seeds are easy to get to with either the boning knife or a spoon. After cutting them out, quickly cut the seedless melon into chunks and eat them without frustration.

ORNERY ONIONS

Onions can fall into two camps: innocuous salad ingredients or lethal weapons. Cooking tames the mighty onion, but serving it raw in salads leaves its powerful kick unchecked. What to do?

This trick won't calm the onion's roar to a whisper, but it will quiet the pungent flavor just a bit. An hour before serving onions in a salad, slice and separate them into rings in a bowl, pour milk (yes, milk) over to cover, and chill. At salad time, drain the milk, rinse the onions, and crown the greenery with them.

JUST SCRAPING BY

Okay, dumping corn kernels from a can or a freezer bag is a lot quicker than shucking, washing, and then scraping fresh corn off the cob. But come on – it's summer. You can't eat the canned or frozen stuff now. (At the very least, enjoy fresh corn in its simplest form – on the cob – and save the recipes calling for kernels for later.)

We acknowledge the time, trouble, and mess. It usually goes like this: You grip a slippery ear of corn, stand it up in a bowl, and then start scraping down the cob with a knife, hoping all your fingers are out of the blade's way when the corn cob slips in the bowl. Plan B: You put the cob on a wooden cutting board for better traction. That works, but there's nothing to keep the kernels and juice from leaping into the next county, or at least over the counter and onto the floor.

Let us offer a compromise. Get out your tube pan or Bundt cakepan (the one with the hole in the middle, for angel food or pound cakes). Set it on the kitchen counter, right side up. Wedge the bottom of the cob in the hole (there's your traction); then start scraping the kernels into the moat below. We don't promise the pan will catch all flying kernels and juice, but this is as close as you'll get to having your cake, er, corn, and eating it, too.

TURNING THE TABLES

Knife on the right, fork on the left, plate smack-dab in the middle as usual. Not this time. Summer begs to break the rules, so shelve that etiquette book and set a whimsical table.

- Forget ironing a tablecloth. Spread white butcher paper over the table, arm guests with crayons, and encourage doodling throughout the meal. At evening's end, cut out the best works for framing or laminating into lighthearted coasters or place mats. For a reusable tablecloth, buy cheap canvas fabric and let guests autograph it with paint pens.

- Serve a spoonable dessert from a plastic beach pail with a matching sand shovel. Use baking shells from kitchen shops as tiny dessert plates to complete the beach theme.

- Use Oriental take-out cartons for eating in. (You can find a variety of colors and sizes at import stores.) Bring individual servings in cartons to the table and place on chargers.

- If you don't have enough plates to feed a crowd but hate to use paper ones, plan an outdoor supper served in baskets lined with cloth napkins. Shop garage sales for small baskets and discount housewares stores for affordable napkins.

- For a simple centerpiece, use cuttings from your garden's bedding plants and accent them with greenery like ivy.

AUGUST

THE FIGS OF SUMMER

Figs are fragile and bruise easily. Their tender flesh surrounds a center of tiny edible seeds, which give the fruit a poppy seed-like crunch. If you can resist eating the figs right off the tree, you can use them to make anything from inviting appetizers to delicious desserts. If you can't wait, consider this: It's said that figs are sweeter when their stems are "popped" off by hand rather than cut off with a knife. Now there's some food for thought.

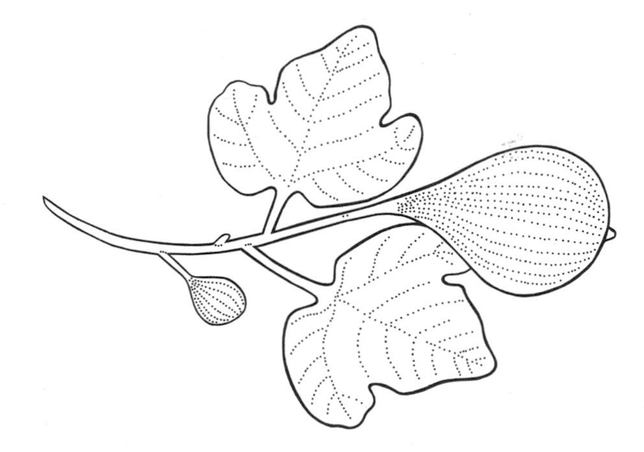

FIGS WITH PROSCIUTTO, WALNUTS, AND CREAM

We enjoyed this appetizer so much that we gave it our best rating.

1 tablespoon fresh mint leaves
2 tablespoons fresh lemon juice
¾ cup whipping cream
12 fresh figs, stemmed
12 thin slices prosciutto or ham (4 ounces)
24 walnut halves

• **Combine** mint leaves and lemon juice in a small bowl; crush mint with back of a spoon. Let stand 20 minutes; remove and discard mint.
• **Stir** whipping cream into lemon juice, and let stand until mixture is slightly thickened.
• **Cut** figs in half lengthwise; cut prosciutto in half.
• **Place** a walnut half on each fig half, and wrap each fig with a slice of prosciutto. Place figs on rack of a broiler pan.
• **Broil** 5½ inches from heat (with electric oven door partially opened) 2 to 3 minutes.
• **Pour** cream mixture onto individual serving plates, and arrange wrapped fig halves over cream mixture. **Yield:** 6 appetizer servings.

Frank Stitt
Birmingham, Alabama

MARINATED GRILLED FIGS

1 cup dry red wine
1 cup orange juice
½ teaspoon ground ginger
2 cloves garlic, pressed
12 large fresh figs, stemmed
¼ cup whipping cream

• **Combine** first 4 ingredients in a heavy-duty, zip-top plastic bag. Pierce figs several times, and place in bag. Seal and chill 1 to 2 hours.
• **Remove** figs from marinade, reserving marinade. Place marinade in a heavy saucepan.
• **Cook** marinated figs, covered with grill lid, over medium-hot coals (350° to 400°) about 5 minutes, turning figs once.
• **Bring** marinade to a boil over medium-high heat; cook 10 minutes or until reduced to ¼ cup. Stir in whipping cream, and spoon over figs. **Yield:** 4 servings.

Note: You can broil figs 5½ inches from heat (with electric oven door partially opened) 3 to 5 minutes.

QUICK STRAWBERRY-FIG PRESERVES

3 cups mashed fresh figs (about 2 pounds)
1½ cups sugar
1 (3-ounce) package strawberry-flavored gelatin

• **Combine** figs and sugar in a heavy saucepan; cook over medium heat 2 minutes, stirring constantly. Gradually stir in gelatin, and cook over low heat 15 minutes, stirring constantly.
• **Spoon** preserves into hot, sterilized jars, filling to ¼ inch from top. Remove air bubbles; wipe jar rims. Cover at once with metal lids, and screw on bands.
• **Process** in boiling-water bath 5 minutes. Store in refrigerator after opening. **Yield:** 4 half-pints.

Nora Henshaw
Okemah, Oklahoma

FIG FLOWERS

A small sharp knife works best for cutting figs. If you don't want to make flowers, just cut the figs in half lengthwise; they'll taste just as good.

12 large fresh figs, stemmed
¼ cup orange liqueur *
1 (8-ounce) package cream cheese, softened
2 tablespoons honey
2 tablespoons whipping cream
2 tablespoons sour cream
Garnish: orange rind strips

• **Stand** figs upright; slice from stem end into 5 or 6 wedges, cutting to, but not through, bottom. Gently separate wedges to resemble a flower. Place figs on a serving plate; drizzle with liqueur.
• **Beat** cream cheese at medium speed with an electric mixer about 2 minutes or until fluffy. Add honey, whipping cream, and sour cream; beat 1 minute. Pipe or dollop mixture onto center of each fig. Garnish, if desired. **Yield:** 4 servings.

* You can substitute ¼ cup orange juice for liqueur.

SUGAR-CRUSTED FIGS

¼ cup water
1 tablespoon vanilla extract
1½ pounds fresh figs, stemmed
1¼ cups superfine sugar
1 cup whipping cream
1 teaspoon vanilla extract

• **Combine** water and 1 tablespoon vanilla in a 1-cup liquid measuring cup. Dip each fig in mixture, and dredge in sugar, coating each thickly. Place figs into lightly greased individual shallow baking dishes.
• **Bake** at 425° for 15 to 20 minutes.
• **Combine** whipping cream and 1 teaspoon vanilla; beat at high speed with an electric mixer until soft peaks form. Spoon mixture over warm figs. **Yield:** 4 servings.

Fig trees are important to Southerners. When the old family homestead is put up for sale, the relatives are usually out back, digging up the fig tree to put in their yard. Fig trees just don't go with the house.

If you're not lucky enough to have a tree of your own, depend on the generosity of others. Folks are often quite willing to share a pint or two of fruit. If you want more, you'd better go to the farmers market or grocery store and try your luck.

FIG PRESERVES

3½ cups sugar
2 cups water
4 thin slices lemon, divided
2 pounds fresh figs, stemmed

• **Bring** sugar, water, and 1 lemon slice to a boil in a Dutch oven, stirring constantly. Cook 5 minutes, stirring occasionally. Add figs, a few at a time; cook 12 minutes or until a candy thermometer registers 220° and figs are clear, stirring occasionally. Add remaining 3 lemon slices, and cook 1 minute. Remove from heat.
• **Pack** figs in hot, sterilized jars, filling to ¼ inch from top. Cover fruit with hot syrup, filling to ¼ inch from top. Remove air bubbles; wipe jar rims. Cover at once with metal lids, and screw on bands.
• **Process** in boiling-water bath 5 minutes. Store in refrigerator after opening. **Yield:** 5 half-pints.

Zada Stafford
Salisbury, North Carolina

Fresh Catch

Jump off the deep end and try different types of fish prepared in fresh ways. For starters take a look at the recipes featured here, including specialties from Chef Chris McDonald of the Atlanta Fish Market. You're sure to be hooked on seafood in no time.

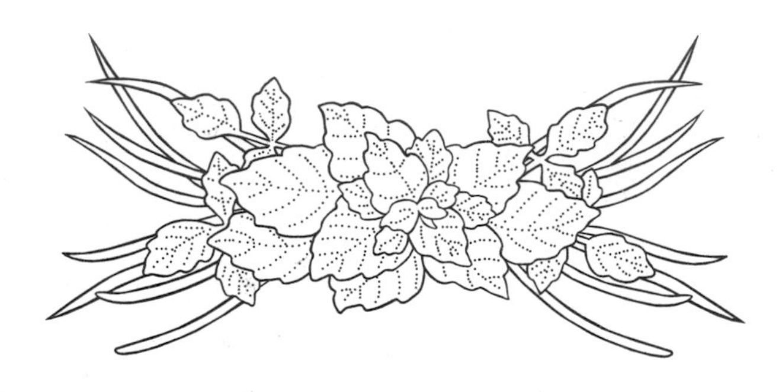

SWORDFISH WITH CASHEW-AND-CRACKED PEPPER CRUST

1½ cups cashews
2 tablespoons cracked pepper
4 (8-ounce) swordfish steaks
2 tablespoons olive oil
Garnish: fresh basil sprigs

• **Position** knife blade in food processor bowl; add cashews, and process until ground, stopping once to scrape down sides. Combine cashews and pepper in a shallow dish; coat both sides of swordfish with mixture.
• **Pour** oil into a large skillet; place over medium heat until hot. Add swordfish, and cook 10 minutes on each side or until fish flakes easily when tested with a fork. Garnish, if desired. Serve with grits, green beans, mushrooms, and bell pepper strips. **Yield:** 4 servings.

Chef Chris McDonald
Atlanta Fish Market
Atlanta, Georgia

HONG KONG-STYLE SEA BASS

1 (2-inch) piece fresh ginger
3 green onions
½ cup vegetable oil, divided
4 cloves garlic, crushed
1 pound fresh spinach, washed and trimmed
4 (6-ounce) sea bass or grouper fillets
¼ cup sesame oil
⅓ cup reduced-sodium soy sauce
⅓ cup dry sherry
⅓ cup water
2 teaspoons sugar

• **Peel** ginger, and cut into thin strips. Cut green onions into 2-inch thin strips; set ginger and green onions aside.
• **Pour** ¼ cup vegetable oil into a large skillet; place over high heat until hot. Add garlic, and cook 5 to 7 seconds, stirring constantly; remove and discard garlic. Add spinach to skillet; cook, stirring constantly, until lightly wilted. Spoon spinach onto individual serving plates, and keep warm.
• **Place** fish in a steamer basket or bamboo steamer over boiling water; cover and steam 8 minutes or until fish flakes easily when tested with a fork. Place fish on spinach; top with ginger and green onions.
• **Combine** remaining ¼ cup vegetable oil and sesame oil in skillet; place skillet over high heat until hot. Drizzle evenly over fish.
• **Bring** soy sauce and next 3 ingredients to a boil in skillet. Drizzle half of mixture over fish, and serve immediately with remaining mixture. **Yield:** 4 servings.

Chef Chris McDonald
Atlanta Fish Market
Atlanta, Georgia

QUICK FISH FILLETS

This quick and easy recipe results in fantastic fish from the oven or microwave.

1 pound orange roughy fillets
¼ cup fine, dry breadcrumbs
1 teaspoon chopped fresh parsley
½ teaspoon paprika
¼ cup plain yogurt
1 teaspoon prepared mustard
Vegetable cooking spray
Lemon wedges

• **Cut** orange roughy into serving-size pieces.
• **Combine** breadcrumbs, parsley, and paprika in a shallow dish.
• **Combine** yogurt and mustard. Dip fillets in yogurt mixture, and dredge in breadcrumb mixture; place in a 9-inch square baking dish coated with cooking spray.
• **Bake** at 450° for 20 minutes. Or microwave, covered with a paper towel, at HIGH 4 minutes or until fish flakes easily when tested with a fork. Serve with lemon wedges. **Yield:** 2 servings.

Laura Morris
Bunnell, Florida

INLAND GRILLED TUNA

1/4 cup soy sauce
1 tablespoon maple syrup
1 tablespoon prepared horseradish
4 (6-ounce) tuna steaks
Vegetable cooking spray

• **Combine** first 3 ingredients in a shallow dish; add tuna, turning to coat. Cover tuna and chill 1 hour, turning occasionally.
• **Remove** tuna from marinade, discarding marinade. Coat food rack with cooking spray.
• **Place** tuna on rack over medium-hot coals (350° to 400°); cook, covered with grill lid, 2 minutes on each side or to desired degree of doneness. **Yield:** 4 servings.

Joel Knox
Inland Seafood Company
Atlanta, Georgia

BATTER-FRIED GROUPER SANDWICHES

(pictured on page 222)

The Dill Mayonnaise is also great with crab cakes or cold steamed lobster.

1 cup all-purpose flour
1/4 cup cornstarch
1 tablespoon garlic powder
1/2 teaspoon pepper
4 (4-ounce) grouper fillets
1/2 to 3/4 cup buttermilk
Canola oil
4 onion sandwich buns, toasted
Dill Mayonnaise
Lettuce leaves
2 large tomatoes, sliced
Garnishes: fresh chives, lemon twists

• **Combine** first 4 ingredients in a shallow dish. Dredge grouper in flour mixture; dip in buttermilk, and dredge in flour mixture again.
• **Pour** oil to depth of 3 inches into a Dutch oven; heat to 350°. Fry fillets in hot oil 5 minutes or until golden; drain on paper towels.
• **Spread** Dill Mayonnaise on buns; place each fillet on a bun with lettuce and tomato, and add top half of bun. Garnish, if desired. Serve immediately. **Yield:** 4 sandwiches.

Dill Mayonnaise

1/2 cup mayonnaise
1 tablespoon chopped fresh parsley
1 tablespoon lemon juice
1 teaspoon chopped fresh dill
1 teaspoon capers
1 teaspoon chopped sweet pickle
1/8 teaspoon ground red pepper

• **Combine** all ingredients in a bowl, stirring well; cover and chill. **Yield:** about 2/3 cup.

Chef Chris McDonald,
Atlanta Fish Market
Atlanta, Georgia

FUSSY ABOUT FISH

Be sure to follow these guidelines when you shop for fresh seafood.

▪ While firmer fish fillets such as white fish are safe lying directly on ice, place a protective barrier (either paper or plastic) between finer fillets and the ice.

▪ Look for fish with clear eyes and reddish gills, signs of freshness.

▪ For best results, cook seafood the same day you buy it.

▪ When a recipe calls for a medium-textured, mild fish, try orange roughy, flounder, or tilapia. For rich flavor try thick, firm steaks of tuna, salmon, or swordfish.

▪ Many markets that have crab and lobster will steam your purchase while you shop.

▪ If your cooking method for fish is only fried, try serving it poached, steamed, baked, blackened, or grilled.

PERFECT PRIME RIB

We think the recipe for Perfect Prime Rib really *is* perfect. Reader Lyn Mulhearn Delcaro instructed us to cook it under a blanket of rock salt sprinkled with water. She also suggested using a hammer to crack into the rock salt because it gets *rock hard* when cooked. This coating keeps the meat tender. And the end result isn't too salty.

The disposable roasting pan is a must. You'll be thankful you don't have to scrub the clingy rock salt from your favorite pan.

PERFECT PRIME RIB

1 (4- to 6-pound) boneless beef rib roast
1 tablespoon Worcestershire sauce
1 teaspoon garlic powder
3 tablespoons cracked pepper
2 (4-pound) packages rock salt
1/2 cup water

• **Brush** roast with Worcestershire sauce; sprinkle with garlic powder. Rub pepper on all sides of roast.
• **Pour** rock salt to depth of 1/2 inch in a disposable aluminum foil roasting pan; place roast in center of pan. Add remaining rock salt, covering roast. Sprinkle with water.
• **Bake** at 500° for 12 minutes per pound or until meat thermometer registers 145° (medium-rare) or to desired degree of doneness. Crack salt with a hammer; remove roast, and brush away rock salt. **Yield:** 8 servings.

Lyn Mulhearn Delcaro
Starkville, Mississippi

Fresh Ideas for Fettuccine

When testing these saucy fettuccine recipes, we tried several flavors of pasta, including spinach, tomato-basil, tomato, lemon-pepper, squid ink, and saffron. We especially liked the tomato-basil flavor in Cajun Chicken Fettuccine. Use your favorite flavored pasta, and turn supper into a special occasion.

SCALLOP-MUSHROOM FETTUCCINE

6 ounces fettuccine, uncooked
4 slices bacon
1 tablespoon butter or margarine
1 pound sea scallops
½ pound sliced fresh mushrooms
¼ cup dry white wine
1 tablespoon diced pimiento
1 cup whipping cream
½ cup freshly grated Parmesan cheese
½ teaspoon garlic powder
¼ teaspoon salt
¼ teaspoon pepper
Grated Parmesan cheese (optional)

• **Cook** pasta according to package directions; drain and keep warm.
• **Cook** bacon in a large skillet until crisp; remove bacon, reserving 1 tablespoon drippings in skillet. Crumble bacon, and set aside.
• **Add** butter to drippings in skillet, and cook over medium-high heat until melted. Add scallops and sliced mushrooms; cook 4 to 5 minutes or until scallops are opaque. Remove scallops, and keep warm.
• **Add** wine to skillet; bring to a boil. Reduce heat, and simmer 15 minutes or until reduced by half.
• **Stir** in bacon, pimiento, and whipping cream, and cook 10 minutes or until mixture is slightly thickened, stirring occasionally.
• **Add** ½ cup Parmesan cheese and next 3 ingredients, stirring until cheese melts; stir in scallops. Spoon over pasta, and sprinkle with additional Parmesan cheese, if desired. Serve immediately. **Yield:** 2 to 3 servings.

Janie Baur
Spring, Texas

FETTUCCINE WITH SHRIMP AND TOMATOES

1½ pounds unpeeled medium-size fresh shrimp
8 ounces fettuccine, uncooked
2 (14.5-ounce) cans diced tomatoes, undrained
1 teaspoon dried basil
3 cloves garlic, minced
2 tablespoons minced shallot
½ teaspoon freshly ground pepper
¼ teaspoon salt
¼ cup olive oil
Freshly grated Romano cheese

• **Peel** shrimp, and devein, if desired.
• **Cook** pasta according to package directions; drain and keep warm.
• **Drain** diced tomato, reserving ¼ cup liquid.
• **Cook** shrimp, tomato, reserved liquid, basil, and next 4 ingredients in oil in a large skillet 5 to 7 minutes or until shrimp turn pink, stirring often. Spoon over pasta; sprinkle with cheese. Serve immediately. **Yield:** 4 servings.

Gail B. Weller
St. Louis, Missouri

CAJUN CHICKEN FETTUCCINE

1 (10-ounce) package tomato-basil fettuccine
1 teaspoon Cajun seasoning
½ teaspoon cracked pepper
4 skinned and boned chicken breast halves
1 cup water
½ teaspoon salt
1 pound broccoli, cut into flowerets
¼ cup butter or margarine
1 clove garlic, minced
1 tablespoon cornstarch
1½ tablespoons water
2 cups half-and-half
¼ teaspoon salt
¼ teaspoon ground red pepper
¼ teaspoon ground black pepper
⅓ cup freshly grated Parmesan cheese
Grated Parmesan cheese (optional)

• **Cook** pasta according to package directions; drain and keep warm.
• **Sprinkle** Cajun seasoning and cracked pepper over chicken; place chicken in a lightly greased 13- x 9- x 2-inch pan.
• **Bake** at 350° for 15 to 20 minutes or until done; cool slightly. Cut chicken crosswise into thin strips.
• **Combine** 1 cup water and ½ teaspoon salt in a large skillet; bring to a boil. Add broccoli; cover and cook 3 to 4 minutes or until crisp-tender. Drain.
• **Melt** butter in skillet; add minced garlic, and cook 2 minutes, stirring often. Set aside 1 cup broccoli flowerets; add remaining broccoli flowerets to garlic in skillet, and cook 2 minutes.
• **Combine** cornstarch and 1½ tablespoons water, stirring until smooth; stir in half-and-half. Gradually add cornstarch mixture to broccoli mixture.
• **Bring** to a boil over medium heat, stirring constantly. Boil 1 minute, stirring constantly. Add ¼ teaspoon salt, red pepper, black pepper, and ⅓ cup Parmesan cheese, stirring until cheese melts. Spoon over pasta; top with remaining 1 cup broccoli. Sprinkle with additional Parmesan cheese, if desired. Serve immediately. **Yield:** 4 servings.

Jill Ann Kelley
Essex, Missouri

QUICK & EASY

SALADS FOR SANDWICHES

Some of the hottest days of summer are still ahead. But with these cool salad sandwich recipes in hand, you'll never have to touch the cooktop or oven.

HAM-AND-PINEAPPLE SLAW SANDWICHES

2 cups chopped cooked ham
3 cups shredded cabbage
1 (8-ounce) can pineapple tidbits, undrained
⅔ cup mayonnaise
1 cup (4 ounces) shredded Cheddar cheese
½ teaspoon salt
½ teaspoon pepper
4 French sandwich rolls

• **Combine** first 7 ingredients, stirring gently. Spoon onto bottoms of rolls; cover with tops, and serve immediately. **Yield:** 4 servings.

Dorsella Utter
Louisville, Kentucky

VEGETABLE PITA SANDWICHES

1 (3-ounce) package cream cheese, softened
1 cup buttermilk
1 cup mayonnaise
1 (8-ounce) carton sour cream
1 (1-ounce) envelope Ranch-style salad dressing mix
2 tablespoons chopped fresh or frozen chives
2 pita rounds, cut in half
Lettuce leaves
1 cucumber, thinly sliced
2 tomatoes, chopped
1 medium onion, chopped
2 carrots, shredded (optional)

• **Beat** cream cheese at medium speed with an electric mixer until fluffy; beat in buttermilk and next 4 ingredients. Set dressing aside.
• **Line** pita halves with lettuce leaves; fill with cucumber, tomato, onion, and carrot, if desired. Serve with dressing, and fruit kabobs, if desired. **Yield:** 4 servings.

Note: You can use dressing on salads, as a dip for vegetables, or as a topping for baked potatoes.

Jim Griffith
Guntersville, Alabama

TUNA ROLL SANDWICHES

Brown bag tip: Pita bread pockets make this sandwich faster to prepare.

1 (3-ounce) package cream cheese, softened
2 tablespoons mayonnaise
1 tablespoon lemon juice
½ teaspoon pepper
¼ teaspoon salt
1 (10-ounce) can solid white tuna in spring water, drained and flaked *
½ cup chopped purple onion
6 large lettuce leaves
6 (8-inch) flour tortillas

• **Combine** first 5 ingredients, stirring until smooth; add tuna and onion, stirring well.
• **Place** lettuce on tortillas, and trim to fit. Spoon tuna mixture onto lettuce. Roll tortilla up, and tie with kitchen string. (Remove string before serving.) Serve with marinated vegetables. **Yield:** 6 servings.

* You can substitute 1 (10-ounce) can white chicken, drained and flaked, for the tuna.

Edith Askins
Greenville, Texas

SPREAD OUT

Wake up your meat-and-cheese sandwiches with one of these flavorful spreads. They'll stay fresh up to one week in the refrigerator.

Dijon-Mayo Spread: Combine ½ cup mayonnaise, ¼ cup Dijon mustard, 1 tablespoon prepared horseradish, 1 tablespoon Worcestershire sauce, 1 teaspoon pepper, ¼ teaspoon salt, and a dash of hot sauce, stirring well.

Darryl R. Turgeon
New Orleans, Louisiana

Garlic-Butter Spread: Combine ½ cup butter or margarine, softened; 1 clove garlic, minced; 2 teaspoons grated Parmesan cheese; and 1 teaspoon finely chopped fresh parsley. This spread is also great for garlic bread.

Patricia Clark
Baton Rouge, Louisiana

Add Avocado

When you want to add a layer of flavor and texture to salads or sandwiches, try an avocado. The creamy green flesh is mild, allowing it to blend well with other flavors. Bacon, chicken, cheese, and citrus all pair well with it. Select fruit that yields to gentle pressure from your hand; or let avocados ripen at room temperature for several days. Cut and peel avocado just before serving to prevent browning.

AVOCADO-POTATO SALAD WITH HORSERADISH DRESSING

1 pound baking potatoes
3 avocados, peeled and cubed
2 medium-size red apples, cubed
¾ cup chopped green onions
½ cup chopped walnuts or pecans, toasted
1 tablespoon chopped fresh parsley
Horseradish Dressing

• **Cook** potatoes in boiling salted water to cover 20 to 30 minutes or until tender; drain. Cool; peel and cube.
• **Combine** potato, avocado, apple, and green onions in a large bowl; toss gently. Sprinkle with walnuts and parsley; cover and chill. Serve immediately with Horseradish Dressing. **Yield:** 6 servings.

Horseradish Dressing

1 (8-ounce) carton sour cream
1 tablespoon prepared horseradish
1 tablespoon lemon juice
½ teaspoon salt
½ teaspoon freshly ground pepper

• **Combine** all ingredients; cover and chill. **Yield:** 1 cup.

ROYAL CURRIED CHICKEN SALAD

½ cup sliced almonds, toasted
2 cups chopped cooked chicken
¼ cup chopped water chestnuts
½ pound seedless green grapes, halved
1 (8-ounce) can pineapple chunks, drained
½ cup chopped celery
¾ cup mayonnaise
1 teaspoon curry powder
2 teaspoons lemon juice
2 teaspoons soy sauce
2 avocados

• **Combine** first 6 ingredients; set aside.
• **Combine** mayonnaise, curry powder, lemon juice, and soy sauce in a bowl; spoon mixture over chicken mixture, and toss gently to coat. Cover and chill at least 4 hours.
• **Peel** and chop avocados; sprinkle over salad, and serve immediately. **Yield:** 6 servings.

Cindy Sullivan
Tallahassee, Florida

CHICKEN-AVOCADO DAGWOODS

(pictured on page 185)

Mash avocados the clean and easy way: Place peeled halves in a heavy-duty, zip-top plastic bag; seal and squeeze.

8 slices sourdough bread, toasted
2 tablespoons mayonnaise
2 avocados, peeled and mashed
8 slices purple onion
4 (1-ounce) slices Monterey Jack or provolone cheese
8 slices bacon, cooked
8 lettuce leaves
8 slices tomato
8 (¼-inch-thick) slices roasted chicken breast
⅛ teaspoon salt
⅛ teaspoon pepper

• **Spread** 1 side of each bread slice evenly with mayonnaise; spread half of slices with mashed avocado, and top with onion and next 5 ingredients. Sprinkle with salt and pepper. Top with remaining bread slices; serve sandwiches immediately. **Yield:** 4 servings.

Karen Lesemann
Charleston, South Carolina

Easy Edibles

- For a simple, elegant appetizer, fill the center of an avocado half with balsamic vinegar.
- Wrap avocado slices with ham or smoked salmon slices.
- Marinate mixed vegetables and avocado cubes in French or Italian salad dressing; serve in pita bread halves.
- Smooth avocado and crispy bacon are great together. You can add avocado slices to a BLT; sprinkle cooked, crumbled bacon on salads containing avocado; or simply add bacon to your favorite guacamole recipe.
- Spread mashed avocado on toast, and sprinkle with salt and pepper for a tasty snack.

HOOKED ON TUNA

Not many menus are planned around a pantry standby like tuna. But take another look at this budget staple. We wouldn't exactly call any of the following recipes *gourmet*, but they do show that canned tuna has plenty of taste-pleasing potential.

The secret to these recipes is thoroughly draining the tuna.

HOT TUNA MELTS

If you're hooked on coffee shop tuna salad sandwiches, you'll love these heated versions.

1 (6-ounce) can solid white tuna in spring water, drained and flaked
1/3 cup mayonnaise
1/4 cup sliced pimiento-stuffed olives, drained
3 hard-cooked eggs, chopped
3 tablespoons sweet pickle relish
2 tablespoons finely chopped onion
2 English muffins, split and lightly toasted
4 (1-ounce) slices sharp Cheddar cheese

• **Combine** first 6 ingredients, stirring well. Spoon evenly onto muffin halves; place on a baking sheet.
• **Broil** 5½ inches from heat (with electric oven door partially opened) 2 minutes. Top each with a cheese slice; broil 1 minute or until cheese melts. **Yield:** 4 servings.

Southwestern Tuna Melt: Prepare tuna mixture as directed, substituting 2 to 4 tablespoons chopped pickled jalapeño peppers for olives. Omit English muffins. Lightly brush 1 side of 4 (6-inch) flour tortillas with ¾ teaspoon melted butter; place, buttered side up, on an ungreased baking sheet, and bake at 400° for 3 minutes. Turn tortillas over, and bake 1 additional minute. Spread buttered sides evenly with tuna mixture, and broil as directed for 1 minute. Top each with a cheese slice, and broil 1 minute or until cheese melts. **Yield:** 4 servings.

TUNA TAPENADE

Tuna makes a lower fat substitute for the traditional amount of ripe olives in this Mediterranean-inspired appetizer spread.

½ pound fresh mushrooms, chopped
2 tablespoons olive oil
1/3 cup chopped onion
2 cloves garlic, chopped
½ teaspoon dried thyme
1 tablespoon lemon juice
1 (6-ounce) can solid white tuna in spring water, drained
¼ teaspoon salt
½ teaspoon freshly ground pepper
½ (8-ounce) package cream cheese, softened
2 tablespoons sliced ripe olives
2 tablespoons capers
2 tablespoons chopped fresh parsley

• **Cook** mushrooms in olive oil in a heavy skillet over medium-high heat 5 minutes, stirring constantly.
• **Stir** in onion, garlic, and thyme; reduce heat to medium, and cook until onion is tender.
• **Add** lemon juice, and cook until liquid is absorbed.
• **Position** knife blade in food processor bowl, and add mushroom mixture, tuna, salt, and pepper. Pulse 4 times.
• **Add** cream cheese to processor bowl, and pulse 4 times or until mixture is blended. Shape mixture into a mound on a serving plate; top with ripe olives, capers, and parsley. Serve spread with toasted baguette slices or melba toast. **Yield:** 1½ cups.

Z. Stiff
Birmingham, Alabama

TUNA NACHOS

To make a lighter version, use baked tortilla chips, reduced-fat cheese, and light sour cream.

1 (10-ounce) bag tortilla chips
1 (8-ounce) package shredded colby-Monterey Jack cheese blend
2 (6-ounce) cans solid white tuna in spring water, drained and flaked
1 cup chopped tomato
¼ to ½ cup pickled jalapeño pepper slices
½ cup sliced green onions
Salsa
Guacamole
Sour cream
Garnish: pickled jalapeño pepper slices

• **Arrange** tortilla chips in a single layer, overlapping edges, in a 15- x 10- x 1-inch jellyroll pan or on ovenproof plates. Sprinkle evenly with 1 cup cheese, tuna, tomato, jalapeño pepper slices, and sliced green onions. Top with remaining cheese.
• **Bake** at 375° for 8 minutes or until cheese melts. Top with salsa, guacamole, and sour cream. Garnish, if desired. **Yield:** 8 appetizer or 4 main-dish servings.

Pam Hamby
St. Petersburg, Florida

All-Star Almonds

Almonds can be star makers. Trout amandine is a perfect example: The addition of buttery almonds turns basic fish into a timeless classic. Try Debbie Slatter's version, along with these other recipes that display the subtle charm of almonds, and we're sure that you'll be pleased.

CLASSIC TROUT AMANDINE

A perfect marriage – delicate trout with buttery almonds and a rich sauce.

2 cups milk
2 teaspoons salt, divided
2 dashes of hot sauce
6 trout fillets
3/4 cup all-purpose flour
1/2 teaspoon pepper
1 1/4 cups butter or margarine, divided
1 tablespoon olive oil
1/2 cup sliced almonds
2 tablespoons lemon juice
2 teaspoons Worcestershire sauce
1/4 cup chopped fresh parsley

• **Combine** milk, 1 teaspoon salt, and hot sauce in a 13- x 9- x 2-inch baking dish; add fillets, turning to coat. Cover and chill 2 hours. Drain, discarding marinade.
• **Combine** flour and pepper in a shallow dish.
• **Melt** 1/4 cup butter in a large skillet over medium heat; add oil. Dredge fillets in flour mixture; add to skillet, and cook 2 minutes on each side or until golden. Remove to a serving platter; keep warm.
• **Combine** remaining 1 cup butter and almonds in a saucepan; cook over medium heat until lightly browned. Add lemon juice, Worcestershire sauce, and remaining 1 teaspoon salt; cook 2 minutes. Remove from heat; stir in parsley. Pour over fillets, and serve immediately. **Yield:** 6 servings.

Debbie Slatter
Kenner, Louisiana

INDIAN RICE

If you don't have saffron on hand or can't find it at your grocery store, use 1/8 teaspoon ground turmeric.

1 1/2 cups basmati rice or other long-grain rice *
3 cups chicken broth
3 tablespoons butter or margarine
3 cups chopped onion
1 clove garlic, minced
1/4 cup finely chopped mango chutney
1/3 cup slivered almonds, toasted
1/2 cup currants or raisins
1/4 teaspoon threads of saffron or 1/8 teaspoon ground saffron
1/4 teaspoon salt
1/4 teaspoon pepper

• **Combine** all ingredients in a large saucepan; bring mixture to a boil over high heat, stirring occasionally. Cover, reduce heat, and simmer 20 to 25 minutes or until liquid is absorbed. **Yield:** 6 servings.

* Substitute 1 1/2 cups yellow rice for basmati rice; omit saffron.

Myrna M. Ruiz
Marietta, Georgia

ALMOND BRITTLE COOKIES WITH ICE CREAM BALLS

1 cup butter or margarine, softened
2 teaspoons instant coffee granules
1 teaspoon salt
3/4 teaspoon almond extract
1 cup sugar
2 cups all-purpose flour
1 cup (6 ounces) semisweet chocolate mini-morsels
4 1/2 cups finely chopped almonds, toasted and divided
1 gallon vanilla ice cream
Fudge topping

• **Beat** first 4 ingredients in a large mixing bowl at medium speed with an electric mixer; gradually add sugar, beating well. Stir in flour, morsels, and 1/2 cup almonds with a wooden spoon.
• **Press** dough into an ungreased 15- x 10- x 1-inch jellyroll pan.
• **Bake** at 350° for 15 minutes. Cut into triangles, and cool cookies in pan on a wire rack.
• **Scoop** ice cream into 12 balls; roll balls in remaining 4 cups chopped almonds, and place on a baking sheet. Freeze until firm.
• **Spoon** topping onto individual serving plates; top with ice cream balls, and serve immediately with cookies. **Yield:** 12 servings.

Elaine McVinney
Alexandria, Virginia

Garden Greens

If you planted a crop of greens, you have a good reason to hurry autumn along. The sweetest greens are those that have been kissed by frost. But if you can't wait, check with local markets for early arrivals. A pinch of sugar will help tame any bitterness.

CREAMY KALE SOUP

Be sure to use green kale – variegated kale is better for garnishing than eating.

1¼ pounds fresh kale
2 (14½-ounce) cans ready-to-serve chicken broth
1 cup water
1½ pounds red potatoes, chopped
1½ cups chopped cooked ham
¾ teaspoon salt
2 to 3 teaspoons pepper
1 large onion, cut in half and sliced
2 cups whipping cream
2 (15-ounce) cans white beans, rinsed and drained
2 tablespoons butter or margarine, softened
2 tablespoons all-purpose flour

• **Remove** and discard stems and discolored spots from kale; rinse with cold water, and drain. Tear into bite-size pieces; set aside.
• **Combine** broth, 1 cup water, and next 4 ingredients in a large Dutch oven; bring to a boil. Reduce heat, and simmer 20 minutes, stirring occasionally. Stir in kale and onion; simmer 20 minutes, stirring occasionally. Add whipping cream and beans; bring to a boil, stirring often.
• **Combine** butter and flour, stirring until blended. Stir into soup, and simmer 10 minutes, stirring occasionally. **Yield:** 16 cups.

Pat Pittman
Boone, North Carolina

RISOTTO WITH COLLARDS

Arborio rice adds a creamy texture.

½ pound fresh collard greens
1 small onion, finely chopped
1 small carrot, finely chopped
2 tablespoons olive oil
1 cup uncooked Arborio rice
3 cloves garlic, finely chopped
2 (14½-ounce) cans ready-to-serve chicken broth
½ teaspoon salt
¼ teaspoon pepper
1 cup grated Parmesan cheese

• **Remove** and discard stems and discolored spots from collards; rinse with cold water. Drain and coarsely chop.
• **Cook** onion and carrot in oil in a large Dutch oven 2 minutes, stirring often. Add rice, and cook 5 minutes or until golden. Add collards and garlic, and cook 1 minute.
• **Stir** in broth; cover and cook over low heat until liquid is absorbed, stirring occasionally. Stir in salt, pepper, and cheese; serve immediately. **Yield:** 4 to 6 servings.

SPINACH PIE PARMA

2 cups garlic-onion croutons, crushed
¼ cup butter or margarine, melted
1 pound fresh spinach, torn *
¼ cup water
3 large eggs, lightly beaten
1 cup small-curd cottage cheese
¼ cup freshly grated Parmesan cheese
¼ cup chopped onion
2 tablespoons sour cream
2 to 3 cloves garlic, pressed
½ teaspoon salt
⅛ teaspoon ground red pepper
4 ounces Monterey Jack cheese, cut into ¼-inch cubes
2 tablespoons freshly grated Parmesan cheese

• **Combine** croutons and butter, stirring well; press into bottom of an 8-inch square baking dish.
• **Combine** spinach and ¼ cup water in a skillet; cover and cook over medium heat 4 minutes or until wilted. Drain well on paper towels.
• **Combine** spinach, eggs, and next 7 ingredients, stirring well; stir in Monterey Jack cheese, and spoon over prepared crust.
• **Bake** at 350° for 35 minutes or until knife inserted in center comes out clean. Sprinkle with 2 tablespoons Parmesan cheese, and let stand 5 minutes. **Yield:** 6 servings.

* You can substitute 1 (10-ounce) package frozen chopped spinach, thawed and well drained, for fresh.

COME HOME TO BREAKFAST

Eat your breakfast . . . for supper. "Breakfast dinners" are fantastic meals created from just a few ordinary ingredients. With these savory recipes, breakfast will become your favorite meal – no matter which time you eat it.

CREAM CHEESE QUICHE

½ (15-ounce) package refrigerated piecrusts
1 tablespoon butter or margarine
¼ cup chopped onion
1 (8-ounce) package cream cheese, cubed
¾ cup milk
4 large eggs, lightly beaten
1 cup finely chopped ham
1 (2-ounce) jar diced pimiento, undrained
¼ teaspoon dried dillweed
⅛ teaspoon pepper

• **Fit** piecrust into a 9-inch quiche dish according to package directions; prick bottom and sides with a fork.
• **Bake** piecrust at 425° for 12 minutes; set aside.
• **Melt** butter in a small saucepan over medium-high heat; add onion, and cook until tender. Add cream cheese and milk; cook over low heat, whisking until cheese melts. Gradually whisk about one-fourth of hot mixture into eggs; add to remaining hot mixture, whisking constantly. Whisk in ham and remaining ingredients; pour into prepared crust.
• **Bake** at 350° for 35 to 40 minutes or until set. **Yield:** 6 to 8 servings.

BELL PEPPER FRITTATA

This earned our highest rating – it's delicious and beautiful. A baking sheet will catch any liquid that leaks from the springform pan.

3 cloves garlic, minced
1 large purple onion, sliced
2 red bell peppers, cut into thin strips
1 yellow bell pepper, cut into thin strips
3 tablespoons olive oil, divided
2 yellow squash, thinly sliced
2 zucchini, thinly sliced
½ pound fresh mushrooms, sliced
6 large eggs
¼ cup whipping cream
2½ to 3 teaspoons salt
2 teaspoons freshly ground pepper
8 slices sandwich bread, cubed
1 (8-ounce) package cream cheese, cubed
2 cups (8 ounces) shredded Swiss cheese

- **Cook** first 4 ingredients in 1 tablespoon oil in a large skillet until tender. Drain and pat dry; set aside.
- **Cook** squash and zucchini in 1 tablespoon oil in skillet until tender. Drain and pat dry; set aside.
- **Cook** mushrooms in remaining tablespoon oil in skillet until tender. Drain and pat dry; set aside.
- **Whisk** together eggs and next 3 ingredients in a large bowl; stir in vegetables, half of bread cubes, cream cheese, and Swiss cheese. Press remaining bread cubes in bottom of a lightly greased 10-inch springform pan, and place on a baking sheet. Pour vegetable mixture into pan.
- **Bake** at 325° for 1 hour, covering with aluminum foil after 45 minutes to prevent excessive browning. Serve warm. **Yield:** 8 servings.

Yvonne Greer
Mauldin, South Carolina

VEGETABLE-EGG SAUTÉ

3 tablespoons butter or margarine
2 medium onions, sliced
3 green bell peppers, thinly sliced
2 medium tomatoes, thinly sliced
½ cup chopped fresh parsley
¾ teaspoon salt
½ teaspoon pepper
6 large eggs
½ cup (2 ounces) shredded Muenster cheese

- **Melt** butter in a 12-inch cast-iron skillet over medium-high heat; add onion, and cook 7 minutes, stirring often. Add bell pepper, tomato, and parsley; cook 7 minutes, stirring constantly. Drain. Stir in salt and pepper.
- **Make** 6 shallow wells in vegetables with back of a spoon; break an egg into each well.
- **Cook** 6 minutes or until set. Sprinkle evenly with cheese; cover and cook 1 to 2 minutes or until cheese melts. Serve on toast or English muffins. **Yield:** 6 servings.

Note: For firmer eggs, cook 6 minutes; then broil 5½ inches from heat (with electric oven door partially opened) 2 additional minutes. Sprinkle with cheese; broil 1 additional minute or until cheese melts.

Martha Smith Vaughn
Tarrant, Alabama

FRENCH BREAD FIX-UPS

Bread alone is just bread. But thick, crusty French bread with butter, herbs, and cheese is an *event*.

Here we've transformed loaves into appetizers and snacks – even a container for dip. These bread winners will give a boost to weeknight meals and can be the life of a spontaneous party.

TENNESSEE SIN

With a name like this, it's got to be good. The bread loaf is the container for a rich, cheesy ham dip.

2 (16-ounce) loaves French bread
1 (8-ounce) package cream cheese, softened
1 (8-ounce) carton sour cream
2 cups (8 ounces) shredded Cheddar cheese
½ cup chopped cooked ham
⅓ cup chopped green onions
⅓ cup chopped green bell pepper
¼ teaspoon Worcestershire sauce
Paprika

- **Slice** off top fourth of 1 bread loaf. Hollow out bottom section, leaving a 1-inch shell.
- **Cut** bread top, inside pieces, and remaining bread loaf into 1-inch cubes; place bread shell and cubes on a large baking sheet.
- **Bake** at 350° for 12 minutes or until lightly browned.
- **Beat** cream cheese at medium speed with an electric mixer until smooth; add sour cream, beating until creamy.
- **Stir** in Cheddar cheese and next 4 ingredients. Spoon into bread shell, wrap in heavy-duty aluminum foil, and place on a baking sheet.
- **Bake** at 350° for 30 minutes; unwrap and place on a serving platter. Sprinkle with paprika; serve with toasted bread cubes. **Yield:** 1 loaf.

Christina Gray
Hohenwald, Tennessee

GARLIC BREAD

The addition of cheese and herbs perks up this familiar favorite.

½ cup butter or margarine, softened
¼ cup grated Parmesan cheese
2 cloves garlic, pressed
¼ teaspoon dried marjoram
¼ teaspoon dried oregano
1 (16-ounce) loaf French bread, cut into 1-inch slices

- **Combine** first 5 ingredients, and spread between bread slices.
- **Reassemble** loaf, and wrap in heavy-duty aluminum foil; place on a baking sheet.
- **Bake** at 350° for 20 minutes. Open foil, and bake 5 additional minutes or until crisp and golden. Slice crosswise into 1-inch slices. Serve immediately. **Yield:** 1 loaf.

Jane Krebs
Fernandina Beach, Florida

CHEESY FRENCH BREAD

1 (8-ounce) package shredded Mexican cheese blend
¾ cup mayonnaise
1½ teaspoons dried parsley flakes
⅛ teaspoon garlic powder
1 (16-ounce) loaf French bread, cut in half horizontally

- **Combine** first 4 ingredients, stirring well. Spread evenly on cut sides of bread; place on a baking sheet.
- **Bake** at 350° for 15 to 20 minutes or until melted and lightly browned. Slice crosswise into 1-inch slices. Serve immediately. **Yield:** 1 loaf.

Lisa Lock
Fort Worth, Texas

DILLY GARLIC BREAD

½ cup butter or margarine, softened
2 cloves garlic, pressed
¼ cup finely chopped fresh dill
1 (16-ounce) loaf French bread, cut in half horizontally
¼ cup grated Parmesan cheese

- **Combine** first 3 ingredients, and spread mixture evenly on cut sides of bread. Sprinkle with Parmesan cheese. Place on a baking sheet.
- **Bake** at 375° for 8 minutes or until golden. Slice crosswise into 1-inch slices. Serve immediately. **Yield:** 1 loaf.

Joy Knight Allard
San Antonio, Texas

PANE CUNSADO (SICILIAN FOR "FIXED BREAD")

Leonard Loria shares a taste from childhood.

1 (16-ounce) loaf French bread, cut in half horizontally
3 tablespoons olive oil
¼ teaspoon freshly ground pepper
1 (5-ounce) package Romano cheese, grated

- **Brush** cut sides of bread with olive oil. Sprinkle bottom half with pepper and cheese.
- **Reassemble** loaf, and wrap in heavy-duty foil; place on a baking sheet.
- **Bake** at 350° for 25 minutes. Slice crosswise into 1-inch slices. Serve immediately. **Yield:** 1 loaf.

Leonard Loria
Birmingham, Alabama

MARVELOUS MANGOES

The best place to eat a mango is in the bathtub. That way, the juice goes down the drain, not down your shirt. For more civilized dining, we offer these recipes to enjoy one of summer's finest tropical fruits.

MANGO BREAD

2 cups all-purpose flour
2 teaspoons baking soda
½ teaspoon salt
1½ cups sugar
2 teaspoons ground cinnamon
3 large eggs, lightly beaten
¾ cup vegetable oil
2 cups finely chopped mango
½ cup chopped pecans or walnuts
1 tablespoon lime juice
½ cup raisins (optional)

- **Combine** first 5 ingredients, and make a well in center of ingredients.
- **Combine** eggs and oil; add to dry ingredients, stirring just until moistened. Stir in mango, pecans, and lime juice. Add raisins, if desired.
- **Spoon** batter into two greased and floured 8½- x 4½- x 3-inch loafpans.
- **Bake** at 375° for 1 hour or until a wooden pick inserted in center comes out clean. Cool in pans on wire racks 10 minutes; remove from pans, and let cool completely on wire racks. **Yield:** 2 loaves.

Carrie Treichel
Johnson City, Tennessee

CHILLED MANGO-CANTALOUPE SOUP

¼ cup sugar
¼ cup boiling water
2 mangoes, peeled and cut into chunks
½ medium cantaloupe, peeled, seeded, and cut into chunks
1½ cups milk, divided
¾ cup whipping cream, divided
2 tablespoons lemon juice
⅛ teaspoon ground cinnamon

- **Dissolve** sugar in boiling water; set aside to cool.
- **Position** knife blade in food processor bowl; add half of fruit and ¼ cup milk, and process until smooth, stopping once to scrape down sides.
- **Pour** fruit mixture through a wire-mesh strainer into a large bowl, discarding pulp. Set fruit mixture aside.
- **Repeat** procedure with remaining fruit and ¼ cup milk.
- **Stir** sugar mixture, remaining 1 cup milk, ½ cup whipping cream, lemon juice, and cinnamon into fruit mixture. Cover and chill until ready to serve.
- **Pour** remaining ¼ cup whipping cream into a heavy-duty, zip-top plastic bag; snip a tiny hole in one corner of bag. Drizzle horizontal lines across each serving, and pull a wooden pick vertically through lines to make a wavy design. **Yield:** 5½ cups.

Carol Lundy
New Tazewell, Tennessee

living *light*

Savor Summer Later

Spicing up dinner without adding fat probably was *not* on your grandmother's mind when she spent the dog days of summer putting up relish. But the idea of keeping a supply of fat-free condiments now seems as up-to-date as salsa. Take a step back in time and create a pantry of vibrant flavors for your kitchen. Come autumn, Peach Chutney served with grilled pork tenderloin will seem very modern indeed.

BLUE-RIBBON MANGO CHUTNEY

3 large mangoes, peeled and chopped (about 2 pounds) *
1½ cups chopped onion
½ cup peeled, chopped cooking apple
½ cup raisins
1 cup cider vinegar
1¼ cups firmly packed brown sugar
½ cup sugar
¼ cup finely chopped fresh ginger
½ teaspoon grated lime rind
2 tablespoons lime juice
1 tablespoon mustard seeds
1½ teaspoons celery seeds
¾ teaspoon salt
¼ teaspoon ground cinnamon
¼ teaspoon ground cloves

• **Combine** all ingredients in a glass bowl; cover and chill 8 hours.
• **Transfer** mango mixture to a Dutch oven; bring to a boil over medium heat. Reduce heat, and cook 1½ hours, stirring occasionally.
• **Divide** mango mixture into airtight containers; chill up to 1 week or freeze up to 6 months. **Yield:** 3 cups.

* Substitute 1 (26-ounce) jar mango, drained and chopped for fresh.

Kathryn McKelvey Smith
Durham, North Carolina

MINTED MANGO SALSA

2 mangoes, peeled and finely chopped
⅔ cup finely chopped red bell pepper
⅔ cup finely chopped purple onion
⅔ cup finely chopped tomato
2 tablespoons chopped fresh mint
2 tablespoons lime juice
1 tablespoon rice wine vinegar

• **Combine** all ingredients; cover and chill. Serve with grilled fish or chicken. **Yield:** 3 cups.

Penny Caughfield
Cocoa, Florida

SWEET ONION RELISH

5 pounds sweet onions, chopped
1 cup sugar
2¼ cups white vinegar (5% acidity)
2 tablespoons salt
2 tablespoons celery seeds

• **Combine** all ingredients in a Dutch oven; bring to a boil over medium heat. Reduce heat, and simmer 20 minutes, stirring occasionally.
• **Spoon** relish into hot jars, filling to ½ inch from top. Remove air bubbles; wipe jar rims. Cover at once with metal lids, and screw on bands.
• **Process** in boiling-water bath 10 minutes. Let stand 1 week before serving. Store in refrigerator after opening. **Yield:** 5 pints.

Mary Reidling
Commerce, Georgia

♥ Per 2-tablespoon serving:
Calories 22 (3% from fat)
Fat 0.1g (0g saturated) Cholesterol 0mg
Sodium 177mg Carbohydrate 5.3g
Fiber 0.5g Protein 0.4g

LIME PICKLES

7 pounds (4-inch-long) cucumbers
1 cup pickling lime
6 cups white vinegar (5% acidity)
6 cups sugar
2 tablespoons pickling spice
1 tablespoon salt

• **Cut** cucumbers lengthwise into ¼-inch-thick slices.
• **Combine** cucumber slices, pickling lime, and water to cover in a nonaluminum stockpot; stir well. Cover and let stand at room temperature 12 hours.
• **Drain** cucumbers; rinse with cold water, and return to stockpot. Add fresh cold water to cover, and let stand 1 hour. Repeat procedure two times. Drain cucumbers, and return to stockpot.
• **Combine** vinegar and next 3 ingredients in a saucepan; bring to a boil over medium heat, stirring until sugar dissolves. Pour vinegar mixture over cucumbers in stockpot; cover and let stand 6 hours or overnight.

YOU CAN DO IT, TOO

CAN CORRECTLY

■ Never reuse canning lids. You can reuse the metal bands if they're not bent or rusty.

■ To keep jars hot before processing, heat them in boiling water or wash them through a complete cycle in the dishwasher and remove them as needed, keeping the dishwasher closed.

■ To remove air bubbles from jars, run a plastic spatula around the jar between food and side of the jar.

■ If you don't have a water-bath canner, improvise with a large Dutch oven. Be sure it's deep enough to have 1 to 2 inches of water covering the jars. Place a rack or a folded towel in the pot to keep the jars from touching the bottom during processing.

■ After processing, let jars cool 24 hours. Then check to see if a vacuum seal has formed by making sure that the lid is concave and that you cannot lift the lid with your fingertips. Because the bands may become rusty, remove them before storing.

■ For additional food preservation tips and recipes, call 1-800-240-3340, ext. 300 to order the 120-page *Ball Blue Book®* Guide to Home Canning, Freezing and Dehydration. The cost is $4.95 plus $1 shipping. All phone orders must be placed with a credit card.

PRESERVING PESTO

If the garden rewards you with a bumper crop of basil, make a batch of pesto for the freezer. Thaw 1 cube of pesto at room temperature for a few minutes, and toss it with 2 ounces hot cooked pasta for dinner in an instant. And pesto is great to have on hand for dressing up vegetable soups, pizzas, sandwiches, omelets, and baked potatoes. A tablespoon serving of pesto has 124 calories.

Pesto: Process ¼ cup olive oil, 2 cups loosely packed fresh basil, 2 tablespoons pine nuts, 2 cloves garlic, and 1 teaspoon salt in an electric blender until mixture is smooth. Stir ¼ cup freshly grated Parmesan cheese and 2 tablespoons freshly grated Romano cheese into mixture.

Spoon 2 tablespoons pesto into each section of an ice cube tray; cover and freeze up to 3 months. **Yield:** ¾ cup or 6 cubes.

Bly Brown
Harrisonburg, Virginia

• **Bring** cucumbers and vinegar mixture to a boil over medium heat; cover, reduce heat, and simmer 35 minutes, stirring gently occasionally.
• **Pack** cucumbers into hot, sterilized jars. Pour vinegar mixture over cucumbers, filling to ½ inch from top. Remove air bubbles; wipe jar rims. Cover at once with metal lids, and screw on bands.
• **Process** in boiling-water bath 5 minutes. Store in refrigerator after opening. **Yield:** 8 pints.

Emily Ingram
Troy, Alabama

❤ Per serving (3 pickles): Calories 56
Fat 0g Cholesterol 0mg
Sodium 77mg Carbohydrate 14.6g
Fiber 0.3g Protein 0.2g

PEACH CHUTNEY

5 pounds firm peaches, peeled and chopped
1 lemon
1⅔ cups golden raisins
1 (8-ounce) package chopped dates
2 cups white vinegar (5% acidity)
3 cups sugar
½ cup chopped pecans
1 (2.7-ounce) jar crystallized ginger (½ cup)
1 teaspoon ground ginger
½ teaspoon ground allspice
½ teaspoon ground cinnamon
½ teaspoon ground cloves

• **Place** peaches in a large nonaluminum saucepan.
• **Cut** lemon into fourths, and thinly slice. Add lemon slices, raisins, dates, and vinegar to peaches; bring to a boil over medium heat. Reduce heat, and simmer 5 minutes or until peaches are soft, stirring occasionally.
• **Add** sugar; return to a boil. Reduce heat, and simmer 15 minutes or until mixture is thickened, stirring occasionally. Add pecans and remaining ingredients; cook 5 minutes, stirring occasionally.
• **Pack** chutney into hot jars, filling to ½ inch from top. Remove air bubbles; wipe jar rims. Cover at once with metal lids, and screw on bands.
• **Process** in boiling-water bath 10 minutes. Serve with chicken or pork. Store in refrigerator after opening. **Yield:** 8 half-pints.

Paula Patterson
Cantonment, Florida

❤ Per 2-tablespoon serving:
Calories 85 (7% from fat)
Fat 0.7g (0g saturated) Cholesterol 0mg
Sodium 2mg Carbohydrate 20.7g
Fiber 1.2g Protein 0.5g

VEGETABLE SALSA

3¼ pounds tomatoes, peeled
12 jalapeño peppers
1 green bell pepper
1 large onion
2 stalks celery
4 cloves garlic
3½ teaspoons salt, divided
2 tablespoons chopped fresh cilantro
2 (6-ounce) cans tomato paste
¼ cup lime juice
2 tablespoons olive oil

• **Chop** first 6 ingredients.
• **Combine** chopped vegetables, 1 teaspoon salt, and next 4 ingredients in a large Dutch oven; cook mixture over medium-high heat until hot (do not boil), stirring often.
• **Pack** salsa into hot jars, filling to ½ inch from top. Add ½ teaspoon salt to each jar. Remove air bubbles; wipe jar rims. Cover at once with metal lids, and screw on bands.
• **Process** in pressure canner at 10 pounds pressure (240°) for 40 minutes. Store in refrigerator after opening. **Yield:** 5 pints.

Ruth Rippetoe
Canton, North Carolina

♥ Per 2-tablespoon serving:
Calories 13 (26% from fat)
Fat 0.4g (0g saturated) Cholesterol 0mg
Sodium 107mg Carbohydrate 2.2g
Fiber 0.3g Protein 0.4g

FROM OUR KITCHEN TO YOURS

KEEP YOUR COOL

So you don't have a wire cooling rack? The next time you bake a pie or cheesecake, just move the metal grate from a burner of your gas cooktop to a cool place on the counter. The grate is the perfect height and size to hold a warm dessert above the counter so air can circulate underneath it and keep your sweet from sweating.

SNAP OUT OF IT

Peeved over puny produce? Either the grocer left nothing but lifeless parsley and wimpy carrots on the shelves or you lost last week's broccoli in the back of the fridge. Regardless, we offer resuscitation advice to make your veggies at least somewhat snappy again.

To perk up tired cauliflower, shriveled green beans, and the like, drop them into a bowl of water with a few ice cubes. We found that a half-hour soak will usually do for most sliced or chopped produce, and overnight is best for sturdier broccoli and cauliflower cut into large pieces. Squash took on water like a sinking ship, so give it only a quick dip at best. And if you don't want to use all your bowls as veggie dunking booths, heavy-duty, zip-top plastic bags work fine and take up less space in the fridge.

A MATTER OF MANNERS

Awkward situations at formal dinners and fine restaurants can happen. But don't let them catch you offguard. Here are some tips from those who've been there – and lived to tell about it.

Someone entertained us with a tale of her worry through three courses as the man next to her used *her* bread plate, leaving her with none. A lighthearted joke halfway through the entrée soon yielded her a fresh one, all to herself.

The greatest debate arose over rescuing bits of food that fall overboard onto the tablecloth. We decided you can't just leave them there as though you didn't notice or don't care. Someone suggested to whisk them under the plate rim, then feign surprise when they're left exposed as the plate is removed. Another advised to hide them in your napkin. But unless you're consciously strategic in your moves, they can fall out into your lap or onto the floor later.

We concluded that you should inconspicuously pick them up from the table and perch them on the part of the plate rim farthest from you. That way they're off the cloth, not back in the food you're eating, and they won't haunt you later in the meal.

EGGPLANT ON OUR FACE

Leonard Loria of Birmingham, Alabama, learned how to turn a near fiasco in his kitchen into a winning dish. He regularly cooks eggplant parmigiana for his wife and daughters. Routinely emptying leftover spaghetti sauce into the skillet, he realized his mistake with one whiff: It was enchilada sauce instead.

He remembered that he had Cheddar and mozzarella cheeses in the refrigerator. So he took the Mexican fork in the road and vowed that he would head that way intentionally next time. Corn oil versus olive oil, a few jalapeños, some chili powder or cumin in the breading, and olé!

PASTA PICKS

The pasta aisle is nearly as overwhelming as the cereal aisle. Next to the familiar spaghetti, lasagna, and fettuccine, you'll find dozens of other shapes including penne, mostaccioli, rotini, and shells in several sizes. It's all about variety, and here are a few pointers to prevent mismatches in your kitchen adventures.

▪ Spoon heavy sauces on sturdy pasta that can hold up to them. You can stir thick, cheesy Alfredo sauce into sturdy fettuccine, but try mixing it in delicate angel hair and you've got a gloppy mess. Use thin, brothy sauces for fine pastas.

▪ When adding pasta to soup, pick shapes that will easily fit into a soup spoon for a graceful bite. Who wants to slosh around the bowl chasing long, stringy noodles and then try to cut a bite without splashing?

▪ Pasta in chunks or pieces, such as ziti, will toss more easily and coat more evenly with most sauces than long strands like vermicelli. If you insist on sauce-covered ribbons, toss them in a sealed zip-top plastic bag rather than stirring in a bowl.

SEPTEMBER

SHRIMP ON THE BAYOU

On a radiator-hot south Louisiana morn, shell-lined, bumpy roads sizzle and twist their way through Houma into Bayou Cocodrie ("Crocodile Bayou"). The *West Wind* chugs away from the marina. On board, shrimper Jimmy Lirette has high hopes for netting a good week's work. After long days skirting the eastern Louisiana coast, Jimmy brings home the treasure: loads of fresh shrimp to sell to local distributors. But some of it he saves.

BARBECUE SHRIMP

¼ cup butter or margarine
½ cup Italian salad dressing
2 tablespoons Worcestershire sauce
2 tablespoons barbecue sauce
1 tablespoon lemon pepper
1 tablespoon pepper
2 bay leaves
2 lemons, sliced
1 large onion, sliced
4 cloves garlic, pressed
3 pounds unpeeled medium-size fresh shrimp

• **Melt** butter in a roasting pan. Add salad dressing and remaining ingredients; stir to coat.
• **Bake** at 400° for 20 minutes or until shrimp turn pink, stirring occasionally. Remove and discard bay leaves. **Yield:** 10 appetizer servings.

SHRIMP FETTUCCINE

2 pounds unpeeled large fresh shrimp
1 (16-ounce) package fettuccine
¾ cup butter or margarine
½ cup chopped green bell pepper
¼ cup chopped onion
2 stalks celery, chopped
1 teaspoon all-purpose flour
¼ cup chopped fresh parsley
1 (8-ounce) loaf process cheese spread, cubed
1 cup half-and-half
1 cup grated Parmesan cheese

• **Peel** shrimp, and devein, if desired; set aside.
• **Cook** pasta according to package directions; drain and keep warm.
• **Melt** butter in a heavy skillet; add bell pepper, onion, and celery, and cook 3 minutes or until tender, stirring often. Add flour, stirring until blended.
• **Stir** in shrimp and parsley; reduce heat, and cook 10 to 15 minutes or until shrimp turn pink, stirring often. Remove from heat; add cheese spread and half-and-half, stirring until cheese spread melts.
• **Combine** pasta and shrimp mixture, stirring gently; serve immediately, or spoon into a lightly greased 13- x 9- x 2-inch baking dish. Sprinkle with Parmesan cheese.
• **Bake** at 350° for 15 minutes or until Parmesan cheese melts. Serve immediately. **Yield:** 8 servings.

SHRIMP CREOLE

1½ pounds unpeeled medium-size fresh shrimp
1 large onion, finely chopped
½ cup chopped green bell pepper
½ cup chopped red bell pepper
½ cup chopped celery
¼ cup chopped green onions
2 cloves garlic, minced
3 tablespoons vegetable oil
1 (16-ounce) can stewed tomatoes, undrained
1 (8-ounce) can tomato sauce
2 bay leaves
1 teaspoon Creole seasoning
¼ teaspoon ground red pepper (optional)
Hot cooked rice

• **Peel** shrimp, and devein, if desired; set aside.
• **Cook** onion and next 5 ingredients in oil in a large skillet over medium-high heat 3 minutes or until tender, stirring often. Stir in tomatoes and next 4 ingredients; bring to a boil. Reduce heat; cook 20 minutes, stirring occasionally.
• **Add** shrimp; cook 5 minutes or until shrimp turn pink. Remove and discard bay leaves; serve shrimp mixture over rice. **Yield:** 4 to 6 servings.

SHRIMP PUFFS

⅔ cup uncooked rice
1½ pounds unpeeled medium-size fresh shrimp
1 cup all-purpose flour
1½ teaspoons baking powder
1 tablespoon Creole seasoning
½ teaspoon garlic powder
2 large eggs, separated
¾ cup milk
1 tablespoon vegetable oil
1 medium onion, chopped
½ cup chopped green onions
Vegetable oil

- **Cook** rice according to package directions; set aside.
- **Peel** shrimp, and devein, if desired; chop shrimp, and set aside.
- **Combine** flour and next 3 ingredients in a large bowl. Combine egg yolks, milk, and 1 tablespoon oil, stirring well; gradually stir into dry ingredients just until blended. Add rice, shrimp, and onions, stirring gently.
- **Beat** egg whites at high speed with an electric mixer until stiff peaks form, and gently fold into shrimp mixture.
- **Pour** oil to depth of 3 inches into a Dutch oven; heat to 375°. Drop shrimp mixture by heaping teaspoonfuls into hot oil; cook 3 to 4 minutes or until golden, turning once. Drain on paper towels, and serve immediately with rémoulade or tartar sauce. **Yield:** 5 dozen.

"You know how it goes, 'Laissez les bon temps rouler' *[let the good times roll] and all that. Let's eat!"*

Jimmy Lirette

Family and friends gather for a taste of Jimmy's catch. The secret to great boiled shrimp? Add salt after it's boiled to keep it from getting tough. Celebrate the sweet smell of success at a shrimper's family feast.

SHRIMP-AND-POTATO SALAD

2 medium potatoes, unpeeled
6 cups water
2 pounds unpeeled medium-size fresh shrimp
½ cup finely chopped green onions
4 stalks celery, finely chopped
4 large hard-cooked eggs
½ cup mayonnaise
2 tablespoons prepared mustard
¼ teaspoon salt
½ teaspoon pepper
½ teaspoon hot sauce
Lettuce leaves

- **Cube** potatoes, and place in a saucepan; add enough water to cover, and bring to a boil over medium-high heat. Cook 6 to 7 minutes or until tender. Drain and place in a large bowl; cool.
- **Bring** 6 cups water to a boil in saucepan; add shrimp, and cook 3 to 5 minutes or just until shrimp turn pink. Drain shrimp, and rinse with cold water.
- **Peel** shrimp, and devein, if desired. Coarsely chop shrimp, if desired. Add shrimp, green onions, and celery to potato.
- **Chop** egg whites, and add to shrimp mixture. Mash egg yolks; stir in mayonnaise and mustard. Add mayonnaise mixture, salt, pepper, and hot sauce to shrimp mixture, tossing gently to coat; cover and chill. Serve on lettuce leaves with fresh fruit and tomato wedges. **Yield:** 6 to 8 servings.

PICNIC IN THE GROVE

This group of Ole Miss alums led by P.T. and Joe Ross of Jackson, Mississippi, has long cherished The Grove, a wooded carpet of grass in the heart of the Ole Miss campus in Oxford, Mississippi. It's THE place to picnic before cheering on the team.

TAILGATING MENU
Serves 12

Fiesta Dip
Marinated Pork Tenderloin With Jezebel Sauce
Miss Mary's Chicken Strips With "Come Back" Dipping Sauce
Marinated Vegetables
Brown Sugar Wafers

Dawn has just peeped in Oxford as Michael Ross rubs drowsy eyes, focusing on the piratelike map of The Grove his mother drew for him the night before. Along with other tailgaters, he waits just outside the boundaries of the gathering place. An official gun pops, releasing them to race for the best picnic spot.

After securing the party site for his mother, Michael knows he can take a well-deserved late-morning snooze. Meanwhile, his parents, P.T. and Joe, and their Ole Miss friends finish preparing the spread they began the day before.

On game days, parked cars loop The Grove like a beaded necklace, but they aren't used for tailgating. Instead trunks open, relinquishing sturdy tables and flowing cloths, silver platters and candelabras, crystal pitchers and pottery vases – to be hauled to the perfect tree.

As everyone nibbles sweets and savories and sips from mint julep cups, morning rolls into afternoon when Ole Miss takes to the field against . . . well, who really cares? For these avid football fans, it's just another glorious Saturday in The Grove.

FIESTA DIP

1 (10½-ounce) package corn chips, crushed
¼ cup butter or margarine, melted
2 (16-ounce) cans refried beans
1 (1¼-ounce) package taco seasoning mix
1 (6-ounce) container frozen avocado dip, thawed
1 (8-ounce) carton sour cream
3 (2¼-ounce) cans sliced ripe olives, undrained
2 medium tomatoes, seeded and chopped
2 (4.5-ounce) cans chopped green chiles, drained
1 (8-ounce) package Monterey Jack cheese with peppers, shredded
Garnish: fresh cilantro sprigs

• **Combine** crushed corn chips and butter; press onto bottom and 1 inch up sides of a lightly greased 9-inch springform pan.
• **Bake** at 350° for 10 minutes. Cool on a wire rack.
• **Combine** refried beans and taco seasoning mix, stirring well; spread over prepared crust. Layer avocado dip and next 5 ingredients over refried bean mixture; cover and chill 8 hours.
• **Place** on a serving plate, and remove sides of springform pan; garnish, if desired. Serve with large corn chips. **Yield:** 18 to 20 appetizer servings.

MARINATED PORK TENDERLOIN WITH JEZEBEL SAUCE

¼ cup lite soy sauce
¼ cup dry sherry or Madeira wine
2 tablespoons olive oil
1 tablespoon dry mustard
1 teaspoon ground ginger
1 teaspoon sesame oil
8 drops of hot sauce
2 cloves garlic, minced
2 (¾-pound) pork tenderloins
½ cup apple cider vinegar
3 dozen party rolls
Jezebel Sauce

• **Combine** first 8 ingredients in a shallow dish or heavy-duty, zip-top plastic bag; add tenderloins. Cover or seal, and chill 8 hours, turning tenderloins occasionally.
• **Remove** tenderloins from marinade, reserving ½ cup marinade; combine reserved marinade and ½ cup apple cider vinegar.
• **Cook** tenderloins, covered with grill lid, over medium-hot coals (350° to 400°) about 20 minutes or until a meat thermometer inserted into thickest portion registers 160°, turning occasionally and basting with marinade mixture during first 15 minutes of cooking time. Remove from heat; slice and serve warm or chilled with party rolls and Jezebel Sauce. **Yield:** 10 to 12 appetizer servings.

Jezebel Sauce

1 cup apple jelly
1 cup pineapple-orange marmalade or pineapple preserves
1 (6-ounce) jar prepared mustard
1 (5-ounce) jar prepared horseradish
¼ teaspoon pepper

• **Beat** apple jelly in a mixing bowl at medium speed with an electric mixer until smooth. Add marmalade and remaining ingredients; beat at medium speed until blended. Cover and chill. **Yield:** 3 cups.

MISS MARY'S CHICKEN STRIPS WITH "COME BACK" DIPPING SAUCE

A friend shared this recipe with P. T. Ross. It's a regular at their tailgating feast. The sauce got its name because it's so good, people "come back" for more.

8 skinned and boned chicken breast halves
2 cups milk
1 teaspoon salt
½ teaspoon pepper
½ teaspoon lemon pepper
2 cups all-purpose flour
Vegetable oil or shortening
"Come Back" Dipping Sauce

• **Cut** chicken into strips.
• **Combine** chicken and next 4 ingredients; cover and chill 4 hours.
• **Drain** chicken; coat with flour.
• **Pour** oil or melt shortening to depth of 3 inches into a large Dutch oven; heat to 350°. Cook chicken, a few pieces at a time, until golden. Drain on paper towels; keep warm or chill. Serve with "Come Back" Dipping Sauce. **Yield:** 16 appetizer servings.

"Come Back" Dipping Sauce

½ cup mayonnaise
¼ cup olive oil
3 tablespoons chili sauce
2 tablespoons ketchup
1 tablespoon water
2 teaspoons Worcestershire sauce
2 teaspoons prepared mustard
1 teaspoon coarsely ground pepper
Dash of paprika
Dash of hot sauce
1 small onion, minced
1 clove garlic, minced

• **Combine** all ingredients; cover and chill. **Yield:** 2 cups.

MARINATED VEGETABLES

1 cup red wine vinegar
½ cup vegetable oil
½ cup olive oil
1 tablespoon salt
1 teaspoon garlic powder
1 teaspoon cracked pepper
1 teaspoon dried oregano
1 (10-ounce) package frozen brussels sprouts
2 green bell peppers
1 yellow onion
2 zucchini
4 small yellow squash
1 pound fresh broccoli
1 (5.75-ounce) can jumbo pitted ripe olives, drained
1 (6-ounce) jar jumbo pimiento-stuffed olives, drained
1 (14-ounce) can quartered artichoke hearts, drained
½ pound fresh small mushrooms
1 pint cherry tomatoes

• **Combine** first 7 ingredients in a saucepan; bring to a boil. Cool.
• **Cook** brussels sprouts according to package directions; drain.
• **Cut** bell peppers into thin strips. Slice onion, zucchini, and yellow squash; separate onion into rings. Cut broccoli into flowerets. Place vinegar mixture, vegetables, olives, and artichokes in a large heavy-duty, zip-top plastic bag. Seal and chill 8 hours, turning occasionally.
• **Add** mushrooms and tomatoes; toss gently. Serve immediately. **Yield:** 20 to 25 appetizer servings.

BROWN SUGAR WAFERS

1 cup butter or margarine, softened
¾ cup firmly packed dark brown sugar
1 egg yolk
1 tablespoon vanilla extract
1¼ cups all-purpose flour
¼ teaspoon salt

• **Beat** butter at medium speed with an electric mixer until creamy, and gradually add sugar, beating well. Add egg yolk and vanilla, beating until blended.
• **Add** flour and salt; beat at low speed until blended. Shape dough into a ball; seal in plastic wrap, and chill dough 2 hours.
• **Shape** dough into 1-inch balls, and place 2 inches apart on cookie sheets. Flatten each cookie to ⅛-inch thickness, using bottom of a glass buttered and dipped in granulated sugar.
• **Bake** at 350° for 10 to 12 minutes or until golden. Carefully remove wafers to wire racks to cool. **Yield:** 2 dozen.

PARTY SIPPERS: MILD OR WILD

Cheering the team to victory leaves fans parched. If you're hosting a football party, offer a variety of thirst quenchers. Here we give several to choose from – fruity punches to spirited concoctions. Kickoff time and temperature may help determine your beverage selections.

HOT BUTTERED RUM

1 teaspoon sugar
½ teaspoon butter
3 tablespoons light rum
4 whole cloves
½ cup apple juice
1 (4-inch) stick cinnamon

• **Combine** first 5 ingredients in a small saucepan; cook just until thoroughly heated. Remove and discard cloves; pour into a mug, and add cinnamon stick. **Yield:** ⅔ cup.

Glenda Marie Stokes
Florence, South Carolina

SPIRITED APPLE CIDER

To intensify the flavor and aroma of whole spices, such as cloves, roast them in a 350° oven for about 10 minutes. Cool completely before using.

12 whole cloves
6 whole allspice
3 (2½-inch) sticks cinnamon, broken
1 tablespoon grated orange rind
4 blades of mace (optional)
8 cups apple cider
1 cup fresh orange juice
1 cup cranberry juice cocktail
1 cup pineapple juice
½ cup dark rum
½ cup apple-flavored brandy

• **Place** first 4 ingredients and mace, if desired, in a cheesecloth bag; combine spice bag and cider in a Dutch oven. Bring mixture to a boil; reduce heat to medium, and cook 15 minutes or until reduced to 4 cups.

• **Remove** and discard spice bag; stir in orange juice and remaining ingredients. Simmer until thoroughly heated. **Yield:** 2 quarts.

PIMM'S CUP

(pictured on page 223)

Imported from England, Pimm's No. 1 Cup is a blend of liqueurs and fruit extracts sold at liquor stores.

2 cups Pimm's No. 1 Cup
1 (2-liter) bottle lemon-lime carbonated beverage
8 cucumber spears

• **Combine** Pimm's No. 1 Cup and carbonated beverage in a large pitcher; mix well. Serve over ice with cucumber spears. **Yield:** 2½ quarts.

TENNESSEE HOT CHOCOLATE

For a richer, darker cup of hot chocolate, try Dutch-processed cocoa. The cocoa has a lower natural acidity, which is perfect for this recipe.

3 cups milk
¾ cup half-and-half
½ cup sugar
½ cup cocoa
1 teaspoon vanilla extract
⅓ to ½ cup bourbon
Marshmallows (optional)

• **Combine** milk and half-and-half in a medium saucepan; cook over medium heat until thoroughly heated (do not boil). Add sugar and cocoa, whisking until blended. Remove from heat; whisk in vanilla and bourbon. Pour into mugs; top with marshmallows, if desired. **Yield:** 4½ cups.

Wylene B. Gillespie,
Gallatin, Tennessee

HOT SPICED PUNCH

When brewed, this punch sends a wonderful aroma throughout your house.

3 (¼-inch-thick) slices fresh ginger
1 stick cinnamon
8 whole cloves
4 cardamom seeds
1 gallon apple cider
1 quart pineapple juice
6 lemons, peeled and sliced
6 small oranges, peeled and sliced

• **Place** first 4 ingredients in a cheesecloth bag; combine spice bag, cider, and remaining ingredients in a large Dutch oven. Bring to a boil; reduce heat, and simmer 15 minutes, stirring occasionally. Discard spice bag. Serve warm. **Yield:** about 5 quarts.

Hot Spiced Rum Punch: Stir in 1½ cups rum before serving. **Yield:** 5½ quarts.

Ellie Wells
Lakeland, Florida

FRUIT JUICE PUNCH

(pictured on page 223)

3 cups pineapple juice
2 cups water
2 cups apple juice
1 (6-ounce) can frozen lemonade concentrate, undiluted
1 (6-ounce) can frozen orange juice concentrate, undiluted
2 teaspoons lemon instant tea mix
2 cups ginger ale, chilled

• **Combine** first 6 ingredients in a large bowl, stirring well; cover and chill at least 2 hours.

• **Stir** in ginger ale. **Yield:** about 2½ quarts.

Fruit Juice-and-Vodka Punch: Add 1½ cups vodka to juice mixture before chilling. **Yield:** 3 quarts.

Liz Randall
Spindale, North Carolina

GAME-DAY BUFFET

Show your team spirit with a party. Celebrate the win or debate the defeat over a generous buffet. This hearty appetizer assortment is perfect because it keeps you in the game and out of the kitchen.

CHUNKY SHRIMP DIP

4½ cups water
1½ pounds unpeeled medium-size fresh shrimp
3 stalks celery
6 green onions
2 large pickled jalapeño peppers
2 (8-ounce) packages cream cheese, softened
½ teaspoon pickled jalapeño pepper liquid
1 tablespoon prepared mustard
½ cup mayonnaise

• **Bring** water to a boil; add shrimp, and cook 3 to 5 minutes or just until shrimp turn pink. Drain; rinse with cold water.
• **Peel** shrimp, and devein, if desired. Finely chop shrimp, celery, green onions, and jalapeño peppers; place in a large bowl.
• **Add** cream cheese and remaining ingredients, stirring well. Cover and chill at least 30 minutes. Serve with crackers or crostini. **Yield:** 5 cups.

SPICY ORIENTAL-STYLE WINGS

3 pounds chicken wings
1 (8-ounce) can pineapple tidbits, undrained
½ cup chunky peanut butter
¼ cup chopped green onions
1 cup white wine Worcestershire sauce
½ cup honey
½ cup soy sauce
¼ cup orange juice
1 tablespoon minced garlic
1 tablespoon dried grated orange rind
1 teaspoon hot sauce
Garnishes: toasted sesame seeds, green onion fans

• **Place** chicken in a 13- x 9- x 2-inch baking dish.
• **Combine** pineapple and next 9 ingredients in an electric blender; process until smooth, stopping once to scrape down sides. Pour 2½ cups of pineapple mixture over chicken. Cover and chill chicken and remaining pineapple mixture 8 hours.
• **Cover** and bake chicken at 350° for 1 hour, basting often with reserved pineapple mixture. Garnish, if desired. **Yield:** 6 appetizer servings.

Laurie McIntyre
Houston, Texas

ORIENTAL CRUNCH
(pictured on page 223)

4 cups crisp oat cereal squares
2 cups crisp corn cereal squares
2 cups crisp rice cereal
1 (3-ounce) can chow mein noodles
1 cup mixed nuts
½ cup vegetable oil
¼ cup soy sauce
1¼ teaspoons garlic powder
1¼ teaspoons onion powder

• **Combine** first 5 ingredients in a roasting pan. Combine oil and next 3 ingredients; pour over cereal mixture, stirring to coat.
• **Bake** at 250° for 1 hour, stirring every 20 minutes; cool. Store in an airtight container. **Yield:** about 10 cups.

STUFFED JALAPEÑO PEPPERS

2 (11-ounce) cans whole pickled jalapeño peppers
1 cup (4 ounces) shredded Cheddar cheese
1 cup (4 ounces) shredded mozzarella cheese
1½ cups all-purpose flour, divided
2 large eggs
1 cup milk
½ cup cornmeal
1½ tablespoons seasoned salt
Vegetable oil

• **Drain** peppers, reserving ¼ cup liquid; rinse peppers with cold water. Cut in half lengthwise, and remove seeds. Pat peppers dry with paper towels.
• **Combine** reserved pepper liquid and cheeses. Spoon cheese mixture into pepper halves, and roll in ½ cup flour to coat. Place on baking sheets; cover and freeze 1 hour.
• **Combine** eggs and milk, stirring well. Combine ½ cup flour, cornmeal, and seasoned salt in a shallow dish.
• **Roll** stuffed peppers in remaining ½ cup flour; dip in egg mixture, and dredge in cornmeal mixture to coat. Cover and freeze peppers up to 2 days.
• **Pour** oil to depth of 3 inches into a Dutch oven; heat to 350°. Fry peppers in hot oil 3 to 4 minutes or until light golden (do not overcook). Serve with sour cream or guacamole. **Yield:** 3 to 4 dozen.

Jan Bryan
Garland, Texas

SIMPLE NIBBLES

All you need are just a few ingredients for this speedy appetizer. It's great as a snack or for a party.

SWISS-BLUE CHEESE CROSTINI

1 French baguette
4 cloves garlic, pressed
¼ cup olive oil
12 oil-packed dried tomatoes, halved
1 cup (4 ounces) shredded Swiss cheese
1 (4-ounce) package crumbled blue cheese
¼ cup chopped fresh parsley

• **Slice** bread into 24 (¼- to ½-inch) slices, and place on an aluminum foil-lined baking sheet.
• **Bake** at 400° for 5 minutes or until lightly browned.
• **Combine** garlic and oil; brush on bread slices. Top each slice with a tomato half; set aside.
• **Combine** cheeses and parsley; spoon on top of tomatoes.
• **Bake** at 400° for 5 minutes or until cheese melts. Serve immediately. **Yield:** 2 dozen.

Helen Maurer
Christmas, Florida

Bountiful Fall Squash

Ridged emerald acorn squash and club-shaped golden butternut squash celebrate the chill in the fall air. You'll discover sweet flavor inside these vegetables. Winter squash are reasonably priced now, so buy several. Bake and freeze the cooked, mashed pulp up to six months. Then you can easily create this variety of recipes anytime of year.

BUTTERNUT SQUASH CASSEROLE

2 cups cooked, mashed butternut squash
3 large eggs
¾ cup sugar
⅓ cup butter or margarine, softened
⅓ cup milk
1 teaspoon ground ginger
½ teaspoon coconut flavoring
Crunchy Cereal Topping

• **Combine** first 7 ingredients; pour into a lightly greased 8-inch square baking dish.
• **Bake** at 350° for 35 minutes. Sprinkle with Crunchy Cereal Topping, and bake 10 additional minutes. **Yield:** 6 to 8 servings.

Crunchy Cereal Topping

1½ cups corn flake crumbs
¾ cup firmly packed brown sugar
½ cup chopped pecans
¼ cup butter or margarine, melted

• **Combine** all ingredients in a bowl. **Yield:** 2½ cups.

Fay Redding
Gastonia, North Carolina

CREAMY BUTTERNUT SOUP

4 cups cooked, mashed butternut squash
2 (14½-ounce) cans ready-to-serve chicken broth
½ teaspoon sugar
½ teaspoon salt
¼ teaspoon pepper
1 cup whipping cream, divided
¼ teaspoon ground nutmeg

• **Combine** half of first 5 ingredients in container of an electric blender or food processor, and process until smooth, stopping once to scrape down sides; pour into a large saucepan. Repeat procedure with remaining half.
• **Bring** to a boil over medium heat; gradually stir in half of whipping cream, and cook until thoroughly heated. Remove from heat.
• **Beat** remaining whipping cream at high speed with an electric mixer until firm peaks form. Dollop on soup; sprinkle with nutmeg. **Yield:** 7 cups.

Creamy Acorn-Butternut Soup: Substitute 2 cups cooked, mashed acorn squash for 2 cups cooked, mashed butternut squash.

Acorn Squash Bowls: Cut off tops of squash; cut a thin slice from bottoms to stand squash upright. Remove seeds, and brown top of shells in a hot greased skillet.

Sandra Holmes-Kennedy
Atlanta, Texas

ACORN SQUASH CAKE

¼ cup butter, softened
¾ cup firmly packed light brown sugar
1 large egg
1 cup cooked, mashed acorn squash
½ teaspoon vanilla extract
2 cups all-purpose flour
2 teaspoons baking soda
1 teaspoon ground cinnamon
½ teaspoon salt
1 cup chopped pecans
Streusel Topping

• **Beat** butter and sugar at medium speed with an electric mixer until creamy. Add egg, beating well. Stir in squash and vanilla.
• **Combine** flour and next 4 ingredients; gradually add to squash mixture, beating at low speed after each addition. Pour batter into a greased 9-inch square pan, and sprinkle with Streusel Topping.
• **Bake** at 350° for 40 minutes. Cool cake in pan on a wire rack. **Yield:** 9 servings.

Streusel Topping

½ cup firmly packed light brown sugar
⅓ cup all-purpose flour
½ teaspoon ground cinnamon
¼ cup butter, softened
½ cup chopped pecans

• **Combine** all ingredients in a bowl. **Yield:** 1½ cups.

Valerie G. Stutsman
Norfolk, Virginia

Ode to Onions

Onions are "the rose of roots," as Robert Louis Stevenson aptly mused. Their thin translucent wrappings shed to reveal fragrant, full-bodied flavor – from mild (shallots, chives, green onions) to strong (rustic white or yellow) to sweet (Vidalias or Texas sweets). Onions easily and inexpensively add flair to any dish.

SWEET-AND-SOUR PEARL ONIONS

1 pound pearl onions *
1 tablespoon olive oil
2 tablespoons balsamic vinegar
2 tablespoons frozen apple juice concentrate
⅛ teaspoon salt

• **Cook** onions in boiling water to cover 3 minutes; drain and plunge immediately into cold water to stop the cooking process. Drain.
• **Combine** onions and oil in a skillet; toss to coat. Cook over low heat 8 minutes or until browned, stirring often.
• **Stir** in vinegar, apple juice concentrate, and salt; cook over medium heat 4 to 5 minutes or until most of liquid evaporates, stirring often. Serve at room temperature. **Yield:** 4 servings.

* Substitute 1 (16-ounce) package frozen pearl onions, thawed, for fresh.

LaJuan Coward
Jasper, Texas

GRILLED ONION FLOWERS WITH PECANS

½ cup chopped pecans
8 large yellow onions (3½ pounds)
½ cup olive oil, divided
¼ cup balsamic vinegar
1 tablespoon chopped fresh parsley
1 tablespoon chopped fresh sage
1 tablespoon chopped fresh rosemary
1 tablespoon chopped fresh thyme
¼ teaspoon salt
¼ teaspoon pepper
Garnishes: fresh sage, rosemary, and thyme sprigs

• **Bake** pecans in a shallow pan at 350° for 5 to 10 minutes or until toasted, stirring occasionally; set aside.
• **Peel** onions carefully, leaving root end intact. Cut each onion into eighths, cutting to, but not through, root end. Drizzle with half of oil.
• **Cook** onions, covered with grill lid, over low coals (under 300°) about 40 minutes or until tips are brown and onions are soft, brushing with remaining oil as needed.
• **Remove** onions to a serving platter; drizzle with vinegar, and sprinkle with pecans, parsley, and next 5 ingredients. Serve at room temperature. Garnish, if desired. **Yield:** 8 servings.

Ray Overton
Roswell, Georgia

SOUTH-OF-THE-BORDER ONION RINGS

(pictured on page 222)

The batter's spicy sweetness stems from the unexpected – sweetened condensed milk.

2 medium onions
1 cup self-rising flour
⅓ cup self-rising cornmeal
1 large egg, lightly beaten
½ cup sweetened condensed milk
¼ cup club soda
⅓ cup minced jalapeño peppers
Vegetable oil
Salt

• **Cut** onions into ¼-inch-thick slices, and separate into rings.
• **Combine** flour and cornmeal in a bowl. Combine egg, condensed milk, and club soda; add to dry ingredients, stirring until smooth. Stir in pepper.
• **Pour** oil to depth of 3 inches into a Dutch oven; heat to 375°.
• **Dip** onion rings in batter, coating well; fry, a few rings at a time, until golden. Drain on paper towels, and sprinkle with salt. Serve immediately. **Yield:** 4 to 6 servings.

Charlotte Pierce
Greensburg, Kentucky

THREE-ONION SOUP

1 large yellow onion
1 medium-size purple onion
4 shallots
¼ cup butter or margarine
1 tablespoon olive oil
2 (14½-ounce) cans ready-to-serve chicken broth
½ teaspoon ground cumin
1 teaspoon dried oregano
½ teaspoon dried thyme
3 tablespoons Madeira wine or dry white wine
1 (8-ounce) carton plain yogurt

• **Chop** first 3 ingredients coarsely.
• **Cook** butter and olive oil in a large Dutch oven over low heat until butter melts; add onions, shallot, chicken broth, and next 3 ingredients. Bring mixture to a boil; reduce heat, and simmer 20 minutes, stirring often. Stir in wine; simmer 20 minutes, stirring often. Cool slightly.
• **Spoon** mixture into container of an electric blender or food processor; process until smooth, stopping once to scrape down sides. Return to pan; cook just until thoroughly heated, stirring often. Stir in yogurt. **Yield:** 6 servings.

Sandra Russell
Gainesville, Florida

DREAM BEANS

Dried beans are the heart of some great recipes. Here, imaginative cooks do delicious things with the versatile legumes, like bake limas with molasses or give black-eyed peas a Cajun twist.

BAKED LIMA BEANS

1 (16-ounce) package large dried lima beans
7 cups water
1 medium onion, quartered
1 pound chopped ham
½ cup molasses
2 to 3 tablespoons brown sugar
4 cups water

• **Sort** and wash beans. Place beans and 7 cups water in a large Dutch oven; bring to a boil, and boil 1 minute. Cover, remove from heat, and let stand 1 hour; drain.
• **Spoon** half of beans into an ovenproof Dutch oven; top with onion and chopped ham. Add remaining beans, molasses, and brown sugar; pour 4 cups water over brown sugar. Cover with aluminum foil.
• **Bake** at 350° for 3 to 3½ hours or until beans are tender, removing foil after 1½ hours. **Yield:** 8 to 10 servings.

Carolyne M. Carnevale
Ormond Beach, Florida

Bean Basics

Here are a few tips to make sure your beans are terrific.

- Store dried beans in an airtight container up to 1 year. Never store them in the refrigerator.

- Do not cook beans in the liquid they soaked in.

- Add tomatoes *after* beans are tender; acid toughens them and they may never get done.

CAJUN BLACK-EYED PEAS

1 pound dried black-eyed peas
8 cups water
6 slices bacon
1 bunch green onions, chopped
1 large onion, chopped
1 green bell pepper, chopped
1 cup chopped fresh parsley
1 small jalapeño pepper, seeded and minced
3 cloves garlic, pressed
2 tablespoons Worcestershire sauce
¼ teaspoon hot sauce
1½ teaspoons salt
1 teaspoon pepper
¼ teaspoon dried oregano
¼ teaspoon dried thyme
1 pound smoked sausage, sliced
1½ cups chopped smoked ham (about ½ pound)
1 (14½-ounce) can Cajun-style stewed tomatoes, undrained

• **Sort** and wash peas; place in a large Dutch oven, and add water to depth of 2 inches above peas. Cover and let stand 8 hours or overnight.
• **Drain** peas, and return to Dutch oven. Add 8 cups water; bring to a boil. Cover, reduce heat, and simmer 30 minutes, stirring occasionally.
• **Add** bacon and next 12 ingredients; return to a boil. Cover, reduce heat, and simmer 30 minutes or until peas are tender.
• **Add** sausage, ham, and tomatoes; return to a boil. Cover, reduce heat, and simmer 30 minutes. Remove bacon, if desired. **Yield:** 14 cups.

RED BEANS AND RICE

(pictured on page 221)

2 pounds dried red beans
6 cups water
2 large onions, chopped
4 cloves garlic, minced
1 large green bell pepper, chopped
1 large red bell pepper, chopped
½ pound salt pork
1 cup dry red wine
½ cup chopped fresh parsley
1 tablespoon chopped fresh oregano
1 tablespoon Old Bay seasoning
3 bay leaves
1 teaspoon celery seeds
1 teaspoon salt
1 teaspoon freshly ground black pepper
1 teaspoon paprika
½ to 1 teaspoon ground red pepper
½ to 1 teaspoon dried crushed red pepper
1 teaspoon hot sauce
1 pound smoked beef sausage, cut into ½-inch pieces
1 pound andouille sausage, cut into ½-inch pieces
2 (11-ounce) cans diced tomatoes and green chiles, undrained
1 tablespoon gumbo filé
Hot cooked rice

• **Sort** and wash beans. Combine beans and next 18 ingredients in a large Dutch oven; bring to a boil. Cover, reduce heat, and simmer 3 hours or until thickened and beans are tender.
• **Add** sausages and tomatoes; cook 30 minutes.
• **Remove** and discard salt pork and bay leaves; stir in filé. Serve over rice. **Yield:** 10 to 12 servings.

Dail "Duke" Mullins, Jr.
Birmingham, Alabama

Simple Soufflés

Soufflés have long been one of the great culinary mysteries. In pursuit of recipe-friendly soufflés, we found that the unbaked soufflé mixture can be spooned into individual baking dishes or custard cups and frozen up to a week. These smaller versions can be baked either all at once or one at a time at a later date. (This timesaving trick does not work with larger soufflés.) In addition our petite soufflés don't require foil collars.

When we whip up gauzy clouds of egg whites (the key to superior puffing power), we find that they perform best when beaten until stiff but not dry. They're ready when they no longer slip when the bowl is tilted – one culinary mystery solved.

BROCCOLI SOUFFLÉS

2 (10-ounce) packages frozen chopped broccoli, thawed
¼ cup butter or margarine
¼ cup all-purpose flour
1¼ cups milk
⅔ cup (2.6 ounces) shredded sharp Cheddar cheese
5 large eggs, separated
1½ teaspoons salt
¼ teaspoon minced garlic
2 tablespoons lemon juice

• **Cook** broccoli in a small amount of boiling water 5 minutes, and drain.
• **Melt** butter in a heavy saucepan over low heat; add flour, whisking until smooth. Cook 1 minute, whisking constantly. Gradually add milk, and cook over medium heat, whisking constantly, until thickened and bubbly. Add cheese, stirring until it melts. Remove from heat.
• **Beat** egg yolks at medium speed with an electric mixer until thick and pale. Add cooked broccoli, salt, garlic, and lemon juice, beating until blended. Gradually stir about one-fourth of hot

cheese mixture into yolk mixture; add to remaining hot mixture, stirring mixture constantly.
• **Beat** egg whites at high speed until stiff; fold one-third of egg whites into broccoli mixture. Fold in remaining egg whites. Pour into eight buttered individual soufflé dishes or 6-ounce custard cups. Seal in aluminum foil, and freeze up to 1 week.
• **Unwrap** soufflés, and place in a 13- x 9- x 2-inch pan; add hot water to pan to depth of 1 inch.
• **Bake** at 400° for 10 minutes; reduce heat to 350°, and bake 35 to 40 additional minutes or until puffed and golden. Serve immediately. **Yield:** 8 servings.

Note: If not freezing soufflés, bake as directed at 350° for 35 to 40 minutes.

CHILE-CHEESE SOUFFLÉS

1/4 cup butter or margarine
1/4 cup all-purpose flour
1 3/4 cups milk
3/4 cup (3 ounces) shredded sharp Cheddar cheese
3/4 cup (3 ounces) shredded Monterey Jack cheese
1 (4.5-ounce) can chopped green chiles, drained
1 teaspoon salt
6 large eggs, separated

• **Melt** butter in a heavy saucepan over low heat; add flour, whisking until smooth. Cook 1 minute, whisking constantly. Gradually add milk, and cook over medium heat, whisking constantly, until thickened and bubbly.
• **Add** Cheddar and Monterey Jack cheeses, chiles, and salt, stirring until cheese melts.
• **Beat** egg yolks at medium speed with an electric mixer until thick and pale. Gradually stir about one-fourth of hot mixture into yolks; add to remaining hot mixture, stirring constantly. Bring to a boil; remove from heat.
• **Beat** egg whites at high speed until stiff but not dry; fold into cheese mixture. Pour into nine buttered individual soufflé dishes or 6-ounce custard cups. Seal in aluminum foil, and freeze up to 1 week.
• **Unwrap** soufflés, and place in a 13- x 9- x 2-inch pan. Add hot water to pan to depth of 1 inch.
• **Bake** at 400° for 10 minutes; reduce heat to 350°, and bake 25 additional minutes or until puffed and golden. Serve immediately. **Yield:** 9 servings.

Note: If not freezing soufflés, bake as directed at 350° for 25 minutes.

THREE-CHEESE SOUFFLÉS

2 tablespoons grated Parmesan cheese
4 large eggs, separated
1 cup (4 ounces) shredded sharp Cheddar cheese
1 (3-ounce) package cream cheese, cubed
1/3 cup half-and-half
1/4 cup grated Parmesan cheese
1/2 teaspoon onion salt
1/2 teaspoon dry mustard
1/4 teaspoon ground red pepper

• **Sprinkle** 2 tablespoons Parmesan cheese evenly into five buttered individual soufflé dishes or 6-ounce custard cups. Set aside.
• **Beat** egg whites at high speed with an electric mixer until stiff.
• **Combine** egg yolks, Cheddar cheese, and next 6 ingredients in container of an electric blender; process 30 seconds or until smooth, stopping once to scrape down sides. Process at high speed 10 to 15 seconds; pour into a bowl. Fold in egg whites; pour into prepared dishes. Seal in aluminum foil, and freeze up to 1 week.
• **Unwrap** soufflés, and place in an 8-inch square pan. Add hot water to pan to depth of 1 inch.
• **Bake** at 400° for 10 minutes; reduce heat to 350°, and bake 20 to 25 additional minutes or until puffed and golden. Serve immediately. **Yield:** 5 servings.

Note: If not freezing soufflés, bake as directed at 350° for 20 to 25 minutes.

SAY CHEESE

Split Creek Farm in Anderson, South Carolina, got our goat with this creamy soup. Goat dairy farm owner Evin J. Evans shared partner Patricia Bell's recipe for a rich, satisfying appetizer. It's so easy you'll want to try it, too.

HERBED CHEESE SOUP

1/4 cup butter or margarine
3 tablespoons all-purpose flour
1 tablespoon chopped fresh chives
1 1/2 teaspoons paprika
1/2 teaspoon dry mustard
1/4 teaspoon salt
Dash of freshly ground pepper
2 cups chicken broth
2 cups half-and-half
8 ounces fresh goat cheese (chèvre), crumbled *
1 clove garlic, minced
1/4 teaspoon caraway seeds, crushed
1 teaspoon dried basil
1 teaspoon dried dillweed
Garnish: fresh chives

• **Melt** butter in a large saucepan over medium-high heat. Whisk in flour and next 5 ingredients. Cook 3 minutes, whisking constantly. Gradually add broth and half-and-half, and cook, whisking constantly, until smooth.
• **Add** cheese and next 4 ingredients; reduce heat to low, and cook 10 minutes, whisking constantly. Garnish, if desired. **Yield:** 4 servings.

* You can substitute 1 (8-ounce) package cream cheese, cubed, for fresh goat cheese.

QUICK & EASY

Tomato Pasta Toppers

Some foods, including pasta and tomatoes, lend themselves to speedy supper preparation. During this busy back-to-school season, a fast meal for the whole family is a wonderful treat.

DRIED TOMATO SAUCE

1 (8-ounce) jar oil-packed dried tomatoes
3 cloves garlic
2 tablespoons white wine vinegar
1 (2¼-ounce) can sliced ripe olives
¼ teaspoon salt
Hot cooked fettuccine

• **Drain** tomatoes, reserving ¼ cup oil in a large skillet; chop tomatoes and garlic, and add to skillet.
• **Cook** over medium-high heat 3 minutes, stirring constantly; stir in vinegar, olives, and salt. Serve sauce over fettuccine. **Yield:** 1½ cups.

TOMATO-BASIL SAUCE

1 pint cherry tomatoes, cut in half
1 cup fresh basil leaves, chopped
¼ cup olive oil
½ teaspoon salt
½ teaspoon pepper
Hot cooked angel hair pasta

• **Combine** first 5 ingredients in a large bowl, tossing gently to coat; let stand 30 minutes. Serve over angel hair pasta. **Yield:** 2 cups.

Hilda Marshall
Culpeper, Virginia

SPICY GINGERED TOMATO SAUCE

5 serrano chile peppers, chopped
3 jalapeño peppers, chopped
2 cloves garlic, chopped
½ onion, chopped
½ green bell pepper, chopped
¼ cup minced fresh ginger
2 (8-ounce) cans tomato sauce
1 teaspoon garlic salt
1 teaspoon lemon pepper
Hot cooked spaghetti

• **Combine** first 9 ingredients in container of an electric blender, and process until smooth, stopping once to scrape down sides. Serve over spaghetti. **Yield:** 2¾ cups.

Judy Carter
Winchester, Tennessee

VEGETABLE SALSA

½ cup fresh or frozen whole kernel corn, thawed
2 medium tomatoes, chopped
1 small cucumber, chopped
2 to 4 tablespoons Italian salad dressing
Hot cooked rotini

• **Combine** first 4 ingredients, tossing gently. Serve over rotini. **Yield:** 4 cups.

June Latimer
Lancaster, South Carolina

PICANTE-BEAN SAUCE

1 (15-ounce) can Mexican beans, drained
1 cup chunky picante sauce
¼ cup chopped fresh cilantro
Hot cooked orzo

• **Cook** beans and picante sauce in a large saucepan over medium heat, stirring gently, until thoroughly heated; stir in cilantro. Serve over orzo. **Yield:** 2½ cups.

Denise Corr
Sugarland, Texas

PASTA PARTICULARS

Angel hair: Long, delicate pasta, thinner than spaghetti

Fettuccine: Egg noodles cut into ¼-inch-wide flat ribbons

Orzo: Rice-shaped pasta

Rotini: From rotelle, meaning little corkscrews; 1- to 2-inch-long spirals

Spaghetti: From the Italian word for strings; long, thin, round strands

This Red Beans and Rice dish (recipe, page 218) owes its fiery goodness to andouille sausage and lots of peppery seasonings.

Above: *The Dill Mayonnaise slathered on Batter-Fried Grouper Sandwich (recipes, page 197) is also great with crab cakes or cold steamed lobster.*

Right: *You'll get a kick from the jalapeño-dotted batter of South-of-the-Border Onion Rings (recipe, page 217).*

Left: *This light Grilled Seafood Po'boy (recipe, page 244) will top any fried seafood sandwich you've ever had.*

Below left: *Oven frying is the secret to spicy, low-fat Seasoned French Fries (recipe, page 245).*

Below: *Refresh parched party guests with Fruit Juice Punch, and Pimm's Cup, while they nibble on Oriental Crunch. (Recipes begin on page 214.)*

Come home to a piece of Peanut Butter-Fudge Cake (recipe, page 254) and a glass of cold milk.

LASAGNA

Making lasagna can either be a time-consuming assembly of scratch ingredients or a quick layering of convenience products. Either way, lasagna is always a hit. Add a tossed green salad and hot, crusty bread for a hearty, satisfying family meal or casual supper with friends.

MICROWAVE LASAGNA

1 pound ground beef
1 (28-ounce) jar spaghetti sauce
½ cup water
1½ cups cottage cheese
1 large egg, lightly beaten
1½ teaspoons pepper
8 lasagna noodles, uncooked
1 (10-ounce) package frozen chopped spinach, thawed
2 cups (8 ounces) shredded mozzarella cheese
½ cup grated Parmesan cheese

• **Crumble** beef in a 2-quart bowl. Microwave at HIGH 4 minutes or until browned, stirring once; drain. Stir in spaghetti sauce and water.
• **Combine** cottage cheese, egg, and pepper.
• **Spread** ½ cup meat sauce in a 13- x 9- x 2-inch baking dish. Top with half each of noodles, cottage cheese mixture, spinach, meat sauce, and mozzarella cheese. Repeat layers with remaining noodles, cottage cheese mixture, spinach, meat sauce, and mozzarella cheese; cover with heavy-duty plastic wrap.
• **Microwave** at HIGH 8 minutes; microwave at MEDIUM (50% power) 30 to 32 minutes or until noodles are tender, turning dish occasionally.
• **Sprinkle** with Parmesan cheese; cover and let stand 15 minutes before serving. **Yield:** 6 servings.

Queever Bronssard
New Iberia, Louisiana

ITALIAN SAUSAGE LASAGNA

12 lasagna noodles, uncooked
1 pound Italian sausage
1 medium onion, chopped
1 clove garlic, pressed
3 tablespoons dried parsley flakes, divided
1 (16-ounce) can whole tomatoes, chopped and undrained
1 (15-ounce) can tomato sauce
1 teaspoon sugar
1 teaspoon dried basil
½ teaspoon salt
1 (16-ounce) carton ricotta cheese
¼ cup grated Parmesan cheese
1½ teaspoons dried oregano
2 cups (8 ounces) shredded mozzarella cheese
2 tablespoons grated Parmesan cheese

• **Cook** noodles according to package directions; drain and set aside.
• **Remove** and discard casings from sausage. Cook sausage, onion, and garlic in a large skillet, stirring until sausage crumbles; drain.
• **Stir** in 2 tablespoons parsley, tomatoes, tomato sauce, sugar, basil, and salt; bring to a boil. Reduce heat, and simmer 45 minutes or until mixture is slightly thickened, stirring occasionally.
• **Combine** remaining 1 tablespoon parsley, ricotta cheese, ¼ cup grated Parmesan cheese, and oregano; set aside.
• **Spread** 1 cup meat mixture in a lightly greased 13- x 9- x 2-inch baking dish. Top with 4 noodles, 1 cup ricotta cheese mixture, ⅔ cup mozzarella cheese, and 4 more noodles. Spread remaining ricotta cheese mixture over noodles, and top with 1 cup meat mixture, ⅔ cup mozzarella cheese, and remaining 4 noodles. Top with remaining meat mixture and mozzarella cheese; sprinkle with 2 tablespoons Parmesan cheese.
• **Bake** at 350° for 45 minutes or until bubbly. Let stand 10 minutes before serving. **Yield:** 6 servings.

Sandra Enwright
Winter Park, Florida

GOURMET WHITE LASAGNA

8 lasagna noodles, uncooked
1 pound ground beef
½ pound ground pork sausage
1 cup chopped onion
½ cup chopped celery
1 clove garlic, minced
2 teaspoons dried basil
1 teaspoon dried oregano
½ teaspoon dried Italian seasoning
½ teaspoon salt
1 cup half-and-half
1 (3-ounce) package cream cheese, softened
½ cup dry white wine
2 cups (8 ounces) shredded Cheddar cheese
1½ cups (6 ounces) shredded Gouda cheese
1 (12-ounce) carton small-curd cottage cheese
1 large egg, lightly beaten
2 cups (8 ounces) shredded mozzarella cheese

• **Cook** noodles according to package directions; drain and set aside.
• **Cook** ground beef and next 4 ingredients in a large skillet, stirring until meats crumble; drain. Stir in basil and next 5 ingredients. Stir in wine and Cheddar and Gouda cheeses; cook, stirring constantly, until cheese melts. Set aside.
• **Combine** cottage cheese and egg; set aside.
• **Arrange** half of noodles in a lightly greased 13- x 9- x 2-inch baking dish; top with half each of meat mixture, cottage cheese mixture, and mozzarella cheese. Repeat layers with remaining meat mixture, cottage cheese mixture, and mozzarella cheese.
• **Bake** at 350° for 40 minutes; let stand 10 minutes before serving. **Yield:** 6 servings.

Mrs. Larry Coppernoll
Linden, North Carolina

UNDER COVER

It's no wonder people quickly change their minds when they switch to low-fat foods. Eating naked fish or chicken night after night will drive most anyone to the nearest drive-through. But adding a coat of flavor can make healthy dinners a welcome routine. Try our recipes to dress up ordinary entrées with rubs, marinades, and crusts.

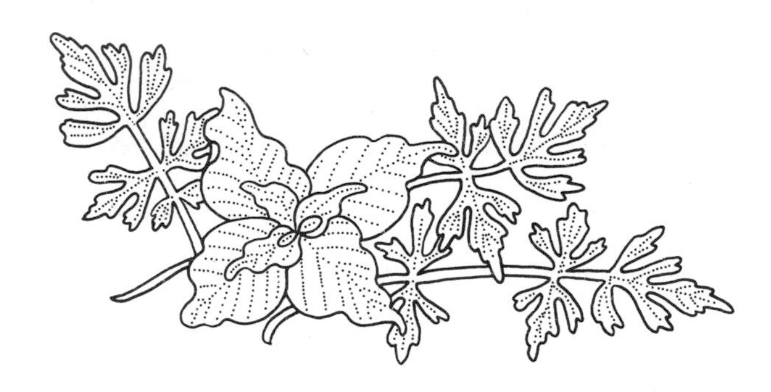

PORK CHOPS WITH WHITE BEAN PUREE

2 (6-ounce) boneless pork loin chops (½ inch thick)
2 teaspoons Cajun spice for pork and veal
1 teaspoon olive oil
½ cup chopped onion
2 cloves garlic, minced
½ cup chicken broth
¼ cup currant jelly
2 tablespoons balsamic vinegar
2 cloves garlic
1 (15-ounce) can Great Northern beans, rinsed and drained
2 tablespoons chicken broth
1 tablespoon chopped fresh cilantro
½ teaspoon pepper

• **Rub** chops with Cajun spice; cook in oil in a large skillet over medium-high heat until browned on both sides. Remove from skillet, reserving drippings in skillet. Add onion and 2 minced cloves garlic to drippings; cook until tender. Return chops to skillet.
• **Add** ½ cup broth, jelly, and vinegar; cover and simmer 10 to 15 minutes or until chops are tender. Transfer to a serving plate; keep warm.
• **Combine** 2 garlic cloves and next 4 ingredients in container of an electric blender or food processor; process until smooth, stopping once to scrape down sides. Pour into a heavy saucepan; cook over low heat, stirring constantly, until thoroughly heated. Serve with chops. **Yield:** 2 servings.

Note: For Cajun spice for pork and veal we used Paul Prudhomme brand.

Mrs. William Alvine
Casselberry, Florida

❤ Per serving: Calories 576 (23% from fat) Fat 14.5g (4.1g saturated) Cholesterol 93mg Sodium 167mg Carbohydrate 61.1g Fiber 8.9g Protein 47.5g

SESAME-CRUSTED CHICKEN WITH PINEAPPLE SALSA

½ cup sesame seeds
2 tablespoons minced fresh ginger
2 teaspoons vegetable oil
4 (4-ounce) skinned and boned chicken breast halves
½ teaspoon salt
Pineapple Salsa

• **Bake** sesame seeds in a shallow pan at 350° for 5 minutes or until toasted, stirring frequently; cool.
• **Combine** sesame seeds, ginger, and oil, stirring well.
• **Sprinkle** chicken with salt; coat with sesame seed mixture, and place on a lightly greased rack in broiler pan.
• **Bake** at 400° for 20 to 25 minutes or until tender. Top evenly with Pineapple Salsa, and serve immediately. **Yield:** 4 servings.

❤ Per serving: Calories 572 (25% from fat) Fat 15.5g (2.4g saturated) Cholesterol 196mg Sodium 519mg Carbohydrate 22.7g Fiber 1.2g Protein 81.7g

Pineapple Salsa

1 (15¼-ounce) can pineapple tidbits, drained
½ cup chopped red bell pepper
1 teaspoon grated fresh ginger
1 tablespoon fresh lime juice
Pinch of ground cloves
¼ cup chopped fresh cilantro
¼ teaspoon hot sauce

• **Combine** all ingredients in a medium bowl; cover and chill 15 minutes. **Yield:** 1½ cups.

Judy Carter
Winchester, Tennessee

Living Light: It's a Family Thing

About five years ago, Scott Roark and Jennifer Chasedunn of Mount Pleasant, South Carolina, made a big change in the way that their family ate. Scott shares their story about what they learned from the metamorphosis.

■ "I had withdrawal symptoms when I gave up ice cream and potato chips," he admits. "But if you do it gradually, eliminating one high-fat food at a time, it's easier."

■ Scott advises, "Don't let your kids grow up with bad eating habits, and they won't have to break them years from now."

■ "Get the family together for dinner every night," he suggests. "It takes extra effort, but the time you spend teaching your children to eat right will pay off in the future."

■ Here are more words of wisdom from their family: Eliminate cream sauces; cook on the grill often; eat pasta, seafood, chicken, and lean pork; do not buy junk food; make dessert an occasional treat; and splurge when you go out to dinner.

TAME HORSERADISH

Combined with breadcrumbs, horseradish loses some of its pungent bite, making it a fitting crust for fresh fish. This easy dish has about 300 calories and 10 grams of fat per serving.

Horseradish-Crusted Red Snapper: Combine ½ cup prepared horseradish, 1 cup soft breadcrumbs, and 2 tablespoons olive oil in a small bowl. Sprinkle 4 (1¾-inch-thick) red snapper fillets (1½ pounds) evenly with ¼ teaspoon salt and ¼ teaspoon freshly ground pepper. Coat fillets with horseradish mixture, and place on a lightly greased rack in broiler pan. Bake at 400° for 20 minutes or until fish flakes easily when tested with a fork. **Yield:** 4 servings.

JAVA FAJITAS

Brewed coffee gives these fajitas their unique flavor.

⅓ cup tomato paste
1¼ cups strongly brewed coffee
½ cup Worcestershire sauce
1 tablespoon sugar
2 teaspoons ground red pepper
1 teaspoon ground black pepper
3 tablespoons fresh lime juice
1 tablespoon vegetable oil
2 (1½-pound) flank steaks
24 (10-inch) flour tortillas
Pico de Gallo
Garnishes: fresh cilantro sprigs, lime wedges, serrano chile peppers, avocado slices

• **Combine** first 8 ingredients in a shallow dish or large heavy-duty, zip-top plastic bag; add steaks. Cover or seal; chill 8 hours, turning occasionally.
• **Remove** steaks from marinade, reserving marinade.
• **Cook** steaks, covered with grill lid, over hot coals (400° to 500°) about 6 minutes on each side or to desired degree of doneness.
• **Cut** steaks diagonally across grain into thin slices; keep warm.
• **Bring** reserved marinade to a boil in a skillet; boil 10 to 15 minutes or until reduced to 1 cup.
• **Place** steak down center of tortillas; drizzle with reduced marinade, and top with Pico de Gallo. Roll up, and serve immediately. Garnish, if desired. **Yield:** 12 servings.

Pico de Gallo

2 medium tomatoes, chopped
½ onion, chopped
3 serrano chile peppers, chopped
½ cup fresh cilantro, chopped
¼ teaspoon salt
¼ teaspoon ground white pepper
2 tablespoons lemon juice

• **Combine** all ingredients in a medium bowl. Cover and chill at least 3 hours. **Yield:** 3 cups.

Janie Baur
Spring, Texas

❤ Per serving: Calories 590 (32% from fat) Fat 20.7g (6.9g saturated) Cholesterol 62mg Sodium 1038mg Carbohydrate 67.7g Fiber 5g Protein 33.5g

Jewish Holiday Traditions

As the sun sets on September 13, Rosh Hashanah begins a new year. This celebration ends 10 days later with the fast of Yom Kippur, the Day of Atonement and most solemn Jewish holiday. On September 27, Succot, a harvest festival, continues the fall festivities.

Holiday tables have long been laden with symbolic foods, such as apples, honey, and sweet-tasting vegetables, which represent hope for a good year and appreciation for the harvest.

The practice of abiding by kosher laws, which are dictated by biblical laws, is part of some Jewish traditions. Although these laws fill volumes, the basics in kosher cooking prohibit eating shellfish, fish without scales, and pork, and eating meat with dairy products at the same meal.

BRISKET

1 (5-pound) beef brisket
½ teaspoon salt
½ teaspoon pepper
1 pound carrots, scraped and cut into chunks
4 pounds small new potatoes
2 cups water
¼ cup Worcestershire sauce
1 (1-ounce) envelope onion soup mix

• **Trim** fat from brisket; place brisket in a large Dutch oven. Sprinkle with salt and pepper. Add carrot and next 3 ingredients; sprinkle with soup mix.
• **Cover** and bake at 350° for 4 hours. **Yield:** 8 servings.

Stephanie Fierman
Birmingham, Alabama

VEGETABLE-NOODLE KUGEL

Traditionally, kugel is served as a side dish on the Jewish Sabbath. Our version adds carrots and zucchini to the baked pudding.

1 (8-ounce) package medium egg noodles
1 onion, chopped
2 carrots, scraped and coarsely shredded
1 zucchini, coarsely shredded
1 tablespoon vegetable oil
1 (16-ounce) carton sour cream
1 (12-ounce) carton cottage cheese
1 teaspoon dried rosemary, crushed
½ teaspoon salt
¾ teaspoon pepper
¼ cup grated Parmesan cheese

• **Cook** noodles according to package directions; drain.
• **Cook** onion, carrot, and zucchini in oil in a large skillet until tender; stir in noodles, sour cream, and next 4 ingredients. Spoon into a lightly greased 2-quart baking dish.
• **Cover** and bake at 350° for 25 minutes; sprinkle with Parmesan cheese, and bake, uncovered, 5 additional minutes. **Yield:** 6 to 8 servings.

APPLE-CREAM CHEESE TART

Cream Cheese Pastry
½ (8-ounce) package cream cheese, softened
¼ cup sour cream
1 egg yolk
2 tablespoons honey
⅛ teaspoon grated lemon rind
1 large Granny Smith apple, peeled and thinly sliced
1 tablespoon apple jelly
1½ teaspoons water
½ cup whipping cream
1½ teaspoons honey
⅛ teaspoon vanilla extract

• **Roll** Cream Cheese Pastry to ⅛-inch thickness on a lightly floured surface; fit into a 7½-inch round tart pan with removable bottom. Trim excess pastry along edges; freeze 10 minutes. Line pastry with aluminum foil, and fill with pie weights or dried beans.
• **Bake** at 400° for 10 minutes. Remove weights and foil, and prick bottom of crust with a fork. Bake 10 additional minutes. Cool on a wire rack (pastry will shrink).
• **Beat** cream cheese and next 4 ingredients in a mixing bowl at medium speed with an electric mixer until smooth. Spoon into tart shell, and arrange apple slices on top.
• **Combine** apple jelly and water in a small saucepan; cook over low heat, stirring constantly, until jelly melts. Brush half of jelly mixture over apples.
• **Bake** at 400° on lower oven rack 35 minutes. Cool on wire rack 15 minutes. Brush with remaining jelly mixture; cool.
• **Beat** whipping cream at medium speed until soft peaks form; stir in 1½ teaspoons honey and vanilla. Serve with tart. **Yield:** 1 (7½-inch) tart.

Cream Cheese Pastry

The food processor makes quick work of this flaky pastry.

¼ cup butter, cut up
½ (8-ounce) package cream cheese, cut up
1 cup all-purpose flour
¼ teaspoon salt

• **Combine** all ingredients with pastry blender or in a food processor. Shape into a ball; seal in plastic wrap, and chill at least 30 minutes (pastry will be dry). **Yield:** enough for 1 (7½-inch) tart shell.

Elizabeth Berek Ellis
Austin, Texas

Food Processor Cakes

A food processor is unbeatable for chopping and slicing, but it can also do more delicate tasks like whipping cake batter and frosting. It's quicker than a mixer and, because the processor bowl has a lid, there's no wiping batter off the wall.

We tested these recipes with a full-size food processor, but if you don't have one, an electric mixer will do just as well. Follow recipe directions, beating just until blended after each additional ingredient.

CHOCOLATE CAKE LAYERS

Freeze cake layers, wrapped tightly in plastic wrap and foil, up to 1 month. Thaw before frosting.

1⅓ cups sifted cake flour
1 teaspoon baking soda
¼ teaspoon salt
½ cup butter or margarine, softened
1⅓ cups sugar
2 large eggs
3 (1-ounce) squares unsweetened chocolate, melted
⅔ cup milk
1 teaspoon vanilla extract

• **Grease** three 8-inch round cakepans; line with wax paper. Grease and flour wax paper; set pans aside.
• **Combine** cake flour, soda, and salt; set aside.
• **Position** knife blade in food processor bowl; add butter and sugar, and process 1 to 2 minutes or until well blended, stopping twice to scrape down sides.
• **Add** eggs, and pulse twice, stopping to scrape down sides of bowl after each pulse. Add chocolate, and pulse twice, stopping to scrape down sides after each pulse.
• **Add** milk and vanilla; process 2 seconds. Add flour mixture; pulse twice, stopping to scrape down sides after each pulse. Pour batter evenly into prepared pans.
• **Bake** at 350° for 18 to 20 minutes or until a wooden pick inserted in center comes out clean. Cool in pans on wire racks 10 minutes; remove from pans, and cool completely on wire racks. **Yield:** 3 (8-inch) cake layers.

Choco-Cherry Cake: Spread 1 (21-ounce) can cherry pie filling between Chocolate Cake Layers; spread top and sides of cake with Whipped Cream Frosting. Cover and chill. **Yield:** 1 (3-layer) cake.

Hooray Parfaits: Crumble 1 Chocolate Cake Layer; set aside. Prepare 1 (3.4-ounce) package vanilla instant pudding mix according to package directions. Layer crumbled cake, pudding, 1½ cups candy-coated chocolate pieces, 1 (6-ounce) container frozen whipped topping, thawed, and 1 cup semisweet chocolate morsels in parfait glasses. Cover and chill. **Yield:** 6 to 8 servings.

PEANUT BUTTER FILLING

¼ cup butter or margarine, softened
1½ cups sifted powdered sugar
¼ cup creamy peanut butter
1½ tablespoons milk
1 teaspoon vanilla extract

• **Position** knife blade in food processor bowl; add butter and half of powdered sugar, and process until creamy.
• **Add** remaining sugar, peanut butter, milk, and vanilla; process until smooth, stopping once to scrape down sides. **Yield:** about 1 cup.

Note: For a 3-layer cake, double filling recipe.

MINT-CREAM FILLING

1 cup whipping cream
2 or 3 drops of green liquid food coloring *
2 tablespoons powdered sugar
¼ teaspoon peppermint extract *

• **Position** knife blade in food processor bowl; add whipping cream and food coloring, and process until foamy. Gradually add sugar, processing until soft peaks form, stopping once to scrape down sides. Stir in peppermint extract. **Yield:** 1½ cups.

* You can substitute 2 tablespoons green crème de menthe for food coloring and peppermint extract.

WHIPPED CREAM FROSTING

2 cups whipping cream
2 tablespoons powdered sugar
1 teaspoon vanilla extract

• **Position** knife blade in food processor bowl; add all ingredients. Process until soft peaks form, stopping once to scrape down sides. **Yield:** 4 cups.

CHOCOLATE BUTTERCREAM FROSTING

1½ cups butter or margarine, softened
4 cups sifted powdered sugar
¼ cup cocoa
2 tablespoons milk
1 teaspoon vanilla extract

• **Position** knife blade in food processor bowl; add butter and half of powdered sugar, and process until creamy.
• **Add** remaining sugar and cocoa; process until light and fluffy, stopping once to scrape down sides. Add milk and vanilla, and process until spreading consistency. **Yield:** 3 cups.

Vanilla Buttercream Frosting: Prepare as directed, omitting cocoa.

From Our Kitchen to Yours

CRISSCROSS YOUR FLOSS

Bettie K. Chastain wrote us from her Ooltewah, Tennessee, kitchen after reading about slicing cookie dough with dental floss in our May column (page 140). Instead of using a sawing motion, Bettie places a 20-inch piece of floss under the dough (about ¼ inch from the end for each slice), brings the floss ends up, crisscrosses them, and pulls the ends down in opposite directions. She says she's been getting clean cuts for years on cinnamon rolls and cheese logs as well as cookie dough. (Either method works on rolls of soft goat cheese, too.)

CALIBRATION CELEBRATIONS

Ovens can develop hot spots and bake unevenly, or the actual oven temperature can stray from what the dial or indicator registers.

For a home remedy approach, buy an oven thermometer to leave in the oven. If the thermometer reads the same as the temperature you set on the oven, then you're fine. If there's a discrepancy, go with the thermometer reading. In the future, set the dial higher or lower to compensate. (If you set the dial at 350° and the thermometer reads 400°, then set it at 300° to get the desired 350°.)

If all that math is harrowing, you can skip the thermometer and resolve the problem by having your oven professionally calibrated. This not only solves your temperature differences but also prevents uneven baking from hot spots. Call an appliance service company or your local electric company to schedule this service.

TAKE LEAVE OF YOUR SENSES

Garnishes from the garden, such as chocolate leaves on desserts, are popular for entertaining. You simply paint melted chocolate on the underside of leaves with a paintbrush, let it dry, then peel the real leaves away. Beware of two drawbacks: Real leaves may be poisonous, and they might tear easily. If you'd rather skip the risk *and* the frustration, use silk greenery for this project instead.

A JUICY SECRET

After you finish a jar of pickled jalapeño peppers, okra, or pepperoncini, there's a lot of juice left in the jar. If your frugal side gets the best of you, pour the juice into a shallow container or heavy-duty, zip-top plastic bag and add a carrot or two and a celery stalk cut into sticks. Now you have a quick snack, and you've gotten your conscience out of a pickle.

MORE STARRING ROLES

Here are a few easy ways to make even the plainest desserts twinkle.

- Melt semisweet chocolate squares or morsels in a sealed heavy-duty, zip-top plastic bag in the microwave. (Microwave at HIGH for 30-second intervals, kneading the bag gently between zaps, until melted.) Snip a tiny hole in one corner from the bottom of the bag and squirt star shapes on dessert plates. Chill until hardened and then stack plates with wax paper between them until time to serve.

- Cut sugar cookie dough or piecrust pastry with a star-shaped cutter. Bake the stars and then dip halfway into melted chocolate. Serve ice cream in a stemmed glass with cookies or pastries stuck vertically into the ice cream.

- Peel oranges in large pieces. Cut rind into star shapes with a paring knife. Float citrus stars in a punch bowl or freeze with juice in ice cubes for individual drinks.

STAR LIGHT, STAR BRIGHT

Create this sparkling make-ahead plate garnish from stellar cowboy cook and creative chef Stephan Pyles of Star Canyon restaurant in Dallas. Billing his fare as new Texas cuisine, Stephan rethinks the old idea of branding with a rosette iron.

Sprinkle 2 to 3 tablespoons granulated sugar off-center on each dessert plate. Then hold a star-shaped rosette iron over the flame on a gas cooktop or directly on a smooth-surface electric cooktop for a few minutes. Immediately place the hot iron on the sugar and hold until you see the sugar browning around the edges of the iron. Remove the iron and turn the plate up over the sink, letting the loose sugar fall away.

You can brand your plates a day ahead and stack them with wax paper between each.

HONK IF YOU'RE A TAILGATER

Tailgating can be hazardous in 5 o'clock traffic, but tailgating of another kind is a must on game day. During this season of football parties, follow these guidelines for food safety so the big game isn't, pardon the pun, spoiled.

- Keep hot foods HOT: Don't depend on warming units that use small candles to keep foods hot. Use electric skillets, chafing dishes, or hot trays. Always keep hot foods at least 140° to avoid the risk of food poisoning.

- Hot foods being transported should be kept at 140° or hotter, too. Take advantage of casserole quilts, baking dish baskets, or cardboard boxes lined with several thicknesses of newspaper to help hold the heat.

- Keep cold foods COLD: Serve food in small dishes, refilling frequently from refrigerator. Bacterial growth starts very quickly above 40°.

- Use an insulated cooler to transport food, and avoid storing it in the trunk of your vehicle.

- Include a cold source such as ice, commercial ice packs, or frozen water or juice as you pack your coolers.

October

A Taste of the Ozarks

Join us in this culinary journey through picturesque northern Arkansas and southern Missouri. These regional dishes from the area's best restaurants reflect the Ozark mountains' innovative fare as well as down-home classics. Enjoy a taste of the good life.

■ Sprawling Big Cedar Lodge, owned by the Bass Pro Shops, celebrates bass fishing in sumptuous but rustic elegance. Its **Devil's Pool Restaurant** overlooks Table Rock Lake – a 43,000-acre angler's playground – and features woodsy delights crafted by Chef Robert Sticklin.

MAPLE-GLAZED QUAIL WITH WHITE BEAN RAGOÛT

4 (4-ounce) dressed quail
2 medium onions, diced
1 tablespoon sugar
4 fresh mushrooms, sliced
1 teaspoon white vinegar
⅓ cup fine, dry breadcrumbs
¼ teaspoon salt
¼ teaspoon pepper
¼ teaspoon dried thyme
3 tablespoons butter or margarine, melted
White Bean Ragoût
Maple Brown Sauce

• **Remove** breast and back bones from quail; set quail aside.
• **Cook** onion in a nonstick skillet over low heat 10 minutes or until browned, stirring often; add sugar and mushrooms, and cook until tender, stirring often. Stir in vinegar and next 4 ingredients. Spoon into quail cavities, and secure with wooden picks. Tuck wings under, and place, breast side up, in a buttered 2-quart casserole. Brush with melted butter.
• **Bake** at 350° for 20 minutes or until done. Serve over a bed of White Bean Ragoût; drizzle with Maple Brown Sauce. **Yield:** 2 servings.

White Bean Ragoût

1 cup dried Great Northern or navy beans
½ cup diced onion
1 bay leaf
3 tablespoons diced carrot
2 cups beef broth

• **Sort** and wash beans; drain.
• **Combine** beans and water to cover in a large saucepan; let stand 1 hour. Drain beans, and return to pan. Add onion and remaining ingredients; bring to a boil. Reduce heat, and simmer 2 hours or until beans are tender, stirring occasionally. Remove and discard bay leaf. **Yield:** 2 cups.

Maple Brown Sauce

1 teaspoon butter or margarine
1 teaspoon all-purpose flour
½ cup beef broth
1 tablespoon maple syrup

• **Melt** butter in a small heavy saucepan over low heat; whisk in flour until smooth. Cook 1 minute, whisking constantly. Whisk in broth; cook over medium heat 5 minutes or until thickened and bubbly, whisking constantly. Stir in maple syrup. **Yield:** ½ cup.

Devil's Pool Restaurant
Big Cedar Lodge
Ridgedale, Missouri

■ At **Gaston's White River Resort** trout is the guest of honor. The ice-cold White River is full of elusive rainbows and browns that hook fishermen to the rustic resort. The menu offers trout everything, and every seat in the riverfront restaurant offers a view.

GASTON'S TROUT AMANDINE

4 medium rainbow or brook trout, dressed
2 tablespoons fresh lemon juice
Cracked pepper
½ cup butter or margarine, divided
1½ cups slivered almonds
¼ cup fresh lemon juice
2 tablespoons minced fresh parsley
Garnish: lemon slices

• **Brush** trout with 2 tablespoons lemon juice, and sprinkle with cracked pepper.
• **Melt** 2 tablespoons butter in a large nonstick skillet over medium-high heat; add 2 trout, and cook 6 to 8 minutes or until fish flakes easily when

tested with a fork, turning once. Remove to serving platter; keep warm. Repeat procedure with remaining 2 tablespoons butter and trout. Wipe skillet with a paper towel.

• **Melt** remaining ¼ cup butter in skillet; add almonds. Cook until golden, stirring often. Stir in ¼ cup lemon juice and parsley; pour over trout. Garnish, if desired. **Yield:** 4 servings.

Gaston's White River Resort
Lakeview, Arkansas

> *"If we should press our ears to the ground we might hear the pulsing of a heart."*
>
> *Ozark novelist Ward Dorrance*
>
> Once touched by the ancient sound of a dulcimer, a part of you never leaves the Ozarks of northern Arkansas and southern Missouri. "It's a very healing, spiritual place," says one Arkansan. Such feelings also surround the area's foodways. With an abundance of trout, catfish, wild game, fresh herbs, and local vineyards, the good life follows. And so do we.

▪ A gas station attendant in Yellville, Arkansas, let us in on the best place to eat in town: the **Front Porch Restaurant**. The secret to their fried catfish? "We use a cornbread mix for our batter," reveals cook Sandy Sheilds.

FRONT PORCH FRIED CATFISH

- **2½ cups cornbread mix**
- **1 tablespoon garlic powder**
- **2 tablespoons dried thyme**
- **6 (¾- to 1-pound) farm-raised catfish fillets**
- **1 cup buttermilk**
- **1 tablespoon salt**
- **2 teaspoons ground black pepper**
- **2 teaspoons ground red pepper**
- **Peanut oil**

• **Combine** first 3 ingredients in a shallow dish. Dip fillets in buttermilk, allowing excess to drip off; sprinkle with salt and peppers, and dredge in cornbread mixture.

• **Pour** oil to depth of 4 inches into an electric fryer or Dutch oven; heat to 400°. Fry fillets, two at a time, 2 to 3 minutes or until they float; drain on paper towels. Serve immediately. **Yield:** 6 servings.

Front Porch Restaurant
Yellville, Arkansas

▪ Holding its chin up amongst wedding chapels and budget motels on the outskirts of Eureka, the **Cottage Inn** with its five one-bedroom cottages surrounds Linda Hager's Mediterranean-style restaurant. Here the emphasis is on flavor not fat.

SPANAKOPITA

- **2 (10-ounce) packages frozen chopped spinach, thawed and drained**
- **1 (8-ounce) package feta cheese, crumbled**
- **1 tablespoon dried oregano**
- **1 tablespoon dried dillweed**
- **1 (16-ounce) package frozen phyllo pastry, thawed**
- **⅓ cup butter or margarine, melted**
- **Garnishes: crumbled feta cheese, tomato wedges, pepperoncini peppers, and kalamata olives**

• **Combine** first 4 ingredients in a bowl, stirring well.

• **Unfold** phyllo, and cut into 2 (13- x 9-inch) rectangles, keeping phyllo covered with a slightly damp towel.

• **Place** 1 phyllo sheet in a buttered 13- x 9- x 2-inch baking dish; brush with melted butter. Place a phyllo sheet on top, allowing half of sheet to drape over one side of dish; brush portion in dish with melted butter. Repeat procedure with 15 more phyllo sheets, alternating sides of dish after each sheet so that each side of dish is covered.

• **Spread** spinach mixture evenly in dish; top with a phyllo sheet, and brush with melted butter. Fold 1 overhanging sheet on each side toward center; brush with butter. Top with a phyllo sheet; brush with butter. Repeat folding procedure with remaining overhanging phyllo sheets, topping each layer with a phyllo sheet and brushing with butter. Cut into 4 or 8 squares.

• **Bake** at 425° for 20 minutes or until golden. Garnish, if desired. **Yield:** 4 main-dish or 8 appetizer servings.

The Cottage Inn
Eureka Springs, Arkansas

▪ A sleek restaurant with even sleeker entrées, **James At The Mill** is tucked behind a restored pre-1835 mill-turned-hotel, Inn at the Mill. "I take the close-to-the-earth foods of the Ozarks to new heights," says Ozark native Miles James.

WARM GOAT CHEESE AND POTATO SALAD

4 large Yukon gold or red potatoes
Vegetable or corn oil
1 teaspoon salt, divided
1 teaspoon cracked pepper, divided
1 cup balsamic vinegar
8 bacon slices
1½ tablespoons balsamic vinegar
½ pound torn frisée or gourmet salad greens
1 tablespoon chopped fresh parsley
1 tablespoon chopped chives
1 tablespoon chopped fresh thyme
1 Granny Smith apple, cut into thin wedges
Warm Goat Cheese Fondue
Parsley Oil
Chili Oil

• **Cut** potatoes into rectangular blocks; dice trimmings.
• **Pour** oil to a depth of 3 inches into a Dutch oven; heat to 375°. Fry diced potato in oil 2 minutes or until golden. Drain and set aside. Fry potato blocks 6 minutes or until golden. Drain and place in a shallow pan.
• **Bake** at 375° for 10 minutes or until tender.
• **Sprinkle** diced potato and potato blocks with ½ teaspoon salt and ½ teaspoon pepper; cool.
• **Boil** 1 cup balsamic vinegar in a heavy nonstick skillet until reduced to ½ cup; set aside.
• **Cook** bacon in skillet until crisp; remove bacon, reserving 1½ tablespoons drippings in skillet. Crumble bacon, and set aside.
• **Add** remaining ½ teaspoon salt, ½ teaspoon pepper, and 1½ tablespoons balsamic vinegar to reserved drippings, stirring balsamic dressing well.
• **Combine** diced potato, bacon, frisée, and next 3 ingredients in a large salad bowl; drizzle with balsamic dressing, and toss gently.
• **Arrange** salad evenly on individual salad plates; stand potato blocks upright in center. Cut a slit in top of potato blocks; insert 3 or 4 apple wedges into each slit.
• **Spoon** Warm Goat Cheese Fondue onto plates; spoon over potato, if desired. Drizzle plate with reduced vinegar, Parsley Oil, and Chili Oil. Serve immediately. **Yield:** 4 servings.

Warm Goat Cheese Fondue

2 tablespoons minced shallot
1 tablespoon corn oil
2 tablespoons chopped fresh thyme
¾ cup whipping cream
1 (5.3-ounce) package goat cheese, crumbled
½ teaspoon salt
½ teaspoon cracked pepper

• **Cook** shallot in oil in a large nonstick skillet until tender, stirring often; stir in chopped thyme and whipping cream. Bring to a boil, stirring constantly; remove from heat. Whisk in goat cheese, salt, and pepper until smooth. **Yield:** about 1½ cups.

Parsley Oil

1 bunch Italian parsley, chopped
½ cup corn oil

• **Combine** parsley and oil in container of an electric blender, and process until combined, stopping once to scrape down sides; pour through a wire-mesh strainer into a small bowl, discarding parsley. **Yield:** ¼ cup.

Chili Oil

1 tablespoon chili powder
½ cup corn oil

• **Cook** chili powder in a nonstick skillet over high heat 1 minute, stirring constantly; remove from heat. Stir in oil; let stand 30 minutes.
• **Pour** mixture through a fine-mesh strainer into a small bowl, discarding chili powder. **Yield:** ½ cup.

James At The Mill
Johnson, Arkansas

HERE'S THE BEEF: WINNER DINNERS

First came the bad news: Budget cutbacks at Fran Yuhas's company in Pennsylvania left the 17-year employee and mother of two searching for a new job opportunity. Then came the good news: She received a check for $25,000 when her recipe for Grecian Skillet Rib Eyes garnered the top prize at the National Beef Cook-Off.

Fran's recipe is an original beef main dish with a total preparation time of less than 1 hour. It uses eight ingredients (excluding salt and pepper) and 1¾ to 2 pounds of beef. All of these winning recipes are easy and delicious.

GRECIAN SKILLET RIB EYES

You'll find that this olive-feta-herb topping works great on chicken and lamb, too.

1½ teaspoons garlic powder
1½ teaspoons dried basil, crushed
1½ teaspoons dried oregano, crushed
½ teaspoon salt
⅛ teaspoon pepper
2 (1-inch-thick) rib-eye steaks (1¾ to 2 pounds)
1 tablespoon olive oil
1 tablespoon fresh lemon juice
2 tablespoons crumbled feta cheese
1 tablespoon chopped kalamata or ripe olives

• **Combine** first 5 ingredients; rub onto all sides of steaks.
• **Pour** oil into a large nonstick skillet; place over medium heat until hot. Add steaks, and cook 10 to 14 minutes or to desired degree of doneness, turning once. Sprinkle with lemon juice; top with cheese and olives. **Yield:** 2 to 4 servings.

Fran Yuhas
Scotrun, Pennsylvania

SAVORY BEEF AND CHEESE ROLL-UPS

This unique sandwich won third prize (and $5,000).

2 (5-ounce) containers vegetable-flavored soft spreadable cheese
4 (10-inch) flour tortillas
1 cup shredded carrot
1 cup (4 ounces) shredded Monterey Jack cheese
8 lettuce leaves
1 pound thinly sliced roast beef

• **Spread** vegetable-flavored cheese evenly over 1 side of each tortilla; top each evenly with carrot, shredded cheese, lettuce, and roast beef, leaving a ½-inch border around edges.
• **Roll** up tortillas tightly, and wrap in plastic wrap. Store in refrigerator up to 8 hours.
• **Unwrap** roll-ups, and cut in half before serving. **Yield:** 4 servings.

Note: For spreadable cheese, we used Rondelé.

Jill Hilton
Cedar Rapids, Iowa

QUICK ITALIAN BEEF AND VEGETABLE SOUP

This ultra easy vegetable-packed soup took second-place honors (and $10,000).

1 medium zucchini
1 pound lean ground beef
1 clove garlic, pressed
½ teaspoon pepper
¼ teaspoon salt
2 (14½-ounce) cans ready-to-serve beef broth
1 (14½-ounce) can Italian-style stewed tomatoes, undrained
1 cup sliced carrots
1 (15.8-ounce) can cannellini or Great Northern beans, rinsed and drained
2 cups loosely packed torn fresh spinach, washed and trimmed

• **Cut** zucchini in half lengthwise; cut each half crosswise into ¼-inch-thick slices. Set aside.
• **Brown** ground beef and garlic in a large Dutch oven, stirring until beef crumbles; drain. Stir in pepper, salt, beef broth, stewed tomatoes, and carrot; bring to a boil. Cover, reduce heat, and simmer 10 minutes.
• **Stir** chopped zucchini and beans into liquid mixture in Dutch oven; cover and cook 4 to 5 minutes or until zucchini is crisp-tender, stirring mixture occasionally.
• **Remove** from heat, and stir in spinach. **Yield:** 3 to 4 servings.

Darol Wetzel
Manhattan, Montana

BEST BUY ON BEEF

Beef lovers agree that lower priced ground beef cooks up juicy and flavorful. And higher priced leaner ground beef makes a less-fatty burger, but is it as flavorful? And which lean-to-fat ratio in ground beef is the best buy?

We compared grilled ground beef, ground chuck, and low-fat ground beef. For the money, we preferred the flavor and texture of 80% lean ground chuck (see chart).

▪ Cover and store ground beef up to two days in the refrigerator, or freeze in the original packaging up to two weeks. For longer storage, wrap in heavy-duty aluminum foil, plastic wrap, or freezer paper, and freeze up to four months.

▪ Wash hands immediately before and after handling raw ground beef.

▪ Thaw frozen ground beef in the refrigerator. Allow 24 hours to thaw a 1- to 1½-inch-thick package.

▪ To freeze ground beef patties, place uncooked patties in a single layer on a baking sheet, and freeze until firm (about 30 minutes). Stack frozen patties, layering with wax paper in between layers; place in an airtight container. Freeze up to four months.

Ground beef packages are labeled according to USDA standards and by supermarket preference. Lean-to-fat ratios vary; however, if a package is labeled ground beef, it must be at least 70% lean. These figures are based on a burger weighing 3 ounces after cooking.

BEEF	CALORIES	FAT	OUR COST	INSIDERS' TIPS
73% lean (ground beef)	248	18g	$1.69/lb *	moist, juicy
80% lean (ground chuck)	228	15g	$1.79/lb *	juicy, firm, best flavor
93% lean (low-fat ground beef)	169	8g	$2.49/lb *	compact, drier, very firm

* Prices in your area may vary.

Sweet and Savory Grits

Grits for dessert? Definitely. With liver? Luscious. Humble hominy is showing up on dinner tables and restaurant menus across the country. The principle is simple: Serve grits in place of mashed potatoes, rice, or even noodles. Or if you're feeling adventuresome, consider grits as a base for a creamy, sweet dessert.

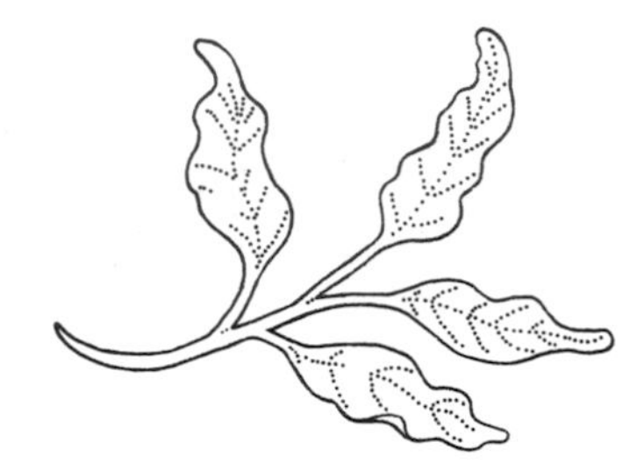

CREOLE LIVER

2 tablespoons all-purpose flour
½ teaspoon dried thyme
¼ teaspoon pepper
1 pound thinly sliced beef liver
2 tablespoons vegetable oil
1 medium onion, chopped
1 large green bell pepper, chopped
1 clove garlic, pressed
1 (14.5-ounce) can diced tomatoes, undrained
1 bay leaf
½ teaspoon salt
Hot cooked grits

• **Combine** first 3 ingredients in a shallow dish; dredge liver in flour mixture.
• **Cook** liver in oil in a large skillet over medium-high heat until browned, turning once. Remove liver, reserving drippings in skillet.
• **Add** onion, bell pepper, and garlic to reserved drippings, and cook until tender, stirring often. Add liver, tomatoes, bay leaf, and salt; cover, reduce heat, and simmer 10 minutes. Remove and discard bay leaf. Serve over grits. **Yield:** 4 servings.

Debbie E. Ipock
Charlotte, North Carolina

SPOONBREAD GRITS WITH SAVORY MUSHROOM SAUCE

(pictured on page 260)

1 (14½-ounce) can ready-to-serve chicken broth
½ cup uncooked quick-cooking grits
¼ cup butter or margarine
1 cup milk
1 cup buttermilk
3 large eggs, lightly beaten
1 cup yellow cornmeal
1 teaspoon baking powder
1 teaspoon salt
¼ teaspoon baking soda
⅛ teaspoon ground red pepper (optional)
Savory Mushroom Sauce
Garnish: fresh thyme sprigs

• **Bring** broth to a boil in a saucepan; stir in grits. Reduce heat, and simmer 5 to 7 minutes or until thickened, stirring occasionally. Stir in butter and next 3 ingredients.
• **Combine** cornmeal and next 4 ingredients; stir into grits mixture. Pour into a lightly greased 11- x 7- x 1½-inch baking dish.
• **Bake** at 425° for 45 minutes or until lightly browned. Cut into triangles, if desired, and serve with Savory Mushroom Sauce; garnish, if desired. **Yield:** 4 to 6 servings.

Savory Mushroom Sauce

2 tablespoons butter or margarine
3 (3½-ounce) packages fresh shiitake mushrooms, sliced
1 clove garlic, minced
2 tablespoons all-purpose flour
¼ cup dry white wine
1 cup chicken broth
½ teaspoon salt
¼ teaspoon pepper

• **Melt** butter in a skillet; add mushrooms and garlic, and cook until tender, stirring often. Remove mushrooms with a slotted spoon, reserving drippings in skillet.
• **Whisk** flour into reserved drippings until smooth. Cook, whisking constantly, until lightly browned. Gradually add wine and broth; cook over medium heat, whisking constantly, until thickened and bubbly. Stir in salt and pepper. Add mushrooms; cook, stirring constantly, until thoroughly heated. **Yield:** 2 cups.

Mrs. Charles DeHaven
Owensboro, Kentucky

PINEAPPLE-GRITS PIE

If you think grits are only a receptacle for redeye gravy, this recipe will make you think again.

2 cups water
½ cup uncooked quick-cooking grits
¼ teaspoon salt
1 (8-ounce) can crushed pineapple, drained
½ (8-ounce) package cream cheese, softened
3 large eggs
1 cup sugar
½ cup milk
¼ teaspoon vanilla extract
2 (9-inch) graham cracker crusts

• **Bring** water to a boil; add grits and salt, and return to a boil. Cover, reduce

heat to low, and cook 5 minutes, stirring occasionally. Remove from heat.
• **Combine** grits, pineapple, and cream cheese in container of an electric blender; process until smooth, stopping once to scrape down sides. With blender running, add eggs, one at a time. Add sugar, milk, and vanilla; process until smooth, stopping once to scrape down sides. Pour into crusts.
• **Bake** at 300° for 1 hour or until mixture is set; cool on a wire rack. **Yield:** 2 (9-inch) pies.

FALL FOR FLAVOR

Autumn is the vegetable garden's last hurrah. Greens have lost their bitter bite after a brush with the season's first frost. And root vegetables, now unearthed, bring rustic flavor to a chilly night's dinner.

Sturdy leaves of sage and rosemary have endured a season of summer heat. When brought to the kitchen, the herbs announce fall as much as a pumpkin does. Savor the final freshness of the season in these recipes at your harvest table.

VEAL CUTLETS WITH LEEKS AND ZINFANDEL CREAM

Wrap leftover leek tops in cheesecloth and use them to flavor soups.

3 leeks
3 tablespoons all-purpose flour
¾ teaspoon salt
½ teaspoon freshly ground pepper
1 pound veal cutlets
3 tablespoons olive oil, divided
½ cup white Zinfandel
½ cup whipping cream

• **Remove** and discard green tops from leeks. Cut white portions diagonally into thin slices; set aside.
• **Combine** flour, salt, and pepper in a shallow bowl; dredge cutlets in flour mixture.
• **Cook** cutlets in 2 tablespoons olive oil in a large skillet 2 minutes on each side or until cutlets are golden. Remove cutlets from pan to a serving platter, and keep warm.
• **Cook** leeks in remaining 1 tablespoon olive oil in skillet 1 minute; add wine, and cook 1 minute or until most of liquid evaporates, stirring often.
• **Add** whipping cream to leek mixture, and cook, stirring constantly, about 2 minutes or until mixture is reduced by half. Serve with veal. **Yield:** 4 servings.

Louise Mayer
Richmond, Virginia

PEPPER-SAGE CHICKEN

(pictured on page 258)

While the chicken marinates, wash a bunch of your favorite greens and put them on to boil. Peel, chop, and roast a few sweet potatoes, and you've got a meal your whole family will enjoy.

¼ cup water
¼ cup lemon juice
2 tablespoons white wine vinegar
2 tablespoons olive oil
2 teaspoons Dijon mustard
¼ cup chopped fresh sage
1 teaspoon cracked pepper
4 skinned and boned chicken breast halves
Vegetable cooking spray
Garnish: fresh sage sprigs

• **Combine** first 7 ingredients in a large heavy-duty, zip-top plastic bag, and add chicken. Seal and chill 1 hour, turning occasionally.
• **Remove** chicken from marinade, reserving marinade.
• **Cook** chicken in a skillet coated with cooking spray over medium-high heat until browned, turning once. Add reserved marinade, and bring to a boil. Reduce heat, and simmer 15 minutes. Slice chicken into strips. Garnish, if desired. **Yield:** 4 servings.

Patsy Bell Hobson
Liberty, Missouri

POTATO-AND-RUTABAGA GRATIN

(pictured on page 259)

1 large rutabaga
4 medium-size red potatoes
¼ cup butter or margarine
¼ cup all-purpose flour
2 cups whipping cream
1 teaspoon salt
¼ teaspoon ground white pepper
¼ teaspoon ground red pepper
Dash of ground nutmeg
½ cup grated Parmesan cheese
Garnishes: fresh sage and rosemary sprigs

• **Peel,** quarter, and thinly slice rutabaga. Peel and thinly slice potatoes; set aside.
• **Melt** butter in a heavy saucepan over low heat, and add flour, stirring until smooth. Cook 1 minute, stirring constantly. Gradually add whipping cream, and cook over medium heat, stirring constantly, until mixture is thickened and bubbly. Stir in salt and next 3 ingredients. Set sauce aside.
• **Sprinkle** Parmesan cheese in a 10-inch cast-iron skillet lined with parchment paper or aluminum foil, and arrange half of rutabaga slices over cheese.
• **Layer** ¾ cup sauce, potato slices, and ¾ cup sauce over rutabaga. Arrange remaining rutabaga slices on top, and add remaining sauce. Cover skillet tightly with aluminum foil.
• **Bake** at 400° for 1 hour; uncover and bake 20 additional minutes. Let stand 15 minutes. Invert onto a serving platter, and garnish, if desired. To serve, cut into wedges. **Yield:** 8 servings.

Steve Oldecker
Brunswick, Georgia

SWEET POTATO CROQUETTES

3 large sweet potatoes
⅓ cup sugar
2 tablespoons all-purpose flour
¼ teaspoon ground cinnamon
¼ teaspoon ground allspice
1 large egg, lightly beaten
18 large marshmallows
4 cups crushed corn flakes cereal
Vegetable oil

• **Cook** sweet potatoes in boiling water to cover 30 minutes or until tender. Drain; cool. Peel sweet potatoes; mash.
• **Combine** sugar and next 3 ingredients; stir sugar mixture and egg into mashed sweet potatoes. Shape mixture around marshmallows, and roll in crushed cereal; place in a single layer on a baking sheet. Cover and freeze 2 hours.
• **Pour** oil into a large skillet to depth of ½ inch; heat to 350°.
• **Fry** croquettes until golden, turning once. Serve immediately. **Yield:** 1½ dozen.

Betty Wall
Huntsville, Alabama

WHAT'S FOR SUPPER?

STUFFED BAKED POTATOES

Split open a hot baked potato and top its fluffy goodness with mounds of mouth-watering stuffings. Start with large russet potatoes. Wash, dry, and prick them with a fork. Then place them directly on an oven rack, and bake at 425° for 45 to 60 minutes. (Forget the foil because foil-wrapped potatoes steam rather than bake.)

Your perfectly baked potatoes will be hearty foundations for any of these recipes. Add a salad or fresh fruit to complete a weeknight meal.

CHICKEN FAJITA SPUDS

2 teaspoons ground cumin
1 teaspoon dried oregano, crushed
¼ teaspoon ground red pepper
½ teaspoon salt
6 skinned and boned chicken breast halves
6 large baked potatoes
1½ cups (6 ounces) shredded Mexican-style cheese blend, divided
1 (8-ounce) carton sour cream, divided
2 tablespoons butter or margarine
3 tablespoons milk
½ teaspoon salt
¼ teaspoon ground black pepper
1 (16-ounce) jar chunky salsa
Garnishes: chopped fresh cilantro, fresh cilantro sprigs

• **Combine** first 4 ingredients; rub onto all sides of chicken. Place chicken in a lightly greased 13- x 9- x 2-inch baking dish, and let stand 15 minutes.
• **Bake** at 400° for 6 minutes on each side. Cut into strips.
• **Cut** a 1-inch-wide strip from top of each baked potato. Carefully scoop out pulp, leaving shells intact; set shells aside. Mash pulp; stir in 1 cup cheese blend, ½ cup sour cream, butter, and next 3 ingredients. Spoon into shells, and place on a baking sheet.
• **Bake** potatoes at 350° for 20 minutes. Sprinkle with remaining cheese blend, and top with chicken. Bake 5 additional minutes or until cheese melts. Serve with remaining sour cream and salsa. Garnish, if desired. **Yield:** 6 servings.

Molly Connally
Annandale, Virginia

MUSHROOM-SWISS SPUDS

½ pound fresh mushrooms, sliced
1 teaspoon olive oil
6 small baked potatoes, split
1 (4-ounce) package shredded Swiss cheese
3 tablespoons chopped fresh parsley
3 tablespoons cooked, crumbled bacon
¼ cup sour cream
¼ teaspoon salt

• **Cook** mushrooms in hot oil in a large skillet 5 minutes, stirring constantly.
• **Sprinkle** each split baked potato evenly with cheese; microwave at HIGH 40 seconds or until cheese melts. Top with mushrooms, chopped parsley, and remaining ingredients. **Yield:** 6 servings.

Emelia Marx-Carman
Louisville, Kentucky

PAPA'S RELLENOS POTATOES

3 large baked potatoes
2 tablespoons butter or margarine
2 tablespoons milk
½ cup grated Parmesan cheese
½ cup frozen English peas, thawed
1 canned chipotle chile pepper, minced
½ cup chopped cooked chicken
½ cup chopped ham
Béchamel Sauce
½ cup (2 ounces) shredded Cheddar cheese

• **Cut** baked potatoes in half lengthwise, and scoop out pulp, leaving shells intact; set shells aside. Mash pulp; stir in butter and milk, and set aside.
• **Stir** Parmesan cheese and next 4 ingredients into Béchamel Sauce; spoon evenly into shells. Top with mashed potato, and place on a baking sheet. Sprinkle with Cheddar cheese.
• **Bake** at 325° for 15 to 20 minutes or until potatoes are thoroughly heated. **Yield:** 6 servings.

Béchamel Sauce

3 tablespoons butter or margarine
3 tablespoons all-purpose flour
1¼ cups milk
¼ teaspoon salt
¼ teaspoon pepper

• **Melt** butter in a heavy saucepan over low heat; whisk in flour until smooth. Cook 1 minute, whisking constantly. Gradually add milk; cook, whisking constantly, over medium heat until thickened. Whisk in salt and pepper. **Yield:** 1¼ cups.

Mary Perrow
Talisco, Mexico

A New Look at Lentils

Instead of black-eyed peas or lima beans, serve lentils. In Middle Eastern and Mediterranean countries, lentils are a staple used in a wide variety of dishes, from marinated salads to deep-fried pies called Samosas. Lentils are widely available, very affordable, and they cook quickly. Keep them on hand for an easy, economical change of pace.

MEDITERRANEAN LENTIL SALAD

1 cup dried lentils
1 small onion, chopped
1 quart water
1 small red bell pepper
1 small green bell pepper
1 tomato
3 green onions
1 (2¼-ounce) can sliced ripe olives, drained
½ cup Italian salad dressing
2 tablespoons lemon juice
½ teaspoon pepper
1 (4-ounce) package crumbled tomato-basil feta cheese

• **Bring** first 3 ingredients to a boil in a Dutch oven; reduce heat, and simmer, partially covered, 15 to 20 minutes or just until lentils are tender. Drain.
• **Chop** bell peppers, tomato, and green onions; add to lentil mixture. Stir in olives and next 3 ingredients; cover and chill. Sprinkle with cheese; serve immediately. **Yield:** 5 cups.

Donna F. Bearden
Gibsonville, North Carolina

SPANISH-STYLE LENTIL SOUP

1 pound dried lentils
2 bay leaves
¼ pound ham, diced
1 large onion, chopped
2 carrots, scraped and sliced
4 cloves garlic, chopped
3 tablespoons olive oil
1 large potato, peeled and chopped
½ pound smoked sausage, sliced
1 (14½-ounce) can ready-to-serve chicken broth
3 tablespoons red wine vinegar
½ teaspoon salt
½ teaspoon pepper
2 teaspoons paprika
2 tablespoons chopped fresh parsley

• **Combine** first 3 ingredients and enough water to cover in a Dutch oven; bring to a boil. Cover, reduce heat, and simmer 30 minutes.
• **Cook** onion, carrot, and garlic in olive oil in a large skillet until tender, stirring often; stir into lentil mixture. Add potato and next 6 ingredients. Cover and simmer 45 minutes or until done, stirring occasionally. Stir in parsley. Remove and discard bay leaves. **Yield:** 2 quarts.

SAMOSAS

(pictured on page 259)

½ cup dried lentils
2 cloves garlic, minced
2 carrots, scraped and diced
1 medium onion, diced
½ teaspoon salt
1 teaspoon dried crushed red pepper
1 to 2 teaspoons curry powder
1 teaspoon ground cumin
2 to 3 tablespoons chopped fresh cilantro
9 egg roll wrappers
Vegetable oil
1 (9-ounce) jar mango chutney

• **Cook** lentils according to package directions, adding garlic and next 6 ingredients; drain. Stir in cilantro.
• **Cut** each wrapper into 4 squares; spoon about 1 teaspoon lentil mixture on half of each square. Moisten edges with water, and fold in half diagonally, pressing edges with a fork to seal.
• **Pour** oil to depth of 1 inch into a large skillet or Dutch oven; heat to 375°. Fry, three at a time, 30 seconds or until golden, turning once; drain on paper towels. Serve immediately with mango chutney. **Yield:** 3 dozen.

Dempse McMullen
Natchez, Mississippi

Take a Look at Lentils

Mention dried peas or beans to a Southerner, and lentils come to mind, right? More like a simmering pot of black-eyed peas. But the versatility of lentils makes them a good choice for soup, an entrée, or in a salad.

Dried lentils keep up to one year in unopened packages or tightly covered containers. Store them in a cool, dry place – not in the refrigerator. Unlike other dried beans, lentils do not require soaking and cook in less than an hour.

Cool Weather, Sunny Flavor

The season for sweet, juicy watermelon may have ended, but don't assume you can't have fruit salad again until next summer.

Although the melons might be sparse and the fresh berries and cherries long gone, you can still enjoy the citrus squirts of sunshine, the welcome tang of pineapple, and the sweet nuggets of flavor packed into dried fruits. We've used these delectable jewels to brighten both grains and lettuces in the following recipes.

And autumn's apples don't belong only in pies. We have freed them from predictable pastry – and saved sweet potatoes from ending up in typical casseroles – for a chilly, cheery surprise.

CURRIED RICE SALAD

1 cup uncooked rice
¼ cup dried Bing cherries, chopped
¼ cup mayonnaise
2 tablespoons mango chutney
½ teaspoon curry powder
1 (2.25-ounce) package slivered almonds
1 pear, chopped
½ cup seedless grapes, cut in half
1½ teaspoons fresh lemon juice

• **Cook** rice according to package directions; drain and cool.
• **Combine** rice, cherries, and next 3 ingredients, stirring well. Cover and chill.
• **Bake** almonds in a shallow pan at 350° for 5 to 10 minutes or until toasted, stirring occasionally; cool.
• **Stir** almonds, pear, grapes, and lemon juice into rice mixture; serve immediately. **Yield:** 4 servings.

CRACKED WHEAT-FRUIT SALAD

3 cups apple cider
1½ cups bulgur wheat
2 small apples, cut into 1-inch chunks
2 oranges, sectioned
1 (8-ounce) package pitted dates, sliced
2 tablespoons vegetable oil
2 tablespoons honey
2 tablespoons lemon juice
2 teaspoons grated orange rind
½ cup chopped pecans

• **Bring** cider to a boil in a medium saucepan; stir in bulgur wheat. Cover, remove from heat, and let stand 2 hours. Pour mixture through a wire-mesh strainer, pressing with back of a spoon; discard cider.
• **Transfer** bulgur wheat to a bowl. Stir in apple chunks, orange sections, and dates.
• **Whisk** oil and next 3 ingredients until blended; pour over salad, and toss gently. Cover and chill.
• **Bake** pecans in a shallow pan at 350° 5 to 10 minutes or until toasted, stirring occasionally; cool. Stir pecans into salad; serve immediately. **Yield:** 8 to 10 servings.

Marsha Littrell
Sheffield, Alabama

SWEET POTATO-APPLE SALAD

8 large sweet potatoes (5¼ pounds)
4 Granny Smith apples
4 green onions
Poppy Seed Dressing

• **Cook** sweet potatoes in boiling water to cover 25 to 30 minutes or until tender; drain and cool. Peel sweet potatoes, and cut into ½-inch-thick slices. Cut apples into thin wedges; slice green onions.
• **Arrange** one-fourth sweet potato slices, apple wedges, and green onions in a large salad bowl; drizzle with one-fourth of Poppy Seed Dressing.
• **Repeat** layers 3 times with remaining ingredients; cover and chill. **Yield:** 12 to 15 servings.

Poppy Seed Dressing

½ cup orange juice
2 tablespoons white wine vinegar
2 tablespoons Dijon mustard
2 tablespoons minced onion
2 tablespoons grated orange rind
1 tablespoon grated lemon rind
1 cup olive oil
1 tablespoon poppy seeds

• **Combine** all ingredients in a jar; cover tightly, and shake vigorously. **Yield:** about 2 cups.

Jennifer Schair
Woodstock, Georgia

CITRUS AND GREENS WITH ORANGE-GINGER DRESSING

3 oranges
2 pink grapefruit
1 pineapple
½ cup orange marmalade
¼ cup raspberry vinegar
1 tablespoon grated fresh ginger
1 (16-ounce) package mixed salad greens (8 cups torn)

• **Section** oranges and grapefruit; peel and cut pineapple into chunks.
• **Melt** marmalade in a small saucepan over low heat, stirring constantly; remove from heat, and stir in vinegar and ginger.
• **Arrange** salad greens evenly on individual serving plates; top with fruit, and drizzle with marmalade mixture. **Yield:** 4 servings.

P'S & Q'S OF NATURE

When moms warn children to mind their p's and q's, they don't mean persimmons, pomegranates, and quince. They want the little ones to be on their best behavior. In the marketplace the same phrase cautions merchants to deliver the full measure of pints and quarts purchased. In other words, don't cheat the buyer. Persimmons, pomegranates, and quince follow both rules. They never cheat on flavor and are always good.

Eat persimmons when they're bright orange and quite soft. Peel them and use the soft pulp. Pomegranates make you work through tough skin, rewarding you with sweet, juicy seeds. Quince looks like a green apple, but do *not* eat it raw. This fruit behaves best when cooked; it turns a lovely pink in the process.

Bring fall color inside with these often overlooked fruits and enjoy nature's p's and q's.

BAKED QUINCE COMPOTE

4 medium quince, unpeeled, cored, and sliced
½ cup firmly packed dark brown sugar
½ cup orange juice
2 tablespoons lemon juice
¼ cup butter or margarine, cut up
2 (3-inch) sticks cinnamon
4 whole cloves

• **Place** quince in an 8-inch square baking dish.
• **Combine** brown sugar and next 5 ingredients; pour over quince.
• **Cover** and bake at 375° for 45 minutes or until tender, stirring every 15 minutes. Remove cinnamon sticks and cloves. Serve compote warm. **Yield:** 4 servings.

POMEGRANATE SYRUP

You can use this syrup as a drink mixer or as a topping for vanilla ice cream.

4 cups pomegranate seeds (4 large pomegranates)
3½ cups sugar

• **Combine** seeds and sugar in a large glass bowl; cover and chill at least 8 hours.
• **Transfer** mixture to a heavy nonaluminum saucepan; bring to a boil over medium heat. Reduce heat, and simmer 3 minutes.
• **Pour** mixture through a cheesecloth-lined colander; press against sides of colander with back of a spoon to squeeze out juice. Discard pulp.
• **Pour** juice into a 1-quart sterilized jar; cover with lid, and screw on band. Cool; store in refrigerator up to 2 weeks. **Yield:** 3 cups.

TEX-MEX WREATH

3 large pink grapefruit
3 oranges
1 large jícama
3 Granny Smith apples
1 cup pomegranate seeds (1 large pomegranate)
Pomegranate Salad Dressing

• **Peel** and slice grapefruit, oranges, and jícama; core and slice apples.
• **Alternate** grapefruit, oranges, jícama, and apples on a serving platter to resemble a wreath;.sprinkle with pomegranate seeds. Serve with Pomegranate Salad Dressing. **Yield:** 6 servings.

Pomegranate Salad Dressing

½ cup Pomegranate Syrup (see recipe)
¼ cup olive oil
2 tablespoons red wine vinegar
1 tablespoon lemon juice
⅛ teaspoon salt

• **Combine** all ingredients in a jar; cover tightly, and shake vigorously. Chill. **Yield:** ⅔ cup.

Marilyn Houghton Kayton
Mission, Texas

PERSIMMON COOKIES

2 large ripe persimmons, peeled and coarsely chopped
1 cup sugar
⅔ cup vegetable oil
1 large egg
2 cups all-purpose flour
1 teaspoon baking soda
1 teaspoon ground cinnamon
1 cup raisins
1 cup chopped walnuts
1 cup sifted powdered sugar
3 tablespoons lemon juice

• **Position** knife blade in food processor bowl; add persimmon, and process until smooth, stopping once to scrape down sides. Measure 1 cup pulp.
• **Combine** pulp, sugar, oil, and egg, stirring until smooth.
• **Combine** flour, soda, and cinnamon in a large bowl; add persimmon mixture, stirring until blended. Stir in raisins and walnuts.
• **Drop** dough by rounded teaspoonfuls onto lightly greased cookie sheets.
• **Bake** at 375° for 9 minutes. Transfer to wire racks placed on wax paper.
• **Combine** powdered sugar and lemon juice, stirring until smooth; drizzle over warm cookies. Cool. **Yield:** 5 dozen.

Cheryl Hodges
Lilburn, Georgia

CAN-DO PUMPKIN

You can really get into the fall season when you're up to your elbows in a pumpkin-carving project. It's something everyone should do . . . once. When those brilliant orange globes beckon at the grocery store, forget all the carving, the seed roasting, the pulp chopping, *and* the pie making. Grab a few convenient cans of pumpkin instead, and you're ready for these easy recipes.

CURRIED PUMPKIN SOUP

(pictured on page 257)

2 tablespoons butter or margarine
1 (8-ounce) package sliced fresh mushrooms
½ cup chopped onion
2 tablespoons all-purpose flour
1 tablespoon curry powder
3 cups chicken broth
2 cups canned pumpkin
1 tablespoon honey
½ teaspoon salt
¼ teaspoon ground nutmeg
¼ teaspoon pepper
1 (12-ounce) can evaporated milk
Garnishes: sour cream, chopped fresh chives

• **Melt** butter in a large saucepan; add mushrooms and onion, and cook until tender, stirring often.
• **Stir** in flour and curry powder; gradually add chicken broth, and cook over medium heat, stirring constantly, until mixture is thickened.
• **Stir** in pumpkin and next 4 ingredients; reduce heat, and simmer 10 minutes, stirring occasionally. Stir in milk, and cook, stirring constantly, until thoroughly heated. Garnish, if desired. **Yield:** 6½ cups.

Nancy Wilson
Houston, Texas

PUMPKIN-APPLE MUFFINS

1⅔ cups all-purpose flour
1 teaspoon baking soda
¼ teaspoon baking powder
¼ teaspoon salt
1 tablespoon pumpkin pie spice
1 cup sugar
1 cup canned pumpkin
½ cup butter or margarine, melted
2 large eggs, lightly beaten
1 Granny Smith apple, peeled and finely chopped
3 tablespoons sugar
1 teaspoon pumpkin pie spice

• **Combine** first 6 ingredients in a large bowl; make a well in center of mixture.
• **Combine** pumpkin, butter, and eggs, and add to dry ingredients, stirring just until moistened. Fold in chopped apple, and spoon into greased muffin pans, filling two-thirds full.
• **Combine** 3 tablespoons sugar and 1 teaspoon pumpkin pie spice; sprinkle evenly over muffins.
• **Bake** at 350° for 20 minutes. Remove from pans immediately, and cool on wire racks. **Yield:** 2 dozen.

June Silver
Morristown, Tennessee

MAMA'S PUMPKIN PIE

Mary White, who shared this recipe, usually makes pastry from scratch, but we give you the easy way out here with refrigerated piecrusts. We use them a lot in our own homes.

½ (15-ounce) package refrigerated piecrusts
1¾ cups canned pumpkin
1¾ cups sweetened condensed milk
2 large eggs, lightly beaten
⅔ cup firmly packed light brown sugar
2 tablespoons sugar
1¼ teaspoons ground cinnamon
½ teaspoon salt
½ teaspoon ground ginger
½ teaspoon ground nutmeg
¼ teaspoon ground cloves

• **Fit** piecrust into a 9-inch pieplate according to package directions; fold edges under, and crimp.
• **Combine** pumpkin and remaining ingredients in a large bowl; beat at medium speed with an electric mixer 2 minutes. Pour into prepared piecrust.
• **Bake** at 425° for 15 minutes. Reduce heat to 350°; bake 50 additional minutes or until a knife inserted in center comes out clean. Cool on a wire rack. **Yield:** 1 (9-inch) pie.

Note: You should always store pumpkin pie in the refrigerator.

Mary White
Birmingham, Alabama

Cracking the Walnut

We adore walnuts for their rich, deep flavor and earthy crunch. They grace everything they touch, which most often is dessert.

But let's not overlook their main-course appeal. Walnuts are a hearty addition to soups, salads, spreads – even meatless "hamburgers." Read on to discover some outstanding original recipes that showcase the many qualities of walnuts.

WALNUT-CHICKEN SALAD

(pictured on page 296)

4 skinned and boned chicken breast halves
3 tablespoons buttermilk
1 cup finely ground walnuts
½ cup fine, dry breadcrumbs
1 teaspoon salt
2 tablespoons vegetable oil
6 cups torn mixed salad greens
4 cups torn fresh spinach
1 cup (4 ounces) shredded colby-Monterey Jack cheese blend
16 cherry tomatoes, cut in half
Buttermilk-Honey Dressing

• **Place** chicken between two sheets of heavy-duty plastic wrap; flatten to ¼-inch thickness, using a meat mallet. Brush buttermilk over chicken.
• **Combine** walnuts, breadcrumbs, and salt in a shallow dish; dredge chicken in mixture.
• **Pour** oil into a large skillet; place over medium-high heat until hot. Add chicken, and cook 3 minutes on each side or until golden. Remove from heat; cool slightly. Cut chicken crosswise into thin slices.
• **Combine** salad greens and spinach, and arrange on each of 4 individual plates. Sprinkle with cheese, and top with tomato halves and chicken slices. Serve with Buttermilk-Honey Dressing. **Yield:** 4 servings.

Buttermilk-Honey Dressing

⅓ cup honey
⅓ cup buttermilk
¼ cup chopped fresh chives
2 tablespoons lemon juice
½ teaspoon pepper

• **Combine** all ingredients in a small bowl, stirring well with a wire whisk. **Yield:** 1 cup.

MEATLESS WALNUT HAMBURGERS

2 large eggs
3 tablespoons water
1 cup quick-cooking oats, uncooked
½ cup walnuts, ground
½ cup finely chopped onion
½ teaspoon salt
½ teaspoon rubbed sage
1 clove garlic, pressed
2 tablespoons soybean oil
½ cup water
4 whole wheat sandwich buns

• **Combine** eggs and 3 tablespoons water in a large bowl, stirring with a fork. Stir in oats and next 5 ingredients. Shape mixture into 4 patties.
• **Pour** oil into a large nonstick skillet, and heat over medium-high until hot. Add patties, and cook 3 minutes on each side or until lightly browned. Add ½ cup water to skillet; cover, reduce heat, and simmer 10 minutes or until water evaporates.
• **Serve** patties on buns with lettuce, tomato slices, and mayonnaise or salad dressing. **Yield:** 4 servings.

Leonard Loria
Birmingham, Alabama

RED BEAN SOUP WITH WALNUTS

1 pound dried red beans
7 cups chicken broth
½ teaspoon salt
2 large onions, finely chopped
3 cloves garlic, minced
¼ cup olive oil
½ cup finely chopped walnuts
3 to 4 tablespoons tarragon vinegar or red wine vinegar
2 teaspoons coriander seeds, crushed
½ teaspoon pepper
½ cup chopped fresh cilantro
¼ cup chopped fresh parsley

• **Sort** and wash beans; place in a Dutch oven. Cover with water 2 inches above beans; let stand at least 8 hours. Drain.
• **Combine** beans, chicken broth, and salt in Dutch oven; bring to a boil over medium heat. Cover, reduce heat, and simmer 1 hour or until beans are tender.
• **Drain** beans, reserving 3 cups liquid. Mash beans with back of a spoon, and return to Dutch oven. Stir in reserved liquid.
• **Cook** onion and garlic in hot oil in a skillet over medium-high heat, stirring constantly, until tender. Stir in walnuts and next 3 ingredients.
• **Add** walnut mixture to beans, and cook until thoroughly heated. Sprinkle with cilantro and parsley. **Yield:** 9 cups.

Marge Clyde
San Antonio, Texas

Nutin' To It

Walnuts can be, pardon the pun, a tough nut to crack. For easier shelling, cover the walnuts with water, and bring to a boil. Remove from heat, cover and set aside for at least 15 minutes or until cool. Drain walnuts, and blot dry with paper towels. The nuts should crack easily from end to end.

living *light*

TRICKS FOR TREATS

If you're trying to lighten up, po'boy sandwiches and creamy soups and dips top your list of rare indulgences. Instead, pasta salads, angel food cake, and chicken breasts make up everyday fare. These recipes give you the best of both worlds. They'll turn forbidden foods into possibilities and mundane dinners into special occasions.

GRILLED SEAFOOD PO'BOY

(pictured on page 223)

Grilling the seafood and using reduced-fat mayonnaise make this sandwich a low-fat possibility.

1 pound unpeeled medium-size fresh shrimp
1 (10-ounce) farm-raised catfish fillet
2 teaspoons Creole seasoning
¼ cup lemon juice
1 teaspoon olive oil
½ cup roasted red peppers
1 jalapeño pepper
½ cup reduced-fat mayonnaise
2 tablespoons Creole mustard
2 tablespoons chopped fresh parsley
1 clove garlic, minced
2 tablespoons sliced green onions
8 slices tomato
8 lettuce leaves
4 French sandwich rolls, split and toasted

• **Peel** shrimp, and devein, if desired. Cut fish crosswise into 1-inch slices. Combine shrimp and fish in a shallow dish, and sprinkle with Creole seasoning. Cover and chill 2 hours.
• **Combine** lemon juice and oil; pour mixture over seafood. Cover and chill 30 additional minutes.
• **Cut** red peppers into thin strips; pat dry. Seed and chop jalapeño pepper. Combine red pepper strips, jalapeño pepper, mayonnaise, and next 4 ingredients; set aside.
• **Drain** seafood, and place in a grill basket coated with cooking spray.
• **Cook,** covered with grill lid, over medium-hot coals (350° to 400°) 7 to 10 minutes, turning once.
• **Place** seafood, tomato, and lettuce evenly on bottom halves of rolls; spread top halves of rolls evenly with mayonnaise mixture, and place on sandwiches. Serve with fat-free potato chips. **Yield:** 4 servings.

Clemie Barron
Panama City, Florida

❤ Per serving: Calories 405 (34% from fat)
Fat 15g (1.3g saturated) Cholesterol 112mg
Sodium 711mg Carbohydrate 39.7g
Fiber 2.3g Protein 25.8g

COUSCOUS SALAD WITH DRIED TOMATO VINAIGRETTE

Toasted spices and dried tomatoes give this salad added flavor. You can substitute rice or orzo for the couscous or add chopped cooked chicken or shrimp to make it a main dish.

1 red bell pepper
½ medium-size purple onion
1 medium cucumber
¼ cup olive oil
3 tablespoons red wine vinegar
¼ teaspoon salt
⅛ teaspoon ground red pepper
1 tablespoon mustard seeds
1 tablespoon cumin seeds
⅓ cup minced dried tomato
¼ cup minced fresh cilantro
1½ cups water
½ teaspoon salt
½ teaspoon pepper
1 clove garlic, pressed
1 cup uncooked couscous

• **Place** bell pepper on an aluminum foil-lined baking sheet.
• **Broil** 5½ inches from heat (with electric oven door partially opened) about 5 minutes on each side or until pepper looks blistered.
• **Place** pepper in a heavy-duty, zip-top plastic bag; seal and let stand 10 minutes to loosen skin. Peel pepper; remove and discard seeds. Dice pepper and onion; peel, seed, and dice cucumber. Set vegetables aside.
• **Whisk** oil and next 3 ingredients in a small bowl.
• **Cook** mustard and cumin seeds in a small skillet over medium heat, stirring constantly, 5 minutes or until toasted; immediately stir into oil mixture. Add tomato and cilantro, stirring well.
• **Bring** water and next 3 ingredients to a boil in a saucepan; stir in couscous. Remove from heat; cover and let stand 5 minutes or until liquid is absorbed. Transfer to a serving bowl; stir in diced vegetables. Drizzle with dressing; toss gently. **Yield:** 6 servings.

❤ Per serving: Calories 231 (39% from fat)
Fat 10.2g (1.3g saturated) Cholesterol 0mg
Sodium 364mg Carbohydrate 30.1g
Fiber 0.9g Protein 5.5g

ROASTED RED PEPPER SOUP

4 red bell peppers
1 large onion, chopped
2 cloves garlic, minced
2 (16-ounce) cans, reduced-sodium chicken broth, divided
¾ cup dry sherry
2 tablespoons all-purpose flour
1 tablespoon butter-flavored granules
1 (16-ounce) can whole tomatoes, drained
1 cup skim milk
1 (8-ounce) carton light sour cream
2 tablespoons lemon juice
½ teaspoon salt
½ teaspoon pepper

• **Place** peppers on an aluminum foil-lined baking sheet.
• **Broil** peppers 5½ inches from heat (with electric oven door partially opened) about 5 minutes on each side or until blistered.
• **Place** peppers in a large heavy-duty, zip-top plastic bag; seal and let stand 10 minutes to loosen skins. Peel peppers; remove and discard seeds.
• **Combine** onion, garlic, and ¼ cup broth in a saucepan; cook, stirring constantly, until tender. Stir in sherry; simmer 15 minutes, stirring occasionally.
• **Whisk** in flour and butter granules; stir in remaining broth and tomatoes. Simmer 15 minutes, stirring occasionally. Stir in peppers and milk, and cook 2 minutes, stirring constantly.
• **Process** soup in batches in container of an electric blender until smooth, stopping once to scrape down sides. Stir in sour cream and remaining ingredients. Return to saucepan, and cook over low heat just until thoroughly heated. (Do not boil.) **Yield:** 8 cups.

♥ Per 1-cup serving:
Calories 97 (24% from fat)
Fat 2.4g (0g saturated) Cholesterol 11mg
Sodium 289mg Carbohydrate 13.4g
Fiber 1.2g Protein 3.7g

CUT THE FAT – FOREVER

When Suzy Thompson's husband, Gary, had triple bypass surgery, she had to make some lifestyle changes fast. Try this Fort Worth, Texas, cook's tips in your low-fat kitchen.

▪ Don't change what you eat, just change the way you cook it.

▪ Use fat-free salad dressing instead of butter for sautéing vegetables.

▪ Make fruit-based desserts. Suzy and Gary love fresh fruit with baked meringues or fat-free pound cake served with a fruit sauce.

▪ Grow your own herbs. They give your cooking a taste of freshness.

▪ Buy a few low-fat cookbooks. Even if you don't follow the recipes exactly, they'll give you ideas on new things to cook.

APPLE CIDER SAUCE

Charles Walton of Birmingham, Alabama, offers his recipe for a rich-tasting, low-fat sauce for pork or ham. Store it in the refrigerator up to one week. A 2-tablespoon serving has 106 calories and 2 grams of fat.

Cider-Port Wine Reduction Sauce: Bring 1 quart apple cider, ½ cup port wine, and 1 vegetable bouillon cube to a boil in a heavy saucepan over high heat. Reduce heat to medium, and simmer 1½ hours or until reduced to ¾ cup. Remove from heat; stir in ½ teaspoon instant coffee granules and 1 tablespoon butter. **Yield:** ¾ cup.

LOW-FAT FRIES

Peggy E. St. Marie of Dunkirk, Maryland, shares this recipe for oven-fried French fries. Her secret is tossing the potatoes with a minimum amount of olive oil and then coating them with a crust of flavorful seasonings. They're even good reheated in the oven the next day. A serving contains 177 calories and 5 grams of fat.

Seasoned French Fries: (Pictured on page 223) Cut 2 large baking potatoes (1½ pounds) into ½-inch-wide strips. Combine potatoes and 1½ tablespoons olive oil in a large heavy-duty, zip-top plastic bag, and shake to coat. Combine 1 teaspoon garlic salt, 1 teaspoon seasoned pepper, 1 teaspoon dried onion flakes, and 1 teaspoon dried Italian seasoning; add to potatoes. Seal bag, and shake until evenly coated. Spread potatoes in a 15- x 10- x 1-inch jellyroll pan coated with cooking spray. Bake at 450° for 25 to 28 minutes or until done, stirring after 15 minutes. **Yield:** 4 servings.

ORANGE ANGEL FOOD CAKE

One taste of this updated standby proves that fat-free desserts can be terrific.

1 cup sugar
2 tablespoons orange liqueur
½ cup water
½ teaspoon lemon juice
15 orange sections
10 egg whites
1 teaspoon cream of tartar
¼ teaspoon salt
1½ cups sugar
1 teaspoon vanilla extract
¾ cup all-purpose flour
1 (18-ounce) jar orange marmalade
½ cup sifted powdered sugar

• **Combine** first 4 ingredients in a heavy saucepan; cook over medium-high heat, stirring constantly, 5 minutes or until a candy thermometer registers 200°. Remove from heat.
• **Dip** orange sections, one at a time, into syrup, and place on parchment paper until cool.
• **Beat** egg whites, cream of tartar, and salt at high speed with an electric mixer until foamy. Add 1½ cups sugar, 2 tablespoons at a time, beating until stiff peaks form and sugar dissolves (2 to 4 minutes). Fold in vanilla and flour, ¼ cup at a time.
• **Line** a 15- x 10- x 1-inch jellyroll pan with parchment paper; spread marmalade over paper. Pour batter over marmalade.
• **Bake** at 325° for 25 minutes; cool in pan on a wire rack. Sprinkle with powdered sugar. Invert onto a large cutting board or baking sheet; peel off parchment paper, and cut cake into circles with a 2½-inch round cutter. Serve with orange sections. **Yield:** 5 servings.

Sara Quattlebaum
Columbia, South Carolina

❤ Per serving: Calories 287 (1% from fat) Fat 0.2g (0g saturated) Cholesterol 0mg Sodium 79mg Carbohydrate 70.1g Fiber 4.2g Protein 3.2g

QUICK & EASY

FUN LUNCHES

You can prepare creative and substantial meals for weekday lunches with a little effort and planning. Consider these recipes when answering the inevitable question, "What am I taking for lunch tomorrow?"

HAMWICHES

1 (8-ounce) can refrigerated crescent rolls
1 tablespoon mayonnaise
1 teaspoon prepared mustard
1 cup finely chopped ham
½ cup (2 ounces) shredded Swiss cheese

• **Unroll** dough, and separate into 4 rectangles; press seams to seal.
• **Combine** mayonnaise and mustard; spread over rectangles, leaving a ½-inch border. Sprinkle ham and cheese evenly over half of each rectangle; moisten edges with water. Fold dough over, and pinch edges to seal.
• **Bake** at 375° for 10 minutes or until Hamwiches are puffed and golden. **Yield:** 4 sandwiches.

Note: You can store baked Hamwiches in an airtight container in the refrigerator up to 1 week.

BARBECUE MUFFINS

1 (12-ounce) can refrigerated buttermilk biscuits
½ pound lean ground beef
¼ cup ketchup
1½ tablespoons brown sugar
1½ teaspoons apple cider vinegar
¼ teaspoon chili powder
½ cup (2 ounces) shredded Cheddar cheese

• **Separate** biscuits; pat or roll biscuits into 5-inch circles on a lightly floured surface, and press into lightly greased muffin pans.
• **Brown** ground beef in a large skillet, stirring until it crumbles; drain. Stir in ketchup and next 3 ingredients; spoon into muffin cups.
• **Bake** at 375° for 15 minutes; sprinkle with cheese, and bake 5 additional minutes or until cheese melts. Cool in pan on a wire rack 5 minutes. **Yield:** 10 muffins.

Note: You can store baked muffins in an airtight container up to 1 week.

PEPPERONI PINWHEELS

1 (10-ounce) can refrigerated pizza crust
1 cup (4 ounces) shredded mozzarella cheese
¼ cup grated Parmesan cheese
½ (3.5-ounce) package sliced pepperoni, chopped
½ cup spaghetti sauce

• **Unroll** refrigerated pizza crust on a cutting board; sprinkle with cheeses and pepperoni. Roll up, starting with long side; moisten edge with water, and pinch seam to seal. Cut into 2-inch slices, and place 1 inch apart in a lightly greased 15- x 10- x 1-inch jellyroll pan; flatten slightly.
• **Bake** at 400° for 15 to 20 minutes; serve with warm spaghetti sauce. **Yield:** 8 servings.

Note: You can store baked pinwheels in an airtight container up to 1 week.

YOGURT FRUIT SALAD

1 (8-ounce) can pineapple chunks, drained
1 (11-ounce) can mandarin oranges, drained
1 cup miniature marshmallows
1 (8-ounce) container vanilla yogurt

• **Combine** all ingredients, tossing gently to coat; cover and chill. **Yield:** 4 servings.

Terri Simpson
Midlothian, Virginia

CAKE MIX OATMEAL COOKIES

1 (18.25-ounce) package yellow cake mix
2 cups quick-cooking oats, uncooked
1 cup sugar
1 cup vegetable oil
2 large eggs
1 cup chopped pecans
1½ teaspoons vanilla extract

• **Combine** first 3 ingredients in a large bowl. Combine oil and eggs; add to dry ingredients, stirring well. Stir in pecans and vanilla.
• **Drop** dough by rounded teaspoonfuls 2 inches apart onto ungreased cookie sheets.
• **Bake** at 350° for 12 minutes or until lightly browned. Remove to wire racks to cool. **Yield:** 5 dozen.

Nancy Williams
Starkville, Mississippi

AN "AUTOMATIC" APPETITE FOR WEAVER D'S

Rock group R.E.M. named their 1992 release *Automatic for the People* after the slogan of their favorite hometown eatery, Weaver D's Delicious Fine Foods in Athens, Georgia. Soon the restaurant began to boom as R.E.M. fans and University of Georgia football fans joined locals and students at this cozy corner of downtown's Broad Street. And, true to his slogan, owner Dexter Weaver replies "automatic" after each order.

SWEET POTATO SOUFFLÉ

Attention R.E.M. fans: This home-style casserole is reportedly lead singer Michael Stipe's favorite side dish at Weaver D's.

6 small sweet potatoes (about 3 pounds)
¾ cup sugar
3 large eggs, lightly beaten
½ cup butter or margarine, melted
3 tablespoons milk
2 teaspoons ground nutmeg
2 teaspoons vanilla extract
¾ teaspoon lemon extract

• **Peel** sweet potatoes, and cut into cubes. Cook sweet potato in boiling water to cover 15 to 20 minutes or until tender; drain and mash.
• **Combine** sweet potato, sugar, and remaining ingredients, stirring mixture until smooth. Spoon mixture into a lightly greased 11- x 7- x 1½-inch baking dish.
• **Bake** at 350° for 30 minutes or until bubbly. **Yield:** 6 to 8 servings.

SQUASH CASSEROLE

4 pounds yellow squash, cut into ¼-inch slices
2 tablespoons butter or margarine
1 large onion, finely chopped
2 cloves garlic, pressed
1 (10¾-ounce) can cream of mushroom soup, undiluted
1 cup (4 ounces) shredded sharp Cheddar cheese
2 large eggs
1 teaspoon salt
½ teaspoon pepper

• **Cook** squash in boiling water to cover 8 to 10 minutes or until tender. Drain squash, and press between paper towels.
• **Melt** butter in a large skillet; add chopped onion and garlic, and cook until tender, stirring often.
• **Combine** onion mixture, squash, soup, and remaining ingredients; spoon mixture into a lightly greased 11- x 7- x 1½-inch baking dish.
• **Bake** at 350° for 30 minutes or until bubbly. **Yield:** 8 to 10 servings.

CORNMEAL MUFFINS

You can buy cornmeal plain or in the self-rising or mix form. Self-rising cornmeal contains baking powder and salt.

1⅓ cups self-rising white cornmeal
1 tablespoon sugar
1 large egg, lightly beaten
1⅓ cups buttermilk
¼ cup butter, melted

• **Combine** cornmeal and sugar; make a well in center of mixture.
• **Combine** egg, buttermilk, and butter; add to dry ingredients, stirring until smooth. Spoon into greased muffin pans, filling two-thirds full.
• **Bake** at 425° for 20 minutes or until golden. Serve immediately. **Yield:** 1 dozen.

WEAVER D'S SEASONING MIX

Dexter uses his mix for battered fried chicken and pork chops. This recipe is enough for about 3½ pounds of fryer pieces. Tip: Just before serving, sprinkle fried chicken or pork with seasoned salt for added zest.

3½ cups all-purpose flour
3 tablespoons garlic powder
3 tablespoons seasoned salt
3 tablespoons pepper
1 tablespoon salt

• **Combine** all ingredients; store in an airtight container. **Yield:** 4 cups.

A TASTE OF SWEETNESS

Coconut's chewy texture and sweet flavor lend themselves to a variety of dishes. Fresh coconuts are plentiful this time of year, but to make these recipes more convenient, we used flaked coconut.

You can store unopened plastic bags of coconut at room temperature up to six months, and canned coconut up to 18 months. Be sure to store any leftover coconut in the refrigerator in airtight containers.

COCONUT FRIED SHRIMP

1 pound unpeeled medium-size fresh shrimp
¾ cup biscuit mix
1 tablespoon sugar
¾ cup beer
¾ cup all-purpose flour
2½ cups flaked coconut
Vegetable oil
Orange-Lime Dip

• **Peel** shrimp, leaving the tails intact; devein, if desired, and set shrimp aside.
• **Combine** biscuit mix, sugar, and beer, stirring until smooth; set aside.
• **Coat** shrimp with flour; dip into beer mixture, allowing excess coating to drain. Gently roll coated shrimp in flaked coconut.
• **Pour** oil to depth of 3 inches in a large saucepan; heat to 350°. Cook shrimp, a few at a time, 1 to 2 minutes or until golden; drain on paper towels, and serve immediately with Orange-Lime Dip. **Yield:** about 3 dozen.

Orange-Lime Dip

1 (10-ounce) jar orange marmalade
3 tablespoons spicy brown mustard
1 tablespoon fresh lime juice

• **Combine** all ingredients in a small saucepan; cook over medium heat, stirring constantly, until marmalade melts. Remove from heat; cool. Cover and store dip in refrigerator up to 1 week. **Yield:** about 1¼ cups.

HIBISCUS-NECTAR CAKE

The genesis of this enchanting title comes from the recipe creator, Janie Wallace. She made up the recipe title to name her prize-winning entry in a cake bake-off for a family reunion. Not surprisingly, the cake won second place.

½ cup butter or margarine, softened
½ cup shortening
2 cups sugar
5 large eggs, separated
1¼ teaspoons vanilla extract
1 teaspoon coconut extract
1 cup buttermilk
¼ cup sour cream
2 cups all-purpose flour
1 teaspoon baking soda
½ teaspoon salt
2 cups flaked coconut, toasted
1 cup chopped pecans
½ cup chopped maraschino cherries, drained
Cherry-Nut Cream Cheese Frosting

• **Beat** butter and shortening at medium speed with an electric mixer until fluffy; gradually add sugar, beating well.
• **Add** egg yolks, one at a time, beating until blended after each addition. Add flavorings; beat just until blended. Set mixture aside.
• **Combine** buttermilk and sour cream, stirring until blended. Combine flour, soda, and salt; add to butter mixture alternately with buttermilk mixture, beginning and ending with flour mixture. Beat at low speed with an electric mixer until blended after each addition.
• **Beat** egg whites until stiff peaks form; fold into batter. Fold in coconut, pecans, and cherries. Pour batter into

three greased and floured 9-inch round cakepans.
• **Bake** at 350° for 20 minutes or until a wooden pick inserted in center comes out clean. Cool in pans on wire racks 10 minutes; remove from pans, and cool completely on wire racks.
• **Spread** Cherry-Nut Cream Cheese Frosting between layers and on top and sides of cake. Cover and store in refrigerator. **Yield:** 1 (3-layer) cake.

Cherry-Nut Cream Cheese Frosting

½ cup butter or margarine, softened
1 (8-ounce) package cream cheese, softened
1 teaspoon vanilla extract
½ teaspoon coconut extract
1 (16-ounce) package powdered sugar, sifted
1 cup chopped pecans
½ cup chopped maraschino cherries, drained

• **Beat** butter and cream cheese in a mixing bowl at medium speed with an electric mixer until creamy; add flavorings. Gradually add powdered sugar, beating well.
• **Fold** in pecans and maraschino cherries. **Yield:** 4½ cups.

Janie Wallace
Seguin, Texas

Crazy for Coconuts

For the adventurous who like fresh coconut, here's the scoop.

▪ Choose coconuts that, when shaken, make a sloshing noise. The milk inside tells you that it's fresh.

▪ To open, tap the coconut all over with a hammer. It should split lengthwise. Beware: Be ready to catch the clear milk inside.

▪ You can grate coconut by hand or in a blender.

Building on Bagels

Bagels are far more versatile than their pastry look-alike, the doughnut. Plain or toasted, bagels are the perfect foundation for a sandwich.

MUSHROOM BAGEL SANDWICHES WITH CURRY-MUSTARD SAUCE

3 tablespoons olive oil
1 tablespoon red wine vinegar
1 tablespoon lemon juice
2 teaspoons Dijon mustard
½ teaspoon Worcestershire sauce
1 clove garlic, pressed
⅛ teaspoon salt
⅛ teaspoon dried oregano
⅛ teaspoon dried tarragon
⅛ teaspoon pepper
Dash of hot sauce
2 (8-ounce) packages sliced fresh mushrooms
1 small purple onion, thinly sliced
6 bagels, sliced
Curry-Mustard Sauce
2 cups (8 ounces) shredded Swiss cheese

• **Whisk** first 11 ingredients in a large bowl. Add mushrooms and onion, tossing to coat.
• **Arrange** bagels, cut side up, on a baking sheet; top bagels evenly with mushroom mixture, Curry-Mustard Sauce, and cheese.
• **Bake** at 350° for 10 to 15 minutes or until bubbly. **Yield:** 6 servings.

Curry-Mustard Sauce

2 tablespoons butter or margarine
2 tablespoons all-purpose flour
¾ cup milk
½ cup chicken broth
2 tablespoons dry sherry
2 teaspoons Dijon mustard
1 teaspoon curry powder

• **Melt** butter in a small saucepan over medium heat. Whisk in flour, and cook 1 minute, whisking constantly.
• **Whisk** in milk and remaining ingredients, and cook, whisking constantly, 1 to 2 minutes or until thickened. **Yield:** 1⅓ cups.

Marie H. McNeil
Roswell, Georgia

STEAK BAGEL SANDWICHES

⅔ cup beer
⅓ cup vegetable oil
1 teaspoon salt
¼ teaspoon garlic powder
¼ teaspoon pepper
1 (1½-pound) flank steak
2 tablespoons butter or margarine
2 large onions, sliced and separated into rings
¼ teaspoon salt
½ teaspoon paprika
6 bagels, sliced and toasted

• **Combine** first 5 ingredients in a heavy-duty, zip-top plastic bag; add steak, turning to coat. Seal and chill 8 hours, turning occasionally.
• **Remove** steak from marinade, discarding marinade. Place steak in a shallow pan.
• **Broil** 3 inches from heat (with electric oven door partially opened) 5 to 7 minutes on each side or to desired degree of doneness. Cut into thin slices; keep warm.
• **Melt** butter in a medium saucepan. Add onion, salt, and paprika; cook until tender, stirring often.
• **Arrange** steak and onion on bagel bottoms. Cover with tops. Serve with horseradish. **Yield:** 6 servings.

Joann J. McKoane
Sarasota, Florida

REMEMBER ROAST

Grandma sure knew, but in case you don't, roast is an easy, affordable way to feed a crowd. And it's still a natural for Sunday dinner in the South.

We give you meatier details than grandma's "about this much liquid" and "cook it till it falls apart," but the flavor will bring back fond memories of her roast with just one bite.

CHICKEN-BENEDICT BAGEL SANDWICHES

4 skinned and boned chicken breast halves
1 (8-ounce) bottle Italian salad dressing, divided
1 pound fresh asparagus *
1 (0.9-ounce) envelope hollandaise sauce mix
8 Canadian bacon slices
4 bagels, sliced and toasted
1 cup (4 ounces) shredded Monterey Jack cheese

• **Place** chicken and half of dressing in a heavy-duty, zip-top plastic bag; seal. Chill 2 hours, turning occasionally.
• **Snap** off tough ends of asparagus; remove scales with a vegetable peeler, if desired. Place asparagus and remaining dressing in a heavy-duty, zip-top plastic bag; seal and chill 2 hours, turning bag occasionally.
• **Prepare** hollandaise sauce according to package directions, and set aside.
• **Remove** chicken and asparagus from dressing, discarding dressing.
• **Cook** chicken, asparagus, and Canadian bacon, without grill lid, over medium-hot coals (350° to 400°) about 5 minutes. Remove asparagus and Canadian bacon, and keep warm. Turn chicken, and cook 5 additional minutes or until done. Cut chicken into thin slices, and keep warm.
• **Place** Canadian bacon on cut side of bagels; top evenly with chicken, asparagus, and hollandaise sauce. Sprinkle with cheese, and serve immediately. **Yield:** 4 servings.

* You can substitute 1 (15-ounce) can asparagus spears, drained, for fresh; do not grill the canned asparagus.

Kathleen A. Cipolla
East Brunswick, New Jersey

GRANDMA RUTH'S GRILLED PORK LOIN

The marinade for this pork loin makes it so easy.

1 (3- to 4-pound) boneless pork loin roast
1 (8-ounce) bottle Italian salad dressing
1 cup dry white wine
3 cloves garlic, minced
10 black peppercorns
Vegetable cooking spray

• **Pierce** roast at 1-inch intervals with a fork; set aside. (Piercing allows marinade to penetrate the meat better.)
• **Combine** salad dressing and next 3 ingredients in a large heavy-duty, zip-top plastic bag. Reserve ½ cup mixture in refrigerator for basting during grilling.
• **Add** roast to white wine mixture in bag; seal bag, and chill 8 hours, turning bag occasionally.
• **Remove** roast from marinade, discarding marinade.
• **Coat** a grill rack with cooking spray, and place over medium-hot coals (350° to 400°); place roast on rack.
• **Cook,** covered with grill lid, 35 minutes or until meat thermometer inserted in thickest portion reaches 160°, turning and basting with reserved ½ cup dressing mixture after 20 minutes. **Yield:** 8 to 10 servings.

Diane Buescher
Jackson, Missouri

MUSHROOM POT ROAST

1 (2- to 3-pound) boneless beef chuck roast
1 teaspoon salt
½ teaspoon freshly ground pepper
2 tablespoons all-purpose flour
2 tablespoons vegetable oil
¼ cup water
¼ cup ketchup
½ teaspoon dried marjoram
½ teaspoon dried rosemary
½ teaspoon dried thyme
¼ teaspoon dry mustard
2 cloves garlic, minced
½ cup dry sherry
1 bay leaf
1 medium onion, thinly sliced
½ pound fresh mushrooms, thinly sliced
¼ cup water
2 tablespoons all-purpose flour

• **Sprinkle** roast with salt, pepper, and 2 tablespoons flour. Brown all sides of roast in hot oil in a large Dutch oven.
• **Combine** ¼ cup water and next 8 ingredients; pour over roast. Add onion. Bring to a boil over medium heat; cover, reduce heat, and simmer 1½ hours.
• **Add** mushrooms; cover and simmer 1 additional hour or until roast is tender.
• **Remove** roast, reserving liquid in Dutch oven. Remove and discard bay leaf from Dutch oven.
• **Combine** ¼ cup water and 2 tablespoons flour, stirring until smooth. Add flour mixture to liquid in Dutch oven, stirring constantly. Bring to a boil over medium heat; boil, stirring constantly, until gravy thickens. Serve gravy with roast. **Yield:** 4 servings.

Note: A pressure cooker will cook this roast in about 40 minutes. Prepare roast as directed, adding all ingredients to cooker. Close lid, and follow manufacturer's directions.

Georgie O'Neill-Massa
Welaka, Florida

HONEY-ROASTED PORK

1 (2- to 3-pound) boneless pork loin roast
1/4 cup honey
2 tablespoons Dijon mustard
2 tablespoons mixed or black peppercorns, crushed
1/2 teaspoon dried thyme, crushed
1/2 teaspoon salt
Garnishes: watercress, apple and orange slices

• **Place** roast on a lightly greased rack in a shallow roasting pan.
• **Combine** honey and next 4 ingredients; brush about half of mixture over roast.
• **Bake** at 325° for 1 hour; brush with remaining honey mixture. Bake 30 additional minutes or until a meat thermometer inserted in thickest portion of roast reaches 160°. Garnish, if desired. **Yield:** 8 servings.

Janie Wallace
Seguin, Texas

GREEN WITH ENVY

Parsley usually plays an understudy role, the supporting ingredient in many dishes. But here we give it star billing in everything from pancakes to meat loaf. Use parsley lavishly and you'll find it's an herb as vivid in taste as it is in color.

WALNUT-PARMESAN PESTO SAUCE

1/2 cup olive oil
1 tablespoon lemon juice
2 cups fresh basil leaves
1 cup fresh parsley leaves
1/4 cup chopped walnuts
2 medium cloves garlic
1/2 cup freshly grated Parmesan cheese
1/2 teaspoon salt

• **Combine** all ingredients in container of an electric blender; process until smooth, stopping to scrape down sides as needed. Stir into hot cooked pasta, or spoon over cream cheese, and serve with crackers. **Yield:** 1 1/4 cups.

Nora Henshaw
Okemah, Oklahoma

GREEK MEAT LOAF

Serve leftovers in pita bread with yogurt sauce.

2 1/2 pounds lean ground lamb
1 large onion, diced
1 green bell pepper, diced
1 (8-ounce) can tomato sauce
1/2 cup uncooked quick-cooking oats
1/4 cup chopped fresh parsley
2 1/2 teaspoons dried oregano
2 teaspoons chopped fresh mint or 1/2 teaspoon dried mint flakes
2 teaspoons pepper
1/2 teaspoon salt
1 (8-ounce) can tomato sauce
2 large eggs, lightly beaten

• **Combine** all ingredients in a large bowl; shape into a loaf, and place in a lightly greased 9- x 5- x 3-inch loafpan.
• **Bake** at 350° for 1 1/2 hours or until done, and serve immediately. **Yield:** 8 servings.

Toni Reed Rashid
Birmingham, Alabama

PARSLEY-POTATO PANCAKES

1 medium onion, diced
Olive oil
2 cups mashed cooked potato
1 tablespoon fresh lemon juice
1/2 cup all-purpose flour
2 large eggs, lightly beaten
1 cup minced fresh parsley
3/4 teaspoon salt
1/2 teaspoon freshly ground black pepper
1/2 teaspoon ground red pepper
Garnish: Italian parsley

• **Cook** onion in 1 teaspoon oil in a large nonstick skillet until tender, stirring often; remove from heat.
• **Combine** onion, potato, and next 3 ingredients, stirring well; stir in parsley and next 3 ingredients.
• **Pour** 1 teaspoon oil into a nonstick skillet; place over medium heat until hot. Drop potato mixture by rounded tablespoonfuls into skillet, and flatten slightly; cook 3 minutes on each side or until golden. Drain on paper towels.
• **Repeat** procedure with remaining potato mixture, adding oil as needed. Garnish, if desired. Serve immediately. **Yield:** 14 (4-inch) pancakes.

TABBOULEH COUSCOUS

1 (14 1/2-ounce) can ready-to-serve chicken broth
1/4 cup fresh lemon juice
1 1/2 cups uncooked couscous
10 plum tomatoes, seeded and chopped
1 cup diced green onions
1 cup minced fresh Italian parsley
1 cup minced fresh mint
1/2 cup frozen whole kernel corn, thawed
2 cloves garlic, pressed
1 tablespoon grated lemon rind
1/3 cup olive oil
1/4 cup fresh lemon juice
1 teaspoon salt
Garnish: Italian parsley

• **Bring** chicken broth and 1/4 cup lemon juice to a boil in a large saucepan; stir in couscous. Cover, remove from heat, and let stand 5 minutes. Stir with a fork, and cool.
• **Stir** in chopped tomato and next 9 ingredients; garnish, if desired. **Yield:** 4 servings.

Jolie Peacock
Birmingham, Alabama

VEGETABLE OPTIONS

For a fresh take on the vegetable plate, serve this buffet on any night. These recipes are fast, fun, and delicious. Each one allows the vegetable flavors to come through by adding just the right amount of seasonings. Pass around loaves of hot, crusty bread with butter to make the meal complete.

SQUASH CASSEROLE

2½ pounds yellow squash, sliced *
½ cup butter or margarine
2 large eggs
¼ cup mayonnaise
1 (8-ounce) can sliced water chestnuts, drained
1 (4-ounce) jar diced pimiento, drained
½ cup chopped onion
¼ cup chopped green bell pepper
2 teaspoons sugar
1½ teaspoons salt
10 round buttery crackers, crushed (about ½ cup)
½ cup (2 ounces) shredded sharp Cheddar cheese

• **Cover** and cook squash in a small amount of boiling water 8 to 10 minutes or until tender; drain well, pressing between paper towels.
• **Combine** squash and butter in a bowl; mash until butter melts. Stir in eggs and next 7 ingredients; spoon into a lightly greased shallow 2-quart baking dish. Sprinkle squash with crushed crackers.
• **Bake** at 325° for 30 minutes. Sprinkle with cheese; bake 5 additional minutes or until cheese melts. **Yield:** 8 servings.

* You can substitute 2½ pounds zucchini, sliced, for the squash.

Judy Frazer
Sylacauga, Alabama

MARINATED BRUSSELS SPROUTS

3 (10-ounce) packages frozen brussels sprouts, thawed *
½ cup olive oil
¼ cup white vinegar
1 (2-ounce) jar sliced pimiento, drained
2 tablespoons diced onion
2 tablespoons minced fresh parsley
1 teaspoon dried thyme
1 teaspoon pepper
¾ teaspoon salt

• **Cook** brussels sprouts according to package directions, omitting salt, and drain well.
• **Whisk** oil and next 7 ingredients until blended; pour over brussels sprouts, stirring gently to coat. Cover and chill 2 hours. **Yield:** 8 servings.

* You can substitute 2 pounds fresh brussels sprouts for frozen brussels sprouts. Cook fresh brussels sprouts in 1 cup boiling water 8 minutes or until tender.

Leisla Sansom
Alexandria, Virginia

CABBAGE-ONION-SWEET PEPPER MEDLEY

½ small red bell pepper
½ small yellow bell pepper
½ small green bell pepper
1 onion
2 bacon slices
2 cups shredded cabbage
3 tablespoons white vinegar
1 tablespoon vegetable oil
1 tablespoon water
1½ teaspoons brown sugar
1½ teaspoons Dijon mustard
½ teaspoon salt
½ teaspoon pepper

• **Cut** bell peppers into 2-inch-long thin strips; chop onion, and cut bacon into 1-inch pieces.
• **Cook** bacon in a large skillet until crisp. Add bell pepper, onion, and cabbage, tossing gently.
• **Combine** vinegar and next 6 ingredients in a jar; cover tightly, and shake vigorously. Add to vegetable mixture, stirring gently.
• **Bring** to a boil; cover, reduce heat, and simmer 8 minutes or until cabbage is tender, stirring occasionally. Serve immediately. **Yield:** 2 to 4 servings.

Dorothy J. Callaway
Thomasville, Georgia

CREAMED SPINACH

¼ cup pine nuts
½ cup butter or margarine
2 cups whipping cream
⅔ cup grated Parmesan cheese
½ teaspoon salt
½ teaspoon freshly ground pepper
½ teaspoon freshly grated nutmeg
2 (10-ounce) packages fresh spinach, washed, trimmed, and shredded

• **Place** pine nuts in a shallow pan; bake at 350° for 5 minutes or until toasted, stirring occasionally. Set aside.
• **Bring** butter and whipping cream to a boil over medium-high heat; reduce heat to medium, and cook 15 minutes or until thickened, stirring often.
• **Stir** in Parmesan cheese and next 3 ingredients. Add shredded spinach, and cook over low heat until wilted, stirring often. Spoon over grits or cornbread; sprinkle with pine nuts. **Yield:** 4 servings.

Ronda Carman
Houston, Texas

MAKE MINE CHOCOLATE

Life without chocolate is not worth living, we always say.

These recipes are guaranteed to bring even the most

calorie-conscious cooks around to our way of thinking.

Trust us, they're worth the splurge.

MISSISSIPPI MUD

1½ cups all-purpose flour
2 cups sugar
½ cup cocoa
2 teaspoons baking powder
½ teaspoon salt
1 cup butter or margarine, melted
4 large eggs, lightly beaten
1 cup chopped pecans, divided
3 cups miniature marshmallows
Chocolate Frosting

• **Combine** first 5 ingredients in a large bowl. Add butter and eggs, stirring until smooth. Stir in ½ cup pecans. Pour mixture into a greased and floured 13- x 9- x 2-inch baking pan.
• **Bake** at 350° for 25 to 30 minutes or until a wooden pick inserted in center comes out clean. Immediately sprinkle marshmallows over top; return to oven, and bake 1 additional minute. Remove from oven; spread marshmallows on top. Let stand 5 minutes.
• **Spread** Chocolate Frosting evenly over marshmallows, and sprinkle with remaining ½ cup pecans. Cool completely, and cut into squares. **Yield:** 24 servings.

Chocolate Frosting

½ cup butter or margarine, melted
⅓ cup cocoa
⅓ cup evaporated milk
1 teaspoon vanilla extract
1 (16-ounce) package powdered sugar, sifted

• **Combine** all ingredients in a large mixing bowl; beat at medium speed with an electric mixer until dry ingredients are moistened. Beat at high speed until spreading consistency. **Yield:** 2½ cups.

Note: If marshmallows do not spread easily after 1 minute in oven, do not bake longer. Let stand 1 to 2 minutes to soften.

Dee Elkins
Little Rock, Arkansas

CHOCOLATE-ALMOND TORTE

3 shortbread finger cookies, crushed
3 tablespoons slivered almonds
⅓ cup walnut pieces
1 cup sugar
1 (8-ounce) packagc semisweet chocolate squares, chopped
½ cup butter, cut into pieces
1 tablespoon almond liqueur
4 large eggs
1 cup whipping cream
2 tablespoons powdered sugar

• **Press** crushed cookies evenly into bottom of a buttered 8-inch springform pan; set aside.
• **Position** knife blade in food processor bowl, and add almonds, walnuts, and 1 cup sugar; process until ground, stopping once to scrape down sides. Transfer mixture to a bowl; set aside.
• **Combine** chocolate and butter in a 1-quart liquid measuring cup; microwave at MEDIUM (50% power) 3 to 4 minutes or until melted, stirring after each minute. Let mixture stand 15 minutes.
• **Stir** almond liqueur into nut mixture. Add eggs, one at a time, stirring just until blended after each addition. Stir in chocolate mixture. Pour over crushed cookies in pan.
• **Bake** at 325° for 35 to 40 minutes or until set; cool completely. Remove sides from pan.
• **Beat** whipping cream and powdered sugar until soft peaks form, and serve with torte. **Yield:** 6 to 8 servings.

Note: You can chill torte. Remove from refrigerator 30 minutes before serving. For testing, we used Walker Shortbread Fingers.

Liz Lorber
Atlanta, Georgia

PEANUT BUTTER-FUDGE CAKE

(pictured on page 224)

Whether you serve it as an after-school snack or for dessert, this recipe is sure to be a favorite of kids of all ages.

2 cups all-purpose flour
1 teaspoon baking soda
2 cups sugar
1 cup butter or margarine
¼ cup cocoa
1 cup water
½ cup buttermilk
2 large eggs, lightly beaten
1 teaspoon vanilla extract
1½ cups creamy peanut butter
Chocolate Frosting

• **Combine** first 3 ingredients in a large bowl; set aside.
• **Melt** butter in a heavy saucepan; stir in cocoa. Add water, buttermilk, and eggs, stirring well.
• **Cook** over medium heat, stirring constantly, until mixture boils. Remove from heat; add to flour mixture, stirring until smooth. Stir in vanilla. Pour batter into a greased and floured 13- x 9- x 2-inch baking pan.
• **Bake** at 350° for 20 to 25 minutes or until a wooden pick inserted in center comes out clean. Cool 10 minutes on a wire rack. Carefully spread peanut butter over warm cake. Cool completely.
• **Spread** Chocolate Frosting over peanut butter; cut into squares. **Yield:** 20 to 25 servings.

Chocolate Frosting

½ cup butter or margarine
¼ cup cocoa
⅓ cup buttermilk
1 (16-ounce) package powdered sugar, sifted
1 teaspoon vanilla extract

• **Bring** butter, cocoa, and buttermilk to a boil in a small saucepan over medium heat, stirring constantly. Pour hot mixture over powdered sugar in a bowl, stirring until smooth. Stir in vanilla. **Yield:** 2½ cups.

Marian T. Talley
Huntsville, Alabama

FROZEN CHOCOLATE-MACADAMIA NUT PIE

1 (8-ounce) package cream cheese, softened
½ cup sugar
1 teaspoon vanilla extract
1 cup (6 ounces) semisweet chocolate morsels, melted
1½ cups macadamia nuts, finely chopped
1½ cups whipping cream
½ cup sugar
Chocolate-Macadamia Crumb Crust
Garnish: sweetened whipped cream

• **Combine** first 3 ingredients; beat at high speed with an electric mixer until smooth and creamy. Add chocolate morsels; beat at lowest speed just until blended. Stir in chopped nuts.
• **Beat** whipping cream at high speed until foamy. Gradually add sugar, beating until firm peaks form; fold into chocolate mixture. Pour into Chocolate-Macadamia Crumb Crust; cover and freeze 8 hours. Garnish, if desired. **Yield:** 1 (9-inch) pie.

Chocolate-Macadamia Crumb Crust

1¼ cups chocolate wafer crumbs
½ cup macadamia nuts, finely chopped
⅓ cup butter or margarine, melted

• **Combine** all ingredients, and press into bottom and up sides of a 9-inch pieplate.
• **Bake** at 350° for 8 minutes; cool. **Yield:** 1 (9-inch) piecrust.

Kim McCully
Knoxville, Tennessee

SPIDERS AND SNAKES

Invite the neighborhood kids to your house for a Halloween party and serve these "frightful" treats. If spooky crawlers give you the creeps, here's your chance to bite the things that scare you. Our snakes are individual pizzas, and our spiders are sweet apricots with licorice legs.

Let your guests make their own pizza snakes with refrigerated pizza crust, pizza sauce, and your choice of toppings. Half the fun is watching the kids roll and decorate the tasty creatures on baking sheets. Then you only have to bake the snakes at 425° for 6 to 8 minutes.

Chocolate-dipped apples, caramel corn, and pumpkin-shaped cake and ice cream bring the party to a sweet end. But don't forget to buy lots of chewy candy worms, spiders, and snakes to fill goody bags as favors. It'll be the most fun you've ever had with creepy crawlers.

CHOCOLATE PUMPKIN

1 (18.25-ounce) package devil's food cake mix
1 (5.9-ounce) package chocolate instant pudding mix
1¼ cups water
½ cup vegetable oil
4 large eggs
2 cups (12 ounces) semisweet chocolate morsels
1 (7½-ounce) package fluffy white frosting mix
Orange liquid food coloring
Garnish: worm- and snake-shaped chewy candies

• **Combine** first 5 ingredients in a large mixing bowl; beat at medium speed with an electric mixer 2 minutes. Stir in morsels. Pour batter into a greased and floured 12-cup Bundt pan.

• **Bake** at 350° for 55 minutes. Cool in pan on a wire rack 10 minutes; remove from pan, and cool on wire rack.
• **Prepare** frosting according to package directions; beat in desired amount of food coloring. Spread frosting over cooled cake, and garnish, if desired. **Yield:** 1 (10-inch) cake.

CHOCOLATE APPLES ON A STICK

6 wooden craft sticks
6 medium apples
1 cup (6 ounces) semisweet chocolate mini-morsels
1 cup (6 ounces) peanut butter morsels
1 tablespoon vegetable oil
1 cup chopped peanuts (optional)

• **Insert** a wooden stick into the top of each apple.
• **Cook** morsels and oil in a heavy saucepan over low heat until morsels melt, stirring often.
• **Dip** apples in chocolate mixture, coating well; roll in peanuts, if desired. Place on a wax paper-lined baking sheet; chill until firm. **Yield:** 6 servings.

Charlotte Pierce
Greensburg, Kentucky

DRIED APRICOT SPIDERS

1 (6-ounce) package dried apricot halves
1 (8-ounce) carton pineapple cream cheese
16 feet thin licorice rope, cut into 2-inch pieces

• **Spread** half of apricot halves with cream cheese; top with remaining apricots. Insert licorice pieces into filling to resemble spider legs. **Yield:** 14 spiders.

CARAMEL CRUNCH POPCORN

6 quarts popped popcorn
1¾ cups salted Spanish peanuts
1 cup butter or margarine
1 (16-ounce) package light brown sugar
¼ cup light corn syrup
¼ cup molasses
½ teaspoon salt
1 teaspoon vanilla extract

• **Place** popcorn and peanuts in a large bowl; set aside.
• **Melt** butter in a large heavy saucepan. Stir in brown sugar and next 3 ingredients; bring to a boil over medium heat, stirring constantly.
• **Boil** 5 minutes, stirring occasionally. Remove from heat; stir in vanilla.
• **Pour** mixture over popcorn mixture; stir until evenly coated. Pour into two lightly greased large roasting pans or four (13- x 9- x 2-inch) pans, spreading into a thin layer.
• **Bake** at 250° for 45 to 50 minutes, stirring every 15 minutes. Cool in pans on wire racks. **Yield:** about 5 quarts.

Jane Maloy
Wilmington, North Carolina

ICE CREAM PUMPKIN

3 quarts vanilla ice cream, slightly softened
2 teaspoons pumpkin pie spice
2 cups whipping cream
½ cup sifted powdered sugar
1 teaspoon vanilla extract
6 drops of red liquid food coloring
5 drops of yellow liquid food coloring
1 (1½-inch) piece candied citron

• **Line** 2 (1½-quart) bowls with aluminum foil. Spoon ice cream evenly into bowls; smooth top with back of a spoon. Sprinkle with pie spice. Cover and freeze at least 8 hours.
• **Beat** whipping cream until foamy; gradually add powdered sugar, beating until soft peaks form. Stir in vanilla and food coloring.
• **Remove** ice cream from bowls, and remove foil. Place ice cream halves together to resemble a ball, and place on a serving plate. Spread with tinted whipped cream to resemble a pumpkin. Place citron on top to resemble a stem. Store in freezer until ready to serve. Serve with chocolate sauce, if desired. **Yield:** 16 servings.

A HEALTHY HALLOWEEN

If Halloween gives you nightmares of trips to the dentist, here are a few ideas that'll help you sleep.

▪ Form a pact with your neighbors to pass out nutritious treats. Granola bars, cheese crackers, and boxes of raisins are kid-approved ideas.

▪ And who says Halloween treats have to be edible? Pencils, erasers, and shaped straws are alternatives that won't send little goblins to the dentist.

▪ If your kids still end up with mountains of sweets, let them use some to decorate a gingerbread house for the upcoming holidays. Candy corn makes great eaves, stacked Tootsie Rolls look a lot like wood piles, and miniature candy bars resemble window shutters.

From Our Kitchen to Yours

QUICK GETAWAY

If you've wondered why chefs usually tie their aprons in the front instead of the back, Chef Joe Cairns says it's for survival under fire, literally. He learned in culinary school (before teaching cooking classes at The House on Bayou Road in New Orleans) that should a gas flame or grease flare-up catch your apron front, you can yank the string or cut it with a knife much quicker in front than you can fumble behind your back to escape the heated situation. Not a bad idea for the home cook either.

CAN'T BEAT BEATEN

Sometimes you just can't take shortcuts. We recently tried to speed up beaten biscuits, that age-old recipe for literally beating biscuit dough on a wooden table with a hammer for a half-hour or more, until it blisters. We tried overworking the dough with a nineties method, the food processor.

We rescued the poor machine, which began to smoke from exhaustion after just one minute. Beaten biscuits, we decided, are a treat enjoyed at someone else's house.

A FLOUR BY ANY OTHER NAME

Cooking is an art, but baking is a science. When it comes to carefully calibrated bread and cake recipes, a flour *isn't* a flour *isn't* a flour, and using the wrong one is your first clue as to why your bread or cake never rose. Without getting into a whole lot of chemistry gobbledy-gook about gluten, we suggest matching the flour label's description to your recipe's ingredient list as closely as possible.

For example, if the recipe calls for all-purpose, use all-purpose. If you use self-rising just because it's in the pantry, you could be sunk – or puffed. It already has the baking powder and salt added, and when you stir in more of those according to the recipe, you've got baked goodies gone bad.

We often specify soft wheat flour in our recipes. Your calls and letters have let us know that we've led some of you astray. This isn't whole wheat flour. Believe it or not, wheat grown in the South is softer than that grown in the North. That means it measures differently than all-purpose and gives a different texture.

Staunch native Southern cooks such as author and television personality Nathalie Dupree and Williams-Sonoma founder Chuck Williams (to name just two) firmly believe in this soft flour's difference. They recommend White Lily flour, milled in Knoxville, Tennessee, for over a century and available at most Southern grocery stores. If you can't find it call 1-800-264-5459 to mail order.

GET A GRIP

When you're serving fish for company, there's a polite way to pick out the bones without fingering everyone's food. Use a pair of tweezers from your kitchen tool drawer to debone those fillets with finesse.

BANANAS FOR PEANUT BUTTER

Virginia's passion for peanuts is perhaps surpassed only by the fervor of that famous former President from Georgia. In those two states, residents eat that lovely, lowly crop in any form and swear it'll make any good recipe even better. We believe it when Marge Killmon from Annandale, Virginia, utters the promise. She opens a jar of peanut butter and goes beyond plain banana pudding: Secret-Ingredient Banana Pudding, North Virginia Style. Before layering vanilla wafers in her favorite recipe, she spreads peanut butter on the flat sides, and then sandwiches them together in pairs. Hmmm, wonder if that was a secret leaked from the White House? Marge's lips are sealed . . . with peanut butter.

IT'S IN THE BAG

Artsy drizzles and drips have pushed perky sprigs of parsley right off the garnishing line in lots of restaurants in the last few years. Plates seemingly inspired by the artist Jackson Pollock (a.k.a. "Jack the Dripper") bring fun to fancy dining, and you can easily do the same in your kitchen.

And you don't need any high-tech equipment. Grab a heavy-duty, zip-top plastic bag and a pair of scissors, and you're in business. (If you want to get really sophisticated, purchase a plastic ketchup or mustard squirt bottle like you see in old-fashioned hamburger joints.) Just spoon or pour your sweet or savory sauce into the plastic bag (or bottle), seal the "zipper," and snip a tiny hole in one corner of bag with the scissors. Hold the bag with the open corner pointed up until you get a plate under it (unless you're ready to paint the kitchen), and then gently squirt the sauce in haphazard patterns. Shake a little powdered sugar or cocoa on desserts for texture if you like.

For instant chocolate sauce, put a few semisweet squares into a plastic bag, seal, and drop into a bowl of hot or boiling water. Take out after a few minutes, let cool to the touch, and then gently knead with your fingers to finish the melting. Snip, squirt, and then toss the bag. No scrubbing stubborn chocolate from a bowl, spatula, sink, counter, and dishcloth.

THE GREAT PUMPKIN

This time of year roadside pumpkin stands beckon.

Small pumpkins are usually best for cooking. They have more edible flesh. Look for a pumpkin with the stem attached; if the stem is off the flesh might be dried out.

To prepare a fresh pumpkin for cooking, first slice in half crosswise, and remove the seeds (but don't discard those jewels). Put the halves, cut side down, on a jellyroll pan, and bake at 325° for 45 minutes or until the pumpkin is tender. When it's cool, remove the skin, and mash the pulp. A 5-pound pumpkin will yield about 4½ cups of cooked, mashed pulp.

And the seeds – they're perfect for snacking. Just bake them in an 8-inch square baking dish at 300° for 25 minutes. Stir in a little butter or margarine, and seasoning salt for flavor, if you like, before baking.

Curried Pumpkin Soup (recipe, page 242) gets its full flavor from canned pumpkin, without all the mess. So you can leave the fresh pumpkins out on the front porch.

Host a harvest dinner with a menu of Pepper-Sage Chicken (recipe, page 237), mustard greens, and roasted sweet potatoes.

Left: *Serve lentil-filled Samosas with mango chutney (recipe, page 239), for a taste of India in an exotic appetizer.*

Below: *A crusty coating of cheese covers layers of root vegetables in Potato-and-Rutabaga Gratin (recipe, page 237).*

Spoonbread Grits With Savory Mushroom Sauce (recipe, page 236) is an easy dish that's elegant enough for a white-tablecloth restaurant.

NOVEMBER

THE SOUTH'S FAMILY TREE

Pecans provide the perfect complement to many foods, both sweet and savory. But there is no ingredient that pairs more perfectly with pecans than sugar. Our Bourbon-Chocolate-Pecan Tarts and Italian Cream Cake prove this theory lusciously.

ROASTED BACON PECANS
(pictured on page 335)

2 cups pecan halves
2 tablespoons butter or margarine, melted
6 slices bacon, chopped
2 tablespoons sugar
½ teaspoon salt

• **Combine** first 3 ingredients, stirring well; spread in a 15- x 10- x 1-inch jellyroll pan.
• **Bake** at 350° for 25 minutes or until pecans are toasted and bacon is done, stirring occasionally. Sprinkle with sugar and salt; stir to coat. Let cool; cover and store in refrigerator. **Yield:** 2 cups.

Sherry Collins
Robbinsville, North Carolina

PEAR-PECAN APPETIZERS

1 cup finely chopped pecans
2 ripe pears
1 quart water
2 tablespoons lemon juice
½ cup butter or margarine, softened
2 tablespoons crumbled blue cheese

• **Place** pecans in a shallow pan; bake at 350° for 5 to 10 minutes or until toasted, stirring occasionally. Set aside.
• **Cut** each pear into thin slices. Combine pear slices, water, and lemon juice in a large bowl.
• **Beat** butter and blue cheese at medium speed with an electric mixer until smooth.
• **Drain** pear slices on paper towels. Spread bottom half of pear slices with butter mixture; coat with pecans, and place on a serving plate. Cover and chill 30 minutes. **Yield:** 2½ dozen.

PECAN PASTA SAUCE

1 (12-ounce) package linguine
1½ cups chopped pecans
4 to 6 cloves garlic, minced
2 tablespoons olive oil
½ teaspoon ground red pepper
1 (15-ounce) carton ricotta cheese
1 cup milk
1 teaspoon salt
1 teaspoon pepper
1 cup grated Parmesan cheese
¼ cup chopped fresh parsley

• **Cook** linguine according to package directions; drain and keep warm.
• **Cook** pecans and garlic in hot oil in a large skillet 1 to 2 minutes or until pecans are lightly browned, stirring often; stir in red pepper. Reserve ⅓ cup pecan mixture.
• **Combine** remaining pecan mixture, ricotta cheese, and next 3 ingredients in container of an electric blender or food processor; process until well blended, stopping once to scrape down sides.
• **Toss** with linguine and ¾ cup Parmesan cheese. Sprinkle with reserved pecan mixture, remaining Parmesan cheese, and parsley. Serve immediately. **Yield:** 4 servings.

Victoria Miller
James Island, South Carolina

ITALIAN CREAM CAKE
(pictured on page 334)

This cake is sure to win raves from your family – as it did in our Test Kitchens.

½ cup butter or margarine, softened
½ cup shortening
2 cups sugar
5 large eggs, separated
1 tablespoon vanilla extract
2 cups all-purpose flour
1 teaspoon baking soda
1 cup buttermilk
1 cup flaked coconut
Nutty Cream Cheese Frosting
Garnishes: toasted pecan halves, chopped pecans

• **Beat** butter and shortening at medium speed with an electric mixer until fluffy; gradually add sugar, beating well. Add egg yolks, one at a time, beating until blended after each addition. Add vanilla; beat until blended.
• **Combine** flour and soda; add to butter mixture alternately with buttermilk, beginning and ending with flour mixture. Beat at low speed until blended after each addition. Stir in coconut.
• **Beat** egg whites until stiff peaks form; fold into batter. Pour batter into three greased and floured 9-inch round cakepans.
• **Bake** at 350° for 25 minutes or until a wooden pick inserted in center comes out clean. Cool in pans on wire racks 10 minutes; remove from pans, and cool on wire racks.
• **Spread** Nutty Cream Cheese Frosting between layers and on top and sides of cake. Garnish, if desired. **Yield:** 1 (3-layer) cake.

Nutty Cream Cheese Frosting

1 cup chopped pecans
1 (8-ounce) package cream cheese, softened
½ cup butter or margarine, softened
1 tablespoon vanilla extract
1 (16-ounce) package powdered sugar, sifted

• **Place** pecans in a shallow pan; bake at 350° for 5 to 10 minutes or until toasted, stirring occasionally. Cool.
• **Beat** cream cheese, butter, and vanilla at medium speed with an electric mixer until creamy. Add sugar, beating at low speed until blended. Beat at high speed until smooth; stir in pecans. **Yield:** about 4 cups.

Donna Willcut
Pryor, Oklahoma

There's an old joke that if you shake the family tree hard enough, you're bound to find a couple of nuts. In the South, those nuts will surely be pecans (or perhaps your great-uncle Thaddeus).

Pecan trees are found throughout most of the South, where growers and homeowners alike collect their autumn bounty. In October and November, when the nuts fall (or are shaken) from the trees, pecan lovers get busy. They squirrel away pecan-filled containers in closets, freezers, and pantries until the nuts can be transformed into delectable dishes. Family members of all ages are pressed into nut-cracking service.

Bake pecans for snacking, toss them into creamy pasta, or simply eat them out of hand, and you'll know without a doubt why the pecan is the South's family tree.

PICK A PECK OF PECANS

Imagine – no more kneeling, crawling, sitting, or stooping to harvest your pecan crop. Special equipment now makes that a reality. **The Better Pecan Picker Upper** and the **Pecan Picker Upper** let you harvest your crop from an upright position. When rolled or pressed against the ground, the tools trap the nuts inside the coils. Then you can easily release them into another container. For even greater ease, **Bag-A-Nut** markets a harvester about the size (and cost) of a small lawnmower. All are available by mail order.

▪ **The Better Pecan Picker Upper,** Kingston, Georgia; call (770) 336-9221 or 1-800-922-6065.

▪ **Pecan Picker Upper,** Willis, Texas; call (409) 856-4052.

▪ **Bag-A-Nut,** Jacksonville, Florida; call 1-800-940-2688.

PECAN PEARLS

▪ Pecan trees take up to 20 years to produce a full crop of nuts.

▪ Pecans are native to the Southern states, although they are now grown commercially in California, New Mexico, and Mexico.

▪ Bases of the 10,000 torches used in the cross-country Olympic relay were made of pecan wood.

▪ Okmulgee, Oklahoma, holds the record for the world's largest pecan pie. The 40-foot-wide pie – made in 1989 – contained 3,044 pounds of pecans, 64,280 eggs, and 6,000 pounds of piecrust dough.

▪ You can store pecans in the refrigerator up to nine months or freeze up to two years.

▪ Pecans, a member of the hickory family, have the highest fat content of any nut – over 70 percent of their calories are from fat.

▪ To shell pecans in large pieces, soak the nuts in cold water for two hours. Then drain and allow to sit overnight. Crack shells open by hitting one end with a hard object.

BOURBON-CHOCOLATE-PECAN TARTS

(pictured on page 335)

Try this wonderfully rich twist on a favorite Southern dessert.

Cream Cheese Pastry
¾ cup semisweet chocolate morsels
3 large eggs, lightly beaten
⅓ cup sugar
3 tablespoons firmly packed light brown sugar
1 tablespoon all-purpose flour
¾ cup light corn syrup
¼ cup butter or margarine, melted
3 tablespoons bourbon
2 teaspoons vanilla extract
2 cups pecan halves
Garnishes: whipped cream, pecan halves, chopped pecans

• **Divide** Cream Cheese Pastry into 6 equal portions; shape each portion into a ball, and press into a 4½-inch tart pan. Sprinkle chocolate morsels into tart shells; chill 30 minutes.
• **Beat** eggs and next 7 ingredients at medium speed with an electric mixer until blended. Pour batter into tart shells, filling each half full. Arrange pecan halves over filling; drizzle with remaining filling.
• **Bake** at 350° for 30 to 35 minutes or until set; cool. Garnish, if desired.
Yield: 6 tarts.

Cream Cheese Pastry

1 (3-ounce) package cream cheese, softened
½ cup butter or margarine, softened
1 cup all-purpose flour

• **Beat** cream cheese and butter at medium speed with an electric mixer until smooth. Add flour, and beat at low speed until a soft dough forms.
Yield: pastry for 6 (4½-inch) tarts.

Note: You can bake tart filling in a 9-inch tart pan fitted with pastry crust. Prepare as directed, and bake at 350° for 55 minutes or until set.

Trenda Leigh
Richmond, Virginia

STEWARDS OF THE BLUE RIDGE

It's late October in Virginia's Blue Ridge. The only thing darker than the approaching cloud bank is the scowl on Jim Law's face. Twenty acres of wine grapes, nearly perfect for picking, await the harvest. Heavy rain now could dilute their sugar, cause them to swell, and eventually burst. "There is nothing more frightening than standing in your vineyard and watching it explode," says Peggy, Jim's wife and partner.

This is Linden Vineyards, Jim and Peggy's home, the scenic and sometimes frantic source of some of the tastiest wines in the South.

OUT OF AFRICA

The vineyard's story begins in the rain forests of central Africa. As a Peace Corps volunteer, Jim journeyed to Zaire. While there, he took his first crack at making wine. But not from grapes – from palm trees.

Quaffing palm wine inspired Jim to make the real stuff. Upon returning to the States, he joined a now-defunct winery in Virginia, where he met Peggy. After the pair's joint apprenticeship, they struck out on their own. In 1983, they bought 76 acres of wooded hillside south of Linden, Virginia. Clearing the land took two full years. They planted their first vines in 1985 and sold their first bottle in 1988. Production now runs at 5,000 cases a year.

The ancient volcanic soil of the Blue Ridge supplies good drainage and rich minerals. Moreover, the 1,350-foot elevation protects the plants from early spring frosts. It also delays ripening well into fall, intensifying the flavors.

"Wine tastes best when grapes ripen over a long period of time," says Jim. "In California, they call it 'long hang time.' Grapes need to ripen when the nights are cool and the days warm and sunny." Peggy adds, "Coolness helps the fruit retain acidity. Without acidity, you end up with something very bland. We call 'em 'wimpy grapes.' "

The Laws make wines from mainstream European grapes (Cabernet Sauvignon, Chardonnay, Riesling), lesser known European grapes (Cabernet Franc, Petit Verdot), and French-American hybrids (Seyval, Vidal). Critics agree there isn't a wimpy wine among them. *Wine Spectator, Food & Wine,* and *Bon Appétit* have praised Linden's wines.

GOOD WINE, GOOD FOOD

November arrives and another successful harvest rests in the crusher. Buckets of red juice, blood of the vine, splash in the press. Family and friends lend hands to the work; the moment's emotion is laughter.

A smile expands Jim's face, recalling the words of food writer M. F. K. Fisher, " 'With good friends and good food on the board, and good wine in the pitcher, we may well ask, when shall we live if not now?' "

Linden Vineyards: off State 638, near the intersection of I-81 and I-66. Tours and tastings: 11 a.m.-5 p.m. Wednesday-Sunday April-December; 11 a.m.-5 p.m. weekends only January-March. For information call (540) 364-1997.

LIGHT BY THE FIRE

Crisp autumn nights call for making your fireplace the centerpiece of an evening's entertainment. Draw the dining table close to the fire, and warm your guests with this light fall menu and other seasonal ideas that follow.

FIRESIDE MENU
Serves Eight

Feta Cheese Spread
Molasses-Grilled Pork Tenderloin
Grilled Acorn Squash With Rosemary **Steamed Green Beans**
Chocolate-Almond Silk Pudding

FETA CHEESE SPREAD

Paula's spread can be made ahead. "My husband is Greek and loves feta cheese, so I'm always looking for ways to use it," Paula says.

1 (8-ounce) package reduced-fat cream cheese, softened
2 (4-ounce) packages crumbled feta cheese
2 tablespoons skim milk
10 fresh mint leaves
1 to 2 cloves garlic
Garnishes: chopped tomato, cucumber, green onions

• **Position** knife blade in food processor bowl. Add cheeses, skim milk, mint, and garlic, and process until smooth. Transfer to a serving bowl. Garnish, if desired.

• **Serve** with toasted baguette slices and fresh vegetables. **Yield:** 2 cups.

Paula Covault
LaGrange, Kentucky

♥ Per 2-tablespoon serving:
Calories 76 (75% from fat)
Fat 6.4g (4.2g saturated) Cholesterol 24mg
Sodium 216mg Carbohydrate 1.2g
Fiber 0g Protein 3.5g

MOLASSES-GRILLED PORK TENDERLOIN

(pictured on page 297)

¼ cup molasses
2 tablespoons coarse-grained Dijon mustard
1 tablespoon apple cider vinegar
4 (¾-pound) pork tenderloins, trimmed

• **Combine** first 3 ingredients; brush over tenderloins. Cover and marinate in refrigerator 8 hours.
• **Cook,** covered with grill lid, over medium-hot coals (350° to 400°) about 20 minutes or until a meat thermometer inserted in thickest portion registers 160°, turning once. **Yield:** 8 servings.

♥ Per serving: Calories 254 (25% from fat)
Fat 6.7g (2.2g saturated) Cholesterol 125mg
Sodium 130mg Carbohydrate 7.2g
Fiber 0g Protein 38.9g

GRILLED ACORN SQUASH WITH ROSEMARY

(pictured on page 297)

When buying acorn squash, choose ones that are heavy for their size and have unblemished skin. Unlike summer squash, the hard skin of acorn squash enables it to be stored in a cool, dark place instead of the refrigerator.

2 tablespoons olive oil, divided
¼ cup white wine vinegar
1 tablespoon fresh rosemary
½ teaspoon salt
4 cloves garlic, pressed
2 pounds acorn squash, thinly sliced
Garnish: fresh rosemary sprigs

• **Combine** 1 tablespoon oil and next 4 ingredients in a large heavy-duty, zip-top plastic bag; add squash. Seal and turn to coat. Marinate in refrigerator 2 hours.
• **Remove** squash from marinade; reserving marinade. Brush squash with remaining tablespoon oil.
• **Cook** squash, covered with grill lid, over medium-hot coals (350° to 400°) about 10 minutes on each side. Place on a serving dish, and drizzle with reserved marinade. Cover and let stand 10 minutes. Garnish, if desired. **Yield:** 8 servings.

♥ Per serving: Calories 79 (37% from fat)
Fat 3.5g (0.5g saturated) Cholesterol 0mg
Sodium 151mg Carbohydrate 12.4g
Fiber 1.4g Protein 1g

CHOCOLATE-ALMOND SILK PUDDING

4 cups skim milk
½ cup amaretto
1½ cups sugar
½ cup cocoa
½ cup cornstarch
1½ teaspoons vanilla extract

• **Combine** milk and liqueur in a heavy saucepan; cook over medium heat until hot (do not boil).
• **Sift** sugar, cocoa, and cornstarch together in a large heavy saucepan; add hot milk mixture, whisking until smooth. Bring to a boil over medium heat; boil 1 minute. Stir in vanilla.
• **Pour** into 10 custard cups or stemmed glasses; cover with wax paper, and chill. **Yield:** 5 cups.

Sandi Pichon
Slidell, Louisiana

♥ Per ½-cup serving:
Calories 210 (3% from fat)
Fat 0.7g (0.4g saturated) Cholesterol 4mg
Sodium 59mg Carbohydrate 47.5g
Fiber 0.1g Protein 3.8g

A THANKSGIVING MOUNTAIN RETREAT

For the Swirles-Hryharrow family, enjoying the holiday means relaxing. "But the only way to do that is to mess up someone else's house," laughs Sudi Swirles, along with husband Jan Hryharrow. Each year, the Durham, North Carolina, couple hooks up with family and friends and heads west to a rented house on Lake Summit in Tuxedo, near Hendersonville.

The couple formerly owned Sudi's, a gourmet restaurant in Durham; Jan's mother, Dee Hryharrow, is a noted Beaufort cookbook author. So it's not surprising that the group is treated to a mix of innovative and traditional fare.

A LAKESIDE REPAST

Serves Six to 10

Roasted Turkey With Sausage-and-Wild Mushroom Stuffing
Gingered Acorn Squash With Spiced Cranberry Sauce
Butterbeans With Bacon and Green Onions
Wild Rice
Pumpkin Cheesecake
Apple-Nut Cake

ROASTED TURKEY WITH SAUSAGE-AND-WILD MUSHROOM STUFFING

(pictured on page 296)

1 cup butter or margarine, softened
1 tablespoon dried thyme, crushed
1 (14- to 16-pound) turkey
1 tablespoon salt
1 tablespoon pepper
Sausage-and-Wild Mushroom Stuffing
2 tablespoons soy sauce
2 tablespoons sesame oil
½ cup dry white wine
¼ cup all-purpose flour
1 (16-ounce) carton half-and-half
½ teaspoon soy sauce
½ teaspoon salt
½ teaspoon pepper
Garnish: fresh sage

• **Combine** butter and thyme in a bowl, mixing well.
• **Remove** giblets and neck from turkey; set aside. Rinse turkey with cold water, and pat dry. Loosen skin from breast without detaching it; carefully spread butter mixture under skin. Rub outside of turkey with 1 tablespoon salt and 1 tablespoon pepper.
• **Spoon** 4 cups Sausage-and-Wild Mushroom Stuffing into turkey; truss

turkey, and tie ends of legs together with string. Lift wingtips up and over back, and tuck under bird. Place turkey, breast side up, in a large roasting pan; rub with 2 tablespoons soy sauce and oil.

• **Bake** at 375° for 2½ hours or until meat thermometer inserted in turkey thigh registers 180° and stuffing registers 165°, shielding turkey with aluminum foil after 1 hour and basting with pan juices every 30 minutes.

• **Cook** giblets and neck in boiling water to cover 45 minutes or until tender. Drain, reserving 1 cup broth. Chop neck meat and giblets; chill.

• **Transfer** turkey to a serving platter, reserving drippings in pan. Remove and discard fat from drippings; pour ¼ cup drippings into a heavy saucepan. Stir wine and reserved broth into roasting pan, stirring to loosen particles that cling to bottom.

• **Place** ¼ cup drippings over medium heat. Add flour, and cook, whisking constantly, until browned. Gradually add wine mixture and half-and-half; cook, whisking constantly, until bubbly. Stir in neck meat and giblets, ½ teaspoon soy sauce, ½ teaspoon salt, and ½ teaspoon pepper; simmer to desired thickness, stirring often. Serve with turkey. Garnish, if desired. **Yield:** 8 servings.

Sausage-and-Wild Mushroom Stuffing

½ pound ground pork sausage
½ cup butter or margarine
3 pounds mixed wild mushrooms (shiitake, portobello, enoki), sliced
1 large onion, sliced
1 bunch green onions, sliced
1 (14½-ounce) can ready-to-serve chicken broth
1 (8-ounce) package herb-seasoned stuffing mix
1 poultry herb bouquet, chopped (see note)
½ teaspoon salt
½ teaspoon pepper

• **Brown** sausage in a large skillet, stirring to crumble. Drain and set aside.

• **Melt** butter in skillet; add mushrooms, onion, and green onions, and cook until tender, stirring often. Stir in sausage, broth, and remaining ingredients. Spoon 4 cups stuffing into turkey, if desired; place remaining stuffing into a lightly greased 13- x 9- x 2-inch baking dish.

• **Bake** stuffing at 375° for 45 minutes or until lightly browned. **Yield:** 8 to 10 servings.

Note: A poultry herb bouquet contains 2 sprigs each of fresh sage, rosemary, and thyme. Or you can substitute 1 teaspoon of each dried herb for fresh.

GINGERED ACORN SQUASH WITH SPICED CRANBERRY SAUCE

(pictured on page 296)

6 small acorn squash
1 cup water
½ cup butter or margarine
2 cloves garlic, minced
¼ cup whipping cream
1½ tablespoons minced fresh ginger
¾ teaspoon salt
¼ teaspoon ground white pepper
Spiced Cranberry Sauce

• **Cut** squash in half crosswise; remove and discard seeds. Place, cut side down, in a 15- x 10- x 1-inch jellyroll pan, and add 1 cup water.

• **Bake** at 350° for 1 hour or until tender; drain. Scoop pulp from bottom halves, leaving ½-inch shells; set shells aside. Scoop all pulp from remaining squash halves; mash all pulp.

• **Melt** butter in a large skillet; add garlic, and cook until tender, stirring often. Stir in squash pulp, whipping cream, and next 3 ingredients; cook over low heat, stirring constantly, until thoroughly heated.

• **Spoon** into squash shells; top and serve with Spiced Cranberry Sauce. **Yield:** 6 servings.

Spiced Cranberry Sauce

1 cup water
1 cup sugar
1 (3-inch) piece fresh ginger, peeled
1 firm pear, diced
1 teaspoon grated lemon rind
1 (12-ounce) package fresh or frozen cranberries
2 tablespoons fresh lemon juice

• **Bring** first 3 ingredients to a boil in a heavy saucepan, stirring constantly; boil 5 minutes.

• **Add** pear and lemon rind; return mixture to a boil, and cook 3 minutes, stirring occasionally. Stir in cranberries. Reduce heat, and simmer, without stirring, 3 to 5 minutes or until cranberry skins pop. Remove from heat; cool. Cover and chill.

• **Remove** and discard ginger; cover and chill sauce up to 2 days. Stir in lemon juice just before serving. **Yield:** 2½ cups.

BUTTERBEANS WITH BACON AND GREEN ONIONS

(pictured on page 296)

2 (10-ounce) packages frozen butterbeans
6 lean slices bacon
4 green onions, chopped
2 cloves garlic, minced
½ cup chopped fresh parsley
½ teaspoon salt
½ teaspoon pepper

• **Cook** beans according to package directions, and set aside.

• **Cook** bacon in a large skillet over medium-high heat until crisp; remove bacon, reserving drippings in skillet. Crumble bacon, and set aside.

• **Cook** green onions and garlic in drippings until tender, stirring often. Stir in beans, chopped parsley, salt, and pepper; cook just until thoroughly heated. Sprinkle with crumbled bacon. **Yield:** 8 to 10 servings.

PUMPKIN CHEESECAKE

1¼ cups gingersnap crumbs (25 to 30 cookies)
3 tablespoons butter or margarine, melted
3 (8-ounce) packages cream cheese, softened
1¼ cups sugar, divided
1 tablespoon vanilla extract
6 large eggs, separated
2 (16.25-ounce) cans pumpkin pie mix
2 large eggs
1 cup whipping cream
1 tablespoon powdered sugar

• **Combine** cookie crumbs and butter; press in bottom and 1 inch up sides of a lightly greased 12-inch springform pan. Set aside.
• **Beat** cream cheese at medium speed with an electric mixer until smooth; add 1 cup sugar and vanilla, beating until creamy. Stir in 6 egg yolks. Pour 2½ cups mixture into prepared crust; set aside.
• **Add** pumpkin pie mix and 2 eggs to remaining cream cheese mixture, stirring well; set aside.
• **Beat** egg whites at high speed until foamy. Add remaining ¼ cup sugar, 1 tablespoon at a time, beating until stiff peaks form and sugar dissolves. Fold into pumpkin mixture; pour over cream cheese mixture in crust.
• **Bake** at 300° for 1½ hours. Turn oven off, and gently run a knife around edge of pan to release sides. Let stand in oven with door partially open for 1½ hours. Remove sides of pan; cover and chill.
• **Beat** whipping cream and powdered sugar at high speed until soft peaks form; spread on sides of cheesecake. **Yield:** 12 to 14 servings.

APPLE-NUT CAKE

Rome and York apples are best for cooking because they retain their flavor while cooking. Rome apples have a mild tart flavor; York have a winelike taste.

1½ cups vegetable oil
1½ cups sugar
½ cup firmly packed brown sugar
3 large eggs
3 cups all-purpose flour
1 teaspoon baking soda
2 teaspoons ground cinnamon
½ teaspoon freshly grated nutmeg
½ teaspoon vanilla extract
3½ cups peeled, diced cooking apple (about 3 large)
1 cup coarsely chopped walnuts
Brown Sugar Glaze

• **Beat** first 3 ingredients in a mixing bowl at medium speed with an electric mixer until blended. Add eggs, one at a time, beating after each addition.
• **Combine** flour and next 3 ingredients; stir into sugar mixture. Stir in vanilla; fold in apple and walnuts. Pour batter into a greased and floured 10-inch tube pan or 12-cup Bundt pan.
• **Bake** at 325° for 1 hour and 30 to 35 minutes or until a long wooden pick inserted in center of cake comes out clean.
• **Cool** in pan on a wire rack 20 minutes. Remove from pan, and cool on wire rack. Drizzle with warm Brown Sugar Glaze. **Yield:** 1 (10-inch) cake.

Brown Sugar Glaze

⅓ cup butter or margarine
⅓ cup firmly packed light brown sugar
⅓ cup sugar
⅓ cup whipping cream
½ teaspoon vanilla extract

• **Combine** first 4 ingredients in a heavy saucepan. Bring to a boil over medium heat, stirring constantly; boil 1 minute. Stir in vanilla. **Yield:** 1 cup.

SAGE ADVICE

Remember sage? Rub its soft, feather-shaped gray-green leaves together and a heady camphor aroma greets you. Open up a jar of dried sage and one whiff reminds you of its very potent flavoring powers.

History honors the worldly plant as a multipurpose herb. Ancient herbalists believed that using sage strengthened the memory. Greeks and Romans prescribed it as medicine. The Chinese prized it as a base for a mood-lifting tea. And American Indians used it to clean their teeth.

Southerners know sage best for the distinctive flavor it imparts to cornbread dressing and the character it adds to pork sausage. Wise cooks continue to find new reasons to celebrate the venerable herb.

TURKEY CUTLETS WITH SAGE GRAVY

Turkey cutlets for company? You bet. A rich, creamy sauce, well worth the calories and time invested, makes this dish fit for any special occasion.

4 (5-ounce) boneless turkey breast cutlets
1 tablespoon finely chopped fresh sage leaves or 1 teaspoon dried leaf sage, crumbled
¼ teaspoon salt
⅛ teaspoon pepper
⅛ teaspoon paprika
½ cup all-purpose flour
2 tablespoons butter
2 tablespoons olive oil
Sage Gravy
Garnish: fresh sage leaves

• **Place** cutlets between two sheets of heavy-duty plastic wrap; flatten to ¼-inch thickness, using a meat mallet or rolling pin.

• **Combine** sage, salt, pepper, and paprika; rub evenly on each side of cutlets. Cover and chill 1 to 2 hours.
• **Dredge** cutlets in flour, and shake off excess.
• **Melt** butter in a large nonstick skillet over medium heat; add olive oil. Add cutlets; cook 3 minutes on each side or until lightly browned. Transfer cutlets to a serving plate; keep warm.
• **Reserve** drippings in skillet for Sage Gravy. Garnish, if desired.
• **Serve** cutlets with Sage Gravy. **Yield:** 4 servings.

Sage Gravy

½ cup finely chopped onion
½ cup finely chopped carrot
¼ cup finely chopped celery
1 tablespoon finely chopped fresh sage leaves or 1 teaspoon dried leaf sage, crumbled
Reserved drippings
⅓ cup dry white wine
½ cup chicken broth
1 cup half-and-half
½ teaspoon lemon juice
½ teaspoon salt
½ teaspoon pepper
2 tablespoons cold butter, cut into pieces

• **Add** first 4 ingredients to reserved drippings in skillet.
• **Cook** over medium heat, stirring constantly, until onion is tender. Add wine; bring mixture to a boil, and cook until liquid in skillet is reduced to about 2 tablespoons.
• **Add** broth, and cook until liquid is reduced by half. Stir in half-and-half. Return to a boil; cook until slightly thickened.
• **Pour** mixture through a wire-mesh strainer into a bowl; discard vegetables. Return mixture to skillet. Stir in lemon juice, salt, and pepper.
• **Add** butter pieces, one at a time, stirring with a wire whisk until blended. (If butter is difficult to work into gravy, place skillet over low heat for a few seconds, being careful not to get mixture too hot.) **Yield:** 1 cup.

PORK CHOPS WITH SWEET POTATOES

4 (½-inch-thick) butterflied boneless pork chops
1 cup apple cider, divided
4 sweet potatoes, peeled and cut into ½-inch-thick slices
2 green onions, chopped
2 tablespoons chopped fresh sage leaves
¾ teaspoon salt
¼ teaspoon pepper
2 large Rome or other cooking apples, cored and sliced
1 teaspoon cornstarch

• **Brown** pork chops on both sides in a large nonstick skillet; remove chops from skillet, and set aside.
• **Place** ¾ cup apple cider and next 5 ingredients in skillet. Bring to a boil; cover, reduce heat, and simmer 10 minutes.
• **Add** apple and pork chops; cover and simmer 10 to 15 minutes or until sweet potato is tender and pork chops are done. Remove apple, sweet potato, and pork chops to serving platter, reserving drippings in skillet.
• **Combine** remaining ¼ cup cider with cornstarch, stirring until smooth. Stir into drippings. Cook over medium heat, stirring constantly, until mixture thickens and boils. Boil, stirring constantly, 1 minute. Pour over pork chops. **Yield:** 4 servings.

Janie Wallace
Seguin, Texas

SAGE BUTTER

Try on grilled chicken or fish, or tossed with steamed vegetables.

½ cup fresh sage leaves, loosely packed
1 large shallot
½ cup butter, softened
1 teaspoon grated lemon rind
½ teaspoon fresh lemon juice
¼ teaspoon freshly ground pepper

• **Position** knife blade in food processor bowl; add sage and shallot, and process until chopped.
• **Add** butter and remaining ingredients; process until mixture is thoroughly blended, stopping occasionally to scrape down sides. **Yield:** ½ cup.

Ian Tarica
Alabaster, Alabama

SAGE-GRILLED EGGPLANT

1 large eggplant, unpeeled
1½ teaspoons salt
⅓ cup Sage Butter (see recipe)
¼ teaspoon pepper

• **Cut** eggplant crosswise into ½-inch slices; sprinkle cut sides with salt. Place in a single layer on paper towels; let stand 1 hour.
• **Rinse** eggplant with water, and pat dry. Arrange in a single layer in a lightly greased grill basket.
• **Melt** Sage Butter in a small saucepan over low heat; stir in pepper. Brush on eggplant.
• **Cook,** covered with grill lid, over medium-hot coals (350° to 400°) 12 to 15 minutes or until lightly browned, turning and brushing with butter mixture. **Yield:** 4 servings.

MORE SAGE ADVICE

▪ Fresh sage can be cut year-round. It's best when gathered while the leaves are still green and just before the plant starts to bloom.

▪ To extract the oils, crush or grind sage just before using.

▪ The flavor of dried herbs is more pronounced than fresh; use one-third the amount of dried sage to replace fresh.

SASSY BUT CLASSY

Even if you're tired of the same old turkey and trimmings, the holiday meal probably isn't the best time to radically overhaul tradition. Here, two creative Southern chefs refrain from extremes and take a calm, classy look at the usual menu prospects.

▪ John Fleer pulls from the Smoky Mountain region's pantry as he cooks for guests at **The Inn at Blackberry Farm** in Walland, Tennessee. He shares an innovative nod to Southern staples in Country Ham with Grits Stuffing, Tasso Gravy, and Sweet Potato Pones.

COUNTRY HAM WITH GRITS STUFFING

John suggests ordering boneless country ham (as we did) from S. Wallace Edwards & Sons, Inc.'s, Virginia Traditions *catalog at 1-800-222-4267 (cost about $60). You'll carve out the center of the ham to stuff it.*

1 (6-pound) country ham half, bone removed
4 cups unbaked Grits Stuffing
2 cups apple cider

• **Soak** ham in water to cover 24 hours; drain and pat dry. Remove center portion of ham with a sharp knife, leaving a 1½-inch border. Reserve center portion for another use, or chop and substitute for oysters in stuffing, if desired.
• **Spoon** 4 cups unbaked Grits Stuffing into ham cavity; tie ham at 1-inch intervals with kitchen string. Wrap ham in cheesecloth, and place, small end down, in a large roasting pan. Add cider to pan.
• **Spoon** remaining Grits Stuffing into a lightly greased 2-quart shallow baking dish.
• **Bake** ham at 325° for 1 hour, basting ham every 20 minutes with pan drippings; place dish of stuffing into oven, and bake ham and stuffing 30 minutes or until stuffing is lightly browned and a meat thermometer inserted in ham registers 140°. Remove dish of stuffing, and keep warm.
• **Remove** cheesecloth from ham, and return ham to roasting pan; baste ham with pan drippings.
• **Broil** 8 inches from heat (with electric oven door partially opened) until browned. Serve with baked stuffing. **Yield:** 12 servings.

Grits Stuffing

If you don't care for oysters, try this stuffing without them. Also, you can use fresh oysters if the smoked flavor is too strong for your taste. Additionally, you can substitute the ham removed from the cavity for the oysters.

3 cups water
1½ teaspoons salt
¼ teaspoon ground red pepper
½ cup butter or margarine
1 cup regular grits, uncooked
1 pound smoked or fresh oysters, drained (optional)
½ cup grated Parmesan cheese
1 red bell pepper, diced
1 bunch green onions, chopped
3 large eggs, lightly beaten
1 cup fine, dry breadcrumbs

• **Bring** first 4 ingredients to a boil in a large saucepan. Stir in grits; return to a boil. Cover, reduce heat, and simmer 10 minutes or until grits are cooked and all liquid is absorbed, stirring occasionally. Remove from heat; cool. Stir in oysters, if desired.
• **Combine** Parmesan cheese and remaining 4 ingredients; stir into grits. **Yield:** about 12 cups.

Note: You can bake Grits Stuffing in a greased 3-quart baking dish at 325° for 45 minutes.

TASSO GRAVY

If you can't find tasso – lean, cured pork or highly seasoned beef – you can use the country ham you removed to make room for the stuffing in Country Ham With Grits Stuffing.

2 tablespoons butter or margarine
½ pound tasso, diced
3 tablespoons all-purpose flour
1 cup brewed coffee
2 cups chicken broth
1 fresh thyme sprig, minced
¼ teaspoon salt
¼ teaspoon pepper

• **Melt** butter in a skillet; add tasso, and cook until browned, stirring often. Whisk in flour, and cook, whisking constantly, until lightly browned.
• **Whisk** coffee and broth into tasso mixture; simmer 20 minutes, whisking occasionally. Stir in thyme, salt, and pepper. **Yield:** 3¼ cups.

SWEET POTATO PONES

John makes a sweet potato casserole, chills it, and cuts it into "pones" that he then bakes. He acknowledges his creative license in the loose application of the traditional term "pone."

7 sweet potatoes
2 tablespoons butter or margarine
1 onion, chopped
1 tablespoon salt
3 cups whipping cream
6 egg yolks
2 large eggs
2 teaspoons salt
½ teaspoon cracked pepper
3 tablespoons grated orange rind
1 tablespoon chopped fresh sage or 1 teaspoon rubbed sage
1 teaspoon grated lemon rind
½ teaspoon ground ginger
½ teaspoon Chinese five spice *
½ cup chopped walnuts

• **Peel** sweet potatoes, and cut into ⅛-inch-thick slices; set aside.

• **Melt** butter in a skillet; add onion, and cook until tender, stirring often. Remove onion from skillet, reserving drippings.
• **Sprinkle** sweet potato with 1 tablespoon salt. Cook in batches in skillet until browned and almost tender, turning once. Place potato in a greased 13- x 9- x 2-inch baking dish.
• **Combine** whipping cream, egg yolks, and eggs in a bowl; stir in 2 teaspoons salt, chopped onion, and remaining 7 ingredients. Pour over potato. Place dish in a shallow roasting pan; add hot water to pan to depth of 1 inch.
• **Bake** at 350° for 45 minutes. Remove dish from water; cool. Cover and chill 8 hours.
• **Remove** from dish, and cut into desired shapes. Place on a lightly greased baking sheet.
• **Bake** at 400° for 12 minutes or until thoroughly heated. **Yield:** 10 to 12 servings.

* Substitute a pinch of ground nutmeg and 1/4 teaspoon ground cinnamon for Chinese five spice.

SECRET TO SUCCESS

John Fleer's philosophy for preparing both a visual and a flavorful feast: "Use things for decorating that are involved in the menu." For example, when he served his ham dinner at the James Beard Foundation in New York recently, he added holiday touches to the party site as well. Guests entering the foyer glimpsed hints of the meal to come, including a wild boar's head surrounded by shapely fruits and vegetables and glimmering gold ribbon. John decorated the tables with produce featured as ingredients in the menu.

▪ Allen Susser combines his Jewish background with the tropical ingredients at his fingertips in North Miami Beach for some flavor surprises at his restaurant, **Chef Allen's**.

POTATO LATKES WITH LEMON-DATE RELISH

2 pounds baking potatoes, peeled
1 medium-size sweet onion
1 bunch green onions
2 large eggs, lightly beaten
2/3 cup matzo meal
1 teaspoon kosher salt
1/2 teaspoon cracked pepper
1/2 cup olive oil
Lemon-Date Relish

• **Grate** potatoes and onion, and place in a large bowl. Chop green onions, and add to potato mixture. Stir in eggs and next 3 ingredients.
• **Drop** mixture by heaping tablespoonfuls into hot oil in a large skillet over medium-high heat; fry 5 minutes, turning once. Drain on paper towels. Serve with Lemon-Date Relish. **Yield:** 6 to 8 servings.

Lemon-Date Relish

2 large lemons
1 teaspoon ground coriander
1/2 cup pine nuts
2 tablespoons olive oil
1 (8-ounce) package chopped pitted dates
3 tablespoons diced purple onion

• **Peel** lemons with a vegetable peeler; cut rind into thin strips, and place in a small saucepan. Add water to cover; bring to a boil. Reduce heat; simmer 5 minutes. Drain and cool.
• **Squeeze** lemons, reserving 1/2 cup juice.
• **Cook** coriander and pine nuts in a heavy skillet over low heat, stirring constantly, until lightly browned. Stir in lemon rind, reserved lemon juice, and oil; cook 2 minutes, stirring often.
• **Combine** dates and onion in a bowl; stir in lemon mixture. Let stand 30 minutes. **Yield:** 3 cups.

SWEET POTATO PANCAKES WITH GOAT CHEESE

After Allen pairs the pancakes and goat cheese on an ovenproof dish, he bakes the combination to soften the cheese.

2 tablespoons butter or margarine
1 medium Granny Smith apple, sliced
3 tablespoons light brown sugar
3 tablespoons applejack brandy
3 medium-size sweet potatoes, peeled
1/2 medium onion
1 large egg
3 tablespoons matzo meal
1/2 teaspoon kosher salt
1/2 teaspoon pepper
1/2 cup peanut oil
3 ounces creamy goat cheese

• **Melt** butter in a skillet; add apple and brown sugar, and cook until tender, stirring often. Stir in brandy; cook just until heated (do not boil). Remove from heat, and ignite with a long match; let flame 1 minute. Keep warm.
• **Grate** sweet potatoes and onion; combine vegetables, egg, and next 3 ingredients.
• **Drop** mixture by tablespoonfuls into hot oil in a large skillet over medium-high heat; fry 5 minutes or until crisp, turning once. Drain on paper towels, and place in a shallow baking dish.
• **Cut** goat cheese into 1/4-inch-thick slices, and place slices over pancakes.
• **Bake** at 350° for 5 minutes. Serve pancakes with apple mixture. **Yield:** 6 to 8 servings.

Note: You can substitute apple juice for applejack brandy and omit the flaming step.

Happy Lucky New Year

Southerners have been downing a dose of good fortune with their New Year's meals for centuries. Black-eyed peas, collards, and cabbage are traditional lucky foods. The peas are said to bring prosperity, the greens money.

We've added a twist to tradition with Elsa Havinga's red cabbage recipe that will add spritely flavor and color to your New Year's table. "Red Cabbage was one of my mother's recipes," she says, "and I've been making it for 50 years. You can easily make it ahead and reheat it – I think the flavor improves overnight."

CORN-AND-BLACK BEAN CAKES WITH SMOKED SALMON SALSA

Allen cooks fresh corn and dried black beans when possible, but he offers shortcuts here.

1 cup all-purpose flour
1 teaspoon baking powder
2 large eggs
¼ cup butter or margarine, melted
¾ cup milk
¾ cup frozen whole kernel corn, thawed
¾ cup canned black beans, rinsed and drained
¾ teaspoon salt
¾ teaspoon coarsely ground pepper
Smoked Salmon Salsa

• **Combine** the first 5 ingredients in a large bowl; stir in corn, beans, salt, and pepper.
• **Pour** about ¼ cup batter for each pancake into a nonstick skillet over medium-high heat. Cook until tops are covered with bubbles and edges look cooked; turn and cook other side. Serve with Smoked Salmon Salsa. **Yield:** 6 servings.

Smoked Salmon Salsa

1 (8-ounce) package smoked salmon, diced
¼ cup diced purple onion
3 tablespoons chopped fresh cilantro
3 tablespoons chopped fresh parsley
1 tablespoon diced jalapeño pepper
2 tablespoons olive oil

• **Combine** all ingredients; let stand 30 minutes before serving. **Yield:** 2 cups.

HOPPING JOHN

(pictured on page 1)

2 cups dried black-eyed peas
¾ pound ham, chopped
1 quart water
1 cup chopped onion
1 teaspoon salt
½ teaspoon pepper
½ teaspoon hot sauce
2 cups hot cooked rice
½ cup chopped green onions

• **Sort** and wash beans; place in a Dutch oven. Cover with water 2 inches above beans; bring to a boil, and cook 2 minutes. Remove from heat; cover and let stand 1 hour. Drain.
• **Bring** ham and 1 quart water to a boil in saucepan; boil 15 minutes. Add peas; cover, reduce heat, and simmer 45 minutes, stirring occasionally.
• **Add** onion and next 3 ingredients; return to a boil. Cover, reduce heat, and simmer 15 minutes or until peas are tender. Stir in rice and green onions. **Yield:** 6 to 8 servings.

Lauri Huss
Charleston, South Carolina

COLLARD GREENS

(pictured on page 1)

1 gallon water
½ pound smoked pork neck bones
5 pounds collard greens
2 tablespoons salt
2 dried red chile peppers (optional)

• **Combine** water and pork neck bones in a large Dutch oven; bring to a boil, and cook neckbones 30 minutes, stirring occasionally.
• **Remove** and discard stems from greens. Coarsely chop leaves. Add greens, salt, and peppers, if desired, to pork broth. Bring to a boil. Reduce heat, and simmer 2 hours or until tender. Serve with hot peppers in vinegar. **Yield:** 10 to 12 servings.

John Martin Taylor
Charleston, South Carolina

RED CABBAGE

1 medium-size red cabbage, shredded
1 cup water
¼ cup white vinegar
⅓ cup butter or margarine
¼ cup firmly packed light brown sugar
1 teaspoon salt
½ teaspoon ground nutmeg
4 medium Granny Smith apples

• **Combine** first 7 ingredients in a Dutch oven; bring to a boil. Reduce heat, and simmer 30 minutes, stirring occasionally.
• **Peel** and cut apples into fourths; add to cabbage mixture. Simmer 30 minutes or until liquid evaporates and apples are tender, stirring occasionally. **Yield:** 8 servings.

Elsa Havinga
Richmond, Virginia

Choosing Sides

Selecting side dishes is often the most difficult part of menu planning. If you're stuck on potatoes, why not try something new? Expand your choices to include caramelized onions or portobello mushrooms. These recipes are a delicious change of pace.

MEDITERRANEAN CARAMELIZED ONIONS

4 medium onions (1½ pounds)
1½ teaspoons salt
½ teaspoon pepper
Dash of saffron *
1 tablespoon chopped fresh parsley
1 tablespoon chopped fresh chives
1 tablespoon chopped fresh thyme
1 teaspoon butter or margarine
1 teaspoon olive oil

• **Cut** onions into ¼-inch-thick slices, and separate into rings. Combine onion, salt, and next 5 ingredients, tossing to coat.
• **Melt** butter in a large heavy skillet over medium heat; add oil and onion, and cook, stirring constantly, 25 minutes or until onion is lightly browned and tender. **Yield:** 4 to 6 servings.

* You can substitute a dash of turmeric for saffron.

SAUTÉED PORTOBELLO MUSHROOMS

3 pounds fresh portobello mushrooms *
12 cloves garlic, minced
⅔ cup olive oil
¾ cup chopped fresh Italian parsley, divided
¼ teaspoon salt
⅛ teaspoon pepper

• **Cut** mushrooms into ¼-inch-thick slices.
• **Cook** half of garlic in half of oil in an electric or extra large skillet over medium heat until tender, stirring often. Add half of mushroom slices and ¼ cup parsley; cook 3 to 5 minutes or until tender and browned, turning once. Remove to a serving dish; sprinkle with half each of salt and pepper. Repeat procedure; sprinkle with remaining ¼ cup parsley, and serve immediately. **Yield:** 12 servings.

* Substitute 3 pounds fresh mushrooms for portobello. Do not slice; stir constantly during cooking.

TANGY MIXED VEGETABLES

1 (8-ounce) package sliced fresh mushrooms
1 green bell pepper, cut into 1-inch pieces
1 medium onion, chopped
1 (8-ounce) can pineapple chunks, undrained
4 medium carrots, scraped and sliced
½ teaspoon ground ginger
½ teaspoon curry powder
½ teaspoon dried basil
1 (8-ounce) can sliced water chestnuts, drained
1 tablespoon brown sugar
¼ teaspoon salt

• **Cook** first 3 ingredients in a large nonstick skillet 5 minutes or until tender, stirring often. Drain and set aside.
• **Drain** pineapple, reserving juice. Pour juice into skillet; set pineapple chunks aside. Add carrot and next 3 ingredients to juice; bring to a boil. Cover, reduce heat, and simmer 10 to 15 minutes or until carrot is tender.
• **Stir** in mushroom mixture, pineapple chunks, water chestnuts, and remaining ingredients; cook over medium-high heat until thoroughly heated. **Yield:** 4 servings.

Hilda Marshall
Culpeper, Virginia

Nutty Salads

When the salad dressing is just right, but you want something extra, add nuts. You get much more than just crunch. The intense, earthy flavor of toasted nuts perfectly complements crisp greens. Try some of our readers' favorite salads featuring almonds, walnuts, and pine nuts.

GREEN BEAN, WALNUT, AND FETA SALAD

1 cup coarsely chopped walnuts
¾ cup olive oil
¼ cup white wine vinegar
1 tablespoon chopped fresh dill
½ teaspoon minced garlic
¼ teaspoon salt
¼ teaspoon pepper
1½ pounds fresh green beans
1 small purple onion, thinly sliced
1 (4-ounce) package crumbled feta cheese

• **Place** walnuts in a shallow pan, and bake at 350° for 5 to 10 minutes or until toasted, stirring occasionally; set aside.
• **Combine** oil and next 5 ingredients; cover and chill.
• **Cut** green beans into thirds, and arrange in a steamer basket over boiling water. Cover and steam 15 minutes or until crisp-tender. Immediately plunge into cold water to stop the cooking process; drain and pat dry.
• **Combine** walnuts, beans, onion, and cheese in a large bowl; toss well. Cover and chill.
• **Pour** oil mixture over bean mixture 1 hour before serving; toss just before serving. **Yield:** 6 servings.

Judi Grant
El Paso, Texas

ALMOND-CITRUS SALAD

- ⅔ cup vegetable oil
- 2 teaspoons grated grapefruit rind
- ½ cup fresh grapefruit juice
- 1 (0.7-ounce) envelope Italian salad dressing mix
- 1 grapefruit
- 2 oranges
- 1 avocado, peeled and sliced
- 3 cups torn spinach
- 3 cups torn leaf lettuce
- 3 cups torn iceberg lettuce
- ½ cup sliced celery
- ½ cup chopped green bell pepper
- ¼ cup Sweet-and-Spicy Almonds

• **Combine** oil, grapefruit rind, grapefruit juice, and salad dressing mix in a jar; cover tightly, and shake vigorously.
• **Peel** and section grapefruit and oranges, and place in a large bowl. Add avocado and next 5 ingredients.
• **Add** dressing, tossing to coat. Sprinkle with Sweet-and-Spicy Almonds. **Yield:** 8 servings.

Sweet-and-Spicy Almonds

Make a double batch of these almonds to serve as an appetizer or hostess gift.

- 1 cup sliced almonds
- 1 tablespoon butter or margarine, melted
- 1½ teaspoons sugar
- ¼ teaspoon ground cumin
- ¼ teaspoon chili powder
- ⅛ teaspoon dried crushed red pepper
- Pinch of salt

• **Combine** almonds and butter, stirring well. Combine sugar and remaining 4 ingredients; sprinkle over almonds, tossing to coat. Spread on a lightly greased baking sheet.
• **Bake** at 325° for 15 minutes, stirring occasionally; cool. **Yield:** 1 cup.

Nora Henshaw
Okemah, Oklahoma

BALSAMIC-PESTO SALAD

- ½ cup pine nuts
- 1 (0.5-ounce) package pesto sauce mix
- ½ cup water
- ¼ cup balsamic vinegar
- 3 tablespoons olive oil
- 8 cups mixed salad greens

• **Place** pine nuts in a shallow pan, and bake at 350° for 5 to 10 minutes or until toasted, stirring occasionally; set aside.
• **Combine** sauce mix and next 3 ingredients in a jar; cover tightly, and shake vigorously. Pour over greens, tossing to coat. Sprinkle with pine nuts; serve immediately. **Yield:** 6 servings.

Donna M. DiRicco
Woodbridge, Virginia

DASHING DIPS

Turn a gathering into a party with these hot dips. They're easy, savory ways to entertain a hungry crowd. Serve them with baskets of chicken fingers, breadsticks, tortilla chips, and vegetables for dipping.

SWEET-AND-SPICY MUSTARD DIP

- 3 tablespoons mayonnaise
- 3 tablespoons coarse-grained mustard
- 1 tablespoon prepared horseradish
- 2 teaspoons sugar

• **Combine** all ingredients in a 1-cup liquid measuring cup; microwave at HIGH 30 seconds, stirring once. Serve with chicken fingers. **Yield:** ⅓ cup.

Charlene Barton
Dora, Alabama

BLACK-EYED PEA CON QUESO

- ½ cup butter or margarine
- 1 large onion, finely chopped
- 2 cloves garlic, pressed
- 1 (16-ounce) loaf process cheese spread, cubed
- 5 jalapeño peppers, unseeded and chopped
- 2 (15.8-ounce) cans black-eyed peas, drained

• **Melt** butter in a Dutch oven; add onion and garlic, and cook until tender, stirring often.
• **Add** cheese, and cook over low heat, stirring constantly, until cheese melts.
• **Stir** in peppers and peas; cook until thoroughly heated, stirring often. Serve with tortilla chips. **Yield:** 3 cups.

FLORENTINE ARTICHOKE DIP

- 1 (10-ounce) package frozen chopped spinach, thawed
- 2 (6-ounce) jars marinated artichoke hearts
- 3 large cloves garlic, minced
- ½ cup mayonnaise
- 1½ (8-ounce) packages cream cheese, softened
- 2 tablespoons lemon juice
- 1 cup grated Parmesan cheese
- 1½ cups fine, dry breadcrumbs

• **Drain** spinach; press between layers of paper towels. Drain and chop artichoke hearts.
• **Combine** spinach, artichoke hearts, garlic, and next 4 ingredients, stirring well. Spoon into a lightly greased 11- x 7- x 1½-inch baking dish; sprinkle with breadcrumbs.
• **Bake** at 375° for 25 minutes; serve with assorted crackers or breadsticks. **Yield:** 4 cups.

Tamora Cornwall
Charlotte, North Carolina

EGGPLANT DIP

3 cups peeled, chopped eggplant
1 medium onion, chopped
1 cup sliced fresh mushrooms
⅓ cup chopped green bell pepper
2 to 3 cloves garlic, pressed
⅓ cup olive oil
1 (6-ounce) can tomato paste
1 (5¾-ounce) jar chopped green olives
2 tablespoons red wine vinegar
1½ teaspoons sugar
1 teaspoon salt
½ teaspoon cracked black peppercorns
¼ teaspoon hot sauce

• **Cook** first 5 ingredients in oil in a large skillet over medium-high heat 10 minutes or until tender, stirring often. Stir in tomato paste and remaining ingredients; bring to a boil.
• **Reduce** heat, and simmer 30 to 40 minutes or to desired thickness, stirring occasionally. Serve with French bread. **Yield:** 4 cups.

Judy H. Loveless
Memphis, Tennessee

SEASONED GREETINGS

It's easy to Christmas shop for friends and family, but when the list turns to teachers, the postman, and your hairdresser, you usually have run out of ideas, money, and patience. We suggest spending a few hours in the kitchen – not the mall – to make these simple, affordable gifts.

These well-seasoned condiments bring refreshing, sometimes spicy, flavor changes to the usual stockpiles of holiday sweets. Add glittery bows to jars or cruets, and write our serving suggestions on the gift cards.

QUICK JALAPEÑO PEPPER JELLY

Serve as an easy appetizer with cream cheese and crackers.

4 (16-ounce) jars lime marmalade or apple jelly
6 to 8 jalapeño peppers, minced
¼ cup apple cider vinegar

• **Combine** all ingredients in a large saucepan; bring mixture to a boil. Reduce heat, and simmer 5 minutes. Remove from heat, and cool. Cover and store in refrigerator up to 2 weeks. **Yield:** 4½ cups.

Judi Grigoraci
Charleston, West Virginia

SOUTHWESTERN SALSA WITH BLACK BEANS AND CORN

Serve with tortilla chips, fajitas, fish, or steak.

2 teaspoons cumin seeds
4 (15-ounce) cans black beans, rinsed and drained
2 (15¼-ounce) cans whole kernel corn, drained
2 red bell peppers, seeded and minced
1 purple onion, minced
1 cup minced fresh cilantro
1 cup minced fresh parsley
⅔ cup lime juice
½ cup olive oil
6 cloves garlic, pressed
2 teaspoons dried crushed red pepper
1 teaspoon ground black pepper

• **Cook** cumin seeds in a small cast-iron skillet over medium heat 2 to 3 minutes or until browned, stirring often.
• **Combine** cumin seeds, black beans, and remaining ingredients; toss well. Cover and store in refrigerator up to 2 weeks. **Yield:** 10 cups.

Sheila Fogle
Huntsville, Alabama

CRANBERRY CHUTNEY
(pictured on page 293)

Serve with turkey or as an appetizer with gingersnaps and cream cheese.

8 (16-ounce) cans jellied whole-berry cranberry sauce
2 cups firmly packed light brown sugar
2 cups chopped dates
2 cups currants or raisins
2 cups slivered almonds
2 cups apple cider vinegar
¼ cup minced crystallized ginger
2 teaspoons ground allspice

• **Combine** all ingredients in a large Dutch oven. Bring to a boil, stirring constantly; reduce heat, and simmer 30 minutes, stirring occasionally.
• **Cool,** place in jars, and store in refrigerator up to 2 weeks. For longer storage, pack chutney into hot, sterilized jars, filling to ½ inch from top; remove air bubbles, and wipe jar rims. Cover at once with metal lids, and screw on bands. Process in boiling-water bath 5 minutes. **Yield:** 10 pints.

Louise Mayer
Richmond, Virginia

RASPBERRY VINAIGRETTE
(pictured on page 293)

Serve with fresh spinach salad or as a marinade for chicken.

1⅓ cups raspberry vinegar
1⅓ cups seedless raspberry jam
1½ tablespoons ground coriander
2 teaspoons salt
1 teaspoon pepper
3 cups olive oil

• **Combine** first 5 ingredients in container of an electric blender; process until smooth. Turn blender on high; gradually add oil in a slow, steady stream. Cover and store in refrigerator up to 2 weeks. **Yield:** 4½ cups.

Gaye Christmas
Columbia, South Carolina

Easy-Does-It Casseroles

During the hectic holiday season, a casserole can be a cook's best friend. To prepare, chop meats and vegetables large enough so that they don't get lost in the sauce. You can assemble a casserole ahead and later serve it with a green salad or fresh fruits.

CHOW MEIN CHICKEN CASSEROLE

1 tablespoon butter or margarine
1 small red bell pepper, chopped
2 cloves garlic, minced
2 (8-ounce) packages sliced fresh mushrooms
1/3 cup slivered almonds
3 green onions, chopped
1 (10 3/4-ounce) can cream of mushroom soup, undiluted
3/4 cup mayonnaise
2 teaspoons soy sauce
3 cups chopped cooked chicken
1/4 teaspoon pepper
1 (3-ounce) can chow mein noodles

• **Melt** butter in a large skillet. Add bell pepper, garlic, and mushrooms; cook until tender, stirring often. Stir in almonds and next 6 ingredients; pour into a lightly greased 11- x 7- x 1 1/2-inch baking dish. Sprinkle with chow mein noodles.

• **Bake** at 350° for 30 minutes or until bubbly. **Yield:** 6 servings.

Louise Mayer
Richmond, Virginia

DAY-AFTER-THE-HOLIDAY CASSEROLE

1 (7-ounce) package spaghetti, cooked
1 3/4 cups (7 ounces) shredded Monterey Jack cheese
1 1/2 cups chopped cooked turkey
1 (2-ounce) jar diced pimiento, undrained
1 small green bell pepper, chopped
1 small onion, chopped
1 (10 3/4-ounce) can cream of celery soup, undiluted
1/2 cup chicken broth
1/2 teaspoon salt
1/4 teaspoon pepper

• **Combine** spaghetti, 1 1/4 cups cheese, and remaining 8 ingredients, stirring gently; spoon into a lightly greased 11- x 7- x 1 1/2-inch baking dish. Sprinkle with remaining 1/2 cup cheese.

• **Bake** at 350° for 45 minutes or until bubbly. **Yield:** 6 to 8 servings.

Patty McCoy Horton
Demopolis, Alabama

MEXICAN VEGETARIAN CASSEROLE

This was originally a dip idea; Margaret added the rice and made it a meatless one-dish meal.

1 (15 1/4-ounce) can whole kernel corn, drained
1 (15-ounce) can black beans, rinsed and drained
1 (10-ounce) can whole tomatoes and green chiles
1 (8-ounce) carton sour cream
1 (8-ounce) jar picante sauce
2 cups (8 ounces) shredded Cheddar cheese
2 cups cooked rice
1/4 teaspoon pepper
1 bunch green onions, chopped
1 (2 1/4-ounce) can sliced ripe olives
1 (8-ounce) package Monterey Jack cheese, shredded

• **Combine** first 8 ingredients; spoon into a lightly greased 13- x 9- x 2-inch baking dish. Sprinkle with remaining ingredients.

• **Bake** at 350° for 50 minutes. **Yield:** 6 servings.

Margaret Monger
Germantown, Tennessee

Souper Starters

Add a soup course to special dinners. Serve small portions of these rich potages to excite the taste buds and whet the appetite. We offer plenty of variations.

OYSTER BISQUE

1/4 cup butter or margarine
3 cloves garlic, minced
2 shallots, finely chopped
3 tablespoons all-purpose flour
1 (8-ounce) bottle clam juice
1/2 cup dry sherry
1/4 cup lemon juice
1 tablespoon Worcestershire sauce
1/8 teaspoon hot sauce
1/4 teaspoon freshly ground pepper
1 quart whipping cream
2 (12-ounce) containers fresh oysters, drained

• **Melt** butter in a large Dutch oven over medium heat; add garlic and shallot, and cook until tender, stirring often.

• **Add** flour, and cook 1 minute. Add clam juice, sherry, and lemon juice; cook 2 to 3 minutes or until thickened and bubbly.

• **Stir** in Worcestershire sauce and next 3 ingredients; add oysters, and cook over medium heat 10 minutes or until oysters are done, stirring occasionally. **Yield:** 9 cups.

MEXICAN CHOCOLATE SOUP

½ onion
1 carrot, scraped
2 stalks celery
1 medium zucchini
1 green bell pepper
1 jalapeño pepper
2 tablespoons vegetable oil
1 to 2 tablespoons tequila
2 tablespoons cocoa
1 tablespoon all-purpose flour
½ teaspoon ground cinnamon
1 quart chicken broth
½ cup chopped fresh cilantro
½ teaspoon salt
½ teaspoon pepper

• **Dice** first 6 ingredients.
• **Cook** vegetables in vegetable oil in a large Dutch oven until crisp-tender, stirring often. Add tequila, and remove from heat.
• **Combine** cocoa, flour, and cinnamon; stir into vegetable mixture. Add broth. Bring to a boil over medium-high heat, stirring constantly; reduce heat, and simmer 5 to 10 minutes or until vegetables are tender, stirring occasionally. Stir in cilantro, salt, and pepper. **Yield:** 6 cups.

William N. Cottrell II
New Orleans, Louisiana

CREAM OF CAULIFLOWER SOUP

1 large onion
2 shallots
1 clove garlic
1 tablespoon olive oil
2 (14½-ounce) cans ready-to-serve chicken broth
1 large cauliflower, cut into flowerets
1½ cups whipping cream
1 teaspoon salt
⅛ teaspoon ground white pepper
Garnishes: asparagus tips, cracked black pepper

• **Slice** first 3 ingredients; cook in oil in a Dutch oven until tender, stirring often. Stir in broth; bring to a boil. Add cauliflower; cook 15 minutes or until tender, stirring occasionally.
• **Process** soup in batches in container of an electric blender until smooth; return to pan. Stir in whipping cream, salt, and white pepper; cook over low heat until thoroughly heated, stirring often. Ladle into soup bowls; garnish, if desired. **Yield:** 8 cups.

Julia Rutland
Cordova, Tennessee

PARTIES WITH PUNCH

Planning beverages for holiday parties doesn't have to be a chore – simply serve punch. A big batch can streamline your party by taking the place of sodas, fruit drinks, and several kinds of liquor and mixers.

You can choose punches either with or without alcohol. One solution is to serve a dry bowl for children and nondrinkers and a spiked one for imbibers. One hostess we know places a beribboned railroad spike next to the spirited bowl to notify her guests of its heady contents.

AUTUMN HARVEST PUNCH

2 cups water
1½ to 2 cups sugar
4 (3-inch) sticks cinnamon
36 whole cloves
2 quarts cranberry juice cocktail
1 quart orange juice
1½ to 2 cups lemon juice
1 lemon, sliced
1 orange, sliced
1 cup rum or 2 tablespoons rum flavoring

• **Combine** first 4 ingredients in a large Dutch oven; bring to a boil over high heat. Reduce heat, and simmer 7 minutes. Remove and discard spices.
• **Add** cranberry juice cocktail and remaining ingredients; cook over medium heat until thoroughly heated. **Yield:** about 5 quarts.

Carole Radford
Lincolnton, Georgia

BERRY-COLADA PUNCH

1 (16-ounce) package frozen strawberries, thawed
1 (15-ounce) can cream of coconut
3 cups pineapple juice, chilled
3 cups club soda, chilled
2 cups rum (optional)

• **Combine** strawberries and cream of coconut in container of an electric blender, and process until smooth; pour into a pitcher or large bowl. Stir in pineapple juice, club soda, and rum, if desired. Serve over crushed ice. **Yield:** 2½ quarts.

Judi Grigoraci
Charleston, West Virginia

CHAMPAGNE PUNCH

6 oranges, unpeeled and thinly sliced
1 cup sugar
2 (750-milliliter) bottles dry white wine
3 (750-milliliter) bottles sparkling wine, chilled

• **Place** orange slices in a large nonmetallic container; sprinkle with sugar. Add white wine; cover and chill at least 8 hours. Stir in sparkling wine just before serving. **Yield:** 1 gallon.

Patty Strawmyer
Houston, Texas

GOLDEN FRUIT PUNCH

⅔ cup boiling water
2 regular-size tea bags
1½ cups pineapple juice
1 cup grapefruit juice
1 cup orange juice
½ cup lemon juice
1¼ cups sugar
4 cups ginger ale, chilled
2 cups ice water

• **Pour** boiling water over tea bags; cover and let stand 5 minutes. Remove and discard tea bags.
• **Combine** tea and fruit juices in a large pitcher or bowl; add sugar, stirring until it dissolves. Cover and chill.
• **Stir** in ginger ale and ice water; serve immediately. **Yield:** 2½ quarts.

Maxine Beckwith
Lebanon, Tennessee

SUNSET PUNCH

1 quart cranberry juice cocktail
1 quart pink lemonade
1 quart orange juice
1 quart pineapple juice
1 quart ginger ale, chilled
1 quart raspberry sherbet or sorbet

• **Combine** first 4 ingredients in a large bowl; chill. Stir in ginger ale; scoop sherbet into punch. Serve immediately. **Yield:** 1½ gallons.

Bernadette Colvin
Houston, Texas

WHAT A PARTY!

Marty Sprague is never at a loss for holiday party themes, thanks to a long list of friends who contributed ideas to her book, *36 Best Christmas Party Ideas* (The Summit Publishing Group, Ltd., $12.95). "Since my husband's a pastor, we've traveled a good deal, and have met a lot of folks who like to entertain as much as we do."

Marty says the first lesson is to *relax*, "and let friends be friends," not just house guests. Her ideas range from trim-the-tree and progressive block parties, to caroling hayride and midnight buffet parties.

Note: You can find *36 Best Christmas Party Ideas* in bookstores or you can order it from The Summit Publishing Group, Ltd., 1112 East Copeland Road, Fifth Floor, Arlington, TX 76011; 1-800-875-3346 (ext. 132).

CHESTNUTS ROASTING ON AN OPEN FIRE PARTY

Make your fireplace the center of attention. "It's the perfect place to gather for a meal," Marty says. Decorate your home with wreaths and garlands, and serve roasted chestnuts in bowls around the room. "Background music can include 'The Christmas Song' (the inspiration for the party's theme), 'White Christmas', and other holiday favorites," Marty says.

WHITE ELEPHANT CHRISTMAS PARTY

Search for last season's gift from Cousin Fritz that only a flea market would love, decorate it beautifully, and bring it to the party. This way, "old friends and new experience the wilder, crazier side of Christmas," Marty says. Let appetizer and dessert pickups feed your guests around the fest's focal point, the Christmas tree, where the exchange of wacky gifts is sure to inspire laughter.

IT'S A WONDERFUL LIFE PARTY

What better way to celebrate the season than with the movie *It's a Wonderful Life.* This low-cost party requires only a video rental and bowls of hot, savory Turkey-Corn Chowder (see recipe) served with crusty bread.

CAJUN CHRISTMAS FEAST

For this party, Marty suggests serving a fabulous New Orleans-style dinner (such as jambalaya, crawfish étouffée, pralines) to the tune of zydeco music. To keep palates cool, serve Twenty-Four-Hour Fruit Salad (see recipe) as a side dish. Then read guests "The Night Before Christmas" with a Cajun accent ("hilarious!") and have a gift exchange of Cajun food products or souvenir T-shirts.

FROSTY'S FAVORITE CHRISTMAS PARTY

Parents will love this party's simplicity: With Frosty the Snowman as the theme, buy or make invitations in the shape of snowpeople, have children arrive in snowcaps and scarves (even if it's not snowing). Sing Christmas carols after dining on Frosty Pumpkin Pie (see recipe, next page).

GOLDEN WASSAIL

1 quart unsweetened pineapple juice
1 (11.5-ounce) can apricot nectar
1 quart apple cider
1 cup orange juice
2 (2-inch) sticks cinnamon
1 teaspoon whole cloves
¼ teaspoon salt
¼ teaspoon ground cardamom
Garnish: cinnamon sticks

• **Combine** first 8 ingredients in a large Dutch oven; bring to a boil over medium-high heat, stirring occasionally. Reduce heat, and simmer 15 minutes.
• **Remove** cinnamon sticks and cloves; garnish, if desired. Serve immediately. **Yield:** 9 cups.

TURKEY-CORN CHOWDER

4 medium onions, sliced
1/4 cup butter or margarine, melted
5 medium potatoes, cubed
2 stalks celery, chopped
1 tablespoon salt
1/2 teaspoon pepper
1 chicken-flavored bouillon cube
2 cups water
5 cups milk
2 (15 1/4-ounce) cans whole kernel corn, drained
1 (14 3/4-ounce) can cream-style corn
1 cup half-and-half
1 1/2 teaspoons paprika
1/4 teaspoon dried thyme
3 cups chopped cooked turkey *
Chopped fresh parsley

• **Cook** onion in butter in a Dutch oven until tender, stirring often. Add cubed potato and next 5 ingredients; bring to a boil. Cover, reduce heat, and simmer 15 minutes or until vegetables are tender.
• **Add** milk and next 6 ingredients; cook until heated. Sprinkle with parsley. **Yield:** 5 quarts.

* You can substitute 3 cups chopped cooked chicken for turkey.

TWENTY-FOUR-HOUR FRUIT SALAD

1 (20-ounce) can crushed pineapple in juice, undrained
1 (16 1/2-ounce) can pitted white cherries, drained
1 (11-ounce) can mandarin oranges, drained
3 egg yolks, lightly beaten
2 tablespoons sugar
2 tablespoons white vinegar
1 tablespoon butter or margarine
1/4 teaspoon salt
2 1/2 cups miniature marshmallows
1 cup whipping cream, whipped

• **Drain** pineapple, reserving 2 tablespoons juice. Combine pineapple, cherries, and oranges; cover and chill.
• **Combine** reserved juice, egg yolks, and next 4 ingredients in a saucepan; cook over medium heat, stirring constantly, until mixture boils and thickens (about 5 minutes). Cool completely.
• **Stir** fruit into egg yolk mixture; fold in marshmallows and whipped cream. Cover and chill 24 hours. **Yield:** 8 servings.

FROSTY PUMPKIN PIE

1 cup canned pumpkin
1/2 cup firmly packed brown sugar
1/8 teaspoon salt
1 teaspoon ground cinnamon
1/4 teaspoon ground nutmeg
1/8 teaspoon ground cloves
1 quart vanilla ice cream, softened
Gingersnap Crumb Crust
Garnishes: whipped cream, gingersnaps

• **Combine** first 6 ingredients in a large bowl, stirring well. Fold in ice cream.
• **Spoon** mixture into Gingersnap Crumb Crust; cover and freeze at least 8 hours. Let stand at room temperature 10 minutes before slicing; garnish, if desired. **Yield:** 1 (9-inch) pie.

Gingersnap Crumb Crust

1 1/2 cups gingersnap crumbs
1/4 cup sifted powdered sugar
1/3 cup butter or margarine, melted

• **Combine** all ingredients, stirring well. Firmly press crumb mixture evenly on bottom and up sides of a 9-inch pieplate. Bake at 375° for 4 to 5 minutes. **Yield:** 1 (9-inch) crust.

GOOD MORNING MUFFINS

Delight your family with a variety of muffins during the busy holiday season. If time is short, bake several batches a week or two in advance, and freeze for later use. Be sure to cool them to room temperature and seal tightly before freezing. Thaw frozen muffins, and then pop them into a warm oven for 7 to 10 minutes for just-baked taste and texture.

JELLY-TOPPED PEANUT BUTTER MUFFINS

These muffins make a quick breakfast or snack for even young finicky eaters.

1 1/2 cups all-purpose flour
2 teaspoons baking powder
1/2 teaspoon salt
1/2 cup cornmeal
3 tablespoons sugar
3/4 cup chunky peanut butter
2 tablespoons honey
2 large eggs
1 cup milk
1/4 cup grape or other flavor jelly

• **Combine** first 5 ingredients in a large bowl; make a well in center of mixture.
• **Combine** peanut butter and honey, stirring well; add eggs and milk, stirring until blended. Add to dry ingredients, stirring just until moistened.
• **Spoon** batter into greased muffin pans, filling three-fourths full. Spoon 1 teaspoon jelly in center of each.
• **Bake** at 375° for 20 minutes or until golden. Remove from pans immediately, and cool on wire racks. Serve warm with additional jelly, if desired. **Yield:** 1 dozen.

Mary Louise Lever
Rome, Georgia

TWIN MOUNTAIN MUFFINS

¼ cup butter or margarine, softened
¼ cup sugar
1 large egg
2 cups all-purpose flour
4 teaspoons baking powder
½ teaspoon salt
1 cup milk

• **Beat** butter and sugar at medium speed with an electric mixer until creamy; add egg, beating just until blended.
• **Combine** flour, baking powder, and salt; add to butter mixture alternately with milk, ending with flour mixture.
• **Spoon** batter into greased muffin pans, filling two-thirds full.
• **Bake** at 375° for 25 minutes. Remove from pans immediately, and cool on wire racks. **Yield:** 1 dozen.

Pepper-Cheese Muffins: Reduce the sugar to 2 tablespoons; stir in 1 cup shredded Monterey Jack cheese with jalapeño peppers with the flour mixture.

Bacon-Cheese Muffins: Reduce sugar to 2 tablespoons; stir in ½ cup shredded Cheddar cheese and 3 slices bacon, cooked and crumbled, with the flour mixture.

Herb Muffins: Reduce sugar to 2 tablespoons; stir in 1 teaspoon instant minced onion, 2 teaspoons dried parsley flakes, 1 teaspoon dried oregano, and ½ teaspoon pepper with the flour mixture.

Lee Ann Robinson
La Grange, Georgia

POPPY SEED-LEMON MUFFINS

1 (18.5-ounce) package yellow cake mix with pudding
⅔ cup vegetable oil
⅔ cup apricot nectar
4 large eggs
⅓ cup poppy seeds
½ teaspoon grated lemon rind
2½ tablespoons fresh lemon juice

• **Combine** all ingredients, stirring until blended. Spoon into greased muffin pans, filling two-thirds full.
• **Bake** at 400° for 18 to 20 minutes or until done. Remove from pans immediately, and cool on wire racks. **Yield:** about 2 dozen.

Glyna Meredith Gallrein
Louisville, Kentucky

HOT BUTTERED RUM MUFFINS

½ cup butter or margarine, softened
½ cup sugar
2 large eggs
2 cups all-purpose flour
2 teaspoons baking powder
½ teaspoon salt
⅛ teaspoon ground cloves
⅛ teaspoon ground nutmeg
½ cup milk
5 tablespoons rum, divided
3 tablespoons sugar

• **Beat** butter at medium speed with an electric mixer until creamy. Add ½ cup sugar, beating well. Add eggs, one at a time, beating just until blended after each addition.
• **Combine** flour and next 4 ingredients. Combine milk and 3 tablespoons rum. Add flour mixture to butter mixture alternately with milk mixture, beginning and ending with flour mixture. Beat at low speed until blended after each addition.
• **Spoon** into greased muffin pans, filling three-fourths full.
• **Bake** at 375° for 20 to 25 minutes or until golden. Remove from pans immediately; place on a wire rack.
• **Combine** remaining 2 tablespoons rum and 3 tablespoons sugar in a small saucepan; cook over low heat, stirring constantly, until sugar dissolves. Brush over warm muffins. **Yield:** 1 dozen.

Sandra Souther
Gainesville, Georgia

SOUTHERNERS DIP INTO BISCOTTI

Coffee shop lingo can be tricky. Just about the time you've figured out cappuccino, espresso, and latte, your server asks, "Would you like biscotti with that?" You figure it must be Italian for curve ball. Actually, it's a not-too-sweet, crunchy cookie just right for dunking in any coffee (or dessert wine) you choose.

Biscotti literally means twice baked – first in a loaf and then in slices. You end up with rugged but refined cookies. Keep them on your counter or wrap some up with a bow and give to friends for the holidays. And biscotti is easy to make at home.

COCOA-ALMOND BISCOTTI

½ cup butter or margarine, softened
1 cup sugar
2 large eggs
1½ tablespoons coffee-flavored liqueur *
2¼ cups all-purpose flour
1½ teaspoons baking powder
¼ teaspoon salt
1½ tablespoons cocoa
1 (6-ounce) can whole almonds (1 cup)

• **Combine** butter and sugar in a large bowl; beat at medium speed with an

electric mixer until light and fluffy. Add eggs, beating well. Mix in liqueur.
• **Combine** flour and next 3 ingredients; add to butter mixture, beating well. Stir in almonds.
• **Divide** dough in half; shape each portion into a 9- x 2-inch log on a lightly greased cookie sheet.
• **Bake** at 350° for 30 minutes or until firm. Cool on cookie sheet 5 minutes. Remove to wire racks to cool.
• **Cut** each log diagonally into ½-inch-thick slices with a serrated knife, using a gentle sawing motion. Place on ungreased cookie sheets.
• **Bake** at 350° for 5 to 7 minutes. Turn cookies over, and bake 5 to 7 additional minutes. Remove to wire racks to cool. **Yield:** 2½ dozen.

* Substitute 1½ tablespoons chocolate syrup for coffee liqueur.

Judy Cederholm
Bardstown, Kentucky

CHOCOLATE CHIP-CINNAMON BISCOTTI

⅓ cup butter or margarine, softened
½ cup firmly packed brown sugar
½ cup sugar
1 tablespoon instant coffee or espresso granules
2 large eggs
2 cups all-purpose flour
1½ teaspoons baking powder
⅛ teaspoon salt
½ teaspoon ground cinnamon
1 cup chopped walnuts or pecans
1 cup (6-ounces) semisweet chocolate mini-morsels
2 (2-ounce) squares vanilla-flavored candy coating, melted

• **Combine** first 4 ingredients in a large mixing bowl; beat at medium speed with an electric mixer until light and creamy. Add eggs, one at a time, beating until blended.
• **Combine** flour and next 3 ingredients; add to butter mixture, stirring until blended. Fold in nuts and chocolate morsels.
• **Divide** dough in half; shape each portion into a 10- x 2-inch log on a lightly greased cookie sheet.
• **Bake** at 350° for 25 minutes or until firm. Let cool on cookie sheet 5 minutes. Remove to wire racks to cool completely.
• **Cut** each log diagonally into ½-inch-thick slices with a serrated knife, using a gentle sawing motion. Place slices on ungreased cookie sheets.
• **Bake** at 350° for 10 minutes; turn cookies over, and bake 10 additional minutes. Remove to wire racks to cool.
• **Dip** 1 side of each cookie into candy coating; chill until set. **Yield:** 2½ dozen.

Carol Y. Chastain
San Antonio, Texas

FRUITCAKE BISCOTTI

It's a fresh look at tradition – the flavors of fruitcake in a crunchy cookie. But don't worry about that old stigma. These are so good, there's no chance they'll still be hanging around after the New Year.

½ cup butter or margarine, softened
2 cups sugar
4 large eggs
1½ teaspoons grated lemon rind
½ teaspoon vanilla extract
¼ teaspoon almond extract
5 cups all-purpose flour
2 teaspoons baking soda
1 teaspoon baking powder
½ teaspoon salt
¾ cup dried cranberries
¾ cup dried tart cherries
½ cup candied orange rind
¾ cup whole blanched or slivered almonds, coarsely chopped

• **Beat** butter at medium speed with an electric mixer until creamy; gradually add sugar, beating well. Add eggs, one at a time, beating after each addition. Add grated lemon rind and flavorings, mixing well.
• **Combine** flour and next 3 ingredients in a bowl; add to butter mixture, beating just until dry ingredients are moistened.
• **Turn** dough out onto a lightly floured surface; lightly flour hands, and knead in cranberries, cherries, orange rind, and almonds.
• **Divide** dough in half; shape each portion into a 14- x 2-inch log on a lightly greased cookie sheet. Flatten logs slightly.
• **Bake** at 325° for 30 to 35 minutes or until golden. Cool on cookie sheet 5 minutes. Transfer to a wire rack to cool completely.
• **Cut** each log diagonally into ½-inch-thick slices with a serrated knife, using a gentle sawing motion. Place slices on ungreased cookie sheets.
• **Bake** at 325° for 10 minutes; turn cookies over, and bake 10 additional minutes. Remove to wire racks to cool. **Yield:** 3½ dozen.

Note: If you can't find dried cranberries and cherries at your supermarket, substitute raisins, dates, or chopped dried apricots.

Cindy Briscoe
Birmingham, Alabama

SECRET TO SUCCESS

"Be a relaxed hostess. If you're nervous, it rubs off on your guests," says Maxine Buchanan of Dunwoody, Georgia. That's why she loves to serve Anise Biscotti (see recipe, next page) for dessert. She can make it a day or two before company comes and keep it in a jar or tin, or bake and freeze even a month or two earlier. No last-minute scurrying allowed.

ANISE BISCOTTI

A traditional flavor for biscotti, anise tastes like sweet licorice. You can find anise seeds at gourmet grocery stores or order from Spices etc. Call 1-800-827-6373 to receive a free catalog or place an order. A 1.4-ounce container costs $1.60 plus shipping and handling. Anise flavoring is available in the spice section of your supermarket.

4 large eggs
1⅓ cups sugar
1 tablespoon anise seeds, crushed
1 tablespoon anisette liqueur or 2 teaspoons anise flavoring
2 cups all-purpose flour

• **Beat** eggs at high speed with an electric mixer until foamy; gradually add sugar, beating 5 minutes or until mixture is thickened.
• **Add** anise seeds and liqueur, mixing until blended. Stir in flour. Spoon batter into two lightly greased 8½- x 4½- x 3-inch loafpans.
• **Bake** at 375° for 30 minutes or until a wooden pick inserted in center comes out clean.
• **Cool** in pans on wire racks 5 minutes; remove from pans, and cool completely on wire racks.
• **Cut** each loaf diagonally into ½-inch-thick slices with a serrated knife, using a gentle sawing motion. Place on lightly greased cookie sheets.
• **Bake** at 350° for 8 minutes; turn cookies over, and bake 8 additional minutes. Remove to wire racks to cool. **Yield:** 2 dozen.

Maxine Buchanan
Dunwoody, Georgia

RED VELVET REDO

Red Velvet Cake is undeniably a Southern tradition. But we've come up with some new uses for those stunning red layers and creamy white frosting.

Bet you never thought of taking this classic recipe and making petits fours with tiny dollops of frosting on top. Or how about a quick-as-a-wink sheet cake – bake, frost, and serve it from the same pan? These desserts sport a new look, but they have the same scrumptious flavor as the original – maybe even better.

RED VELVET CAKE

(pictured on page 336)

½ cup shortening
1½ cups sugar
2 large eggs
1 (1-ounce) bottle red liquid food coloring
1 teaspoon vanilla extract
2½ cups sifted cake flour
½ teaspoon salt
2 teaspoons cocoa
1 cup buttermilk
1 tablespoon white vinegar
1 teaspoon baking soda
Cream Cheese Frosting
Garnish: chopped pecans

• **Beat** shortening at medium speed with an electric mixer until fluffy; gradually add sugar, beating well. Add eggs, one at a time, beating until blended after each addition.
• **Stir** in food coloring and vanilla, blending well.
• **Combine** flour, salt, and cocoa; set aside.
• **Combine** buttermilk, vinegar, and soda in a 4-cup liquid measuring cup. (Mixture will bubble.)
• **Add** flour mixture to shortening mixture, alternately with buttermilk mixture, beginning and ending with flour mixture. Beat at low speed until blended after each addition. Beat at medium speed 2 minutes; pour batter into three greased and floured 8-inch round cakepans.
• **Bake** at 350° for 25 minutes or until a wooden pick inserted in center comes out clean.
• **Cool** in pans on wire racks 10 minutes; remove from pans, and cool completely on wire racks.
• **Spread** Cream Cheese Frosting between layers and on top of cake. Garnish, if desired. **Yield:** 1 (3-layer) cake.

Cream Cheese Frosting

1 (8-ounce) package cream cheese, softened
½ cup butter or margarine, softened
1 (16-ounce) package powdered sugar, sifted
1 teaspoon vanilla extract

• **Beat** cream cheese and butter until creamy. Gradually add powdered sugar, beating at low speed until blended; add vanilla, beating until blended. **Yield:** 3½ cups.

Sheet Cake: Pour batter into a greased and floured 13- x 9- x 2-inch baking pan. Bake at 350° for 30 minutes or until a wooden pick inserted in center comes out clean. Cool completely in pan on a wire rack. Spread Cream Cheese Frosting on top of cake. Garnish, if desired. **Yield:** 1 (13- x 9- x 2-inch) cake.

Petits Fours: Pour half of batter into a greased and floured 15- x 10- x 1-inch jellyroll pan; cover and refrigerate remaining batter. Bake at 350° for 10 minutes or until center of cake springs back when lightly touched (do not overbake). Cool in pan on a wire rack 10 minutes; remove from pan, and let cool completely on wire rack. Repeat baking and cooling procedure with remaining batter. Reserve ½ cup Cream Cheese Frosting. Place 1 cake layer on a large cutting board or baking sheet; spread with remaining 3 cups frosting.

Top with remaining cake layer; cover and chill. Using a round cutter or knife, cut into 1½-inch circles or squares. Pipe or dollop reserved ½ cup frosting on tops of cakes. Garnish, if desired. **Yield:** about 3 dozen.

Georgana McNeil
Houston, Texas

Simple, Sweet Comfort

Puddings soothe like a warm hug at the end of a busy day. These dessert pleasers win extra credit for their uncomplicated flavors.

A bit of yesterday's bread or refrigerated cinnamon-raisin rolls together with basics such as milk, eggs, and sugar yield a variety of sweets from glamorous to down-home. Puddings are sure to satisfy your yearnings for life's simpler pleasures.

STEAMED GINGER PUDDING

(pictured on page 300)

2 cups all-purpose flour
1 cup whole wheat flour *
1¼ teaspoons baking soda
2 tablespoons ground ginger
2 (2.7-ounce) jars crystallized ginger, finely chopped **
1 cup butter or margarine
¾ cup firmly packed brown sugar
½ cup sugar
5 large eggs
1 tablespoon brandy
1 tablespoon grated orange rind
¼ cup fresh orange juice
Lemon Sauce
Garnishes: unsweetened whipped cream, lemon slices, orange rind strips, fresh mint sprigs

• **Combine** first 5 ingredients, tossing to coat chopped ginger. Set aside.
• **Position** knife blade in food processor bowl; add butter and sugars, and process 1 minute.
• **Add** eggs, one at a time, through food chute with processor running; process just until mixture is blended. Scrape down sides of bowl, if necessary; add brandy, grated orange rind, and orange juice. Gradually add flour mixture through food chute, pulsing 3 or 4 times or just until blended.
• **Pour** batter into a greased 8-cup fluted pudding mold, and cover tightly with greased aluminum foil.
• **Place** mold on a small wire rack in an 8-quart Dutch oven; add enough hot water to Dutch oven to come two-thirds up sides of mold. Bring water to a boil; cover, reduce heat, and simmer 1½ hours, adding additional hot water as needed. Serve with Lemon Sauce. Garnish, if desired. **Yield:** 12 servings.

* Substitute 1 cup all-purpose flour for whole wheat.

** You can substitute 1 (2.7-ounce) jar crystallized ginger and ½ cup golden raisins, finely chopped, for the crystallized ginger.

Lemon Sauce

1 cup sugar
1 large egg, lightly beaten
⅓ cup water
¼ cup butter or margarine
½ teaspoon lemon extract
⅛ teaspoon ground nutmeg

• **Combine** all ingredients in a small, heavy nonaluminum saucepan. Cook over medium-low heat, stirring constantly, 5 minutes or until thickened. **Yield:** 1⅓ cups.

Louise Jackson
Shreveport, Louisiana

LEMON-PEAR PUDDING

3 large pears, peeled and thinly sliced
¼ cup fresh lemon juice
¼ cup sugar
1 cup self-rising flour
¾ cup firmly packed brown sugar
1 teaspoon grated lemon rind
½ cup butter or margarine
Unsweetened whipped cream

• **Combine** first 3 ingredients, and place in a lightly greased 8-inch square baking dish.
• **Combine** flour, brown sugar, and lemon rind; cut in butter with pastry blender until mixture is crumbly, and sprinkle evenly over pear mixture.
• **Bake** at 400° for 30 to 35 minutes. Serve warm with whipped cream. **Yield:** 6 servings.

Wylene B. Gillespie
Gallatin, Tennessee

SWEET ROLL PUDDING

1 (7-ounce) can refrigerated cinnamon-raisin rolls *
2 large eggs
1½ cups milk
¾ cup sugar
1 teaspoon vanilla extract
¼ cup butter or margarine, melted
2 tablespoons honey

• **Bake** rolls according to package directions; cool and crumble. Sprinkle 3 cups crumbs into a lightly greased 1½-quart baking dish.
• **Combine** eggs and milk; stir in sugar and vanilla, and pour over crumbs.
• **Combine** butter and honey; pour over crumb mixture.
• **Bake** at 300° for 1 hour or until golden. **Yield:** 4 to 6 servings.

* Substitute 3 cups leftover cinnamon rolls or coffee cake crumbs for refrigerated rolls.

Virginia Landers
Memphis, Tennessee

CINNAMON TOAST PUDDING WITH CARAMEL SAUCE

8 slices white sandwich bread
3 tablespoons butter or margarine, softened
¼ cup sugar
2 teaspoons ground cinnamon
2½ cups milk
⅔ cup sugar
Pinch of salt
1¼ cups egg substitute
1 tablespoon vanilla extract
Caramel Sauce

• **Spread** 1 side of each bread slice evenly with butter.
• **Combine** ¼ cup sugar and cinnamon; sprinkle evenly over buttered side of bread. Place on a baking sheet.
• **Broil** 3½ inches from heat (with electric oven door partially opened) 2 minutes or until browned and bubbly. Remove from oven; cool.
• **Cut** each toast slice into 4 triangles. Arrange triangles, sugared side up, on bottom and around the sides of a well-buttered 9-inch quiche dish, overlapping, if necessary. Set aside.
• **Cook** milk in a saucepan over low heat until hot; remove from heat, and add ⅔ cup sugar and next 3 ingredients, stirring until sugar dissolves.
• **Spoon** half of custard into quiche dish; let stand 5 minutes.
• **Pour** in remaining custard, and place dish in a large shallow pan. Add hot water to pan to depth of ¾ inch.
• **Bake** at 350° for 30 to 35 minutes or until a knife inserted in center comes out clean. Serve warm with Caramel Sauce. **Yield:** 8 servings.

Caramel Sauce

1 cup sugar
½ cup dark corn syrup
1 tablespoon butter or margarine
Pinch of salt
¼ cup evaporated milk
1½ teaspoons vanilla extract

• **Combine** first 4 ingredients in a heavy saucepan; bring to a boil over medium heat, stirring constantly. Boil 1 minute, stirring constantly. Remove from heat.
• **Stir** in evaporated milk and vanilla. **Yield:** 1½ cups.

SINGULAR SENSATIONS

When the finale for your special occasion has to be grand, bake one of these creations.

Choose tarts made from ordinary apples or cakes that showcase autumn's pears, rich chocolate pudding, or goat cheese – yes, goat cheese!

Each recipe makes individual servings, so guests can have their own sweet ending to the evening.

BRANDIED APPLE TARTS
(pictured on page 299)

1 (17¼-ounce) package frozen puff pastry sheets, thawed
½ cup butter or margarine, softened
2 tablespoons sugar
1 cup sugar
6 Rome apples, thinly sliced
¼ teaspoon ground cinnamon
½ cup brandy
Vanilla ice cream

• **Cut** pastry into 6 (5-inch) circles, and place on a baking sheet. Spread evenly with butter, and sprinkle with 2 tablespoons sugar. Lightly grease bottom of another baking sheet, and place directly on pastry circles.
• **Bake** at 400° for 10 minutes or until pastry is golden. Remove to wire racks to cool.
• **Sprinkle** 1 cup sugar in a large skillet; cook over medium heat, stirring constantly, until golden. Stir in apple slices and cinnamon; cook until tender, stirring occasionally. Remove apples with a slotted spoon.
• **Stir** brandy into sugar mixture; cook 10 to 15 minutes or until thickened, stirring occasionally.
• **Place** pastry circles on individual dessert plates. Arrange apple slices on top; drizzle with brandy mixture. Top with vanilla ice cream, and serve immediately. **Yield:** 6 servings.

PEAR CAKES WITH PRALINE SAUCE
(pictured on page 299)

8 pears
3 cups sugar
2 cups water
¾ cup vegetable oil
1 cup sugar
1 large egg
1½ cups all-purpose flour
½ teaspoon baking soda
½ teaspoon salt
½ teaspoon ground cinnamon
½ cup chopped pecans
1 teaspoon vanilla extract
⅓ cup flaked coconut (optional)
Praline Sauce
Garnish: chopped pecans

• **Cut** 6 very thin slices lengthwise from center of each pear (do not core pears). Chop remainder of pears to measure 1½ cups.
• **Combine** 3 cups sugar and water in a medium saucepan; bring to a boil, stirring constantly. Add pear slices, and boil 20 minutes, stirring occasionally.
• **Drain** and arrange 8 slices on parchment paper-lined baking sheets, overlapping wide edges. Repeat procedure with remaining pear slices.
• **Bake** at 350° for 5 minutes or until edges begin to brown. Let stand overnight.
• **Beat** oil, 1 cup sugar, and egg at medium speed with an electric mixer until blended. Combine flour and next 3 ingredients; gradually add to oil mixture, beating at low speed after each addition. Add chopped pear, pecans,

vanilla, and coconut, if desired; beat at low speed just until blended.
• **Grease** and sugar six 6-ounce custard cups; spoon batter into cups.
• **Bake** at 325° for 40 minutes or until a wooden pick inserted in center comes out clean. Cool in cups on a wire rack.
• **Remove** cakes from cups; press a band of pear slices around sides of each cake. Serve with Praline Sauce, and garnish, if desired. **Yield:** 6 servings.

Praline Sauce

½ cup sugar
1 cup whipping cream
3 egg yolks
¼ cup praline liqueur

• **Combine** sugar and whipping cream in a heavy saucepan, and cook over low heat, stirring constantly, until sugar dissolves.
• **Beat** egg yolks until thick and pale. Gradually stir about one-fourth of hot mixture into yolks; add to remaining hot mixture, stirring constantly.
• **Cook** over medium heat, stirring constantly, until thickened. Remove from heat; stir in liqueur. Pour through a wire-mesh strainer into a bowl; cool. **Yield:** 1⅔ cups.

Rita W. Cook
Corpus Christi, Texas

GOAT CHEESE CUSTARD

1 large egg
⅓ cup sugar
1 teaspoon cornstarch
1½ teaspoons lemon juice
1 teaspoon vanilla extract
3 (5.3-ounce) containers creamy goat cheese
¼ cup milk
1 (16-ounce) package frozen strawberries, thawed
¼ cup amaretto
2 tablespoons sugar

• **Combine** first 5 ingredients in a large bowl; whisk together until mixture is smooth.
• **Whisk** goat cheese and milk until smooth; add to egg mixture, whisking until smooth.
• **Pour** into four lightly greased 6-ounce custard cups, and place cups in a 9-inch square pan. Add hot water to pan to depth of 1 inch.
• **Bake** at 375° for 10 minutes; reduce heat to 325°, and bake 35 additional minutes or until almost set. Transfer to a wire rack to cool. Cover and chill 8 hours.
• **Combine** strawberries, liqueur, and 2 tablespoons sugar in container of an electric blender or food processor; process until smooth, stopping once to scrape down sides. Pour through a wire-mesh strainer into a bowl, pressing with back of a spoon; discard seeds. Cover and chill.
• **Spoon** ¼ cup strawberry sauce on each serving plate; unmold custards onto plates. **Yield:** 4 servings.

Note: Serve leftover strawberry sauce over ice cream.

FUDGY CHOCOLATE PUDDING

2 (4-ounce) bars dark sweet chocolate bars
⅔ cup strongly brewed coffee
1 cup sugar
1 cup butter
4 large eggs
½ cup whipping cream
1 tablespoon powdered sugar

• **Combine** chocolate and coffee in top of a double boiler; bring water to a boil. Reduce heat to low; cook until chocolate melts, stirring occasionally. Gradually whisk in sugar. Add butter, 1 tablespoon at a time, whisking until melted.
• **Whisk** eggs until thick and pale. Gradually stir about one-fourth of hot mixture into eggs; add to remaining hot mixture, whisking constantly. Pour into six 6-ounce greased custard cups, and place cups in a 13- x 9- x 2-inch pan. Add hot water to pan to depth of 1 inch. Cover pan with aluminum foil.
• **Bake** at 350° for 45 minutes or until set. Remove cups from pan, and cool on a wire rack. Cover and chill at least 8 hours.
• **Beat** whipping cream at high speed with an electric mixer until foamy; gradually add powdered sugar, beating until soft peaks form. Pipe or dollop onto pudding. **Yield:** 6 servings.

William N. Cottrell II
New Orleans, Louisiana

TABLE ETIQUETTE FOR KIDS OF ALL AGES

Having dinner together as a family is an important part of the holidays. It can also be the perfect time to teach table manners. Here are some specifics.

■ As soon as you are seated, place the napkin in your lap. Never tuck it in a collar or belt. Remove napkin from your lap only to pat your lips or to cover a cough or sneeze. When leaving the table, lay the napkin on the left side of your plate or if the plate has been removed, lay it in the center of your place.

■ Keep hands in your lap or your hands and wrists on the table's edge when you're eating. Always remember to keep elbows off the table.

■ Before eating, wait until everyone has been served and the hostess picks up a piece of flatware. Begin with the piece of flatware that is farthest from your plate; just remember "from the outside in." If you're unsure, follow the hostess's lead.

■ Always keep table conversation about pleasant subjects, and maintain voices at a moderate level.

DRIED AND TRUE

The recipe for Dried Fruit Mix has many talents. You can leave the fruit whole to make Brandied Fruit Compote or a dessert paired with whipped cream or ice cream. You can chop the prunes, apricots, apples, and figs to make Fruitcake Loaf, a fruited dressing to accompany holiday meats, or a salsa for pork.

For an imaginative gift, package the fruit mix in a pretty jar, and attach recipes and serving suggestions.

DRIED FRUIT MIX

¾ cup pitted prunes
½ cup dried apricot halves
½ cup dried apple slices
5 dried figs
1 orange
1 cup dried cranberries
½ cup dried cherries
½ cup flaked coconut
¼ cup raisins
¼ cup golden raisins
½ cup brandy
½ cup honey
½ teaspoon ground cinnamon
¼ teaspoon ground cloves

• **Place** first 4 ingredients in a bowl.
• **Peel** orange with a vegetable peeler, reserving sections for another use. Cut rind into very thin strips; stir rind and next 5 ingredients into prune mixture.
• **Combine** brandy and remaining 3 ingredients in a small saucepan; cook over medium heat 3 minutes or until warm. Pour over fruit mixture, stirring gently.
• **Serve** warm or at room temperature. Store in an airtight container in refrigerator up to 1 month. **Yield:** 3½ cups.

BRANDIED FRUIT COMPOTE

(pictured on page 298)

3½ cups Dried Fruit Mix (see recipe)
2 cups water
¾ cup sugar
½ cup brandy

• **Combine** all ingredients in a heavy saucepan, stirring well. Cook over low heat 15 minutes, stirring occasionally; cool. Cover and store in refrigerator up to 1 month; serve at room temperature. **Yield:** 5 cups.

FRUITCAKE LOAF

1 cup all-purpose flour, divided
2 cups Dried Fruit Mix (see recipe)
1 cup pecan pieces
¾ cup butter or margarine, softened
½ cup firmly packed brown sugar
2 large eggs
½ teaspoon baking soda
½ teaspoon ground nutmeg
½ cup light corn syrup

• **Line** a 5- x 3- x 2-inch loafpan with brown paper; grease paper, and set pan aside.
• **Combine** ½ cup flour, Dried Fruit Mix, and pecans, tossing gently to coat; set aside.
• **Beat** butter at medium speed with an electric mixer until creamy. Gradually add brown sugar, beating well. Add eggs, one at a time, beating well after each addition.
• **Combine** remaining ½ cup flour, soda, and nutmeg; gradually add to butter mixture, beating at low speed until blended. Add corn syrup, beating just until blended. Stir in fruit mixture; spoon into prepared pan.
• **Bake** at 350° for 1½ hours. Cool in pan on a wire rack 10 minutes; remove from pan, and peel off paper. Cool completely on wire rack. **Yield:** 1 loaf.

PLAYFUL PILGRIMS' FEAST

Jan Downs, a preschool teacher in Shreveport, Louisiana, imagines that there were surely young children involved in the first thankful celebration. So she continues that tradition.

"Thanksgiving is all about sharing and making memories," Jan says. "Creating a space especially for the children adds to the spirit of celebration."

Jan finds that children often inspire the most successful kid-pleasing ideas for the holidays. "If you're planning on setting aside an area for the children, let them decide where to locate their table. Just make sure it's within sight, or at least earshot, of the adult table," she advises.

We asked Jan – and daughters Mary Amelia and Emmie, ages 7 and 4 – to share some of their favorite holiday ideas. Their recipes and hints offer even more reasons to give thanks.

TURKEY-IN-THE-STRAW SALAD

6 stalks celery
5 carrots, scraped
6 raisins
2 maraschino cherries
1 (29-ounce) can pear halves, drained
1 cup (4 ounces) finely shredded Cheddar cheese

• **Cut** celery into 3- x ½-inch pieces. Cut 4 thin slits from center of celery to end; place in ice water 15 minutes to separate slits. Drain on paper towels.
• **Cut** 4 carrots into 3- x ¼-inch pieces, and cut remaining carrot into ½-inch triangles.
• **Cut** raisins in half; cut cherries into thin strips.
• **Place** 1 pear half, cut side down, on an individual serving plate. Arrange

celery and carrot sticks around pear to resemble feathers. Arrange 2 raisin halves and a cherry strip on narrow end of pear to resemble eyes and gobbler.
• **Place** 2 carrot triangles at large end of pear to resemble feet. Sprinkle cheese around large end to resemble straw. **Yield:** 6 servings.

Indian Chief Salad: Substitute peach halves for pear halves; use chewy fruit rolls for headband; use carrot and celery sticks for feather headdress; use raisin halves for eyes; use cherry strip for mouth; use miniature marshmallow for nose.

MAYFLOWER SANDWICHES

1 small carrot, scraped
4 (6-inch) sandwich rolls, split
Mustard (optional)
Mayonnaise (optional)
64 slices ripe olive
32 pretzel sticks
Leaf lettuce
24 thin slices turkey
8 plastic drinking straws
8 slices process Swiss cheese
8 wooden picks

• **Cut** long strips from carrot, using a vegetable peeler. Trim strips into 3-inch triangles to resemble a pennant. Place triangles into bowl of ice water for 15 minutes or until triangles become slightly wavy.
• **Spread** rolls, if desired, with mustard and mayonnaise. Place an olive slice on each end of pretzel sticks; place 4 sticks on each roll half to resemble portholes. Place lettuce leaves over pretzels; arrange turkey over lettuce.
• **Cut** straws into 6-inch lengths; insert straws into cheese slices to resemble a sail. Insert straw into sandwich.
• **Drain** carrot triangles on paper towels. Insert a wooden pick through wide end of each carrot triangle; place pick in straw to resemble flag.
• **Serve**, if desired, with mustard or mayonnaise. **Yield:** 8 sandwiches.

INDIAN CORN

These candied ears of corn can be made several days ahead and then stored in an airtight container.

3 tablespoons butter or margarine
1 (10-ounce) package marshmallows
6 cups crisp rice cereal
1 cup (6-ounces) peanut butter-flavored morsels
1 cup candy corn
Vegetable cooking spray
Yellow plastic wrap
Wooden craft sticks
Raffia
Craft paper twine

• **Melt** butter in a large saucepan over low heat. Add marshmallows, stirring until melted. Remove from heat; stir in cereal, peanut butter morsels, and candy corn.
• **Coat** six 7-inch pieces of yellow plastic wrap with cooking spray; divide cereal mixture into 6 equal portions. Wrap each portion in plastic wrap, rolling tightly and shaping to resemble ears of corn. Insert a wooden craft stick 1 inch into larger end of ear; cool completely.
• **Untwist** craft paper twine to form crinkled paper; cut paper to resemble corn husks. Attach husks to larger end of ear with raffia. **Yield:** 6 ears.

LET'S GIVE THANKS

▪ Local libraries offer a good selection of seasonal children's books. Read Thanksgiving stories with your children before the big day.

▪ Let children help make place cards and place mats for the tables several days ahead, using construction paper, markers, and water-based paints.

▪ Fashion a tablecloth from crepe paper or a sheet draped over the table; tie excess fullness to legs of table, using raffia.

▪ Help create a special place for the children to gather for the meal. "Child-size tables and chairs are ideal, but any flat surface will do. A tablecloth or large piece of brown paper spread picnic style on the floor works just as well. Children can sit Indian style around the edges," suggests Jan Downs.

▪ As children arrive, have construction paper, crayons, and markers available. Ask them to draw a picture of what they are most thankful for. Before the meal, ask each guest – young and old – to share what he's most thankful for. Children can show their artwork at this time.

living *light*

HOME ON THE RANGE

Somewhere in the distant past a strong-legged holiday reveler decided that for the last six weeks of the year, everyone would eat standing up. From late November until New Year's Eve, there'll be standing-room-only cocktail parties and meals balanced on trays. Escape the season's chaos and reward yourself with the comfort of a healthy dinner at home. These easy cooktop recipes range from slow-simmered stews to quick sautés. Whatever your schedule, there's a meal to fit into your sit-down dinner plans.

SAUTÉED SHRIMP AND PASTA

8 ounces linguine, uncooked
2 pounds unpeeled medium-size fresh shrimp
1 small onion, chopped
2 cloves garlic, minced
1 tablespoon hot sesame oil
6 plum tomatoes, peeled and chopped
1 teaspoon dried oregano
½ teaspoon salt
½ teaspoon dried basil
½ teaspoon freshly ground pepper
¼ cup chopped fresh parsley
¼ cup kalamata olives, sliced
¼ cup lemon juice
2 ounces crumbled feta cheese

• **Cook** linguine according to package directions; drain and keep warm.
• **Peel** shrimp, and devein, if desired.
• **Cook** onion and garlic in oil in a large skillet until tender, stirring often. Stir in tomato and next 4 ingredients; cook 3 minutes, stirring constantly. Add shrimp, and cook 3 minutes or until shrimp turn pink, stirring occasionally.
• **Stir** in parsley, olives, and lemon juice; cook just until thoroughly heated. Serve over linguine; sprinkle with cheese. **Yield:** 4 servings.

Carol Barclay
Portland, Texas

♥ Per serving: Calories 449 (21% from fat)
Fat 10.6g (3.3g saturated) Cholesterol 185mg
Sodium 708mg Carbohydrate 54.1g
Fiber 3.7g Protein 33.9g

CHICKEN-AND-BLACK BEAN QUESADILLAS

The ubiquitous Tex-Mex appetizer becomes a hearty meal with main-dish ingredients.

1 tablespoon fajita seasoning
2 (4-ounce) skinned and boned chicken breast halves, cut into thin strips
Vegetable cooking spray
½ onion, cut into strips
½ green bell pepper, cut into strips
2 cloves garlic, minced
1 to 2 jalapeño peppers, minced
1 (15-ounce) can black beans, rinsed and drained
½ cup chopped fresh cilantro
4 (10-inch) flour tortillas
1½ cups (6 ounces) shredded reduced-fat Monterey Jack cheese

• **Rub** fajita seasoning on all sides of chicken; cover and chill 30 minutes.
• **Cook** chicken in a large nonstick skillet over medium-high heat, stirring constantly, 4 minutes or until done. Remove from skillet, and keep warm.
• **Coat** skillet with cooking spray; add onion and next 3 ingredients, and cook until tender, stirring often. Stir in black beans and cilantro; cook, stirring constantly, until thoroughly heated.
• **Coat** 1 side of each tortilla with cooking spray; layer chicken, vegetable mixture, and cheese evenly on uncoated side of 2 tortillas. Top with remaining tortillas, coated side up. Cook in skillet over medium heat until lightly browned, turning once. Serve immediately. **Yield:** 2 servings.

Patty Messer
Middlesboro, Kentucky

♥ Per serving: Calories 697 (28% from fat)
Fat 22.2g (10.4g saturated) Cholesterol 93mg
Sodium 911mg Carbohydrate 70.5g
Fiber 7.7g Protein 58.3g

VEGETABLE TAGINE

1 onion
1 green bell pepper
3 carrots, scraped
2 sweet potatoes
1 eggplant
4 plum tomatoes
3 zucchini
1 tablespoon olive oil
3 cloves garlic, minced
5 (16-ounce) cans fat-free reduced-sodium chicken broth
2 tablespoons lemon juice
1 tablespoon honey
½ cup golden raisins
½ teaspoon ground cumin
½ teaspoon ground coriander
½ teaspoon ground turmeric
¼ teaspoon ground cinnamon
1 (15.5-ounce) can chick-peas, rinsed and drained
1 teaspoon salt
1 teaspoon pepper
2 tablespoons sambal oelek *
Hot cooked couscous

• **Chop** onion and bell pepper; cut carrots and next 4 ingredients into 2-inch pieces.
• **Cook** onion and bell pepper in oil in a Dutch oven 6 minutes or until tender, stirring often. Add garlic, and cook 1 minute, stirring often; stir in carrot, sweet potato, eggplant, tomato, broth, and next 7 ingredients. Bring to a boil over medium-high heat; cover, reduce heat, and simmer 30 minutes, stirring occasionally.
• **Stir** in zucchini, chick-peas, salt, and pepper; simmer 10 to 15 minutes or until zucchini is tender. Remove 1 cup cooking liquid; stir sambal oelek into liquid, and serve sauce with tagine. Serve with couscous. **Yield:** 2 quarts.

* Sambal oelek is a hot chile paste. You can substitute any Asian or Mexican chile paste.

Liz Lorber
Atlanta, Georgia

♥ Per 2-cup serving:
Calories 205 (13% from fat)
Fat 2.8g (0.4g saturated) Cholesterol 0mg
Sodium 421mg Carbohydrate 39.2g
Fiber 5.2g Protein 5.4g

EATING OUT, EATING RIGHT

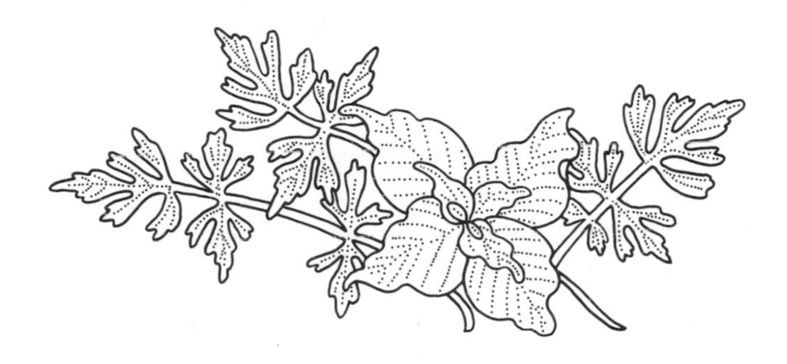

Katie Klauber Moulton of Longboat Key, Florida, grew up in a family where exercise and healthy meals were a part of the daily routine. She shares her tips for a lifetime of healthy living.

■ When eating out, Katie recommends that you "look at the menu briefly, choose the first thing that catches your eye, and then close the menu. The longer you take to decide, the more food you're likely to order."

■ "Question waiters about how dishes are prepared," she says. "You never know where the cream sauce is hiding until you ask."

■ "Watch calories, not just fat," Katie cautions.

■ "When you feel full, stop eating," she advises. "And always leave some food on your plate."

■ Katie tries to exercise at least three times a week. "It's as good for your mental health as it is for your physical health."

FRESH MEX

Tony Brown, owner of The Burro restaurant in Washington, D.C., has built a thriving business around his commitment to serving fresh food. He prepares black beans for his vegetable burritos every day. Try the beans on their own, in the Chicken-and-Black Bean Quesadillas (on previous page) or in Tony's Veggie Burritos (below).

Tony's Black Beans: To cook dried black beans for Tony's Veggie Burritos, sort and wash beans; soak 1 pound dried beans in water to cover 8 hours, and drain. Bring beans and water to cover to a boil in a Dutch oven; reduce heat, and simmer 1 hour, adding water as needed. Position knife blade in food processor bowl; add 2 medium onions, quartered; 6 cloves garlic; 4 jalapeño peppers; and 1 cup water, and process until mixture is finely chopped, stopping once to scrape down sides of bowl. Add to beans, and cook 30 minutes or until beans are tender. Stir in 2 teaspoons salt and ¼ cup chopped fresh cilantro. **Yield:** 6 cups.

Tony's Veggie Burritos: Cut 1 onion and 1 green bell pepper into strips, and slice 1 zucchini. Cook vegetables in 1 tablespoon olive oil until crisp-tender, stirring often.

Spoon vegetables evenly down centers of 4 (10-inch) warm flour tortillas; top each with ¼ cup Tony's Black Beans, and roll up. Serve with salsa, chopped fresh cilantro, and chopped tomato. Each burrito contains 250 calories and 8 grams of fat. **Yield:** 4 burritos.

PASTA!

Remember when we called it macaroni? We'd stir cheese into it and dinner was ready.

Now it's called pasta, the shapes are fancier, and there's nothing we won't add to it.

CRABMEAT LASAGNA

6 lasagna noodles, uncooked
¼ cup butter or margarine
1 cup shredded carrot
½ cup finely chopped celery
½ cup finely chopped onions
⅓ cup chopped yellow bell pepper
⅓ cup chopped red bell pepper
3 cloves garlic, minced
1 teaspoon coriander seeds, crushed
1 (8-ounce) carton plain yogurt
¼ cup chopped fresh cilantro
¼ teaspoon salt
⅛ teaspoon ground white pepper
⅛ teaspoon ground nutmeg
1 pound fresh lump crabmeat, drained
2 cups (8 ounces) shredded mozzarella cheese
2 cups (8 ounces) shredded process American cheese

• **Cook** noodles according to package directions; drain.
• **Melt** butter in a large skillet over medium-high heat; add carrot and next 6 ingredients. Cook 4 to 5 minutes or until vegetables are tender, stirring often.
• **Combine** yogurt and next 4 ingredients in a bowl; stir in vegetable mixture. Add crabmeat; toss.
• **Combine** shredded cheeses.
• **Arrange** 3 lasagna noodles in bottom of a lightly greased 13- x 9- x 2-inch baking dish; top with half of crabmeat mixture. Sprinkle half of cheese mixture on top. Repeat layers with remaining noodles and crabmeat mixture.
• **Cover** and bake at 350° for 30 minutes or until thoroughly heated. Sprinkle with remaining cheese mixture, and bake, uncovered, 5 additional minutes. **Yield:** 6 servings.

Carolene and Richard Martinez
Natchez, Mississippi

CRAWFISH AND TASSO FETTUCCINE

12 ounces fettuccine, uncooked
3 tablespoons butter or margarine, melted
3 cloves garlic, minced
3 ounces tasso, chopped (½ cup)
1 cup sliced green onions
1 cup fresh mushrooms, sliced
1 medium-size green bell pepper, seeded and chopped
3 tablespoons all-purpose flour
2 cups whipping cream
1 teaspoon dried oregano
1 teaspoon dried thyme
¼ teaspoon ground red pepper
¼ teaspoon freshly ground pepper
¼ teaspoon salt
1 pound frozen cooked crawfish tails, thawed and drained
½ cup freshly grated Parmesan cheese

• **Cook** pasta according to package directions; drain and keep warm.
• **Melt** butter in a skillet over medium heat; add garlic, and cook, stirring constantly, 3 minutes or until tender. Stir in tasso and next 3 ingredients; cook 5 minutes, stirring constantly.
• **Stir** in flour; gradually stir in whipping cream and next 5 ingredients. Bring to a boil; cook, stirring constantly, 1 minute or until smooth and thickened.
• **Add** crawfish tails; cook just until thoroughly heated, stirring mixture occasionally.
• **Pour** over pasta, tossing gently to coat. Sprinkle evenly with Parmesan cheese, and serve immediately. **Yield:** 6 servings.

Carla Wells
Mandeville, Louisiana

HOT BROWN PASTA CASSEROLES

8 ounces penne pasta, uncooked (2½ cups)
6 ounces sliced ham, cut into ½-inch strips
6 ounces sliced smoked turkey, cut into ¼-inch strips
1 (10¾-ounce) can Cheddar cheese soup, undiluted
½ cup milk
¼ teaspoon pepper
8 slices tomato
8 slices bacon, cooked
¼ cup freshly grated Parmesan cheese

• **Cook** pasta according to package directions; drain. Combine pasta, ham, and turkey in a bowl.
• **Combine** soup, milk, and pepper; stir into pasta mixture. Spoon into four lightly greased individual baking dishes; top with tomato slices.
• **Bake** at 350° for 15 minutes. Top with bacon slices, sprinkle with cheese; bake 5 additional minutes or until casseroles are thoroughly heated. Serve immediately. **Yield:** 4 servings.

Lillian Harris
Mayfield, Kentucky

SHELLY GREENS AND BACON

8 ounces shell pasta, uncooked
5 slices salt-cured bacon
2 cloves garlic, minced
1 medium onion, chopped
1 tablespoon country Dijon mustard
1 (10-ounce) package frozen chopped collard greens, thawed and drained
1 (14-ounce) can diced tomatoes
¼ teaspoon freshly ground pepper
Freshly grated Parmesan cheese

• **Cook** pasta according to package directions; drain and keep warm in a serving bowl.
• **Cook** bacon in a large skillet until crisp. Drain, reserving 1 tablespoon drippings in skillet. Crumble bacon, and set aside.

• **Cook** garlic and onion in drippings over medium-high heat, stirring constantly, until tender.
• **Add** mustard, collard greens, and tomatoes to skillet; reduce heat to medium, and cook 10 minutes. Add pepper; pour over pasta, tossing to coat. Top with bacon and cheese. **Yield:** 3 to 4 servings.

Katie Williams
Montgomery, Alabama

BOW TIES, BLACK BEANS, AND KEY LIMES

6 ounces bow tie pasta, uncooked (2½ cups)
4 cloves garlic, minced
2 tablespoons olive oil
⅓ cup fresh Key lime juice
¼ cup dry sherry
1 cup sliced green onions
½ pound plum tomatoes, peeled and chopped
1 (15-ounce) can black beans, rinsed and drained
½ teaspoon salt
¼ teaspoon freshly ground pepper
2 teaspoons grated Key lime rind
¼ cup chopped fresh Italian parsley
Garnish: Italian parsley sprig

• **Cook** pasta according to package directions; drain and keep warm in a serving bowl.
• **Cook** garlic in oil in a skillet over medium-high heat, stirring constantly, 2 minutes or until tender. Add lime juice and sherry; cook over high heat 5 minutes or until mixture is reduced to ¼ cup.
• **Add** green onions and chopped tomato; cook over medium heat 5 to 8 minutes, stirring occasionally.
• **Stir** in beans and next 3 ingredients; pour over pasta, tossing to coat. Sprinkle with chopped parsley, and garnish, if desired. Serve immediately. **Yield:** 3 servings.

Mike Adams
Naples, Florida

BOURBON-PECAN ALFREDO

6 ounces linguine, uncooked
2 tablespoons butter or margarine
3 cloves garlic, minced
¾ cup bourbon, divided
1 cup whipping cream
1 cup freshly grated Parmesan cheese
½ cup pecan pieces, toasted
2 tablespoons chopped parsley

• **Cook** linguine according to package directions; drain and keep warm.
• **Melt** butter in a skillet over medium-high heat; add garlic, and cook, stirring constantly, until tender.
• **Add** ½ cup bourbon, and cook 3 to 5 minutes, stirring constantly. Stir in whipping cream and cheese. Cook over low heat, stirring constantly, until cheese melts. Gradually stir in remaining ¼ cup bourbon; stir in pecans and parsley. Pour over pasta; toss. Serve immediately. **Yield:** 2 main-dish or 4 side-dish servings.

Megen McCully
Knoxville, Tennessee

PERFECT PASTA

▪ Cook pasta in plenty of water – about 6 quarts for each pound of pasta – and you won't need to add oil to keep it from sticking together. However, a little oil does help keep the water from foaming over during cooking.

▪ Salting the cooking water is purely a matter of taste. If you choose to add salt, use 1 to 2 teaspoons for 8 ounces of pasta.

▪ The best way to tell when pasta is done is to taste a piece of it. It should be "al dente," tender yet firm to the bite.

▪ For short pasta, such as macaroni or shells, 2 ounces uncooked equals just over ½ cup dry pasta or 1 cup cooked. For long pasta, such as spaghetti or fettuccine, 2 ounces uncooked equals ½-inch bunch dry or 1 cup cooked.

▪ To store cooked pasta, drain and toss with a drizzle of oil to keep it from sticking together. Then cover and store in the refrigerator up to 5 days.

▪ Know your noodles. Noodles contain eggs or egg yolks; pastas do not.

▪ You may have heard that pasta makes you fat, but nothing could be further from the truth. Pasta is packed with B vitamins, provides an excellent source of complex carbohydrates, and is low in fat and cholesterol free. It's the butter and some sauces added to pasta that give it an undeserved "fat" reputation.

Holy Jalapeños!

Texans approach a lot of things with near-religious fervor, and home cooking is one of them. Outside the Lone Star State, pantry staples are usually mild ingredients: flour, sugar, and salt. But sixth-generation San Antonio native and cookbook author Candy Wagner tops her grocery list with lively jalapeños.

Candy and her sister (and coauthor) Sandra Marquez offer plenty of recipes to spice up your diet with these power-packed peppers, including ones that gently disarm them. We've adapted these favorites from their recently updated volume, *Cooking Texas Style* (University of Texas Press, Austin).

Jalapeño Cheese Pie

This is a good recipe for the timid. The heat of the peppers is soothingly coated with cheese. Stir in chicken or sausage for an easy brunch dish.

1 (11.5-ounce) jar whole jalapeño peppers, drained
4 cups (16 ounces) shredded Cheddar cheese
6 large eggs, lightly beaten

• **Cut** peppers in half lengthwise; remove seeds. Rinse with cold water; drain on paper towels. Mince peppers.
• **Sprinkle** half of cheese in a lightly greased 11- x 7- x 1½-inch pan; top with peppers and remaining cheese. Pour eggs over top.
• **Bake** at 350° for 30 to 40 minutes or until lightly browned and set. Cool 5 to 10 minutes, and cut into squares. **Yield:** 12 servings.

Fried Jalapeños

You can buy these frozen at some warehouse foods stores, but this homemade version is much better. For a quick dip, stir a little green jalapeño hot sauce into sour cream.

2 (11.5-ounce) jars whole jalapeño peppers, drained
4 ounces Muenster cheese
½ cup yellow cornmeal
1 cup all-purpose flour
1 teaspoon baking powder
½ teaspoon salt
1 tablespoon vegetable oil
1¼ cups beer
Vegetable oil
½ cup all-purpose flour

• **Cut** a small slit in each pepper; carefully remove seeds. Rinse peppers with cold water; drain on paper towels.
• **Cut** cheese into 18 pieces; insert 1 piece into each pepper.
• **Combine** cornmeal and next 3 ingredients in a small bowl; add 1 tablespoon oil and beer, stirring until smooth. Let stand 10 to 15 minutes.
• **Pour** oil to depth of 3 inches into a skillet or deep-fat fryer; heat to 350°.
• **Dredge** peppers in ½ cup flour; then dip in batter. Fry 3 to 4 minutes or until golden, turning occasionally. Serve immediately. **Yield:** 1½ dozen.

Jalapeño Jelly

We've skipped the canning process to make an easy, small-batch, keep-in-the-fridge jelly. It's a cool appetizer (or relish) with just a little heat.

3 fresh jalapeño peppers, seeded and coarsely chopped
½ green bell pepper, coarsely chopped
3 cups sugar
½ cup cider vinegar
½ (6-ounce) package liquid fruit pectin
2 tablespoons fresh lime juice

• **Position** knife blade in food processor bowl; add jalapeño and bell peppers. Process until smooth, stopping once to scrape down sides.
• **Combine** pepper puree, sugar, and cider vinegar in a large nonaluminum saucepan. Bring mixture to a boil over medium-high heat, stirring constantly. Boil 3 minutes; stir in pectin and lime juice. Boil 1 minute, stirring constantly. Remove from heat, and skim off foam with a metal spoon.
• **Pour** into hot, sterilized jars, filling to ¼ inch from top; wipe jar rims. Cover at once with metal lids, and screw on bands; cool.
• **Store** in refrigerator. Serve over cream cheese with crackers or toast as an appetizer or with meats as a relish. **Yield:** 3 half-pints.

Burning Issues

▪ Wear disposable gloves when working with jalapeño peppers.

▪ To reduce most of a pepper's heat, remove seeds and membranes with a paring knife.

▪ Keep a jar of pickled jalapeños on your pantry shelf for emergencies. They'll substitute for the same amount of fresh.

Cranberry Chutney and Raspberry Vinaigrette (recipes, page 275) make great gifts for seasoning the holidays.

Celebrate the holidays in the company of friends with our Supper Club Menu. (Menu begins on page 306.)

Above: *Crown Pork Roast With Cranberry-Pecan Stuffing, Carrot Soufflé, and steamed green beans with Herb Butter.*

Left: *Caramelized Shallot Salad.*

Far Left: *Crown Pork Roast With Cranberry-Pecan Stuffing.*

Right: *Traditional Thanksgiving dinner partners take on an innovative look with Roasted Turkey With Sausage-and-Wild Mushroom Stuffing, Gingered Acorn Squash With Spiced Cranberry Sauce, wild rice, and Butterbeans With Bacon and Green Onions. (Recipes begin on page 266.)*

Below: *A crisp coating of ground walnuts and a bit of buttermilk create the sweet, nutty flavor of Walnut-Chicken Salad (recipe, page 243).*

Serve Molasses-Grilled Pork Tenderloin, Grilled Acorn Squash With Rosemary, and steamed green beans against a backdrop of firelight. (Recipes begin on page 265.)

Keep Brandied Fruit Compote (recipe, page 286) on hand for an instantly elegant finish to your holiday meals.

Left: *Baked pear slices make a stunning presentation for Pear Cakes With Praline Sauce (recipe, page 284).*

Below: *Brandied Apple Tarts (recipe, page 284) are easier than pie to make – puff pastry sheets are the secret.*

A fluted pudding mold lends elegance to Steamed Ginger Pudding atop a pool of Lemon Sauce (recipes, page 283). The dense, spicy dessert, slow cooked on a rack in boiling water, can also be steamed in a stainless steel bowl.

BOUNTIFUL HARVEST

We are, by nature, gatherers. We gather together for family time, intimate occasions, and large celebrations. Autumn brings the harvest, and we gather its abundant yield to celebrate fall.

Rich colors, wonderful textures, and golden days are autumn's gifts to us. Use them all to bring the harvest home. Everywhere you look there are piles of pumpkins waiting for an owner and a face. Gourds of every shape, size, and color abound in markets and grocery stores. Bunches of tangled bittersweet and clusters of Indian corn hang at farmers markets. Sunflowers' heavy heads wait to decorate a wreath or serve as a snack for birds.

WARM WELCOME

You can begin saying welcome to all who come to visit by placing a big basket of apples on the doorstep. A cluster of odd-shaped pumpkins brings autumn in a hurry. And don't think that they're just for carving. Unblemished pumpkins will last on a doorstep for over a month, provided the temperature stays above freezing.

Dressing a vine wreath for fall is a breeze. Keep items compatible in size. Use small gourds, miniature pumpkins, Indian corn, sunflower heads, and bittersweet for a variety of color and texture. Resist the temptation to scatter these around the wreath; cluster them instead, and avoid overwhelming the wreath with too many decorations. By poking a hole in a gourd or small pumpkin, you can push a piece of florist wire through it and wire it to the wreath. Remember, leaving a sunflower head outdoors is an open invitation to birds.

For a simple front door dress-up, hang a flat-backed basket, place a container of water inside (a jelly jar works well), and fill the basket with autumn leaves. The leaves can also make their way indoors. A few branches of sugar maple with blazing autumn color are nothing short of breathtaking. Norman Kent Johnson, a garden consultant in Birmingham, Alabama, also recommends using sourwood, beech, black gum, and Chinese tallow.

Norman points out that while cut branches are magnificent, once cut they will last only a day or two. For maximum longevity, he recommends taking a bucket of water with you when you cut branches. Use sharp pruners and immediately place the cut end of the branch in water. Then cut the stem again under water to prevent any sap from clogging the cut.

TASTEFUL TABLES

Entertaining can easily take on autumn's natural finery. Arrange your menu and your table with fall's bounty.

- Use baskets and pottery as the base of your table arrangements – the more rustic, the better. For the look of abundance, let the treasures you've collected spill from a container and onto the table.

- Combine mini-pumpkins, gourds, apples, nuts, artichokes, and pears. Lay some on the table for a loose, abundant look. A few candles in small clay pots will add a touch of warmth.

- Maple leaves bring the fiery colors of autumn to the hearth. When it's too warm for a real fire, there's no hazard placing the cut leaves here.

- The mantel is a perfect home to swan gourds, Indian corn, and bittersweet. A late-blooming sunflower in a water vial adds a touch of freshness.

INVENT YOUR OWN CASSEROLE

During the cold winter months, churches in Gainesville, Georgia, take turns feeding and housing the homeless. Janine Todaro's group from St. Michael's Catholic Church uses this basic mix-and-match recipe, switching ingredients for variety.

We added a few of our own ideas – sour cream, milk, and seasonings – and liked the following 4 combinations. Each casserole bakes 1 hour and 20 minutes, eliminating the need to precook the pasta or rice. Don't limit yourself to these recipes – experiment with different flavors and invent your own casseroles.

Chicken Casserole: cream of chicken soup, broccoli, rice, chicken, Parmesan cheese, and breadcrumbs

Ham Casserole: cream of celery soup, Italian green beans, wide egg noodles, ham, garlic, and 2 portions Swiss cheese

Turkey Casserole: Italian-style diced tomatoes, spinach, medium pasta shells, turkey, onion, garlic, mozzarella cheese, and breadcrumbs

Vegetarian Casserole: Italian-style diced tomatoes, yellow squash, rice, olives, 4 portions celery, 4 portions bell pepper, garlic, Parmesan cheese, and breadcrumbs

CHOOSE ONE SAUCE MAKER

- 1 (10¾-ounce) can cream of mushroom soup, undiluted
- 1 (10¾-ounce) can cream of celery soup, undiluted
- 1 (10¾-ounce) can cream of chicken soup, undiluted
- 1 (10¾-ounce) can Cheddar cheese soup, undiluted
- 2 (14½-ounce) cans Italian-style diced tomatoes, undrained

CHOOSE ONE FISH/MEAT/POULTRY

- 2 (6-ounce) cans solid white tuna, drained and flaked
- 2 cups chopped cooked chicken
- 2 cups chopped cooked ham
- 2 cups chopped cooked turkey
- 1 pound ground beef, browned and drained

CHOOSE ONE PASTA/RICE

- 2 cups uncooked elbow macaroni
- 1 cup uncooked rice
- 4 cups uncooked wide egg noodles
- 3 cups uncooked medium shells

CHOOSE ONE OR TWO TOPPINGS

- ½ cup (2 ounces) shredded mozzarella cheese
- ½ cup (2 ounces) shredded Swiss cheese
- ½ cup grated Parmesan cheese
- ½ cup fine, dry breadcrumbs

CHOOSE ONE FROZEN VEGETABLE

- 1 (10-ounce) package frozen chopped spinach, thawed
- 1 (10-ounce) package frozen cut broccoli
- 1 (10-ounce) package frozen Italian green beans
- 1 (10-ounce) package frozen English peas
- 1 (16-ounce) package frozen sliced yellow squash
- 1 (10-ounce) package frozen whole kernel corn

CHOOSE ONE OR MORE EXTRAS (OPTIONAL)

- 1 (3-ounce) can sliced mushrooms, drained
- ¼ cup sliced ripe olives
- ¼ cup chopped bell pepper
- ¼ cup chopped onion
- ¼ cup chopped celery
- 2 cloves garlic, minced
- 1 (4.5-ounce) can chopped green chiles
- 1 (1¼-ounce) envelope taco seasoning mix

• **Combine** 1 (8-ounce) carton sour cream, 1 cup milk, 1 cup water, 1 teaspoon salt, and 1 teaspoon pepper with Sauce Maker (omit sour cream and milk when using tomatoes). Stir in Pasta/Rice, Frozen Vegetable, Fish/Meat/Poultry, and if desired, Extras.

• **Spoon** casserole mixture into a lightly greased 13- x 9- x 2-inch baking dish; sprinkle with your choice of toppings.

• **Cover** and bake casserole at 350° for 1 hour and 10 minutes; uncover and bake 10 additional minutes. **Yield:** 6 servings.

HOT FOR HAM

Thanks to packaged ham slices, you can satisfy a craving without buying the whole hog. Pan fry, bake, or grill these ½-inch pieces for a weeknight change of pace. Grab a slice or two on your way home and ham it up with these fast-flavor options.

PRALINE HAM

⅓ cup chopped pecans
2 (½-inch-thick) ham slices (about 2½ pounds)
½ cup maple syrup
3 tablespoons sugar
2 teaspoons butter or margarine

• **Place** pecans in a shallow pan, and bake at 325° for 5 to 10 minutes or until toasted, stirring occasionally; set aside.
• **Bake** ham slices in a shallow pan at 325° for 10 minutes.
• **Bring** syrup, sugar, and butter to a boil in a small saucepan, stirring often. Stir in pecans, and spoon over ham.
• **Bake** 30 additional minutes. **Yield:** 4 servings.

Nancy Woodall
Bellaire, Texas

GRILLED HAM AND APPLES

½ cup orange marmalade
2 teaspoons butter or margarine
¼ teaspoon ground ginger
2 (½-inch-thick) ham slices (about 2½ pounds)
4 apples, cut into ½-inch-thick slices

• **Combine** first 3 ingredients in a 1-cup liquid measuring cup; microwave at HIGH 1 minute or until melted, stirring once.
• **Cook** ham and apple, covered with grill lid, over medium-hot coals (350° to 400°), turning occasionally and basting with marmalade mixture, 20 minutes or until thoroughly heated. **Yield:** 4 servings.

CROISSANTS STEP-BY-STEP

When you're eager to bake something special, these recipes will satisfy. Definitely a hands-on food, croissants require kneading, rolling, punching, and folding to achieve ultimate tenderness. Most of the ingredients are probably already in your kitchen.

CROISSANTS

1 cup butter, softened
2 packages active dry yeast
3 tablespoons sugar, divided
½ cup warm water (105° to 115°)
⅔ cup milk
4 to 4½ cups all-purpose flour, divided
¼ cup vegetable oil
2 teaspoons salt
2 large eggs

• **Spread** butter into a 10- x 8-inch rectangle on wax paper; cover and chill.
• **Combine** yeast, 1 tablespoon sugar, and water in a 2-cup liquid measuring cup; let stand 5 minutes.
• **Heat** milk to 105° to 115°. Combine yeast mixture, warm milk, remaining 2 tablespoons sugar, 2 cups flour, and remaining 3 ingredients in a large mixing bowl. Beat at medium speed with an electric mixer until smooth. Gradually stir in enough remaining flour to make a soft dough.
• **Turn** dough out onto a lightly floured surface, and knead until smooth and elastic (about 10 minutes). Place dough in a well-greased bowl, turning to grease top.
• **Cover** and let rise in a warm place (85°), free from drafts, 1 hour or until doubled in bulk.
• **Punch** dough down. Cover with plastic wrap, and chill 1 hour.
• **Punch** dough down; turn out onto a lightly floured surface, and roll into a 24- x 10-inch rectangle. Place chilled butter rectangle in center of dough rectangle; gently fold dough over butter. Pinch edges to seal.
• **Roll** dough into an 18- x 10-inch rectangle; fold into thirds, beginning with short side. Cover and chill 1 hour.
• **Repeat** rolling and folding procedure twice, chilling dough 30 minutes each time. Wrap dough in aluminum foil, and chill 8 hours.
• **Divide** dough into 4 equal portions. Roll 1 portion into a 12-inch circle on a lightly floured surface, and cut into 6 wedges (keep remaining dough chilled). Roll up each wedge tightly, beginning at wide end. Place, point side down, on greased baking sheets, curving into crescent shapes.
• **Cover** and let rise in a warm place, free from drafts, 30 minutes or until doubled in bulk.
• **Bake** at 425° for 8 minutes or until golden. Cool slightly on baking sheets; transfer to wire racks to cool. Repeat procedure with remaining dough portions. **Yield:** 2 dozen.

Chocolate-Filled Croissants: Place 2 or 3 tiny rectangles of a milk chocolate candy bar on wide end of each wedge; roll up, and proceed as directed.

Strawberry or Apricot Croissants: Spread 1 teaspoon strawberry or apricot preserves over each wedge, leaving a ¼-inch border; roll up, and proceed as directed.

Cinnamon-Sugar Croissants: Sprinkle wedges with a mixture of ground cinnamon and sugar; roll up, and proceed as directed. Combine sifted powdered sugar and milk, stirring until drizzling consistency. Spoon glaze over croissants after baked.

From Our Kitchen to Yours

TIPTOE THROUGH THE TULIPS

Most of us put more fuss and frills into our entertaining during the holidays, sometimes tossing flower petals and fresh sprigs of greenery onto serving plates with festive abandon. Two seasonal favorites should be left far from the kitchen: poinsettias and holly berries. (Sorry, they're both toxic.)

But you can snip pansy blossoms from your winter garden for garnishing or use carnations and roses from the florist. Other times of year, feel free to add tulips, nasturtiums, daylilies, and herb blossoms to your culinary creations. Just be sure that neither the florist flowers nor your home-grown varieties has been chemically treated.

SO WHERE'S TAHINI?

No, it's not a Polynesian island, but it once came from a faraway place. Tahini is a Middle Eastern ingredient made from ground sesame seeds and often used in the appetizer spreads like hummus and baba ghanoush. Like its cousin, sesame oil, it has an intense flavor, so recipes call for just a dollop here and there. Look for the jars in the ethnic foods or peanut butter section of larger grocery stores. (They're about $4 to $5, but you use only a little at a time.)

SANE OVER STAINS

Homemade cranberry sauce with its brilliant strawberry red color really stands out on the Thanksgiving table – and on the tablecloth, napkins, and clothes.

Not to worry, though. A soak in club soda and the stains vanish. Just pour the fizzy magic potion into a large bowl and submerge the stained cloth and napkins for a few minutes. Like magic, stains are gone. Linens are fresh as new.

GET A GRIP ON GREENS

Before you simmer thin, leathery autumn greens to a tender surrender, you first have to corral the unwieldy bunches into the pot. They're a lot of trouble, with all the washing, stemming, chopping, and cooking. But most devout Southerners have their own kitchen folkways – and a lot of patience – when it comes to their beloved collard, mustard, and turnip greens.

One way is to pull the leaves from the stems by hand like shucking corn. Another is to hold the greens, one by one, over the kitchen sink, slashing the leaves from the stem with a knife. Then, toss away the stems and wash the leaves in the sink.

You can use a pair of kitchen scissors to trim the leaves from the stems, and then chop the leaves – all with the scissors. Wash the greens by hand, once in warm water, three times in cold to get rid of all the grit.

FOR LOVE OF GARLIC

Some on the Foods Staff just love garlic. They may even go so far as to think it belongs in every kind of food. In their opinion, the famous bread pudding soufflé at Commander's Palace in New Orleans would be perfect if only it had a little garlic in it.

To make sure you never run out, why not grow garlic in your backyard vegetable garden. You may question the wisdom of this, seeing as how it's so available in supermarkets. But homegrown just tastes better, and you can grow unusual types you can't find at most stores.

Garlic comes in three basic types.

- **Softneck garlic** is the strongest tasting and most familiar. Each bulb produces both an inner and outer layer of cloves and is the kind you use for decorative braiding.

- **Stiffneck garlic** forms a single layer of milder tasting cloves and also sends up a coiled spike of bulblets that are perfect for stir-frying.

- **Elephant garlic** gets its name from its huge cloves, more than twice the size of the other types of garlic. It has a mild taste, too.

You can order all three types from Johnny's Selected Seeds, (207) 437-4301, or Burpee, 1-800-888-1447. Or you can plant cloves bought at the supermarket.

Plant garlic cloves in October or November. A good rule is to put them in the ground after your first frost. You can grow garlic where it seldom frosts, but your harvested bulbs will likely be smaller. Break each bulb into individual cloves. Plant the cloves, pointed end up, about 2 inches deep and 6 inches apart in fertile, well-drained soil. You may want to stir a teaspoon of cottonseed meal into each hole at planting. But Holland Bulb Booster would probably do fine. Make sure the bed receives plenty of sun. Mulch with an inch of pine straw, shredded leaves, or shredded bark.

Leaves appear in late winter. Harvest the bulbs in summer when the foliage starts yellowing and flopping over. Brush off the soil and then dry the bulbs by hanging them in a braid or laying them on a screen. Store in a cool, dry, well-ventilated place. They should keep for four to six months.

And what should you do with your home-grown bounty? Here's a recipe anybody can do.

Roasted Garlic: You'll need a head of garlic, a garlic roaster or aluminum foil, olive oil, and a knife. Cut off the pointed end of the head, leaving outer covering intact; then place garlic in the roaster dish or on a piece of aluminum foil, cut side up. Drizzle garlic with olive oil, cover with the roaster lid or wrap in foil; bake at 425° for 30 minutes. After it cools, squeeze the pulp from the cloves. It's delicious spread on bread dipped in a little olive oil.

DECEMBER

Dinner at The White House

Unwrap our gift to you this season – a Christmas of family and memories. Charles and Mary White of Birmingham, Alabama, share their traditions, and we share our favorite suggestions to make the holidays more fun – and maybe a little less hectic.

Supper Club Celebration

Serves 12

Hot Burgundy Cider **Party Mix**
Miniature Crab Cake Sandwiches
Caramelized Shallot Salad
Crown Pork Roast With Cranberry-Pecan Stuffing
Carrot Soufflés **Steamed Green Beans With Herb Butter**
Cream Puffs **Berliner Kranse**

The Whites' supper club menu is easy to recreate. Friends arrive to the welcoming aroma of hot cider. Mary serves some of the Party Mix with the cider and packages the rest in bags so no guest leaves empty-handed. Our make-ahead tips with each recipe will help you enjoy dinner in the dining room with your guests – not in the kitchen.

Hot Burgundy Cider

2 cups water
2 family-size tea bags
3 quarts apple cider
½ cup lemon juice
1 cup sugar
6 whole allspice
6 whole cloves
6 (3-inch) sticks cinnamon
6 whole star anise
1 (1-liter) bottle Burgundy
Garnishes: lemon slices, cinnamon sticks

• **Bring** 2 cups water to a boil in a large Dutch oven; remove from heat, and add tea bags. Cover tea, and let stand 5 minutes; remove tea bags, squeezing gently, and discard.
• **Add** cider and next 6 ingredients to Dutch oven; bring to a boil over high heat. Reduce heat, and simmer 10 minutes; remove and discard spices. Stir in wine; cook just until thoroughly heated. Ladle into mugs; garnish, if desired. **Yield:** 4½ quarts.

Party Mix

1 cup butter or margarine, melted
1 tablespoon Worcestershire sauce
1 teaspoon curry powder
½ teaspoon garlic salt
⅛ teaspoon hot sauce
6 cups corn chips
4 cups cheese crackers
3 cups mixed nuts
6 cups popped popcorn
1½ cups walnut pieces

• **Combine** first 5 ingredients in a bowl, stirring well.
• **Combine** corn chips and remaining 4 ingredients in a large roasting pan; add butter mixture, stirring to coat.
• **Bake** at 250° for 1 hour, stirring every 15 minutes. Spread on paper towels to cool. **Yield:** 16 cups.

Miniature Crab Cake Sandwiches

2 cups biscuit mix
1 teaspoon dried dillweed
1 (8-ounce) carton sour cream
½ cup butter or margarine, melted
Miniature Crab Cakes

• **Combine** first 4 ingredients, stirring until blended. Turn dough out onto a lightly floured surface, and knead lightly 5 or 6 times.
• **Roll** dough to ½-inch thickness; cut with a 1-inch round cutter, and place on lightly greased baking sheets.
• **Bake** at 450° for 6 to 8 minutes or until lightly browned. Cool.
• **Split** biscuits, and place a Miniature Crab Cake in each. Serve with tartar sauce. **Yield:** 4½ dozen.

Miniature Crab Cakes

1 pound fresh lump crabmeat
½ cup fine, dry breadcrumbs
2 tablespoons mayonnaise
2 teaspoons Old Bay seasoning
2 tablespoons chopped fresh parsley

• **Drain** crabmeat, removing any bits of shell. Combine crabmeat, breadcrumbs, and remaining ingredients; shape into 1-inch patties, and place on lightly greased baking sheets.
• **Bake** at 400° for 8 to 10 minutes or until golden. **Yield:** 4½ dozen.

"It's time for us to make our own traditions. We no longer travel to South Carolina or Mississippi to our parents' homes. Our families come to see us."

Mary White

Like many young families, Mary and Charles are striving to build traditions, to create a home of love, security, and values for their children. This year, they're staying home to decorate, entertain friends, and celebrate as a family.

Charles and Mary White invited us to share their first Christmas in their new Birmingham home – and to be part of a family celebration for Elizabeth, 7, Matthew, 3½, and Virginia, 18 months. Their family traditions incorporate beloved memories from Mary's childhood, baking from family recipes, hosting parties for friends, and repeating special rituals. They start the first Sunday in Advent, when Charles lights an Advent candle and reads a Bible passage to the family. "We turn out the lights," Mary says. "The children all look forward to this time of just our family being together."

Other rituals are whimsical reminders of the magic Christmas holds for little ones. "We do special things like putting shoes at the fireplace for Santa's elves to fill with candy," adds Mary. "And we put out 'reindeer food' on the steps." Elizabeth and Matthew, with a little help from their mother, make the reindeer snack of straw and Cheerios. Santa's cookie plate is a treasured gift from the children's paternal grandmother.

"Every year, my mother and I make cookies from my grandmother's recipes," says Mary. Tatti Samuelson, Mary's mother, visiting from Greenville, South Carolina, makes her mother's special Christmas Berliner Kranse (see recipe on page 311). "And we keep my childhood tradition of going to church on Christmas Eve, then reading the Christmas story before we hang stockings."

Of their family traditions, both old and new, giving is the most important. Charles says, "As a child, I learned from my grandfather that those who are blessed should share with others. Hopefully, somehow what we do with our own children now will help them make that connection."

The Whites have adopted a family every Christmas since Elizabeth was a toddler. "We shop and fill their list," Mary says. "It's really fun, and the children learn the joy of helping others."

And Mary helps Elizabeth give a party, complete with cake, to celebrate the birth of Jesus. This year, she and Elizabeth are hosting her daughter's Bible club. "I got a list of needy children from a Civitans child development center," Mary says. "We asked each girl in the club to bring an unwrapped gift. The party activity is wrapping the gifts for the children. We read the Christmas story and share a birthday cake. We don't have gift bags for the girls or anything like that. We want them to know what it is to give, not always to receive." Charles says, "There's no greater gift than to make someone else happy at Christmas. Giving out of love is what Christmas is all about."

Decorations That Say Welcome

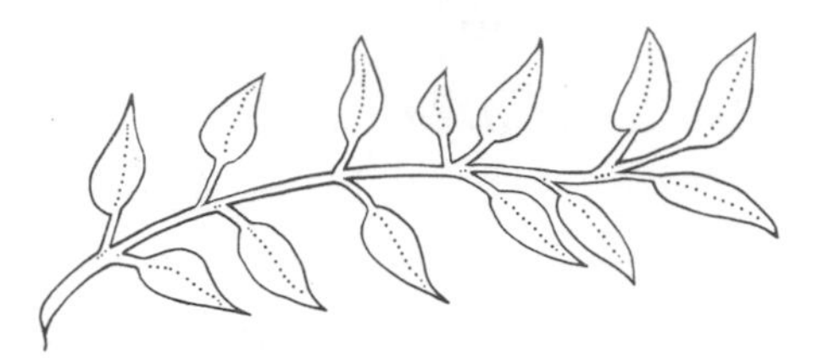

It wouldn't seem like Christmas without festive decorations at the entry of your home. Here we give several suggestions to welcome friends.

▪ **Framing Your Entry:** Mother Nature can lend a hand to frame your entry way. Lengths of woody grapevine can wrap a column and appear to grow up and across a porch. Magnolia leaves inserted among the vines will bring them alive. Sprays of possumhaw add shining red berries to the decor.

▪ **Decor Express:** When there's much to do, purchasing a ready-made wreath from a Christmas tree lot is a real time-saver. You can personalize it by attaching ribbon and greenery. Select ribbon in traditional holiday colors or choose shades that coordinate with your home's exterior. If your door is protected by a porch or overhang, you can use any kind of ribbon. But if the areas you're decorating are open to the elements, choose a waterproof ribbon that's made for exterior use.

▪ **Door Decor:** Take cuttings of various kinds of greenery like elaeagnus, holly, cedar, juniper, boxwood, smilax, and nandina; collect pinecones and various kinds of colorful berries. Hang a wreath on your door, and attach the extra pieces of greenery with florist wire. Start at one point, such as the upper right corner or lower left, and position several long pieces so that they extend from the point you've chosen. Use clippers to shape and trim excess foliage or twigs. Now open the door to see if you can easily step inside the house. Make a plump bow and wire it to the wreath. Next, work shorter cuttings of other materials under the ribbon and among the longer pieces of greenery. Step back, checking to see if the wreath appears well-balanced. If it doesn't, you can quickly add a few pieces where needed.

▪ **Light the Way:** Use lanterns made of glass hurricane shades, terra-cotta pots, red candles, and greenery to highlight the front steps or to illuminate a pathway to your home. First cover the pot's drainage hole with tape; then fill the pot with sand. Place a red pillar candle securely down into the sand and cover it with a glass hurricane shade. Tuck clusters of magnolia leaves around the edge of the pot. If you use yucca leaves, snip off the sharp tips of the spearlike foliage. Magnolia and yucca leaves are good choices because they won't wilt once you've lit the candles.

▪ **Garden in a Pot:** Choose a large container to serve as a base for a distinctive arrangement. Fill the pot with plants such as white ornamental kale and autumn fern, and insert 3- and 4-foot branches of possumhaw into the center to give the arrangement height. Encircle your container with slender grapevines. Then add color by inserting the berries of holly, nandina, or Carolina moonseed among the vines.

Caramelized Shallot Salad

(pictured on page 295)

Caramelize the shallots, make the dressing, and wash the greens a day ahead.

2 pounds shallots
1 cup chicken broth
2 tablespoons brown sugar
½ cup balsamic vinegar
2 cloves garlic, minced
½ teaspoon salt
½ teaspoon freshly ground pepper
¾ cup olive oil
2 heads romaine lettuce
2 heads Bibb lettuce
2 heads Belgian endive
12 radicchio leaves
2 (4-ounce) packages crumbled blue cheese

• **Place** shallots in a large skillet; add broth and brown sugar. Cover and cook over medium heat 25 minutes or until shallots are tender, stirring occasionally with a rubber spatula.
• **Uncover,** reduce heat, and simmer 20 minutes or until shallots are golden, stirring often. Carefully transfer shallots to a large shallow dish.
• **Whisk** together vinegar and next 3 ingredients; add oil in a slow, steady stream, whisking constantly. Reserve ½ cup mixture; pour remaining vinegar mixture over shallots. Cover and chill 8 hours.
• **Tear** romaine and Bibb lettuces, and shred 6 small endive leaves; toss with reserved ½ cup vinegar mixture.
• **Arrange** whole endive leaves, lettuces, and radicchio leaves on individual serving plates; drain shallots, and place in radicchio leaves. Sprinkle with blue cheese. **Yield:** 12 servings.

CROWN PORK ROAST WITH CRANBERRY-PECAN STUFFING

(pictured on pages 294 and 295)

1 tablespoon salt
1 tablespoon pepper
2 teaspoons dried thyme
1 (16-rib) crown pork roast, trimmed
2 cups Cranberry-Pecan Stuffing
¼ cup butter or margarine
⅓ cup all-purpose flour
2 (14½-ounce) cans ready-to-serve chicken broth
2 tablespoons orange liqueur *
2 tablespoons grated orange rind
¼ teaspoon salt
¼ teaspoon pepper
Garnishes: kumquat leaves, sugared kumquats, grape clusters, crabapples

• **Combine** first 3 ingredients; rub over all sides of roast.
• **Fold** a piece of aluminum foil into an 8-inch square; place on a rack in a roasting pan. Place roast, bone ends up, on foil-lined rack.
• **Bake** at 350° for 1 hour.
• **Spoon** 2 cups Cranberry-Pecan Stuffing into center of roast; cover with a 12-inch square of heavy-duty foil, and fold over tips of ribs.
• **Bake** at 350° for 1½ hours or until a meat thermometer registers 160°. Remove foil; let roast stand 15 minutes before slicing.
• **Pour** pan drippings into a skillet; add butter, and cook over medium heat until butter melts. Add flour, whisking until smooth; cook, whisking constantly, until caramel colored.
• **Stir** in chicken broth and next 4 ingredients; cook, whisking constantly, until smooth and thickened. Serve with roast. Garnish, if desired. **Yield:** 12 servings.

Note: To make sugared fruit, sprinkle 4 envelopes unflavored gelatin over 4 cups warm water; stir with a wire whisk until gelatin dissolves. Dip fruit into gelatin mixture, shaking to remove excess; sprinkle all sides of fruit with superfine sugar, covering completely. Place on baking sheets; let stand 30 minutes or until dry and firm.

Cranberry-Pecan Stuffing

You can make the stuffing the day before the party. Place it in a large bowl; cover and chill until ready to bake. If not preparing a roast, spoon all stuffing into two lightly greased 11- x 7- x 1½-inch baking dishes; bake as directed.

2 cups dried cranberries
1 cup orange liqueur *
2 pounds mild ground pork sausage
4 cups coarsely chopped celery
1½ cups chopped onion
½ cup butter or margarine
2 (14½-ounce) cans ready-to-serve chicken broth
1 teaspoon salt
½ teaspoon pepper
1 teaspoon dried thyme
2 (6-ounce) packages pork stuffing mix
2 tablespoons grated orange rind
2 cups chopped pecans

• **Combine** cranberries and liqueur in a small saucepan; bring to a boil over medium-high heat. Remove from heat, and set aside.
• **Brown** sausage in a large skillet, stirring until it crumbles; drain, reserving 2 tablespoons drippings in skillet. Set sausage aside.
• **Add** celery and onion to reserved drippings; cook over medium-high heat 10 minutes, stirring constantly. Add butter and next 4 ingredients; cook, stirring constantly, 3 minutes or until butter melts.
• **Combine** the cranberry mixture, sausage, stuffing mix and seasoning packet, orange rind, and pecans in a large bowl, stirring well.
• **Spoon** 2 cups stuffing into crown pork roast; spoon remainder of stuffing into a lightly greased 13- x 9- x 2-inch baking dish.
• **Cover** and bake at 350° for 20 minutes; uncover and bake 10 additional minutes or until lightly browned. **Yield:** 12 servings.

* You can substitute an equal amount of orange juice for liqueur.

CARROT SOUFFLÉS

(pictured on page 295)

Cook sliced carrots the day before the party; cover and chill. When you're ready to bake the soufflés, process all ingredients, spoon into dishes, and bake.

3 pounds carrots, sliced
1½ cups butter or margarine
6 large eggs
½ cup all-purpose flour
1 tablespoon baking powder
3 cups sugar
¼ teaspoon ground cinnamon

• **Cook** carrot in boiling water to cover 15 minutes or until tender; drain.
• **Position** knife blade in food processor bowl; add carrot, butter, and remaining ingredients, and process until smooth, stopping once to scrape down sides.
• **Spoon** into 2 lightly greased 1½-quart soufflé or baking dishes.
• **Bake** at 350° for 1 hour or until set and lightly browned. Serve immediately. **Yield:** 12 servings.

HERB BUTTER

(pictured on page 295)

This butter develops better flavor if you make it a day ahead.

1 cup butter, softened
1 teaspoon dried marjoram
1 teaspoon dried rosemary, crushed
1 teaspoon dried thyme
⅛ teaspoon dried basil
⅛ teaspoon rubbed sage

• **Combine** all ingredients, stirring until blended. **Yield:** 1 cup.

■ If ever a dessert deserved a standing ovation, our holiday Cream Puff Tree certainly does. It's a fairytale confection, and the main ingredient is patience, not professional pastry skills. Serve one or all four easy-to-make sauces with the airy puffs, and expect little hands at your table to reach up for an edible ornament.

CREAM PUFF TREE

(pictured on page 333)

A holiday Cream Puff Tree is a dazzling dessert to crown your holiday meal – it's spectacular in presentation and sensational in taste. A foil-wrapped cone provides the base for the elegant Cream Puff Tree. A simple sugar mixture provides the "glue" to attach the pastry puffs to the cone. Once the tree has cooled, remove the foil-wrapped plastic cone. (Leave cone in place if using tree as decoration.)

3 cups water
1½ cups butter
3 cups all-purpose flour
1½ teaspoons salt
12 large eggs
2 cups sugar
½ cup water
1 cup light corn syrup
Dark Chocolate Sauce
White Chocolate Sauce
Caramel Sauce
Raspberry Sauce

• **Bring** 3 cups water and butter to a boil in a large saucepan over medium-high heat; reduce heat to low.
• **Add** flour and salt, and beat with a wooden spoon until mixture leaves sides of pan. Remove from heat, and cool slightly.
• **Add** eggs, one at a time, beating until smooth.
• **Spoon** batter into a decorating bag fitted with a large star tip; pipe 1½-inch mounds, 2 inches apart, onto lightly greased baking sheets.
• **Bake** at 450° for 10 minutes; reduce heat to 375°, and bake 30 additional minutes or until puffed and golden. Pierce warm puffs on 1 side with a small sharp knife to let steam escape. Let cool.
• **Cover** a 12- or 15-inch plastic foam cone with aluminum foil, and place on an 18- x 12-inch piece of foil. Lightly grease foil.
• **Combine** sugar, ½ cup water, and corn syrup in a heavy saucepan; cook over low heat, stirring constantly, until sugar melts.
• **Bring** to a boil over high heat; cook, stirring constantly, 5 minutes or until mixture is light amber. Remove from heat; cool 2 minutes or until slightly thickened.
• **Dip** bottom of each cream puff into hot sugar mixture, using tongs; press puffs onto cone, starting at bottom and working toward top. Attach more cream puffs over first layer, hiding any gaps, and evenly shaping tree. If sugar mixture hardens, cook over low heat just until it melts. (Freeze any remaining cream puffs for another use.)
• **Drizzle** any remaining sugar mixture over top of tree, allowing it to flow down sides; cool.
• **Remove** and discard cone and foil. Serve with Dark Chocolate Sauce, White Chocolate Sauce, Caramel Sauce, or Raspberry Sauce. **Yield:** 12 servings.

Note: You can drop batter by rounded tablespoonfuls rather than piping it. Recipe makes about 3 dozen puffs.

Dark Chocolate Sauce

¾ cup whipping cream
8 (1-ounce) squares dark sweet or semisweet chocolate
2 tablespoons light corn syrup

• **Cook** whipping cream in a small heavy saucepan over medium-low heat just until thoroughly heated, stirring often. Add chocolate and corn syrup, stirring until chocolate melts. **Yield:** 1½ cups.

White Chocolate Sauce

¾ cup whipping cream
8 (1-ounce) squares white chocolate or baking bar
2 tablespoons light corn syrup

• **Cook** whipping cream in a small heavy saucepan over medium-low heat just until thoroughly heated, stirring often.
• **Add** white chocolate and corn syrup, stirring until chocolate melts. **Yield:** 1½ cups.

Caramel Sauce

This sauce can also be used over ice cream.

½ cup butter
1 cup sugar
½ cup whipping cream
2 teaspoons vanilla extract

• **Combine** butter and sugar in a small heavy saucepan; cook over medium heat, stirring constantly, until sugar melts.
• **Stir** in whipping cream. Bring to a boil, and cook 1 minute, stirring constantly. Stir in vanilla. **Yield:** 1¼ cups.

Raspberry Sauce

This ruby sauce can also be drizzled over ice cream and is especially pretty coupled with fresh berries.

2 (10-ounce) packages frozen raspberries, thawed
4 teaspoons cornstarch

• **Place** raspberries in container of an electric blender; process until smooth, stopping once to scrape down sides. Pour through a wire-mesh strainer into a small saucepan, discarding seeds. Stir in cornstarch.
• **Bring** to a boil over medium heat, stirring constantly; boil 1 minute, stirring constantly. Cool. **Yield:** 1 cup.

BERLINER KRANSE

Although some of the Whites' traditions are new, some have been passed down through generations. Baking from family recipes revives beloved memories from Mary's childhood. We share her grandmother's recipe for her favorite Christmas cookies. Share them with guests, but make sure to save some for Santa.

1 cup butter or margarine, softened
¼ cup butter-flavored shortening
1 cup sugar
2 large eggs
4 cups all-purpose flour
2 teaspoons grated orange rind
1 egg white
2 tablespoons sugar
Red candied cherries, cut into fourths
Chopped green citron

- **Beat** butter and shortening at medium speed with an electric mixer until creamy; gradually add 1 cup sugar, beating well.
- **Add** eggs, one at a time, beating until blended after each addition. Gradually add flour and orange rind, beating mixture at low speed after each addition.
- **Divide** dough into 4 portions; shape each portion into a ball, and wrap in plastic wrap. Chill 2 hours.
- **Remove** 1 ball of dough from refrigerator; divide dough into 18 portions. Roll each portion into a 6-inch rope. Loop each rope into a circle, crossing ends to resemble an "X"; place on ungreased cookie sheets.
- **Beat** egg white at high speed until foamy; gradually add 2 tablespoons sugar, beating until stiff peaks form and sugar dissolves.
- **Brush** egg white mixture over tops of cookies; arrange cherries and citron where dough overlaps to resemble holly, and lightly press into dough.
- **Bake** at 400° for 10 minutes or until golden (do not brown). Let stand on cookie sheets 5 minutes; transfer to wire racks to cool completely. Repeat with remaining dough. **Yield:** 6 dozen.

DECK THE HALLS

Come in to a house house full of holiday cheer. Here we give you decorating suggestions to get you in the Christmas spirit.

■ **Garland ABCs:** A swagged garland can bring holiday cheer to any entry hall. You can recreate this classic treatment of a stairway by using a cedar garland purchased from a florist or at a Christmas tree lot. First wrap colorful ribbon around a long piece of the garland and wire one end to the top of the banister. Swag the garland down the staircase and attach it with wire to the banister at regular intervals; use wire to connect additional lengths of the cedar as necessary. You can also swag a door or window with the garland. Insert small nails into molding above the window or door; then wire a length of the garland to the nails.

■ **A (Paper) White Christmas:** Unsurpassed for their fresh fragrance, paperwhites are available at garden centers throughout the holidays. Group several pots on the floor or a table. Place waterproof (not terracotta) saucers under each pot, and you can add water without moving them. If exposed to sunlight and kept evenly moist, they should last well into the New Year.

■ **Dining Room Decorations:** Seasonal fruit adds a festive touch to your dining room. Tie oranges and limes with French ribbon, stud with upholstery tacks, and then arrange inside a large serving bowl or soup tureen for a simple centerpiece. The crowning touch is a chandelier swag. To make your own, thread kumquats, crabapples, and dried orange slices on florist wire, and attach to the chandelier. Finish the look with streamers of French ribbon.

■ **The Stockings Are Hung:** Keep your Christmas stockings naturally shaped by weighting the feet with small bags of dried black-eyed peas that you can put to good use on New Year's Day.

■ **Trim a Mini-Tree:** You can create your own miniature Christmas tree from any cone-shaped plant. Velvet makes a pretty wrap for a pot containing a small conifer. Cut a piece of velvet that's large enough to surround the pot. Place a waterproof saucer in the center of the fabric, and set the pot in the saucer. Pull the velvet up around the pot, and secure it by wrapping wire around the container. Turn raw fabric edges to the inside. Cover the wire with ribbon, and add a generous bow. Wrap strands of Christmas lights around the foliage. Display the tree on a table that's protected by a trivet or waterproof mat. In a week or two, you can transplant the conifer to a container in your garden.

SWEET FINALES

Consider the indomitable marshmallow-topped sweet potato casserole. There it sits on your holiday plate, stealing the show from cornbread dressing and English peas. Why? It's like a dessert you eat *with* the main course. It's delicious but predictable. So let's celebrate the sweet potato as dessert in grand style.

CARAMEL-SWEET POTATO TORTE

6 large eggs, separated
1⅓ cups mashed cooked sweet potato
1½ teaspoons vanilla extract
¾ teaspoon ground cinnamon
½ teaspoon ground nutmeg
¼ teaspoon ground cloves
¾ cup chopped pecans
¾ cup chopped dates
¾ cup crushed round buttery crackers
½ teaspoon cream of tartar
¾ cup sugar
Caramel Whipped Cream Filling
Garnish: pecan halves

• **Beat** egg yolks and next 5 ingredients at medium speed with an electric mixer until smooth. Stir in pecans, dates, and crackers.
• **Beat** egg whites and cream of tartar at high speed until foamy. Add sugar, 2 tablespoons at a time, beating until soft peaks form and sugar dissolves. Fold into yolk mixture.
• **Line** three 8-inch round cakepans with wax paper; grease and flour wax paper. Pour batter into prepared pans.
• **Bake** at 350° for 25 minutes or until a wooden pick inserted in center comes out clean.
• **Cool** in pans on wire racks 10 minutes. Remove from pans, peeling off wax paper; cool on wire racks.
• **Spread** Caramel Whipped Cream Filling between layers and on top of cake. Garnish, if desired. Chill 3 to 4 hours. **Yield:** 1 (3-layer) torte.

Caramel Whipped Cream Filling

2 tablespoons butter
1 tablespoon all-purpose flour
⅔ cup firmly packed brown sugar
⅓ cup light corn syrup
2 tablespoons half-and-half
1½ cups whipping cream

• **Melt** butter in a heavy saucepan over low heat; whisk in flour until smooth. Cook 1 minute, whisking constantly. Stir in brown sugar and corn syrup; cook 5 minutes, whisking constantly.
• **Remove** from heat; cool 15 minutes. Gradually whisk in half-and-half.
• **Beat** whipping cream at high speed with an electric mixer until soft peaks form; fold into caramel mixture. **Yield:** about 4 cups.

SWEET POTATO CHEESECAKE

1½ cups graham cracker crumbs
⅓ cup chopped pecans
3 tablespoons sugar
¼ teaspoon pumpkin pie spice
⅓ cup butter or margarine, melted
1 (16-ounce) carton cream-style cottage cheese
2½ (8-ounce) packages cream cheese, softened
¾ cup sugar
1 teaspoon grated orange rind
1 teaspoon pumpkin pie spice
¼ teaspoon salt
3 large eggs
2 cups mashed cooked sweet potato
1 (16-ounce) carton sour cream
⅓ cup orange marmalade
Garnishes: orange rind strips, fresh mint

• **Combine** first 5 ingredients in a bowl, stirring until blended; press in bottom and 1 inch up sides of a 10-inch springform pan.
• **Bake** at 350° for 6 minutes; cool.
• **Beat** cottage cheese at medium speed with an electric mixer until smooth. Add cream cheese and next 4 ingredients; beat at medium speed until mixture is smooth.
• **Add** eggs, one at a time, beating until blended after each addition. Fold in mashed sweet potato, and pour into prepared crust.
• **Bake** at 300° for 1½ hours. Combine sour cream and marmalade, stirring until blended; spread over cheesecake. Bake 10 additional minutes; cool on a wire rack. Cover and chill 8 hours. Garnish, if desired. **Yield:** 12 servings.

Lisa Varner
Fairborn, Ohio

Coffee Break

Take a coffee break. We mean a real one, not the usual last drops from an hours-old pot and a half-eaten candy bar from the fridge. Set aside time to spend with a friend, sipping this spiked cup-o'-joe and nibbling these hint-of-coffee meringue cookies.

You can make Chocolate-Dipped Coffee Kisses a day or two ahead and keep them at room temperature in an airtight container. The recipe makes three dozen, so you might want to invite a few more friends. Just double or triple the Orange Coffee, and make it in a Dutch oven.

Chocolate-Dipped Coffee Kisses

3 egg whites
¼ teaspoon cream of tartar
1 tablespoon instant coffee granules
1 cup sugar
½ teaspoon vanilla extract
½ cup chopped walnuts
3 (2-ounce) squares chocolate candy coating, melted
½ cup finely chopped walnuts, toasted

• **Combine** first 3 ingredients; beat at high speed with an electric mixer just until foamy.
• **Add** sugar, 1 tablespoon at a time, beating until stiff peaks form and sugar dissolves (2 to 4 minutes). Stir in vanilla and ½ cup walnuts. Drop by tablespoonfuls onto brown paper-lined cookie sheets.
• **Bake** at 225° for 1 hour and 15 minutes. Turn oven off, and leave cookies in oven 2 hours.
• **Dip** bottom of each cookie in melted coating; dip again in toasted walnuts. Place on wax paper until dry. **Yield:** 3 dozen.

Sandi Pichon
Slidell, Louisiana

Orange Coffee

4 sugar cubes
1 large orange
2 tablespoons butter or margarine
¼ cup sugar
¼ cup orange-flavored liqueur
½ cup brandy
4 cups brewed coffee
Garnishes: sweetened whipped cream, orange zest

• **Rub** sugar cubes over surface of orange until cubes are light yellow; place cubes in a large saucepan. Cut orange in half, and squeeze juice into saucepan, discarding orange halves; add butter and ¼ cup sugar.
• **Cook** over medium-high heat until sugar dissolves. Add liqueur and brandy, and bring to a boil. Remove from heat.
• **Ignite** mixture carefully with a long match, and let burn until flames die. Stir in coffee, and pour into cups. Garnish, if desired. **Yield:** about 5 cups.

Mike Singleton
Memphis, Tennessee

How to Set Up a Coffee Bar

For a warming touch at your holiday gathering, treat your guests to a coffee bar, and let them choose the flavors.

To set up a coffee bar, place a coffeemaker on a countertop or sideboard, where you'll have room for cups, saucers, spoons, and a variety of flavoring ingredients. For brewing basics see our tips at right. In addition to plenty of fresh coffee, serve liqueurs to add a spirited kick to coffee. A well-stocked coffee bar should include the following:

Liqueurs
Kahlúa (coffee flavor)
Crème de cacao (chocolate flavor)
Truffles (a mild chocolate flavor)
Amaretto (almond flavor)
Cointreau (orange flavor)
Grand Marnier (orange flavor)
Irish Mist (whiskey-honey flavor)
Frangelico (hazelnut flavor)

Other Ingredients
Half-and-half
Granulated raw sugar
Sugar cubes
Chocolate shavings
Ground nutmeg
Cinnamon sticks
Whipped cream

For Fresh Brewed Coffee

Follow these guidelines for a perfect cup every time.

▪ Remove residual coffee oils by cleaning and rinsing coffeemaker with hot water before each use.

▪ Start coffee with fresh cold water. Water high in minerals or chlorine or treated with chemical softeners won't make as flavorful coffee. Use bottled water if you don't like the way your water tastes.

▪ Select a variety of flavored coffees as well as a few basic types. And be sure to include some varieties of decaffeinated coffees.

▪ When possible, buy coffee beans and grind them just before use. Store beans in an airtight container in the refrigerator two to three weeks or in the freezer two to three months. Grind the beans (at home or where you buy them) as directed for your coffeemaker. If the grind is too coarse or too fine you won't get the best flavor.

▪ Use two level tablespoons (one standard coffee measure) for each six ounces of water. Adjust to taste.

Cookie Traditions

Cookies are the heart of holiday baking. Here are some of our long-time favorite recipes to help you start your own cookie tradition.

CHRISTMAS SPRITZ COOKIES

Bertha Bareuther, 92, has been making these cookies at Christmastime since her children were small. "We give containers of them as gifts. Our friends really look forward to them," she says. Butter gives the cookies their rich flavor.

1 cup butter, softened
1 cup sugar
2 large eggs
2 teaspoons vanilla extract
2½ cups all-purpose flour
⅛ teaspoon salt
10 drops of yellow liquid food coloring
Red and green decorator candies

• **Beat** butter at medium speed with an electric mixer until creamy; gradually add sugar, beating well. Add eggs and vanilla, beating until blended.
• **Combine** flour and salt; add to butter mixture, beating at low speed until blended. Add food coloring, beating until blended.
• **Use** a cookie gun with a bar-shaped disc, and shape dough into 1½-inch cookies following manufacturer's instructions; or shape dough into 1-inch balls, and flatten to ¼-inch thickness with a flat-bottomed glass. Place on greased cookie sheets; sprinkle with candies.
• **Bake** at 375° for 8 minutes or until edges are lightly browned. Transfer to wire racks to cool. **Yield:** about 8 dozen.

Bertha Bareuther
Cambridge, Maryland

GINGER COOKIES

Eloise Pope, who is known for her unique "water-whipped pastry" ("From Our Kitchen to Yours," Annual Recipes, 1995, *page 246), has been making 1,500 of these delicious cookies each Christmas for almost 50 years. "I am confident that I have made at least 50,000 of these," she reports. Her cookies are so popular that the neighborhood kids call her the "Ginger Cookie Lady."*

1½ cups shortening
2 cups sugar
2 large eggs
½ cup molasses
4 cups all-purpose flour
2 teaspoons baking soda
1 teaspoon ground cinnamon
1 teaspoon ground cloves
1 teaspoon ground ginger
Sugar

• **Combine** first 9 ingredients in a large mixing bowl; beat at medium speed with an electric mixer until mixture is blended.
• **Shape** into 1-inch balls, and roll in additional sugar. Place on greased cookie sheets, and flatten slightly with a flat-bottomed glass.
• **Bake** at 375° for 8 to 10 minutes. Transfer to wire racks to cool. **Yield:** 7 dozen.

Eloise Pope
Milton, West Virginia

FRUITCAKE COOKIES

Carrie Treichel, 90, has been making these cookies since 1949 "because everyone likes them so much." She cooks for herself and friends, paints prize-winning pictures, makes quilts, and plays the organ.

½ cup shortening
1 cup firmly packed light brown sugar
1 large egg
¼ cup buttermilk
2 cups all-purpose flour
½ teaspoon baking soda
½ teaspoon baking powder
½ teaspoon salt
1 cup chopped dates
1 cup chopped pecans
1 cup chopped candied cherries
5 dozen pecan halves (optional)

• **Combine** first 3 ingredients in a large bowl, stirring well; stir in buttermilk.
• **Combine** flour and next 3 ingredients; stir into brown sugar mixture. Stir in dates, pecans, and cherries; cover and chill 1 hour.
• **Drop** dough by rounded teaspoonfuls, 2 inches apart, onto lightly greased cookie sheets. Top each cookie with a pecan half, if desired.
• **Bake** at 375° for 10 minutes or until lightly browned. Transfer to wire racks to cool. **Yield:** 5 dozen.

Carrie Treichel
Johnson City, Tennessee

Crazy for Cookies

■ Use shiny cookie sheets for baking. Dark pans absorb more heat and can cause overbrowning on the cookie bottoms.

■ Use vegetable cooking spray or solid shortening (not butter or margarine) to grease cookie sheets.

■ For chewy cookies, choose the low range of the baking time.

■ To loosen cookies that have been left on the cookie sheet too long, return them to a 350° oven for 1 minute; then remove cookies from the cookie sheet immediately.

BENNE SEED WAFERS

Benne seed (sesame seed) wafers are traditional in Charleston, South Carolina. Clementa "Ment" Florio makes huge cans of these papery thin, crisp cookies every year for Christmas. "Make the cookies as thin as possible," Ment advises.

½ cup sesame seeds
½ cup butter or margarine, softened
1 cup sugar
1 large egg
½ teaspoon vanilla extract
1¾ cups all-purpose flour
2 teaspoons baking powder
½ teaspoon baking soda
½ teaspoon salt

• **Cook** sesame seeds in a heavy skillet over medium heat 5 minutes or until toasted, stirring often.
• **Beat** butter at medium speed with an electric mixer until creamy; gradually add sugar, beating well. Stir in sesame seeds, egg, and vanilla.
• **Combine** flour and remaining 3 ingredients; stir into butter mixture. Cover and chill at least 1 hour.
• **Shape** dough into ½-inch balls, and place on lightly greased cookie sheets. Flatten to 1/16-inch thickness with floured fingers or a flat-bottomed glass.
• **Bake** at 325° for 10 minutes or until lightly browned. Transfer to wire racks to cool. **Yield:** 10 dozen.

Note: Purchase sesame or benne seeds in bulk at natural food stores; store leftovers in the freezer.

Clementa Florio
Wadmalaw Island, South Carolina

COOKIE SWAP

The hustle and bustle that accompany December rarely leave time for baking more than a batch or two of your family's favorite holiday cookies. But a cookie swap party a few weeks before Christmas ensures that you'll have plenty of homemade goodies, while spending only an hour or so in the kitchen.

Here's how the cookie swap works. Each person involved in the cookie swap bakes a batch of her favorite holiday cookies. Sources for the sweets range from old family standbys to the newest magazine features. Cookies are shared at a festive get-together, and participants leave with a variety of treats to keep their cookie jar full through the holiday season. Your own cookie swap party can be as simple or as detailed as you'd like. Here's how to begin.

▪ Choose a theme for the cookie swap and carry it out in the invitations and the recipe booklet. A gingerbread man is a great start. Use a gingerbread man cookie cutter to make a pattern design for the invitation and to decorate the recipe booklet.

▪ Include a blank recipe card with the invitation to the party so that you can compile a "Cookie Swap Recipe Booklet" after the holidays. (The hostess or hostesses are responsible for the recipe booklet.)

▪ Have enough of the same size cookie containers for each person. Baskets work well, so do decorated tins and Shaker boxes. Line the containers with grease-proof paper like cellophane, wax paper, or aluminum foil.

▪ To make it easier for your guests to carry home their cookie-filled containers, place the containers in paper or plastic bags and label each with a name tag. (You can make the name tags ahead.)

▪ Take turns hosting the party each year. Let a guest at the cookie swap volunteer to host the next one or draw a name from among guests, and designate her as the hostess for the next cookie swap.

▪ After the cookie swap and the holidays, assemble the guests' cookie recipes for the booklet. Mail the booklet to the guests who attended the cookie swap.

living *light*

TINY TEMPTATIONS

Even if you refuse to eat anything low fat during the holidays, rethink dessert. A selection of small sweets instead of a large cake or pie diminishes the temptation to overdo. Display these edible works of art for a tea or dessert buffet. Make a variety, and mix them on small dessert plates as an understated finish to your next dinner party. Or place an assortment in a beautiful box for a special gift. The only thing reduced in these desserts is their size. So enjoy them in moderation.

ORANGE FILLING

Each of these fillings has about 80 calories and 7 fat grams per 2-tablespoon serving. You can use them to fill tarts, Chocolate-Coffee Cones, or Praline Horns.

1 (8-ounce) package cream cheese, softened
¼ cup sifted powdered sugar
1½ teaspoons vanilla extract
¼ cup crème de Grand Marnier *
½ cup whipping cream

• **Combine** first 3 ingredients; beat at high speed with an electric mixer until light and fluffy. Add liqueur to cream cheese mixture, beating at medium speed until blended.
• **Beat** whipping cream at high speed until soft peaks form; gently fold into cream cheese mixture. **Yield:** about 2½ cups.

* You can substitute Irish cream liqueur for the Grand Marnier.

Almond Filling: Omit vanilla and Grand Marnier; add ¼ cup almond liqueur.

Chocolate Filling: Omit Grand Marnier; add 4 (1-ounce) squares semisweet chocolate, melted.

Coffee Filling: Omit vanilla and Grand Marnier; add ¼ cup coffee liqueur.

PRALINE HORNS

¼ cup unsalted butter
¼ cup firmly packed light brown sugar
¼ cup light corn syrup
1 teaspoon vanilla extract
½ teaspoon almond extract
¼ cup sliced almonds, coarsely chopped
3 tablespoons all-purpose flour
2 recipes Almond Filling (see recipe)

• **Combine** first 3 ingredients in a small saucepan; bring to a boil over medium-high heat, stirring constantly. Remove from heat, stirring until sugar dissolves. Stir in flavorings, almonds, and flour; let cool.
• **Drop** mixture by ½ teaspoonfuls, 3 inches apart, onto lightly greased cookie sheets (only 2 cookies on each sheet).
• **Bake** at 350° for 7 minutes or until browned; cool on cookie sheets 1 minute. Remove and quickly roll into cones. Cool completely on wire racks.
• **Pipe** or spoon Almond Filling into cones. **Yield:** 2½ dozen.

♥ Per horn (includes filling):
Calories 105 (70% from fat)
Fat 8.1g (4.9g saturated) Cholesterol 25mg
Sodium 40mg Carbohydrate 6.7g
Fiber 0.1g Protein 1.2g

CHOCOLATE-COFFEE CONES

A lot of the white chocolate adheres to the brush, so we've called for more chocolate than you'll really use.

6 (1-ounce) squares semisweet chocolate
12 (1-ounce) squares white baking chocolate
Coffee Filling (see recipe)

• **Cut** 9 (6-inch) circles from wax paper; cut circles in half, and shape each into a cone. Secure edges of cone with tape.
• **Place** semisweet chocolate in a small heavy-duty, zip-top plastic bag; seal and submerge in hot water until chocolate melts. Let cool until slightly thickened. Snip a tiny hole in one corner of bag; drizzle melted chocolate into lower 2 inches of each cone. Chill until firm.
• **Place** white chocolate in a 1-cup liquid measuring cup. Microwave at HIGH 1 to 2 minutes or until melted, stirring every 30 seconds; cool until slightly thickened. Brush a thin layer over semisweet chocolate inside each cone; chill until firm.

• **Pipe** or spoon Coffee Filling into cones; chill. Remove wax paper from cones just before serving. **Yield:** 1½ dozen.

❤ Per cone (includes filling):
Calories 111 (70% from fat)
Fat 8.4g (5.2g saturated) Cholesterol 23mg
Sodium 43mg Carbohydrate 6.9g
Fiber 0g Protein 1.4g

ORANGE TARTS

Use any flavor of filling and any shape tartlet tins for these tiny pastries.

3 cups all-purpose flour
½ cup sugar
1 cup butter
½ cup cold water
6 (1-ounce) squares semisweet chocolate, melted
Orange Filling (see recipe)
Garnish: orange zest

• **Combine** flour and sugar in a large bowl; cut in butter with pastry blender until crumbly. Sprinkle cold water, 1 tablespoon at a time, evenly over flour mixture; stir with a fork just until dry ingredients are moistened.
• **Divide** dough into 4 equal portions; wrap each in plastic wrap, and chill 8 hours.
• **Roll** each portion to ⅛-inch thickness on a lightly floured surface, and cut into 12 equal portions. Fit dough into 1- or 2-inch tartlet tins; trim excess pastry from edges, and prick bottoms with a fork. Place tins on a baking sheet.
• **Bake** at 400° for 10 to 15 minutes or until lightly browned. Cool in tins. Carefully remove from tins, and brush chocolate inside tart shells; pipe or spoon Orange Filling into shells; chill. Garnish, if desired. **Yield:** 4 dozen.

Diane Woodall
Houston, Texas

❤ Per tart (includes filling):
Calories 119 (58% from fat)
Fat 7.7g (4.8g saturated) Cholesterol 19mg
Sodium 56mg Carbohydrate 11.4g
Fiber 0.2g Protein 1.4g

MERINGUE MUSHROOMS

You can choose from several flavors of chocolate morsels at your local supermarket. Try mint flavored for variety.

3 egg whites
¼ teaspoon cream of tartar
⅛ teaspoon salt
¼ teaspoon vanilla extract
¼ teaspoon almond extract
½ cup superfine sugar
⅔ cup (4 ounces) semisweet chocolate morsels, melted
2 teaspoons cocoa

• **Combine** first 5 ingredients; beat at high speed with an electric mixer until foamy. Add sugar, 1 tablespoon at a time, beating until stiff peaks form and sugar dissolves (2 to 4 minutes).
• **Spoon** mixture into a decorating bag fitted with a large round tip. Pipe 32 (1¼-inch-wide) mounds to resemble mushroom caps and 32 (1-inch-tall) columns to resemble stems onto a parchment paper-lined baking sheet.
• **Bake** at 200° for 1 hour and 30 minutes; turn oven off. Let meringues stand in closed oven 2 hours.
• **Spread** a thin layer of melted chocolate on flat side of caps. Trim rounded end of stems to make flat; press against chocolate to attach stems to caps. Sprinkle lightly with cocoa. **Yield:** 32 mushrooms.

❤ Per mushroom: Calories 33 (28% from fat)
Fat 1g (0g saturated) Cholesterol 0mg
Sodium 15mg Carbohydrate 5.4g
Fiber 0g Protein 0.5g

BEST-DRESSED BERRIES

These delicate gems aren't just for the holidays. They're perfect for wedding receptions or any other special occasion.

1 (6-ounce) package white chocolate baking squares
24 large fresh strawberries
6 (1-ounce) squares semisweet chocolate

• **Melt** white chocolate baking squares in a small heavy saucepan over low heat, stirring constantly. Dip each strawberry into melted chocolate, and place on wax paper-lined cookie sheets. Chill until firm.
• **Melt** semisweet chocolate in a small heavy saucepan over low heat, stirring constantly. Dip 1 side of each coated strawberry halfway into chocolate; dip half of opposite side, forming a "V" with chocolate. Chill until firm.
• **Spoon** remaining semisweet chocolate into a small heavy-duty, zip-top plastic bag; seal. (If necessary, submerge bag in hot water until piping consistency.)
• **Prick** a tiny hole in one corner of bag with a round wooden pick; pipe a bow tie and 3 buttons onto strawberries to resemble tuxedos. Chill until firm. **Yield:** 2 dozen.

❤ Per strawberry: Calories 76 (48% from fat)
Fat 4.3g (2.5g saturated) Cholesterol 0mg
Sodium 7mg Carbohydrate 9.9g
Fiber 0.4g Protein 0.8g

A BAKER'S DOZEN

Take your party over the top with our 13 ways to WOW. Turn an appetizer cheese spread into a work of art, let your guests see their names in lights, or let onions bloom alongside the entrée. Or to give guests an extravagant finale, make them a Gift Box Cake. You can wrap it up in no time. Here, we show you how.

1. Boursin Cheese Basket: Prepare 3 recipes of Buttery Boursin Cheese Spread (recipe below). Press 6 cups spread in an 8-inch round cakepan; chill cakepan and remaining spread. Unmold onto a serving plate; fit decorating bag with basket-weave tip, and spoon remaining spread into bag. Pipe basket-weave pattern around sides; pipe ruffle around top, using smooth side of tip. Form handle from florist wire, attaching fresh herbs to handle with florist tape. Serve with assorted vegetables.

BUTTERY BOURSIN CHEESE SPREAD

1 clove garlic, minced
2 (8-ounce) packages cream cheese, softened
1 cup butter or margarine, softened
1 teaspoon dried oregano
1/4 teaspoon dried basil
1/4 teaspoon dried dillweed
1/4 teaspoon dried marjoram
1/4 teaspoon dried thyme
1/4 teaspoon pepper

• **Position** knife blade in food processor bowl; add all ingredients, and process until smooth, stopping once to scrape down sides. **Yield:** about 3 cups.

2. Miniature Topiary Place Cards: For animal shapes, cut 1/2-inch-thick plastic foam with 3- to 4-inch cookie cutters or use plastic foam cows or balls; glue sphagnum moss to shapes. Fill tiny decorative clay pots with plastic foam. Glue moss to cover foam. Attach cutouts to pots with cinnamon sticks. Glue place cards to pots.

3. Personalized Stocking Place Cards: Decorate miniature stockings with lace, ribbon, and trim. Paint names on stockings, and stuff with candy and small gifts.

4. Wine and Cheese: Arrange chives, basil leaves, and thin slices of grapes over a Brie round in a grapevine design. Sprinkle 3 envelopes unflavored gelatin over 3 cups dry white wine in a saucepan. Let stand 1 minute. Cook over low heat, stirring constantly, until gelatin dissolves; cool. Spoon gelatin over cheese in a thin coat; chill 10 minutes. Repeat procedure with remaining gelatin. Cover loosely and chill. Serve with grapes and crackers.

5. Personalized Candle Lights: Insert a small piece of cardboard into a tiny decorative bag; fold bag flat. Cut out names and designs with a sharp knife. Remove cardboard, and open bags. Stabilize bags on table; insert tea candles, and light. Do not leave unattended.

6. Sweet Things in Small Packages: Wrap small gift boxes, bottom and tops separately, and line with decorative cellophane; fill with desserts. For some holiday cookie recipes see page 314.

7. Fancy Flatware: Set each place at your holiday table with a different flatware pattern, and let guests select the pattern that best matches their style.

8. Herb and Spice Tree: Glue fresh herbs, dried cranberries, whole nutmeg, cinnamon sticks, dried rosebuds, acorns, and tiny bows on a plastic foam cone for a beautiful centerpiece that remains fragrant up to one week.

9. Christmas Crackers: Decorate 6- to 7-inch cardboard tubes (from gift wrap or paper towels) with fabric, ribbon, and trim. Place small gifts such as chocolates, mints, and party favors in folds of cloth napkins, and insert into tubes. Have guests pull napkins out of tubes for a surprise.

10. Onion Mums: Peel an onion. Starting at root end, cut v-shaped petals around base of onion, taking care to cut outer layer only. Peel off large top portion of outer layer. Repeat cutting and peeling procedure just above last row of petals until all of onion is cut. Place onion in water, and store in refrigerator up to one day. Place on a lettuce-lined plate to add a festive touch to your table.

11. Dessert in a Nutshell: Melt 2 tablespoons butter and 2 tablespoons brown sugar in a skillet over low heat; add 2 sliced bananas, and cook until browned and glazed, stirring often. Add 2 tablespoons rum, if desired. Arrange ice cream and bananas in 2 coconut halves; sprinkle with toasted flaked coconut. **Yield:** 2 servings.

12. Gift Box Cake: This year, surprise your guests with a cake whimsically decorated as a gift box. It's sure to become a holiday tradition the entire family will want to help adorn. Recipe is on opposite page.

GIFT BOX CAKE

(pictured on cover)

Short on time? Make your cake with 2 (18.25-ounce) packages white cake mix and 4 (16-ounce) containers ready-to-spread frosting. The layers will be taller if you use cake mix. Make the gingerbread men using your favorite recipe or a gingerbread mix or buy the cookies from a bakery.

½ cup butter or margarine, softened
½ cup shortening
2 cups sugar
⅔ cup water
⅔ cup milk
3 cups all-purpose flour
1 tablespoon baking powder
1 teaspoon salt
2 tablespoons vanilla extract
1 teaspoon almond extract
6 egg whites
Powdered Sugar Frosting
3 (4.5-ounce) packages strawberry-flavored chewy fruit rolls by the foot
⅓ cup clear sparkling sugar or edible glitter *
8 gingerbread men

• **Beat** butter and shortening at medium speed with an electric mixer 2 minutes or until creamy; gradually add sugar, beating well.
• **Combine** water and milk. Combine flour, baking powder, and salt; add to butter mixture alternately with milk mixture, beginning and ending with flour mixture. Stir in vanilla and almond extracts.
• **Beat** egg whites at high speed until stiff peaks form; fold into batter. Pour into three greased and floured 8-inch square pans.
• **Bake** at 350° for 20 minutes or until a wooden pick inserted in center comes out clean. Cool in pans on wire racks 10 minutes; remove from pans, and cool on wire racks.
• **Set** aside 2 cups frosting.
• **Spread** ½ cup frosting into an 8-inch square on cake plate.
• **Spread** remaining 4½ cups frosting between cake layers and on top and sides of cake.
• **Unroll** fruit rolls (do not remove paper backing), and brush with water. Sprinkle with sparkling sugar or edible glitter; let dry 15 minutes.
• **Cut** 4 (12-inch) pieces from fruit rolls. Remove paper backing, and arrange on top and sides of cake, pressing gently into frosting, to resemble ribbon.
• **Spoon** ½ cup reserved frosting onto center of cake, forming a 3-inch mound.
• **Cut** remaining fruit rolls into 4-inch pieces, and remove paper backing. Fold each piece in half, resembling the loop of a bow; press cut ends into frosting mound, creating a large bow on top of cake. Place 2 gingerbread men on each side of cake.
• **Spoon** 1½ cups frosting into a decorating bag fitted with a large star tip. Pipe a border around the bottom edge of cake. **Yield:** 1 (8-inch) cake.

Powdered Sugar Frosting

2 cups shortening
1 teaspoon salt
1 teaspoon almond extract
1 teaspoon vanilla extract
3 (16-ounce) packages powdered sugar, sifted
1 cup evaporated milk

• **Combine** first 4 ingredients; beat at medium speed with a heavy-duty electric mixer until blended.
• **Add** powdered sugar alternately with milk, beating at low speed until blended after each addition. Beat at medium speed 8 minutes or until light and fluffy. **Yield:** 7 cups.

* Edible glitter is available at baking-supply stores.

Note: You can store frosting, covered, in refrigerator up to 2 weeks. If using a portable mixer, prepare the frosting in 2 batches.

13. Napkin Fanfare: Give your table flair with beautifully folded napkins by using our step-by-step instructions below.

• **Fold** and crease napkin as shown.

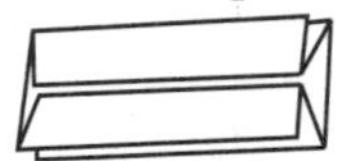

• **Fold** in half, keeping folded edges toward you.

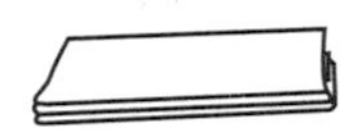

• **Fold** sides toward center as shown.

• **Lift** one fold, and press down center to form a triangle.

• **Repeat** with remaining folds.

• **Open** folds slightly; place napkin on plate or table. Drape with ribbon or decorative cord.

CRAZY OVER CRANBERRIES

Just before the holidays, the grocery stores stock up on fresh and canned cranberries. And, in a panic, so do you. If you still have a heap of the store-bought crop after the feast, use the leftovers in these refreshing recipes. We offer cookies and pastries you can freeze for later, so you don't have to look at the berries again for a few months. You'll also find the requisite leftover turkey sandwich, and a sweet pizza the kids will put away in no time.

TURKEY-CRANBERRY CROISSANT

1 (8-ounce) package cream cheese, softened
¼ cup orange marmalade
½ cup chopped pecans
6 large croissants, split
Lettuce leaves
1 pound thinly sliced cooked turkey
¾ cup whole-berry cranberry sauce

• **Combine** first 3 ingredients, stirring well. Spread evenly on cut sides of croissants.
• **Place** lettuce and turkey on croissant bottoms; spread with cranberry sauce, and cover with tops. **Yield:** 6 servings.

Patricia Jones
Fairmont, North Carolina

CRANBERRY POCKETS

1 (15-ounce) package refrigerated piecrusts
1 (8-ounce) carton soft cream cheese
⅓ cup sugar
½ cup chopped fresh cranberries
½ cup chopped pecans
1 teaspoon grated orange rind
2 tablespoons powdered sugar

• **Unfold** piecrusts, and press out fold lines. Cut each piecrust into 4 squares, discarding scraps.
• **Combine** cream cheese and next 4 ingredients; spread ¼ cup mixture onto each pastry square, leaving a ½-inch border. Moisten edges with water; fold pastry diagonally over filling, pressing edges to seal.
• **Crimp** edges with a fork. Place on lightly greased baking sheets.
• **Bake** at 350° for 15 to 18 minutes or until golden. Sprinkle with powdered sugar; serve warm or at room temperature. **Yield:** 8 servings.

Note: You can freeze unbaked pockets in airtight containers up to 1 month. Bake frozen pastries at 350° for 25 minutes or until golden.

CRANBERRY DESSERT PIZZAS

Use any leftover holiday cranberries in this recipe. (For perfect streusel stripes lay strips of wax paper on the pizzas before sprinkling the topping.)

3½ cups all-purpose flour, divided
2½ cups sugar, divided
2 teaspoons cream of tartar
1 teaspoon baking soda
½ teaspoon salt
1 cup butter or margarine, softened
2 large eggs
½ teaspoon ground cinnamon
4 cups fresh cranberries
½ cup orange juice
1 tablespoon cornstarch
¼ cup uncooked regular oats
¼ cup firmly packed light brown sugar
2 tablespoons butter or margarine, softened
¼ cup chopped pecans

• **Combine** 3 cups flour, 1 cup sugar, and next 3 ingredients; cut in 1 cup butter with pastry blender until crumbly. Stir in eggs with a fork until dry ingredients are moistened.
• **Shape** dough into a ball. Divide dough in half, and press into two greased 12-inch pizza pans.
• **Combine** ¼ cup sugar and cinnamon; sprinkle over dough.
• **Bake** at 350° for 15 minutes.
• **Combine** 1 cup sugar, cranberries, orange juice, and cornstarch in a saucepan, stirring well; bring to a boil over medium-high heat, stirring often. Cook 10 to 12 minutes or until thickened, stirring occasionally. Spread evenly over crusts.
• **Combine** remaining ½ cup flour, remaining ¼ cup sugar, oats, and brown sugar in a bowl; cut in 2 tablespoons butter with pastry blender until crumbly. Stir in pecans.
• **Cut** narrow strips of wax paper with scissors; lay at intervals over cranberry mixture. Sprinkle topping over pizzas; remove wax paper.
• **Bake** at 350° for 12 minutes; serve warm. **Yield:** 2 (12-inch) pizzas.

Agnes Stone
Ocala, Florida

Lighter-Than-Air Rolls

Lighten up your holidays with airy, easy yeast rolls. The feathery texture and delicate taste of Overnight Yeast Rolls belie their simple preparation – they require only one rising and no kneading. You can also make sweet rolls from the dough – Cinnamon Rolls and Orange Rolls are two delicious variations.

For faster results, 60-Minute Rolls will fill the house with the rich aroma of baking bread and grace your table with tasty, tender, flavorful results.

Overnight Yeast Rolls

2 packages active dry yeast
1 cup warm water (105° to 115°)
1 cup shortening
1 cup sugar
1 teaspoon salt
1 cup boiling water
2 large eggs
6 cups all-purpose flour

• **Combine** yeast and warm water in a 2-cup liquid measuring cup; let stand 5 minutes.
• **Place** shortening, sugar, and salt in a large mixing bowl. Add boiling water, and beat at medium speed with an electric mixer until smooth. Add eggs and yeast mixture, beating at low speed until blended; gradually beat in flour. Cover and chill 8 hours.
• **Shape** dough into 1-inch balls, and place 3 balls in each lightly greased muffin cup.
• **Cover** and let rise in a warm place (85°), free from drafts, 45 minutes or until doubled in bulk.
• **Bake** at 400° for 12 minutes or until lightly browned. **Yield:** 3 dozen.

Cinnamon Rolls: Divide chilled dough in half; roll each portion into a 12- x 10-inch rectangle. Brush each rectangle with 2 tablespoons melted butter. Combine ⅔ cup firmly packed light brown sugar, ½ cup raisins, and 1 tablespoon ground cinnamon; sprinkle evenly over dough rectangles. Starting with a long side, roll up, jellyroll fashion, pressing edges to seal. Cut logs into 1-inch slices, and place in a lightly greased 13- x 9- x 2-inch pan. Let rise, and bake as directed. Cool slightly. Combine 2 cups sifted powdered sugar, 3 to 4 tablespoons milk, and 1 teaspoon vanilla extract. Drizzle over warm rolls. **Yield:** 2 dozen.

Orange Rolls: Divide chilled dough in half; roll each portion into a 12- x 10-inch rectangle. Combine 2½ cups sifted powdered sugar, 2 teaspoons grated orange rind, ¼ cup melted butter, and 3 tablespoons fresh orange juice; spread evenly over dough rectangles. Starting with a long side, roll up, jellyroll fashion, pressing edges to seal. Cut logs into 1-inch slices, and place in a lightly greased 13- x 9- x 2-inch pan. Let rise, and bake as directed. Cool slightly. Combine 2 cups sifted powdered sugar, ½ teaspoon grated orange rind, and 2 to 3 tablespoons orange juice, stirring well. Drizzle over warm rolls. **Yield:** 2 dozen.

Christine H. Morrow
Bossier City, Louisiana

60-Minute Rolls

2 packages active dry yeast
½ cup warm water (105° to 115°)
2 tablespoons butter
3 tablespoons sugar
1¼ cups milk
1½ teaspoons salt
4½ to 5 cups all-purpose flour

• **Combine** yeast and warm water in a 1-cup liquid measuring cup; let stand 5 minutes.
• **Combine** butter and next 3 ingredients in a heavy saucepan; cook over medium heat, stirring constantly, just until butter melts. Pour into a large bowl; cool. Stir in yeast mixture; gradually stir in enough flour to make a soft dough.
• **Turn** dough out onto a well-floured surface; knead until smooth and elastic (about 5 minutes). Place in a well-greased bowl, turning to grease top.
• **Cover** and let stand in a warm place (85°), free from drafts, 15 minutes.
• **Divide** dough in half; shape each portion into 12 balls, and place in two greased 9-inch square pans. Cover and let rise in a warm place, free from drafts, 15 minutes.
• **Bake** at 425° for 10 to 12 minutes. **Yield:** 2 dozen.

Barbara Wagner
Gainesville, Florida

Roll-Shaping Techniques

Cloverleaf Rolls: Lightly grease muffin pans. Shape dough into 1-inch balls; place 3 dough balls in each muffin cup. Cover and let rise until doubled in bulk. Bake as directed.

S Rolls: Divide dough in several small portions. Roll each portion into a 9-inch rope about ¾ to 1 inch thick. Place on greased baking sheets; curl ends in opposite directions, forming an S shape. Cover and let rise until doubled in bulk. Bake as directed.

Bow Ties: Roll dough into several long ropes about ½ inch in diameter. Cut ropes into 8-inch strips. Carefully tie each dough strip into a knot. Place bow ties on a lightly greased baking sheet. Cover and let rise until doubled in bulk. Bake as directed.

Catering to Southern Living

When *Southern Living* magazine has a party, we call Kathy G. Mezrano. Her Birmingham-based catering company produces some of the most fabulous parties in our region. In addition to private parties, Kathy G. & Co. caters for the Terrace Cafe at the Birmingham Museum of Art.

Kathy and her talented team have a flare for design and adventurous palates. If you can't book Kathy for your next party, you can serve some of her favorite appetizers.

BRIE IN BRAIDED BREAD RING

⅓ cup sliced almonds
⅓ cup sesame seeds *
1 (35.2-ounce) round Brie
3 tablespoons apricot or pineapple preserves
½ cup dried cranberries
½ cup diced candied pineapple
Braided Bread Ring

• **Place** almonds and sesame seeds in shallow pans; bake at 350° for 5 to 10 minutes or until toasted, stirring occasionally (do not burn).

• **Trim** rind from top of Brie; brush preserves over top. Arrange almonds, sesame seeds, cranberries, and pineapple over preserves. Place Brie in center of Braided Bread Ring; serve with toasted French baguette slices. **Yield:** 20 servings.

Braided Bread Ring

½ (32-ounce) package frozen bread dough, thawed

• **Place** two large baking sheets on oven rack, overlapping edges so that width of baking sheets is at least 15 inches; grease and set aside.

• **Divide** dough into thirds; roll each portion into a 36-inch rope and braid. Grease outside of a 9-inch round cakepan; place in center of prepared baking sheets. Wrap braid around cakepan, pinching ends to seal.

• **Cover** and let rise in a warm place (85°), free from drafts, 1 hour or until doubled in bulk.

• **Bake** at 375° for 18 to 20 minutes or until golden. Remove from oven, and let cool on a wire rack. **Yield:** 1 (15-inch) loaf.

* You can substitute poppy seeds for sesame seeds; do not toast poppy seeds.

BASIL-CHEESE TERRINE

1 (8-ounce) package cream cheese, softened
1 (4-ounce) package crumbled blue cheese
1 cup loosely packed spinach leaves
¾ cup loosely packed Italian parsley leaves
¼ cup loosely packed basil leaves
2 cloves garlic, minced
¼ teaspoon salt
¼ cup olive oil
¼ cup chopped pine nuts
1 cup freshly grated Parmesan cheese
½ cup dried tomatoes in oil, sliced
Garnishes: fresh basil sprigs, cherry tomato wedges

• **Position** knife blade in food processor bowl; add cream cheese and blue cheese, and process until smooth, stopping once to scrape down sides. Spoon into a small bowl, and set aside.

• **Process** spinach and next 4 ingredients in processor; with processor running, pour oil in a slow, steady stream through food chute. Stir in pine nuts and Parmesan cheese.

• **Line** a 7½- x 3- x 2-inch loafpan with plastic wrap, allowing edges to extend over sides of pan. Spread half of cheese mixture in loafpan; top with half of tomatoes. Spread with pesto mixture; top with remaining tomatoes, and spread with remaining cheese mixture. Cover with plastic wrap; chill 24 hours.

• **Let** stand at room temperature 30 minutes; invert onto serving platter. Serve with crackers and breadsticks. Garnish, if desired. **Yield:** 16 servings.

DATE-WALNUT-CHEESE SPREAD

2 cups chopped walnuts, divided
6 (8-ounce) packages cream cheese, softened
⅓ cup sifted powdered sugar
⅓ cup dark rum
1 (8-ounce) package chopped dates
Garnish: walnut halves

• **Place** chopped walnuts in a shallow pan; bake at 350° for 5 to 10 minutes or until toasted, stirring occasionally; let cool.

• **Beat** cream cheese at medium speed with an electric mixer until fluffy. Add sugar and rum, beating until smooth. Stir in dates and 1 cup chopped walnuts; spoon into a 9-inch springform pan. Cover and chill 8 hours.

• **Remove** sides of pan carefully; press remaining 1 cup chopped walnuts on sides and around top edges of spread. Garnish, if desired. Serve with gingersnaps and sliced apples and pears. **Yield:** 50 servings.

MANGO CHUTNEY TORTA

1 cup low-fat cottage cheese
2 (8-ounce) packages cream cheese, softened
1 teaspoon curry powder
1 (9-ounce) jar mango chutney, divided
1 cup dry roasted peanuts
1 cup sliced green onions
1 cup golden raisins
Garnishes: sliced green onions, chopped peanuts, toasted coconut

• **Position** knife blade in food processor bowl; add cottage cheese, and

process until smooth. Add cream cheese and curry; process until mixture is smooth. Set aside half of cottage cheese mixture.
• **Add** 2 tablespoons chutney and half each of peanuts, green onions, and raisins to remaining cheese mixture; pulse 3 or 4 times or until coarsely chopped.
• **Spoon** mixture into an 8½- x 4½- x 3-inch loafpan lined with plastic wrap; spread with ¼ cup chutney.
• **Pulse** reserved cheese mixture, 2 tablespoons chutney, and remaining peanuts, green onions, and raisins 3 or 4 times or until coarsely chopped; spoon over torta. Cover and chill 8 hours.
• **Invert** onto serving plate; garnish, if desired. Serve with crackers. **Yield:** 25 servings.

CHOP AND TOP

Add interest to a plain main dish with homemade relish. Try Fruited Onion Marmalade for distinctly Southern style or Apple Relish for sweet-but-tart flavor. Only one of these condiments requires cooking – most of the effort is in the chopping.

EYE-OF-ROUND ROAST WITH FRUITED ONION MARMALADE

1 (2- to 3-pound) eye-of-round roast
1 teaspoon salt
½ teaspoon pepper
½ cup all-purpose flour
2 tablespoons vegetable oil
2 to 3 cloves garlic, sliced
1 (14½-ounce) can ready-to-serve beef broth
1 (12-ounce) bottle dark beer
Fruited Onion Marmalade

• **Sprinkle** roast with salt and pepper; dredge in flour.
• **Cook** roast in hot oil in a Dutch oven over medium heat until browned on all sides.
• **Add** garlic, broth, and beer; bring to a boil. Cover, reduce heat, and simmer 1½ hours or until tender. Serve with Fruited Onion Marmalade. **Yield:** 6 to 8 servings.

Fruited Onion Marmalade

1 tablespoon butter or margarine
1 tablespoon light brown sugar
2 onions, sliced
1 (8-ounce) package chopped dried fruit
1 cup beef broth
1½ teaspoons apple cider vinegar
¼ teaspoon ground ginger

• **Cook** butter and sugar in a large skillet over medium-low heat, stirring constantly, until sugar dissolves. Stir in sliced onion, and cook 20 minutes or until onion is tender, stirring mixture occasionally.
• **Stir** in chopped dried fruit and remaining ingredients.
• **Cover** reduce heat, and simmer 20 minutes or until fruit is tender. **Yield:** about 2 cups.

Nora Henshaw
Okemah, Oklahoma

APPLE RELISH

4 apples, diced
2 dill pickles, minced
1 onion, chopped
¼ cup apple cider vinegar
½ cup sugar
¼ teaspoon salt

• **Combine** all the ingredients in a medium bowl.
• **Cover** and chill relish at least 2 hours. Serve with chicken or pork. **Yield:** about 4 cups.

Lauri Ingham
Largo, Florida

PINEAPPLE-COCONUT RELISH

This tropical topping stays fresh in the refrigerator up to one week.

1 fresh pineapple, chopped *
1 (7-ounce) can flaked coconut
1 large red bell pepper, chopped
¼ cup minced purple onion
2 jalapeño peppers, seeded and minced
3 tablespoons rice wine vinegar
1 teaspoon salt
1¼ teaspoons chili powder

• **Combine** all ingredients in a bowl.
• **Cover** and chill at least 4 hours. Serve with pork, chicken, or fish. **Yield:** 5½ cups.

* You can substitute 1 (20-ounce) can of pineapple tidbits in juice, drained and chopped.

Linda Marco
Chapel Hill, North Carolina

GREEN OLIVE RELISH WITH CORIANDER

1 (12-ounce) jar pimiento-stuffed olives, drained and chopped
¼ cup olive oil
¼ cup red wine vinegar
2 cloves garlic, pressed
1 tablespoon ground coriander

• **Combine** all ingredients in a bowl.
• **Cover** and chill at least 8 hours. Serve with cream cheese and crackers. **Yield:** about 2 cups.

Caroline Kennedy
Newborn, Georgia

A GRAND ENTRÉE

Some dishes just demand attention – witness our Mustard Greens-Stuffed Tenderloin. This showy roast is fork tender and tastes as wonderful as it looks. You don't have to be a talent in the kitchen to prepare it, but your guests will think you are. If frozen mustard greens are not available in your area, collards will do just as well.

MUSTARD GREENS-STUFFED TENDERLOIN

1 (16-ounce) package frozen chopped mustard greens
3 tablespoons butter or margarine, divided
1 cup thinly sliced green onions
¾ pound country ham slices
1 cup soft breadcrumbs
¼ teaspoon ground red pepper
1 (3- to 4-pound) trimmed beef tenderloin
¼ teaspoon ground black pepper
2 to 3 tablespoons cracked black pepper
1 tablespoon all-purpose flour
1 cup beef broth
½ cup dry red wine
¼ teaspoon ground black pepper
Garnish: fresh mustard greens

- **Cook** greens according to package directions; drain. Press between layers of paper towels to remove excess moisture; transfer to a large bowl.
- **Melt** 1 tablespoon butter in a skillet; add green onions, and cook until tender, stirring often. Add to greens.
- **Melt** remaining 2 tablespoons butter in skillet; add ham, and cook over medium-high heat 4 minutes, turning once. Remove ham from skillet, reserving drippings in skillet; chop ham. Stir ham, breadcrumbs, and red pepper into greens.
- **Preheat** oven to 500°.
- **Make** a lengthwise cut down center of tenderloin, cutting to, but not through, bottom. Starting from center cut, slice horizontally toward 1 side, stopping ½ inch from edge. Repeat on opposite side. Unfold meat so that it's flat. Lay between two pieces of heavy-duty plastic wrap. Flatten to ½-inch thickness, using a meat mallet.
- **Sprinkle** ¼ teaspoon ground black pepper over tenderloin; spread with greens mixture. Roll up, jellyroll fashion, starting with a long side; secure with string at 4-inch intervals.
- **Press** cracked pepper on tenderloin, and place, seam side down, on a lightly greased rack in a roasting pan. Place tenderloin in oven, and reduce heat to 350°.
- **Bake** 40 minutes or until meat thermometer inserted in thickest portion registers 145° (medium-rare) to 160° (medium). Cover loosely with aluminum foil, and let stand 15 minutes.
- **Stir** flour into reserved ham drippings in skillet; cook over medium-low heat, stirring constantly, 4 to 5 minutes or until caramel colored.
- **Add** broth and wine gradually, and cook over medium-low heat, stirring constantly, until gravy is thickened and bubbly. Stir in ¼ teaspoon ground black pepper.
- **Slice** tenderloin, and garnish, if desired. Serve with gravy. **Yield:** 8 to 10 servings.

WINE SELECTION MADE EASY

Consider the food and its preparation when choosing wine.

FOR STEAKS, GAME, LAMB, STEWS

A mildly seasoned lamb chop calls for a delicate red like Pinot Noir. Merlot, a smoother wine such as Cabernet Sauvignon, is perfect for broiled steaks, chops, and game. But a rich stew or a grilled steak requires a hearty red like Zinfandel, Cabernet, or Shiraz. We recommend:

Cabernet, De Loach, Sonoma (CA), 1992
Merlot, Forest Glen, Sonoma (CA), 1995
Pinot Noir, Mountain View (CA), 1993
Shiraz/Cabernet, Rosemount Estate (Australia), 1995
Zinfandel, Mountain View (CA), 1994

FOR SPICY ORIENTAL DISHES

These highly flavored foods are best balanced with medium-dry wines. We recommend:

Gewürztraminer, The Hogue Cellars, Columbia Valley (WA), 1994
Johannisberg Riesling, Chateau Ste. Michelle (WA), 1995

FOR APPETIZERS, CHICKEN, PASTA, SEAFOOD

Serve these dishes with light white or a lightly chilled Beaujolais. We recommend:

Chardonnay, Undurraga, Santa Ana, Maipo Valley (Chile), 1995
Chenin Blanc, Callaway, Temecula (CA), 1995
Signature White, Llano Estacado (TX), 1994
White Bordeaux, Marquis de Chasse (France), 1993

FOR GO-WITH-ANYTHING SIPPING WINES

We recommend:

Cabernet Rosé, Dry Creek Vineyards, Sonoma (CA), 1993
Ca'del Solo Big House White, Livermore (CA), 1995
Grenache Rosé, McDowell, Mendocino (CA), 1994
Rosé of Cabernet Sauvignon, Simi (CA), 1995
White Zinfandel, Belvedere, Sonoma (CA), 1993

FEAST FOR KWANZA

Kwanza is a nonreligious celebration of family, home, and the cultural heritage of African Americans. Each day of the event, December 26 through January 1, participants focus on one of the holiday's seven principles – unity, self-determination, collective work and responsibility, cooperative economics, purpose, creativity, and faith. The holiday comes to a delicious end with a potluck feast that features fresh fruits, vegetables, and grains. It's a time to sample new dishes and enjoy familiar foods cooked different ways.

On this 30th anniversary of the holiday, host a Kwanza celebration for family and friends. No special equipment or costumes are required. A simple candelabra with seven candles in the traditional colors of red, green, and black that represent the seven principles of Kwanza is the only ornamental celebration symbol. Just use these easy recipes to help plan the menu, and then be as exotic as your imagination allows. Remember, unity of family and community is the focus, so let everybody help. Join the fun and reap the benefits.

OKRA SOUP WITH FOU-FOU

1 onion, diced
2 dried red chile peppers (optional)
2 tablespoons vegetable oil
2 cups sliced fresh okra *
1 tomato, chopped
2 cups water
1 (14½-ounce) can ready-to-serve chicken broth
2 (6-ounce) cans tomato paste
1 (10-ounce) package frozen chopped spinach, thawed
½ teaspoon salt
½ teaspoon pepper
¼ teaspoon rubbed sage
Fou-Fou

• **Cook** onion and peppers, if desired, in hot oil 1 minute. Add okra and tomato; bring to a boil.
• **Reduce** heat, and simmer 5 minutes, stirring occasionally.
• **Add** water, broth, and tomato paste; return to a simmer, and cook 7 minutes, stirring occasionally.
• **Stir** in spinach and next 3 ingredients; simmer 10 minutes, stirring occasionally. Serve soup with Fou-Fou. **Yield:** 8 cups.

* You can substitute 1 (10-ounce) package frozen sliced okra for fresh.

Fou-Fou

6 cups water
1 teaspoon salt
2½ cups cream of wheat

• **Bring** 6 cups water to a boil; add salt. Gradually add cream of wheat, stirring constantly.
• **Reduce** heat to low; cook 3 to 4 minutes or until mixture is very thick, stirring vigorously.
• **Press** into a 1-quart bowl sprinkled with cold water; invert onto a serving plate, and serve immediately. **Yield:** 8 servings.

Adaora Schmiedl
Montgomery, Alabama

COLLARD GREENS SALAD

2 pounds fresh collard greens, washed and shredded
3 small carrots, shredded
1 onion, minced
3 cloves garlic, minced
½ teaspoon dried oregano
3 tablespoons apple cider vinegar
¼ cup olive oil

• **Combine** all ingredients in a large bowl; tossing gently. Cover and chill 1 hour. **Yield:** 8 to 10 servings.

Ellen Byrd
Furman, Alabama

SWEET POTATO PIE

2 large sweet potatoes (1½ pounds)
½ (15-ounce) package refrigerated piecrusts
¾ cup sugar
¼ cup firmly packed light brown sugar
2 tablespoons all-purpose flour
2 large eggs
½ cup evaporated milk
1 teaspoon ground nutmeg
½ teaspoon ground allspice
¼ teaspoon salt
Dash of ground cinnamon
1 teaspoon vanilla extract
½ teaspoon lemon extract

• **Cook** sweet potatoes in boiling water to cover 45 to 50 minutes or until tender; drain. Cool.
• **Fit** piecrust into a 9-inch pieplate according to package directions; fold edges under, and crimp. Line pastry with aluminum foil, and fill with pie weights or dried beans.
• **Bake** at 450° for 8 minutes. Remove weights and foil; bake 4 additional minutes.
• **Peel** potatoes, and place in a mixing bowl; beat at medium speed with an electric mixer until smooth. Add sugars and remaining 9 ingredients, beating until blended. Pour into piecrust.
• **Bake** at 375° for 45 to 50 minutes or until a knife inserted in center comes out clean; shield edges with strips of aluminum foil the last 15 minutes to prevent excessive browning. Serve warm or at room temperature. **Yield:** 1 (9-inch) pie.

Note: You can substitute a food processor for an electric mixer.

Karen Taylor
Montgomery, Alabama

SPLASHY GIFTS

Tired of the usual holiday gifts? Give these salad dressings and toppings a try. These dressings offer a flavorful change from grocery store brands, while the toppings add crunch to tossed salads.

Select pretty cruets or olive oil bottles for the dressings, and clear bags or attractive tins for the toppings. Remind your friends to store the dressings, covered, in the refrigerator to keep them fresh and safe.

■ **Curried Salad Gift:** Package Curry Salad Dressing, Curry Salad Topping, and directions to serve with mixed salad greens.

CURRY SALAD DRESSING

1 cup olive oil
¼ cup lemon juice
1 tablespoon white wine vinegar
1 tablespoon mango chutney
1 teaspoon Dijon mustard
½ teaspoon curry powder
¼ teaspoon salt
¼ teaspoon pepper

• **Combine** all ingredients in container of an electric blender; process until smooth, stopping once to scrape down sides. Cover and chill. **Yield:** 1¾ cups.

Carol Scheder
Roswell, Georgia

CURRY SALAD TOPPING

½ cup flaked coconut
1 (2.25-ounce) package sliced almonds
1 (3-ounce) package banana chips or chopped dried apple

• **Place** coconut and almonds in shallow pans; bake at 350° for 5 to 10 minutes or until toasted, stirring occasionally; cool. Combine coconut, almonds, and banana chips; store in an airtight container. **Yield:** 1½ cups.

■ **Caesar Salad Gift:** Package Creamy Caesar Salad Dressing, Seasoned Croutons, and ½ cup freshly grated Parmesan cheese with directions to serve with Romaine lettuce.

CREAMY CAESAR SALAD DRESSING

This dressing contains egg substitute and must be kept chilled.

1 cup olive oil
½ cup egg substitute
½ cup apple cider vinegar
¼ cup lemon juice
1 tablespoon Worcestershire sauce
1 (2-ounce) can anchovies, undrained
4 cloves garlic
2 teaspoons dry mustard
1 teaspoon salt

• **Combine** all ingredients in container of an electric blender; process until smooth, stopping once to scrape down sides. Cover and store in refrigerator up to 1 week. **Yield:** 3 cups.

SEASONED CROUTONS

2½ cups large French bread cubes
Olive oil-flavored cooking spray
1 teaspoon fines herbes

• **Coat** bread cubes with cooking spray; place bread cubes in a heavy-duty, zip-top plastic bag. Add herbs; seal and shake to coat. Spread in a single layer on a baking sheet; spray with cooking spray.
• **Bake** at 400° for 9 minutes or until croutons are browned, stirring occasionally. **Yield:** 2½ cups.

Angela Mathias
Tampa, Florida

THE GIFT OF GIVING

■ Small beautifully wrapped goodies placed in a basket near the front door are a pleasure, both to view and to give. Prepare a few extras and you'll be ready for unexpected callers.

■ Wrap up individual packages of our Party Mix (recipe on page 306) in festive bags for guests.

■ Holiday guests will enjoy steaming mugs of hot cider, a spicy brew infused with the aromas of the season. It's easy to create a thoughtful gift by bundling the spices in decorative fabric or a festive container and attaching the recipe on page 306.

■ Use lightly wired ribbon, available at craft and florist supply stores, to dress up inexpensive wrapping paper. Add an ornament for a festive touch.

■ Embellish a plain gift bag with a Christmas card, ornament, and brightly colored ribbon.

■ Adorn a special package with not one but two colors of ribbon. Tie on some candy canes or Christmas candy for a sweet treat.

■ Fashion gift cards from scraps of paper, linen, and laces. If you want to make a card even more personal, choose a subject the recipient is interested in: sheet music, old photographs, newspaper, or even natural items like leaves and berries.

■ Put your personal seal on a gift with colorful wax seals. Ribbons add a regal flair when fastened underneath the wax seal.

■ Give holiday dinner guests a sweet treat *before* dinner. Assemble napkin rings for your holiday dinner table to resemble British party crackers. Glue paper, trimmings, and beads on the cylinder of toilet tissue rolls, and let dry. Wrap mints, chocolates, and other small party favors in colorful paper napkins and pull through the ends.

■ An addition to a silver collection such as antique sterling napkin rings makes a Christmas memory. Or you can start a new tradition and give something you know guests will enjoy collecting for years to come.

■ Give the gift of photographs. Knowing that the North Pole takes a dim view of young squirmers and squinters, children will be on their best behavior this time of year. So take a family portrait that your family will cherish for years to come.

■ **Asian Salad Gift:** Package Asian Salad Dressing, Asian Crumble Mix, and directions to serve with mixed salad greens.

ASIAN SALAD DRESSING

1 cup vegetable oil
⅓ cup rice wine vinegar
2 tablespoons soy sauce
2 tablespoons dark sesame oil
2 teaspoons dry mustard
4 teaspoons sugar
2 teaspoons grated fresh ginger

• **Combine** all ingredients in a jar; cover tightly, and shake vigorously. Chill. **Yield:** about 1½ cups.

ASIAN CRUMBLE MIX

1 (3-ounce) package ramen noodle soup mix
1 (2.6-ounce) jar sesame seeds, toasted
⅔ cup cashews

• **Remove** flavor packet from soup mix, and reserve for another use.
• **Crumble** noodles in a shallow pan; add sesame seeds.
• **Bake** at 350° for 3 to 5 minutes or until toasted, stirring occasionally. Let cool.
• **Combine** noodle mixture and cashews; store in an airtight container up to 1 month. **Yield:** 1½ cups.

A TRIO OF EASY MEALS

This column in each monthly chapter throughout the book provides you with food for thought for the dinner dilemma. Some meals are a rush job of convenience products, while others take the slow route to the table. For even more mealtime ideas, add this trio of delicious entrées to your recipe stash.

CORNED BEEF AND CABBAGE

1 (4-pound) corned beef brisket
3 tablespoons pickling spice
2 cups water
6 small round red potatoes (about 2 pounds)
1 cabbage, cut into 6 wedges
3/4 cup sour cream
2 tablespoons prepared horseradish

• **Combine** first 3 ingredients in a 6-quart pressure cooker.
• **Cover** with lid, and seal securely; place pressure control over vent tube. Cook over high heat until pressure control rocks back and forth quickly. Reduce heat until pressure control rocks occasionally; cook 50 minutes.
• **Remove** from heat, run cold water over cooker to reduce pressure. Carefully remove lid.
• **Remove** corned beef to a serving platter, and keep warm. Add potatoes and cabbage to cooker. Cook as directed 5 minutes. Arrange potatoes and cabbage around corned beef.
• **Combine** sour cream and horseradish; serve with corned beef, potatoes, and cabbage. **Yield:** 6 servings.

Barbara Rutyna
Louisville, Kentucky

SAGE LAMB CHOPS

Lamb chops from the microwave? We were pleasantly surprised.

1 tablespoon red wine vinegar
1 teaspoon dark brown sugar
1/2 teaspoon rubbed sage
1/8 teaspoon garlic powder
1/8 teaspoon salt
1/8 teaspoon pepper
4 (1-inch-thick) lamb chops

• **Combine** first 6 ingredients in a 9-inch pieplate or microwave-safe dish. Add chops, turning to coat; arrange chops with bones toward center of dish. Cover and chill 2 to 3 hours.
• **Microwave** at MEDIUM-HIGH (70% power) 3 to 5 minutes or until chops are pink in the center (do not overcook). Cover with aluminum foil; let stand 3 minutes. **Yield:** 2 servings.

LaJuan Coward
Jasper, Texas

KENTUCKY-STYLE OVEN-BARBECUED CHICKEN

1/4 cup butter or margarine
1 (3- to 3 1/2-pound) broiler-fryer, cut up
1/2 cup white vinegar
1 tablespoon Worcestershire sauce
1 teaspoon salt
1/2 teaspoon dry mustard
1/2 teaspoon ground black pepper
1/2 teaspoon ground red pepper
Hot cooked rice

• **Melt** butter in a large nonstick skillet over medium heat; add chicken, and brown on all sides. Remove from skillet, reserving drippings. Place chicken in an 11- x 7- x 1 1/2-inch baking dish.
• **Add** vinegar and next 5 ingredients to reserved drippings in skillet, stirring to loosen browned particles that cling to bottom. Pour over chicken.
• **Cover** and bake chicken at 325° for 45 minutes; uncover and bake 15 additional minutes. Serve over rice. **Yield:** 4 servings.

Note: You can skin chicken before cooking.

Lillian B. Harris
Mayfield, Kentucky

COZY CASSOULET

The French have given us many good things, but none so comforting as cassoulet. Meats and white beans baked together in a casserole define the classic version of cassoulet (ka-soo-LAY). It's peasant food, meant to be eaten with gusto, using crusty bread to mop up the rich sauce that envelopes the beans.

Cassoulet served with a green salad and a loaf of bread makes a warming winter dinner for at least eight.

CASSOULET

1 pound dried Great Northern beans
2 1/2 quarts water
1/2 pound salt pork with skin
3 cloves garlic, crushed
1 onion
2 carrots, scraped and cut in half
2 stalks celery, cut in half
1 teaspoon dried thyme
1 bay leaf
1 (6- to 7-pound) chicken
1 teaspoon salt
2 teaspoons freshly ground pepper
1 pound andouille sausage, cut into 2-inch pieces *
2 pounds boneless center-cut pork chops
1 medium onion, chopped
4 cloves garlic, minced
1 cup dry white wine
1 (14.5-ounce) can diced tomatoes, undrained
1/2 teaspoon dried thyme
2 teaspoons freshly ground pepper
1 cup fresh French breadcrumbs
1/4 cup chopped fresh parsley

• **Sort** and wash beans; place in an 8-quart ovenproof Dutch oven. Cover with water 2 inches above beans; let soak 8 hours. Drain.

• **Add** 2½ quarts water to beans; stir in salt pork and next 6 ingredients. Bring to a boil; cover and cook 2 hours or until beans are tender, adding water if necessary. Remove and discard salt pork, onion, carrot, celery, and bay leaf; set beans aside.

• **Place** chicken in a roasting pan; sprinkle with salt and 2 teaspoons pepper.

• **Bake** at 350° for 2 hours or until meat thermometer registers 180°; cool completely, reserving 3 tablespoons drippings. Cut chicken into serving-size pieces; set aside.

• **Cook** sausage in a skillet over medium-high heat until browned; remove sausage, reserving drippings in skillet. Set sausage aside.

• **Add** pork chops to skillet, and cook until browned on both sides; remove pork chops, reserving drippings in skillet. Set pork chops aside.

• **Add** reserved chicken drippings to skillet. Add chopped onion and minced garlic, and cook over medium-high heat, stirring constantly, until tender. Add wine, and cook 6 minutes or until reduced by half.

• **Add** tomatoes, ½ teaspoon thyme, and 2 teaspoons pepper; stir into beans.

• **Spoon** half each of beans, sausage, chicken, and pork chops into a Dutch oven; repeat layers with remaining ingredients. Sprinkle with breadcrumbs.

• **Bake** at 325° for 1½ hours. Sprinkle with parsley. **Yield:** 8 to 10 servings.

* Substitute any spicy smoked sausage for andouille.

STREAMLINE CASSOULET

We offer two versions of cassoulets. One is a takeoff on the French classic, using chicken, andouille sausage, and boneless pork chops. The other version is vegetarian and starts with chick-peas (garbanzo beans).

Yes, both cassoulets take hours to make. But the recipes are easy, the ingredients are ordinary, and the time spent will reward you with perfectly mingled flavors.

Once the beans are cooked, you're halfway to cassoulet. To streamline the process, cook the beans in a pressure cooker or cook them overnight in a slow cooker. You can even cook them a day ahead, and then cook and assemble the remaining ingredients the following day.

Bring cassoulet to the table in its baking dish for a casual get-together.

VEGETARIAN CASSOULET

1 (16-ounce) package dried chick-peas (garbanzo beans)
3 quarts water
3 tablespoons minced garlic, divided
1 bay leaf
¼ cup butter or margarine
½ pound whole fresh mushrooms
½ teaspoon dried thyme
¼ teaspoon dried rosemary, crushed
½ teaspoon dried oregano
1 cup dry white wine
3 tablespoons tomato paste
6 turnips, peeled and cut into fourths
4 large red potatoes, peeled and cut into fourths
1 rutabaga, peeled and cut into 1-inch pieces
2 onions, cut into eighths
6 carrots, scraped and cut into 2-inch pieces
½ teaspoon salt
½ teaspoon pepper
¼ cup olive oil
2 (14½-ounce) cans ready-to-serve vegetable broth
½ cup fine, dry breadcrumbs

• **Sort** and wash chick-peas; place in an ovenproof 6-quart Dutch oven. Cover with water 2 inches above beans; let soak 8 hours. Drain.

• **Add** 3 quarts water, 1 tablespoon garlic, and bay leaf; cook over medium-high heat 2 hours or until beans are tender. Remove and discard bay leaf. Set beans aside.

• **Melt** butter in a large skillet over medium-high heat; add 1 tablespoon garlic, mushrooms, and next 3 ingredients. Cook 5 minutes, stirring constantly. Add wine and tomato paste; cook 2 minutes, stirring constantly. Add to beans.

• **Combine** remaining 1 tablespoon garlic, turnip, and next 7 ingredients; place in an aluminum foil-lined roasting pan.

• **Bake** at 500° for 20 minutes, stirring once. Spoon vegetables over beans in Dutch oven; pour broth over vegetables. Sprinkle with breadcrumbs.

• **Bake** at 325° for 1½ hours or until vegetables are tender. **Yield:** 8 servings.

QUICK & EASY

DINNER EXPRESS

If you shop for supper on your way home from work, then you really don't have time to stand in a long line at the grocery store. We've created this no-hassle meal plan that serves at least four to help you zip through the 12-items-or-less express lane so you can get back on the road toward home. Pantry staples not included in the ingredient count are salt, sugar, hot sauce, and fresh garlic.

FAR EAST FEAST
Serves Four to Six

Japanese Tortellini Soup
Broiled Fish
Chinese Green Beans
Lemon-Pineapple Sherbet

SHOPPING LIST

- 2 (14½-ounce) cans ready-to-serve Oriental broth
- 1 (16-ounce) package frozen broccoli, Sugar Snap peas, water chestnuts, and red peppers with teriyaki sauce
- 1 (9-ounce) package refrigerated cheese-filled tortellini
- 4 whitefish fillets
- 1 pound fresh green beans
- 2 green onions
- 1 (1-inch) piece fresh ginger
- 3 tablespoons sesame oil
- 2 tablespoons soy sauce
- 1 lemon
- ½ gallon pineapple sherbet

JAPANESE TORTELLINI SOUP

2 (14½-ounce) cans ready-to-serve Oriental broth
1 (16-ounce) package frozen broccoli, Sugar Snap peas, water chestnuts, and red peppers with teriyaki sauce, thawed
1 (9-ounce) package refrigerated cheese-filled tortellini
¼ teaspoon hot sauce

• **Combine** broth, seasoning packet from vegetables, tortellini, and hot sauce in a large saucepan; bring mixture to a boil.
• **Add** vegetables; return to a boil. Cover, reduce heat, and simmer 10 minutes or until vegetables are crisp-tender. **Yield:** 6 cups.

Note: For frozen vegetables, we used Green Giant.

Jerry Nugent
Virginia Beach, Virginia

CHINESE GREEN BEANS

1 pound fresh green beans
1 tablespoon chopped green onions
2 cloves garlic, pressed
6 thin slices fresh ginger
3 tablespoons sesame oil
1 teaspoon sugar
½ teaspoon salt
2 tablespoons soy sauce
¼ cup water

• **Cook** beans in boiling water to cover 3 to 4 minutes; drain and plunge into cold water to stop the cooking process. Drain on paper towels.
• **Cook** green onions, garlic, and ginger in hot oil in a skillet 1 minute, stirring often; add sugar, salt, and soy sauce, and cook until sugar dissolves, stirring often.
• **Add** beans and water; reduce heat to medium, and stir-fry 3 minutes. Serve immediately. **Yield:** 4 to 6 servings.

Kathy Sea
Lubbock, Texas

LEMON-PINEAPPLE SHERBET

1 lemon
½ gallon pineapple sherbet, softened

• **Grate** 1 teaspoon rind from lemon; squeeze lemon, reserving 3 tablespoons juice.
• **Combine** rind, juice, and sherbet, stirring well; cover and freeze until firm. **Yield:** ½ gallon.

A Christmas Album

Creating a scrapbook is a project your family can enjoy. Start a new tradition by following our step-by-step instructions to begin your own keepsake. We created an album you can add pages to each Christmas – one that would eventually hold a holiday history of your family.

Begin by pasting in a family photograph and inscribing the year on a title page. Let children draw borders and glue collages of invitations, Christmas cards, and their own art. Add a short narrative or funny comments with colorful pens.

TOOLS & MATERIALS

From an art-supply store

- 2 (11- x 15-inch) watercolor paper tablets
- foam-core board (approximately 18 x 24 inches)
- 1 sheet of decorative paper for binding
- 2 sheets of heavy decorative paper for inside covers

From a fabric store

- 5 yards of ribbon in each of four colors (3 colors ⅞ inch wide and 1 color 1½ inches wide)
- 1⅓ yards of ⅞-inch-wide ribbon for ties
- fusible interfacing

Tools

- hot-glue gun
- scissors
- ruler
- pencil
- straight pins
- iron
- ice pick

Choose Your Colors: Begin by choosing four colors of grosgrain ribbon and coordinating decorative paper for the binding and lining of the covers. You will find all materials at an art-supply store and a fabric store.

Construct the Scrapbook: Have a printer trim the binding from the two watercolor tablets and drill two holes for the scrapbook binding. One hole should be positioned ¾ inch in from the short side and 2½ inches from the top; the second hole should be ¾ inch in from the short side and 2½ inches from the bottom. The trimmed and drilled tablets should measure approximately 11 x 14½ inches. Discard the front covers of each pad. Set the watercolor pages aside. The chipboard backing from each tablet becomes the scrapbook covers.

Weave Ribbon for Front Cover: Make a surface to weave ribbons on by drawing a 15- x 18-inch rectangle in the center of a large piece of foam-core board. Cut eight 18-inch strips of ribbon in colors A and B (both should be ⅞ inch wide). Pin ends A and B across the 15-inch markings, alternating colors. Cut seven 15-inch strips of ribbon in colors C and D (C should be ⅞ inch wide and D should be 1½ inches wide). Beginning at the corner of one long end, weave one length of the ribbon C under and over horizontal ribbons, pinning ends to secure. Weave one length of ribbon D over and under horizontal ribbons; pin end. Continue weaving, alternating colors C and D, until your penciled area is completely covered. Adjust pins and ribbons so that ribbons are as tightly woven as possible and the pins are holding ribbons taut. Following manufacturer's instructions, fuse a 14½- x 17½-inch piece of interfacing to woven ribbons. Remove pins.

Attach Ribbon to Cover: Position chipboard cover on wrong side of woven ribbons so that one short side of chipboard is at the edge of the ribbons and the long sides of the board are centered between the edges of the ribbons. (This means you will have ribbon showing on three of the four sides of the chipboard.) Fuse board front to ribbons following manufacturer's instructions for the interfacing. Wrap top and bottom ribbon edges to inside of board, and fuse. Wrap remaining side to inside, and fuse. Hot glue may also be needed for corners.

Bind and Line Scrapbook: Cut a sheet of decorative paper 14 x 10 inches to create the binding. Fold in half lengthwise to 14 x 5 inches. Glue folded edge of paper to front cover, overlapping ribbon by 2½ inches. Turn cover over and fold paper to other side. Glue short sides to board and then fold corners of paper as if you were wrapping a present, and glue remaining edge. Cut heavier paper 14 x 10½ inches, and glue in center of inside cover for lining. Repeat above steps for back cover.

Assemble Scrapbook: Use an ice pick or other pointed object to pierce paper binding through the drilled holes of both covers. Cut two pieces of ribbon 24 inches long to use as binding ties. Assemble the scrapbook by placing watercolor pages between the covers, threading ribbons through holes and making the bows.

From Our Kitchen to Yours

SIZING UP YOUR PAN

There you are in the kitchen, the cake batter mixed or the casserole ingredients assembled, and you read that line of doom in the recipe: "Use a so-and-so-size pan." Then the hunt begins, only to determine you don't have one. So what's plan B?

We can help you somewhat with our chart of pan sizes (below) and their capacities. If a pan you have isn't listed in the chart, fill it with water, measuring cup by measuring cup, to find out how much it holds. And then consult the chart for pans that accommodate the same amounts and, therefore, may be interchangeable.

Now, here's a friendly warning: When you substitute a pan that holds the same amount but is a different *shape,* the cooking time on the recipe will vary. Generally, the deeper the pan is, the longer the cooking time will be. But you'll need to experiment with your particular recipes.

MELTING POTLESS

Thank goodness the days of melting chocolate in a cumbersome double boiler are long gone. You can use a heavy saucepan over low heat, eliminating one of the two pots. Or, get rid of the pot altogether with the handy plastic bag method that follows.

For velvety, melted chocolate, put chocolate squares or morsels into a heavy-duty, zip-top plastic bag, and drop the bag in a small bowl. Pour very hot tap water or boiling water over the bag, and let it sit a few minutes until the chocolate melts and the water cools a little.

Then fish out the bag, gently knead it to be sure the chocolate is smooth, and snip a tiny hole in one corner of the bag with scissors. You can squirt the chocolate decoratively onto dessert plates, over ice cream, or into the other ingredients of a recipe; then toss the bag. No scrubbing stubborn chocolate from a bowl, a spatula, the sink, the counter, and the dishcloth. If this dashes the plans of a devoted bowl-licker, you can always leave just enough chocolate in the bag for the moment when no one's looking.

INDUCTION TO REDUCTION

Do you shy away from menu listings in fine restaurants that try to lure you with an irresistible reduction sauce? (If it's so wonderful, then why would you want a reduced amount?) Or does that term in a recipe spur you to quickly flip the page with an intimidated "I dunno" shrug? Actually, reduction is just a fancy culinary word for a simple kitchen task.

It all boils down to, well, boiling down a liquid to concentrate its flavor. If you can turn on the burner under a pot and take a peek and stir every few minutes, you have mastered reduction sauce techniques.

The process starts with a good sauce mixture, stock or wine, and evaporates the extra moisture to make a rich treasure suitable for sopping to the very last drop.

USING YOUR NOODLE

If you don't own a cake tester, and you discover just as the timer rings that you don't have any wooden picks for your baking cake's trial, Charlotte Bryant of Greensburg, Kentucky, offers emergency help. Grab a piece of uncooked spaghetti from your pantry, and take the cake plunge. If the tester, pick, or noodle comes out clean, the cake's done. If bits of cake batter stick to it, leave the cake in a few more minutes, and try again.

CHARTING THE COURSE

For best results, always use the size and type of pan or baking dish called for in a recipe. It can be the difference between success or failure.

PAN SIZES	PAN CAPACITIES
13- x 9- x 2-inch baking dish	12 to 15 cups
10- x 4-inch tube pan	12 cups
10- x 3½-inch Bundt pan	12 cups
9- x 3-inch tube pan	9 cups
9- x 3-inch Bundt pan	9 cups
11- x 7- x 1½-inch baking dish	8 cups
8- x 8- x 2-inch square baking dish	8 cups
9- x 5- x 3-inch loafpan	8 cups
9- x 2-inch deep-dish pieplate	6 to 8 cups
9- x 1½-inch cakepan	6 cups
7½- x 3-inch Bundt pan	6 cups
9- x 1½-inch regular pieplate	5 cups
8- x 1½-inch cakepan	4 to 5 cups
8½- x 4½- x 2½-inch loafpan	4 cups

There will be a chorus of oohs and aahs when you bring this Cream Puff Tree (recipe, page 310) to your holiday table. A dramatic finale, this spiral of heavenly sweets only looks difficult to make.

Rich Bourbon-Chocolate-Pecan Tarts, Italian Cream Cake, and Roasted Bacon Pecans deliciously showcase the South's favorite nut. (Recipes begin on page 262.)

Show off Red Velvet Cake's ruby layers by spreading Cream Cheese Frosting (recipes, page 282) only between the layers and on top of the cake.

Metric Equivalents

The recipes that appear in this cookbook use the standard United States method for measuring liquid and dry or solid ingredients (teaspoons, tablespoons, and cups). The information in the following charts is provided to help cooks outside the U.S. successfully use these recipes. All equivalents are approximate.

METRIC EQUIVALENTS FOR DIFFERENT TYPES OF INGREDIENTS

A standard cup measure of a dry or solid ingredient will vary in weight depending on the type of ingredient. A standard cup of liquid is the same volume for any type of liquid. Use the following chart when converting standard cup measures to grams (weight) or milliliters (volume).

Standard Cup	Fine Powder (ex. flour)	Grain (ex. rice)	Granular (ex. sugar)	Liquid Solids (ex. butter)	Liquid (ex. milk)
1	140 g	150 g	190 g	200 g	240 ml
¾	105 g	113 g	143 g	150 g	180 ml
⅔	93 g	100 g	125 g	133 g	160 ml
½	70 g	75 g	95 g	100 g	120 ml
⅓	47 g	50 g	63 g	67 g	80 ml
¼	35 g	38 g	48 g	50 g	60 ml
⅛	18 g	19 g	24 g	25 g	30 ml

USEFUL EQUIVALENTS FOR LIQUID INGREDIENTS BY VOLUME

¼ tsp							=	1 ml		
½ tsp							=	2 ml		
1 tsp							=	5 ml		
3 tsp	=	1 tbls			=	½ fl oz	=	15 ml		
		2 tbls	=	⅛ cup	=	1 fl oz	=	30 ml		
		4 tbls	=	¼ cup	=	2 fl oz	=	60 ml		
		5⅓ tbls	=	⅓ cup	=	3 fl oz	=	80 ml		
		8 tbls	=	½ cup	=	4 fl oz	=	120 ml		
		10⅔ tbls	=	⅔ cup	=	5 fl oz	=	160 ml		
		12 tbls	=	¾ cup	=	6 fl oz	=	180 ml		
		16 tbls	=	1 cup	=	8 fl oz	=	240 ml		
		1 pt	=	2 cups	=	16 fl oz	=	480 ml		
		1 qt	=	4 cups	=	32 fl oz	=	960 ml		
						33 fl oz	=	1000 ml	=	1 l

USEFUL EQUIVALENTS FOR DRY INGREDIENTS BY WEIGHT

(To convert ounces to grams, multiply the number of ounces by 30)

1 oz	=	1/16 lb	=	30 g
4 oz	=	¼ lb	=	120 g
8 oz	=	½ lb	=	240 g
12 oz	=	¾ lb	=	360 g
16 oz	=	1 lb	=	480 g

USEFUL EQUIVALENTS FOR LENGTH

(To convert inches to centimeters, multiply the number of inches by 2.5)

1 in					=	2.5 cm		
6 in	=	½ ft			=	15 cm		
12 in	=	1 ft			=	30 cm		
36 in	=	3 ft	=	1 yd	=	90 cm		
40 in					=	100 cm	=	1 m

USEFUL EQUIVALENTS FOR COOKING/OVEN TEMPERATURES

	Fahrenheit	Celcius	Gas Mark
Freeze Water	32° F	0° C	
Room Temperature	68° F	20° C	
Boil Water	212° F	100° C	
Bake	325° F	160° C	3
	350° F	180° C	4
	375° F	190° C	5
	400° F	200° C	6
	425° F	220° C	7
	450° F	230° C	8
Broil			Grill

Equivalent Weights and Yields

FOOD	WEIGHT (OR COUNT)	YIELD
Apples	1 pound (3 medium)	3 cups sliced
Bacon	8 slices cooked	½ cup crumbled
Bananas	1 pound (3 medium)	2½ cups sliced or about 2 cups mashed
Bread	1 pound	12 to 16 slices
	About 1½ slices	1 cup soft crumbs
Butter or margarine	1 pound	2 cups
	¼- pound stick	½ cup
Cabbage	1 pound head	4½ cups shredded
Candied fruit or peels	½ pound	1¼ cups chopped
Carrots	1 pound	3 cups shredded
Cheese, American or Cheddar	1 pound	About 4 cups shredded
cottage	1 pound	2 cups
cream	3- ounce package	6 tablespoons
Chocolate morsels	6- ounce package	1 cup
Cocoa	1 pound	4 cups
Coconut, flaked or shredded	1 pound	5 cups
Coffee	1 pound	80 tablespoons (40 cups perked)
Corn	2 medium ears	1 cup kernels
Cornmeal	1 pound	3 cups
Crab, in shell	1 pound	¾ to 1 cup flaked
Crackers, chocolate wafers	19 wafers	1 cup crumbs
graham crackers	14 squares	1 cup fine crumbs
saltine crackers	28 crackers	1 cup finely crushed
vanilla wafers	22 wafers	1 cup finely crushed
Cream, whipping	1 cup (½ pint)	2 cups whipped
Dates, pitted	1 pound	3 cups chopped
	8- ounce package	1½ cups chopped
Eggs	5 large	1 cup
whites	8 to 11	1 cup
yolks	12 to 14	1 cup
Flour, all-purpose	1 pound	3½ cups
cake	1 pound	4¾ to 5 cups sifted
whole wheat	1 pound	3½ cups unsifted
Green pepper	1 large	1 cup diced
Lemon	1 medium	2 to 3 tablespoons juice; 2 teaspoons grated rind
Lettuce	1- pound head	6¼ cups torn
Lime	1 medium	1½ to 2 tablespoons juice; 1½ teaspoons grated rind
Macaroni	4 ounces dry (1 cup)	2 cups cooked
Marshmallows	10 large	1 cup
	10 miniature	1 large marshmallow
Marshmallows, miniature	½ pound	4½ cups
Milk, evaporated	5- ounce can	½ cup
evaporated	12- ounce can	1½ cups
sweetened, condensed	14- ounce can	1¼ cups
Mushrooms	3 cups raw (8 ounces)	1 cup sliced cooked

EQUIVALENT WEIGHTS AND YIELDS *(continued)*

FOOD	WEIGHT (OR COUNT)	YIELD
Nuts, almonds	1 pound	1 to 1¾ cups nutmeats
	1 pound shelled	3½ cups nutmeats
peanuts	1 pound	2¼ cups nutmeats
	1 pound shelled	3 cups
pecans	1 pound	2¼ cups nutmeats
	1 pound shelled	4 cups
walnuts	1 pound	1⅔ cups nutmeats
	1 pound shelled	4 cups
Oats, quick cooking	1 cup	1¾ cups cooked
Onion	1 medium	½ cup chopped
Orange	1 medium	½ cup juice; 2 tablespoons grated rind
Peaches	2 medium	1 cup sliced
Pears	2 medium	1 cup sliced
Potatoes, white	3 medium	2 cups cubed cooked or 1¾ cups mashed
sweet	3 medium	3 cups sliced
Raisins, seedless	1 pound	3 cups
Rice, long-grain	1 cup	3 to 4 cups cooked
precooked	1 cup	2 cups cooked
Shrimp, raw in shell	1½ pounds	2 cups (¾ pound) cleaned, cooked
Spaghetti	7 ounces	About 4 cups cooked
Strawberries	1 quart	4 cups sliced
Sugar, brown	1 pound	2⅓ cups firmly packed
powdered	1 pound	3½ cups unsifted
granulated	1 pound	2 cups

EQUIVALENT MEASURES

3 teaspoons .... 1 tablespoon
4 tablespoons .... ¼ cup
5⅓ tablespoons .... ⅓ cup
8 tablespoons .... ½ cup
16 tablespoons .... 1 cup
2 tablespoons (liquid)...... 1 ounce
1 cup.......................... 8 fluid ounces

2 cups .... 1 pint (16 fluid ounces)
4 cups.............. 1 quart
4 quarts .... 1 gallon
⅛ cup .... 2 tablespoons
⅓ cup............... 5 tablespoons plus 1 teaspoon
⅔ cup............... 10 tablespoons plus 2 teaspoons
¾ cup .... 12 tablespoons

Party Planner

Copy these worksheets for each party you plan.

EVENT		GUESTS	TOTAL NUMBER	R.S.V.P.
DATE	TIME			
PLACE				
THEME				
BUDGET				
NOTES				

Menu

RECIPES	RECIPE SOURCES	GROCERY LIST
Appetizers:		
Soups/Salads:		
Entrées:		
Side Dishes:		
Breads:		
Desserts:		
Beverages:		
Garnishes:		

CHECK LIST

TO DO	DONE	ITEMS NEEDED
		Paper Goods
☐	☐	invitations
☐	☐	guest book
☐	☐	other:
☐	☐	
		Decor
☐	☐	lighting, candles
☐	☐	flowers
☐	☐	music
☐	☐	entertainment, games
☐	☐	tent
☐	☐	other:
☐	☐	
		Table Matters
☐	☐	napkins
☐	☐	tablecloth(s)
☐	☐	place mats
☐	☐	place cards
☐	☐	china
☐	☐	glassware
☐	☐	serving pieces
☐	☐	menu display
☐	☐	other:
☐	☐	
		Miscellaneous
☐	☐	photography
☐	☐	party favors
☐	☐	trash receptacles
☐	☐	other:
☐	☐	
☐	☐	
☐	☐	

TIMETABLE

One Week Before:

Three Days Before:

The Day Before:

Three Hours Before:

One Hour Before:

Last Minute:

RECIPE TITLE INDEX

An alphabetical listing of every recipe by exact title

All microwave recipe page numbers are preceded by an "M."

MONTH-BY-MONTH INDEX

An alphabetical listing within the month of every food article and accompanying recipes

All microwave recipe page numbers are preceded by an "M."

JANUARY

FEBRUARY

FEBRUARY
(continued)

MARCH

APRIL

MAY

JUNE

JULY

July
(continued)

August

September

OCTOBER

NOVEMBER

NOVEMBER
(continued)

DECEMBER

General Recipe Index

A listing of every recipe by food category and/or major ingredient

All microwave recipe page numbers are preceded by an "M."

FAVORITE RECIPES

Jot down your family's and *your* favorite recipes for quick and handy reference. And don't forget to include the dishes that drew rave reviews when company came for dinner.

RECIPE	SOURCE/PAGE	REMARKS
Appetizers & Beverages		
Breads		
Desserts		

FAVORITE RECIPES *(continued)*

RECIPE	SOURCE/PAGE	REMARKS
Main Dishes		
Side Dishes		
Soups & Salads